Introduction to Law and the Legal System

Third Edition

Introduction to Law and the Legal System

Third Edition

Harold J. Grilliot

University of Cincinnati

Houghton Mifflin Company   Boston

Dallas   Geneva, Illinois   Hopewell, New Jersey   Palo Alto   London

Printed in the U.S.A.
Library of Congress Catalog Card Number: 82-83383
ISBN: 0-395-32701-6

Preface

This book provides an introduction to what every educated citizen should know about law and the American legal system. It gives students an interesting and exciting means of developing an understanding of the strengths and weaknesses of law. Students of the law can decide for themselves whether the lawmaking institutions—the legislative, executive, judicial, and administrative agencies—are dealing adequately with social and business problems. An interesting, concisely written, and relevant text is self-motivating and makes the instructor's job easy. With the instructor's leadership and direction, a course becomes complete.

As President Woodrow Wilson said, "Every citizen should know what the law is, how it came into existence, what relation its form bears to its substance, and how it gives to society its fiber and strength and pose of fame." A basic understanding of the law and the legal system in one's community promotes a better understanding of the role law plays in a complex modern society. This text is designed to stimulate students to exercise their powers of reasoning. An analysis of the facts of the various real-world case situations, along with descriptions of the numerous approaches, develops an appreciation of the theory of legal problem solving. Evaluating the alternative solutions and opposing views presented sharpens the students' sense of justice. Case analysis stimulates thinking and consideration of the extent to which the law addresses itself to the social and business problems of the time.

Educated persons are thought of as those who have exposed themselves to many different areas of study, even though their academic pursuits may not go beyond acquiring a basic understanding of most of the areas. The Parker-Ehrlich Carnegie Commission Report has suggested that "a course taught or designed by an academic lawyer and making use of basically legal materials can both convey knowledge and understanding about law and convey insight into and practice in various useful methods of thought.''

This book is designed for one-term basic law courses offered in any graduate or undergraduate program. It is a survey of the American legal system which can be used in courses such as Survey of Law, Introduction to Law and the Legal System, Legal Environment of Business, and Legal Process. The course could be an integral part of a business, political science, police science, or any other program offered in an institution of higher education.

The text is succinctly written, making use of the most current, controversial court cases available, cases that have been edited and classroom tested with outstanding results. The cases are followed by case questions for class discussions and suggested readings for those who want more depth. There are between ten and seventeen questions at the end of each chapter. These questions are based on actual court cases which apply and expand the chapter material.

Law, like other disciplines, has a language of its own. A glossary of some 350 terms is included at the end of the book to help the reader. A copy of the United States Constitution can also be found there.

The book is a complete educational package. The materials are organized so that each chapter builds on the previous one. However, if an instructor should wish to use the material in a different order, it would not seriously detract from the value of the text.

There are twelve chapters. The first chapter is the introduction, which includes an explanation of the case-study method and some basic legal terminology. The heart of the American legal system is the constitutional guarantee of due process. Chapter II explains the systems of courts in the United States, their jurisdiction and function. The roles of judge and jury during the trial and appellate procedures are included. The third chapter identifies the limitations in seeking judicial relief. A suit must be brought within the statute of limitations, based on a genuine dispute, must be brought only once, and cannot be against one who is immune to suit. Chapter IV discusses the courts' role in following previous cases as precedent and what happens when more than one jurisdiction is involved. The fifth chapter identifies the various judicial remedies available, when they are available, and how they are computed.

The sixth chapter contains a description of the procedures followed in a civil case from the time one decides to bring a suit until a final court judgment is received. Chapter VII describes the procedures that are followed in a criminal proceeding and the constitutional guarantees that are applicable at each stage. Legislation and the courts are explained in the eighth chapter, which also includes interpretation and constitutionality of statutes, along with the power to legislate. The ninth chapter explains the investigative, rulemaking, and adjudicatory functions of administrative agencies, along with the scope of judicial review of agencies' findings. Chapter X deals with some of the major attempts by the federal government to regulate business activity. It discusses antitrust, employment, and consumer legislation. The eleventh chapter describes the substantive law of torts. Negligence and various intentional torts are explained, as well as some trends toward no-fault and strict liability. Chapter XII, a chapter that is new in this third edition, covers contract law, with emphasis on the elements of an enforceable contract.

The third edition contains new material as well as a rewrite and update of materials in the second edition. Materials on due-process guarantee, injunctions, legislative process, the adjudicatory power of agencies, and comparative negligence have been expanded. New material on property has been added. Chapter X (Government Regulation of Business) has been expanded and rewritten and a section on consumer credit has been added.

Thirty-seven new and interesting court cases have been added in the third edition in order to update the book and make it an even more effective teaching tool. The book now presents a total of 113 cases. Of the 152 end-of-chapter questions, 34 are new; the best ones from the second edition have been retained.

Many new illustrations have been included. Copies of a subpoena, a search warrant, and an indictment have been added so that students can see actual documents used by the courts. An important addition is the comprehensive chart of the statute of limitations for the various contract and tort actions for all the states. The subject of agencies, which some find difficult, has been made easier to visualize by an illustration explaining the structure and function of one of the federal administrative agencies. A chart of the various steps in the federal legislative process has been included.

I would like to express my gratitude to all those who have made a genuine contribution to the preparation of the third edition: Professors Ann Selover, of Kent State University; Steven Dow, of Michigan State University; Billie Brandon, of Northern Kentucky University; Irwin F. Flack, of the State University College at Oswego, N.Y.; and Gene Evans, of Western Kentucky University. Their helpful criticism assisted in the preparation of the final manuscript. William Mattingly checked the accuracy of the case citations. I also want to acknowledge the encouragement and friendly criticism of my colleagues at the University of Cincinnati. And I really appreciate the efforts of my research assistants: Ruth Miltimore, Nancy Nies, Ed Rizer, and Marcia Van Pelt. Diane Anando typed most of the manuscript.

H.J.G.

Contents

Introduction   I

Role of Law in Society

Law is a dynamic force for maintaining social order and preventing chaos in society. It is difficult to imagine the existence of a community without law. Lawmakers, courts, and other officials of the law help to preserve a harmonious society. A basic understanding of the law and the legal process of one's community promotes a better understanding of society.

Law embodies the story of a nation's development through the centuries. From primitive customs, codes, and practices, the law of a nation evolves, becoming a sophisticated system administered by highly trained jurists. That which makes up our present-day law should not be taken for granted. It represents years of struggle and thought. To fully appreciate the American legal process, it is necessary to understand its past.

The law and the legal system of the United States are based on the British system. In the colonial period, a system of law was needed to maintain social order. Since law was not to be found on the new continent, it had to be imported. The adoption of English law was not a sweeping process. It was done gradually so that by the time of the Revolution, English law had become generally accepted. The principles derived from the common law system of England form the basis of the legal rights of the American people and are responsible for the laws governing the nation.

Law is not merely a body of static rules to be obeyed by all citizens who are subject to its sanctions. It is a dynamic process by which rules are constantly being adopted and changed to fit the complex situations of a developing society. A community of people uses legal institutions to create and administer law. In the United States, the legislative, executive, and judicial branches and the administrative agencies of the federal and local governments perform the lawmaking and law-administering function.

Law may be divided into the following categories: constitutional law, case law, statute law, treaties, executive orders, regulations of administrative agencies, and local ordinances. The United States Constitution is the supreme law of the land. Any state constitutional provision, or federal, state, or local law that conflicts with the Constitution is invalid. Case law is developed by the application of rules to controversies by courts. Legislative bodies make substantial changes in the law by enacting statutes. Executive orders are regulations issued by the executive branch of government at the federal and state levels. Administrative agencies regulate the activities of certain industries and the activities of persons in certain categories.

To view the law only as a technical institution used for economic and political purposes would be to overlook an important aspect of its function: It reflects society's articulated values. Because moral and legal questions overlap, the law of a democratic society mirrors the people's basic values. This repository of moral knowledge is continuously being reworked and revised as its norms are questioned by various segments of the population. Critics claim that our legal and political institutions are too slow to respond to the need for change. They argue that the law's rate of development does not match society's rate of change. In its attempt to maintain stability in the law, yet be dynamic and accommodating to change, the legal system must consider the complexity of life, the various contradictory demands for reform, and the consequences of its actions. It cannot reach the ''icy stratosphere of certainty'' that is demanded of mathematics and science. Fairness, not perfection, is its goal. It remains accountable to the workaday world, which sometimes does not understand its baffling procedures and mechanisms. It has a duty to prove to this world that truth has been found and justice reached in the fairest possible way.

Today, many people want a better understanding of the law and the legal process. One reason for this interest is the extent to which all phases of one's life are affected by law. Legal concepts and legal rights and duties play an important role in business, governmental activities, educational affairs, family life, recreation, religious affairs. Appreciation of the law is necessary, not to handle one's own legal problems or to make one's personal legal decisions, but rather to understand the important roles that law plays in life and in society. A basic understanding of law also helps one recognize when a legal problem exists for which advice should be sought. It enhances one's capacity to communicate with one's attorney and to understand legal advice. Remember, however, that an understanding of the materials presented in this text is not a substitute for professional legal advice. There are many generalizations about law made throughout the text. No attempt has been made to cover the myriad exceptions. Bear in mind that for each source of law—federal, state, local—there is a corresponding legal system with its own laws and procedures. Even if one could learn all the rules of every system, this knowledge would be of little value, because those rules are constantly changing. The law continues to evolve to fulfill the metamorphic needs of society.

The application of law to factual situations is necessary when there is a controversy between two or more persons or when parties seek guidance concerning the consequences of their conduct or proposed conduct. The court cases in this text are opinions written by judges in disputes where the parties resorted to the courts for the solution to their controversies. However, most disputes are settled by the parties outside court based on professional predictions of what a court would do. In fact, most of a lawyer's time is spent in legal research and guidance in the total absence of controversy—for example, in preparing wills and contracts, and in giving advice concerning such proposed conduct as corporate mergers.

By analyzing actual court cases, students of the law develop an understanding of the legal process and the relationship between judicial theories and practical legal problems. The study of legal principles is necessary. But to absorb information without application is valueless. The recently decided cases presented here illustrate particular points of law. In addition, they convey current legal theory. These cases should stimulate consideration of the extent to which judges address themselves to the social problems of the time. It is important to develop an understanding of the strengths and weaknesses of the law as an instrument of social change.

In analyzing each case decision, focus attention on (1) the underlying fact situation, (2) the law that was applied by the court, (3) whether justice was accomplished by the decision, and (4) the future impact of the decision when it is used as precedent. This method of analysis will help you develop a comprehension of the kind of reasoning used in reaching decisions. Judges apply legal principles to fact situations and test these applications in terms of their potential consequences. The case decisions are official explanations of how the judge responsible for each decision reached it.

One of the great virtues of case law is its dynamic nature—that which makes it adaptable to the requirements of society at the time of its application in court. The law has come a long way since the horse-and-buggy days when it was concerned with one person stealing another's horse. Today, courts are still protecting the right of ownership, but the disputes involve modern inventions and technology. When photographs of a competitor's secret process can be taken from an airplane with the use of a telephoto lens, the ensuing dispute will require more than a horse-and-buggy analysis. In such a situation, the court will have to decide whether to condone such a modern competitive practice or to enforce a higher standard of commercial morality on the business community. Commercial morality has become a vital interest of society because of the size and power of modern business organizations. In determining what standards the law will require of business, one has to use some system of ethics. Religion, moral feeling of the judges, and community standards are some of the factors considered.

E. I. Du Pont De Nemours & Co., Inc. v. Christopher
431 F.2d 1012
United States Court of Appeals, Fifth Circuit
August 25, 1970

GOLDBERG, JUSTICE
This is a case of industrial espionage in which an airplane is the cloak and a camera the dagger. The defendants-appellants, Rolfe and Gary Christopher, are photographers in Beaumont, Texas. The Christophers were hired by an unknown third party to take aerial photographs of new construction at the Beaumont plant of E. I. Du Pont de Nemours & Company, Inc. Sixteen photographs of the Du Pont facility were taken from the air on March 19, 1969, and these photographs were later developed and delivered to the third party.

Du Pont employees apparently noticed the airplane on March 19 and immediately began an investigation to determine why the craft was circling over the plant. By that afternoon the investigation had disclosed that the craft was involved in a photographic expedition and that the Christophers were the photographers. Du Pont contacted the Christophers that same afternoon and asked them to reveal the name of the

person or corporation requesting the photographs. The Christophers refused to disclose this information, giving as their reason the client's desire to remain anonymous.

Having reached a dead end in the investigation, Du Pont subsequently filed suit against the Christophers, alleging that the Christophers had wrongfully obtained photographs revealing Du Pont's trade secrets which they then sold to the undisclosed third party. Du Pont contended that it had developed a highly secret but unpatented process for producing methanol, a process that gave Du Pont a competitive advantage over other producers. This process, Du Pont alleged, was a trade secret developed after much expensive and time-consuming research, and a secret that the company had taken special precautions to safeguard. The area photographed by the Christophers was the plant designed to produce methanol by this secret process, and because the plant was still under construction, parts of the process were exposed to view from directly above the construction area. Photographs of that area, Du Pont alleged, would enable a skilled person to deduce the secret process for making methanol. Du Pont thus contended that the Christophers had wrongfully appropriated Du Pont trade secrets by taking the photographs and delivering them to the undisclosed third party. In its suit Du Pont asked for damages to cover the loss it had already sustained as a result of the wrongful disclosure of the trade secret and sought temporary and permanent injunctions prohibiting any further circulation of the photographs already taken and prohibiting any additional photographing of the methanol plant.

The Christophers answered with motions to dismiss for lack of jurisdiction and failure to state a claim upon which relief could be granted. Depositions were taken during which the Christophers again refused to disclose the name of the person to whom they had delivered the photographs. Du Pont then filed a motion to compel an answer to this question and all related questions.

On June 5, 1969, the trial court held a hearing on the pending motions. The court denied the Christophers' motions to dismiss for want of jurisdiction and failure to state a claim. The court granted Du Pont's motion to compel the Christophers to divulge the name of their client. Agreeing with the trial court's determination that Du Pont had stated a valid claim, we affirm the decision of that court.

This is a case of first impression, for the Texas courts have not faced this precise factual issue, and sitting as a diversity court we must sensitize our *Erie* antennae to decide what the Texas courts would do if such a situation were presented to them. The only question involved in this interlocutory appeal is whether Du Pont has asserted a claim upon which relief can be granted. The Christophers argued both at trial and before this court that they committed no "actionable wrong" in photographing the Du Pont facility and passing these photographs on to their client because they conducted all of their activities in public airspace, violated no government aviation standard, did not breach any confidential relation, and did not engage in any fraudulent or illegal conduct. In short, the Christophers argue that for an appropriation of trade secrets to be wrong there must be a trespass, other illegal conduct, or breach of a confidential relationship. We disagree.

It is true, as the Christophers assert, that the previous trade secret cases have contained one or more of these elements. However, we do not think that the Texas courts would limit the trade secret protection exclusively to these elements. On the contrary, in *Hyde Corporation v. Huffines*, 1958, 158 Tex. 566, 314 S.W.2d 763, the Texas Supreme Court specifically adopted the rule found in the Restatement of Torts which provides:

One who discloses or uses another's trade secret, without a privilege to do so, is liable to the other if

a. he discovered the secret by improper means, or

b. his disclosure or use constitutes a breach of confidence reposed in him by the other in disclosing the secret to him. . . .

Thus, although the previous cases have dealt with a breach of a confidential relationship, a trespass, or other illegal conduct, the rule is much broader than the cases heretofore encountered. Not limiting itself to specific wrongs, Texas adopted subsection (a) of the Restatement which recognizes a cause of action for the discovery of a trade secret by any "improper" means.

The question remaining, therefore, is whether aerial photography of plant construction is an improper means of obtaining another's trade secret. We conclude that it is and that the Texas courts would so hold. The supreme court of that state has declared that "the undoubted tendency of the law has been to recognize and enforce higher standards of commercial morality in the business world." *Hyde Corporation v. Huffines*, 314 S.W.2d at 773. That court has quoted with approval articles indicating that the *proper* means of gaining possession of a competitor's secret process is "through inspection and analysis" of the product in order to create a duplicate. Later another Texas court explained:

The means by which the discovery is made may be obvious, and the experimentation leading from known factors to presently unknown results may be simple and lying in the public domain. But these facts do not destroy the value of the discovery and will not advantage a competitor who by unfair means obtains the knowledge *without paying the price expended by the discoverer.* (*Brown v. Fowler*, Tex. Civ. App. 1958, 316 S.W.2d 111.)

We think, therefore, that the Texas rule is clear. One may use his competitor's secret process if he discovers the process by reverse engineering applied to the finished product; one may use a competitor's process if he discovers it by his own independent research. But one may not avoid these labors by taking the process from the discoverer without his permission at a time when he is taking reasonable precautions to maintain its secrecy. To obtain knowledge of a process without spending the time and money to discover it independently is *improper* unless the holder voluntarily discloses it or fails to take reasonable precautions to ensure its secrecy.

In the instant case the Christophers deliberately flew over the Du Pont plant to get pictures of a process which Du Pont had attempted to keep secret. The Christophers delivered their pictures to a third party who was certainly aware of the means by which they had been acquired and who may be planning to use the information contained therein to manufacture methanol by the Du Pont process. The third party has a right to use this process only if he obtains this knowledge through his own research efforts. But thus far all information indicates that the third party has gained this knowledge solely by taking it from Du Pont, at a time when Du Pont was making reasonable efforts to preserve its secrecy. In such a situation Du Pont has a valid cause of action to prohibit the Christophers from improperly discovering its trade secret and to prohibit the undisclosed third party from using the improperly obtained information.

We note that this view is in perfect accord with the position taken by the authors of the Restatement. In commenting on improper means of discovery, the savants of the Restatement of Torts said:

f. *Improper Means of Discovery.* The discovery of another's trade secret by improper means subjects the actor to liability independently of the harm to the interest in the secret. Thus, if one uses physical force to take a secret formula from another's pocket, or breaks into another's office to steal the formula, his conduct is wrongful and subjects him to liability apart from the rule stated in this section. Such conduct is also an improper means of procuring the secret under this rule. But means may be improper under this rule even though they do not cause any other harm than that to the interest in the trade secret. Examples of such means are fraudulent misrepresentations to induce disclosure, tapping of telephone wires, eavesdropping or other espionage. A complete catalogue of improper means is not possible. In general they are means which fall below the general accepted standards of commercial morality and reasonable conduct.

In taking this position, we realize that industrial espionage of the sort here perpetrated has become a popular sport in some segments of our industrial community. However, our devotion to freewheeling industrial competition must not force us into accepting the law of the jungle as the standard of morality expected in our commercial relations. Our tolerance of the espionage game must cease when the protections required to prevent another's spying cost so much that the spirit of inventiveness is dampened. Commercial privacy must be protected from espionage that could not have been reasonably anticipated or prevented. We do not mean to imply, however, that everything not in plain view is within the protected vale, nor that all information obtained through every extra optical extension is forbidden. Indeed, for our industrial competition to remain healthy there must be breathing room for observing a competing industrialist. A competitor can and must shop his competition for pricing and examine his products for quality, components, and methods of manufacture. Perhaps ordinary fences and roofs must be built to shut out incursive eyes. But we need not require the discoverer of a trade secret to guard against the unanticipated, the undetectable, or the unpreventable methods of espionage now available.

In the instant case Du Pont was in the midst of constructing a plant. Although after construction the finished plant would have protected much of the process from view, during the period of construction the trade secret was exposed to view from the air. To require Du Pont to put a roof over the unfinished plant to guard its secret would impose an enormous expense to prevent nothing more than a schoolboy's trick. We introduce here no new or radical ethic, since our ethos has never given moral sanction to piracy. The marketplace must not deviate far from our mores. We should not require a person or corporation to take unreasonable precautions to prevent another from doing that which he ought not to do in the first place. Reasonable precautions against predatory eyes we may require. But an impenetrable fortress is an unreasonable requirement, and we are not disposed to burden industrial inventors with such a duty in order to protect the fruits of their efforts. ''Improper'' will always be a word of many nuances, determined by time, place, and circumstances. We therefore need not proclaim a catalogue of commercial improprieties. Clearly, however, one of its commandments does say "thou shalt not appropriate a trade secret through deviousness under circumstances in which countervailing defenses are not reasonably available."

Having concluded that aerial photography, from whatever altitude, is an improper method of discovering the trade secrets exposed during construction of the Du Pont plant, we need not worry about whether the flight pattern chosen by the Christophers violated any federal aviation regulations. Regardless of whether the flight was legal or illegal in that sense, the espionage was an improper means of discovering Du Pont's trade secret.

The decision of the trial courts is affirmed and the case remanded to that court for proceedings on the merits.

CASE QUESTIONS

1. The court in *Hyde Corporation v. Huffines*, cited in the *Du Pont* opinion, stated that the law has tended to "recognize and enforce higher standards of commercial morality." Should the law perform that function?

2. What conflicting social values was the court presented with in *Du Pont?* How did the court resolve this conflict?

3. How strongly was the court in *Du Pont* influenced by the argument that commercial espionage is a prevailing practice in American commerce? Does this suggest that courts may reject certain customary trade practices as standards for the development of the law when those practices are in conflict with other accepted social values?

4. Most disputes are settled outside of court by the parties to the dispute based on a prediction of what the court would do if the case went before it. Would a lawyer be able to predict the result of *Du Pont* with a high degree of certainty?

5. What is the issue or question of the *Du Pont* case?

SUGGESTED READINGS

L. L. FULLER, THE MORALITY OF LAW (1964).

R. POUND, LAW AND MORALS (1926).

Aldisert, *Role of the Courts in Contemporary Society*, 38 U. PITT L. REV. 437 (1977).

Bok, *Lying to Enemies: Lawyer's Moral Choice*, 52 N.Y. ST. B.J. 552 (1980).

Byron, *Ideas and Images of Justice*, 26 Loy. L. Rev. 439 (1980).

Hart, *Social Solidarity and the Enforcement of Morality*, 35 U. Chi. L. Rev. 1 (1967).

Schwartz, *Law and Its Developments: A Synoptic Survey*, 1978 S. Ill. U. L.J. 44.

Tedeschi, *Custom and Modern Law*, 15 U.W.O. L. Rev. 1 (1976).

Case Analysis

Since the *Du Pont* case is the first reported judicial decision of this book, a brief analysis of it is appropriate. The heading consists of four items. The first line contains the names of the parties to the suit. E. I. du Pont de Nemours & Company, Inc., the party that brought the suit, is the *plaintiff*. Rolfe and Gary Christopher are the *defendants*. When there is more than one plaintiff or defendant, it is appropriate to include only one name. This is the reason the heading reads ''Christopher'' rather than ''Christophers.'' The Christophers are the *appellants*, the parties who appealed to a higher court from the decision of a lower court. The other party to an appeal is called the *appellee*.

The next item in the heading describes the volume and page where the case can be found. The *Du Pont* case is reported in volume 431 of the second series of the Federal Reporter on page 1012. The name of the court that decided the dispute is next in the heading. It is followed by the date the decision was reached. The first item in the body of the court opinion is the name of the judge who wrote the court opinion. Usually, only one judge is selected to write the majority opinion, even though several judges may have participated in reaching the decision.

In the suit, Du Pont asked for *damages* (money to cover the loss sustained as a result of the defendant's action) and for an *injunction* (an order by the court prohibiting the action of the defendants). What the plaintiff really wanted was to know for whom the defendants were taking the pictures. The defendants made a motion to *dismiss for lack of jurisdiction*. This means that the defendants asked the court not to hear the case because it did not have the authority to do so. The defendants also asked that the court dismiss the complaint against them for the plaintiff's failure to state a claim, meaning that there was no legal basis for granting relief. The court denied both motions. Since the case was on *appeal*, a judicial review of a decision rendered by a lower court, the appellate court could have affirmed, remanded, reversed, or dismissed the appeal. The court rejected the motion to dismiss and chose to affirm and remand the case. By *affirming*, the appellate court rules that the lower court's decision is valid and reasserts the judgment. To render a judgment of *reversal* is to vacate and set aside the lower court's judgment. Note that reversals can be in part. When a case is *remanded*, it is returned to the lower court, generally with instructions, so that further proceedings may be taken.

The issue that the court had to decide in this case was whether aerial photography of plant construction is an improper means of obtaining another's trade secret. This was a case of *first impression*, meaning that no decision in Texas had been reached on the point at issue. The federal court tried to determine the law for the state of Texas. The court searched for factual situations in previously decided Texas cases comparable to the factual situation of the case before it. The court extracted from the previously decided comparable cases the principle on which those cases were decided and applied those principles of law to the case at hand.

Learning about law through the case-study method can result in an understanding of the law and the legal process that cannot be obtained through other methods. In order to reap the benefits of the case-study method, one must read each case accurately and pay close attention to detail. After reading a case, one should have not merely a general sense or the gist of what the case says, but a precise understanding of what the court did. Careful attention should be given to the *holding* of the case—what the court decided on the facts of the case.

Opinions are often discursive. Judges often discuss issues they need not decide. Their statements on these issues are labeled *dictum*. Although these statements may be important, they lack the authority of the case's holding.

Most students find it helpful to *brief* a case. After careful reading and analysis of a case, one can write a brief without referring to the case again. Briefing with the book aside provides a check on understanding as well as an incentive to careful reading. A brief should contain the parts of the case selected as important, organized for the purpose at hand rather than in the haphazard order in which they may be reported. Generally a brief includes the briefer's attempt to formulate the important questions raised by the case. Each of the cases in this book should be carefully studied and analyzed with the following questions in mind.

Parties: Who is suing whom? Who is the plaintiff? Who is the defendant?

Legal Proceedings: What is the nature of the litigation, civil or criminal? What remedies are sought? What was the result in the trial court? What particular ruling of the trial judge became crucial on appeal? Was there any prior review of the case, and, if so, what was the result of that review? How did the case come before the court currently considering the matter?

Facts: What happened? This requires not a recitation of all the details that can be learned, but a selection of those events that are relevant to the decision.

Legal Provisions: What rules of law are applicable? Are any constitutional provisions relied upon?

Issue: What issue (or question) is presented for decision?

Decision: How is the issue decided? Who won? What did the winner gain?

Rule of the Case: What general rule does the case lay down?

Reasons: What explanation does the court give to justify its decision?

Concurring and Dissenting Opinions: If there are any concurring or dissenting opinions, what do they say?

Legal Terminology: Legal terms must be looked up in the Glossary, because the definitions in an ordinary dictionary are not sufficient. For words not defined in the Glossary, consult law dictionaries by Ballentine, Black, and Gilmer.

Due-Process Guarantee

The Fifth Amendment of the federal Constitution states that no person shall be "deprived of life, liberty, or property without due process of law." This is a limitation on the powers of the federal government. The same limitation on the power of the states is contained in the Fourteenth Amendment, which declares that no state shall "deprive any person of life, liberty, or property without due process of law."

The guarantee of due process of law contained in the federal Constitution binds and restrains the federal and state governments and each of their branches. This fundamental principle of justice applies to every governmental proceeding that may interfere with property or personal rights, whether the proceeding is legislative, judicial, executive, or administrative.

There is no exact, comprehensive definition of due process that applies to all possible situations. The guarantee is meant to ensure a fundamental fairness for all. What it is depends on circumstances. It varies with the subject matter and situation. If, in certain situations, a government proceeding is found to be arbitrary, oppressive, or unjust, it is declared to violate the due-process guarantee. A proceeding that results in the denial of fundamental fairness and is shocking to the universal sense of justice is considered an unconstitutional exercise of power.

The purpose of the due-process guarantee is to ensure the fair and orderly administration of the laws. Everyone is entitled to the protection of those fundamental principles of liberty and justice. No person can be deprived of life, liberty, property, or any right granted by statute unless first adjudicated against by an orderly proceeding conducted according to established rules, and given reasonable notice and the opportunity to be heard and to present any claim or defense. That every human being has an inherent right to due process of law is the very essence of our concept of law and government. Under both the Fifth and Fourteenth Amendments, a corporation, as well as a partnership or unincorporated association, is a person to whom the protection applies.

Due process of the law focuses on life, liberty, and property. "Liberty" covers a vast scope of rights, including those freedoms guaranteed by the First Amendment: free speech, press, and religion. It infers the absence of arbitrary and unreasonable restraint on an individual conducting business or using property. "Life" can be defined as all personal rights that are judicially protected. These are—but are not limited to—the right to marry, establish a home, rear children, worship according to one's preferred religion, and to voice one's opinion without fear of reprisal. "Property" is everything that may be subject to ownership, including real and personal property, obligations, rights, and other untangibles.

The due-process guarantee protects citizens from unfairness in the operation of both substantive law and procedural law. *Substantive law* is the part of the law that creates, defines, and regulates rights. It defines the legal relationship between the citizen and the state and among citizens themselves. The primary responsibility of the legislative branch of the government is the enactment of substantive law. *Procedural law* prescribes the methods and means of enforcing legal rights. It provides the machinery by which citizens can maintain suits to enforce these rights or to obtain redress for the invasion of such rights. The judicial branch of the government, in its administration of justice, must follow the procedures set forth by the Constitution.

Substantive Due Process

The guarantee of due process of law is a limitation on legislation. It demands that the law not be unreasonable, arbitrary, or capricious. Every legislative act must have a legitimate purpose that justifies its enactment. The means selected—that is, the legislation enacted—must have a substantial relation to the desired end and must operate evenhandedly. An act that is so vague in its terms that persons of ordinary intelligence must guess at its meaning violates the due-process clause.

Village of Hoffman Est. v. Flipside, Hoffman Est., Inc.
102 S.Ct. 1186
United States Supreme Court
March 3, 1982

MR. JUSTICE MARSHALL
This case presents a pre-enforcement facial challenge[1] to a drug paraphernalia ordinance on the ground that it is unconstitutionally vague and overbroad under the due-process clause.

---

[1] A *facial challenge* is a challenge of the language used in the act only, without the inclusion of extrinsic facts or evidence. —*Ed.*

The ordinance in question requires a business to obtain a license if it sells any items that are "designed or marketed for use with illegal cannabis or drugs." Village of Hoffman Estates Ordinance No. 969–1978. The United States Court of Appeals for the Seventh Circuit held that the ordinance is vague on its face. 630 F.2d 373 (1980). We noted probable jurisdiction, and now reverse.

For more than three years prior to May 1, 1978, appellee The Flipside, Hoffman Estates, Inc. (Flipside), sold a variety of merchandise, including phonographic records, smoking accessories, novelty devices, and jewelry, in its store located in the village of Hoffman Estates, Illinois (the village). On February 20, 1978, the village enacted an ordinance regulating drug paraphernalia, to be effective May 1, 1978. The ordinance makes it unlawful for any person "to sell any items, effect, paraphernalia, accessory or thing which is designed or marketed for use with illegal cannabis or drugs, as defined by Illinois Revised Statutes, without obtaining a license therefor." The license fee is $150. A business must also file affidavits that the licensee and its employees have not been convicted of a drug-related offense. Moreover, the business must keep a record of each sale of a regulated item, including the name and address of the purchaser, to be open to police inspection. No regulated item may be sold to a minor. A violation is subject to a fine of not less than $10 and not more than $500, and each day that a violation continues gives rise to a separate offense. A series of licensing guidelines prepared by the village attorney define "Paper," "Roach Clips," "Pipes,"

and "Paraphernalia," the sale of which is required to be licensed.

On May 30, 1978, instead of applying for a license or seeking clarification via the administrative procedures that the village had established for its licensing ordinances, Flipside filed this lawsuit in the United States District Court. The complaint alleged, *inter alia*, that the ordinance is unconstitutionally vague and overbroad, and requested injunctive and declaratory relief and damages. The court issued an opinion upholding the constitutionality of the ordinance, and awarded judgment to the village defendants.

The Court of Appeals reversed, on the ground that the ordinance is unconstitutionally vague on its face. The court reviewed the language of the ordinance and guidelines and found it vague with respect to certain conceivable applications, such as ordinary pipes or "paper clips sold next to *Rolling Stone* magazine." 639 F.2d, at 382. It also suggested that the "subjective" nature of the "marketing" test creates a danger of arbitrary and discriminatory enforcement against those with alternative lifestyles. *Id.*, at 384. Thus it concluded that the ordinance is impermissibly vague on its face.

A law may be challenged on its face as unduly vague, in violation of due process. To succeed, however, the complainant must demonstrate that the law is impermissibly vague in all its applications. Flipside makes no such showing. The standards for evaluating vagueness were enunciated in *Grayned v. City of Rockford*, 408 U.S. 104, 108 (1972): "Vague laws offend several important values. First, because we assume that man is free to steer between lawful and unlawful conduct, we insist that laws give the person of ordinary intelligence a reasonable opportunity to know what is prohibited, so that he may act accordingly. Vague laws may trap the innocent by not providing fair warning. Second, if arbitrary and discriminatory enforcement is to be prevented, laws must provide explicit standards for those who apply them. A vague law impermissibly delegates basic policy matters to policemen, judges, and juries for resolution on an *ad hoc* and subjective basis, with the attendant dangers of arbitrary and discriminatory applications.''

These standards should not, of course, be mechanically applied. The degree of vagueness that the Constitution tolerates—as well as the relative importance of fair notice and fair enforcement—depend in part on the nature of the enactment. Thus economic regulation is subject to a less strict vagueness test because its subject matter is often more narrow, and because businesses, which face economic demands to plan behavior carefully, can be expected to consult relevant legislation in advance of action. Indeed, the regulated enterprise may have the ability to clarify the meaning of the regulation by its own inquiry, or by resort to an administrative process. The Court has also expressed greater tolerance of enactments with civil rather than criminal penalties because the consequences of imprecision are qualitatively less severe. And the Court has recognized that a scienter[2] requirement may mitigate a law's vagueness, especially with respect to the adequacy

of notice to the complainant that his conduct is proscribed.

Finally, perhaps the most important factor affecting the clarity that the Constitution demands of a law is whether it threatens the exercise of constitutionally protected rights. If, for example, the law interferes with the right of free speech or of association, a more stringent vagueness test should apply.

This ordinance simply regulates business behavior and contains a scienter requirement with respect to the alternative ''marketed for use'' standard. The ordinance nominally imposes only civil penalties. However, the village concedes that the ordinance is ''quasi-criminal,'' and its prohibitory and stigmatizing effect may warrant a relatively strict test. Flipside's facial challenge fails because, under a test appropriate to either a quasi-criminal or a criminal law, the ordinance is sufficiently clear as applied to Flipside.

The ordinance requires Flipside to obtain a license if it sells ''any items, effect, paraphernalia, accessory or thing which is designed or marketed for use with illegal cannabis or drugs, as defined by the Illinois Revised Statutes.'' Flipside expresses no uncertainty about which drugs this description encompasses. As the District Court noted, 485 F.Supp. at 406, Illinois law clearly defines cannabis and numerous other controlled drugs, including cocaine. Ill. Rev. Stat., ch. 56 1/2, para. 703 and 1102(g) (1977). On the other hand, the words ''items, effect, paraphernalia, accessory or thing'' do not identify the type of merchandise that the village desires to regulate. Flip-

---

[2] *Scienter* in this context means defendant's guilty knowledge.—*Ed.*

side's challenge thus appropriately focuses on the language "designed or marketed for use." Under either the "designed for use" or "marketed for use" standard, we conclude that at least some of the items sold by Flipside are covered. Thus Flipside's facial challenge is unavailing.

Designed for use

The Court of Appeals objected that "designed . . . for use" is ambiguous with respect to whether items must be inherently suited only for drug use; whether the retailer's intent or manner of display is relevant; and whether the intent of a third party, the manufacturer, is critical, since the manufacturer is the "designer." 639 F.2d, at 380–81. For the reasons that follow, we conclude that this language is not unconstitutionally vague on its face.

The court of appeals' speculation about the meaning of "design" is largely unfounded. The guidelines refer to "paper of colorful design" and to other specific items as conclusively "designed" or not "designed" for illegal use. Webster's New International Dictionary says that a principal meaning of "design" is "to fashion according to a plan." It is therefore plain that the standard encompasses at least an item that is principally used with illegal drugs by virtue of its objective features, that is, features designed by the manufacturer. A businessperson of ordinary intelligence would understand that this term refers to the design of the manufacturer, not the intent of the retailer or customer. It is also sufficiently clear that items which are principally used for nondrug purposes, such as ordinary

pipes, are not "designed for use" with illegal drugs. Moreover, no issue of fair warning is present in this case, since Flipside concedes that the phrase refers to structural characteristics of an item.

The ordinance and guidelines do contain ambiguities. Nevertheless, the "designed for use" standard is sufficiently clear to cover at least some of the items that Flipside sold. The ordinance, through the guidelines, explicitly regulates "roach clips." Flipside's co-operator admitted that the store sold such items, see Tr. 26, 30, and the village chief of police testified that he had never seen a "roach clip" used for any purpose other than to smoke cannabis. App. 52. The chief also testified that a specially designed pipe that Flipside marketed is typically used to smoke marijuana. App. 52. Whether further guidelines, administrative rules, or enforcement policy will clarify the more ambiguous scope of the standard in other respects is of no concern in this facial challenge.

Marketed for use

Whatever ambiguities the "designed . . . for use" standard may engender, the alternative "marketed for use" standard is transparently clear. It describes a retailer's intentional display and marketing of merchandise. The guidelines refer to the display of paraphernalia, and to the proximity of covered items to otherwise uncovered items. A retail store therefore must obtain a license if it deliberately displays its wares in a manner that appeals to or encourages illegal drug use. The standard requires scienter, since a retailer could scarcely "market" items "for" a particular use without intending that use.

Under this test, Flipside had ample warning that its marketing activities required a license. Flipside displayed the magazine *High Times* and books entitled *Marijuana Grower's Guide*, *Children's Garden of Grass*, and *The Pleasures of Cocaine* physically close to pipes and colored rolling papers, in clear violation of the guidelines. As noted above, Flipside's co-operator admitted that his store sold "roach clips," which are principally used for illegal purposes. Finally, in the same section of the store, Flipside had posted the sign, "You must be 18 or older to purchase any head supplies."

Many American communities have recently enacted laws regulating or prohibiting the sale of drug paraphernalia. Whether these laws are wise or effective is not, of course, the province of this Court. We hold only that such legislation is not facially overbroad or vague if it does not reach constitutionally protected conduct and is reasonably clear in its application to the complainant.

Accordingly, the judgment of the court of appeals is reversed, and the case is remanded for further proceedings consistent with this opinion.

It is so ordered.

CASE QUESTIONS

1. When the Supreme Court determined whether the ordinance of the village of Hoffman Estates was unconstitutionally void for vagueness, what standards of evaluation did the Court use?
2. Did the ordinance limit any rights protected by the Constitution?
3. Why does the ordinance forbid the sale of drug paraphernalia to minors? Under what doctrine may a state or city limit such a sale?

SUGGESTED READINGS

Aigler, *Legislation in Vague or General Terms*, 21 MICH. L. REV. 831 (1923).

Bennion, *The Science of Interpretation*, 130 NEW L.J. 493 (1980).

Bice, *Standards of Judicial Review Under the Equal Protection and Due Process Clauses*, 50 S. CALIF. L. REV. 689 (1977).

Freud, *The Use of Indefinite Terms in Statutes*, 30 YALE L.J. 437 (1921).

Johnson, *Constitutionality of Drug Paraphernalia Laws*, 81 COLUM. L. REV. 581 (1981).

Perry, *Constitutional "Fairness": Notes on Equal Protection and Due Process*, 63 VA. L. REV. 383 (1977).

Note, *The Void-for-Vagueness Doctrine in the Supreme Court*, 109 U. Pa.
  L. Rev. 67 (1960).
Note, *Due-Process Requirements of Definiteness in Statutes*, 62 Harv. L.
  Rev. 77 (1948).

Procedural Due Process

An organized and civilized society must provide an impartial dispute-solving mechanism or legal system. It must be competent and impartial in order to gain the acceptance of society. The decision-making process must be based on fair and rational principles.

The due-process guarantee requires fairness and justice in judicial proceedings. No particular form of procedure is required. Every person is entitled to notice of any proceeding that could result in the deprivation of life, liberty, or property, and there must be a hearing in which he has the opportunity to defend himself. The hearing must be fair, and it must be conducted before an impartial and competent tribunal.

Courts have shown an increased concern for the protection of the rights of individuals. In the past, those rights have been protected from governmental interference, but not from intrusions by private institutions or private persons. Private action has not been restricted by the due-process guarantee, which is applicable only where some sort of governmental action is present.

Courts have only recently begun to protect the rights of students in private academic institutions. The due-process protection has not been applied to expulsion and other disciplinary actions of private schools. Public institutions, on the other hand, have always been required to extend procedural due process in disciplinary actions. Since public colleges and universities are governmental institutions, students of these institutions must be provided with the guarantees of the Fifth and Fourteenth Amendments.

Due process is being invoked with growing frequency whenever a person's liberty or property is in jeopardy and when government is even remotely involved. The years that have seen the expansion of the concept of "state action" have also seen tremendous growth in the connections between private schools and government in the form of grants, scholarships, and research funds. Courts are beginning to require procedural due process in actions of those private colleges and universities in which such governmental involvement is found.

Goss v. Lopez
419 U.S. 565
United States Supreme Court
January 22, 1975

Mr. Justice White
This appeal by various administrators of the Columbus, Ohio, Public School System (CPSS) challenges the judgment of a three-judge federal court, declaring the appellees—various high school students in the CPSS—were denied due process of law contrary to the command of the Fourteenth Amendment in that they were temporarily suspended from their high schools without a hearing either prior to suspension or within a reasonable time thereafter, and enjoining the administrators to remove all references to such suspensions from the students' records.

Ohio law, Rev. Code Ann. §3313.65 (1972), provides for free education to all children between the ages of 6 and 21. §3313.66 of the code empowers the principal of an Ohio public school to suspend a pupil for misconduct for up to 10 days, or to expel him. In either case, he must notify the student's parents within 24 hours and state the reasons for his action. A pupil who is expelled, or his parents, may appeal the decision to the Board of Education and in connection therewith shall be permitted to be heard at the board meeting. The board may reinstate the pupil following the hearing. No similar procedure is provided in §3313.66 or any other provision of state law for a suspended student. Aside from a regulation tracking the statute, at the time of the imposition of the suspensions in this case, the CPSS itself had not issued any written procedure applicable to suspensions. Nor, so far as the record reflects, had any of the individual high schools involved in this case. Each, however, had formally or informally described the conduct for wnich suspension could be imposed.

The nine named appellees, each of whom alleged that he had been suspended from public high school in Columbus for up to 10 days without a hearing pursuant to Section 3313.66, filed an action against the Columbus Board of Education and various administrators of the CPSS. The complaint sought a declaration that Section 3313.66 was unconstitutional in that it permitted public school administrators to deprive plaintiffs of their rights to an education without a hearing of any kind, in violation of the procedural due-process component of the Fourteenth Amendment. It also sought to enjoin the public school officials from issuing future suspensions pursuant to Section 3313.66 and to require them to remove references to the past suspensions from the records of the students in question.

The proof below established that the suspensions arose out of a period of widespread student unrest in the CPSS during February and March 1971. Two named plaintiffs, Dwight Lopez and Betty Crome, were students at the Central High School and McGuffey Junior High School, respectively. The former was suspended in connection with a disturbance in the lunchroom which involved some physical damage to school property. Lopez testified that at least 75 other students were suspended from his school on the same day. He also testified below that he was not a party to the destructive conduct but was instead an innocent bystander. Because no one from the school testified with regard to this incident, there is no evidence in the record indicating the official basis for concluding otherwise. Lopez never had a hearing.

Betty Crome was present at a demonstration at a high school other than the one she was attending. There she was arrested together with others, taken to the police station, and released without being formally charged. Before she went to school on the following day, she was notified that she had been suspended for a 10-day period. Because no one from the school testified with respect to this incident, the record does not disclose how the McGuffey Junior High School principal went about making the decision to suspend Crome, nor does it disclose on what information the decision was based. It is clear from the record that no hearing was ever held.

At the outset, appellants contend that because there is no constitutional right to an education at public expense, the due-process clause does not protect against expulsions from the public school system. This position misconceives the nature of the issue and is refuted by prior decisions. The Fourteenth Amendment forbids the state to deprive any person of life, liberty, or property without due process of law. Protected interests in property are normally not created, and their dimensions are defined by an independent source such as state statutes or rules entitling the citizen to certain benefits.

Although Ohio may not be constitutionally obligated to establish and maintain a public school system, it has nevertheless done so and has required

its children to attend. Those young people do not ''shed their constitutional rights'' at the schoolhouse door. *Tinker v. Des Moines School Dist.*, 393 U.S. 503, 506 (1969). The Fourteenth Amendment, as now applied to the states, protects the citizen against the state itself and all of its creatures—boards of education not excepted. The authority possessed by the state to prescribe and enforce standards of conduct in its schools, although concededly very broad, must be exercised consistently with constitutional safeguards. Among other things, the state is constrained to recognize a student's legitimate entitlement to a public education as a property interest which is protected by the due-process clause and which may not be taken away for misconduct without adherence to the minimum procedures required by that clause.

The due-process clause also forbids arbitrary deprivations of liberty. Where a person's good name, reputation, honor, or integrity is at stake because of what the government is doing to him, the minimal requirements of the clause must be satisfied. School authorities here suspended appellees from school for periods of up to 10 days based on charges of misconduct. If sustained and recorded, those charges could seriously damage the students' standing with their fellow pupils and their teachers, as well as interfere with later opportunities for higher education and employment. It is apparent that the claimed right of the state to determine unilaterally and without due process whether that misconduct has occurred immediately collides with the requirements of the Constitution.

A short suspension is, of course, a far milder deprivation than expulsion. But ''education is perhaps the most important function of state and local governments,'' *Brown v. Board of Education*, 347 U.S. 483, 493 (1954), and the total exclusion from the educational process for more than a trivial period—and certainly if the suspension is for 10 days— is a serious event in the life of the suspended child. Neither the property interest in educational benefits temporarily denied nor the liberty interest in reputation, which is also implicated, is so insubstantial that suspensions may constitutionally be imposed by any procedure the school chooses, no matter how arbitrary.

At the very minimum, therefore, students facing suspension and the consequent interference with a protected property interest must be given *some* kind of notice and afforded *some* kind of hearing. Parties whose rights are to be affected are entitled to be heard. And in order that they may enjoy that right, they must first be notified.

The prospect of imposing elaborate hearing requirements in every suspension case is viewed with great concern. Many school authorities may well prefer the untrammeled power to act unilaterally, unhampered by rules about notice and hearing. But it would be a strange disciplinary system in an educational institution if no communication was sought by the disciplinarian with the student in an effort to inform him of his dereliction and to let him tell his side of the story in order to make sure that an injustice is not done. Fairness can rarely be obtained by secret, one-sided determination of facts decisive of rights. Secrecy is not congenial to truth-seeking and self-righteousness gives too slender an assurance of rightness. No better instrument has been devised for arriving at truth than to give a person in jeopardy of serious loss notice of the case against him and opportunity to meet it.

Students facing temporary suspension have interests qualifying for protection of the due-process clause, and due process requires, in connection with a suspension of 10 days or less, that the student be given oral or written notice of the charges against him and, if he denies them, an explanation of the evidence the authorities have and an opportunity to present his side of the story. The clause requires at least these rudimentary precautions against unfair or mistaken findings of misconduct and arbitrary exclusion from school.

We stop short of construing the due-process clause to require, countrywide, that hearings in connection with short suspensions must afford the student the opportunity to secure counsel, to confront and cross-examine witnesses supporting the charge, or to call his own witnesses to verify his version of the incident. Brief disciplinary suspensions are almost countless. To impose in each such case even truncated trial-type procedures might well overwhelm administrative facilities in many places and, by diverting resources, cost more than it would save in educational effectiveness. Moreover, further formalizing the suspension process and escalating its formality and adversary nature may not only make it too costly as a regular disciplinary tool but also destroy its effectiveness as part of the teaching process.

On the other hand, requiring effective notice and informal hearing permitting the student to give his version of the events will provide a meaningful hedge against erroneous action. At least the disciplinarian will be alerted to the existence of disputes about facts and arguments about cause and effect. He may then determine himself to summon the accuser, permit cross-examination, and allow the student to present his own witnesses. In more difficult cases, he may permit counsel. In any event, his discretion will be more informed and we think the risk of error substantially reduced.

We should also make it clear that we have addressed ourselves solely to the short suspension, not exceeding 10 days. Longer suspensions or expulsions for the remainder of the school term, or permanently, may require more formal procedures. Nor do we put aside the possibility that in unusual situations, although involving only a short suspension, something more than the rudimentary procedures will be required.

The District Court found each of the suspensions involved here to have occurred without a hearing, either before or after the suspension, and that each suspension was therefore invalid and the statute unconstitutional insofar as it permits such suspensions without notice or hearing. Accordingly, the judgment is
Affirmed

MR. JUSTICE POWELL, with whom the CHIEF JUSTICE, MR. JUSTICE BLACKMUN, and MR. JUSTICE REHNQUIST join, dissenting.
The Court today invalidates an Ohio statute that permits student suspensions from school without a hearing "for not more than ten days."

The Court's decision rests on the premise that, under Ohio law, education is a property interest protected by the Fourteenth Amendment's due-process clause and therefore that any suspension requires notice and a hearing. In my view, a student's interest in education is not infringed by a suspension within the limited period prescribed by Ohio law. Moreover, to the extent that there may be some arguable infringement, it is too speculative, transitory, and insubstantial to justify imposition of a *constitutional* rule.

The Court thus disregards the basic structure of Ohio law in posturing this case as if Ohio had conferred an unqualified right to education, thereby compelling the school authorities to conform to due-process procedures in imposing the most routine discipline.

The Ohio suspension statute allows no serious or significant infringement of education. It authorizes only a maximum suspension of eight school days, less than 5% of the normal 180-day school year. Absences of such limited duration will rarely affect a pupil's opportunity to learn or his scholastic performance. Indeed, the record in this case reflects no educational injury to appellees. Each completed the semester in which the suspension occurred and performed at least as well as he had in previous years. Despite the Court's unsupported speculation that a suspended student could be "seriously damaged," there is no factual showing of any such damage to appellees.

Today's opinion holds in effect that government infringement of any interest to which a person is entitled, no

matter what the interest or how inconsequential the infringement, requires *constitutional* protection. As it
is difficult to think of any less consequential infringement than suspension
of a junior high school student for a
single day, it is equally difficult to
perceive any principled limit to the
new reach of procedural due process.

CASE QUESTIONS

1. Do students in a public or private institution have only a *privilege* to
continue their education in that institution, or do they have a *right* to do
so?
2. What minimum standards of procedure do you think should be mandatory in the review of student discipline?
3. If a student's presence endangers persons or property or threatens
disruption of the academic process, should prior notice be given and a
hearing be held before the student is suspended?

SUGGESTED READINGS

Friedman, *Constitutional and Statutory Challenges to Discrimination in
    Employment Based on Sexual Orientation,* 64 IOWA L. REV. 527 (1979).
Ransom, *Procedural Due Process in Public Schools: The "Thicket" of
    Goss v. Lopez,* 1976 WIS. L. REV. 934.
Smith, *Analysis of When Juveniles Must Be Afforded Due Process Rights,*
    58 NEB. L. REV. 136 (1979).
Note, *Beyond the Schoolhouse Gate: Protecting the Off-Campus First
    Amendment Freedoms of Students,* 59 NEB. L. REV. 790 (1980).

Criminal and Civil Law

The distinction between criminal and civil law is a very important concept in our legal system. This text deals primarily with civil law. A civil
suit involves a dispute between private individuals involving either a
breach of an agreement or a breach of a duty imposed by law. A criminal
action is brought by the government against an individual who has
allegedly committed a crime. Crimes are classified as treason, felonies,
and misdemeanors, depending on the punishment attached to the crime.
Treason is a crime defined only by the Constitution, art. III, § 3, clause 1.

Criminal and Civil Law

Law

Criminal
government action against individual
for an act against society

Substantive
rules concerning conduct that is
offensive to society

Procedural
rules governing the proceedings in
determining guilt of the accused

Misdemeanors
less serious crimes
that could involve
imprisonment

Felonies
offenses punishable
by death or by
imprisonment

Treason
a crime defined by the
U.S. Constitution

Civil
dispute between private individuals
(sometimes the government is a party)

Substantive
rules concerning the duty owed by
one individual to another

Procedural
rules governing the proceedings in
deciding the dispute between the
individuals

Other
other duties that
may be imposed by
constitution, statutes,
or property rights

Contract
duty imposed by
agreement

Tort
duty imposed by law

To commit treason—levying war against the United States, or adhering to or giving aid or comfort to its enemies—there must be an overt act and the intent to commit treason. A *felony* is a crime that is classified by statute of the place in which it is committed. That is, the severity of the punishment for a felony varies from place to place. A felony is generally regarded as being any criminal offense for which a defendant may be imprisoned for more than one year, or executed. One determines whether a crime is a felony according to the sentence that might lawfully be imposed, not according to the sentence actually ordered. Felonies do not include *misdemeanors*, which are offenses that are generally punishable by a maximum term of imprisonment of less than one year.

In a civil suit, the court attempts to remedy the controversy between individuals by determining their legal rights, awarding money damages to the injured party, or directing one party to do or refrain from doing a specific act. Since a crime is an act against society, the criminal court punishes a guilty defendant by imposing a fine or imprisonment or both.

Criminal proceedings are completely separate and distinct from civil action. Rules of court procedure differ. In order to meet the burden of proof to find a person guilty of a crime, guilt must be proved beyond a reasonable doubt. The standard in a civil case—preponderance of evidence—is a lesser degree than "beyond a reasonable doubt." When the same act gives rise to both a criminal proceeding and a civil suit, the actions are completely independent of each other.

Katko v. Briney
183 N.W.2d 657
Supreme Court of Iowa
February 9, 1971

MOORE, CHIEF JUSTICE
The primary issue presented here is whether an owner may protect personal property in an unoccupied boarded-up farmhouse against trespassers and thieves by a spring gun capable of inflicting death or serious injury.

We are not here concerned with a man's right to protect his home and members of his family. Defendants' home was several miles from the scene of the incident to which we refer *infra*.

Plaintiff's action is for damages resulting from serious injury caused by a shot from a 20-gauge spring shotgun set by defendants in a bedroom of an old farmhouse which had been uninhabited for several years. Plaintiff and his companion, Marvin McDonough, had broken and entered the house to find and steal old bottles and dated fruit jars which they considered antiques.

At defendant's request, plaintiff's action was tried to a jury consisting of residents of the community where defendants' property was located. The jury returned a verdict for plaintiff and against defendants for $20,000 actual and $10,000 punitive damages.

After careful consideration of defendants' motions for judgment notwithstanding the verdict and for new trial, the experienced and capable trial judge overruled them and entered judgment on the verdict. Thus we have this appeal by defendants.

Most of the facts are not disputed. In 1957 defendant Bertha L. Briney inherited her parents' farmland in Mahaska and Monroe counties. Included was an 80-acre tract in southwest Mahaska County where her grandparents and parents had lived. No one occupied the house thereafter. Her husband, Edward, attempted to care for the land. He kept no farm machinery thereon. The outbuildings became dilapidated.

For about ten years, 1957 to 1967, there occurred a series of trespassing and housebreaking events with loss of some household items, the breaking of windows, and "messing up of the property in general." The latest occurred June 8, 1967, prior to the event on July 16, 1967, herein involved.

Defendants through the years boarded up the windows and doors in an attempt to stop the intrusions. They had posted "no trespass" signs on the land several years before 1967. The nearest one was 35 feet from the house. On June 11, 1967, defendants set a "shotgun trap" in the north bedroom. After Mr. Briney cleaned and oiled his 20-gauge shotgun, the power of which he was well aware, defendants took it to the old house where they secured it to an iron bed with the barrel pointed at the bedroom door. It was rigged with wire from the doorknob to the gun's trigger so it would fire when the door was opened. Briney first pointed the gun so an intruder would be hit in the stomach but at Mrs. Briney's suggestion it was lowered to hit the legs. He admitted he did so "because I was mad and tired of being tormented" but he "did not intend to injure anyone." He gave no explanation of why he used a loaded shell and set it to hit a person already in the house. Tin was nailed over the bedroom window. The spring gun could not be seen from the outside. No warning of its presence was posted.

Plaintiff lived with his wife and worked regularly as a gasoline station attendant in Eddyville, seven miles from the old house. He had observed it for several years while hunting in the area and considered it as being abandoned. He knew it had long been uninhabited. In 1967 the area around the house was covered with high weeds. Prior to July 16, 1967, plaintiff and McDonough had been to the premises and found several old bottles and fruit jars which they took and added to their collection of antiques. On the latter day about 9:30 P.M. they made a second trip to the Briney property. They entered the old house by removing a board from a porch window which was without glass. While McDonough was looking around the kitchen area, plaintiff went to another part of the house. As he started to open the north bedroom door, the shotgun went off, striking him in the right leg above the ankle bone. Much of his leg, including part of the tibia, was blown away. Only by McDonough's assistance was plaintiff able to get out of the house. After crawling some distance, he was put in his vehicle and rushed to a doctor and then to a hospital. He remained in the hospital 40 days.

Plaintiff's doctor testified he seriously considered amputation, but eventually the healing process was successful. Some weeks after his release from the hospital, plaintiff returned to work on crutches. He was required to keep the injured leg in a cast for approximately a year and wear a special brace for another year. He continued to suffer pain during this period.

There was undenied medical testimony plaintiff had a permanent deformity, a loss of tissue, and a shortening of the leg.

The record discloses plaintiff to trial time had incurred $710 medical expense, $2056.85 for hospital service, $61.80 for orthopedic service and $750 as loss of earnings. In addition thereto the trial court submitted to the jury the question of damages for pain and suffering and for future disability.

Plaintiff testified he knew he had no right to break and enter the house with intent to steal bottles and fruit jars therefrom. He further testified he had entered a plea of guilty to larceny in the nighttime of property of less than $20 value from a private building. He stated he had been fined $50 and costs and paroled during good behavior from a 60-day jail sentence. Other than minor traffic charges, this was plaintiff's first brush with the law. On this civil case appeal, it is not our prerogative to review the disposition made of the criminal charge against him.

The main thrust of defendants' defense in the trial court and on this appeal is that "the law permits use of a spring gun in a dwelling or warehouse for the purpose of preventing the unlawful entry of a burglar or thief." They repeated this contention in their exceptions to the trial court's instructions 2, 5, and 6. They took no exception to the trial court's statement of the issues or to other instructions.

In the statement of issues, the trial court stated plaintiff and his companion committed a felony when they broke and entered defendants' house. In instruction 2, the court referred to the early case history of the use of spring guns and stated under the law their use was prohibited except to prevent the commission of felonies of violence and where human life is in danger. The instruction included a statement breaking and entering is not a felony of violence.

Instruction 5 stated: "You are hereby instructed that one may use reasonable force in the protection of his property, but such right is subject to the qualification that one may not use such means of force as will take human life or inflict great bodily injury. Such is the rule even though the injured party is a trespasser and is in violation of the law himself."

Instruction 6 stated: "An owner of premises is prohibited from willfully or intentionally injuring a trespasser by means of force that either takes life or inflicts great bodily injury. And therefore a person owning a premise is prohibited from setting out 'spring guns' and like dangerous devices which will likely take life or inflict great bodily injury, for the purpose of harming trespassers. The fact that the trespasser may be acting in violation of the law does not change the rule. The only time when such conduct of setting a 'spring gun' or a like dangerous device is justified would be when the trespasser was committing a felony of violence or a felony punishable by death, or where the trespasser was endangering human life by his act.''

Instruction 7, to which defendants made no objection or exception, stated: ''To entitle the plaintiff to recover from compensatory damages, the burden of proof is upon him to establish by a preponderance of the evidence each and all of the following propositions:

''1. That defendants erected a shotgun trap in a vacant house on land owned by defendant, Bertha L. Briney, on or about June 11, 1967, which fact was known only by them, to protect household goods from trespassers and thieves.

''2. That the force used by defendants was in excess of that force reasonably necessary and which persons are entitled to use in the protection of their property.

''3. That plaintiff was injured and damaged and the amount thereof.

''4. That plaintiff's injuries and damages resulted directly from the discharge of the shotgun trap which was set and used by defendants.''

The overwhelming weight of authority, both textbook and case law, supports the trial court's statement of the applicable principles of law.

Prosser on Torts, third edition, pages 116–118, states that:

the law has always placed a higher value upon human safety than upon mere rights in property. It is the accepted rule that there is no privilege to use any force calculated to cause death or serious bodily injury to repel the threat to land or chattels, unless there is also such a threat to the defendant's personal safety as to justify a self-defense. . . . Spring guns and other man-killing devices are not justifiable against a mere trespasser, or even a petty thief. They are privileged only against those upon whom the landowner, if he were present in person, would be free to inflict injury of the same kind.

Restatement of Torts, §85, page 180, states that:

The value of human life and limbs, not only to the individual concerned but also to society, so outweighs the interest of a possessor of land in excluding from it those whom he is not willing to admit thereto that a possessor of land has, as is stated in §79, no privilege to use force intended or likely to cause death or serious harm against another whom the possessor sees about to enter his premises or meddle with his chattel, unless the intrusion threatens death or serious bodily harm to the occupiers or users of the premises. . . . A possessor of land cannot do indirectly and by a mechanical device that which, were he present, he could not do immediately and in person. Therefore, he cannot gain a privilege to install, for the purpose of protecting his land from intrusions harmless to the lives and limbs of the occupiers or users of it, a mechanical device whose only purpose is to inflict death or serious harm upon such as may intrude, by giving notice of his intention to inflict, by mechanical means and indirectly, harm which he could not, even after request, inflict directly were he present.

In *Hooker v. Miller*, 37 Iowa 613, we held defendant vineyard owner liable for damages resulting from a spring gun shot, although plaintiff was a trespasser and there to steal grapes. At pages 614, 615, this statement is made: "This court has held that a mere trespass against property other than a dwelling is not a sufficient justification to authorize the use of a deadly weapon by the owner in its defense; and that if death results in such a case it will be murder, though the killing be actually necessary to prevent the trespass. *State v. Vance*, 17 Iowa 138." At page 617 this court said: "[T]respassers and other inconsiderable violators of the law are not to be visited by barbarous punishments or prevented by inhuman inflictions of bodily injuries."

The facts in *Allison v. Fiscus*, 156 Ohio 120, 100 N.E.2d 237, decided in 1951, are very similar to the case at bar. There plaintiff's right to damages was recognized for injuries received when he feloniously broke a door latch and started to enter defendant's warehouse with intent to steal. As he entered, a trap of two sticks of dynamite buried under the doorway by defendant owner was set off and plaintiff seriously injured. The court held the question whether a particular trap was justified as a use of reasonable and necessary force against a trespasser engaged in the commission of a felony should have been submitted to the jury. The Ohio Supreme Court recognized plaintiff's right to recover punitive or exemplary damages in addition to compensatory damages.

In *United Zinc & Chemical Co. v. Britt*, 258 U.S. 268, 275, the Court states: "The liability for spring guns and mantraps arises from the fact that the defendant has . . . expected the trespasser and prepared an injury that is no more justified than if he had held the gun and fired it."

In addition to civil liability, many jurisdictions hold a landowner criminally liable for serious injuries or homicide caused by spring guns or other set devices. *See State v. Childers*, 133 Ohio 508, 14 N.E.2d 767 (melon thief shot by spring gun); *Pierce v. Commonwealth*, 135 Va. 635, 115 S.E. 686 (policeman killed by spring gun when he opened unlocked front door of defendant's shoe repair shop); *State v. Marfaudille*, 48 Wash. 117, 92 P. 939 (murder conviction for death from spring gun set in a trunk); *State v. Beckham*, 306 Mo. 566, 267 S.W. 817 (boy killed by spring gun attached to window of defendant's chili stand); *State v. Green*, 118 S.C. 279, 110 S.E. 145, 19 (intruder shot by spring gun when he broke and entered vacant house).

In Wisconsin, Oregon, and England, the use of spring guns and similar devices is specifically made unlawful by statute. 44 A.L.R., §3, 386, 388.

The legal principles stated by the trial court in instructions 2, 5, and 6 are well established and supported by the authorities cited and quoted *supra*. There is no merit in defendants' objections and exceptions thereto. Defendants' various motions based on the same reasons stated in exceptions to instructions were properly overruled.

Plaintiff's claim and the jury's allowance of punitive damages, under the trial court's instructions relating thereto, were not at any time or in any manner challenged by defendants in the trial court as not allowable. We therefore are not presented with the problem of whether the $10,000 award should be allowed to stand.

We express no opinion as to whether punitive damages are allowable in this type of case. If defendants' attorneys wanted that issue decided, it was their duty to raise it in the trial court.

The rule is well established that we will not consider a contention not raised in the trial court. In other words, we are a court of review and will not consider a contention raised for the first time in this court.

Under our law, punitive damages are not allowed as a matter of right. When malice is shown or when a defendant acted with wanton and reckless disregard of the rights of others, punitive damages may be allowed as punishment to the defendant and as a deterrent to others. Although not meant to compensate a plaintiff, the result is to increase his recovery. He is the fortuitous beneficiary of such an award simply because there is no one else to receive it.

The jury's findings of fact, including a finding that defendants acted with malice and with wanton and reckless disregard, as required for an allowance of punitive or exemplary damages, are supported by substantial evidence. We are bound thereby.

This opinion is not to be taken or construed as authority that the allowance of punitive damages is or is not proper under circumstances such as exist here. We hold only that question of law not having been properly raised cannot in this case be resolved.

Study and careful consideration of defendants' contentions on appeal reveal no reversible error.

Affirmed

Larson, Justice, dissenting.
I respectfully dissent, first, because the majority wrongfully assumes that by installing a spring gun in the bedroom of their unoccupied house the defendants intended to shoot any intruder who attempted to enter the room. Under the record presented here, that was a fact question. Unless it is held that these property owners are liable for any injury to an intruder from such a device regardless of the intent with which it is installed, liability under these pleadings must rest on two definite issues of fact. That is, did the defendants intend to shoot the invader, and if so, did they employ unnecessary and unreasonable force against him?

It is my feeling that the majority oversimplifies the impact of this case on the law, not only in this but other jurisdictions, and that it has not thought through all the ramifications of this holding.

There being no statutory provisions governing the right of an owner to defend his property by the use of a spring gun or other like device, or of a criminal invader to recover punitive damages when injured by such an instrumentality while breaking into the building of another, our interest and attention are directed to what should be the court determination of public policy in these matters. On both issues we are faced with a case of first impression. We should accept the task and clearly establish the law in this jurisdiction hereafter. I would hold there is no absolute liability for injury to a criminal intruder by setting up such a device on his property. Unless done with an intent to kill or seriously injure the intruder, I would absolve the owner from liability other than for negligence. I would also hold the court had no jurisdiction to allow punitive damages when the intruder was engaged in a serious criminal offense such as breaking and entering with intent to steal.

CASE QUESTIONS

1. Suppose that, instead of a spring gun, the Brineys had unleashed on the premises a vicious watchdog that severely injured Katko's leg. Would the result have been different? What if the watchdog were properly chained?
2. How many court suits could be brought as a result of shooting in the *Katko* case? What would the suits be for, and who would be the parties?
3. What effect did Katko's plea of guilty to larceny in a criminal suit have on the outcome of this case?
4. When may one set a spring gun and *not* be subject to liability? What can one do to protect property or life?

SUGGESTED READINGS

Angel, *Substantive Due Process and the Criminal Law*, 9 LOYOLA U.L.J. 61 (1977).
Bennett and Rowe, *Shot in the Dark—Some Reflections on the Law and Lethal Force*, 131 NEW L.J. (1981).
Hall, *Interrelation of Criminal Law and Torts*, 43 COLUM. L. REV. 753 (1943).
Harlow, *Self-Defense: Public Right or Private Privilege?* 1974 CRIM. L. REV. 528.
Levy, *Crime and Punishment*, 130 NEW L.J. 79 (1980).
Note, *Criminal Law: Private Rights and Public Interests in the Balance*, 20 W. & M.L. REV. 655 (1979).

A person can become civilly liable by accidentally injuring another person. However, a court cannot find a defendant guilty of a crime without (1) proof that the defendant committed it and (2) proof that the defendant had the requisite state of mind (*mens rea*). Statutes defining crimes normally include the culpability required. When the culpability is not specified, the court may infer it. The required culpability will be either intentional, knowing, reckless, or negligent, depending on the crime. Before a defendant can be found guilty, state of mind and actual commission of the crime must each be proved beyond a reasonable doubt. Defendants know their own states of mind. But the Fifth Amendment protects the accused against self-incrimination. Under this amendment, a defendant has the privilege of choosing whether to testify, whether the case is being tried under federal or state law. Therefore, the prosecution will try to infer a state of mind from the defendants' actions.

People v. Aaron
409 Mich. 672, 299 N.W.2d 304
Supreme Court of Michigan
November 24, 1980

FITZGERALD, JUSTICE
In this case we must decide whether Michigan has a felony-murder rule that allows the element of malice required for murder to be satisfied by the intent to commit the underlying felony or whether malice must be otherwise found by the trier of fact.

Defendant Aaron was convicted of first-degree felony murder as a result of a homicide committed during the perpetration of an armed robbery. The jury was instructed that they could convict defendant of first-degree murder if they found that defendant killed the victim during the commission or attempted commission of an armed robbery.

If one had to choose the most basic principle of the criminal law in general, it would be that criminal liability for causing a particular result is not justified in the absence of some culpable mental state in respect to that result. The most fundamental characteristic of the felony-murder rule violates this basic principle, in that it punishes all homicides committed in the perpetration or attempted perpetration of proscribed felonies—whether intentional, unintentional or acciden-

tal—without the necessity of proving the relation between the homicide and the perpetrator's state of mind. This is most evident when a killing is done by one of a group of co-felons. The felony-murder rule completely ignores the concept of determination of guilt on the basis of individual misconduct.

The felony-murder rule's most egregious violation of basic rules of culpability occurs when felony murder is categorized as first-degree murder. All other murders carrying equal punishment require a showing of premeditation, deliberation, and willfulness, while felony murder requires a showing of intent to do only the underlying felony. Although the purpose of our degree statutes is to punish more severely the more culpable forms of murder, an accidental killing that occurs during the perpetration of a felony would be punished more severely than a second-degree murder requiring intent to kill, intent to cause great bodily harm, or wantonness and willfulness. Furthermore, a defendant charged with felony murder is permitted to raise defenses only to the mental element of the felony, thus precluding certain defenses available to a defendant charged with premeditated murder who may raise defenses to the mental element of murder (for example, self-defense, accident). Certainly, felony murder is no more reprehensible than premeditated murder.

Little compassion may be felt for the

criminal whose innocent victim dies. However, this does not justify ignoring the principles underlying our system of criminal law. The United States Supreme Court has reaffirmed on several occasions the importance of the relationship between culpability and criminal liability. "The criminal law . . . is concerned not only with guilt or innocence in the abstract, but also with the degree of criminal culpability." *Mullaney v. Wilbur*, 421 U.S. 684 (1975).

In order to understand the operation of any state's felony-murder doctrine, initially it is essential to understand how that state defines murder and malice. In Michigan, murder is not statutorily defined. This court early defined the term as follows: "Murder is where a person of sound memory and discretion unlawfully kills any reasonable creature in being, in the peace of the state, with malice prepense or aforethought, either express or implied." *People v. Potter*, 5 Mich. 1 (1858). Thus malice aforethought is the "grand criterion" that elevates a homicide, which may be innocent or criminal, to murder.

We do not believe that the felony-murder doctrine abolishes the requirement of malice. Nor do we believe that it equates the *mens rea* of the felony with the *mens rea* required for a nonfelony murder. We construe the felony-murder doctrine as providing a separate definition of malice. The effect of the doctrine is to recognize the intent to commit the underlying felony, in itself, as a sufficient *mens rea* for murder.

We believe that it is no longer acceptable to equate the intent to commit a felony with the intent to kill, intent to do great bodily harm, or wanton and willful disregard of the likelihood that the natural tendency of a person's behavior is to cause death or great bodily harm. In *People v. Hansen*, 368 Mich. 344, 350, 118 N.W.2d 422 (1962), this court said that "malice requires an intent to cause the very harm that results or some harm of the same general nature, or an act done in wanton or willful disregard of the plaintiff and strong likelihood that such harm will result." In a charge of felony murder, it is the murder which is the harm which is being punished. A defendant who only intends to commit the felony does not intend to commit the harm that results and may or may not be guilty of perpetrating an act done in wanton or willful disregard of the plain and strong likelihood that such harm will result. Although the circumstances surrounding the commission of the felony may evidence a greater intent beyond the intent to commit the felony, or a wanton and willful act in disregard of the possible consequence of death or serious injury, the intent to commit the felony, of itself, does not connote a "Man-endangering state of mind." Hence we do not believe that it constitutes a sufficient *mens rea* to establish the crime of murder.

Accordingly, we hold today that *malice* is the intention to kill, the intention to do great bodily harm, or the wanton and willful disregard of the likelihood that the natural tendency of defendant's behavior is to cause death or great bodily harm. We further hold that malice is an essential element of any murder, as that term is judicially defined, whether the murder occurs in the course of a felony or otherwise. The facts and circumstances involved in the perpetration of a felony may evidence an intent to kill, an intent to cause great bodily harm, or a wanton and willful disregard of the likelihood that the natural tendency of defendant's behavior is to cause death or great bodily harm. However, the conclusion must be left to the jury to infer from all the evidence.

Abrogation of this rule does not make irrelevant the fact that a death occurred in the course of a felony. A jury can properly *infer* malice from evidence that a defendant intentionally set in motion a force likely to cause death or great bodily harm. Thus, whenever a killing occurs in the perpetration or attempted perpetration of an inherently dangerous felony, in order to estabish malice, the jury may consider the nature of the underlying felony and the circumstances surrounding its commission. If the jury concludes that malice existed, they can find murder. And, if they determine that the murder occurred in the perpetration or attempted perpetration of one of the enumerated felonies, by statute the murder would become first-degree murder.

Finally, in cases in which the death was purely accidental, application of the felony-murder doctrine is unjust and should be precluded. The underlying felony, of course, is still subject to punishment.

Whatever reasons can be gleaned from the dubious origin of the felony-murder rule to explain its existence, those reasons no longer exist today. The felony-murder doctrine is unnecessary and in many cases unjust, in that it violates the basic premise of individual moral culpability upon which our criminal law is based.

We hold that in order to convict a defendant of murder, as that term is defined by Michigan case law, it must be shown that he acted with intent to kill or to inflict great bodily harm or with a wanton and willful disregard of the likelihood that the natural tendency of his behavior is to cause death or great bodily harm. We further hold that the issue of malice must always be submitted to the jury.

In *Aaron*, the judgment of conviction of second-degree murder is reversed. This case is remanded to the trial court for a new trial.

CASE QUESTIONS

1. What is the effect of the felony-murder doctrine?
2. What is the policy reason for requiring proof of a defendant's state of mind before the defendant can be convicted of a crime?
3. Why did the court hold that the "issue of malice must always be submitted to the jury"?

SUGGESTED READINGS

Elkins, *Corporations and the Criminal Law: An Uneasy Alliance*, 65 KY. L.J. 73 (1977).

Hughes, *Morals and the Criminal Law*, 71 YALE L.J. 662 (1962).

Wilson, *Shifting Burdens in Criminal Law: A Burden on Due Process*, 8 HASTINGS CONST. L.Q. 731 (1981).

Note, *Analysis of the Term "Willful" in Federal Criminal Statutes*, 51 NOTRE DAME LAW. 786 (1976).

Comment, *Rethinking the Specific–General Intent Doctrine in California Criminal Law*, 63 CALIF. L. REV. 1352 (1975).

Tort and Contract Law

A person has a right to bring a civil action against another for a wrongful act or omission that causes injury to him. The basis of the suit is a violation of some duty owed to the injured person. Such duty arises either by an agreement of the persons or by operation of law. A *suit in contract* is brought for a cause of action arising from a breach of an agreement. A *suit in tort* is maintained for injury to person, property, or reputation caused by a breach of duty imposed by law.

A *contract* is a promissory agreement between two or more persons that creates, modifies, or destroys a legal obligation. It is a deliberate engagement to do or refrain from doing some act. A *tort* is any wrongful act, not involving a breach of an agreement, for which a civil action may be maintained. There must be a violation of some duty owed to another, and such duty must arise by operation of law and not by contract.

A contractual duty is voluntarily assumed, whereas a tort duty is one imposed by law. The essence of contract law is the enforcement of a promise voluntarily made. Tort liability requires no promissory or consensual relationship. Persons enter into a contract voluntarily to create private duties for mutual advantage. Tort law establishes standards of conduct that all citizens must meet. It creates social duties among all members of society.

A tort is a civil wrong for which the injured party can recover in an action for damages. A tort can be either intentional or unintentional. An intentional tort may result in a criminal action as well as a civil action, as in the case of *Katko v. Briney*. An unintentional tort gives rise only to a civil action. An unintentional tort occurs when a person accidentally breaches a duty imposed by law. Torts will be discussed more fully in Chapter XI.

Those duties that we voluntarily impose on ourselves take the form of contracts. In the legal sense, the term *contract* does not mean the tangible document that contains evidence of an agreement, but the legally enforceable agreement itself. A contract may take many forms: oral, written, express (explicit terms), or implied (inferred from the persons' actions).

There are three parts to a contract: consideration, offer, and acceptance. *Consideration* is the inducement to enter into an agreement. An *offer* is a communication of a promise, with a statement of what is expected in return. An offer is made with the intention of creating an enforceable legal obligation. *Acceptance* is the manifestation of assent to the terms of the offer. A contract is a legally enforceable agreement containing one or more promises. Not every promise is a contract; only a promise enforceable by law is a contract. If a contract is breached, the person who fails to perform the obligation is liable for breach of contract.

Marvin v. Marvin
134 Cal. Rptr. 815, 557 P.2d 106
Supreme Court of California
December 27, 1976

TOBRINER, JUSTICE
During the past 15 years, there has been a substantial increase in the number of couples living together without marrying. Such nonmarital relationships lead to legal controversy when one partner dies or the couple separates. We take this opportunity to declare the principles that should govern distribution of property acquired in a nonmarital relationship.

We conclude that the courts should enforce express contracts between nonmarital partners except to the extent that the contract is explicitly founded on the consideration of meretricious sexual services.

In the instant case, plaintiff, Michelle Marvin, and defendant, Lee Marvin, lived together for seven years without marrying. All property acquired during this period was taken in defendant's name. Plaintiff sued to enforce a contract under which she was entitled to half the property and to support payments. The trial court granted judgment on the pleadings for defen-dant, thus leaving him with all property accumulated by the couple during their relationship.

Plaintiff avers that in October of 1964 she and defendant "entered into an oral agreement" that while "the parties lived together they would combine their efforts and earnings and would share equally any and all property accumulated as a result of their efforts, whether individual or combined." Furthermore, they agreed to "hold themselves out to the general public as husband and wife" and that "plaintiff would further render her services as a companion, homemaker, housekeeper and cook to . . . defendant."

Shortly thereafter plaintiff agreed to "give up her lucrative career as an entertainer and singer" in order to "devote her full time to defendant as a companion, homemaker, housekeeper and cook." In return defendant agreed to "provide for all of plaintiff's financial support and needs for the rest of her life."

Plaintiff alleges that she lived with defendant from October of 1964 through May of 1970 and fulfilled her obligations under the agreement. During this period the parties as a result of their efforts and earnings acquired in defendant's name substantial real and personal property, including motion picture rights worth over $1 million. In May of 1970, however, defendant compelled plaintiff to leave his household. He continued to support plaintiff until November of 1971, but thereafter refused to provide further support.

On the basis of these allegations, plaintiff asserts two causes of action. The first, for declaratory relief, asks the court to determine her contract and property rights. The second seeks to impose a constructive trust on one-half of the property acquired during the course of the relationship.

In *Trutalli v. Meraviglia* (1932) 215 Cal. 698, 12 P.2d 430 we established the principle that nonmarital partners may lawfully contract concerning the ownership of property acquired during the relationship. We reaffirmed this principle in *Vallera v. Vallera* (1943) 21 Cal. 2d 681, 685, 134 P.2d 761, 763, stating that "If a man and woman [who are not married] live together as husband and wife under an agreement to pool their earnings and share equally in their joint accumulations, equity will protect the interests of each in such property."

In the case before us, plaintiff, basing her cause of action in contract on these precedents, maintains that the trial court erred in denying her a trial on the merits of her contention. Although that court did not specify the ground for its conclusion that plaintiff's contractual allegations stated no cause of action, defendant offers some four theories to sustain the ruling. We proceed to examine them.

Defendant first and principally relies on the contention that the alleged contract is so closely related to the supposed "immoral" character of the relationship between plaintiff and himself that the enforcement of the contract would violate public policy. He points to cases asserting that a contract between nonmarital partners is unenforceable if it is "involved in" an illicit relationship. A review of the numerous California decisions concerning contracts between nonmarital partners, however, reveals that the courts have not employed such broad and uncertain standards to strike down contracts. The decisions instead disclose a narrower and more precise standard: A contract between nonmarital partners is unenforceable only to the extent that it explicitly rests on the immoral and illicit consideration of meretricious sexual services.

Although the past decisions hover over the issue in the somewhat wispy form of the figures of a Chagall painting, we can abstract from those decisions a clear and simple rule. The fact that a man and woman live together without marriage, and engage in a sexual relationship, does not in itself invalidate agreements between them relating to their earnings, property, or expenses. Neither is such an agreement invalid merely because the parties may have contemplated the creation or continuation of a nonmarital relationship when they entered into it. Agreements between nonmarital partners fail only to the extent that they rest on a consideration of meretricious sexual services. Thus the rule asserted by defendant, that a contract fails if it is "involved in" or made "in contemplation" of a nonmarital relationship, cannot be reconciled with the decisions.

Defendant secondly relies on the ground suggested by the trial court: that the 1964 contract violated public policy because it impaired the community property rights of Betty Marvin, defendant's lawful wife. Defendant points out that his earnings while living apart from his wife before rendition of the interlocutory decree were community property under 1964 statutory law and that defendant's agreement with plaintiff purported to transfer to her a half interest in that community property. But whether or not defendant's contract with plaintiff exceeded his authority as manager of the community property, defendant's argument fails for the reason that an improper transfer of community property is not void *ab initio*, but merely voidable at the instance of the aggrieved spouse.

In the present case Betty Marvin, the aggrieved spouse, had the opportunity to assert her community property rights in the divorce action. The interlocutory and final decrees in that action fix and limit her interest. Enforcement of the contract between plaintiff and defendant against property awarded to defendant by the divorce decree will not impair any right of Betty's, and thus is not on that account violative of public policy.

Defendant's third contention is noteworthy for the lack of authority advanced in its support. He contends that enforcement of the oral agreement between plaintiff and himself is barred by Civil Code section 5134, which provides that "all contracts for marriage settlements must be in writing. . . ." A marriage settlement, however, is an agreement in contemplation of marriage in which each party agrees to release or modify the property rights that would otherwise arise from the marriage. The contract at issue here does not conceivably fall within that definition, and thus is beyond the compass of section 5134.

Defendant finally argues that enforcement of the contract is barred by Civil Code section 43.5, subdivision (d), which provides that "No cause of action arises for . . . [b]reach of a promise of marriage." This rather strained contention proceeds from the premise that a promise of marriage impliedly includes a promise to support and to pool property acquired after marriage to the conclusion that pooling and support agreements not part of or accompanied by promise of marriage are barred by the section. We conclude that section 43.5 is not reasonably susceptible to the interpretation advanced by defendant, a conclusion demonstrated by the fact that since section 43.5 was enacted in 1939, numerous cases have enforced pooling agreements between nonmarital partners, and in none did court or counsel refer to section 43.5.

In summary, we base our opinion on the principle that unmarried adults who voluntarily live together and engage in sexual relations are nonetheless as competent as any other persons to contract respecting their earnings and property rights. Of course, they cannot lawfully contract to pay for the performance of sexual services, for such a contract is, in essence, an agreement for prostitution and unlawful for that reason. But they may agree to pool their earnings and to hold all property acquired during the relationship in accord with the law governing community property. Conversely they may agree that each partner's earnings and the property acquired from those earnings remain the separate property of the earning partner. So long as the agreement does not rest on illicit meretricious consideration, the parties may order their economic affairs as they choose. No policy precludes the courts from enforcing such agreements.

In the present instance, plaintiff alleges that the parties agreed to pool their earnings, that they contracted to share equally in all property acquired, and that defendant agreed to support plaintiff. The terms of the contract as alleged do not rest on any unlawful consideration. We therefore conclude that the complaint furnishes a suitable basis on which the trial court can render declaratory relief. The trial court consequently erred in granting defendant's motion for judgment on the pleadings.[2]

CASE QUESTIONS

1. If there had never been an *express* agreement between the parties, how could plaintiff have recovered half the property?
2. Would the Supreme Court of California have come to the same decision if the parties had agreed to prorate the division of property on the basis of the number of times they had sexual relations during the time they lived together? What if Lee Marvin promised to divide the property but plaintiff had promised nothing in exchange?
3. If the plaintiff had sought money damages from the defendant for defaming her reputation or striking her or negligently injuring her, could she have recovered in tort or in contract?

SUGGESTED READINGS

Childers and Jennings, *Legal Theories Available for a* Marvin *Case*, 3 FAM. ADVOC. 30 (1980).

MacNeil, *Essays on the Nature of Contract*, 10 N.C. CENTRAL L.J. 159 (1979).

Note, 90 HARV. L. REV. 1708 (1977).

Comment, *Contractual Relations: When Are They Also a Tort?* 28 BAYLOR L. REV. 687 (1976).

---

[2] Michelle Triola Marvin and Lee Marvin had their trial. The trial judge, Arthur Marshall, denied that Michelle had an explicit or implied contract with Lee that entitled her to a portion of his property. Even though the judge reached this decision, he awarded her $104,000 "for rehabilitation purposes" to re-educate herself and to learn a new profession. On appeal, the California Court of Appeal for the Second District nullified Michelle Triola's award of $104,000. However, the precedent that unmarried persons may sue each other, upon separation, for distribution of property was not disturbed by the 2–1 decision. —*Ed.*

Property

Real Property

Property includes real and personal property. *Real property*, which is synonymous with real estate, consists of land and things that are permanently attached to land. The law of real property has developed out of concern for settling disputes over the ownership of land and things attached to the land in an orderly manner. Real property is distinguishable from *personal property* in that real property is generally immovable. This sets it apart from money, goods, and movable chattels, which fall under personal property. The laws that govern real property in America have their origins in medieval England.

An *estate* in land is the amount of interest a person has in land, or the manner in which the person may hold and dispose of the land. An *easement* and a *license* are interests in land that do not amount to an estate, but nevertheless have an impact on how the owner can use the land. A landowner's property may increase in value as a result of being benefited by an incidental interest. Or a use of the property may be restricted, thereby benefiting another person, not necessarily the landowner.

An *easement* is a nonpossessory interest in land that gives a person a privilege to enter onto land of another and have limited use or enjoyment of that land. Easements are of less interest than an estate in land, in that easements usually allow the land to be used for a specific purpose, whereas estates provide for a general use of the land, with possible limitations. An *affirmative easement* might allow a person to lay pipeline across one's land, or merely confer a right to walk across the land. A *negative easement* would exist if neighbors were forbidden to burn trash on their own property, or to construct multistory buildings on it. An easement may also be created by *eminent domain*. This happens when the government decides that public interest requires an easement, and justly compensates the landowner for that easement.

A *license* can be distinguished from an easement in that a license is a temporary grant of authority to perform certain acts on the land of another, as opposed to being an actual interest in the land. Licenses to hunt or fish on another's property merely prevent the licensee from becoming a trespasser.

Personal Property

Practically every person in the United States owns personal property. *Personal property* consists of all tangible physical objects that are not land (or attached permanently to the land) and all *in*tangible rights, duties, and obligations arising out of the ownership of physical objects. Personal property also includes intangible property, such as money, stocks, and bonds which are paper substitutes for certain ownership rights. Thus personal property includes not only a physical or representative object, but also the right to own, use, sell, or dispose of it as regulated by law.

Whether personal property is classed as tangible or intangible usually depends on the physical nature of the property. If the property exists as an object, it is tangible. However, if it exists in a representative capacity, then it is intangible.

The term *property* means not only a physical object, but also a set of legal rights defining the bounds of ownership. Tangible personal property consists of those physical objects that in and of themselves embody the rights of ownership. For example, when you buy a shirt at a department store, you obtain legal possession of the shirt. This entitles you to use or dispose of the shirt at your discretion. The shirt is an actual physical thing that you can possess as an object. The shirt is therefore tangible personal property. Other examples are cars, food, furniture, farm animals, and jewelry.

*In*tangible personal property is personal property that is *not* a physical object. Your ownership of intangible personal property is usually evidenced by some type of legal document setting forth the nature of your ownership rights. For example, a bank savings account is personal property. The savings account has a protected legal existence. However, it does not, in and of itself, have a physical existence. The savings account is represented by the passbook that the bank issues to the saver. The passbook, therefore, is evidence of the saver's right to title and right to possession of the funds contained in the particular account. Other examples of intangible personal property are currency, bonds, stock certificates, patents, copyrights, and promissory notes.

An item of personal property can be the subject of both tangible and intangible property rights. For example, suppose that you buy an object, the design of which is protected by a valid federal patent. You have acquired a piece of tangible personal property that you can use and dispose of in any legal manner. One legal restriction on your right to use your property is the intangible property rights held by the patent holder. The patent holder has a legal right to prevent you from selling duplicates of the product without permission, although you have a legal right to possession of the object. Thus both the patent holder and the purchaser have personal property rights to the same object. These rights are protected by the courts.

Davis v. Davis
495 S.W.2d 607
Court of Civil Appeals of Texas
May 10, 1973

CLAUDE WILLIAMS, CHIEF JUSTICE

The sole question presented by this appeal is the validity of that portion of the trial court's judgment in this divorce action wherein the court decreed to the wife a proportionate part of the serviceman husband's future military retirement pay benefits which will not become payable to him under appropriate federal statutes until completion of 20 years' service in 1983, or 11 years after the divorce decree. We hold that, inasmuch as the rights of the husband to the retirement benefits provided by federal statutes had not been acquired at the time of divorce, such did not constitute community property subject to be apportioned by the trial court.

Thomas D. Davis entered the military service of the United States on July 12, 1963. Since that time he has served continuously as an officer on active duty in the United States Air Force. Captain Davis and Sandra Rose Davis were married on July 3, 1965. On September 9, 1971, the husband instituted an action for divorce. The parties had not reached an agreement concerning possible retirement benefits which the husband might receive in the future from the United States Air Force. It was stipulated that this matter would be submitted to the court for decision.

As a member of the United States Air Force, he did not contribute anything to his retirement benefits. To be eligible for receiving retirement pay from the United States Air Force, he must complete a minimum of 20 years on active

duty. Also, during that period of time, he must be continuously promoted, which would require a high standard of performance. As an officer, he could resign from the Air Force at any time. But if he did so prior to the expiration of the 20-year period, he would receive no retirement benefits.

The trial court found that Captain Davis had a total of eight and one-half years in the service as of November 24, 1971 and that of this period of time, 82 months were served during marriage to Mrs. Davis. The court also found that Captain Davis "would earn retirement benefits after 20 years' service, subject to contingent forfeitures." The trial court decided that the right to retirement benefits, though not ripened by cessation of service, is not an expectancy but a property right, and the wife is entitled to receive one-half of 82 over the total number of months served by the husband, times the benefits payable at and during retirement.

When we consider the retirement payments provided by the federal statutes in the light of the characterization of marital property, a determination of whether such retirement pay benefits are a part of the community estate and subject to be divided by the trial court must be resolved by deciding whether such retirement benefits are actually property rights acquired during marriage.

The word *property* has been the subject of many definitions by legislatures and by courts. Courts have variously defined the word property as signifying the physical corporeal thing, or denoting rights and interest. It may reasonably be construed to include obligations, rights, and other intangibles, as well as physical things. And thus the word property means not only the thing possessed, that is, the physical corporeal thing, but also rights in the physical corporeal thing which are created and sanctioned by law. The word property embraces everything which is or may be the subject of ownership, whether a legal ownership, or whether beneficial, or a private ownership.

In the light of these definitions, it is quite evident that the interest acquired by a serviceman in retirement benefits may constitute community property subject to be divided by a divorce court. The question then presents itself: At what point in time was the property "acquired"? The answer to this question is obviously crucial because of the provisions of §5.01 of the Family Code, which expressly states that community property is that which is "acquired" by either spouse during marriage.

The right to retirement benefits is vested upon the date the requisite tenure of service is completed by the serviceman. The completion of 20 years of active duty by appellant would operate as the only condition precedent to the acquisition of the vested right to participate in the retirement benefits. A community property status would attach with the completion of a prescribed number of years in the service and would not depend upon the officer's actual election to retire.

We hold that at the time of the divorce decree in this case, Captain Thomas D. Davis and his wife Sandra Rose Davis had not acquired community property rights in military retirement pay benefits which might possibly become payable to Captain Davis by virtue of his military service in 1983, pursuant to appropriate federal statutes. Since said benefits were not community property subject to division, the trial court was in error in rendering a decree awarding Sandra Rose Davis any part of such potential military retirement benefits.

Reversed and rendered

Case Questions

1. How does the court define the term *property?*
2. When does a member of the military forces acquire the legal right to obtain retirement benefits in terms of such benefits being community property?

Suggested Readings

Goble, *Solar Access and Property Rights: Reply to a "Maverick" Analysis,* 12 Conn. L. Rev. 270 (1980).
Meth, *Guidelines for Sustaining the Special-Use Valuation of Property,* 8 Est. Plan. 30 (1981).

Watt, *How Much Can the Government Take?* 105 Pub. Util. Fort. 8 (1980).

Chapter Questions

1. Define the following terms:
   a. appellant   b. appellee
   c. case law   d. Constitution
   e. contract   f. criminal
   g. damages   h. defendant
   i. due process   j. injunction
   k. plaintiff   l. substantive law
   m. tort   n. trade secret
   o. trespass

2. A Cincinnati, Ohio, ordinance makes it a criminal offense for "three or more persons to assemble, except at a public meeting of citizens, on any of the sidewalks, street corners, vacant lots, or mouths of alleys, and there conduct themselves in a manner annoying to persons passing by, or occupants of adjacent buildings." Coates, a student involved in a demonstration, was arrested and convicted for the violation of this ordinance. His argument on appeal was that the ordinance on its face violated the Fourteenth Amendment. Is this a valid contention?
   Coates v. City of Cincinnati, 402 U.S. 611 (1971)

3. Mrs. Fuentes purchased a stove and stereo from Firestone Tire and Rubber Co. Payment was to be made in monthly installments over a period of time. After two-thirds of the payments were made, Mrs. Fuentes defaulted. Firestone filed an action for repossession and at the same time instructed the sheriff to seize the property pursuant to state law. The sheriff seized the property before Mrs. Fuentes even knew of Firestone's suit for repossession. Mrs. Fuentes claims that she was deprived of due process because her property was taken without notice or a hearing. What should the result be?
   Fuentes v. Shevin, 407 U.S. 67 (1972)

4. Plaintiff brought a class action on behalf of all female welfare recipients residing in Connecticut and wishing divorces. She alleged that such class was prevented from bringing divorce suits by Connecticut statutes that require payment of court fees and costs of service of process as a condition precedent to access to the courts. Plaintiff contended that such statutes violate basic due-process considerations. Is her argument valid?
   Boddie v. Connecticut, 401 U.S. 371 (1970)

5. Like many other states, Connecticut requires nonresidents of the state who are enrolled in the state university system to pay tuition and other fees at higher rates than residents of the state who are so enrolled. A Connecticut statute defined as a nonresident any unmarried student if his "legal address for any part of the one-year period immediately prior to his application for admission . . . was outside of Connecticut," or any married student if his "legal address at the time of his application for admission . . . was outside of Connecticut." The statute also provided that the "status of a student, as established at the time of his application for admission . . . shall be his status for the entire period of his attendance." Two University of Connecticut students who claimed to be residents of Connecticut were by the statute classified as nonresidents for tuition purposes. They claimed that the due-process clause does not permit Connecticut to deny an individual the opportunity to present evidence that he is a *bona fide* resident entitled to in-state rates. They are being deprived of property without due process. Is this a valid argument?
    Vlandis v. Kline, 412 U.S. 441 (1973)

6. Pursuant to an Ohio law that authorizes mayors to sit as judges in cases of ordinance violations and certain traffic offenses, the mayor of Monroeville, Ohio, convicted Clarence Ward for violation of two local ordinances and fined him $50 for each offense. The defendant was convicted under Monroeville ordinance 47–12, section 2 and 29, which are, respectively, failure to comply with a lawful order of a police officer and failure to produce a driver's license on request of a police officer. The mayor of Monroeville has wide executive powers and general supervision of all village affairs, as well as being judge and chief conservator of the peace. A large part of the village income is derived from fines, forfeitures, costs, and fees imposed by the mayor's court—about 40% of the village revenues in the past year. Ward alleges that his right to due process of law has been violated. He contends on appeal that the mayor's court is not an impartial tribunal as required by the Fourteenth Amendment, even though he has a right to a whole new trial in the county court if he wishes. Is Ward correct? Is this a violation of substantive or procedural due process? Why?
    Ward v. Village of Monroeville, Ohio, 409 U.S. 57 (1972)

7. Steve was driving home from his college classes one fine winter day when he saw a snowball coming toward his car. The snowball turned out to be a rock covered with snow, and the impact caused a dent in Steve's orange Volkswagen. Steve stopped his car, and after examining the damage, walked toward Greg, the person he thought threw the snowball. Steve asked to see Greg's gloves. Since Greg's gloves were wet, Steve assumed that Greg was the guilty party and punched him in the mouth. Jay, who was standing about ten feet away behind a

tree, was the person who actually threw the snowball. List and explain the various suits that could result from this happening.

8. Defendant set a spring gun in his barn opposite a stall used as a hen roost in order to protect his chickens from thieves. The hen roost contained only a few chickens. Deceased was killed when he trespassed upon the property and caused the gun to be discharged by disturbing a wire which was attached to the gun and was stretched across the passageway in front of the roost. Is there a possible criminal suit against the defendant? Is there a possible civil suit against the defendant?

State v. Plumlee, 177 La. 687, 149 So. 425 (1933)

9. On June 1, 1975, Ralph's car and Walt's car collided. Each was driving his own car. Walt admitted liability. Ralph and Walt were both covered by the same insurance company, XYZ Mutual. XYZ told Ralph that it would pay for his repairs. Ralph believed the company and did not bring legal action against Walt. XYZ failed to send Ralph a check and kept ignoring his inquiries. On June 1, 1977, Ralph received notice that the repairs would not be paid for. By then the statute of limitations had run out, so Ralph had no recourse against Walt. The state in which Ralph lives imposes a duty on insurance companies to act in good faith toward clients. Ralph brings an action against XYZ. Is the action in tort or contract? Explain.

See Escambia Treating Co. v. Aetna Casualty & Surety Co.. 421 F.Supp. 1367 (1976).

10. The Automatic Canteen Company of America purported to sell a particular vending machine route to the Continental Lake Vendors Corporation. Continental Lake was to supply all machines and foodstuffs, while Automatic Canteen assigned its supply contracts with customers to Continental Lake. Continental Lake defaulted on its payments to Automatic, and Automatic sued Continental Lake under local personal-property law for the debt owed it by Continental Lake. Continental Lake contended that no property ever exchanged hands. Is Continental Lake's contention correct?

Automatic Canteen Co. of America v. Wharton, 358 F.2d 587 (2d Cir., 1966)

11. The city of Tyler, under its power of eminent domain, brought a condemnation proceeding against ARP Nursery Company, the landowners. In arriving at the cash market value of the land, the trial court included small seedlings and grafted trees. These seedlings and grafted trees were planted with the purpose of being subsequently harvested and sold on the market. The city of Tyler appealed the decision, claiming that the seedlings and grafted trees should not be included in the valuation, since they constitute personal property. Should the seedlings and grafted trees be considered real property or personal property? *City of Tyler v. ARP Nursery Co. 451 S. W. 2d 809 (Tex. 1970)*

II   The Judicial System

Courts

Function

A court is a governmental body to which the administration of justice is delegated. In the United States there are 51 court systems: Each state plus the federal government has established its own. Courts are established by constitutions and acts of legislature. The legislative branch of the government has the power to establish and change courts and their procedures as long as its acts are not in violation of a constitutional provision.

Even though the 51 judicial systems are available, very few of the disputes in our society are ever brought before them. In the usual case, a dispute is settled outside the courtroom on the basis of a prediction of what a court would do if the issue were brought before it. Both the expense connected with bringing a suit and the time delay in obtaining judicial relief encourage persons to reach an agreement without using an organized court system. A court does not undertake to adjudicate a dispute by itself. It can do this only when someone brings a controversy before it. A court is without power to initiate proceedings or investigate situations.

Trial Courts

Courts are classified by function; there are trial courts and appellate courts. A trial court hears and decides controversies by determining facts and applying appropriate rules. The opposing parties to a dispute argue

State and Federal Judicial Systems

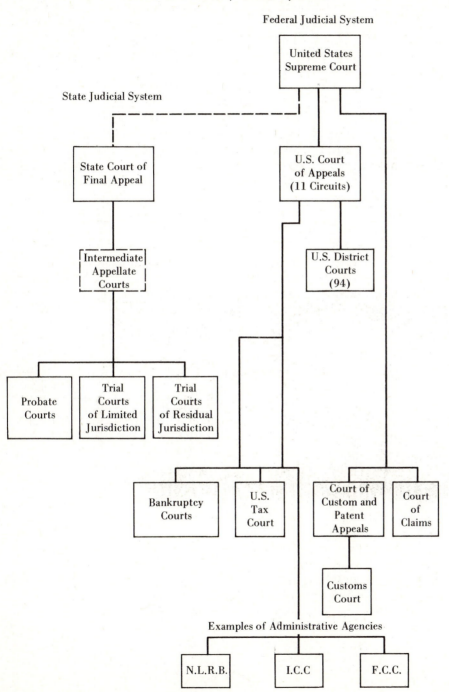

Federal Judicial System

United States
Supreme Court

State Judicial System

State Court of
Final Appeal

U.S. Court
of Appeals
(11 Circuits)

Intermediate
Appellate
Courts

U.S. District
Courts
(94)

Probate
Courts

Trial
Courts
of Limited
Jurisdiction

Trial
Courts
of Residual
Jurisdiction

Bankruptcy
Courts

U.S.
Tax
Court

Court of
Custom and
Patent
Appeals

Court
of
Claims

Customs
Court

Examples of Administrative Agencies

N.L.R.B.   I.C.C   F.C.C.

their positions by presenting arguments on the law and evidence on the facts in the form of documents and testimony from witnesses. This is done before a single judge and sometimes in the presence of a jury. When there is no jury, the judge controls the entire trial and determines the outcome. In a trial with a jury, the decision-making functions are divided between the judge and the jury. This division of responsibility provides a safeguard of checks and balances in the legal process. The judge determines the correct law to be applied and decides the questions of law. The jury decides what the facts are and applies to those facts the law as stated by the judge. The judge controls the entire litigation. The judge's actions and statements are often persuasive in the jury's decision-making process.

Sometimes the judge asks the jury to answer specific factual questions. Their answers are considered a *special verdict*. The judge applies the law to the jury's answers to reach a final judgment. When a *general verdict* is sought, the jury decides who wins and what the recovery will be.

The distinction between questions of fact and questions of law is not easily ascertained. Factual issues, which are decided by the jury, involve a determination based on the special circumstances of each case. A factual issue is presented when reasonable persons could arrive at different results in deciding what happened in an actual event. When an inference is so certain that all reasonable persons must agree on and draw the same conclusion, it becomes a question of law for the judge. The jury must resolve all questions regarding the weight of the evidence and the credibility of the witnesses. In a negligence case, for example, the jury has to decide what really happened (if the facts are disputed). The jury has to decide whether the defendant was negligent under the circumstances, and the amount of money damages to be awarded to the plaintiff. In this example, the judge's function of deciding the questions of law would involve determining the rule of duty. If there were no dispute over the facts, the judge would determine the law that applies, and interpret it.

A jury is traditionally composed of twelve persons, though some states use fewer members in some cases. They are chosen from the community at random, and their qualifications are reviewed before they are seated. At trial, they make their decision in private. The jury system is regarded as being one of the safeguards against judicial corruption. Although the jury system is an accepted part of our legal process, there is some dispute concerning the advisability of retaining it. It has been argued that juries are arbitrary, unpredictable, and subject to passion. Jury trials are time-consuming and contribute to the congestion of court dockets. A jury trial is more expensive. Those who *favor* the jury system argue that juries are less prejudiced and fairer than judges. A jury represents a cross section of the public, whereas judges, who are usually lawyers, do not. Judges may become calloused to human feelings and misery after a period of time on the bench. A jury has a fresh viewpoint. A jury discusses and argues the case and reaches its decision as a group, thus minimizing the effect of individual bias. The system allows citizens to participate in the legal process. Federal and state constitutions guarantee the right to a trial by jury, so it is not likely that right will be eliminated in the near future.

Appellate Courts

Appellate courts review the decisions of trial courts. Usually, an appeal will lie only from a final decision of a lower court. If either person in a civil action is dissatisfied with the decision of the trial court, that person may appeal the decision to an appellate court. In criminal cases, the defendant alone may appeal. The prosecution usually may not.

An appellate court's power is confined to reviewing errors committed in the court below in the case brought up on appeal. It reviews the proceedings of the trial court to ascertain whether it acted in accordance with the law. The appellate court reaches its decision by using only the record of the proceedings in the lower court, the written briefs filed by both parties to the appeal, and the parties' oral arguments given before the appellate judges. The record of the proceedings in the lower court includes the pleadings, pretrial papers, depositions, and a transcript of the trial proceedings and testimony. The court bases its decision solely on the theories argued and evidence presented in the lower court. No new arguments or proof are admissible. There are no witnesses or jury at the appellate level. The appellate court does not retry the facts of the case.

McGowan v. Story
70 Wis.2d 189, 234 N.W.2d 325
Supreme Court of Wisconsin
October 28, 1975

HEFFERNAN, JUSTICE

This negligence action for damages arose out of an accident that occurred in Monroe County on August 4, 1970. The plaintiff, Francis McGowan, was injured by an eruption of hot tar while he was in the process of transferring the hot tar mix from the tanker truck owned by his employer, the Stang Transport Company, to a distributor vehicle owned by the D. L. Gasser Construction Company. The case was tried to a jury, which returned a verdict finding the plaintiff, Francis McGowan, 50% negligent, Duane Story, the operator of the distributor truck, 20% negligent, and Story's employer, the D. L. Gasser Construction Company, 30% negligent. Since the plaintiff was found to be 50% negligent, under the law of Wisconsin he was not entitled to recover anything.

The plaintiff on this appeal argues that the trial judge committed error when he refused to instruct the jury on the effect of its answers to the special verdict questions. As a subsidiary to that issue, plaintiff argues that the case should have been submitted on a general verdict, which would have made clear to the jury the effect of its answer.

The injured plaintiff, Francis Mc-Gowan, drove a tanker truck for the Stang Transport Company. The truck driven by McGowan was used for the hauling of "emulsion," which is a substance composed of tar and a high percentage of water, and MC-5, a hot asphalt mix, which is heated to a temperature of approximately 350 degrees Fahrenheit prior to transportation. In the event that MC-5 and emulsion are allowed to mix at high temperatures, a marked reaction occurs as a result of the sudden superheating of the water in the emulsion.

The day before this accident occurred, the plaintiff delivered a load of emulsion in his tanker to the Fond du Lac area. He then returned to his home base at Green Bay with an empty tank. He stated that, while en route, he opened all the valves and cover of the tanker in order to clean it out and to dry all the emulsion in the tanker. There was evidence that, whatever effect this air drying would have, the external air would not reach a reservoir, which consisted of some piping outside of the shell of the tank proper but within the insulated sheathing of the tanker.

The next morning, the date of the accident, the same tanker truck was loaded with MC-5, which at the time of loading had a temperature of approximately 350 degrees Fahrenheit. At the time the accident occurred, the temperature of the MC-5 remained within a few degrees of that original temperature.

The plaintiff drove the tanker loaded with the hot asphalt to Sparta, where he was met by Polzin, an employee of the D. L. Gasser Construction Company which was intending to use the hot asphalt on road work. He was guided to the location where the MC-5 was to be loaded into an Etnyre blacktopper preparatory to its distribution onto the road surface.

During the transfer process, while McGowan was on the top of his tanker, and after a connection was made to the blacktopper distributor, the MC-5 in the tanker erupted, throwing the superheated tar 20 or 30 feet into the air. To avoid more serious injury, McGowan jumped from the top of the tanker onto the roadway and severely injured his right ankle.

There was conflicting evidence to explain this accident. It was contended by the plaintiff that the defendant had improperly connected the hose from the tanker to the distributor. Instead of attaching that hose to the inlet, he hooked it up to an outlet, which by pump action forced air into the tanker causing a bubbling and the subsequent geyser.

It was the contention, basically, of the defendants that the negligence was on the part of plaintiff. When the tanker hose was in the process of being connected, the defendant Story saw a quantity of liquid resembling cold pork gravy run out of the hose. Defendant Story states that, when he asked McGowan what the liquid was, he was told it was emulsion. This fact, the defendants argue, shows that emulsion was present, at least in the hose. Moreover, there was no evidence to show that opening the hatches and valves the day before would have effectively cleared the emulsion from the reservoir beneath the tank. This evidence, the defendants argue, supports the theory that the plaintiff was negligent in failing to clean the vehicle of emulsion.

The defendant's theory is that this emulsion was already superheated as a result of its location within the insulation of the tanker and, when the valve opened, permitting the hot tar to come in contact with the emulsion, an upward eruption occurred within the tanker.

On this appeal by the plaintiff, he contends that the trial court committed error which prevented a proper jury verdict.

He contends that the trial judge erred in not instructing the jury of the effect of its answers. The record shows that the plaintiff asked for a general verdict, which would have made apparent the effect of the jury's answer. Moreover, during the course of its deliberations, the jury returned to the courtroom and asked to be advised of the effect of its answers on the rights of the parties.

The trial judge declined as a matter of discretion to submit the general verdict and submitted a special verdict in the ultimate fact form. He also refused to advise the jury about the effect of its answers.

The law of this state forecloses the judge from advising the jury on the effect of its answers. We have said:

The fundamental rule in this state is that it is reversible error for either the court or counsel to inform the jury of the effect of their answer on the ultimate result of their verdict. This is true whether the jury is explicitly informed or informed by necessary implication. *Kobelinski v. Milwaukee & Suburban Transport Corp.* (1972), 56 Wis.2d 504, 520, 202 N.W.2d 415, 425.

The rationale of our present rule is explained in *Ryan v. Rockford Ins. Co.* (1890), 77 Wis. 611, 615, 616, 46 N.W. 885, 886, wherein this court said:

The purpose of thus submitting particular controverted questions of fact is to secure a direct answer free from any bias or prejudice in favor of or against either party. It has often been demonstrated in the trial of cases that the non-expert juryman is more liable than the experienced lawyer or judge to be led away from the material issues of fact involved by some collateral circumstances of little or no significance, or by sympathy, bias, or prejudice. . . .

Under our system of jurisprudence, the jury is the finder of fact and it has no function in determining how the law should be applied to the facts found. It is not the function of a jury in a case between private parties on the determination of comparative negligence to be influenced by sympathy for either party, nor should it attempt to manipulate the apportionment of negligence to achieve a result that may seem socially desirable to a single juror or to a group of jurors.

While we recognize the validity of the problem posed by the plaintiff, there is no evidence that the remedy of advising a jury of the effect of its answers would not result in jury confusion and create a situation more to be deplored than that which presently exists.

We suggest that the jury should be admonished, and impressed, that its function in a negligence case is fact-finding only and that it is not its role to usurp the legislative function under the comparative negligence law or the judicial function in interpreting the comparative negligence law. It is the role of the judge, acting under the law, and not the jury, to implement the general policies of the comparative negligence statute. We decline to consider the change in the jury function proposed by the plaintiff.

Under the law as it existed at the time of the accident, August 4, 1970, a plaintiff whose negligence was equal to that of the defendant was foreclosed from any recovery.

The recovery of the plaintiff must be based on the legislation as it existed at the time of the accident.

Judgment affirmed

CASE QUESTIONS

1. Why didn't the judge ask the jury for a general verdict in which they would just determine who wins and the amount of recovery?
2. Was the Wisconsin Supreme Court reviewing the jury's determination of the plaintiff's percentage of negligence? What exactly was it deciding?

SUGGESTED READINGS

Note, *Court Administration: The Newest Profession*, 10 DUQUESNE L. REV. 220 (1971).
Berger, *Do the Courts Communicate?* 55 JUDICATURE 318 (1972).
Wilson, *Use of Jurors*, 62 F.R.D. 211 (1974).
Slater, *System Works . . . or Does It?* 11 TRIAL, July 1975, at 36.
Anderson, *Four Unwritten Rules of Appellate Procedure*, 51 Fla. B.J. 88 (1977).

Jurisdiction

Jurisdiction is the power or authority of a court to determine the merits of a dispute and to grant relief. A court has jurisdiction when it has this power both over the subject matter of the case and over the person of the defendant or property of the case. A court has the power and the duty to determine whether it has jurisdiction over a controversy presented before it even though neither party brings it up. The determination should be made before it concerns itself with other matters involved in the case.

Subject Matter

If a case is of the sort that the court is authorized to hear, the court has jurisdiction over the subject matter. State courts of general jurisdiction are authorized to handle any subject matter. Probate courts, criminal courts, and traffic courts are examples of state courts with limited subject-matter jurisdiction. If, for example, a traffic court decided a controversy involving a probate matter, the judgment would be of no legal consequence, for that court has no jurisdiction over the subject matter. There can never be a waiver by the parties of jurisdiction over the subject matter. Occasionally, jurisdiction over the subject matter is determined by the amount involved in the controversy.

Champion v. Rakes
155 Ga. App. 134, 270 S.E.2d 272
Court of Appeals of Georgia
June 20, 1980

SOGNIER, JUDGE
This is an appeal from a judgment of the state court of Cobb County awarding Rakes $2000 general damages and $4000 punitive damages. Appellants, Ricky Joe and Marie S. Champion, filed a motion to set aside the judgment on the ground that the trial court lacked jurisdiction over the subject matter of this case. The trial court denied the motion and the Champions' appeal.

Rakes filed suit seeking $10,000 damages for personal injury and $25,000 for the willful and malicious conduct of the Champions, and as a deterrent to such conduct by them in the future. The jury returned a verdict in favor of Rakes for $2000 general damages and $4000 punitive damages.

At the time Rakes filed suit, the jurisdictional limit of the state court of Cobb County in personal-injury cases was $25,000. At the time the verdict was returned and judgment was entered, the jurisdictional limits in such cases had been removed. Thus, we are confronted with a question of whether a court that had no jurisdiction of the subject matter when suit was filed can obtain jurisdiction by rendering a judgment that is within such court's jurisdiction. While there appear to be no cases on this specific factual situation, we believe the lack of jurisdiction at the time of filing is determinative of the issue.

Georgia Laws 1977, Volume II, page 3190, provides, in pertinent part: "The State Court of Cobb County . . . shall have jurisdiction to try and dispose of all civil . . . cases regardless of their nature, except cases of injury to the person in which the total amount *sued for* [emphasis ours] in the petition . . . shall exceed $25,000 . . ." The plain meaning of such language is that the jurisdiction of the court is determined by the amount sued for. Thus, the amount of the judgment would play no part in determining whether the court has subject-matter jurisdiction. This view is supported by case law, for the Supreme Court has held that "[i]t is the amount of damages laid in the declaration that fixes the jurisdiction, and not the verdict of the jury. (Cits.)" *Giles v. Spinks*, 64 Ga. 205, 206, 207(1) (1879). Further, jurisdiction of the subject matter cannot be waived, consent cannot confer jurisdiction, and the lack of jurisdiction can be taken advantage of at any time. *McKenzie v. Perdue*, 67 Ga. App. 202, 215(3), 19 S.E.2d 765 (1942). See also *Dix v. Dix, supra; King v. King*, 203 Ga. 811, 817(2), 48 S.E.2d 465 (1948). Lastly, we note that our court has held that jurisdiction of the subject matter is given only by law, *Griffin v. Nix*, 33 Ga. App. 136, 125 S.E. 732 (1924), and a judgment on a matter not within the jurisdiction of the court is void at all times.

It is apparent from the foregoing cases that it is the amount of damages *sued for*, not the amount of the judgment, that fixes the jurisdiction. A judgment on a matter not within the jurisdiction of the court is void *at all times*. Further, as the power of the court over the subject matter is a prerequisite to a valid judgment, and the court in the instant case had no jurisdiction over the subject matter, the judgment is void. Finally, filing suit in an amount exceeding a court's jurisdiction is a nonamendable defect, and thus the court has no subject-matter jurisdiction. Accordingly, it was error for the trial court to deny appellant's motion to set aside the judgment for lack of jurisdiction.

Judgment reversed

CASE QUESTIONS

1. At the time the verdict was returned and judgment was entered, the state court of Cobb County had subject-matter jurisdiction over the case. Why did the court of appeals of Georgia decide that the judgment was void for lack of jurisdiction over the subject matter?
2. If the Champions had not argued the court's lack of subject-matter jurisdiction until after the final judgment was rendered, could they make the argument on appeal?

SUGGESTED READINGS

Moore, *Collateral Attack on Subject Matter Jurisdiction: A Critique of the Restatement (Second) of Judgments*, 66 CORNELL L. REV. 534 (1981).
Cooke, *Waste Not, Wait Not—A Consideration of Federal and State Jurisdiction*, 49 FORDHAM L. REV. 895 (1981).

Person and Property

In personam jurisdiction—jurisdiction over the person of the defendant—may be acquired in one of three ways: by serving process (giving notice of the hearing) on the defendant in person in the state in which the court sits; by serving process to the defendant's residence or domicile in the state in which the defendant is being sued; or by the defendant's voluntary submission or consent to the court's jurisdiction. In many jurisdictions, if defendants wish to challenge the court's jurisdiction over their persons, a special appearance is entered for that purpose. If defendants make a general appearance by arguing the facts of the case, this gives implied consent to jurisdiction. Defendants, in effect, waive the right to jurisdiction over their persons by making a general appearance and failing to raise objection.

There are various other ways in which a state court can acquire personal jurisdiction over a nonresident even though the nonresident was not served personally within the state. Consent is considered to have been given to the court's jurisdiction if the cause of action arises from a defendant's transacting business in the state or from a tort allegedly being committed in the state. The various long-arm statutes automatically give a state jurisdiction over a defendant in such cases. This is true if a defendant—whether an individual or a corporation—has had at least some minimum contacts in the state in which the action is brought and the cause of action arose through the minimum contacts. Contacts are considered adequate for jurisdictional purposes when they are "so continuous and substantial as to make it reasonable for the state to exercise such jurisdiction."

For example, a nonresident motorist who has an automobile accident gives consent to suit in the jurisdiction in which the accident took place. In a civil suit, a party can give consent to jurisdiction over his person by agreement. There is never a problem with jurisdiction over the person of the plaintiff, who submits to the jurisdiction of the court by bringing the suit.

A state court has jurisdiction over property. It can render a decision *in rem* only over property located within the state. An *in rem* decision operates against a particular thing, whereas a decision *in personam* imposes liability on a person, and is personally binding. A decision *in rem* is rendered against the property, regardless of its owner or whether the court has jurisdiction over the owner. For example, suppose that two parties, one of which is out of state, dispute the ownership of a piece of land in a certain state. The court of that state may settle the dispute because it deals with property in that state.

Jurisdiction can be asserted in a third way: *quasi-in rem*. *Quasi-in rem* jurisdiction uses property within the jurisdiction in the same way that *in rem* jurisdiction does. However, the property is not the actual subject matter of the suit. It is merely the method of acquiring jurisdiction over the owner of the property. For example, suppose that *P* wants to sue *D* in Iowa for $1000, and *D* is out of state and refuses to come to Iowa. The court may use *quasi-in rem* jurisdiction to take the property *D* owns in Iowa and use it to satisfy any judgment against *D*.

Whether a court has jurisdiction over a case depends on the situation existing at the time the suit begins. Once a court has acquired jurisdiction, it keeps it throughout the case, even though a party changes domicile or property is removed from the state. When more than one court has jurisdiction, the first to exercise it has exclusive jurisdiction to proceed in the case until the case is completely disposed of. No other court may interfere with the proceedings.

Winward v. Holly Creek Mills, Inc.
83 N.M. 469, 493 P.2d 954
Supreme Court of New Mexico
February 11, 1972

MONTOYA, JUSTICE

Robert W. Winward, hereinafter referred to as plaintiff, brought this suit in the district court of Bernalillo County, New Mexico, to recover wages and commissions allegedly owed by Holly Creek Mills, Inc., hereinafter referred to as defendant. Defendant entered a special appearance for the purpose of contesting jurisdiction of the court over the defendant. Defendant moved to quash service of process, supporting its motion with an affidavit. Plaintiff responded to the motion with an affidavit of his own. After a hearing on the motion, an order was entered quashing the service and dismissing the action for lack of jurisdiction over the defendant. Plaintiff appeals from that order.

From the affidavits of the parties, it appears that defendant is a Georgia corporation engaged in the manufacture of rugs and carpets. It is not qualified to do business in New Mexico. It does not maintain offices, bank accounts, or inventories here; nor does it own real or personal property in this state. Plaintiff bases his action on an oral contract between plaintiff and defendant entered into in Phoenix, Arizona, under which he was retained as an agent for the solicitation of orders for the purchase of defendant's products. Pursuant to the contract, plaintiff solicited orders for defendant's products from three businesses in Albuquerque, New Mexico, and one in Santa Fe, New Mexico. It also appears that plaintiff arranged for advertising of defendant's products through customer price reductions, and that plaintiff was paid a salary by defendant, delivered to him by mail or wire within the state of New Mexico.

The basis upon which plaintiff asserts jurisdiction over defendant is the "long-arm statute." Under the provisions of this statute, the "transaction of any business within this state" is one method by which a person submits himself to the jurisdiction of the courts of New Mexico in any cause arising out of that transaction. Thus, the questions on appeal are whether the acts of defendant were sufficient to bring it within the "transaction of any business" provision of the statute for jurisdictional purposes; and, if so, whether plaintiff's cause of action arose out of those transactions.

This court, in *McIntosh v. Navaro Seed Company*, 81 N.M. 302, 466 P.2d 868 (1970), restated the constitutional principle that, to subject a defendant to *in personam* jurisdiction if he is not within the state, there must be certain "minimum contacts" with the state, so that the maintenance of the suit does not offend traditional notions of fair play and substantial justice. Whether the statute applies must be determined by the facts of each case.

We hold that the actions of defendant in having plaintiff solicit orders, make delivery to purchasers, advertise its products through plaintiff, and pay plaintiff wages and commissions within the state of New Mexico, constitute the transaction of business. These actions are minimum contacts which subject defendant to our courts without offending traditional notions of fair play and substantial justice.

Defendant relies on *Grobark v. Addo Machine Co.*, 16 Ill.2d 426, 158 N.E. 2d 73 (1959), for the proposition that merely shipping orders into a state is not sufficient to subject the shipper to *in personam* jurisdiction under a long-arm statute very much like our own.

However, that case is distinguishable because Addo Machines employed no agents in Illinois, whereas, in the instant case, it is admitted that plaintiff was acting as defendant's agent here in New Mexico. Therefore, defendant had a "presence" in New Mexico through its agent that Addo did not have in the Illinois case.

Having decided that the acts of defendant constituted transacting business in New Mexico, we turn to the question of whether plaintiff's cause arose out of the business transacted. The long-arm statute establishes two requirements for the assertion of jurisdiction over a nonresident not within the state. First, the defendant must have done one of the acts enumerated in the statute. Second, the plaintiff's cause of action must arise from defendant's doing the act.

On appeal, defendant argues that the trial court correctly quashed service because the suit was upon a contract made in Arizona, not upon acts arising out of transaction of business in New Mexico. In support of this contention, defendant relies on *Koplin v. Thomas, Haab & Botts*, 73 Ill. App. 2d 242, 219 N.E.2d 646 (1966), citing the following:

Its purpose arising from language of the long-arm statute is to ensure that there is a close relationship between a nonresident defendant's jurisdictional activities and the cause of action against which he must defend.

We subscribe to this view. There must be a close relationship between jurisdictional activities and the cause of action. Had defendant read that case further, he would have discovered the test employed by the Illinois court to determine whether there is a close relationship between the jurisdictional activity and the plaintiff's claim. There the court stated: "The statutory phrase 'arising from' requires only that the plaintiff's claim be one which lies in the wake of the commercial activities by which the defendant submitted to the jurisdiction of the Illinois courts."

This is the proper method for determining whether a plaintiff's claim arises from defendant's jurisdictional activities. Like the test for determining whether the activities subject a defendant to jurisdiction, the test for determining whether the claims arise from those activities must be decided on a case-by-case basis.

Thus, the question is whether plaintiff's claim for wages and commissions lies in the wake of defendant's commercial activities in New Mexico. Plaintiff's claim meets the requirements of this test. Defendant's jurisdictional activities consisted of the solicitation of business, advertising its products through customer discounts, having its agent physically present in the state for those purposes, and delivering payment to plaintiff within New Mexico. At oral argument, defendant's counsel admitted that the New Mexico courts would have jurisdiction in any action arising out of the sale of defendant's products in New Mexico in a suit brought by its New Mexico customers. It follows that any dispute arising out of payment to the agent for services in representing the defendant's business transactions in New Mexico would be within the wake of defendant's commercial activity. Plaintiff's claim, therefore, is one "arising from" the transaction of business within New Mexico.

The order of the district court in quashing service on the defendant is hereby reversed and the case remanded with direction to reinstate plaintiff's complaint on the docket of said court.

CASE QUESTIONS

1. What are some justifications for the long-arm statute?
2. If the defendant had merely shipped its products to New Mexico without actively promoting them, would this court have declined jurisdiction? Why?
3. What factors might a plaintiff consider in choosing a jurisdiction?

SUGGESTED READINGS

Cahill, *Jurisdiction over Foreign Corporations and Individuals Who Carry on Business Within the Territory*, 30 HARV. L. REV. 676 (1917).
Gavin, *Doing Business as Applied to Foreign Corporations*, 11 TEMP. L.Q. 46 (1936).

Note, *Developments in the Law—State Court Jurisdiction*, 73 Harv. L. Rev. 909, 919–35 (1960).

Foster, *Judicial Economy, Fairness and Convenience of Place of Trial: Long-Arm Jurisdiction in District Courts*, 47 F.R.D. 73 (1969).

Comment, *Long-Arm and Quasi-in Rem Jurisdiction and the Fundamental Test of Fairness*, 69 Mich. L. Rev. 300 (1970).

Martin, *Personal Jurisdiction and Choice of Law*, 78 Mich. L. Rev. 872 (1980).

Venue

There is a difference between *jurisdiction* which is the power to adjudicate, and *venue*, referring to the place in which judicial authority should be exercised. A court may have jurisdiction over a controversy, yet venue in that particular district might not be proper. Parties wishing to challenge venue must assert their objections promptly, or they may waive it. Venue in both civil and criminal cases may be considered not proper for several reasons. Fear of local prejudice, convenience for the litigants and witnesses, and interests of justice are reasons for a court to decline to hear a case.

In a civil case, the most common reason given for a court to decline to exercise jurisdiction is that it believes the case can proceed more conveniently in another court. This is known as the doctrine of *forum non conveniens*. This is an exception to the general rule that a court with jurisdiction has not only the right but the duty to exercise it. The doctrine is applied with discretion and caution. One frequent ground for applying the doctrine occurs when the event that gave rise to the suit took place somewhere other than in the forum state. The difficulties of securing the attendance of out-of-state witnesses and applying foreign law make decision making inconvenient. The court balances the conveniences between the forum court and another court and weighs the obstacles to a fair proceeding and advantage. The plaintiff's choice of forum is not changed except for very good reasons.

Harrison v. Capivary, Inc.
334 F. Supp. 1141
United States District Court, E.D. Missouri
November 3, 1971

Meredith, Chief Judge
This matter is before the court on defendant's motion to dismiss and to quash service of process on grounds of lack of jurisdiction, and a motion in the alternative to dismiss because of *forum*

non conveniens. Defendant has submitted an affidavit with the first motion, and an affidavit and exhibits with the second.

This action is a diversity suit to recover $17,519.12 for various services plaintiff performed for the defendant in his capacity as defendant's vice president and as a manager of a coffee plantation in Paraguay, South America.

The affidavit of J. R. Hutchinson, Jr., president of defendant corporation, dated October 28, 1971, reveals the following facts. The defendant corporation was organized under the laws of Panama, and has its principal place of business in Paraguay, South America.

The cause of action complained of in the complaint arose out of the performance of plaintiff's duties as a manager in Paraguay. It involves the right of set-off by defendant for funds advanced in Paraguay at plaintiff's request and loaned to him by defendant to defray the legal expenses and other costs of the defense of a murder charge against plaintiff. Of the 24 persons defendant lists as having relevant knowledge of the lawsuit and its defense, all reside in Paraguay with the exception of three.

With regard to defendant's motion to dismiss because of *forum non conveniens*, if a federal district court finds that a foreign court is a more convenient forum, it may apply the traditional rules of *forum non conveniens* and dismiss the action. Whether jurisdiction should be declined is deter-

mined by weighing various considerations, but the plaintiff's choice of forum will not be disturbed unless the balance is strongly in favor of the defendant.

In the instant case, the balance is clearly in favor of the defendant. As evidenced by defendant's affidavit, the defendant corporation would be put to great expense and undue hardship if it were required to defend this lawsuit in this forum. Substantially all the material witnesses, and the court records pertaining to the murder charge against plaintiff, are located in Paraguay, South America, well beyond the reach of process of this court. Furthermore, requiring these witnesses to travel from South America for the attendance of a trial in this action would entail a great expense and substantial loss of time to the witnesses. Moreover, it appears that plaintiff could have and should have brought this suit in South America. Therefore, assuming for purposes of this motion, that this court has jurisdiction, it is the opinion of this court that for the convenience of the parties, and in the interest of justice, defendant's motion to dismiss plaintiff's complaint on the ground of *forum non conveniens* should be granted. Thus, plaintiff's complaint will be dismissed without prejudice in order to allow plaintiff to initiate his suit in South America. In light of the above, it is unnecessary for this court to decide defendant's alternative motion.

CASE QUESTIONS

1. If the plaintiff is a resident of the United States, is it not an undue hardship on him to expect him to bring a suit in Paraguay?

2. What two interests should a court weigh in determining whether to decline jurisdiction under the doctrine of *forum non conveniens?*

3. What factors should a court look to in deciding which interest prevails?

SUGGESTED READINGS

Barrett, *The Doctrine of Forum Non Conveniens*, 35 CALIF. L. REV. 380 (1947).

Blair, *The Doctrine of Forum Non Conveniens in Anglo-American Law*, 29 COLUM. L. REV. 1 (1929).

Braucher, *The Inconvenient Federal Forum*, 60 HARV. L. REV. 908 (1947).

Korbel, *The Law of Federal Venue and Choice of the Most Convenient Forum*, 15 RUTGERS L. REV. 607 (1961).

Note, *Forum Non Conveniens and Foreign Plaintiffs in the Federal Courts.* 69 GEO. L. J. 1257 (1981).

The Federal Court System

Article III, section 1, of the federal Constitution is the basis of our federal court system. It provides that "the judicial power of the United States shall be vested in one supreme court, and in such inferior courts as Congress may, from time to time, ordain and establish." Congress has the power to establish courts inferior to the Supreme Court of the United States, to regulate their procedure and practice, and to prescribe their jurisdiction. Congress first exercised this power by passing the Judiciary Act of 1789. This act has been amended and supplemented many times in order to establish the various federal courts, their jurisdiction, and procedure. Federal courts have jurisdiction over disputes that are within the judicial power as defined in the federal Constitution or conferred by an act of Congress.

The federal court system consists of the district courts exercising original federal jurisdiction, courts of appeals exercising intermediate federal jurisdiction, and the United States Supreme Court sitting as the highest court for both federal and state matters. Alongside these courts of general jurisdiction, there are the Court of Claims, which decides non-tort claims filed against the United States; the Customs Court, which reviews the rulings and appraisals of customs collectors; the Court of Customs and Patent Appeals, which reviews decisions of the Customs Court and the Patent Office; the Tax Court, which decides federal tax matters; the newly created Federal Bankruptcy Court, which hears bankruptcy cases;

and the United States Court of Military Appeals, which is a court of final appeal involving military criminal matters.

The United States District Courts

Jurisdiction: There are 94 federal district courts—at least one in each state and territory of the United States. They are courts of original jurisdiction and serve as the trial court in the federal court system. The federal district courts are given jurisdiction by the Constitution and by Congress. In criminal cases, these courts have original jurisdiction, exclusive of the state courts, of all violations of federal laws.

In civil actions, the district courts have subject-matter jurisdiction over the following categories:

1. *Diversity of citizenship cases* in which the amount in controversy exceeds $10,000 and is between citizens of different states or between a citizen of a state and an alien. The diversity of citizenship must be complete—meaning that in a multiple-party suit, no one plaintiff and one defendant can be citizens of the same state. Suppose a citizen of New York brings a suit against two defendants, one a citizen of Ohio and one a citizen of Michigan. There would be diversity of citizenship. A federal district court would have jurisdiction over the subject matter if the plaintiff is suing in good faith for over $10,000. If, however, one of the parties being sued was a citizen of New York, there would not be complete diversity of citizenship necessary for jurisdiction. For purposes of these suits, a corporation is considered a citizen in the state where incorporated and in the state of its principal place of business. For example, a corporation incorporated in Delaware with its principal place of business in New York cannot sue or be sued by citizens of either of the two states in a diversity case in a federal district court. One reason given for the existence of diversity jurisdiction is to avoid exposing the defendant to possible prejudice in the plaintiff's state court. However, there are those who argue against diversity jurisdiction, claiming that the fear of possible local prejudice does not justify the expense of the huge diversity caseload in federal courts.

2. *Federal question cases* which arise under the Constitution, laws, or treaties of the United States. These would include cases involving suits by the United States, and civil rights, patent, copyright, trademark, unfair competition, and admiralty suits.

In order for a district court to hear a civil case, it must have, in addition to jurisdiction over the subject matter, jurisdiction over the property in an *in rem* proceeding or over the person of the defendant in an *in personam* proceeding. Jurisdiction over the person is normally acquired by service of a summons within the territory. In an ordinary civil action, the summons may be properly served anywhere within the territorial limits of the state in which the district court is located.

Cunningham v. Ford Motor Co.
413 F.Supp. 1101
United States District Court, D. South Carolina
April 6, 1976

HEMPHILL, DISTRICT JUDGE

On March 5, 1976, defendant Ford Motor Company (hereinafter Ford) filed in this court its motion for an order dismissing the suit (1) for lack of jurisdiction; and (2) because a similar suit, based on an identical cause or causes of action, has been filed against Charleston Lincoln Mercury, Inc., in the Court of Common Pleas for Charleston County, South Carolina.

The complaint seeks recovery for damages allegedly suffered by the plaintiff because of a purchase of a Lincoln Continental automobile, admittedly manufactured by Ford, which she says was defective. Plaintiff filed in the Court of Common Pleas for Charleston County, South Carolina, an identical complaint against Charleston Lincoln Mercury, Inc., the dealer who sold the vehicle to the plaintiff. Plaintiff's action is twofold: for breach of an express warranty and for breach of implied warranty of merchantability.

It is not disputed that the purchase price of the automobile involved in the suit was $11,221.40, although plaintiff claimed that finance charges increased the total purchase price to $14,075.52. Initially, this posed a question of whether or not the carrying charges can be added as a part of the purchase price of the vehicle, but the decision of this issue is not necessary to the disposition of the motion to dismiss on the ground of lack of jurisdictional amount. Plaintiff admits the costs of the car and admits that the car was driven 12,000 miles, including at least one trip to Florida, despite the fact that plaintiff and her husband testified at their depositions that the car was "worth nothing" to them because of its lack of dependability. Defendant would have the court calculate the cost of $11,221.40 and deduct $1800.00 from the value of the car, as the value of the transportation in the car for the 12,000 miles at 15 cents per mile. It is obvious that if the $1800 were deducted from $11,221.40, there would remain $9,421.40, which is less than the jurisdictional amount.

It is elementary that where an action is brought on the grounds of diversity of citizenship, it is absolutely essential that the amount in controversy exceed the requisite jurisdictional sum. This should appear either by the allegations of the complaint or otherwise from proof as to the loss suffered and sought to be recovered. The amount in controversy is measured, not by the monetary result of determining the principle involved in the litigation, but by its pecuniary consequence to those involved. It has been held that to establish the jurisdictional amount, it is sufficient that there is a probability that the value of the matter in controversy exceeds such amount.

Initially this court had jurisdiction when plaintiff exhibited a good-faith allegation that $10,000 is in issue in this litigation, because, at the time the complaint was filed, it did not appear to a legal certainty that the recovery could not exceed the jurisdictional amount. Before a suit will be dismissed for lack of jurisdiction, it must appear to a legal certainty that the plaintiff cannot recover in the lawsuit more than $10,000, exclusive of interests and costs. The right to recover the jurisdictional amount must exist at the time of the institution of the suit in federal court. Events occurring subsequent to the institution of the suit in federal court do not oust jurisdiction though they reduce the amount recoverable below the statutory limit. Considerable latitude may be given the plaintiff to establish the basis of his claim for damages for the purpose of satisfying the jurisdictional amount requirement in a diversity suit. But there must be something other than pure speculation on which the court and/or jury can rely.

The court here is faced with plaintiff's claim, on the one hand, but under the UCC, she is entitled to a limited measure of damages for breach of the warranty she claims—a difference between the value of the goods accepted and the value the goods would have had if they had been as warranted. Defendant insists that plaintiff's claim is less than $10,000, not only because of the facts above discussed, but also because of the terms of the warranty. This warranty, which is put out by the Ford Customer Service Division of Ford in what is known as the "Warranty Facts Booklet" for "1974 New Car and Light Truck Warranty," provides:

Ford and the Selling Dealer jointly warrant for each 1974 model passenger car or light truck (P400 or lower series) sold by Ford that for the earliest of 12 months or 12,000 miles from either first use or retail delivery, the Selling Dealer will repair or replace free of charge any part except tires that is found to be defective in factory materials or workmanship under normal use in the United States or Canada.

. . .

To the extent allowed by law, THIS WARRANTY IS IN PLACE OF all other warranties, express or implied, including the ANY IMPLIED WARRANTY OF MERCHANTABILITY OR FITNESS. Under this warranty, repair or replacement is the only remedy.

It is admitted that before the 12,000 miles had expired, plaintiff took the automobile back to the dealer for various complaints. But it is the claim of the plaintiff that the dealer never complied with the guarantee set forth in this warranty. The plaintiff, in her brief, states that she will stipulate that the implied warranty of merchantability given by the defendant to the plaintiff was properly limited to the replacement of parts found to be defective under normal use. Plaintiff contends that defendant-Ford failed to comply with the properly limited warranty, that is, to replace defective parts, etc., within the warranty period, and that the limited warranty or exclusive limited remedy has failed in its essential purpose, said being to provide the plaintiff with a new, defect-free automobile.

Under such circumstances, the plaintiff invokes the general remedy provision of the Uniform Commercial Code in regard to breach of warranty. Plaintiff claims damages under the provisions of the UCC, in the amount of the difference between the value of the automobile as it actually was and its value if it had been in the condition warranted, as well as incidental damages, ''including but not limited to plaintiff's loss of use of the automobile in question, expense and inspection, receipt, transportation, care and custody of the automobile in question, and other reasonable expenses. . . .''

It is easily seen that, even if defendant's theory of deduction for mileage driven be allowed and that reduction applied to the actual purchase price, instead of to the inflated price caused by the addition of finance charges, when the other damages which plaintiff claims are included, the amount may well exceed $10,000 under any calculation. It therefore does not appear to a legal certainty that the amount in controversy does not meet the jurisdictional amount required in a diversity action.

It must appear to a legal certainty that the amount of claim is really for less than the jurisdictional amount to justify dismissal. The inability of plaintiff to recover an amount adequate to give the court jurisdiction does not show his bad faith or oust the jurisdiction. Nor does the fact that the complaint discloses the existence of a valid defense of the claim. But if, from the face of the pleadings, it is apparent, to a legal certainty, that the plaintiff cannot recover the amount claimed or if, from the proofs, the court is satisfied to a like

certainty that the plaintiff never was entitled to recover that amount, and that his claim was therefore colorable for the purpose of conferring jurisdiction, the suit will be dismissed. It thus appears that the certainty prerequisite does not exist here, and the motion to dismiss for lack of jurisdiction is denied.

Defendant has also moved for dismissal because of the state court action pending against Charleston Lincoln Mercury and arising out of the same facts and transaction as this suit. Counsel for defendant invokes the doctrine of *forum non conveniens* as a ground for dismissal and, after arguments on the motion for dismissal were heard by the court, moved in the alternative for an order staying the federal action under some form of the abstention doctrine.

Counsel's shift in emphasis from *forum non conveniens* to abstention was well founded, because there appears to be no authority at all for the application of the former doctrine in this case. Defendant in this case would prefer to have plaintiff sue both Ford and its dealer in a single action, but there is nothing in that commendable desire sufficient to warrant invocation of the doctrine of *forum non conveniens* to accomplish it.

The doctrine of abstention, unlike *forum non conveniens*, is intimately connected with the relationship of the state and federal judicial systems. The need for abstention must be clearly shown before the court will decline to exercise its jurisdiction. The diversity jurisdiction was not conferred for the benefit of the federal courts or to serve their convenience. Its purpose was generally to afford to suitors an opportunity in such cases, at their option, to assert their rights in the federal rather than in the state courts. In the absence of some recognized public policy or defined principle guiding the exercise of the jurisdiction conferred, which would in exceptional cases warrant its nonexercise, it has from the first been deemed to be the duty of the federal courts, if their jurisdiction is properly invoked, to decide disputes before them.

Defendant in this action, Ford Motor Company, is not named as a defendant in the state court suit. Although the defendant there is closely related, being a Ford dealer, the parties concede that Ford and its dealer will likely raise dissimilar defenses to some of the allegations of plaintiff's identical state and federal complaints. In these circumstances, there is no justification for a stay of this action under any form of abstention recognized in this circuit or elsewhere, and defendant's motion for a stay must be denied.

Defendant's motion for dismissal is denied as to both grounds alleged, and the alternative motion for a stay is also denied.

And it is so ordered.

CASE QUESTIONS

1. If during the trial of *Cunningham v. Ford* it appears to a certainty that the amount recoverable is less than $10,000, will the federal district court dismiss the suit?
2. Why did Congress impose a $10,000 limitation on diversity of citizenship cases?

SUGGESTED READINGS

C. A. WRIGHT, LAW OF FEDERAL COURTS §§32–37 (3d ed. 1976).
Hart, *The Power of Congress to Limit the Jurisdiction of Federal Courts: An Exercise in Dialectics*, 66 HARV. L. REV. 1362 (1953).
Comment, *Federal Jurisdiction: Amount in Controversy in Suits for Nonmonetary Remedies*, 46 CALIF. L. REV. 601 (1958).
Comment, *Corporate Diversity Jurisdiction: Voluntary Multiple Incorporation and the Forum Doctrine*, 12 GONZ. L. REV. 347 (1977).
Uxa, *Jurisdictional Amount: An Unreasonable Limitation on Diversity Jurisdiction*, 65 ILL. B.J. 78 (1976).

Removal from State to Federal Courts

Except in those areas in which federal courts have exclusive jurisdiction, a suit does not have to be brought in a federal district court just because it has jurisdiction over the subject matter and over the person or property. A plaintiff may bring a dispute in any state or federal court that has jurisdiction.

A defendant sued in a state court may have a right to have the case removed to the federal courts. Any civil action brought in a state court may be moved by the defendant to a federal district court if the district court has jurisdiction. In other words, if the suit is one that could have been initiated in a district court, it is removable. When any of the defendants to a suit are citizens of the state in which the action is brought, it is not removable unless it is a claim arising under the Constitution, treaties, or laws of the United States. For example, if a citizen of New York sues a citizen of Ohio in a state court in Ohio for breach of contract or tort, the defendant could not have the case removed. The defendant could have the case removed if the suit were brought in any other state. Where the basis of jurisdiction is diversity of citizenship, it must exist at the time of filing the original suit and also at the time of petitioning for removal.

Gatch v. Hennepin Broadcasting Associates, Inc.
349 F. Supp. 1180
United States District Court, D. Minnesota
October 7, 1972

NEVILLE, DISTRICT JUDGE
This case comes before the court by way of removal from the Minnesota district court of Hennepin County. Plaintiff alleges in his complaint that he is a radio broadcaster conducting a ''personality talk-radio-host and commentator show'' in the Twin Cities area; that he has a contract to do so with Arrow Broadcasting Company, Inc., which in turn has purchased under a contract certain broadcasting time from the defendant radio station KTCR and KTCR–FM, a duly licensed radio station in Hennepin County, Minnesota; that while both contracts were in full force and effect he was cut off the air on several occasions without justifi-cation or excuse and was not allowed to broadcast. Plaintiff himself has no direct contract with the defendant radio station but sues it in tort for alleged ''illegal and unwarranted interference with defendant's contractual relation'' with Arrow Broadcasting Company, Inc. The latter is not a party-defendant in this lawsuit. The complaint does not purport to and does not allege the presence of any federal question as such, does not assert the violation of any federal statute, and refers only quite incidentally to rules and regulations of the Federal Communications Commission with which he alleges full compliance.

The defendant has filed a one-page answer in the form of a general denial. At the hearing on the motion, however, its counsel orally asserted the defenses (1) that Arrow Broadcasting Company was and is delinquent in the amount of some $7000 to $8000 in its contract payments due defendant; (2) that plaintiff's program was entitled "smut-talk" and engendered certain sex-oriented responses and caused unfavorable and unsavory publicity for the radio station, possibly putting its Federal Communications license in jeopardy if obscene talk and conversations were permitted to be broadcast over its station. This is the only alleged federal question raised, and this is not in fact asserted in either pleading.

The court having considered the matter does not believe it has removal jurisdiction in this case and so has remanded the same to the Minnesota state court. There is no diversity of citizenship here. Even though the jurisdictional limit of $10,000 is alleged, removal jurisdiction would have to depend solely on whether a federal question is involved.

It is well established by a long line of authority in removal proceedings that federal jurisdiction must be disclosed upon the face of the complaint, unaided by the answer or by the petition for removal. It has been held that a suit may be removed where the real nature of the claim asserted in the complaint is federal, irrespective of whether it is so characterized. In this case neither the complaint, nor, for that matter, the answer disclose any real federal question. Collateral federal issues even if asserted by way of answer are not grounds for removal to federal court. In sum, plaintiff here does not seek relief arising under the laws or the Constitution of the United States, but merely asserts a tort action arising out of alleged unlawful interference by a third party with a contractual relationship. No federal question is in any sense alleged to be an essential part of plaintiff's cause of action.

CASE QUESTIONS

1. Since the federal court refused to confer removal jurisdiction of the case, where must the action be entertained?
2. Should the aggrieved party be allowed to appeal an adverse decision on the issue of removal jurisdiction?
3. Is a party to a claim more likely to obtain justice in a federal court than a state court?

SUGGESTED READINGS

Wills and Boyer, *Proposed Changes in Federal Removal Jurisdiction and Procedure*, 9 OHIO ST. L.J. 257 (1948).

Keeffe, *Venue and Removal Jokers in the New Federal Judicial Code*, 38 VA. L. REV. 569 (1952).

Mishkin, *The Federal "Question" in the District Courts*, 53 COLUM. L. REV. 157 (1953).

Cohen, *The Broken Compass: The Requirement That a Case Arise "Directly" under Federal Law*, 115 U. Pa. L. Rev. 890 (1967).
Note, 33 Corn. L.Q. 261 (1947).
Note, 44 Ill. L. Rev. 397 (1949).

Erie Doctrine

Quite often the litigants have a choice of bringing their suit in a federal court or in a state court. Does a federal court follow different rules of law than a state court when adjudicating state matters? Section 34 of the Judiciary Act of 1789 states:

> The laws of the several States, except where the Constitution, treaties, or statutes of the United States otherwise require or provide, shall be regarded as rules of decision in trials at common law, in the courts of the United States, in cases where they apply.

Originally, the federal courts held that "the laws of the several states" meant statutes only. In the absence of any state statute, the federal courts followed their own common law.

The landmark case of *Erie R. Co. v. Tompkins*, 304 U.S. 64 (1938), held that, except in matters governed by the federal Constitution or by acts of Congress, the law to be applied in federal courts is the law of the state. The law of the state includes judicial decisions as well as statutory law. There is no federal general common law concerning state matters. A federal district court is bound by the statutes and precedents of the state in which it sits. This prevents a federal court and a state court from reaching different results on the same issue of state law.

The *Erie* decision, which is one of the most important cases decided by the United States Supreme Court, gave the state courts a power that had formerly been exercised by the federal courts. A large portion of the civil cases brought subsequent to this landmark case have been affected by the decision, which went to the heart of the relations between the state and federal courts.

Carson v. National Bank	Per Curiam[1]
501 F.2d 1082	This case is before the court upon appeal from an order granting judgment in favor of defendants on the first count of a two-count complaint.
United States Court of Appeals, Eighth Circuit	
July 30, 1974	

---

[1] An opinion written by the entire court rather than by just one judge. —*Ed.*

The count which was dismissed was based on diversity of citizenship and alleged that defendants, in advertising a travel tour, used the name and image of the plaintiff without his permission, thereby damaging him. The federal district court dismissed the count on the ground that, under Nebraska law, it failed to state a claim upon which relief could be granted.

The facts are undisputed. Defendants, a bank and its wholly owned subsidiary travel agency, placed an advertisement bearing the name and picture of Johnny Carson, the well-known television personality and nightclub performer, in several newspapers and in a pamphlet distributed to bank customers. The advertisement concerned a travel tour to Las Vegas organized by defendant Travel Unlimited, Inc., which was called "Nebraskan Johnny Carson's Tour of Las Vegas." Mr. Carson was to be performing at a Las Vegas nightclub during the time scheduled for the tour, and tickets to his show were included in the tour package. Mr. Carson did not approve the use of his name and photograph, nor was he connected in any way with the travel venture.

The federal courts must apply the law of the state wherein the United States District Court is located. Here, the applicable principles must, therefore, be determined from an examination of the law of the state of Nebraska. The district court, after examining that law, determined that Count I of the complaint failed to state a claim upon which relief could be granted. The only issue on appeal is whether the trial court was correct in that interpretation of Nebraska law.

We therefore have undertaken our own review of Nebraska law, and particularly the case of *Brunson v. Ranks Army Store*, 161 Neb. 519, 73 N.W.2d 803 (1955). This case formed the basis for the district court's conclusion that plaintiff's first cause of action did not state a claim upon which relief could be granted.

Plaintiff Brunson was an actor who was hired by Ranks Army Store to re-enact the Brinks armed robbery as a publicity device. The store failed to warn the local police of the planned re-enactment, and Mr. Brunson was arrested and jailed during the staged robbery. Thereafter, the store ran advertisements setting forth the story of Brunson's arrest and incarceration, using Brunson's name and picture. Brunson sued the store, charging in one count that his right to privacy, which he had not waived, was violated by the use of the picture and story without his consent and he had thereby been subjected to ridicule, embarrassment, and humiliation. The Nebraska Supreme Court affirmed the lower court's dismissal of the action, stating:

Our research develops no Nebraska case holding that this court has in any form or manner adopted the doctrine of the right of privacy, and there is no precedent in this state establishing the doctrine. Nor has the Legislature of this state conferred such a right of action by statute. We therefore hold that the action of the trial court in sustaining the defendant's demurrer to plaintiff's action based on the right of privacy was correct and needs no further comment.

Brunson, argues plaintiff here, sought damages not for his loss of the opportunity to sell his name for commercial purposes, but for the mental suffering he underwent as a result of the revelation of an embarrassing incident. Both these actions stem from the initial recognition of a right to control the use of one's own name and image, which the Nebraska Supreme Court explicitly rejected in *Brunson.* Plaintiff's characterization of his action as one seeking damages for "misappropriation" cannot serve as a means to escape the rule of the Brunson case. If the Nebraska court had intended to recognize an action for "misappropriation," *Brunson* would certainly have been an appropriate place for some indication of such intention, since Brunson, like Carson, alleged that his picture and name had been used without his permission in an advertising scheme. (Brunson had agreed that his picture could be used in connection with the re-enactment of the robbery, but had not contracted for the use of his name and picture in connection with his actual arrest and incarceration.)

Such a result might seem anomalous today where the vast majority of states have recognized a "right to privacy" by court decision or statute, and where the plaintiff's first cause of action, in most jurisdictions, would clearly state a claim upon which relief could be granted. However, the fact that Nebraska has followed a different course from that of other states is not reason for this court to determine that Nebraska would now wish to judicially change its law. This court must look to Nebraska law as it is and not as one might believe it ought to be.

Plaintiff argues that we need not slavishly adhere to the last ruling of the Nebraska Supreme Court in a similar case, but should determine what the present Supreme Court would do if faced with this case now. We have done so, but we believe that the best method of ascertaining what the Nebraska court would do with this case is to examine what it has done with similar cases in the past. The Brunson case has not been overruled, nor has any subsequent case we have found cast any doubt on its continuing authority. The learned district judge, familiar with the law of Nebraska, has concluded that *Brunson* states the current law of Nebraska. We conclude that his interpretation was, and is, correct.

Affirmed

Case Questions

1. Why did the federal district court have jurisdiction in this case?
2. Since the case was heard in federal court, why didn't the judge apply the law as generally applied in the country rather than the law of Nebraska?

Suggested Readings

Note, *Of Lawyers and Laymen: A Study of Federalism, the Judicial Process, and Erie,* 71 Yale L.J. 344 (1961).

Comment, *State or Federal Law in Federal Courts: The Rise and Fall of Erie*, 42 Miss. L.J. 89 (1971).

Note, *Federal Jurisdiction—Environmental Law—Nuisance—State Ecological Rights Arising Under Federal Common Laws*, 1972 Wis. L. Rev. 597.

Baroni, *The Class Action as a Consumer Protection Device*, 9 Am. Bus. L.J. 141 (1971).

Agata, *Delaney, Diversity and Delay: Abstention or Abdication?* 4 Houston L. Rev. 422 (1966).

United States Courts of Appeals and their Circuits

Circuit	Location of Court	Number of District Courts	States and Territories in the Circuit
D.C.	Washington, D. C.	1	District of Columbia
First	Boston, Mass.	5	Maine, Massachusetts, New Hampshire, Rhode Island, Puerto Rico
Second	New York, N.Y.	6	Connecticut, New York, Vermont
Third	Philadelphia, Pa.	6	Delaware, New Jersey, Pennsylvania, Virgin Islands
Fourth	Richmond, Va.	9	Maryland, North Carolina, South Carolina, Virginia, West Virginia
Fifth	New Orleans, La.	9	Louisiana, Mississippi, Texas
Sixth	Cincinnati, Ohio	9	Kentucky, Michigan, Ohio, Tennessee
Seventh	Chicago, Ill.	7	Illinois, Indiana, Wisconsin
Eighth	St. Louis, Mo.	10	Arkansas, Iowa, Minnesota, Missouri, Nebraska, North Dakota, South Dakota
Ninth	San Francisco, Calif.	15	Alaska, Arizona, Hawaii, California, Idaho, Montana, Nevada, Oregon, Washington, Guam, N. Mariana Islands
Tenth	Denver, Colo.	8	Colorado, Kansas, New Mexico, Oklahoma, Utah, Wyoming
Eleventh	Atlanta, Ga.	9	Alabama, Florida, Georgia
12		94	

The United States Courts of Appeals

The United States is divided into 12 circuits, with one court of appeals sitting in each circuit. These appellate courts hear appeals on questions of law from decisions of the federal district courts in their circuits and review findings of federal administrative agencies. For most litigants, they are the ultimate appellate tribunal of the federal system. Appeal to the courts of appeals is a matter of right, not discretionary, so long as proper procedures are followed in bringing the appeal.

When attorneys wish to appeal decisions of lower tribunals, they must follow the proper procedures to get the cases before the court of appeals. Then they must persuade the judges that the lower tribunals committed errors that resulted in injustices to their clients. Notice of appeal must be filed within 30 days from the entry of judgment, 60 days when the United States or an officer or agent thereof is a party. A cost bond (in civil cases), the record on appeal, and a brief must also be filed. On appeal, the court of appeals does not substitute its judgment for that of the lower tribunal's finding of fact. But it reverses the lower court's decision if it was clearly erroneous.

The long-standing policy of the United States courts of appeals, as well as that of most other appellate courts, is that appeal lies only from final orders or decisions of the lower courts. However, this rule as applied does not mean that a case may be appealed only after final judgment has been rendered by the lower court. The "finality" of a decision or order of the lower court is often determined for purposes of appeal by the nature and subject matter of that decision, as well as by the effect of the decision on the outcome of the case. The United States courts of appeals use a "pragmatic" approach to determine finality in each individual case. Thus appellate review may be available to determine a controlling question of law before the case itself is determined.

Sierra Club v. Froehlke
534 F.2d 1289
United States Court of Appeals, Eighth Circuit
April 23, 1976

TALBOT SMITH, SENIOR DISTRICT JUDGE
This case is an appeal from a district court judgment denying injunctive and declaratory relief. The plaintiffs-appellants, Sierra Club and several named individuals, seek to enjoin construction of the Meramec Park Lake Dam and any other dams planned in the Meramec Basin. The district court denied such relief. We affirm.

Sierra Club is an organization dedicated to the preservation and enjoyment of natural resources. There are also four individual plaintiffs who own land in the Meramec Basin. The three defendants were all officers of the United States Army when this action was filed. Robert F. Froehlke was secretary of the army; Lieutenant General Frederick J. Clarke was chief of the Army Corps of Engineers; and Colonel Guy E. Jester was district engineer of United States Army Engineer District, St. Louis, Missouri. In those positions, the three defendants were responsible for the construction of the Meramec Park Lake Dam and for the overall Meramec Basin Plan.

The original complaint alleged violations of the National Environmental Policy Act of 1969 (hereinafter NEPA). The plaintiffs moved for a summary judgment based on the inadequacy of the original environmental impact statement (hereafter EIS). The motion was denied without prejudice. The final statement is a four-volume work of nine sections which greatly expanded the detail of discussion contained in the original impact statement.

After a two-and-one-half day trial, the district court, in an order and opinion entered March 19, 1975, found against the plaintiffs on all counts and denied their request for declaratory and injunctive relief, holding in part:

In conclusion, this court is of the opinion that it can have no other holding, but to enter judgment for the defendants. In every instance of alleged statutory violation, or other alleged failings of the defendants with regards to the Meramec Park Reservoir, the defendants have carried the burden of proof or have indicated to this court's satisfaction that no violation has occurred. 392 F.Supp. 130, 144 (E.D.Mo. 1975).

This appeal followed. On appeal, Sierra Club has confined its claims of error to alleged violations of NEPA. It argues that the NEPA is being violated in that the revised EIS was inadequate in its discussion of alternatives to the proposed project.

The proposed Meramec Park Lake Dam will be located in the Meramec Basin, encompassing a watershed of some 4000 square miles. Generally speaking, it is in an area running southwest from St. Louis for approximately 120 miles. At the present time there is no major dam or reservoir on the river, or its principal tributaries. It comprises areas of great natural beauty, of rugged terrain, as well as of pastoral sites, and of natural caves and springs. But there is another side to the coin. The flow of the river is extremely variable. During drought periods, the streams in the basin do not carry enough water to provide adequate dilution of the wastes that empty into them. At flood periods it is highly destructive. Major floods have occurred on the average of about once every six years, although portions of the bottom lands have experienced flooding almost annually. "Rural slum" areas are prevalent in some of the river stretches. There is a need to supply the recreational needs of the St. Louis Metropolitan Area. All of these considerations, and more, we find discussed in great detail in the EIS. It is obvious, and has been for years, that the problems presented demand solution, although it is equally obvious that for every weight on one side of the scales, there is at least some counterweight.

The above-described project is part of a comprehensive plan for flood control in the upper Mississippi River Basin first authorized by Congress in the River and Harbor Flood Control Act of 1938. The Meramec Park Lake Project has been in the real-estate-acquisition category since 1968. The project is scheduled to be complete and operational by June of 1980. The primary benefits of the project are expected to be flood control, water supply, water quality (pollution abatement), recreation, fish and wildlife, and navigation.

As to compliance with NEPA, the plaintiffs assert that the EIS "contained an inadequate discussion of the alternative of flood plain acquisition." With specific reference to plaintiff's contention that the statement is inadequate with respect to the alternative of flood plain acquisition, a land-planning expert was present in the court. It was his thinking that the nonstructural alternatives had not been fully analyzed or considered, nor had there been economic analysis of the "costs and benefits of flood plain acquisition." There was contrary testimony, such as that flood plain acquisition was not "a reasonable and viable alternative to the presently planned project" and that its total cost would be approximately $143 million. The defendants' position on this aspect of the case, contained in the EIS, was that flood plain acquisition was impractical because of (a) the difficulty and cost of relocating the residences, utilities, and transportation facilities in the Meramec River flood plain, (b) the vigorous opposition from those in the urbanized lower areas, (c)

the adverse effect on the income-producing capability of the land, and (d) the elimination of private, taxable income from the area, as well as the tax base for government purposes. The EIS contains a full discussion and evaluation of possible alternatives. The reasons for the choice of course of action are clear. We cannot say that the trial court's conclusions, that the EIS discussion of flood plain alternative was adequate and that flood plain acquisition was not a reasonable alternative to the proposed action, are clearly erroneous.

In the courts, the burden is upon the plaintiffs to establish by a preponderance of the evidence that the EIS was inadequate and that the decision to proceed was arbitrary and capricious. It was the holding in the trial court that this burden was not met. In our court, it is the plaintiff's burden to establish that the lower court's findings were clearly erroneous.

It is manifest that the treatment of the issues presented could have been more voluminous. But it is equally clear that the discussion need not be exhaustive, but rather must provide sufficient information that a reasonable choice of alternatives may be made.

So tested, and after a careful study of the record, we find no clear error in the court's findings.

CASE QUESTIONS

1. For an appellate court to reverse the finding of a trial court, the trial court's factual finding must be clearly erroneous. Why should an appellate court not reverse a trial court's decision if it considers it wrong but not clearly erroneous?

2. What were the competing interests that had to be balanced by the trial court?

SUGGESTED READINGS

C. A. WRIGHT, LAW OF FEDERAL COURTS §§ 101–4 (3d ed. 1976).

Parker, *Jury Reversal and the Appellate Court View of Law and Fact*, 14 OSGOODE HALL L.J. 287 (1976).

Comment, *Limits of Judicial Intervention in Criminal Trials and Reversible Error*, 11 GA. L. REV. 371 (1977).

Coleman, *Appellate Proceedings in the United States Court of Appeals*, 38 MISS. L.J. 554 (1967).

Carrington, *Power of District Judges and the Responsibility of Courts of Appeals*, 3 GA. L. REV. 507 (1969).

Klein, *Reviewing the Evidence on Appeal*, 44 LOS ANGELES BAR BULLETIN 159 (1969).

The United States Supreme Court

The Supreme Court has existed since President Washington appointed its first justice. Today the Court consists of a chief justice and eight associate justices. It exercises both appellate and original jurisdiction. Its chief function is to act as the last and final court of review over all cases in the federal system and some cases in the state system. It occupies a singular position within the dual system of federal and state courts in that it reviews certain decisions of the states' highest courts as well as decisions of lower federal courts.

The great majority of the cases that reach the Supreme Court come from the United States courts of appeals on *certiorari*. A review by *certiorari* is not a matter of right but of sound judicial discretion and will be granted only where there are special and important reasons for so doing. The Court thus controls its docket, reserving its time and efforts for the cases that seem to the justices to deserve consideration. In only a few circumstances can one appeal a decision to the Supreme Court as a matter of right. For instance, an appeal to the Supreme Court can be made when a court of appeals invalidates a state law as unconstitutional. The appeal is limited to the federal questions involved.

Unlike other federal courts, the Supreme Court of the United States is named and has its jurisdiction specified in the Constitution. After defining the judicial power of the United States, article III, section 2, granted original jurisdiction to the Supreme Court in certain cases:

In all cases affecting ambassadors, other public ministers and consuls, and those in which a state shall be party, the Supreme Court shall have original jurisdiction. In all the other cases before-mentioned, the Supreme Court shall have appellate jurisdiction, both as to law and fact, with such exceptions, and under such regulations as the Congress shall make.

Original jurisdiction means the power to take cognizance of a suit at its inception, try it, and pass judgment on the law and the facts of the controversy. In addition to the appellate jurisdiction of the Supreme Court, the Constitution has given it the power to perform the function of a trial court in cases affecting ambassadors, public ministers, and consuls, and in controversies in which a state is a party. Usually, the power is not exclusive, nor is the Court required to hear all cases over which it has original jurisdiction.

Ohio v. Wyandotte Chemicals Corporation
401 U.S. 493
United States Supreme Court
March 23, 1971

MR. JUSTICE HARLAN
By motion for leave to file a bill of complaint, Ohio seeks to invoke this Court's original jurisdiction. For reasons that follow, we deny the motion for leave to file.

The action, for abatement of a nuisance, is brought on behalf of the state and its citizens, and names as defendants Wyandotte Chemicals Corporation (Wyandotte), Dow Chemical Company (Dow America), and Dow Chemical Company of Canada, Limited (Dow Canada). Wyandotte is incorporated in Michigan and maintains its principal office and place of business there. Dow America is incorporated in Delaware, has its principal office and place of business in Michigan, and owns all the stock of Dow Canada.

Dow Canada is incorporated, and does business in Ontario. A majority of Dow Canada's directors are residents of the United States.

The complaint alleges that Dow Canada and Wyandotte have each dumped mercury into streams whose courses ultimately reach Lake Erie, thus contaminating and polluting the lake's waters, vegetation, fish, and wildlife and that Dow America is jointly responsible for the acts of its foreign subsidiary. Assuming the state's ability to prove these assertions, Ohio seeks a decree: (1) declaring the introduction of mercury into Lake Erie's tributaries a public nuisance; (2) perpetually enjoining these defendants from introducing mercury into Lake Erie or its tributaries; (3) requiring defendants either to remove the mercury from Lake Erie or to pay the costs of its removal into a fund to be administered by Ohio and used only for that purpose; and (4) directing defendants to pay Ohio monetary damages for the harm done to

Lake Erie, its fish, wildlife, and vegetation, and the citizens and inhabitants of Ohio.

Original jurisdiction is said to be conferred on this Court by article III of the federal Constitution. Section 2, clause 1, of that article, provides: ''The judicial power shall extend . . . to controversies . . . between a state and citizens of another state and between a state . . . and foreign . . . citizens or subjects.'' Section 2, clause 2, provides: ''In all cases . . . in which a state shall be a party, the Supreme Court shall have original jurisdiction.'' Finally, 28 U.S.C. §1251(b) (3) provides: ''The Supreme Court shall have original but not exclusive jurisdiction of . . . all actions or proceedings by a state against the citizens of another state or against aliens.''

That we have jurisdiction seems clear enough. Beyond doubt, the complaint on its face reveals the existence of a genuine ''case or controversy'' between one state and citizens of another, as well as a foreign subject. Diversity of citizenship is absolute. Nor is the nature of the cause of action asserted a bar to the exercise of our jurisdiction.

Ordinarily, the foregoing would suffice to settle the issue presently under consideration: whether Ohio should be granted leave to file its complaint. For it is a time-honored maxim of the Anglo-American common-law tradition that a court possessed of jurisdiction generally must exercise it. Nevertheless, although it may initially have been contemplated that this Court would always exercise its original jurisdiction when properly called upon to do so, it seems evident to us that changes in the American legal system and the development of American society have rendered untenable, as a practical matter, the view that this Court must stand willing to adjudicate all or most legal disputes that may arise between one state and a citizen or citizens of another, even though the dispute may be one over which this Court does have original jurisdiction.

Thus, at this stage, we go no further than hold that, as a general matter, we may decline to entertain a complaint brought by a state against the citizens of another state or country only where we can say with assurance that (1) declination of jurisdiction would not disserve any of the principal policies underlying the article III jurisdictional grant and (2) the reasons of practical wisdom that persuade us that this Court is an inappropriate forum are consistent with the proposition that our discretion is legitimated by its use to keep this aspect of the Court's functions attuned with its other responsibilities.

Two principles seem primarily to have underlain conferring upon this Court original jurisdiction over cases and controversies between a state and citizens of another state or country. The first was the belief that no state should be compelled to resort to the tribunals of other states for redress, since parochial factors might often lead to the appearance, if not the reality, of partiality to one's own. The second was that a state, needing an alternative forum, of necessity had to resort to this Court in order to obtain a tribunal competent to exercise jurisdiction over the acts of nonresidents of the aggrieved state.

Neither of these policies is, we think,

implicated in this lawsuit. The courts of Ohio, under modern principles of the scope of subject matter and *in personam* jurisdiction, have a claim as compelling as any that can be made out for this Court to exercise jurisdiction to adjudicate the instant controversy, and they would decide it under the same common law of nuisance upon which our determination would have to rest. In essence, the state has charged Dow Canada and Wyandotte with the commission of acts, albeit beyond Ohio's territorial boundaries, that have produced and, it is said, continue to produce disastrous effects within Ohio's own domain. While this Court, and doubtless Canadian courts, if called upon to assess the validity of any decree rendered against either Dow Canada or Wyandotte, would be alert to ascertain whether the judgment rested on an evenhanded application of justice, it is unlikely that we would totally deny Ohio's competence to act if the allegations made here are proved true. And while we cannot speak for Canadian courts, we have been given no reason to believe they would be less receptive to enforcing a decree rendered by Ohio courts than one issued by this Court. Thus, we do not believe exercising our discretion to refuse to entertain this complaint would undermine any of the purposes for which Ohio was given the authority to bring it here.

Additionally, Ohio and Michigan are both participants in the Lake Erie Enforcement Conference, convened a year ago by the Secretary of the Interior pursuant to the Federal Water Pollution Control Act. The conference is studying all forms and sources of pollution, including mercury, infecting Lake Erie.

The purpose of this conference is to provide a basis for concerted remedial action by the states or, if progress in that regard is not rapidly made, for corrective proceedings initiated by the federal government.

In view of all this, granting Ohio's motion for leave to file would, in effect, commit this Court's resources to the task of trying to settle a small piece of a much larger problem that many competent adjudicatory and conciliatory bodies are actively grappling with on a more practical basis.

The nature of the case Ohio brings here is equally disconcerting. It can fairly be said that what is in dispute is not so much the law as the facts. And the fact-finding process we are asked to undertake is, to say the least, formidable. We already know, just from what has been placed before us on this motion, that Lake Erie suffers from several sources of pollution other than mercury; that the scientific conclusion that mercury is a serious water pollutant is a novel one; that whether and to what extent the existence of mercury in natural waters can safely or reasonably be tolerated is a question for which there is presently no firm answer; and that virtually no published research is available describing how one might extract mercury that is in fact contaminating water. Indeed Ohio is raising factual questions that are essentially ones of first impression to the scientists. The notion that appellate judges, even with the assistance of a most competent special master, might appropriately undertake at this time to unravel these complexities is to say the least unrealistic. Nor would it suffice to impose on Ohio an unusually high standard of proof. That might serve to mitigate our personal difficulties in seeking a just result that comports with sound judicial administration, but would not lessen the complexity of the task of preparing responsibly to exercise our judgment, nor the serious drain on the resources of this Court it would entail. Other factual complexities abound. For example, the Department of the Interior has stated that eight American companies are discharging, or have discharged, mercury into Lake Erie or its tributaries. We would, then, need to assess the business practices and relative culpability of each to frame appropriate relief as to the one now before us.

To sum up, this Court has found even the simplest sort of interstate pollution case an extremely awkward vehicle to manage. And this case is an extraordinarily complex one, both because of the novel scientific issues of fact inherent in it and the multiplicity of governmental agencies already involved. Its successful resolution would require primarily skills of fact-finding, conciliation, detailed coordination with—and perhaps not infrequent deference to—other adjudicatory bodies, and close supervision of the technical performance of local industries. We have no claim to such expertise nor reason to believe that, were we to adjudicate this case, and others like it, we would not have to reduce drastically our attention to those controversies for which this Court is a proper and necessary forum. Such a serious intrusion on society's interest in our most deliberate and considerate performance of our paramount role as the supreme federal appellate court could, in our view, be justified only by the strictest necessity, an element which is evidently totally lacking in this instance.

What has been said here cannot, of course, be taken as denigrating in the slightest the public importance of the underlying problem Ohio would have us tackle. Reversing the increasing contamination of our environment is manifestly a matter of fundamental import and utmost urgency. What is dealt with above are only considerations respecting the appropriate role this Court can assume in efforts to eradicate such environmental blights. We mean only to suggest that our competence is necessarily limited, not that our concern should be kept within narrow bounds.

Ohio's motion for leave to file its complaint is denied without prejudice to its right to commence other appropriate judicial proceedings.

MR. JUSTICE DOUGLAS dissents.

CASE QUESTIONS

1. Since the United States Supreme Court has jurisdiction to hear and decide the controversy, is it not obligated to decide the case?
2. Does the decision of the Supreme Court to decline jurisdiction mean that the state of Ohio has no possible court remedy?

SUGGESTED READINGS

C. A. WRIGHT, LAW OF FEDERAL COURTS §§105–10 (3d ed. 1976).
F. FRANKFURTER, THE BUSINESS OF THE SUPREME COURT: A STUDY IN THE FEDERAL JUDICIAL SYSTEM (1927).
R. L. STERN, SUPREME COURT PRACTICE (5th ed. 1978).
J. R. SCHMIDHAUSER, THE SUPREME COURT AS FINAL ARBITER IN FEDERAL–STATE RELATIONS (1958).
Bock, *Dealing with the Overload in Article III Courts*, 70 F.R.D. 231 (1976).

State Court Systems

The power to create courts is an attribute of every sovereignty. The various states of the United States have exercised this power either by constitutional provisions or by statutory enactments. The power to create courts includes the authority to organize them, including the establishment of judgeships, and to regulate their procedure and jurisdiction.

It is beyond the scope of this text to describe the court systems of 50 states, because the judicial systems vary considerably from state to state. A general structural pattern, however, does exist among the states, even though the terminology and structures differ. A state court system usually consists of probate courts, a large number of courts with limited jurisdiction, courts with residual jurisdiction, and appellate courts.

Courts of limited jurisdiction—inferior courts—are limited as to subject matter and territory. For example, the justice of the peace court administers justice in minor matters at the local level. A justice of the peace with little or no legal training conducts trials in civil cases involving small sums of money, and in minor criminal matters. A state judicial system also usually includes a probate court to handle deceased persons' estates. The jurisdiction of local courts, such as municipal, city, and county courts, is limited to a specified territory. The jurisdiction of small-claims courts is limited to relatively low maximum amounts. In small-claims proceedings, representation by attorney and ordinary court procedure may be dispensed with.

Trial courts of residual jurisdiction in the state court system may bear the name of common pleas, district, superior, circuit, or even—in New York State—supreme court. These courts have the power to hear all types of cases. The primary function of trial courts is to exercise original jurisdiction. Generally, they also exercise appellate jurisdiction over decisions of courts of limited jurisdiction.

A state's judicial system may provide an intermediate appellate court analogous to the court of appeals in the federal system. Not all states provide this intermediate step. A final appellate court, analogous to the United States Supreme Court, serves as the highest court in the state. It reviews appeals of major questions emanating from the lower state courts, and at the state level its decision is final.

Wilson v. Iowa District Court
297 N.W.2d 223
Supreme Court of Iowa
October 15, 1980

UHLENHOPP, JUSTICE

We granted a writ of *certiorari* to determine whether a district judge possesses subject-matter jurisdiction to hear and decide an appeal from a judgment rendered by a district associate judge in a civil action which began as a small claim but was later transferred and then tried by regular proceedings.

James Wilson had a garage with a leaky roof. Paul T. Rentzel contracted with him to repair the roof for $1250. Rentzel worked on the roof for $1250. Rentzel worked on the roof, but the leaks continued. He then did additional work, but still did not stop the leaks. Wilson thereafter employed another roofer, who fixed the roof for $1000.

Wilson sued Rentzel for $1000 in a small-claims proceeding. Rentzel counterclaimed for $1250. When the case came before the court for hearing, the court entered an order which recited, "Defendant's counsel requests transfer to regular proceeding in district court. Defendant's request *sustained*, clerk directed to transfer cause from Small Claims docket 1 SW 6368 case."

After trial, the district associate judge initially recited in her decision, "The matter was tried by regular formal procedure for the reason that the counterclaim exceeded the $1000 small-claim jurisdiction." The court found for Wilson, awarded him $1000 and interest, and dismissed the counterclaim.

Rentzel thereupon appealed "to the district court of Iowa," stating that "the matter will come on in accordance with the appellate rules governing small-claim matters." The appeal was submitted to a district judge for decision, who found that neither party was entitled to recover and dismissed the claim and the counterclaim.

Wilson filed a posttrial motion. In ruling on the motion, the district judge stated at the outset, "Upon reviewing the motion, it seems to indicate that the case was conducted by ordinary proceedings because of the counterclaim in excess of $1000. If such be the case, it would appear that this should not have been appealed to district court, but should have been appealed to the supreme court, and it was not a small claims case originally. However, it might be pointed out that the counterclaimant did not appeal." The court adhered to its original decision and overruled the motion.

Wilson then sought review by us, and we granted a writ of *certiorari*.

Chapter 631 of the Iowa Code prescribes a simple, swift, and inexpensive procedure for hearing and determining civil claims for money not exceeding $1000 and for some forcible entry cases. Part- and full-time magistrates, district associate judges, and district judges may entertain these cases, but frequently the cases are handled by magistrates. An expeditious form of appeal to a district judge is provided in these cases. Further appeal is permitted to the supreme court, but only on discretionary review. If the present case had involved only a small claim and had been heard and decided as such, the initial course taken by Rentzel would have been correct: appeal to a district judge.

When Rentzel interposed his counterclaim exceeding $1000, however, section 631.8(4) came into play: "4. In small-claims actions, a counterclaim, cross claim, or intervention in a greater amount than that of a small claim shall be in the form of a regular pleading. The court shall either order such counterclaim, cross claim, or intervention to be tried by regular procedure and the other claim to be heard under this division, or order the entire action to be tried by regular procedure."

The judicial officer before whom the case originally came properly transferred the entire case from the small-claims docket, since the claim and counterclaim both arose out of the same transaction and the counterclaim exceeded $1000. This meant that the case was no longer a small claim. It was to be tried by "regular procedure." Since the amount in controversy on one side of the case exceeded $1000, the case exceeded the jurisdiction of a part-time magistrate. The case had to be heard by a full-time magistrate, a district associate judge, or a district judge. Actually it was heard by a district associate judge employing the required regular procedure.

In that situation, section 631.13, authorizing an initial appeal to a district judge, did not apply, for the case was no longer a small claim. For the same reason, section 631.16, authorizing further discretionary review by the supreme court, did not apply. Instead, the initial appeal would be to the supreme court to the extent permitted by rules 1 and 3 of the rules of appellate procedure. Rentzel did not proceed in that manner.

The judgment of the district associate judge for $1000 did not restore the case to small-claims status. The case remained a regular action. The district judge did not possess jurisdiction to entertain Rentzel's attempted appeal of the action. Hence the decision of the district judge is of no effect. The judgment entered by the district associate judge remains in force.

Writ sustained

CASE QUESTION

What are the arguments for and against small-claims courts?

SUGGESTED READINGS

C. W. BUNN, A BRIEF SURVEY OF THE JURISDICTION AND PRACTICE OF THE
    COURTS OF THE UNITED STATES (5th ed. 1949).
F. JAMES, CIVIL PROCEDURE (2d ed. 1977).
Barth, *Perception and Acceptance of Supreme Court Decisions at the
    State and Local Level*, 17 J. PUB. L. 308 (1968).
Newton, *Trial Courts of Limited Jurisdiction: Is the Traditional Jurispru-
    dential Approach Appropriate?* 1977 DET. COLL. L. REV. 279.
Axworthy, *Controlling the Abuse of Small Claims Courts*, 22 MCGILL L.J.
    480 (1976).

Arbitration

Arbitration is an important method of resolving commercial disputes outside the courts. It does not replace the courts, but it is an alternative to formal court litigation in certain types of controversies. *Arbitration* is a proceeding whereby the parties to a dispute select an impartial third person
who hears the arguments and decides the controversy in place of a tribunal
established by law. The parties agree in advance to be bound by the decision (*award*) of the third party (*arbitrator*). The award of the arbitrator in
settlement of the controversy is final and binding on the parties. This process usually results in an inexpensive, speedy, and final disposition of the
matter in dispute. Arbitration performs a valuable service to the community and to the courts, since it relieves court congestion.

In certain disputes, states are beginning to use arbitration as an alternative to trials. For example, the state of Pennsylvania has a compulsory
arbitration law. Plaintiffs with disputes involving less than $5,000 to
$10,000, depending on the county, must submit the dispute to arbitration.
However, these decisions may be appealed. A dissatisfied party may ask
for a trial before a court.

Arbitration should be distinguished from mediation. *Mediation* is used
primarily in labor–management grievances. It helps the parties reach an
agreement and offers recommendations for settlement. The recommendations are not binding on the parties. The function of mediation is basically
advisory, whereas arbitration performs a judicial function and decides
disputes between parties.

The system of arbitration coexists with the judicial system, but there
are many important differences between courts and arbitration. The
strength of arbitration comes from how it differs from the courts. The continuity that exists in the judicial system is not present in arbitration. Arbitrators do not follow precedent in their decision-making process.

Generally, no reasons need be given for their decision. Arbitration is temporarily convened for the sole purpose of deciding a particular dispute. Arbitration hearings are not as formal as cases held in the courts.

Arbitration hearings are essentially fair and impartial, even though the formalities of a court proceeding are dispensed with. Although formalities are not required, an arbitration hearing usually follows the sequence of opening statements by the opposing parties, examination and cross-examination of witnesses, introduction of exhibits, and a summation at the closing. Arbitrators base their decisions on the arguments made before them and are bound by no rules of evidence. The hearing can take place anywhere that is convenient and comfortable. It is generally private and not open to the public, as a trial is. The law provides a review of an award as long as the award is authorized by agreement and principles of justice have been maintained.

People in business agree to arbitrate in order to obtain prompt, expert decisions. Arbitration is geared more to a lay or business sense of justice than to the rules of law governing the courts. Many commercial disputes involve technical facts that are perhaps better handled by an expert in the field than by a jury or an expert in the law. The expediency of the simplified arbitration procedure has induced many persons to surrender the felt advantage of a jury trial.

Arbitrators who make the decisions are generally selected by the parties according to their individual expertise in a specific field that better enables them to render a decision in a specific dispute. Judge and jury are not selected on the basis of their expertise in a particular area. The success of arbitration depends largely on the arbitrator's fairness and ability to understand the dispute and the area involved. Care should be taken to select a person who will conduct the proceedings with integrity in attaining a just decision. Since arbitrators derive their authority from the agreement of the parties, they do not have the power to go beyond the limits of the authority that the parties have vested in them.

In order for arbitration to take place, the parties must have specifically agreed in a binding agreement to use this method for the settlement of their controversies. For the most part, no law or government agency compels persons to arbitrate their disputes. They do so voluntarily. The agreement may be entered into before the dispute arises, possibly as part of a contract, or it may be agreed on after the controversy has arisen. The arbitration agreement, like any other contract obligation, is meant to be carried out voluntarily by the parties as a legal obligation.

In order to enforce an arbitration agreement against an unwilling person, the demanding party may seek the assistance of the court to compel arbitration. Arbitration agreements are effective in places in which the law is expressly favorable to them. In most states and in the federal area, there are statutes that compel arbitration when parties agree to it. This legislation recognizes and enforces arbitration and provides standards of conduct for it. These statutes make arbitration more effective by giving it legislative sanction. They make arbitration agreements irrevocable, state that court action cannot be brought until arbitration is completed, and restrict the court's power to review the arbitrator's finding of facts and application of the law.

In the absence of a statute recognizing arbitration clauses, courts are reluctant to enforce such agreements. One reason for this reluctance is the fact that in an arbitration agreement, the parties agree to bypass the established judicial system. In those states without arbitration legislation, the agreement to arbitrate is revocable at will by either party at any time before the award is rendered. Either party may institute a court action on the contract that contains an arbitration clause.

Arbitration may be administered by a private agency dedicated to arbitration, such as the American Arbitration Association. The AAA is a public service, nonprofit agency organized in 1926 to encourage the resolution of disputes of all kinds through the use of arbitration. It is the only arbitration agency in the United States that is independent of any specific industry or trade. The AAA does not itself act as an arbitrator. It maintains a national panel of arbitrators consisting of some 30,000 men and women, many of whom are experts in a field or profession, who have been nominated for their knowledge and their reputation for impartiality. The parties in a dispute select an arbitrator from the panel, and the AAA provides for the administration of the proceedings. The AAA's tribunal activities include labor grievances, business controversies, and car insurance claims. Although it is not a suitable means of determining every type of dispute, there are some controversies best handled by arbitration.

Garrity v. Lyle Stuart, Inc.
40 N.Y.2d 354, 353 N.E.2d 793
Court of Appeals of New York
July 6, 1976

BREITEL, CHIEF JUDGE
Plaintiff author brought this proceeding to confirm an arbitration award granting her $45,000 in compensatory damages and $7500 in punitive damages against defendant publishing company. Supreme court confirmed the award. The appellate division affirmed, one justice dissenting, and defendant appeals.

The issue is whether an aribtrator has the power to award punitive damages. The order of the appellate division should be modified to vacate the award of punitive damages and otherwise affirmed. An arbitrator has no power to award punitive damages, even if agreed upon by the parties.

Plaintiff is the author of two books published by defendant. While the publishing agreements between the parties contained broad arbitration clauses, neither of the agreements provided for the imposition of punitive damages in the event of breach.

In March 1974, plaintiff brought an action alleging that defendant had wrongfully withheld $45,000 in royalties. Defendant moved for a stay pending arbitration, which was granted, and plaintiff demanded arbitration. The demand requested the $45,000 withheld royalties and punitive damages for defendant's alleged "malicious" withholding of royalties.

Defendant appeared at the arbitration hearing and raised objections concerning plaintiff's standing and the conduct of the arbitration hearing. Upon rejection of these objections by the arbitrators, defendant walked out.

After hearing testimony, and considering an "informal memorandum" on punitive damages submitted by plaintiff at their request, the arbitrators awarded plaintiff both compensatory and punitive damages. On plaintiff's motion to confirm the award, defendant objected on the ground that the award of punitive damages was beyond the scope of the arbitrators' authority.

Arbitrators generally are not bound by principles of substantive law or rules of evidence, and thus error of law or fact will not justify *vacatur* of an award. It is also true that arbitrators generally are free to fashion the remedy appropriate to the wrong, if they find one, but an authentic remedy is compensatory and measured by the harm caused and how it may be corrected.

The court will vacate an award enforcing an illegal agreement or one violative of public policy. Since enforcement of an award of punitive damages as a purely private remedy would violate public policy, an arbitrator's award which imposes punitive damages, even though agreed upon by the parties, should be vacated.

In the instant case, however, there was no provision in the agreements permitting arbitrators to award liquidated damages or penalties. Indeed, the subject apparently had never even been considered.

The prohibition against an arbitrator awarding punitive damages is based on strong public policy indeed. Punitive damages are available only in a limited number of instances. Punitive or exemplary damages have been allowed in cases where the wrong complained of is morally culpable, or is actuated by evil and reprehensible motives, not only to punish the defendant but to deter him, as well as others who might otherwise be so prompted, from indulging in similar conduct in the future. It is a social exemplary "remedy," not a private compensatory remedy.

Even if the so-called "malicious" breach here involved would permit the imposition of punitive damages by a court or jury, it was not the province of arbitrators to do so. Punitive sanctions are reserved to the state, surely a public policy of such magnitude as to call for judicial intrusion. The evil of permitting an arbitrator, whose selection is often restricted or manipulable by the party in a superior bargaining position, to award punitive damages is that it displaces the court and the jury, and therefore the state, as the engine for imposing a social sanction.

The trouble with an arbitration admitting a power to grant unlimited damages by way of punishment is that, if the court treated such an award in the way arbitration awards are usually treated, and followed the award to the letter, it would amount to an unlimited draft on judicial power. In the usual case, the court stops only to inquire if the award is authorized by the contract; is complete and final on its face; and if the proceeding was fairly conducted.

Actual damage is measurable against some objective standard—the number of pounds, or days, or gallons, or yards. But punitive damages take their shape from the subjective criteria involved in attitudes toward correction and reform. Courts do not accept readily the delegation of that kind of power. Where punitive damages have been allowed for those torts that are still regarded somewhat as public penal wrongs as well as actionable private wrongs, they have had rather close judicial supervision. If the usual rules were followed there would be no effective judicial supervision over punitive awards in arbitration.

Parties to arbitration agree to the substitution of a private tribunal for purposes of deciding their disputes without the expense, delay, and rigidities of traditional courts. If arbitrators were allowed to impose punitive damages, the usefulness of arbitration would be destroyed. It would become a trap for the unwary, given the eminently desirable freedom from judicial overview of law and facts. It would mean that the scope of determination by arbitrators, by the license to award punitive damages, would be both unpredictable and uncontrollable.

In imposing penal sanctions in private arrangements, a tradition of the rule of law in organized society is violated. One purpose of the rule of law is to require that the use of coercion be controlled by the state. In a highly developed commercial and economic society, the use of private force is not the danger, but the uncontrolled use of coercive economic sanctions in private ar-

rangements. For centuries the power to punish has been a monopoly of the state, and not that of any private individual. The day is long past since barbaric man achieved redress by private punitive measures.

The parties never agreed or, for that matter, even considered punitive damages as a possible sanction for breach of the agreement. The law does not and should not permit private persons to submit themselves to punitive sanctions of the order reserved to the state. The freedom of contract does not embrace the freedom to punish, even by contract.

That the award of punitive damages in this case was quite modest is immaterial. Such a happenstance is not one on which to base a rule.

Accordingly, the order of the appellate division should be modified, without costs, to vacate so much of the award which imposes punitive damages, and otherwise affirmed.

GABRIELLI, JUDGE, dissenting
The majority reaches a result favoring a guileful defendant and voids a just and rational award of punitive damages to a wholly innocent and deserving plaintiff. Stripped to its essence, the defendant, by willful and fraudulent guises, refused to pay plaintiff royalties known to be due and owing to her; forced her to commence actions claiming fraudulent acts and to enforce arbitration to redress the wrongs done to her and to collect the sums rightfully due; and, finally, defendant waived any objection to the claim for punitive damages, deliberately refused to participate in the arbitration hearing, and abruptly left the hearing without moving against the claim for punitive damages or even so

much as offering any countervailing evidence or argument on the merits of plaintiff's claims. I cannot, therefore, join with the majority and conclude, as they now do, that the ultimate limit of the damages awardable to plaintiff is that sum which was unquestionably due and owing to her in any event under the royalty agreement.

Plaintiff, the author of *The Sensuous Woman* and *The Sensuous Man*, entered into agreements with the defendant to publish the two books. The agreements contained identical, broad arbitration clauses.

The public policy which "favors the peaceful resolutions of disputes through arbitration" outweighs the public policy disfavoring the assessment of punitive damages in this instance, where the unjustifiable conduct complained of is found to be with malice. I would conclude, therefore, that any public policy limiting punitive damages awards does not rise to that level of significance in this case as to require judicial intervention.

An affirmance here would do no violence to precedents in this court. In at least two varied circumstances, we have held that, although public policy would bar a civil suit for relief, that same public policy was not of such overriding import as to preclude confirmation of an arbitration award [Matter of *Staklinski* (*Pyramid Elec. Co.*), 6 N.Y.2d 159, 188 N.Y.S.2d 541, 160 N.E.2d 78; Matter of *Ruppert* (*Egelhofer*), 3 N.Y.2d 576, 170 N.Y.S.2d 785, 148 N.E.2d 129]. In *Ruppert*, we permitted the enjoining of a work stoppage in a labor dispute by arbitration, despite the fact that the issuance of such relief by a court was prohibited by statute (then Civil Practice Act, §876-a). Similarly, in *Staklinski*, citing *Ruppert*, we upheld an arbitration award of specific performance of an employment contract in the face of the public policy against compelling a corporation to continue the services of an officer whose services were unsatisfactory to the board of directors. The rule to be distilled from these cases, therefore, is that only where the public interest clearly supersedes the concerns of the parties should courts intervene and assert exclusive dominion over disputes in arbitration.

Nor can we hold, as defendant also urges, that the arbitrators exceeded their authority in awarding punitive damages to plaintiff. Arbitrators are entitled to "do justice." It has been said that, short of "complete irrationality," they may fashion the law to fit the facts before them. The award made here was neither irrational nor unjust. Indeed, defendant has not denied that its actions were designed to harass and intimidate plaintiff, as she claimed and the arbitrators obviously concluded. Hence, the award was within the power vested in the arbitrator.

Accordingly, the order of the appellate division should be affirmed.

CASE QUESTIONS

1. List some examples of disputes that would be appropriate for arbitration. What types of disputes would *not* be appropriate for arbitration?

2. List some advantages arbitration has over a court proceeding.

3. When a party to arbitration questions an award of an arbitrator, what inquiry into the case will a court make?

Suggested Readings

Note, *Arbitration: The Award of Punitive Damages as a Public Policy Question*, 43 Brooklyn L. Rev. 546 (1977).

Note, *Judicial Deference to Arbitral Determination: Continuing Problems of Power and Finality*, 23 U.C.L.A. L. Rev. 936 (1976).

Note, *Arbitration—A Viable Alternative?* 3 Fordham Urban L.J. 53 (1974).

Naffziger, *All Power to the Arbitrator: Aftermath of the Steelworks Trilogy, Collyer Wire and ENA*, 12 Am. Bus. L.J. 295 (1975).

Poppleton, *Arbitrator's Role in Expediting the Large and Complex Commercial Case*, 36 Arb. J. Dec. 1981, at 6.

Chapter Questions

1. Define the following terms:

   a. affidavit   b. appellate jurisdiction
   c. arbitration   d. cause of action
   e. *certiorari*   f. courts
   g. diversity   h. *forum non conveniens*
   i. *in personam*   j. *in rem*
   k. judge   l. jurisdiction
   m. jury   n. motion
   o. quash   p. venue

2. A man and a woman, both married to others, had been engaged in meretricious relations for some years. The man was a resident of New York and never lived in Florida. She pleaded with him to come to Florida to see her, since her husband had died. She wrote him a letter at his office address telling him that her mother was sick in Ireland and asking him to come to Miami to advise her on her recent state of affairs, slyly hinting that she would arrange accommodations for them. He told her exactly when he would arrive. He arrived at 6 o'clock in the morning at the Miami Airport and saw her standing some 75 feet away. As he approached her, a deputy sheriff stopped him and asked his name. When he replied, the deputy handed him a summons. A suit was brought by her for $500,000 for money loaned to

him and for seduction under promise of marriage. Does the Florida court have jurisdiction over him? Can it render an effective *in personam* judgment against him if he leaves and disregards the complaint? What if he had come to Miami on ordinary business?

Wyman v. Newhouse, 93 F.2d 313 (2d Cir. 1937)

3. Miller sold a gas cooking stove to Nelson at his place of business in Wisconsin. Miller sent one of his employees to deliver the stove to Nelson's home in Illinois. At the request of the employee, Nelson assisted in unloading the stove from the truck. In the course of this operation, the employee negligently pushed the stove, so that it severed one finger on Nelson's right hand and injured another. Could Nelson effectively sue Miller in a state court in Illinois?

Nelson v. Miller, 11 Ill.2d 378, 143 N.E.2d 673 (1957)

4. Mr. and Mrs. Woodson instituted a product-liability action in an Oklahoma state court to recover for personal injuries sustained in Oklahoma in an accident involving a car that they had bought in New York while they were New York residents. The Woodsons were driving the car through Oklahoma at the time of the accident. The defendants were the car retailer and its wholesaler, both New York corporations, who did no business in Oklahoma. The defendants entered a special appearance, claiming that the Oklahoma state court did not have personal jurisdiction. Would there be enough "minimum contacts" between the defendants and the forum state for the forum state to have personal jurisdiction over the defendants?

World-Wide Volkswagen Corp. v. Woodson, 444 U.S. 286 (1980)

5. Mr. and Mrs. Mottley were injured while riding a passenger train on the Short Line Railroad in Kentucky about 20 years ago. As compensation for their injuries, Short Line agreed to issue a lifetime free travel pass to the Mottleys. A year ago, Congress passed a law forbidding railroads to issue free passes. Short Line promptly canceled the Mottleys' pass, in compliance with the law. The Mottleys filed a complaint in federal court in Kentucky alleging that Short Line made a contract with them 20 years ago to issue them a free pass for life and that the railroad had canceled it last year. The complaint further alleged that the reason for this cancellation was the law against free passes; and that unless the law is construed as not requiring the cancellation of the Mottleys' pass, it deprived the Mottleys of their property without due process, in violation of the Fifth Amendment. Why did the Mottleys' complaint fail to confer jurisdiction of the case on the United States District Court in Kentucky, as presenting a federal question?

Louisville & Nashville R. R. v. Mottley, 211 U.S. 149 (1908)

6. In a diversity of citizenship case, federal law requires complete diversity of citizenship between plaintiffs and defendants and an amount in controversy greater than $10,000 in order for federal courts to entertain jurisdiction of an action. Tom Jones and Leonard Woodrock were deep-shaft coal miners in West Virginia, although Leonard lived across the border in Kentucky. Tom purchased a new Corsair, a National Motors' car, from Pappy's Auto Sales, a local firm. National Motors Corp. is a large auto manufacturer with its main factory in South Bend, Indiana, and incorporated in Kentucky. When Tom was driving Leonard home from the mine, the Corsair's steering wheel inexplicably locked. The car hurtled down a 100-foot embankment and came to rest against a tree. The Corsair, which cost $2100, was a total loss. Tom and Leonard suffered damages of $8000 apiece for personal injuries. Can Tom sue National Motors for damages in a federal court? Why? Can Leonard? Can Leonard and Tom join their claims and sue National Motors in federal court?

7. Several Arizona citizens brought a diversity suit in a federal district court against Harsh Building Co., an Oregon corporation. All parties involved in the suit stipulated that the defendant had its principal place of business in Oregon. During the trial, the evidence showed that the only real business activity of Harsh Building Co. was owning and operating the Phoenix apartment complex, which was the subject of the suit. The plaintiffs lost the suit. On appeal, they claimed that the district court did not have jurisdiction because of lack of diversity of citizenship. Did the plaintiffs waive their right to challenge jurisdiction?

   Bialac v. Harsh Building Co., 463 F.2d 1185 (9th Cir. 1972)

8. National Mutual Insurance Co. is a District of Columbia corporation. It brought a diversity action in the U.S. District Court of Maryland against Tidewater Transfer Co., a Virginia corporation doing business in Maryland. National Mutual contends that, for diversity purposes, a D.C. resident may file suit against the resident of a state. Tidewater Transfer disagrees. What should be taken into consideration in deciding whether the District of Columbia can, for diversity purposes, be regarded as a state?

   National Mutual Insurance v. Tidewater Transfer Co., 337 U.S. 582 (1949)

9. A check was drawn on the treasurer of the United States through the Federal Reserve Bank of Philadelphia to the order of Paul Friendly for $324.20, to cover services rendered in his government job. The check was mailed to Friendly's address in Butler, Pa., but for some reason it never reached him. An unknown person presented the check to the J. C. Penney store in Clearfield, Pa., endorsed it, and presented identification. Penney's cashed the check and endorsed it to the Clearfield

Trust Co. for payment. Clearfield endorsed it to the Federal Reserve Bank, guaranteeing all previous endorsements as genuine. When Friendly notified the government that he had not received his check, the forgery was discovered. The Treasury Department waited more than six months before notifying Clearfield Trust and J. C. Penney of the forgery. The United States then sued Clearfield Trust for the $324.20. Clearfield defended on the ground that the government waited too long before giving notice of the forgery. Under Pennsylvania law, the trust company wins. Under federal common law, the United States wins. Which law governs?

Based on *Clearfield Trust Co. v. United States, 318 U.S. 363 (1943)*

10. Mrs. Pike, a black woman, was demoted from her position as high school counselor and offered a job as a teacher. Mrs. Pike refused to accept the teaching position. Instead, she filed a civil-rights action in federal court, alleging that the school board's action was racially motivated and thus invalid. She asked for reinstatement as high school counselor. At trial, evidence was introduced on both sides of the question. The school board's action was sustained on a finding that Mrs. Pike was professionally incompetent. Mrs. Pike appealed the decision of the district court on the racial motivation issue. In addition, for the first time, she alleged that she was denied due process, since no hearing was held prior to her dismissal. Can the court of appeals consider Mrs. Pike's complaint of lack of a hearing? Why? How should the court go about evaluating whether Mrs. Pike's dismissal was based on the fact that she is black?

Board of Education v. Parks, 469 F.2d 1315 (5th Cir. 1972)

11. John Popovici is a citizen of Rumania. As Rumania's vice consul in the United States, he lived in Cleveland, Ohio, where he met and married his wife. Now, unfortunately, the marriage has failed. Mrs. Popovici wants to sue him for divorce in an Ohio state court. Popovici, however, wants the suit brought in a federal district court, since federal courts have original jurisdiction over "suits against . . . consuls or vice consuls." Consider the nature of the suit and the criteria for federal jurisdiction. Can Mrs. Popovici sue her husband for divorce in federal court?

Popovici v. Agler, 280 U.S. 379 (1930)

12. Benson Winston, a wealthy New York tycoon, had long been dealing with Flaherty & Finch, a well-known brokerage house and member of the New York Stock Exchange. In 1969, Winston claimed that Paul Hertz, an agent of Flaherty & Finch, had fraudulently induced him to buy 10,000 shares of International Unicycle. Winston demanded arbitration of the controversy under stock-exchange rules. The stock was sold and Winston signed a submission for arbitration to decide his

damages from the transaction. Winston claimed the damages were $34,000. The arbitration panel held two hearings, heard witnesses, and studied documents. In March 1973, the arbitration panel issued a simple statement awarding $69.35 to Winston as damages. Winston was furious and immediately took the case to court, claiming that the arbitrators at least had to show the basis of their decision in a written opinion. Is Winston correct?

Sobel v. Hertz, Warner & Co., 469 F.2d 1211 (2d Cir. 1972)

Limitations in
Seeking Judicial Relief III

The function of the courts is to furnish an impartial tribunal to decide disputes. Access to judicial tribunals is limited by common-law, constitutional, and statutory requirements. Thus potential litigants are not free to bring an action in any court, for any matter, at any time, as often as they want, or against anyone.

The court that entertains a suit must have the power to hear and decide the controversy. The jurisdictional requirements were discussed in Chapter II. In addition, a genuine dispute between individuals must exist, since courts generally do not give advice or answer theoretical questions. There is a time period within which a suit must be brought, and only one suit may be maintained against a person for any one cause of action. Certain individuals are immune to being sued. For example, governments, their officials in discharge of their duties, and charitable institutions are not ordinarily subject to suit. The law has protected parents from being sued by their children.

Case or Controversy

It is the duty of courts to adjudicate actual controversies existing between parties with adverse interests and conflicting claims. The best way to find truth and do justice is to require disputing parties to put their full faculties in opposition to each other in court. Where the parties are of one interest and desire the same relief, a judicial tribunal does not ordinarily entertain the action. A friendly, arranged suit without adverse interests is not permitted. Collusive cases are not heard by the courts. A suit is *collusive* when one party is financing and controlling both sides of the litigation.

A court will decline to decide an abstract, theoretical, or moot proposition. A controversy appropriate for judicial determination exists only when there is a definite and real dispute. A court does not determine a question that may arise in the future or set rules to guide litigants in their future conduct. A controversy must be ripe for judicial determination. *Ripeness* exists when the subject of a controversy or a government act has a direct adverse effect on the party making the challenge.

The person bringing a court action must have a personal interest in the dispute, in other words, have standing to sue. The person must be adversely affected by the conduct that is the subject of the suit. Only the party harmed by the wrong may bring a suit to challenge the constitutionality of a public law.

To be within the federal judicial power, a matter must be a "case" or "controversy" as required by article III, § 2, of the United States Constitution. The United States Supreme Court has always construed the "case or controversy" requirement as precluding the federal courts from being advisers to the other branches of the government or to anyone else.

In some jurisdictions, the courts issue advisory opinions to government officials concerning matters of law. Unless a constitution imposes this duty on the courts, the giving of advisory opinions is beyond the power of the judiciary. Many state constitutions follow the United States Constitution and do not provide for the rendering of advisory opinions. In this situation, the courts decide only real controversies between individuals. When a constitutional provision requires an advisory opinion, the court of that jurisdiction renders its opinion if the particular question falls within the scope of the authorization. In this capacity the court acts only as an adviser, and its opinion does not have the effect of a judicial decision. When the constitution does not provide for judicial opinions or the question is outside the scope of authorization, the executive and legislative branches must seek advice from the attorney general.

Abele v. Markle
452 F.2d 1121
United States Court of Appeals, Second Circuit
December 13, 1971

MANSFIELD, CIRCUIT JUDGE
Appellants, 858 women, brought suit in the United States District Court for the district of Connecticut challenging the constitutionality of that state's anti-abortion statutes, and seeking a permanent injunction against enforcement of the statutes. Plaintiffs appeal from the district court's dismissal of their complaint. We affirm in part, reverse in part, and remand the case for further proceedings.

Plaintiffs are residents of Connecticut. Each falls within one of three groups: (1) women of child-bearing age, (2) women physicians, nurses, and medical personnel, and (3) women who counsel others concerning abortions. Except for defendant Robert K. Killian, the attorney general of Connecticut, defendants are state's attorneys for nine counties in Connecticut, charged with enforcement of its anti-abortion laws.

Sections 53–29 and 53–30, Conn. Gen. Stats., make it a crime for any person to attempt to procure an abortion upon a woman or for a woman to produce an abortion upon herself unless "necessary to preserve her life or that of her unborn child." Section 53–31 makes it a misdemeanor for any person to encourage the commission of an abortion by any one of various means, including use of publications, lectures, advertisements, or sale or circulation of publications.

The first claim of the complaint alleges that some plaintiffs have physical disabilities making pregnancy and childbearing hazardous to their health, some are subject to the risk of unplanned pregnancies, some do not presently want to bear children, and others have obtained abortions at the risk of prosecution or outside of ordinary medical settings and have suffered injuries or impairment to their health. It is claimed that the aforementioned Connecticut statutes violate plaintiffs' rights under the First, Fourth, Fifth, Eighth, Ninth, Thirteenth and Fourteenth Amendments. More specifically, plaintiffs allege that the Connecticut abortion laws deny equal protection to women who cannot afford psychological and medical evaluations or to pay for out-of-state abortions, that

they are void for vagueness, that they deny plaintiffs their right of privacy and of free speech guarantees, that they discriminate against women on the basis of sex, and that they impose cruel and unusual punishment.

The second claim of the complaint alleges on behalf of women doctors and medical personnel that Connecticut's statutory prohibition against performing, recommending, or disseminating information about abortions violates their constitutional rights by preventing them from practicing their professions, by prohibiting their engaging in free speech with respect to medical abortion procedures, by imposing vague standards contrary to or not correlated with medical diagnoses, and by subjecting them to criminal liability for engaging in such practices. Similar charges are made in claim 3 on behalf of plaintiffs engaged in counseling, advertising, lecturing, and publishing information concerning family planning, health, and guidance.

By decision dated May 12, 1971, the district court dismissed the action, finding that the "suit lacks a jurisdictional basis to be maintained in the federal court." In his opinion Judge Clarie pointed out that the issues as to the constitutionality of the Connecticut anti-abortion statutes "do not arise in the context of specific factual situations. None of the plaintiffs allege that they are pregnant or that the named physicians have performed any abortions. The plaintiffs are not threatened with imminent prosecution nor do they seek to enjoin any state prosecution." He further observed that there were pending in the Connecticut Supreme Court appeals from two convictions, one of a physician and the other of a nonmedical abortionist, in which the constitutionality of the Connecticut abortion statutes was challenged.

The threshold question, as Judge Clarie sensed, was whether the plaintiffs had sufficient standing to present a justiciable case within the meaning of Art. III, § 2, of the Constitution, which limits the judicial power of federal courts to adjudication of "cases" or "controversies." The existence of a case or controversy depends on whether the persons seeking relief have alleged a sufficient personal stake in the outcome to assure that the court will be called on to resolve real issues between genuine adversaries rather than merely to give advisory opinions with respect to abstract or theoretical questions. It is settled that advisory opinions may not be given by federal courts. The constitutionality of laws may be challenged only by those litigants who will suffer some actual or substantial injury from their enforcement, as distinguished from a remote, general, or hypothetical possibility of harm.

The concept of "standing" as a prerequisite is admittedly an amorphous one. However, we are satisfied in the present case that those female plaintiffs who seek to invoke the court's jurisdiction solely on the ground that they are of child-bearing age do not allege a sufficient threat of personal harm to give them standing to attack the constitutionality of Connecticut's anti-abortion laws. Although some of them may in the future become pregnant and may in such event desire an abortion in Connecticut, it is also possible that they will not become pregnant or that if they do they will, upon further reflec-

tion, decide for other reasons against an abortion. We need not explore the many other conditions that might preclude their gaining any stake or interest, such as change of domicile to another state, infertility, or the like. It is clear that any threat of harm to them is remote and hypothetical. Accordingly we hold that nonpregnant female plaintiffs in this category do not show a sufficient nexus or present a sufficiently concrete issue in an adversary setting to give them standing, and we affirm the district court's dismissal of the complaint as to plaintiffs claiming standing solely on the basis of their child-bearing age. However, we grant leave to pregnant plaintiffs to file an amended complaint so alleging. Pregnancy has repeatedly been held to confer standing to challenge anti-abortion laws, since the prospective enforcement of such statutes prevents the mother from deciding not to bear the child.

As distinguished from nonpregnant women claiming standing solely because they are of child-bearing age, the remaining plaintiffs (physicians, nurses, medical and counseling personnel, and those similarly engaged) allege a sufficiently direct threat of personal harm to give them standing. Each asserts that she is qualified as part of the practice of her profession or calling in Connecticut to perform abortions or to give advice and assistance in connection therewith. It is undisputed that the state of Connecticut has enforced the statutes against those performing abortions, including doctors, a factor which has been held to establish standing. Furthermore, the practical effect of such enforcement of the statutes is to bar these plaintiffs from engaging in activities that could be an important source of their livelihood. These circumstances disclose a sufficiently substantial and imminent interest to satisfy the standing requirement. Such professional women should not be forced to undergo the hardship of criminal prosecution as the sole means of seeking relief. Therefore, the complaint should not have been dismissed as to such plaintiffs.

The district court's dismissal of the complaint is affirmed as to all plaintiffs except women physicians, nurses, medical personnel, and others who perform, or assist in the performance of, abortions or who counsel concerning abortions, with leave to file an amended complaint on behalf of any pregnant plaintiffs seeking relief solely on that ground. In all other respects, the judgment of the district court is reversed and remanded for further proceedings in accordance with this opinion.

CASE QUESTIONS

1. Explain what is meant by a *case* or *controversy*.
2. Why did the drafters of the United States Constitution limit the judicial power of federal courts to the adjudication of cases or controversies?
3. Who had standing in *Abele* and why?

SUGGESTED READINGS

Tucker, *Metamorphosis of the Standing to Sue Doctrine*, 17 N.Y.L.F. 911 (1972).

Dugan, *Standing to Sue: A Commentary on Injury in Fact*, 22 CASE W. RES. L. REV. 256 (1971).

Moore, *Abortion and Public Policy: What Are the Issues?* 17 N.Y.L.F. 411 (1971).

Tushnet, *New Law of Standing: A Plea for Abandonment*, 62 CORNELL L. REV. 663 (1977).

A controversy between parties exists when their legal interests are adverse and a definite, existing dispute touches their legal relations. Generally, courts do not have the power to decide questions that do not affect the rights of the litigants before them. Moot cases are outside the judicial power, since there is no case or controversy. The decision as to when a case is moot is sometimes difficult. An actual controversy must not only exist at the date the action was instituted at the trial court level, but also exist at the appellate stage. Mootness is an aspect of ripeness, in that there is no reason to try a case unless there has been some direct adverse effect to some party. Thus there is no case or controversy and the question is moot. An exception to the mootness rule is made when the issue before the court is capable of repetition. If a defendant is "free to return to his old ways," the public interest in having the legality of the practices settled will prevent mootness.

DeFunis v. Odegaard
416 U.S. 312
United States Supreme Court
April 23, 1974

PER CURIAM

In 1971 the petitioner Marco DeFunis, Jr., applied for admission as a first-year student at the University of Washington Law School, a state-operated institution. The size of the incoming first-year class was to be limited to 150 persons, and the law school received some 1600 applications for these 150 places. DeFunis was eventually notified that he had been denied admission. He thereupon commenced this suit in a Washington trial court, contending that the procedures and criteria employed by the law school admissions committee invidiously discriminated against him on account of his race in violation of the equal-protection clause of the Fourteenth Amendment to the United States Constitution.

DeFunis brought the suit on behalf of himself alone, and not as the representative of any class, against the various respondents, who are officers, faculty members, and members of the Board of Regents of the University of Washington. He asked the trial court to issue a mandatory injunction commanding the respondents to admit him as a member of the first-year class entering in September 1971, on the ground that the law school admissions policy had resulted in the unconstitutional denial of his application for admission. The trial court agreed with his claim and granted the requested relief. DeFunis was, accordingly, admitted to the law school and began his legal studies there in the fall of 1971. On appeal, the Washington Supreme Court reversed the judgment of the trial court and held that the law school admissions policy did not violate the Constitution. By this time, DeFunis was in his second year at the law school.

He then petitioned this Court for a writ of *certiorari*, and the judgment of the Washington Supreme Court was stayed pending the "final disposition of the case by this Court." By virtue of this stay, DeFunis has remained in law school, and was in the first term of his third and final year when this Court first considered his petition in the fall of 1973. Because of our concern that DeFunis' third-year standing in the law school might have rendered this case moot, we requested the parties to brief the question of mootness before we acted on the petition. In response, both sides contended that the case was not moot. The respondents indicated that, if the decision of the Washington

Supreme Court were permitted to stand, the petitioner could complete the term for which he was then enrolled, but would have to apply to the faculty for permission to continue in the school before he could register for another term.

We granted the petition for *certiorari* on November 19, 1973. The case was orally argued on February 26, 1974.

In response to questions raised from the bench during the oral argument, counsel for the petitioner has informed the Court that DeFunis has now registered ''for his final quarter in law school.'' Counsel for the respondents have made clear that the law school will not in any way seek to abrogate this registration. In light of DeFunis' recent registration for the last quarter of his final law school year, and the law school's assurance that his registration is fully effective, the insistent question again arises whether this case is not moot, and to that question we now turn.

The starting point for analysis is the familiar proposition that federal courts are without power to decide questions that cannot affect the rights of litigants in the case before them. The inability of the federal judiciary to review moot cases derives from the requirement of Art. III of the Constitution under which the exercise of judicial power depends on the existence of a case or controversy. Although as a matter of Washington state law, it appears that this case would be saved from mootness by ''the great public interest in the continuing issues raised by this appeal,'' 82 Wash. 2d 11,23 n 6, 507 P.2d 1169, 1177 n 6 (1973), the fact remains that under Art. III, even in cases arising in the state courts, the question of mootness is a federal one which a federal court must resolve before it assumes jurisdiction.

The respondents have represented that, without regard to the ultimate resolution of the issues in this case, DeFunis will remain a student in the law school for the duration of any term in which he has already enrolled. Since he has now registered for his final term, it is evident that he will be given an opportunity to complete all academic and other requirements for graduation. If he does so, he will receive his diploma regardless of any decision this Court might reach on the merits of this case. In short, all parties agree that DeFunis is now entitled to complete his legal studies at the University of Washington and to receive his degree from that institution. A determination by this Court of the legal issues tendered by the parties is no longer necessary to compel that result, and could not serve to prevent it. DeFunis did not cast his suit as a class action, and the only remedy he requested was an injunction commanding his admission to the law school. He was not only accorded that remedy, but he now has also been irrevocably admitted to the final term of the final year of the law school course. The controversy between the parties has thus clearly ceased to be definite and concrete and no longer touches the legal relations of parties having adverse legal interests.

It matters not that these circumstances partially stem from a policy decision on the part of the respondent law school authorities. The respondents, through their counsel, the attorney general of the state, have professionally represented that in no event will the status of DeFunis now be affected by any view this Court might express on the merits of this controversy. And it has been the settled practice of the Court, in contexts no less significant, fully to accept representations such as these as parameters for decision.

There is a line of decisions in this Court standing for the proposition that the "voluntary cessation of allegedly illegal conduct does not deprive the tribunal of power to hear and determine the case, i.e., does not make the case moot." These decisions and the doctrine they reflect would be quite relevant if the question of mootness here had arisen by reason of a unilateral change in the admissions procedures of the law school. For it was the admissions procedures that were the target of this litigation, and a voluntary cessation of the admissions practices complained of could make this case moot only if it could be said with assurance that there is no reasonable expectation that the wrong will be repeated. Otherwise, the defendant is free to return to his old ways, and this fact would be enough to prevent mootness because of the public interest in having the legality of the practices settled. But mootness in the present case depends not at all upon a "voluntary cessation" of the admissions practices that were the subject of this litigation. It depends, instead, upon the simple fact that DeFunis is now in the final quarter of the final year of his course of study, and the settled and unchallenged policy of the law school to permit him to complete the term for which he is now enrolled.

It might also be suggested that this case presents a question that is capable of repetition and is thus amenable to federal adjudication even though it might otherwise be considered moot. But DeFunis will never again be required to run the gauntlet of the law school's admission process, and so the question is certainly not "capable of repetition" so far as he is concerned. Moreover, just because this particular case did not reach the Court until the eve of the petitioner's graduation from law school, it hardly follows that the issue he raises will in the future evade review. If the admissions procedures of the law school remain unchanged, there is no reason to suppose that a subsequent case attacking those procedures will not come with relative speed to this Court, now that the supreme court of Washington has spoken. The usual rule in federal cases is that an actual controversy must exist at stages of appellate or *certiorari* review, and not simply at the date the action is initiated.

Because the petitioner will complete his law school studies at the end of the term for which he has now registered regardless of any decision this Court might reach on the merits of this litigation, we conclude that the Court cannot, consistently with the limitations of Art. III of the Constitution, consider the substantive constitutional issues tendered by the parties. Accordingly, the judgment of the supreme court of Washington is vacated, and the cause is remanded for such proceedings as by the Court may be deemed appropriate.

It is so ordered.

MR. JUSTICE BRENNAN, with whom MR. JUSTICE DOUGLAS, MR. JUSTICE WHITE, and Mr. Justice Marshall concur, dissenting.

I respectfully dissent. Many weeks of the school term remain, and petitioner may not receive his degree despite respondents' assurances that petitioner will be allowed to complete this term's schooling regardless of our decision. Any number of unexpected events—illness, economic necessity, even academic failure—might prevent his graduation at the end of the term. Were that misfortune to befall, and were petitioner required to register for yet another term, the prospect that he would again face the hurdle of the admissions policy is real, not fanciful. For respondents warn that Mr. DeFunis would have to take some appropriate action to request continued admission for the remainder of his law school education, and *some discretionary action by the university on such request would have to be taken*. Petitioner might once again have to run the gauntlet of the university's allegedly unlawful admissions policy. The Court therefore proceeds on an erroneous premise in resting its mootness holding on a supposed inability to render any judgment that may affect one way or the other petitioner's completion of his law studies. For surely if we were to reverse the Washington Supreme Court, we could ensure that, if for some reason petitioner did not graduate this spring, he would be entitled to re-enrollment at a later time on the same basis as others who have not faced the hurdle of the university's allegedly unlawful admission policy.

In these circumstances, and because the university's position implies no concession that its admissions policy is unlawful, this controversy falls squarely within the Court's long line of decisions holding that the mere voluntary cessation of allegedly illegal conduct does not moot a case. Since respondents' voluntary representation to this Court is only that they will permit petitioner to complete this term's studies, respondents have not borne the "heavy burden," of demonstrating that there was not even a "mere possibility" that petitioner would once again be subject to the challenged admissions policy. On the contrary, respondents have positioned themselves so as to be "free to return to their old ways."

I can thus find no justification for the Court's straining to rid itself of this dispute. There is no want of an adversary contest in this case. Indeed, the Court concedes that, if petitioner has lost his stake in this controversy, he did so only when he registered for the spring term. But petitioner took that action only after the case had been fully litigated in the state courts, briefs had been filed in this Court, and oral argument had been heard. The case is thus ripe for decision on a fully developed factual record with sharply defined and fully canvassed legal issues.

Moreover, in endeavoring to dispose of this case as moot, the Court clearly disserves the public interest. The constitutional issues that are avoided today concern vast numbers of people, organizations, and colleges and universities, as evidenced by the filing of 26 *amicus curiae* briefs. Few constitutional questions in recent history have stirred as much debate, and they will not disappear. They must inevitably return to the federal courts and ultimately again to this Court. Although the Court should, of course, avoid unnecessary decisions of constitutional questions, we should not transform principles of avoidance of constitutional decisions into devices for sidestepping resolution of difficult cases.

On what appears in this case, I would find that there is an extant controversy and decide the merits of the very important constitutional questions presented.

CASE QUESTIONS

1. If plaintiff had been in his second-to-last quarter of law school when the Supreme Court heard the case, would its decision have been different?
2. The dissenting opinion states, "The constitutional issues that are avoided today concern vast numbers of people, organizations, and colleges and universities. . . ." List some situations that might be affected.
3. Did the United States Supreme Court do a service to society by not deciding the issue, or would it have been better if it *had* decided it?

SUGGESTED READINGS

Note, *DeFunis v. Odegaard: Reverse Discrimination in Law School Admission*, 11 WILLAMETTE L.J. 134 (1974).
Cohen, *End to Affirmative Action?*, 28 LAB. L.J. 218 (1977).
Note, *Article III Justiciability and Class Action: Standing and Mootness*, 59 TEX. L. REV. 297 (1981).

Statute of Limitations

There is a time period within which an action must be brought upon claims or rights to be enforced. This time period is established by the legislature and is known as the *statute of limitations* (see Table III.1, pages 136–137). The statute of limitations compels the exercise of a right of action within a reasonable time, so that the opposing party has a fair opportunity to defend. Undue delay in bringing a suit is prevented so that the defending party will not be surprised by the assertion of a stale claim after evidence has been lost or destroyed. With the lapse of time, memories fade, witnesses may die or move. The prospects for impartial and comprehensive fact-finding diminish.

The statutory time period begins to run immediately upon the accrual of the cause of action. A cause of action accrues when the plaintiff's right to institute a suit arises. The statutory period is counted from the day when a suit first could have been maintained. If the plaintiff brings the suit after the statutory period has run, the defendant may plead the statute of limitations as a defense.

Generally, once the statute of limitations begins to run, it continues to run until the time period is exhausted. However, many statutes of limitation contain a "saving clause," listing conditions and events that "toll" or suspend the running of the statute. The occurrence of one of these conditions may also extend the limitations period for a prescribed period of time. In personal injury cases, the statute may start to run from the date of the injury or from the date when the injury is discoverable, depending on the jurisdiction. Conditions that may serve to toll the running of the statute or extend the time period include infancy, insanity, imprisonment, court orders, war, and fraudulent concealment of a cause of action by a trustee or other fiduciary. The commencement of an action almost universally tolls the running of the statute of limitations. Thus, once an action is commenced on a claim within the statutory time period, it does not matter if judgment is ultimately rendered after the period of limitations has expired.

Hodge v. Service Machine Company
438 F.2d 347
United States Court of Appeals, Sixth Circuit
February 18, 1971

CELEBREZZE, CIRCUIT JUDGE
This appeal is of an order of the United States District Court for the Eastern District of Tennessee dismissing the appellant's complaint. The district court found the appellant's claim for personal injuries, allegedly caused by a defective punch press sold to his employer by the appellees, barred by the applicable Tennessee statute of limitations, Tenn. Code Ann. § 28–304 (1955). Jurisdiction is founded on diversity of citizenship.

The essential allegations of the complaint are as follows. On February 7, 1966, the appellant's employer purchased a high-speed, 60-ton punch press for perforating metal plates to be used in electric heaters. About 18 months later, on August 17, 1967, the appellant, as part of his job, was attempting to correct a malfunction in the press, which required him to position his left hand between the dies. The press had been stopped to allow the appellant to perform these repairs. However, while the appellant's hand was so positioned in the machine, a defect caused the press to activate, amputating the entire portion of the appellant's left hand with the exception of his thumb. The appellant alleges that at the time of the accident, the machine was in the use for which it was intended, but that it contained defects in design and manufacture which created an unreasonable risk of harm to those likely to use it.

Twenty-seven months after the purchase of the machine by his employer, and nine months after the accident, on May 1, 1968, the appellant instituted this action against the appellees, the manufacturer, and selling agent of the punch press. Upon motion, the district court ordered the complaint dismissed, holding that under *Jackson v. General Motors Corporation, Oldsmobile Division*, 441 S.W.2d 482 (Tenn. 1969), the appellant's cause of action "accrued," within the intendment of Tennessee's one-year statute of limitations, when his employer purchased the machine, that is, on February 7, 1966. Therefore, the district court held, the statute of limitations ran against the appellant 6 months before he was injured, and 15 months before he filed his complaint. We reverse.

In federal diversity actions to recover upon a state-created right, jurisdiction being based solely on diversity of citizenship of the parties, the state's statute of limitations applies. The statute of limitations that applies in the instant case is Tenn. Code Ann. § 28–304 (1955), which provides: "Actions for libel, for injuries to the person, false imprisonment, malicious prosecution, criminal conversation, seduction, breach of marriage promise, and statutory penalties, shall be commenced within one (1) year after cause of action accrued."

The latest Tennessee case applying section 28–304 was *Jackson v. General Motors Corporation, Oldsmobile Division, supra,* 441 S.W.2d 482. In *Jackson,* the plaintiff purchased an automobile from the defendants in May of 1963. Some two and one-half years later, in November 1965, the purchaser parked the car on her sloping driveway, set the hand brake, and got out of the car. After alighting from the car, the plaintiff walked behind it. The safety brake, which allegedly was defective, disengaged, and the car rolled backward down the driveway, striking the plaintiff and injuring her. It was alleged in the complaint that the defect that ultimately caused the injury was present in the automobile continuously from the date of sale. The action was commenced in November 1966, approximately one year after the injury and three and one-half years after the sale of the car.

The Tennessee Supreme Court held that the suit was barred by § 28–304 because the plaintiff's cause of action "accrued" at the date of sale of the car. In selling the plaintiff a defective automobile, the court reasoned, the defendants were committing a breach of contractual duty to the plaintiff on which she could sue immediately, her remedy, presumably, being repair of the defect, replacement, recision, restitution, etc. Since the plaintiff could have sued immediately at the time of the breach, i.e., the time of sale, that is the time her cause of action "accrued."

"The cause of action in this case was an alleged breach of contract and duty in respect to a contract of sale of an automobile. Under the allegations of the declaration, this breach occurred at the time of the sale, so that the cause of action accrued at that time and the statute of limitations began to run on it." 441 S.W.2d at 484.

Since the plaintiff did not sue within one year from the time of her cause of action for defendants' breach of contract duty accrued, she was barred from suing thereafter, upon her personal injury, by the one-year statute.[1]

Presumably since the *Jackson* case was the Tennessee Supreme Court's most recent application of § 28–304, the district court felt bound to apply it to the instant case. Thus the district court held that the statute began to run when the press was sold to the appellant's employer. We believe that the *Jackson* case is distinguishable. For reasons which will be considered fully below, in *Jackson*, the plaintiff's cause of action "accrued" on the date of sale of the automobile. In the instant case, the appellant's cause of action did not "accrue" until he was injured; therefore the statute could not begin to run before that date.

A cause of action accrues when a suit may be maintained upon it. A suit may not be brought upon a cause of action until it exists, and a cause of action does not exist until all its elements coalesce. In civil actions for damages, two elements must coalesce before a cause of action can exist: (a) a breach of some legally recognized duty owed by the defendant to the plaintiff; (b) which causes the plaintiff some legally cognizable damage.

In *Jackson*, the statute of limitations ran from the date of sale because the Tennessee Supreme Court found that (a) a breach of duty, and (b) legally cognizable damage coalesced on that date. The breach of duty was a breach of contract: the defendant's failure to provide the plaintiff with an automobile free of defect, as he had promised. The legally significant damage: the plaintiff got less than he paid for. That is, he bargained and paid for an automobile free of defect, and he received a defective one. The cause of action, therefore, accrued at the date of sale.

In *Albert v. Sherman*, 167 Tenn. 133, 67 S.W.2d 140 (1934), a dentist failed to remove the entire root of an extracted tooth. It was not for some 22 months that the plaintiff began to experience pain and swelling. Within a year thereafter she sued the dentist, her cause of action arising out of contract. The Tennessee Supreme Court held that since the breach occurred the day of the extraction, and since the plaintiff incurred damages for which she could have sued at that time, the fact that personal injuries were discovered 22 months later was irrelevant. She could have sued on the day the tooth was improperly extracted. Her cause of action accrued on that day; her failure to bring suit within one year barred her recovery.

The statute begins to run when the cause of action accrues. Later injurious developments are merely elements of damage which may be recovered in the original cause of action. Such later developments attach themselves to the

---

[1] In reaction to the *Jackson* decision, the Tennessee State Legislature amended § 28–304 by adding the following two sentences: "For the purpose of this section, insofar as product-liability cases are concerned, the cause of action for injury to the person shall accrue on the date of the personal injury, not the date of the negligence or the sale of a product. The preceding sentence shall not apply to causes of action accruing prior to May 20, 1969." Tenn. Code Ann. § 28–304 (1969 Supp.).

primary cause of action, and are not individual causes of action in themselves.

It must be emphasized that in every Tennessee case in which the Tennessee Supreme Court held the statute to run from the date of the breach of legal duty, there was also, on that date, some legally cognizable damage, for which the plaintiff could have recovered. The fact that the legally cognizable damage was latent on the date of the breach has been deemed irrelevant, so long as it was there. In *Jackson*, the plaintiff alleged that the defect was present the day she bought the car. In *Albert* the damage was caused the day of the extractions, and suit could immediately have been maintained to correct the faulty dental work.

In the instant case, unlike *Jackson*, the appellant had no legally cognizable damage, therefore no cause of action against the appellee, until his hand was severed by the punch press. He had no cause of action arising out of contract, because there was no contract between the appellant and the appellee.

The appellant did not have a cause of action in tort until he sustained his injury. Actual damage is an indispensable element of any tort action he could have maintained. There was no damage to the appellant on the date of the sale of the machine to his employer. Thus the first date the appellant could have maintained a cause of action in tort was when his hand was severed. That was also the date his cause of action accrued. The statute of limitations could not, therefore, have begun to run against him before that time. Since the appellant brought his action within a year from the date when that action could first have been maintained, he is not barred by § 28–304.

The purpose of a statute of limitations is to compel the exercise of a right of action within a reasonable time. The appellant in the instant case had no "right to action" until 18 months after the machine was sold to his employer. To apply the *Jackson* accrual-at-time-of-sale rule to the facts of the instant case would "compel the exercise of a right of action" before that right existed. This result would be inimical to the purpose of the statute.

Reversed and remanded

CASE QUESTIONS

1. What is the purpose of the statute of limitations?
2. What problem was brought out by the *Jackson* case cited in the *Hodge* opinion, and what was the reaction of the legislature?
3. Distinguish *Hodge* from *Jackson*.

SUGGESTED READINGS

Note, *Tolling of State Statutes of Limitations in Federal Courts*, 71 COLUM. L. REV. 865 (1971).

Note, *Torts—Statute of Limitations—Employee Injured Using Employer's Equipment*, 38 Tenn. L. Rev. 608 (1971).

Note, *Statute of Limitations*, 8 Seton Hall L. Rev. 134 (1976).

McGovern, *Status of Statute of Limitations and Statutes of Repose in Product Liability Actions: Present and Future*, 16 Forum 416 (1981).

Res Judicata

Res judicata literally means that the matter has been decided. A final decision by a competent court on the merits concludes the litigation of the parties and constitutes a bar to a new suit. A matter once judicially decided is finally decided, and the loser may not bring a new suit against the winner for the same cause of action in any court. The loser may, of course, appeal the decision of a lower court to a higher court, but the decision may not be collaterally attacked.

The justification for the principle of *res judicata* is that there must be an end to litigation. If the parties realize that they have only one chance to win, they will make their best effort. The doctrine reduces litigation and prevents harassment or hardship on an individual who otherwise could be sued twice for the same cause of action.

For *res judicata* to apply, two conditions must be met. First, there must be an identity of parties. This means that parties to a successive suit must be the same as, or in privity with, the parties to the original suit. *Privity* exists where there is a relationship between two people that allows one not directly involved in the case to take the place of the one who *is* a party. Thus, if a person dies during a lawsuit, the executor of the estate may take the deceased person's place in the lawsuit. This also means that if the person dies after the lawsuit has concluded, the executor is prevented from bringing another suit for the same cause of action, since the deceased could not have brought the suit again. Privity exists between the person who dies and the executor, so that as far as this litigation is concerned, they are the same person.

Second, there must be an identity of issues. In other words, for *res judicata* to bar (put an end to) the suit, the issue—or cause of action—in the first case must be the same the second time litigation is attempted. For instance, suppose that *A* sues *B* for breach of contract and loses. *Res judicata* prohibits any further action on that same contract by *A* and *B* (except for appeal). *A* could, however, sue *B* for the breach of a different contract, since that would be a different cause of action.

Whitehead v. General Telephone Company
20 Ohio St. 2d 108, 254 N.E.2d 10
Supreme Court of Ohio
December 17, 1969

HERBERT, JUDGE
This action to recover damages for personal injuries was filed by Bobetta A. Whitehead, a minor, through her father, Jess R. Whitehead. Plaintiff-appellee alleged in her petition that the appellant, General Telephone Company of Ohio, negligently installed and maintained a telephone at the Whitehead residence and that defendant Major Materials Corporation of Ohio (which was affixing vinyl siding to the Whitehead residence at the time of the injury) was negligent in dislodging the telephone ground wire, in removing the cover from the telephone fuse box on the side of the house, and in leaving a metal ladder against the house in close proximity to the telephone wire during an electrical storm. The telephone service was installed in the Whitehead residence by General Telephone Company in 1960.

On July 11, 1966, Major Materials Corporation of Ohio commenced work to affix vinyl siding to the Whitehead home. During the morning of July 12, 1966, an employee of Major Materials, preparatory to the installation of the vinyl siding, removed the telephone lightning arrester (fuse box) from the side of the house. In order to dislodge this device, it was necessary to remove the cover, loosen it from the house and allow the fuse box to hang limp, attached only to the wires leading into it. The arrester remained hanging in this exposed condition while the employee left for lunch. A rainstorm developed during the employee's lunch period and because of the storm he was unable to return to the Whitehead residence. While using the telephone at approximately 6:30 P.M. on July 12, 1966, the appellee's left ear was injured by an electrical discharge, which was emitted from the earpiece and caused by a bolt of lightning.

Prior to the trial of this case, the parents of the appellee brought suit against the appellant and Major Materials in Sylvania Municipal Court for the loss of appellee's services and medical expenses, alleging that such loss was the result of defendant's negligence. The municipal court entered a judgment for the telephone company.

In answer to appellee's petition in the case at bar, appellant admitted that it was a corporation doing business under the laws of the state of Ohio, denied each and every other allegation in the appellee's petition, and affirmatively alleged that: "On of the 30th day of September, 1966, plaintiffs Jess R. Whitehead and Bobetta A. Whitehead instituted an action against these same defendants entitled *Jess R. Whitehead and Bobetta A. Whitehead v. General Telephone Company of Ohio and Major Materials Corporation of Ohio*; that plaintiffs sought to recover a money judgment therein against said defendants for loss of services and medical expenses; that after due trial of said action a judgment was entered by the court in favor of defendant General Telephone Company of Ohio; that the issues in the instant case regarding the liability of General Telephone Company of Ohio are identical to the issues adjudicated in the Sylvania Municipal Court and that said issues were resolved adversely to the plaintiff and in favor of the defendant and that plaintiff is thereby estopped by judgment entered in the prior action from relitigating herein the identical issues which were raised in said prior action or which could have been raised therein.''

The trial court sustained the appellee's demurrer to this defense and appellant filed an amended answer. During the trial, the appellee settled her claim against Major Materials for $4000, and it was dismissed as a party-defendant. The jury returned a verdict of $12,500 for the appellee and against appellant, and the trial court entered judgment upon that verdict. The court of appeals affirmed the judgment and the cause is here pursuant to the allowance of a motion to certify the record.

Appellant argues that this injured minor is estopped to relitigate the identical issues involved in her parent's derivative action for loss of services and medical expenses. Thus, this case presents the question whether the defense of collateral estoppel applies to one who was not a party to the prior suit in which the identical issues were determined.

In the instant case, the single alleged wrong gave rise to two separate and distinct causes of action: an action by the minor for her personal injuries and a derivative action in favor of the parents of the child for the loss of her services and her medical expenses.

Res judicata or collateral estoppel are operative in a second suit only when there is an identity of issues and an identity of parties or their privies in both the first and second suit. Never-theless, appellant argues that the present case is one where the defense of collateral estoppel should be appropriate, and urges the definition and use of the word *privity* adopted by the courts of Ohio thwarts the policies of the doctrine of *res judicata*. Appellant further suggests that this court should define privity so as to focus on the relationship of the parties to the subject matter of litigation, thereby lessening the importance of identity of parties in the first and second actions and elevating the emphasis placed on the subject matter of the litigation and the issues raised thereby. Appellant's position would result in the appellee being precluded or estopped from relitigating the issue of appellant's negligence, even though she was not a party or in privity with parties to the prior action, the sole question being whether her interests were adequately represented, therein. The matter of such adequate representation would essentially be a question of whether there was sufficient incentive and opportunity for her parents to adequately litigate the issue in the prior suit in such a manner that the appellee's interests were fully and fairly represented.

This court has consistently held that for a judgment or decree to be *res judicata*, or to operate as estoppel, there must be an identity of issues and an identity of parties or persons in privity with the parties. We have also held that the term ''parties'' includes those who are directly interested in the subject matter of a suit, who have a right to make a defense, or who control the proceedings. It has often been suggested that a person although not technically a party to a prior judgment, may nevertheless be connected with it by his interest in the result of that litigation and by his active participation therein, so as to be bound by that judgment. Moreover, "parties in privity," to the extent that they are bound by a final judgment, includes those who acquire an interest in the subject matter after the beginning of the action or the rendition of the final judgment.

Generally, a person is in privity with another if he succeeds to an estate or an interest formerly held by another. In the present case, the parents' cause of action for loss of services and medical expenses of the minor child, although derivative, does not arise by way of succession from an estate or interest of the minor child. The interest, as well as any possible recovery, was solely that of the parents. Thus the minor child and her parents are not in privity.

Moreover, it cannot be said that this child was, in any sense, a real party in interest in the suit by her parents or had any control over that litigation. For a record to constitute a bar or *res judicata* against one not a party or privy, but who assisted in the prosecution or defense of the action in aid of some interest of his own, the record itself must in some way show such assistance.

In our opinion, the existing Ohio requirement that there be an identity of parties or their privies is founded upon the sound principle that all persons are entitled to their day in court. The doctrine of *res judicata* is a necessary judicial development involving considerations of finality and multiplicity, but it should not be permitted to encroach upon fundamental and imperative rights.

Judgment affirmed

Case Questions

1. Bobetta's parents brought a suit for the loss of Bobetta's services and medical expenses. They lost their case and recovered nothing. The jury returned a verdict in Bobetta's favor in her suit based on identical facts. How is this possible?
2. What is the reason for the doctrine of *res judicata*?
3. Major Materials Corporation of Ohio (one of the two defendants) settled outside of court for $4000. Why would a party to a suit settle outside of court?
4. Why did not Bobetta and her parents bring just one suit rather than two?

Suggested Readings

F. JAMES and G. C. HAZARD, CIVIL PROCEDURE, §§ 11.1–11.5 (2d ed. 1977).
Note, *Developments in the Law—Res Judicata*, 65 HARV. L. REV. 818, 843–45 (1952).

RESTATEMENT OF JUDGMENTS § 79 (1940).

Brousseau, *Reader's Guide to the Proposed Changes in the Preclusion Provisions of the Restatement of Judgments*, 11 TULSA L.J. 305 (1976).

Holland, *Modernizing Res Judicata: Reflections on the Parklane Doctrine*, 55 IND. L.J. 615 (1980).

Immunity from Legal Action

The law provides immunity from tort liability in situations in which it is in the best interest of the public. This is an exception to the rule that there must be a remedy for every wrong. This does not mean that the conduct is not tortious in character, but only that for policy reasons the law denies liability resulting from the tort.

Sovereign Immunity

It is a basic principle of common law that no sovereign may be sued without its express consent. The doctrine of government immunity from tort liability originated from the English notion that the "king can do no wrong." Ironically, whereas most of the courts in the United States have retained the doctrine, England has repudiated it. The immunity applies to government agencies as well as to the sovereignty. Government hospitals, prisons, educational institutions, and water works are examples of government operations that are sheltered from liability.

In 1946 the federal government passed the Federal Tort Claims Act. By this act, the United States Government waived its immunity from tort liability, permitting itself to be sued in federal courts for negligence or wrongful acts committed by its employees within the scope of their employment. Liability is based on the applicable local tort law. Immunity was not waived for all acts of federal employees. Acts within the discretionary function of a federal employee or acts of military and naval forces in time of war are examples of situations in which immunity has not been waived.

Courts have drawn a distinction between functions of the government that are *governmental* and those that are *proprietary*. When a public entity is involved in a governmental function, it is generally immune from tort liability. The legal sovereignty in the United States rests in the people, and the people do not want to be sued in the exercise of their governmental functions. The state would not be liable, for example, for the torts of a police officer in making an arrest. When the government engages in activity that is usually carried on by private individuals or that is commercial in character, it is involved in a proprietary function, and the cloak of immunity is lost. A state is not immune when it provides a service that a corporation may perform, such as providing electricity.

The current trend favors abolition of government immunity. To a greater or lesser extent, all states have given consent to suits by certain individuals in particular cases. An argument often used for the retention of the doctrine of sovereign immunity is that there are no funds designated from which claims can be paid. It would be embarrassing for the government to have to divert public funds, which have been appropriated for legitimate government purposes, for the compensation of private injuries. Perhaps liability insurance can be obtained in order to eliminate the threat of depletion of public funds.

Sousa v. State
341 A.2d 282
Supreme Court of New Hampshire
June 30, 1975

LAMPRON, JUSTICE
Actions by John Sousa and Joseph Evans, driver and passenger in a tractor-trailer truck, to recover damages for the injuries they sustained when the state-owned-and-maintained bridge over the Gale River on Route 117 in Franconia collapsed while they were driving over it. Plaintiffs allege that their injuries were caused by the negligent failure of the state to properly maintain the bridge, to keep it in proper repair, and to post warning signs of load limitation. The state filed motions to dismiss these actions on the ground of sovereign immunity. The motions were granted by the lower court. We are asked by the plaintiffs to reconsider and abolish the existing immunity of the state from liability for such accidents.

The doctrine of sovereign immunity is deeply entrenched in this jurisdic-

tion. State immunity is broader than municipal immunity, which this court has recently abolished. In addition to having immunity from liability for torts, which municipal corporations previously enjoyed as to certain torts, the state is also immune from suit in its courts without its consent, a privilege cities and towns never had.

In many states, the rule that a state cannot be sued without its consent is written into its constitution, which either prohibits the giving of consent, or provides that the legislature will direct the manner, courts, and cases in which suits can be brought. In other jurisdictions, including our own, the state's immunity from suit is traced back to the immunity of the British Crown, carried over to the states by the courts.

The state's immunity for torts, also said to be a carry-over from the British Crown, is generally recognized to be of judicial origin. In most cases, however, no distinction has been made as to whether a tort suit against the state was dismissed because of the state's immunity for torts or its immunity from suit without its consent.

Plaintiffs argue that abolishment of this immunity is mandated by Art. 14, part I, of our constitution. It reads in pertinent part as follows: ''Every subject of this state is entitled to a certain remedy, by having recourse to the laws, for all injuries he may receive in his person, property, or character . . . conformably to the laws.'' As indicated in Art. 14, the remedies provided are to be ''conformable to the laws.'' This means the rules of statutory and common law applicable at the time the injury is sustained. If Art. 14 were to be interpreted as urged by the plaintiffs, contributory or comparable negligence, statutes of limitations, or other defenses that would prevent an injured plaintiff from recovering for his injuries against an individual defendant or the state would be unconstitutional.

Plaintiffs' actions are based on a negligent act of agents of the state and not on an appropriation of their property. Hence the defense of state immunity is not in violation of state and federal constitutional provisions that a man's property is not to be taken by eminent domain without just compensation being awarded. In short, we hold that there is no constitutional provision that confers on the plaintiffs a right to sue and hold the state liable for a tort.

It is not contested that the state may waive its immunities and permit suits to be brought and recovery obtained by plaintiffs injured by the negligence of its agents. As this permission is altogether voluntary on the part of the sovereignty, it follows that it may prescribe the terms and conditions on which it consents to be sued, and the manner in which the suit shall be conducted.

The state has waived its immunities in many instances. It has permitted suits to be brought and judgments entered against it in actions founded on any express or implied contract. The governor and council have been authorized to pay claims against the state arising out of accidents occasioned by the activities of the National Guard. The commissioner of public works and highways may pay claims of less than $150 resulting from accidents due to the activities of his department. State agencies, institutions, and departments are made subject to the workmen's compensation laws. State agencies may procure policies of liability insurance, and the defense of immunity is waived to the extent of the policy limits.

Another avenue of relief for plaintiffs who are damaged by the negligence of state employees, or otherwise, is a petition to the legislature. However, the legislature is not organized to determine the merits of such claims, and the time consumed in their consideration adds materially to the legislative costs. To obviate these difficulties, many states have created a board of claims in which relief for torts committed by agents of the state can be obtained. Our legislature may find it in the best interest of the state itself, and of claimants, to consider and enact legislation creating a board of claims, fixing its membership, and enumerating its powers.

As previously stated, state immunity for torts involves certain factors not present in the immunity of cities and towns. By its magnitude, the striking of a balance between granting relief to injured claimants and protecting the solvency of the state is a more complex problem at that level than it is for most cities and towns. Extremely broad considerations of public policy and government administration are involved. In this respect, the legislature's machinery is well adapted to conduct investigations and give consideration to plans advanced as a solution. Furthermore, the legislature has already enacted certain laws in that area. We are aware that other measures are under

consideration to regulate this field of liability which could lead to additional legislation. For these reasons, we are of the opinion that at this time it would be inappropriate for the court to abrogate by judicial action the existing rules of state immunity.

Because of the result reached, it is unnecessary to consider the other issues raised by the parties. We hold that the state's motions to dismiss were properly granted under the existing law.

All incurred.

CASE QUESTIONS

1. Discuss the pros and cons of government immunity.
2. If someone were driving along a state road in New Hampshire and hit a chuckhole that caused a flat tire, would the state be liable?

SUGGESTED READINGS

Borchard, *Governmental Responsibility in Tort*, 36 YALE L.J. 1 (1926).

Van Alstyne, *Governmental Tort Liability: A Public Policy Prospectus*, 10 U.C.L.A. L. REV. 463 (1963).

Kennedy and Lynch, *Some Problems of a Sovereign Without Immunity*, 36 S.CAL. L. REV. 161 (1963).

Davis, *Tort Liability of Governmental Units*, 40 MINN. L. REV. 751 (1956).

David, *Tort Liability of Local Government: Alternatives to Immunity from Liability or Suit*, 6 U.C.L.A. L. REV. 1 (1959).

Weick, *Erosion of State Sovereign Immunity and the Eleventh Amendment by Federal Decisional Law*, 10 AKRON L. REV. 583 (1977).

Immunity of Government Officials

Executive, legislative, and judicial officers are afforded immunity when they act within the scope of their authority and in the discharge of their official duties. The purpose of the immunity is to protect government officials from being unduly inhibited in the performance of their functions by the threat of legal action. It is in the public interest to shield responsible government officers from harrassment or ill-founded damage suits based on acts done in the exercise of their official responsibility.

The immunity applies only when public officers perform an official function. Public officials are not immune from liability for tortious conduct when they transcend their lawful authority and invade the constitutional rights of others. They are legally responsible for their personal torts and are not shielded from their responsibility merely because they are officers.

Immunity is not the same for all government officials. High-level executive, legislative, and judicial officials with discretionary functions enjoy more immunity than lower-level officials. For example, judges have been held absolutely immune regardless of their motives or good faith, whereas police officers and like officials enjoy a more limited privilege. Immunity is afforded only in those instances in which the official in question has performed a discretionary—as opposed to a ministerial—act, within the scope of official duties.

An argument for not granting immunity to officials is that individual citizens should be protected against damage caused by oppressive or malicious conduct on the part of public officers. Immunity should not be a cloak for the abuse of the power entrusted to them. Government officials may in some jurisdictions lose their immunity if they act maliciously or for an improper purpose rather than honestly or in good faith.

Galella v. Onassis
487 F.2d 986
United States Court of Appeals, Second Circuit
September 13, 1973

J. JOSEPH SMITH, CIRCUIT JUDGE
Ronald Galella, a free-lance photographer, appeals from a summary judgment dismissing his complaint against three Secret Service agents for false arrest, malicious prosecution, and interference with trade.

Galella is a free-lance photographer specializing in the making and sale of photographs of well-known persons. Defendant Onassis is the widow of the late President, John F. Kennedy, mother of the two Kennedy children, John and Caroline, and is the wife of Aristotle Onassis, widely known shipping figure and reputed multimillionaire. John Walsh, James Kalafatis, and John Connelly are U.S. Secret Service agents assigned to the duty of protecting the Kennedy children.

Galella fancies himself as a *paparazzo* (literally a kind of annoying insect, perhaps roughly equivalent to the English gadfly). Paparazzi make themselves as visible to the public and obnoxious to their photographic subjects as possible to aid in the advertisement and wide sale of their works.

Some examples of Galella's conduct brought out at trial are illustrative. Galella took pictures of John Kennedy riding his bicycle in Central Park across the way from his home. He jumped out into the boy's path, causing the agents concern for John's safety. The agents' reaction and interrogation of Galella led to Galella's arrest and his action against the agents. Galella on other occasions interrupted Caroline at tennis, and invaded the children's private schools. At one time he came uncomfortably close in a power boat to Mrs. Onassis swimming. He often jumped and postured around while taking pictures of her party, notably at a theater opening but also on numerous other occasions. He followed a practice of bribing apartment house, restaurant, and nightclub doormen as well as romancing a family servant to keep him advised of the movements of the family.

After detention and arrest following complaint by the Secret Service agents protecting Mrs. Onassis' son and his acquittal in the state court, Galella filed suit against the agents and Mrs. Onassis. Galella claimed that under orders from Mrs. Onassis, the three agents had falsely arrested and maliciously prosecuted him, and that this incident in addition to several others described in the complaint constituted an unlawful interference with his trade.

On a motion for summary judgment, Galella's claim against the Secret Service agents was dismissed, the court finding that the agents were acting within the scope of their authority and thus were immune from prosecution.

We conclude that grant of summary judgment and dismissal of Galella's claim against the Secret Service agents was proper. Federal agents, when charged with duties that require the exercise of discretion, are immune from liability for actions within the scope of their authority. Ordinarily, enforcement agents charged with the duty of arrest are not so immune. The protective duties assigned the agents under this statute, however, require the instant exercise of judgment which should be protected. The agents saw Galella jump into the path of John Kennedy, who was forced to swerve his bike dangerously as he left Central Park and was about to enter Fifth Avenue, whereupon the agents gave chase to the photographer. Galella indicated that he was a press photographer listed with the New York City Police. He and the agents went to the police station to check on the story, where one of the agents made the complaint on which the state court charges were based. Certainly it was reasonable that the agents check out an individual who has endangered their charge, and seek prosecution for apparent violation of state law which interferes with them in the discharge of their duties.

If an officer is acting within his role as a government officer, his conduct is at least within the outer perimeter of his authority. The Secret Service agents were charged with guarding against and preventing any activity by any individual that could create a risk to the safety and well-being of the children or result in their physical injury. It was disputed that the agents were on duty at the time, and there was evidence that they believed John Kennedy to be endangered by Galella's actions. Unquestionably, the agents were acting within the scope of their authority.

To be sure, even where acting within their authority, not all federal agents are immune from liability. Immunity is accorded officials whose decisions involve an element of discretion, so that the decisions may be made without fear or threat of vexations or fictitious suits and alleged personal liability. The issue in each case is whether the public interest in a particular official's unfettered judgments outweighs the private rights that may be violated. The protective duties of the agents on assignments similar to this warrant this protection.

Affirmed

CASE QUESTIONS

1. Consider the following fact pattern: The three Secret Service agents in the above case are at a bar having a drink after work. They see a man who has had too much to drink bothering patrons at the bar. If they physically throw the man out of the bar, can they be sued for assault and battery? What if one of the patrons were a child of the current President?
2. How effective would government officials be if they were subject to suit for official acts within the scope of their authority?
3. When are government officials immune and not immune from tort liability?

SUGGESTED READINGS

McCormack and Kirkpatrick, *Immunities of State Officials under Section 1983*, 8 RUT.-CAM. L. REV. 65 (1976).
Palmer, *Personal Liability for Official Acts*, 18 A.F.L.R. 85 (1976).
Gray, *Private Wrongs of Public Servants*, 47 CALIF. L. REV. 303 (1959).
Rubinstein, *Liability in Tort of Judicial Officers*, 15 U. TORONTO L. J. 317 (1964).
Seng, *Municipal Liability for Police Misconduct*, 51 MISS. L.J. 1 (1980).

Charitable Immunity

The doctrine that excuses charitable institutions from tort liability is based on public policy. The public good is served by recognizing charitable immunity and protecting charitable funds from being depleted by negligence claims. Courts have recognized that charitable funds must be preserved so that charity may carry out its benevolent functions.

The United States has witnessed the rise and fall of the doctrine of charitable immunity. At the time the doctrine was established, charities were supported mainly by small contributors and operated on a relatively small scale. Today, charitable institutions are often big businesses. Liability insurance is easily obtainable to protect their funds. It can be argued that there is nothing charitable in denying recovery to an injured party.

Abernathy v. Sisters of St. Mary's
446 S.W.2d 599
Supreme Court of Missouri
November 10, 1969

HENLEY, CHIEF JUSTICE

This is an action by a patient against a hospital for $35,000 damages for personal injuries allegedly suffered as a result of negligence of defendant. Defendant moved for summary judgment, alleging that it is, and operates the hospital as, a benevolent, religious, nonprofit corporation and charitable institution, and therefore is immune from liability for its torts. The motion was sustained, judgment was entered for defendant, and plaintiff appealed.

The question presented is whether Missouri should continue to adhere to the doctrine that a charitable institution is immune from liability for the tortious acts of its agents and employees. We abolish the doctrine.

Plaintiff's petition alleges, in substance, that while a paying patient in defendant's hospital, he was assisted by Marie Taylor, an employee of the hospital and an original defendant in this action, to move from his bed to his bathroom where he was left by the employee unattended; that due to his weakened condition, he fell to the bath-

room floor and suffered multiple injuries, including a fracture of his right leg; that his injuries were the result of negligence of the hospital in failing (1) to provide handrails for his support in lowering and raising his body to and from the toilet seat; and (2) to furnish a nurse or attendant to remain with and assist him in these necessary body functions.

The doctrine of immunity of charitable institutions from liability for tort was adopted in this state in 1907 by a decision of the Kansas City Court of Appeals in *Adams v. University Hospital*, 122 Mo. App. 675, 99 S.W. 453. Plaintiff Adams, a paying patient, while still under the influence of an anesthetic, suffered postoperative burns from hot water bottles administered by incompetent nurses employed by defendant. Judgment was for plaintiff. The court of appeals reversed, holding in substance, that it is the public policy of this state that a charitable institution is immune from liability for damages for its own negligence in selecting incompetent employees and for the negligence of its employees. In adopting this policy, the court reasoned that it is in the best interest of every member of the public, and the state itself, that charitable institutions designed either for the alleviation of human suffering or for the moral well-being of mankind be built up and maintained by the funds of the benevolent. Those institutions should be protected from any action which might tend either to close the purses of donors or deplete its funds and thereby prevent the institution from performing its functions. In other words, the court said, in effect, that it is better that the individual suffer injury without compensation from the negligent charitable institution than to risk the judicially assumed probability that the public and state would be deprived of the benefits of the charity. The interest of the latter is so supreme that the former must be sacrificed to it.

While resting the immunity doctrine on public policy, the court refers to two legal theories as justification and support. The first theory is that of "implied waiver," that he who accepts the benefit of charity does so on the implied assurance that he will not assert against the institution a claim for damages for injuries resulting from its negligence or the negligence of its employees. The second is the "trust fund" theory, that the funds of the institution are given and held in trust for a charitable purpose. They shall not be used to compensate persons suffering injury resulting from the tortious acts of the institution or its employees, because that use would be contrary to the intent of the donor and beyond the powers of the trustee.

Plaintiff recognizes the state of our law on the subject, but he makes a direct, frontal attack on it, saying it denies basic, substantive rights of the individual; that it is not fair now, has never been fair, and will never be fair; that whatever the reason for the doctrine in its inception, it does not exist today and the doctrine should be abolished. More or less obliquely, he says also that the fact that defendant carries public liability insurance and that its insurer would pay any damages for injury resulting from its negligence removes the reason for and the need, if any ever existed, of protecting the institution from damage claims. Defendants contend that the reasons for the doctrine still exist. Charitable institutions should continue to be immune from tort liability so long as they are operated for the alleviation of human suffering or the moral well-being of mankind, and so long as no part of the institution's funds is profit from operation inuring to the benefit of a private person. The fact that the institution is protected by public liability insurance has no relation to the basic issue of liability. Defendants contend also that the doctrine of immunity is so firmly embedded as public policy that, if it is to be modified or abolished, it properly should be done by the legislature rather than the court.

When Missouri adopted the doctrine, the courts in most of her sister states that had considered the question accorded immunity to charity. In 1942, only six states remained in which full liability was the rule. Since that year, the doctrine has been under continuous attack so devastating that today it lies almost in ruins. Only four states remain in which full immunity was the rule: Massachusetts, Missouri, Rhode Island, and South Carolina. We do not have the time nor space to list or discuss the cases where the rule is full liability or full immunity, or where the rule lies somewhere between these two extremes. We have re-examined and reconsidered the doctrine as a rule of public policy in the light of what is common knowledge of the facts of life today and conclude that it must be abolished.

Plaintiff argues that the general rule is, and always has been, that there must be a remedy for every wrong; that the doctrine of immunity runs directly counter to this basic concept of justice. The court of appeals in the *Adams* case, and this court in subsequent decisions, recognized the rule, but deliberately chose to create an exception to it. There can be no doubt that at the time of its adoption the exception was a rule of expediency justifiable then, and for some time thereafter, to encourage and protect charity as vital to the growth and development of the state, but the reasons for the exception to the rule do not exist today. Today we have a new set of facts, conditions, and circumstances. In the period of our history when the doctrine of immunity arose, charity operated on a small scale. Most persons engaged in the operation of its institutions gave their time free, as their contribution to society. Most gifts to charity were not corporate but private. And the needs of charitable institutions were, for the most part, poorly satisfied. Today charity is big business. It often is corporate both in the identity of the donor and in the identity of the donee who administers the charity. Tax deductions sometimes make it actually profitable for donors to give to charity. Organized corporate charity takes over large areas of social activity which otherwise would have to be handled by

government, or even by private business. Charity today is a large-scale operation with salaries, costs, and other expenses similar to business generally. It makes sense to say that this kind of charity should pay its own way, not only as to its office expenses but as to the expense of insurance to pay for torts as well. Today public liability insurance is available to charitable institutions to indemnify them against losses by way of damages for their negligence. It is common knowledge that most charitable institutions carry such insurance and pay the premiums thereon as a part of their normal cost of operation. In the states where immunity has not been accorded charity, experience has shown that the apprehension expressed here and elsewhere that the purses of donors would be closed and the funds of charity depleted if these institutions were not granted immunity was not well founded. In the quarter century since the doctrine began its decline, there has been no indication in the states that have abolished immunity that its withdrawal has discouraged donations or that the funds of these institutions have been depleted, resulting in their demise.

The public is doubtless still interested in the maintenance of charitable institutions. We acknowledge society's debt to them and recognize their right to every benefit and assistance that the law can justly allow. But the day has arrived when these institutions must acknowledge the injustice of denying compensation to a person injured as a result of their negligence or the negligence of their agents or employees; when they must acknowledge that all persons, organizations, and corporations stand equal before the law and must be bound or excused alike. They must recognize that immunity fosters neglect and breeds irresponsibility, while liability promotes care and caution. The public has an interest also in the protection of life and limb of the individual as a member of society and must require that those who minister to these needs do so carefully. To lift the mantle of immunity will tend to promote care and caution.

For the reasons stated, we hold that a nongovernmental charitable institution is liable for its own negligence and for the negligence of its agents and employees acting within the scope of their employment. *Adams v. University Hospital, supra,* and all other decisions of like effect are overruled.

Having abolished the doctrine of charitable immunity, it remains for us to determine the point of departure from precedent. We are cognizant of the fact that retrospective application of our decision could result in great hardship to those institutions that have relied on our prior decisions upholding the doctrine of charitable immunity. Therefore, feeling that justice will best be served by prospective application of the decision announced today, we hold that the new rule shall apply to this case and to all future causes of action arising after November 10, 1969, the date of the filing of this opinion.

The judgment is reversed and the cause remanded for further proceedings.

CASE QUESTIONS

1. The two legal theories used to justify and support the doctrine of charitable immunity are "implied waiver" and "trust fund." Explain these theories.
2. How are charitable institutions—for example, hospitals—different today from the way they were at the time of the development of the doctrine of charitable immunity?
3. Would revoking charitable immunity be an unsound public policy that would discourage donors to charity with the fear that their gifts might go to pay tort claims?

SUGGESTED READINGS

Appleman, *The Tort Liability of Charitable Institutions,* 22 A.B.A.J. 48 (1936).

Note, 23 Wash. & Lee L. Rev. 109 (1966).

Note, *Charitable Immunity—A Reappraisal,* 39 Tenn. L. Rev. 289 (1972).

Note, *Tort Liability of Non-Profit Charitable Corporations,* 1 U.S.F.V. Rev. 190 (1968).

Note, *The Doctrine of Charitable Immunity—The Persistent Vigil of Out-dated Law*, 4 U. BALT. L. REV. 125 (1974).

Immunity Among Family Members

Traditionally, husbands and wives have been immune from liability for torts committed against their spouses. It is argued that personal tort actions between husband and wife would disrupt the peace and harmony of the home. In old common-law doctrine, husband and wife were considered as one person. Today, of course, they are considered to be separate legal entities. Courts have been developing exceptions to the common-law immunity. Many states have done away with it entirely, seeing no justification for its survival.

It has been considered in the best interest of society to prohibit unemancipated minor children from maintaining actions for negligence or intentional torts against their parents. A child is unemancipated until the parents surrender the right of care, custody, and earnings of such child, and renounce their parental duties. Subjecting the parent to suit by the child might result in interference with domestic harmony, depletion of family funds at the expense of the other members of the family, the encouragement of fraud or collusion, and interference with the discipline and control of children. There is no English common-law doctrine of parental immunity. The doctrine, which is an invention of the United States courts, is gradually being eroded. It is being recognized that the arguments for the retention of the doctrine are extremely weak. Unemancipated minor children have always been able to enforce contracts or property rights against their parents.

Gibson v. Gibson
92 Cal. Rptr. 288, 479 P.2d 648
Supreme Court of California
January 25, 1971

SULLIVAN, JUSTICE
We are asked to re-examine our holding in *Trudell v. Leatherby* (1931), 212 Cal. 678, 300 P. 7, that an unemancipated minor child may not maintain an action against his parent for negligence. That decision, announced 40 years ago, was grounded on the policy that an ac-tion by a child against his parent would "bring discord into the family and disrupt the peace and harmony which should exist between members of the same household." If this rationale ever had any validity, it has none today. We have concluded that parental immun-ity has become a legal anachronism, riddled with exceptions and seriously undermined by recent decisions of this court. Lacking the support of authority and reason, the rule must fall.

James A. Gibson, plaintiff herein, is

the minor son of defendant Robert Gibson. James's complaint alleges in substance as follows. In January 1966, he was riding at night in a car which was being driven by his father and which was towing a jeep. His father negligently stopped the car on the highway and negligently instructed James to go out on the roadway to correct the position of the jeep's wheels. While following these directions, James was injured when another vehicle struck him.

The doctrine of parental immunity for personal torts is only 80 years old, an invention of the American courts. Although the oft-compared rule of interspousal immunity reached back to the early common law, English law books record no case involving a personal tort suit between parent and child. In 1891, however, the Mississippi Supreme Court laid the egg from which parental immunity was hatched. Citing no authorities in *Hewlett v. George* (1891), 68 Miss. 703, 9 So. 885, the Mississippi court barred a minor daughter's false-imprisonment action against her mother who had wrongfully committed her to an insane asylum. The court declared that the "peace of society, and of the families composing society, and a sound public policy, designed to subserve the repose of families and the best interests of society" would be disturbed by such an action, and concluded that a child's only protection against parental abuse was to be found in the criminal law. This "compelling" logic soon led the Washington Supreme Court to conclude that family peace and harmony would be irreparably destroyed if a 15-year-old girl were allowed to sue her father for rape. Other states quickly adopted the rule, applying it to actions for negligence as well as for intentional torts, occasionally with more emotion than reason.

No sooner had American courts, including our own, embraced the parental-immunity doctrine than they began to fashion a number of qualifications and exceptions to it. We allowed an *emancipated* minor to sue her parents for simple negligence. We have held that willful or malicious torts were not within the scope of the immunity. Courts in other states compounded the doctrine's idiosyncrasies in decisions permitting tort actions by minors against the estate of a deceased parent and against the parent's employer under *respondeat superior* for the tort of the parent within the scope of his employment. Although purporting to distinguish the situation of a negligence action directly against a living parent, such cases probably rested as much on growing judicial distaste for a rule of law which in one sweep disqualified an entire class of injured minors.

Apart from this general trend to restrict parental immunity, however, we believe that a trilogy of recent California cases in the area of intra-family tort immunity has weakened, if not eroded, the doctrinal underpinnings of the rule. We recognized the right of an injured minor to sue her father for willful or malicious tort and to sue her brother for negligence. We abrogated *interspousal* immunity for intentional and negligent torts. We think that the reasoning of those decisions has totally destroyed two of the three grounds of parental immunity: (1) disruption of family harmony and (2) fraud or collusion between family "adversaries." The third ground, the threat to parental authority and discipline, although of legitimate concern, cannot sustain a total bar to parent–child negligence suits. We shall examine these arguments one by one.

The danger to family harmony is a rationale for immunity. This argument is illogical and unsound. Observing that spouses commonly sue each other over property matters, we concluded that it would not appear that such assumed conjugal harmony is any more endangered by tort actions than by property actions. The risk of family discord is much less in negligence actions, where an adverse judgment will normally be satisfied by the defendant family member's insurance carrier, than in property actions, where it will generally be paid out of the defendant's pocket. Since the law has long allowed a child to sue his parent over property matters, the rationale is equally applicable to parent–child tort suits.

Arguments based on the fear of fraudulent actions are also adequately answered. While some danger of collusion cannot be denied, the peril is no greater when a minor child sues his parent than in actions between husbands and wives, brothers and sisters, or adult children and parents, all of which are permitted in California. The possibility of fraud or perjury exists to some degree in all cases. But we do not deny a cause of action to a party because of such a danger. It would be a sad commentary on the law if we were to admit that the judicial processes are so ineffective that we must deny relief to a person otherwise entitled because in some future case a litigant may be guilty of fraud or collusion. Once that concept were accepted, then all causes of action should be abolished.

Preservation of the parent's right to discipline his minor children has been the basic policy behind the rule of parental immunity from tort liability. The possibility that some cases may involve the exercise of parental authority does not justify continuation of a blanket rule of immunity. In many actions, no question of parental control will arise. Thus the parent who negligently backs his automobile into his child or who carelessly maintains a lawnmower, which injures the child, cannot claim that his parental role will be threatened if the infant is permitted to sue for negligence. To preserve the rule of immunity in such cases, where the reason for it fails, appears indefensible.

We do recognize, however, that issues of parental discretion and supervision will occasionally be raised when children sue their parents in tort. In such situations, some jurisdictions, although abrogating a broad doctrine of immunity, have nevertheless retained a limited one where basic parental functions are involved. The Wisconsin Supreme Court, while ending parental immunity in general, delineated two areas where immunity should remain: "(1) where the alleged negligent act involves an exercise of parental authority over the child; and (2) where the alleged negligent act involves an exercise of ordinary parental discretion with respect to the provision of food, clothing, housing, medical and dental services, and other care."

We agree with this approach in its recognition of the undeniable fact that the parent–child relationship is unique in some aspects, and that traditional concepts of negligence cannot be blindly applied to it. Obviously, a parent may exercise certain authority over a minor child which would be tortious if directed toward someone else. For example, a parent may spank a child who has misbehaved without being liable for battery, or he may temporarily order the child to stay in his room as punishment, yet not be held responsible for false imprisonment.

Although a parent has the prerogative and the duty to exercise authority over his minor child, this prerogative must be exercised within reasonable limits. The standard to be applied is the traditional one of reasonableness, but viewed in light of the parental role. Thus we think the proper test of a parent's conduct is this: What would an ordinarily reasonable and prudent parent have done in similar circumstances?

In deciding to abrogate parental immunity, we are also persuaded by several policy factors. One is the obvious but important legal principle that "when there is negligence, the rule is liability, immunity is the exception." As we stated in *Klein*, this fundamental doctrine of compensation for injury proximately caused by the act of another governs "in the absence of statute or compelling reasons of public policy." Of course, no statute requires parental immunity. And, as we have already explained, public policy compels liability, not immunity.

Secondly, we feel that we cannot overlook the widespread prevalence of liability insurance and its practical effect on intrafamily suits. Although it is obvious that insurance does not create liability where none otherwise exists, it is unrealistic to ignore this factor in making an informed policy decision on whether to abolish parental negligence immunity. We can no longer consider child–parent actions on the outmoded assumption that parents may be required to pay damages to their children. Recovery by the unemancipated minor child against his parent is almost uniformly denied for a variety of reasons which involve the integrity of the family unit and the family exchequer and the importance of parental discipline. But in truth, virtually no such suits are brought except where there is insurance. And where there is, none of the threats to the family exist at all.

By our decision today, we join ten other states which have already abolished parental tort immunity. We think it is significant that, since 1963, when the Wisconsin Supreme Court drove the first wedge, other jurisdictions have steadily hacked away at this legal deadwood. Other states which now allow children to sue their parents in tort include Kentucky, Alaska, New Jersey, Arizona, New York, Illinois, Minnesota, North Dakota, and New Hampshire.

Applying what we have said above to the case at bench, we hold that the trial court erred in sustaining the defendant's demurrer in reliance on *Trudell v. Leatherby*. We overrule *Trudell*, and hold that an unemancipated minor child may maintain an action for negligence against his parent. Consequently, plaintiff's complaint stated a cause of action and was not vulnerable to demurrer.

The judgment is reversed and the cause is remanded to the trial court.

CASE QUESTIONS

1. List and explain the reasons for parental immunity.
2. Does parental immunity promote peace in the family? Suppose the parent beat or raped the child?
3. Explain the difference between an emancipated and an unemancipated minor child.

SUGGESTED READINGS

W. L. PROSSER, LAW OF TORTS §§ 122–25 (4th ed. 1971).

Sanford, *Personal Torts Within the Family*, 9 VAND. L. REV. 823 (1956).

Herskowitz, *Tort Liability Between Husband and Wife; the Interspousal Immunity Doctrine*, 21 U. MIAMI L. REV. 423 (1966).

Polelle, *Illinois Family Immunity: The Unequal Protection of Junior*, 55 CHI. B. REC. 219 (1974).

Immunity Through Contract

In addition to the immunities imposed by law, parties can create their own immunities by agreeing not to sue. Because of the policy favoring freedom of contract, the agreement may be enforced in a court of law. However, courts are often reluctant to do so. It is construed against the party asserting it and is held invalid if it is against public policy or a result of unfair negotiations. Factors that the court considers in determining whether to enforce the agreement are (1) the subject matter involved, (2) the clause itself, (3) the relation of the parties, and (4) the relative bargaining power of the parties.

One of the basic tenets behind freedom of contract is that both parties are free to negotiate the terms of the contract. As a result, the contract should reflect a real and voluntary meeting of the minds, not merely an objective meeting. Therefore the equality of bargaining power is an important consideration for courts in determining unfair negotiations. Different courts accord different degrees of importance to such elements as superior bargaining power, a lack of meaningful choice by one party, a take-it-or-leave-it proposition, or exploitation by one party of another's known weaknesses.

McCutcheon v. United Homes Corporation

79 Wash. 2d 443, 486 P.2d 1093
Supreme Court of Washington
July 8, 1971

STAFFORD, ASSOCIATE JUSTICE
The two cases involved herein were considered separately by the trial court. Since the issues presented are identical, they have been consolidated on appeal.

Plaintiff Norma McCutcheon, a tenant of defendant United Homes Corporation, was injured one evening when she fell down an unlighted flight of stairs leading from her apartment. She alleged the defendant was negligent because the lights at the top and bottom of the stairwell were not operative.

Plaintiff Douglas R. Fuller, also defendant's tenant, was injured as he descended the outside stairs of his apartment on his way to work. A step pulled loose, causing him to fall. He, too, claimed negligence on the part of the defendant.

Defendant's answer alleged each plaintiff had executed a form "Month to Month Rental Agreement" which contained the following exculpatory clause: "neither the Lessor, nor his Agent, shall be liable for injury to Lessee, his family, guests or employees or any person entering the premises or the building of which the demised [leased] premises are a part."

In each case, the trial court granted a summary judgment of dismissal.

The question is one of first impression. The issue is whether the lessor of a residential unit within a multifamily dwelling complex may exculpate itself from liability for personal injuries sustained by a tenant, which injuries result from the lessor's own negligence in maintenance of the approaches, common passageways, stairways, and other areas under the lessor's dominion and control, but available for the tenants' use (hereinafter called the "common areas").

Basic to the entire discussion is the common-law rule that one who leases a portion of his premises but retains control over the approaches, common passageways, stairways, and other areas to be used in common by the owner and tenants has a duty to use reasonable care to keep them in safe condition for use of the tenant in his enjoyment of the demised premises. The landlord is required to do more than passively refrain from negligent acts. He has a duty of affirmative conduct, an affirmative obligation to exercise reasonable care to inspect and repair the previously mentioned portions of the premises for protection of the lessee.

It is readily apparent that the exculpatory clause was inserted in defendant's form "Month to Month Rental Agreement" to bar its tenants from asserting actions for personal injuries sustained through the landlord's own negligence. It was adopted to negate the result of the lessor's failure to comply with its affirmative duty to the tenants.

The defendant asserts that a lessor may contract, in a rental agreement, to exculpate itself from liability to its lessee, for personal injuries caused by lessor's own negligence. It contends such exculpatory clauses are not contrary to public policy because the landlord–tenant relationship *is not a matter of public interest, but relates exclu-*

sively to the private affairs of the parties concerned, and that the two parties stand upon equal terms. Thus, there should be full freedom to contract.

The importance of "freedom of contract" is clear enough. However, the use of such an argument for avoiding the affirmative duty of a landlord to its residential tenant is no longer compelling in light of today's multifamily dwelling complex, wherein a tenant merely rents some space with appurtenant rights to make it more usable or livable. Under modern circumstances, the tenant is almost wholly dependent on the landlord to provide reasonably for his safe use of the common areas beyond the four walls demised to him.

As early as 1938, Williston recognized that while such exculpatory clauses were recognized as "legal," many courts had shown a reluctance to enforce them. Even then, courts were disposed to interpret them strictly so they would not be effective to discharge liability for the consequences of negligence in making or failing to make repairs. In Williston, *A Treatise on the Law of Contracts*, the author said:

A promise not to sue for the future damage caused by simple negligence may be valid. *Such bargains are not favored*, however, and, if possible, bargains are construed not to confer this immunity.

The key to our problem is found in *Restatement of Contracts* § 574, which reads:

A bargain for exemption from liability for the consequences of negligence *not falling greatly below the standard established by law* for the protection of others against unreasonable risk of harm is legal.

In other words, such an exculpatory clause may be legal, when considered in the abstract. However, when applied to a specific situation, one may be exempt from liability for his own negligence *only when the consequences thereof do not fall greatly below the standard established by law*.

In the landlord–tenant relationship, it is extremely meaningful to require that a landlord's attempt to exculpate itself from liability for the result of its own negligence *not fall greatly below the standard of negligence set by law*. As indicated earlier, a residential tenant who lives in a modern multifamily dwelling complex is almost wholly dependent on the landlord for the reasonably safe condition of the common areas. However, a clause which exculpates the lessor from liability to its lessee, for personal injuries caused by lessor's own acts of negligence, not only lowers the standard imposed by the common law, it effectively *destroys* the landlord's affirmative obligation or duty to keep or maintain the common areas in a reasonably safe condition for the tenant's use.

When a lessor is no longer liable for the failure to observe standards of affirmative conduct, or for *any* conduct amounting to negligence, by virtue of an exculpatory clause in a lease, *the standard ceases to exist*. In short, such a clause *destroys* the concept of negligence in the landlord–tenant relationship. Neither the standard nor negligence can exist in abstraction.

It is no answer to argue that the rental agreement relates exclusively to the "personal and private affairs of two parties on equal footing" and thus is "no matter of public interest." Such a concept had its origin in contracts entered into between *indemnitors and indemnitees*. The theory was first carried from *indemnity* contracts into the landlord–tenant relationship by the Pennsylvania Supreme Court's rather cursory consideration of mere dicta in *Perry v. Payne*, 66 A. 533 (1907). In *Cannon v. Bresch*, 160 A. 595 (1932), the court first used the language now relied on by defendant, applying it to an exculpatory clause concerned with *property damage* arising out of a lease for business purposes:

It is a contract between persons conducting a strictly private business, and relates entirely to their personal and private affairs, and so cannot be opposed to public policy. It would seem to be a matter of no interest to the public or the state.

The foregoing cases and their progeny actually form the basis for the so-called "majority rule." It is safe to say, however, that there is no true majority rule. There are only numerous conflicting decisions, decisions concerned with contracts of indemnity, cases relating to property damage under business leases, and a disposition of the courts to emasculate such exculpatory clauses by means of strict construction. From this, one can reasonably infer that even though such clauses are recognized by some courts, a great number have regarded them with disfavor.

It is inaccurate to characterize the foregoing as a majority rule. Furthermore, one must ignore present-day realities to say that such an exculpatory clause, which relieves a lessor of liability for personal injuries caused by its own negligence, is purely a "personal and private affair" and "not a matter of public interest."

We no longer live in an era of the occasional rental of rooms in a private home or over the corner grocery. In the relatively short span of 30 years, the public's use of rental units in this state has expanded dramatically. In the past 10 years alone, in the state of Washington, there has been an increase of over 77,000 rental units. It takes no imagination to see that a business which once had a minor impact on the living habits of the citizenry has developed into a major commercial enterprise directly touching the lives of hundreds of thousands of people who depend on it for shelter.

Thus, we are not faced merely with the theoretical duty of constructing a provision in an isolated contract specifically bargained for by *one landlord and one tenant* as a purely private affair. Considered realistically, we are asked to construe an exculpatory clause, the generalized use of which may have an impact on thousands of potential tenants.

Under these circumstances, it cannot be said that such exculpatory clauses are "purely a private affair" or that they are "not a matter of public interest." The real question is whether we should sanction a technique of immunizing lessors of residential units within a multifamily dwelling complex from liability for personal injuries sustained by a tenant, which injuries result from the lessor's own negligence in maintaining the common areas, particularly when the technique employed destroys the concept of negligence and the standard of affirmative duty imposed on the landlord for protection of the tenant.

An exculpatory clause of the type here involved contravenes long-established common-law rules of tort liability that exist in the landlord–tenant relationship. As so employed, it offends the public policy of the state and will not be enforced by the courts. It makes little sense for us to insist, on the one hand, that a workman have a safe place in which to work, but, on the other hand, to deny him a reasonably safe place in which to live.

The trial court is reversed and the cause is remanded for trial.

CASE QUESTIONS

1. Did the court view the case before it as one in tort or contract?
2. What fundamental differences are there in viewing a case in tort rather than contract?

SUGGESTED READINGS

Prosser, *The Borderland of Tort and Contract*, in W. L. PROSSER, SELECTED TOPICS ON THE LAW OF TORTS (1954).
W. L. PROSSER, LAW OF TORTS, §§ 92–95 (4th ed. 1971).
Rose, *Responsibility of Landlords for Conditions of Habitability*, 1 REAL ESTATE L.J. 53 (1972).

Chapter Questions

1. Define the following terms:
   a. cases and controversies
   b. collateral attack
   c. demurrer
   d. estoppel
   e. governmental function
   f. insurance
   g. limitations
   h. malice
   i. moot
   j. privity
   k. proprietary function
   l. public policy
   m. *res judicata*
   n. *respondeat superior*
   o. sovereign immunity
   p. statute

2. Sally Vanderbuilt, owner of the Benign Manor Apartments, was dismayed by the building commissioner's decision to place her housing complex into a lower rent bracket under the city's rent-control ordinance. The older tenants were worried that units might be rented to

persons of lower economic and social status, and Sally was afraid that she might lack funds. Mr. Darrow, Sally's attorney, assured her that the rent-control ordinance was patently unconstitutional. After considering Darrow's advice, Sally decided not to lower the rent and to finance a lawsuit by Mr. Smith, an elderly tenant, against herself as landlord. Smith's suit would ask that the rent be lowered and Sally could defend on the ground that the rent-control ordinance was unconstitutional. Does this lawsuit meet the case-or-controversy requirement? Why?

See *United States v. Johnson, 319 U.S. 302 (1943)*

3. After conducting lengthy hearings, the commissioner of Food and Drugs published a regulation in the *Federal Register*, requiring drug manufacturers to label each of their products with its generic name every time the proprietary or trade name is used, including in the drug's advertising. The Pharmaceutical Manufacturers Association fears that profits on drug sales will plunge because the regulation makes consumers aware that certain brand-name drugs can be obtained at a significant savings under their generic names. Although the regulation does not become enforceable for 90 days, the PMA has filed an action seeking (1) a declaratory judgment that the regulation is beyond the powers of the commissioner and (2) an injunction against enforcement of the regulation. Consider whether the case poses concrete issues sufficient to satisfy the case-or-controversy requirements. For purposes of judicial review, is the case "green," "ripe," or "rotten"? Would your answer be different if the PMA sought judicial review after the regulation becomes enforceable?

Abbott Laboratories v. Gardner, 387 U.S. 136 (1967)

4. According to a collective bargaining agreement between the Miami Longshoremen's Union and Bilgeway Fisheries, Inc., the longshoremen agreed to spend June and July of the next two summers working at the Bilgeway cannery on Grand Bahama Island. About half the union's members were native Bahamians domiciled in Miami as resident aliens and hoping to become naturalized citizens. In February, the director of immigration informed the union that the Immigration Act provided that any alien seeking to enter the United States from the Bahamas would be treated as an alien entering the United States for the first time. The union and its alien members sued the director of immigration to enjoin him from interpreting the law so as to include the resident Bahamian longshoremen, claiming that, if so construed, the law is unconstitutional. Is this case appropriate for adjudication as a "case or controversy"?

Int'l Longshoremen's Union v. Boyd, 347 U.S. 222 (1954)

5. On February 1, 1974, John Smith bought a car for $1000. He paid $200 down and signed a promissory note for $800, due in one year. Assume that the note was never paid and the applicable statute of limitations is five years. The plaintiff could wait until what date to bring a civil suit for nonpayment of the note?

6. Armco Recreational Products, Inc., allegedly discriminated against Ernest McKinney on October 6, 1972. Ernest was 19 years old at the time. On July 1, 1973, the age of majority was changed from 21 to 18. Ernest turned 21 on May 5, 1974. Ernest filed a claim under the Civil Rights Act on February 18, 1976. There is a two-year statute of limitations on the Civil Rights Act. Will the court hear Ernest's claim or will it be barred by the statute of limitations?

   McKinney v. Armco Recreational Products, Inc., 419 F.Supp. 464 (1976)

7. Ray Zweily was insured by Nationwide Insurance Co. for his car for $100 deductible property damage. His car collided with a truck driven by Steigerwalt. The damage to Zweily's car was extensive. Pursuant to a subrogation agreement in the policy, Nationwide paid Zweily $2105 for damage to his car, and became subrogated for such amount to Zweily's claim against Steigerwalt. Zweily sued Steigerwalt for personal injuries and the $100 deductible portion of his property damage, alleging that Steigerwalt was negligent in driving his truck. Later, Nationwide also sued Steigerwalt for the $2105 it paid to Zweily. Although Steigerwalt was aware of the two cases against him, he made no motion to join the claims or even to suggest they be joined. In the Zweily case, the jury returned a verdict for defendant, thus finding no negligence on Steigerwalt's part. In Nationwide's action against him, Steigerwalt asserted that the issue of his negligence had been decided in the previous action and that Nationwide, being in privity with Zweily, was barred from trying that issue again. What is your answer to this question? Refer back to the *Whitehead* case.

8. The S.S. *Santo Domingo* was seized by rebels while in port in the city of Santo Domingo in the Dominican Republic. The rebels directed small arms and automatic weapon fire from the ship on an element of the U.S. Army, which had occupied parts of the city to protect United States nationals. The U.S. Army returned the fire and sank the ship. The owner of the ship brought an action against the United States, claiming that the sinking of the ship was taking of private property for public use without just compensation. Should the owner of the ship be entitled to compensation from the United States?

   American Manufacturers Mut. Ins. Co. v. United States, 453 F.2d 1380, 197 Ct. Cl. 99 (1972)

9. Judge Stump of a circuit court in Indiana, a court of general jurisdiction, approved a mother's petition to have her "somewhat retarded" 15-year-old daughter sterilized. The judge approved the mother's petition the same day, without a hearing and without notice to the daughter or appointment of a guardian *ad litem*. The operation was performed on Linda Sparkman, but she was told that she was having her appendix removed. A few years later, after Linda married and discovered that she had been sterilized, she and her husband brought suit against Judge Stump. Should Judge Stump be immune under the circumstances?
   Stump v. Sparkman, 435 U.S. 349 (1978)

10. Peter Constantino was a public defender assigned to defend Mary Spring. Prior to Mary's trial, Peter told the judge he thought Mary was crazy. Bail was set and Mary was placed in a mental institution. Peter failed to tell Mary how she could arrange bail. Claiming that her prolonged stay in the mental institution was caused by Peter's negligence, Mary sued Peter for malpractice. Peter claims that his position as an officer of the court gives him the defense of judicial immunity. Who wins? Why?
    Spring v. Constantino, 362 A.2d 871 (1975)

11. St. Joseph's, a large church maintaining a grade school and involved in much community work, conducted bingo games every Friday night to raise funds for the school and for other projects. The games became very popular and attendance was open to the public. Mrs. Bang, a non–church member who enjoyed playing bingo, walked into the church basement, paid one dollar admission, and received two bingo cards. As she sat down on a metal chair, the chair collapsed and Mrs. Bang fell to the floor, seriously injuring her spine. She is suing the church for personal injuries. Keeping in mind the fact that the church is a charitable institution and that all the proceeds of the bingo games go to charity, will the doctrine of charitable immunity prevent Mrs. Bang's recovery?
    Blankenship v. Alter, 171 Ohio St. 65 (1960)

12. Mrs. Ella O'Callaghan, a tenant in an apartment building, was injured when she fell while crossing the paved courtyard on her way from the garage to her apartment. She instituted an action to recover for her injuries, alleging that they were caused by defective pavement in the courtyard. Before the case was tried, Mrs. O'Callaghan died and her administrator was substituted as plaintiff. The jury returned a verdict in the sum of $14,000. The defendant landlord appealed, contending that the action should have been barred by virtue of an exculpatory

Table III.1
Statutes of Limitations for Civil Actions (in Years)

| | Contract | | | | Tort | | | | | | | | | | | |
| | | | | | Negligence | | | Intentional Torts | | | | | | | | |
	Breach of Sales Contract	Breach of Warranty	Oral	Written	Personal Injury	Wrongful Death	Medical Malpractice	Assault and Battery	Fraud and Deceit	Libel	Slander	Trespass	Damage to Personal Property	Conversion	False Imprisonment	Malicious Prosecution
Alabama	4	4	6	6	1	2	2	6	1	1	1	6	1	6	6	1
Alaska	4	4	6	6	2	2	2	2	2	2	2	6	6	6	2	2
Arizona	4	4	3	6	2	2	3	2	3	1	1	2	2	2	1	1
Arkansas	4	4	3	5	5	3	2	1	5	3	1	3	3	3	1	5
California	4	4	2	4	1	1	3	1	3	1	1	3	3	3	1	1
Colorado	4	4	3	6	6	2	2	1	3	1	1	6	6	6	1	6
Connecticut	4	4	3	6	2	2	2	3	3	2	2	3	3	3	3	3
Delaware	4	4	3	3	2	2	2	2	3	2	2	3	2	3	2	3
D.C.	4	4	3	3	3	1	3	1	3	1	1	3	3	3	1	1
Florida	4	4	4	5	4	2	2	4	4	4	4	4	4	4	4	4
Georgia	4	4	4	6	2	2	2	2	4	1	1	4	4	4	2	2
Hawaii	4	4	6	6	2	2	2	2	6	2	2	2	2	6	6	6
Idaho	4	4	4	5	2	2	2	2	3	2	2	3	3	3	2	4
Illinois	4	4	5	10	2	2	2	2	5	1	1	5	5	5	2	2
Indiana	4	4	6	10	2	2	2	2	6	2	2	6	2	6	2	2
Iowa	5	5	5	10	2	2	2	2	5	2	2	5	5	5	2	2
Kansas	4	4	3	5	2	2	2	1	2	1	1	2	2	2	1	1
Kentucky	4	4	5	15	1	1	1	1	5	1	1	5	5	5	1	1
Louisiana	1	1	10	10	1	1	1	1	1	1	1	1	1	1	1	1
Maine	4	4	6	6	6	2	2	2	6	2	2	6	6	6	2	6
Maryland	4	4	3	3	3	3	3	1	3	1	1	3	3	3	3	3
Massachusetts	4	4	6	6	3	3	3	3	3	3	3	3	3	3	3	3
Michigan	4	4	6	6	3	3	2	2	6	1	1	3	3	3	2	2
Minnesota	4	4	6	6	6	3	2	2	6	2	2	6	6	6	2	2
Mississippi	6	6	3	6	6	6	6	1	6	1	1	1	6	6	1	1

clause in the lease. The administrator contended that the exculpatory clause should be invalidated as against public policy, and pointed to the fact that there was a housing shortage, which caused a disparity of bargaining power. Write an opinion for the appellate court's holding.

O'Callaghan v. Waller & Beckwith Realty Company, 15 Ill. 2d 436, 155 N.E.2d 545 (1959)

Table III.1
Statutes of Limitations for Civil Actions (in Years)

| | Contract | | | | Tort | | | | | | | | | | | |
| | | | | | Negligence | | | Intentional Torts | | | | | | | | |
	Breach of Sales Contract	Breach of Warranty	Oral	Written	Personal Injury	Wrongful Death	Medical Malpractice	Assault and Battery	Fraud and Deceit	Libel	Slander	Trespass	Damage to Personal Property	Conversion	False Imprisonment	Malicious Prosecution
Missouri	4	4	5	10	5	3	2	2	5	2	2	5	5	5	2	5
Montana	4	4	5	8	3	3	3	2	2	2	2	2	2	2	2	5
Nebraska	4	4	4	5	4	2	2	1	4	1	1	4	4	4	1	1
Nevada	4	4	4	6	2	2	2	2	3	2	2	3	3	3	2	2
New Hampshire	4	4	6	6	6	6	6	6	6	6	6	6	6	6	6	6
New Jersey	4	4	6	6	2	2	2	2	6	1	1	6	6	6	2	2
New Mexico	4	4	4	6	3	3	3	3	4	3	3	4	4	4	3	3
New York	4	4	6	6	3	2	2½	1	6	1	1	3	3	3	1	1
North Carolina	4	4	3	3	3	2	3	1	3	1	1	3	3	3	1	3
North Dakota	4	4	6	6	6	2	2	2	6	2	2	6	6	6	2	6
Ohio	4	4	6	15	2	2	1	1	4	1	1	4	2	4	1	1
Oklahoma	5	5	3	5	2	2	2	1	2	1	1	2	2	2	1	1
Oregon	4	4	6	6	2	3	2	2	2	1	1	6	6	6	2	2
Pennsylvania	4	4	6	6	2	2	2	2	6	1	1	2	2	2	2	2
Rhode Island	4	4	10	10	3	2	3	10	10	10	1	10	10	10	3	10
South Carolina	6	6	6	6	6	6	3	2	6	2	2	6	6	6	2	6
South Dakota	4	4	6	6	3	3	2	2	6	2	2	6	6	6	2	6
Tennessee	4	4	6	6	1	1	1	1	3	1	½	3	3	3	1	1
Texas	4	4	2	4	2	2	2	2	2	1	1	2	2	2	2	1
Utah	4	4	4	6	4	2	2	1	3	1	1	3	3	3	1	1
Vermont	4	4	6	8	3	2	3	3	6	3	3	6	3	6	3	3
Virginia	4	4	3	5	2	2	2	2	3	2	2	5	5	5	2	1
Washington	4	4	3	6	3	3	3	2	3	2	2	3	3	3	2	3
West Virginia	4	4	5	10	2	2	2	2	2	1	1	2	2	2	1	1
Wisconsin	6	6	6	6	3	3	3	2	6	2	2	6	6	6	2	2
Wyoming	4	4	8	10	4	2	2	1	4	1	1	4	4	4	1	1

IV   Judicial Decision Making

Following Precedent

Stare Decisis

A rule of law that has been decided by judicial decisions is generally binding on the courts and should be followed where applicable in later cases. This principle is referred to as the doctrine of *stare decisis*. It is a policy, not an absolutely binding rule. Judge-made law, or case law or common law, is created by judicial decisions. The doctrine of *stare decisis* is the basis of common law. It originated in England and was used in the colonies as the basis of their judicial decisions.

A decision on an issue of law by a court is followed in that jurisdiction by the same court or by a lesser ranked court in a future case presenting the same issue of law. A court is not bound by decisions of courts of other states, although such decisions may be considered in the decision-making process. A decision of the United States Supreme Court on a federal question is absolutely binding on state courts as well as on lower federal courts. Similarly, a decision of a state court of final appeal on an issue of state law is binding on lower state courts and federal courts in the state dealing with that issue. The decisions of lower federal courts are generally not binding as precedent.

Courts are bound to follow the common law as it has been judicially declared in previously adjudicated cases. Prior decisions on a point of law are binding on a future case only if the same—or substantially the same—issue is involved. In order to determine whether the issues are the same or substantially the same, one must consider the precedent in light of the facts. Where the facts are substantially different, the principle of *stare decisis* does not apply.

Literally, *stare decisis* means that a court will "stand by its decisions" or those of a higher court. Within one jurisdiction, the law can give but one answer to a given legal question. Even-handed justice requires like cases to be decided alike, regardless of who the parties are. The quality of the law decided on is thereby improved, as more careful and thorough consideration is given to the legal questions than would be the case if the determinations affected only the case before the court.

The principle of *stare decisis* is firmly rooted in American jurisprudence. It is a policy that is based on and promotes predictability, certainty, uniformity, and stability. Our legal system should furnish a clear guide for conduct so that people may plan their affairs with assurance against surprise. It is important to further fair and rapid adjudication by eliminating the need to relitigate every proposition in every case. Public faith in the judiciary should be maintained by furnishing a source of impersonal and reasoned judgment. These factors should be considered by a court before rejecting any established rule.

Stare decisis is not a binding rule, and a court need not feel absolutely bound to follow previous cases. Even though it is only policy, courts are not inclined to deviate from it, especially when the precedents have been treated as authoritative for a long time. The number of decisions announced on a rule of law also has some bearing on the weight of the precedent. It is often said that it is up to the legislature to change long-established precedent. When a principle of law established by precedent is no longer appropriate because of changing economic, political, and sociological conditions, however, courts should recognize this and overrule the precedent to reflect what is best for society.

Only a judicial decision of the majority of a court on a point of law expressed in connection with a reported opinion can have *stare decisis* effect. A dissent has no precedential value, nor does the fact that an appellate court is split make the majority less of a precedent. When judges are equally divided as to the outcome of a particular case, there is no precedent created by that court. This is true even though the decision affirms the decision of the next-lower court. The reason is that the outcome was not reached by a majority.

Furman v. Georgia
408 U.S. 238
United States Supreme Court
June 29, 1972

Per Curiam
William Furman was convicted of murder in Georgia and was sentenced to death. Lucius Jackson was convicted of

rape in Georgia and was sentenced to death. Elmer Branch was convicted of rape in Texas and was sentenced to death. *Certiorari* was granted limited to the following question: "Does the imposition and carrying out of the death penalty in these cases constitute cruel and unusual punishment in violation of the Eighth and Fourteenth Amendments?" The Court holds that the imposition and carrying out of the death penalty in these cases constitute cruel and unusual punishment in violation of the Eighth and Fourteenth Amendments. The judgment in each case is therefore reversed insofar as it leaves undisturbed the death sentence imposed, and the cases are remanded for further proceedings.

So ordered

Mr. Justice Douglas, concurring
The words *cruel and unusual* certainly include penalties that are barbaric. But the words, at least when read in light of the English proscription against selective and irregular use of penalties, suggest that it is "cruel and unusual" to apply the death penalty—or any other penalty—selectively to minorities whose numbers are few, who are outcasts of society, and who are unpopular, but whom society is willing to see suffer, though it would not countenance general application of the same penalty across the board.

A penalty should be considered unusually imposed if it is administered arbitrarily or discriminatorily. The extreme rarity with which applicable death penalty provisions are put to use raises a strong inference of arbitrariness.

Mr. Justice Brennan, concurring
The outstanding characteristic of our present practice of punishing criminals by death is the infrequency with which we resort to it. The evidence is conclusive that death is not the ordinary punishment for any crime.

When a country of over 200 million people inflicts an unusually severe punishment no more than 50 times a year, the inference is strong that the punishment is not being regularly and fairly applied. To dispel the inference would indeed require a clear showing of nonarbitrary infliction.

Although there are no exact figures available, we know that thousands of murders and rapes are committed annually in states where death is an authorized punishment for those crimes. However the rate of infliction is characterized—as "freakishly" or "spectacularly" rare, or simply as "rare"—it would take the purest sophistry to deny that death is inflicted in only a minute fraction of these cases. How much rarer, after all, could the infliction of death be?

When the punishment of death is inflicted in a trivial number of the cases in which it is legally available, the conclusion is virtually inescapable that it is being inflicted arbitrarily. Indeed, it smacks of little more than a lottery system. The states claim, however, that this rarity is evidence not of arbitrariness, but of informed selectivity: Death is inflicted, they say, only in "extreme" cases.

When the rate of infliction is at this low level, it is highly implausible that only the worst criminals or the criminals who commit the worst crimes are selected for this punishment. No one has yet suggested a rational basis that could differentiate the few who die from the many who go to prison. Crimes and criminals simply do not admit of a distinction that can be drawn so finely as to explain, on that ground, the execution of such a tiny sample of those eligible. Certainly the laws that provide for this punishment do not attempt to draw that distinction. All cases to which the laws apply are necessarily ''extreme.'' Nor is the distinction credible in fact. If, for example, petitioner Furman or his crime illustrates the ''extreme,'' then nearly all murderers and their murders are also ''extreme.'' Furthermore, our procedure in death cases, rather than resulting in the selection of ''extreme'' cases for this punishment, actually sanction an arbitrary selection. For this Court has held that juries may, as they do, make the decision whether to impose a death sentence wholly unguided by standards governing that decision. In other words, our procedures are not constructed to guard against the totally capricious selection of criminals for the punishment of death.

MR. JUSTICE STEWART, concurring
Legislatures—state and federal—have sometimes specified that the penalty of death shall be the mandatory punishment for every person convicted of engaging in certain designated criminal conduct. Congress, for example, has provided that anyone convicted of acting as a spy for the enemy in time of war shall be put to death.

If we were reviewing death sentences imposed under these or similar laws, we would be faced with the need to decide whether capital punishment is unconstitutional for all crimes and under all circumstances. We would need to decide whether a legislature—state or federal—could constitutionally determine that certain criminal conduct is so atrocious that society's interest in deterrence and retribution wholly outweighs any considerations of reform or rehabilitation of the perpetrator, and that, despite the inconclusive empirical evidence, only the automatic penalty of death will provide maximum deterrence.

On that score, I would say only that I cannot agree that retribution is a constitutionally impermissible ingredient in the imposition of punishment. The instinct for retribution is part of the nature of man, and channeling that instinct in the administration of criminal justice serves an important purpose in promoting the stability of a society governed by law. When people begin to believe that organized society is unwilling or unable to impose upon criminal offenders the punishment they ''deserve,'' then there are sown the seeds of anarchy—of self-help, vigilante justice, and lynch law.

The constitutionality of capital punishment in the abstract is not, however, before us in these cases. For the Georgia and Texas legislatures have not provided that the death penalty shall be imposed on all those who are found guilty of forcible rape. And the Georgia legislature has not ordained that death shall be the automatic punishment for murder. In a word, neither state has made a legislative determination that forcible rape and murder can be deterred only by imposing the penalty of death on all who perpetrate those offenses.

Instead, the death sentences now before us are the product of a legal system that brings them, I believe, within the very core of the Eighth Amendment's guarantee against cruel and unusual punishments, a guarantee applicable against the states through the Fourteenth Amendment. In the first place, it is clear that these sentences are "cruel" in the sense that they excessively go beyond, not in degree but in kind, the punishments that the state legislatures have determined to be necessary. In the second place, it is equally clear that these sentences are "unusual" in the sense that the penalty of death is infrequently imposed for murder, and that its imposition for rape is extraordinarily rare.

These death sentences are cruel and unusual in the same way that being struck by lightning is cruel and unusual. For, of all the people convicted of rapes and murders in 1967 and 1968, many just as reprehensible as these, the petitioners are among a capriciously selected random handful upon whom the sentence of death has in fact been imposed.

I simply conclude that the Eighth and Fourteenth Amendments cannot tolerate the infliction of a sentence of death under legal systems that permit this unique penalty to be wantonly and so freakishly imposed.

For these reasons I concur in the judgments of the Court.

MR. JUSTICE WHITE, concurring

The facial constitutionality of statutes requiring the imposition of the death penalty for first-degree murder, for more narrowly defined categories of murder, or for rape would present quite different issues under the Eighth Amendment than are posed by the cases before us. In joining the Court's judgments, therefore, I do not at all intimate that the death penalty is unconstitutional *per se* or that there is no system of capital punishment that would comport with the Eighth Amendment. That question, ably argued by several of my Brethren, is not presented by these cases and need not be decided.

The narrower question to which I address myself concerns the constitutionality of capital punishment statutes under which (1) the legislature authorizes the imposition of the death penalty for murder or rape; (2) the legislature does not itself mandate the penalty in any particular class or kind of case (that is, legislative will is not frustrated if the penalty is never imposed), but delegates to judges or juries the decisions as to those cases, if any, in which the penalty will be utilized; and (3) judges and juries have ordered the death penalty with such infrequency that odds are now very much against imposition and execution of the penalty with respect to any convicted murderer or rapist. It is in this context that we must consider whether the execution of these petitioners would violate the Eighth Amendment.

A major goal of the criminal law—to deter others by punishing the convicted criminal—would not be substantially served where the penalty is so seldom invoked that it ceases to be the credible threat essential to influence the conduct of others. For present purposes, I accept the morality and utility of punishing one person to influence another. I accept also the effectiveness of punishment generally and need not reject the death penalty as a more effective deterrent than a lesser punishment. But common sense and experience tell us that seldom-enforced laws become ineffective measures for controlling human conduct and that the death penalty, unless imposed with sufficient frequency, will make little contribution to deterring those crimes for which it may be exacted.

The imposition and execution of the death penalty are obviously cruel in the dictionary sense. But the penalty has not been considered cruel and unusual punishment in the constitutional sense because it was thought justified by the social ends it was deemed to serve. At the moment that it ceases realistically to further these purposes, however, the emerging question is whether its imposition in such circumstances would violate the Eighth Amendment. It is my view that it would, for its imposition would then be the pointless and needless extinction of life with only marginal contributions to any discernible social or public purposes. A penalty with such negligible returns to the state would be patently excessive and cruel and unusual punishment violative of the Eighth Amendment.

It is also my judgment that this point has been reached with respect to capital punishment as it is presently administered under the statutes involved in these cases. Concededly, it is difficult to prove as a general proposition that capital punishment, however administered, more effectively serves the ends of the criminal law than does im-

prisonment. But however that may be, I cannot avoid the conclusion that as the statutes before us are now administered, the penalty is so infrequently imposed that the threat of execution is too attenuated to be of substantial service to criminal justice.

Judicial review, by definition, often involves a conflict between judicial and legislative judgment as to what the Constitution means or requires. In this respect, Eighth Amendment cases come to us in no different posture. It seems conceded by all that the Amendment imposes some obligations on the judiciary to judge the constitutionality of punishment and that there are punishments that the Amendment would bar, whether legislatively approved or not. Inevitably, then, there will be occasions when we will differ with Congress or state legislatures with respect to the validity of punishment.

In this respect, I add only that past and present legislative judgment with respect to the death penalty loses much of its force when viewed in light of the recurring practice of delegating sentencing authority to the jury, and the fact that a jury, in its own discretion and without violating its trust or any statutory policy, may refuse to impose the death penalty no matter what the circumstances of the crime. Legislative ''policy'' is thus necessarily defined not by what is legislatively authorized but by what juries and judges do in exercising the discretion so regularly conferred upon them. In my judgment, what was done in these cases violated the Eighth Amendment.

I concur in the judgments of the Court.

MR. JUSTICE MARSHALL, concurring
Even if capital punishment is not excessive, it nonetheless violates the Eighth Amendment because it is morally unacceptable to the people of the United States at this time in their history.

In judging whether or not a given penalty is morally acceptable, most courts have said that the punishment is valid unless it shocks the conscience and sense of justice of the people.

MR. JUSTICE BLACKMUN, dissenting
To reverse the judgments in these cases is, of course, the easy choice. It is easier to strike the balance in favor of life and against death. It is comforting to relax in the thoughts—perhaps the rationalizations—that this is the compassionate decision for a maturing society; that this is the moral and the "right" thing to do; that thereby we convince ourselves that we are moving down the road toward human decency; that we value life even though that life has taken another or others or has grievously scarred another or others and their families.

This, for me, is good argument, and it makes some sense. But it is a good argument and it makes sense only in a legislative and executive way and not as a judicial expedient. Were I a legislator, I would do all I could to sponsor and to vote for legislation abolishing the death penalty. And were I the chief executive of a sovereign state, I would be sorely tempted to exercise executive clemency, as Governor Rockefeller of Arkansas did recently just before he departed from office. There—on the legislative branch of the state or federal government, and secondarily, on the executive branch—is where the authority and responsibility for this kind of action lies. The authority should not be taken over by the judiciary in the modern guise of an Eighth Amendment issue.

I do not sit on these cases, however, as a legislator, responsive, at least in part, to the will of constituents. Our task here, as must so frequently be emphasized and re-emphasized, is to pass on the constitutionality of legislation that has been enacted and that is challenged. This is the sole task for judges. We should not allow our personal preferences as to the wisdom of legislative and congressional action, or our distaste for such action, to guide our judicial decision in cases such as these. The temptations to cross that policy line are very great. In fact, as today's decision reveals, they are almost irresistible.

CASE QUESTIONS

1. What were the various reasons given by the concurring justices for finding the death penalty unconstitutional?
2. What is Justice Blackmun arguing in his dissenting opinion?
3. What provisions would have had to be included in the law for Justice White to have found it constitutional?

4. What is the precedental value of concurring and dissenting opinions?

SUGGESTED READINGS

Black, *Death Penalty Now*, 51 TUL. L. REV. 429 (1977).

Tao, *Beyond Furman v. Georgia: The Need for a Morally Based Decision on Capital Punishment*, 51 NOTRE DAME LAW 722 (1976).

Comment, *Capital Punishment Statutes after Furman*, 35 OHIO S. L.J. 651 (1974).

Deutsch and Hoeflich, *Legal Duty and Judicial Style: The Meaning of Precedent*, 25 ST. LOUIS U.L.J. 87 (1981).

Court decisions can also influence the actions of legislatures. In *Furman v. Georgia*, the United States Supreme Court held that most capital punishment statutes were unconstitutional. In his concurring opinion to *Furman*, Justice Byron White indicated provisions that should be included in a capital punishment statute for it to be considered constitutional. A number of states rewrote their statutes to fit Justice White's requirements. In *Gregg v. Georgia*, the Supreme Court employed the doctrine of *stare decisis* by determining the constitutionality of the rewritten Texas and Georgia statutes in light of its decision in *Furman*.

Gregg v. Georgia
428 U.S. 153
United States Supreme Court
July 2, 1976

MR. JUSTICE STEWART

The issue in this case is whether the imposition of the sentence of death for the crime of murder under the law of Georgia violates the Eighth and Fourteenth Amendments.

The petitioner, Troy Gregg, was charged with committing armed robbery and murder. In accordance with Georgia procedure in capital cases, the trial was in two stages, a guilt stage and a sentencing stage. The evidence at the guilt trial established that on November 21, 1973, the petitioner and a traveling companion, Floyd Allen, while hitchhiking north in Florida, were picked up by Fred Simmons and Bob Moore. Their car broke down, but they continued north after Simmons purchased another vehicle with some of the cash he was carrying. While still in Florida, they picked up another hitchhiker, Dennis Weaver, who rode with them to Atlanta, where he was let out about 11 P.M. A short time later, the four men interrupted their journey for a rest stop along the highway. The next morning, the bodies of Simmons and Moore were discovered in a ditch nearby. Allen's version of the slayings was as follows. After Simmons and Moore left the car, the petitioner stated that he intended to rob them. The petitioner then took his pistol in hand and positioned himself on the car to improve his aim. As Simmons and Moore came up an embankment toward the car, the petitioner fired three shots and the two men fell near a ditch. The petitioner, at close range, then fired a shot into the head of each. He robbed them of valuables and drove away with Allen.

Gregg testified in his own defense. He confirmed that Allen had made the statements described by the detective, but denied their truth or ever having admitted to their accuracy. He indicated that he had shot Simmons and Moore because of fear and in self-defense, testifying they had attacked Allen and him, one wielding a pipe and the other a knife.

The jury found the petitioner guilty of two counts of armed robbery and two counts of murder.

At the penalty stage, which took place before the same jury, neither the prosecutor nor the petitioner's lawyer offered any additional evidence. Both counsel, however, made lengthy arguments dealing generally with the propriety of capital punishment under the circumstances and with the weight of the evidence of guilt. The trial judge instructed the jury that it could recommend either a death sentence or a life prison sentence on each count. The judge further charged the jury that in determining what sentence was appropriate the jury was free to consider the facts and circumstances presented by the parties, if any, in mitigation or aggravation.

Finally, the judge instructed the jury that it "would not be authorized to consider imposing the sentence of death" unless it first found beyond a reasonable doubt one of these aggravating circumstances:

One—That the offense of murder was committed while the offender was engaged in the commission of two other capital felonies, to wit, the armed robbery of Simmons and Moore.

Two—That the offender committed the offense of murder for the purpose of receiving money and the automobile described in the indictment.

Three—The offense of murder was outrageously and wantonly vile, horrible, and inhuman, in that they involved the depravity of the mind of the defendant.

Finding the first and second of these circumstances, the jury returned verdicts of death on each count.

We granted the petitioner's application for a writ of *certiorari* challenging the imposition of the death sentence in this case as "cruel and unusual" punishment in violation of the Eighth and the Fourteenth Amendments.

Four years ago, the petitioners in *Furman* and its companion cases predicated their argument primarily on the asserted proposition that standards of decency had evolved to the point where capital punishment no longer could be tolerated. The petitioners in those cases said, in effect, that the evolutionary process had come to an end, and that standards of decency required that the Eighth Amendment be construed finally as prohibiting capital punishment for any crime regardless of its depravity and impact on society. This view was accepted by two Justices. Three other Justices were unwilling to go so far. Focusing on the procedures by which convicted defendants were selected for the death penalty rather than on the actual punishment inflicted, they joined in the conclusion that the statutes before the Court were constitutionally invalid.

The petitioners in the capital cases before the Court today renew the "standards of decency" argument, but developments during the four years since *Furman* have undercut substantially the assumptions on which their argument rested. Despite the continuing debate, dating back to the nineteenth century, over the morality and utility of capital punishment, it is now evident that a large proportion of American society continues to regard it as an appropriate and necessary criminal sanction.

The most marked indication of society's endorsement of the death penalty for murder is the legislative response to *Furman*. The legislatures of at least 35 states have enacted new statutes that provide for the death penalty for at least some crimes that result in the death of another person. And the Congress of the United States, in 1974, enacted a statute providing the death penalty for aircraft piracy that results in death. These recently adopted statutes have attempted to address the concerns expressed by the Court in *Furman* primarily (1) by specifying the factors to be weighed and the procedures to be followed in deciding when to impose a capital sentence, or (2) by making the death penalty mandatory for specified crimes. But all of the post-*Furman* statutes make clear that capital punishment itself has not been rejected by the elected representatives of the people.

While *Furman* did not hold that the infliction of the death penalty *per se* violates the Constitution's ban on cruel and unusual punishments, it did recognize that the penalty of death is different in kind from any other punishment imposed under our system of criminal justice. Because of the uniqueness of the death penalty, *Furman* held that it could not be imposed under sentencing procedures that created a substantial risk that it would be inflicted in an arbitrary and capricious manner.

The concerns expressed in *Furman* that the penalty of death not be imposed in an arbitrary or capricious manner can be met by a carefully drafted statute that ensures that the sentencing authority is given adequate information and guidance. As a general proposition, these concerns are best met by a system that provides for a bifurcated proceeding at which the sentencing authority is apprised of the information relevant to the imposition of sentence and provided with standards to guide its use of the information.

We do not intend to suggest that only the above-described procedures would be permissible under *Furman*, or that any sentencing system constructed along these general lines would inevitably satisfy the concerns of *Furman*, for each distinct system must be examined on an individual basis. Rather, we have embarked on this general exposition to make clear that it is possible to construct capital-sentencing systems capable of meeting *Furman's* constitutional concerns.

We now turn to consideration of the constitutionality of Georgia's capital-sentencing procedures. In the wake of *Furman*, Georgia amended its capital punishment statute, but chose not to narrow the scope of its murder provisions. Thus, now as before *Furman*, in Georgia a person commits murder when he unlawfully and with malice aforethought, either express or implied, causes the death of another human being. All persons convicted of murder shall be punished by death or by imprisonment for life.

Georgia did act, however, to narrow the class of murderers subject to capital punishment by specifying ten statutory aggravating circumstances, one of which must be found by the jury to exist beyond a reasonable doubt before a death sentence can ever be imposed. In addition, the jury is authorized to consider any other appropriate aggravating or mitigating circumstances. The jury is not required to find any mitigating circumstance in order to make a recommendation of mercy that is binding on the trial court, but it must find a statutory aggravating circumstance before recommending a sentence of death.

These procedures require the jury to consider the circumstances of the crime and the criminal before it recommends sentence. No longer can a Georgia jury do as *Furman's* jury did: reach a finding of the defendant's guilt and then, without guidance or direction, decide whether he should live or die. Instead, the jury's attention is directed to the specific circumstances of the crime: Was it committed in the course of another capital felony? Was it committed

for money? Was it committed upon a peace officer or judicial officer? Was it committed in a particularly heinous way or in a manner that endangered the lives of many persons? In addition, the jury's attention is focused on the characteristics of the person who committed the crime: Does he have a record of prior convictions for capital offenses? Are there any special facts about this defendant that mitigate against imposing capital punishment (for example, his youth, the extent of his cooperation with the police, his emotional state at the time of the crime). As a result, while some jury discretion still exists, the discretion to be exercised is controlled by clear and objective standards so as to produce nondiscriminatory application.

As an important additional safeguard against arbitrariness and caprice, the Georgia statutory scheme provides for automatic appeal of all death sentences to the state's supreme court. That court is required by statute to review each sentence of death and determine whether it was imposed under the influence of passion or prejudice, whether the evidence supports the jury's finding of a statutory aggravating circumstance, and whether the sentence is disproportionate compared to those sentences imposed in similar cases.

The basic concern of *Furman* centered on those defendants who were being condemned to death capriciously and arbitrarily. Under the procedures before the Court in that case, sentencing authorities were not directed to give attention to the nature or circumstances of the crime committed or to the character or record of the defendant. Left unguided, juries imposed the death sentence in a way that could only be called freakish. The new Georgia sentencing procedures, by contrast, focus the jury's attention on the particularized nature of the crime and the particularized characteristics of the individual defendant. While the jury is permitted to consider any aggravating or mitigating circumstances, it must find and identify at least one statutory aggravating factor before it may impose a penalty of death. In this way the jury's discretion is channeled. No longer can a jury wantonly and freakishly impose the death sentence; it is always circum-scribed by the legislative guidelines. In addition, the review function of the supreme court of Georgia affords additional assurance that the concerns that prompted our decision in *Furman* are not present to any significant degree in the Georgia procedure applied here.

For the reasons expressed in this opinion, we hold that the statutory system under which Gregg was sentenced to death does not violate the Constitution. Accordingly, the judgment of the Georgia supreme court is affirmed.

It is so ordered.

CASE QUESTION

In today's fast-moving society, courts, with their reliance on precedent, have been criticized for being too slow in recognizing changing social values. What reasons justify court reliance on precedent?

SUGGESTED READINGS

Hare and Hare, *Stare Decisis*, 31 ALA. LAW 273 (1970).

Birmingham, *Neutrality of Adherence to Precedent*, 1971 DUKE L.J. 541.

Birnbaum, *Stare Decisis vs. Judicial Activism: Nothing Succeeds Like Success*, 54 A.B.A.J. 482 (1968).

Kelman, *Force of Precedent in the Lower Courts*, 14 WAYNE L. REV. 3 (1967).

Allen, *Importance of Following Precedent in the Development of Law and the Administration of Justice*, 26 MO. B.J. 190 (1970).

Note, *Stare Decisis and the Lower Courts; Two Recent Cases*, 59 COLUM. L. REV. 504 (1959).

Rule of the Case

Under the doctrine of *stare decisis*, only a point of law necessarily decided in a reported judicial opinion is binding on other courts as precedent. A question of fact determined by a court has no binding effect on a subsequent case involving similar questions of fact. The facts of each case are recognized as being unique. The authority of a previous decision as precedent is therefore limited to the rule of law as applied to the particular facts of that case. For the rule of law expressed in a previous case to apply, the factual situations in both cases must be nearly alike. A decision that applies a rule of law to a set of facts different from those in the case in question may not serve as a precedent for that case.

Those points of law decided by a court to resolve a legal controversy constitute the *holding* of the case. In other words, the court holds that a certain rule of law applies to the given factual situation of the case and renders its decision accordingly. The rule of law as applied to the facts of the case express the *rule* of the case. Under *stare decisis*, the rule of the case is applied to decide future cases with the same or closely analogous factual situations. The rule of the case as expressed in a court's holding becomes a precedent that guides courts in their decisions and is generally considered to be the law.

Sometimes, in their opinions, courts make comments that are not necessary to support the decision. These extraneous judicial expressions are referred to as *dictum*. They have no value as precedent because they do not fit the facts of the case. The reason for drawing a distinction between holding and *dictum* is that only the issues before the court have been argued and considered fully. Other principles of law are rarely argued and considered completely. Another reason *dictum* is not considered law is that the judiciary may not make law, for this is the function of the legislature. Even though *dictum* is not binding under the doctrine of *stare decisis*, it is entitled to consideration as being persuasive. Other judges and lawyers can determine what the decision makers are thinking and gain an indication of how the problem may be handled in the future.

State v. Butler
19 Ohio St. 2d 55, 249 N.E.2d 818
Supreme Court of Ohio
July 9, 1969

SCHNEIDER, JUSTICE
The offense for which appellant was indicted, tried, and convicted occurred on August 30, 1964. He struck Annie Ruth Sullivan with a jack handle, causing an injury which resulted in loss of sight of her left eye. Appellant was apprehended and arrested by the Cincinnati police, and while in custody he was interrogated by police officers. Prior to the questioning, the police gave no explanation to appellant as to his rights to remain silent and have an attorney present. The interrogation was recorded and reduced to writing. Over objection by appellant's counsel, these questions and answers were repeated by the prosecutor at trial to impeach statements made by appellant during cross-examination.

Appellant appeared before the municipal court of Hamilton County on November 22, 1965. Probable cause was found and appellant was bound over to the Hamilton County grand jury. Bond was set at $500, which appellant posted. The grand jury returned an indictment for the offense of "maiming." Appellant was arraigned and pleaded not guilty, after which the court appointed counsel. Trial was set. A jury was waived and appellant was found guilty by the court of the lesser included offense of aggravated assault. The court of appeals affirmed the judgment of conviction.

Appellant raises the question in this appeal as to whether, in cross-examination of a defendant, the prosecutor may use prior inconsistent statements of the defendant, made to police without *Miranda* warnings, in order to impeach his credibility.

Appellant's contention is that the prosecution violated his Fifth Amendment right against self-incrimination by using statements of his which were made to police during in-custody interrogation with no warning of his right to silence or to counsel. The questioning occurred after arrest, on November 20, 1965, which was prior to the United States Supreme Court decision in *Miranda v. Arizona* (1966), 384 U.S. 436. It was held there that the prosecution's use of statements of an accused, made to police without prior warnings of his rights to remain silent, to counsel and appointed counsel if indigent, was a violation of the accused's Fourteenth and Fifth Amendment right against self-incrimination. In *Johnson v. New Jersey* (1966), 384 U.S. 719, the court held that the rule of *Miranda* applied to all trials commenced after its date of

announcement, June 13, 1966. The delayed trial in the instant case occurred on May 15, 1968, making *Miranda* applicable.

The appellant took the stand and, on cross-examination by the prosecution, he made assertions as to the facts surrounding the crime. A recorded statement appellant made to a detective after arrest was then read to him to show a prior inconsistent statement. Counsel objected, but the court allowed the statement to be used as evidence to impeach the witness's credibility. Appellant contends that this use of the statements, made without cautionary warnings, violated his Fifth Amendment rights as defined by *Miranda v. Arizona, supra* (384 U.S. 436).

We cannot agree. First, the statements used by the prosecution were not offered by the state as part of its direct case against appellant, but were offered on the issue of his credibility after he had been sworn and testified in his own defense. Second, the statements used by the prosecution were voluntary, no claim to the contrary having been made.

The distinction between admissibility of wrongfully obtained evidence to prove the state's case in chief and its use to impeach the credibility of a defendant who takes the stand was expressed in *Walder v. United States* (1954), 347 U.S. 62, 65: "It is one thing to say that the government cannot make an affirmative use of evidence unlawfully obtained. It is quite another to say that the defendant can turn the illegal method by which evidence in the government's possession was obtained to his own advantage, and provide himself with a shield against contradiction of his untruths. . . ."

Those words of Justice Frankfurter were uttered in regard to evidence inadmissible under the Fourth Amendment exclusionary rule. In the case of the Fifth Amendment, even greater reason exists to distinguish between statements of an accused used in the prosecution's direct case and used for impeachment in cross-examining the accused when he takes the stand. We must not lose sight of the words of the Fifth Amendment: ". . . nor shall be compelled to be a witness against himself . . ." This is a privilege accorded an accused not to be compelled to testify, nor to have any prior statements used by the prosecution to lie with impunity once he elects to take the stand to testify.

We do not believe that the case of *Miranda v. Arizona, supra* (384 U.S. 436), dictates a conclusion contrary to ours. In *Miranda*, the court indicated that statements of a defendant used to impeach his testimony at trial may not be used unless they were taken with full warnings and effective waiver. However, we note that in all four of the convictions reversed by that decision, statements of the accused, taken without cautionary warnings, were used by the prosecution as direct evidence of guilt in the case in chief.

We believe that the words of Chief Justice Marshall regarding the difference between holding and *dictum* are applicable here. "It is a maxim not to be disregarded, that general expressions, in every opinion, are to be taken in connection with the case in which those expressions are used. If they go beyond the case, they may be respected, but ought not to control the judgment in a subsequent suit when the very point is presented for decision. The reason of this maxim is obvious. The question actually before the court is investigated with care, and considered in its full extent. Other principles which may serve to illustrate it, are considered in their relation to the case decided, but their possible bearing on all other cases is seldom completely investigated."

The court, in *Miranda*, was not faced with the facts of this case. Thus, we do not consider ourselves bound by the *dictum* of *Miranda*.

The "linch pin" (as Mr. Justice Harlan put it, 384 U.S. at 513) of *Miranda* is that police interrogation is destructive of human dignity and disrespectful to the inviolability of the human personality. In the instant case, the use of the interrogation to impeach the voluntary testimony of the accused is neither an assault on his dignity nor disrespectful of his personality. He elected to testify, and cannot complain that the state seeks to demonstrate the lack of truth in his testimony.

Finally, we emphasize that the statements used by the prosecution were voluntarily made. The decision in *Miranda* did not discard the distinction between voluntary and involuntary statements made by an accused and used by the prosecution. Lack of cautionary warnings is one of the factors to consider in determining whether statements are voluntary or not. However, appellant here has never claimed that the statements used to impeach were involuntary. Thus, we assume they were voluntary, and hold that voluntary statements of an accused made to police without cautionary warnings are admissible on the issue of credibility after defendant has been sworn and testifies in his own defense. Had the case been tried to a jury and not the court, explicit instructions to consider the statement only on the matter of credibility and not as to guilt would have been necessary.

Judgment affirmed

DUNCAN, JUSTICE, dissenting
The use of statements made by the defendant for impeachment without the warnings set forth in *Miranda v. Arizona*, 384 U.S. 436, having been given, is reversible error.

In *Miranda*, Chief Justice Warren stated, at page 476:

The warnings required and the waiver necessary in accordance with our opinion today are, in the absence of a fully effective equivalent, prerequisites to the admissibility of *any statement made by a defendant*. No distinction can be drawn between statements which are direct confessions and statements which amount to "admissions" of part or all of an offense. The privilege against self-incrimination protects the individual from being compelled to incriminate himself in any manner; it does not distinguish degrees of incrimination. Similarly, for precisely the same reason, *no distinction may be drawn between inculpatory statements and statements alleged to be merely "exculpatory."* If a statement made were in fact truly exculpatory, it would, of course, never be used by the prosecution. *In fact, state-*

ments merely intended to be exculpatory by the defendant are often used to impeach his testimony at trial or to demonstrate untruths in the statement given under interrogation and thus to prove guilt by implication. These statements are incriminating in any meaningful sense of the word and may not be used without the full warnings and effective waiver required for any other statement. . . . [Emphasis supplied.]

This *specific* reference to impeachment, I believe, forecloses the use of defendant's in-custody statement in the instant case.

The United States Court of Appeals for the Second Circuit, in *United States v. Fox*, 403 F.2d 97, arrived at a decision contrary to that arrived at by the majority in this case. Judge Bryan, at page 102, stated:

These pronouncements by the Supreme Court may be technically *dictum*. But it is abundantly plain that the court intended to lay down a firm general rule with respect to the use of statements unconstitutionally obtained from a defendant in violation of *Miranda* standards. The rule prohibits the use of such statements whether inculpatory or exculpatory, whether bearing directly on guilt or on collateral matters only, and whether used on direct examination or for impeachment.

I would reverse.

CASE QUESTIONS

1. Explain the difference between holding and *dictum*.
2. Can the holding of a case be broader than the precedent relied on?

3. Why should *dictum* not be considered binding under the doctrine of *stare decisis?*

4. Was *Miranda* properly relied on by the majority in the *Butler* case?

SUGGESTED READINGS

Oliphant, *A Return to Stare Decisis*, 14 A.B.A.J. 71 (1928).

Goodhart, *Determining the Ratio Decidendi of a Case*, 40 YALE L.J. 161 (1930).

Hare and Hare, *Stare Decisis*, 31 ALA. LAW 273 (1970).

Birnbaum, *Stare Decisis vs. Judicial Activism: Nothing Succeeds like Success*, 54 A.B.A.J. 482 (1968).

Stone, *On the Liberation of Appellate Judges—How Not to Do It!* 35 MODERN L. REV. 449 (1972).

Shapiro, *Toward a Theory of Stare Decisis*, 1 J. LEGAL STUDIES 125 (1972).

Reported Judicial Opinion

In order for a court decision on a legal point to create precedent, it must be the final decision of the majority of the court, and the opinion must be reported. A decision by a court without a reported opinion does not have *stare decisis* effect. A written opinion of a decision not having precedential value is usually not published. In the great majority of decisions, no opinion is written. Appellate courts are responsible for practically all the reported opinions, although occasionally a trial court issues a written opinion. There are approximately 2.5 million reported United States judicial decisions. Part of the task of the lawyer and judge is to find the decision or decisions that set the precedent for a particular factual situation.

Once a reported judicial precedent-setting opinion is found, the effective date of that decision has to be determined. For this purpose, the crucial date is the date of the court decision, not the date of the happening of the events that gave rise to the suit. Whether the court decision should be given retroactive or prospective effect as a precedent has to be determined. Generally, there is no distinction drawn between civil and criminal litigation.

A court has the power to declare in its opinion whether the decision should be given retroactive or prospective application. If there is no such declaration, the precedent-setting decision is given both retroactive and prospective effects. *Retroactive effect* means that the decision controls the legal consequences of a cause of action occurring before the announcement of the decision. The correct new rule decided by a court and presented in its opinion should apply to all questions subsequently coming before that court and the lower courts of the jurisdiction. The chronology of the factual events of the subsequent case should not matter.

The general rule is that unless the precedent-setting court has expressly indicated otherwise, or unless special circumstances warrant the denial of retroactive application, the decision is entitled to retroactive as well as prospective effect. The surrounding circumstances are examined to determine the extent to which a judicially changed rule should be given retroactive effect. The degree of reliance on the rule of law being overruled is probably the most important factor that is considered. Courts examine the purpose of the new rule to determine whether it can be effectuated without giving it retroactive application. The extent to which a retroactive operation of an overruling decision may burden the administration of justice is also considered. Courts have reached different results when giving retroactive effect to judicial decisions, depending on the surrounding circumstances.

Baldonado v. Navajo Freight Lines
90 N.M. 284, 562 P.2d 1138
Court of Appeals of New Mexico
January 18, 1977

SUTIN, JUDGE
This appeal involves only the dismissal of a third-party complaint for the reason that the third-party complaint against the third-party defendant for contribution was barred by the New Mexico "guest statute."

On October 30, 1974, an automobile-truck accident occurred in Gallup, New Mexico. The automobile was driven by Ruth Ann English. Robert Baldonado was a guest in this car. The truck was owned by Navajo Freight Lines and it was operated by Robert A. Whedon.

Baldonado sued Navajo and Whedon for personal injuires. Navajo and Whedon filed a third-party complaint against English. Navajo sued for contribution and property damage. Whedon sued for personal injuries.

The English motion to dismiss was granted. Navajo's claim for contribution was barred by the New Mexico "guest statute." Section 64-24-1 reads: "No person transported by the owner or operator of a motor vehicle as his guest . . . shall have a cause of action for damages against such owner or operator for injury. . . ." Under this statute, Baldonado had no claim for damages against English. English was immune from such suit.

Navajo and Whedon claim that this concept was abolished because the "guest statute" was declared unconstitutional on September 23, 1975. *McGeehan v. Bunch*, 88 N.M. 308, 540 P.2d 238 (1975). The court said:

After due deliberation, it is the opinion of this court that the decision holding our guest statute unconstitutional shall be given modified prospectivity. That is, this newly announced rule shall apply to the case at bar, all similar pending actions and all cases which may arise in the future. [88 N.M. at 314, 540 P.2d at 244].

"Purely prospective" application means that the overruling decision shall not apply to the parties in the case at bar. A "modified prospective" application means a qualified application: (1) that the *McGeehan* decision shall apply to the case at bar, (2) all similar pending actions, and (3) all cases which may arise in the future.

We must determine if the case at bar is a "pending action" or a case that "may arise in the future." It is neither.

1. This is not a "pending action." A civil action is commenced by filing a complaint with the court. An action is to be regarded as pending from the time of its commencement until its final termination. Navajo's third-party complaint was not pending in court at the time of the *McGeehan* decision.
2. This is not a case that "may arise in the future." We are confronted with the meaning of the word "case" and the words "arise in the future." The word "case" in a legal sense means "suit." The word "suit" is more general than the word "action," because it applies to equitable, criminal, and legal proceedings.

Under Rule 3 of the Rules of Civil Procedure, the words "civil action" are broad and used interchangeably with the words "civil case."

A "cause of action" is not easily defined, but for purposes of this case, it means those facts that give rise to a right of action. A cause of action accrues or arises when there is an existing right to sue forthwith. Thus a cause of action arises when it springs up, originates, comes into being, becomes operative, presents itself.

What is meant by a case "that may arise in the future?" It does not mean a case "that may be filed in the future," or "that may be commenced in the future." If this were the intent of the court, it would have so stated. In *Vaughn v. Murray*, 214 Kan. 456, 521 P.2d 262 (1974), the court was confronted with *Henry v. Bauder*, 213 Kan. 751, 518 P.2d 362 (1974), pending in its court, which declared the Kansas "guest statute" unconstitutional without any provision for modified prospectivity. *Vaughn* concluded that *Henry* "be given retroactive application to all similar cases pending in the courts of [Kansas] on January 26, 1974, and to cases filed thereafter regardless of when the causes of action accrued...." [521 P.2d at 271]. If the same language had appeared in *McGeehan*, English would not have the benefit of the "guest statute."

A cause of action or suit arises, according to the universal rule in courts of both law and equity, when and as soon as the party has a right to apply to the proper tribunal for relief.

In the instant case, the accident occurred on October 30, 1974. Navajo's causes of action arose at that time. Navajo's "case" arose at that time out of its rights of action because a civil action could have commenced at that time. This date was long before the *McGeehan* opinion. Modified prospectivity therein granted English the benefit of the "guest statute."

The trial court properly barred the count of Navajo's third-party complaint for contribution.

Affirmed

LOPEZ, JUDGE, dissenting

I dissent. The plaintiff, Robert Baldonado, brought an action for personal injuries and property damage based on the negligence of the defendants, Navajo Freight Lines and Robert A. Whedon. The defendants then filed a third-party complaint against Ruth Ann English Baldonado. This third-party complaint, which sought contribution from a joint tortfeasor [one who commits a tort], was dismissed. The defendants appeal and I would reverse.

For reversal, the defendants present the argument that the claim for contribution is not barred by the New Mexico guest statute.

Facts

Defendants' third-party complaint against Ruth Ann English Baldonado was contained in the answer to plaintiff's complaint. For clarity, we will refer to the third-party defendant as English. The third-party complaint reads as follows:

Count One

2. The third-party claimants have been sued in this cause by Robert Baldonado . . . for injuries allegedly incurred as a result of an accident on the 30th day of October, 1974. . . .
3. The accident alleged in the complaint . . . was caused by third-party defendant's negligent operation of her automobile.
4. If the plaintiff, Robert Baldonado, should recover anything under this complaint against the defendants and third-party claimants, they should have

judgment against the third-party defendant for contribution.

On September 23, 1975, the Supreme Court of New Mexico decided *McGeehan v. Bunch*, 88 N.M. 308, 540 P.2d 238 (1975). *McGeehan* found that unreasonable classifications created by the New Mexico guest statute were an unconstitutional denial of equal protection.

On November 17, 1975, Baldonado sued Navajo and Whedon. The defendants' third-party complaint was filed December 29, 1975.

Navajo's claim for contribution is not barred by the New Mexico guest statute.

The significant wording of *McGeehan* is:

After due deliberation, it is the opinion of this court that the decision holding our guest statute unconstitutional shall be given modified prospectivity. That is, this newly announced rule shall apply to the case at bar, all similar pending actions and all cases which may arise in the future.

The third-party plaintiffs, Navajo and Whedon, argue that *McGeehan* applies to the McGeehan case itself, all cases pending at that time, and all cases filed after the decision. This gives the word "case" its ordinary meaning. I agree.

I must also determine what the supreme court meant by "modified prospectivity." This is a case of first impression in New Mexico and for guidance I look to other states. The Kansas Supreme Court declared the Kansas guest statute unconstitutional in *Henry v. Bauder*, 213 Kan. 751, 518 P.2d 362 (1974). In *Vaughn v. Murray*,

214 Kan. 456, 521 P.2d 262 (1974), the court considered the retroactive effect of the overruling decision. The court noted that the cases fall into four categories: (1) purely prospective, where the law declared will not apply even to the parties to the overruling case; (2) limited retroactive, where the law declared will govern the rights of the parties to the overruling case and apply prospectively in all other cases; (3) general retroactive, governing the rights of the parties to the overruling case and to all pending and future cases, unless further litigation is barred by the statute of limitations or jurisdictional rules of appellate procedure; and (4) retroactive, governing the rights of the parties to the overruling case, other cases pending when the overruling case was decided and all future cases, but limited so the new law will not govern the rights of the parties to cases terminated by a judgment or verdict before the overruling decision was announced. I find the reasoning of the Kansas Supreme Court compelling, and conclude that, by "modified prospectivity," the New Mexico Supreme Court meant categories (3) and (4) above.

English cites *Hicks v. State*, 88 N.M. 588, 544 P.2d 1153 (1975). That case was modified to apply purely prospectively, that is, only to torts arising subsequent to the decision. The general rule is that unless there are special circumstances (such as reliance) which require the denial of retroactive application, an overruling decision will be given retroactive as well as prospective application. Although the traditional policy is in favor of giving unlimited retroactive effect of an overruling decision, it is now recognized that a court has the power to go to the opposite extreme and overrule a case purely prospectively.

But *Hicks* is not relevant to this case. The fault concept of tort liability has generally left little room for reliance. Pure prospectivity has been especially appropriate in cases such as *Hicks*, where sovereign immunity was overruled, because of the high degree of reliance. The agencies losing immunity would have no opportunity to obtain insurance. In *Hicks*, stability and the right to rely on existing law seem to have controlled.

I believe the supreme court of New Mexico intended *McGeehan* to apply to that case itself, to cases pending at the time of the decision, and cases or lawsuits filed subsequent to the ruling. This case was filed subsequent to the ruling of *McGeehan*. Therefore the ruling applies to it. There is no reliance, as in *Hicks*, that would justify purely prospective application.

I hold that the court erred in determining that *McGeehan* did not apply to the instant case. The defense of the guest statute is not applicable and the defendants can implead [sue] English as a third-party defendant.

The district court having erred, I would reverse the summary judgment and would remand this case for proceedings consistent with my opinion.

CASE QUESTION

On what basis does the majority and dissent differ?

SUGGESTED READINGS

Radin, *The Requirement of Written Opinions*, 18 CALIF. L. REV. 486 (1930).

Hanson, *Findings of Fact and Conclusions of Law: An Outmoded Relic of Stage Coach Days*, 32 A.B.A.J. 52 (1946).

Musmanno, *Dissenting Opinions*, 60 DICK. L. REV. 139 (1956).

Stone, *Dissenting Opinions Are Not Without Value*, 26 J. AM. JUD. SOC'Y. 78 (1942).

Absence of Precedent

When judges are confronted by a novel fact situation, they must rely on their own sense of justice. Public interest, tradition, prevailing customs, business usage, and moral standards are also considered in the decision-making process. When precedent is lacking in the forum state, decisions of other state and federal courts, as well as English decisions, may be considered persuasive on the legal point at issue. Judges create new law when they decide a novel case. In so doing, they must recognize the future impact of their decisions.

Strunk v. Strunk
445 S.W.2d 145
Court of Appeals of Kentucky
September 26, 1969

OSBORNE, JUDGE

The specific question involved upon this appeal is: Does a court of equity[1] have the power to permit a kidney to be removed from an incompetent ward of the state upon petition of his commit-tee, who is also his mother, for the purpose of being transplanted into the body of his brother, who is dying of a fatal kidney disease? We are of the opinion it does.

The facts of the case are as follows: Arthur L. Strunk, 54 years of age, and Ava Strunk, 52 years of age, of Williamstown, Kentucky, are the parents of two sons. Tommy Strunk is 28 years of age, married, an employee of the

---

[1] Equity will be discussed in Chapter V. —*Ed.*

Penn State Railroad and a part-time student at the University of Cincinnati. Tommy is now suffering from chronic glomerulus nephritis, a fatal kidney disease. He is now being kept alive by frequent treatment on an artificial kidney, a procedure that cannot be continued much longer.

Jerry Strunk is 27 years of age, incompetent, and through proper legal proceedings has been committed to the Frankfort State Hospital and School, which is a state institution maintained for the feeble-minded. He has an IQ of approximately 35, which corresponds with the mental age of approximately six years. He is further handicapped by a speech defect, which makes it difficult for him to communicate with persons who are not well acquainted with him. When it was determined that Tommy, in order to survive, would have to have a kidney, the doctors considered the possibility of using a kidney from a cadaver if and when one became available, or one from a live donor if this could be made available. The entire family, his mother, father, and a number of collateral relatives were tested. Because of incompatibility of blood type or tissue, none was medically acceptable as a live donor. As a last resort, Jerry was tested and found to be highly acceptable. This immediately presented the legal problem as to what, if anything, could be done by the family, especially the mother and the father, to procure a transplant from Jerry to Tommy. The mother as a committee petitioned the county court for authority to proceed with the operation. The court found that the operation was necessary, that under the peculiar circumstances of this case, it

would not only be beneficial to Tommy but also beneficial to Jerry because Jerry was greatly dependent on Tommy, emotionally and psychologically, and that his well-being would be jeopardized more severely by the loss of his brother than by the removal of a kidney.

Appeal was taken to the Franklin Circuit Court where the chancellor reviewed the record, examined the testimony of the witnesses, and adopted the findings of the county court.

A psychiatrist, in attendance to Jerry, who testified in the case, stated in his opinion the death of Tommy under these circumstances would have ''an extremely traumatic effect upon him [Jerry].''

The Department of Mental Health of this commonwealth has entered the case as *amicus curiae* and on the basis of its evaluation of the seriousness of the operation as opposed to the traumatic effect on Jerry as a result of the loss of Tommy, recommended to the court that Jerry be permitted to undergo the surgery. Its recommendations are as follows: ''It is difficult for the mental defective to establish a firm sense of identity with another person. The acquisition of this necessary identity is dependent on a person whom one can conveniently accept as a model and who at the same time is sufficiently flexible to allow the defective to detach himself with reassurances of continuity. His need to be social is not so much the necessity of a formal and mechanical contact with other human beings as it is the necessity of a close intimacy with other men, the desirability of a real community of feeling, an urgent need for a unity of understanding. Purely mechanical and formal contact with other men does not offer any treatment for the behavior of a mental defective. Only those who are able to communicate intimately are of value to hospital treatment in these cases. And this generally is a member of the family.

"In view of this knowledge, we now have particular interest in this case. Jerry Strunk, a mental defective, has emotions and reactions on a scale comparable to that of a normal person. He identifies with his brother Tom. Tom is his model, his tie with his family. Tom's life is vital to the continuity of Jerry's improvement at Frankfort State Hospital and School. The testimony of the hospital representative reflected the importance to Jerry of his visits with his family and the constant inquiries Jerry made about Tom's coming to see him. Jerry is aware he plays a role in the relief of this tension. We the Department of Mental Health must take all possible steps to prevent the occurrence of any guilt feelings Jerry would have if Tom were to die.

"The necessity of Tom's life to Jerry's treatment and eventual rehabilitation is clearer in view of the fact that Tom is his only living sibling and at the death of their parents, now in their fifties, Jerry will have no concerned, intimate communication so necessary to his stability and optimal functioning.

"The evidence shows that at the present level of medical knowledge, it is quite remote that Tom would be able to survive several cadaver transplants. Tom has a much better chance of survival if the kidney transplant from Jerry takes place."

Upon this appeal, we are faced with the fact that all members of the immediate family have recommended the transplant. The Department of Mental Health has likewise made its recommendation. The county court has given its approval. The circuit court has found that it would be to the best interest of the ward of the state that the procedure be carried out. Throughout the legal proceedings, Jerry has been represented by a guardian *ad litem*, who has continually questioned the power of the state to authorize the removal of an organ from the body of an incompetent who is a ward of the state. We are fully cognizant of the fact that the question before us is unique. Insofar as we have been able to learn, no similar set of facts has come before the highest court of any of the states of this nation or the federal courts. The English courts have apparently taken a broad view of the inherent power of the equity courts with regard to incompetents. *Ex parte Whitebread* (1816), 2 Mer. 99, 35 E.R. 878, holds that courts of equity have the inherent power to make provisions for a needy brother out of the estate of an incompetent. This case was followed in this country. The inherent rule in these cases is that the chancellor has the power to deal with the estate of the incompetent in the same manner as the incompetent would if he had his faculties. This rule has been extended to cover not only matters of property but also to cover the personal affairs of the incompetent.

The right to act for the incompetent in all cases has become recognized in this country as the doctrine of substituted judgment and is broad enough not only to cover property but also to cover all matters touching on the well-being of the ward.

The medical practice of transferring tissue from one part of the human body to another (autografting) and from one human being to another (homografting) is rapidly becoming a common clinical practice. In many cases, the transplants take as well when the tissue is dead as when it is alive. This has made practicable the establishment of tissue banks where such material can be stored for future use. Vascularized grafts of lungs, kidneys, and hearts are becoming increasingly common. These grafts must be of functioning, living cells with blood vessels remaining anatomically intact. The chance of success in the transfer of these organs is greatly increased when the donor and the donee are genetically related. It is recognized by all legal and medical authorities that several legal problems can arise as a result of the operative techniques of the transplant procedure.

The renal transplant is becoming the most common of the organ transplants. This is because the normal body has two functioning kidneys, one of which it can reasonably do without, thereby making it possible for one person to donate a kidney to another. Testimony in this record shows that there have been over 2500 kidney transplants performed in the United States up to this date. The process can be effected under present techniques with minimal danger to both the donor and the donee.

Review of our case law leads us to believe that the power given to a committee under KRS 387.230 would not extend so far as to allow a committee to subject his ward to the serious surgical techniques here under consideration unless the life of his ward be in jeopardy. Nor do we believe the powers delegated to the county court by virtue of the above statutes would reach so far as to permit the procedure which we are dealing with here.

We are of the opinion that a chancery court does have sufficient inherent power to authorize the operation. The circuit court having found that the operative procedures in this instance are to the best interest of Jerry Strunk and this finding having been based on substantial evidence, we are of the opinion the judgment should be affirmed. We do not deem it significant that this case reached the circuit court by way of appeal as opposed to a direct proceeding in that court.

Judgment affirmed

HILL, C.J., MILLIKEN, *and* REED, JJ., concur.

NEIKIRK, PALMORE, and STEINFELD, JJ., dissent.

STEINFELD, JUDGE, dissenting

Apparently because of my indelible recollection of a government which, to the everlasting shame of its citizens, embarked on a program of genocide and experimentation with human bodies, I have been more troubled in reaching a decision in this case than in any other. My sympathies and emotions are torn between a compassion to aid an ailing young man and a duty to fully protect unfortunate members of society.

The opinion of the majority is predicated on the authority of an equity court to speak for one who cannot speak for himself. However, it is my opinion that in considering such right in this instance, we must first look to the power and authority vested in the committee, the appellee herein. KRS 387.060 and KRS 387.230 do nothing more than give the committee the power to take custody of the incompetent and the possession, care, and management of his property. Courts have restricted the activities of the committee to that which is for the best interest of the incompetent. The authority and duty have been to protect and maintain the ward, to secure that to which he is entitled and preserve that which he has.

The wishes of the members of the family or the desires of the guardian to be helpful to the apparent objects of the ward's bounty have not been a criterion. A curator or guardian cannot dispose of his ward's property by donation, even though authorized to do so by the court on advice of a family meeting, unless a gift by the guardian is authorized by statute.

Two Kentucky cases decided many years ago reveal judicial policy. In *W. T. Sistrunk & Co. v. Navarra's Committee*, 268 Ky. 753, 105 S.W.2d 1039 (1937), this court held that a committee was without right to continue a business which the incompetent had operated prior to his having been declared a person of unsound mind. More analogous is *Baker v. Thomas*, 272 Ky. 605, 114 S.W.2d 1113 (1938), in which a man and woman had lived together out of wedlock. Two children were born to them. After the man was adjudged incompetent, his committee, acting for him, together with his paramour, instituted proceedings to adopt the two children. In rejecting the application and refusing to speak for the incompetent, the opinion stated: "The statute does not contemplate that the committee of a lunatic may exercise any other power than to have the possession, care, and management of the lunatic's or incompetent's estate."

The majority opinion is predicated on the finding of the circuit court that there will be psychological benefits to the ward but points out that the incompetent has the mentality of a six-year-old child. It is common knowledge beyond dispute that the loss of a close relative or a friend to a six-year-old child is not of major impact. Opinions concerning psychological trauma are at best most nebulous. Furthermore, there are no guarantees that the transplant will become a surgical success, it being well known that body rejection of transplanted organs is frequent. The life of the incompetent is not in danger, but the surgical procedure advocated creates some peril.

It is written in *Prince v. Massachusetts*, 321 U.S. 158 (1944), that "Parents may be free to become martyrs themselves. But it does not follow they are free, in identical circumstances, to make martyrs of their children before they have reached the age of full and legal discretion when they can make the choice for themselves." The ability to fully understand and consent is a prerequisite to the donation of a part of the human body.

Unquestionably, the attitudes and attempts of the committee and members of the family of the two young men whose critical problems now confront us are commendable, natural, and beyond reproach. However, they refer us to nothing indicating that they are privileged to authorize the removal of one of the kidneys of the incompetent for the purpose of donation, and they cite no statutory or other authority vesting such right in the courts. The proof shows that less compatible donors are available and that the kidney of a cadaver could be used, although the odds of operational success are not as great in such cases as they would be with the fully compatible donor brother.

I am unwilling to hold that the gates should be open to permit the removal of an organ from an incompetent for transplant, at least until such time as it is conclusively demonstrated that it will be of significant benefit to the incompetent. The evidence here does not rise to that pinnacle. To hold that committees, guardians, or courts have such awesome power, even in the persuasive case before us, could establish legal precedent, the dire result of which we cannot fathom. Regretfully I must say no.

NEIKIRK and PALMORE, JJ., join with me in this dissent.

CASE QUESTIONS

1. The Court of Appeals of Kentucky is the court of last resort in Kentucky. The *Strunk* decision is now the law of the commonwealth of Kentucky. Does the decision make mental institutions a storehouse of human bodies available for distribution to the more productive members of society whenever the state decides that someone's need outweighs the danger to the incompetent?
2. Do you think the justice who wrote the dissenting opinion was influenced by his background?
3. Which opinion, the majority or dissent, was more persuasive?
4. Where there are no legal cases that have a direct bearing upon the issue of a case, should the court turn to other disciplines for authority?

SUGGESTED READINGS

Spaeth, *An Approach to the Study of Attitudinal Differences as an Aspect of Judicial Behavior*, 5 MIDWEST J. POL. SCI. 165–80 (1961).

A. M. PAUL, CONSERVATIVE CRISIS AND THE RULE OF LAW: ATTITUDES OF BAR AND BENCH, 1887–1895 (1960).

K. N. LLEWELLYN, THE COMMON LAW TRADITION: DECIDING APPEALS (1960).

Nagel, *Political Party Affiliation and Judges Decisions*, 55 AM. POL. SCI. REV. 843 (1961).

Recognizing Foreign Law

Conflict of Laws

Each of the 50 states is an individual sovereignty that creates its own common and statutory law. Frequently there are inconsistencies among the laws of the various states. A conflict-of-laws problem is presented whenever a legal controversy arises in which there is a foreign element. When the facts of a case under consideration have occurred in more than one state or country, and it becomes necessary for a court to make a choice between the laws of the different states or nations, a conflict case is presented. Another type of conflict-of-laws case involves a situation in which an event occurred in one state and the suit is brought in another state. In this situation, the court must decide whether to apply its own substantive law, the law of the state in which the events occurred, or possibly the law of some other state. A court always follows its own procedural law.

Conflict-of-laws rules have been developed by each state to assist its courts in determining whether and when foreign substantive law should be given effect within the territory of the forum. A lawyer uses these rules to predict the outcome of a case. The rules afford some assurance that a case will be treated in the same way under the appropriate law, no matter where the suit is brought.

Every person within the territorial limits of a government is bound by its laws. It is well recognized that law does not of its own force have any effect outside the territory of the sovereignty from which its authority is derived. Foreign law may be enforced or given effect elsewhere when the conflict-of-laws rule determining such enforcement or recognition is part of the law of the local jurisdiction.

TORT CASES

In tort cases, the traditional approach is to apply the law of the place where the wrong was committed—*lex loci delicti*. The place of the wrong is the place where the last event necessary to make the actor liable takes place or where the person or thing harmed is situated at the time of the wrong. In recent years, some courts have declined to apply the *lex loci delicti* rule and apply the more flexible *significant relationship* rule. This approach is used in contract cases as well as tort cases. It requires application of the law of the place that has the most significant contacts with the incident or event in dispute. Most states apply the law of the place of the wrong in determining the law to be applied in tort cases.

Hardly Able Coal Co., Inc., v. International Harvester
494 F. Supp. 249
United States District Court, N.D. Illinois
July 23, 1980

SHADUR, DISTRICT JUDGE
Defendant has moved to strike the allegations of ''economic loss'' in plaintiff's complaint and to dismiss the case. For the reasons stated in this opinion and order, that motion is denied.

Two legal questions are posed by defendant's motion:

1. What state's substantive law is applicable to plaintiff's cause of action in this diversity case?
2. Does the applicable state law permit a tort cause of action based on either strict liability or negligence where the only damage claimed is to the product that was allegedly designed and manufactured defectively or negligently—that is, where no injury to other property or to persons is charged?

Facts

Plaintiff's complaint charges that a bulldozer designed, manufactured, and sold by defendant was either improperly or negligently designed and manufactured. When the hoist ram hydraulic crossover hose failed on the bulldozer unit, hydraulic fluid escaped under pressure and sprayed upon the engine and turbocharger housing, causing a subsequent fire and explosion which seriously, severely, and substantially damaged and destroyed the entire International Harvester Model. As a result of the damage, the plaintiff has been unable to repair said bulldozer and the same has been scrapped. As a result of the foregoing damage to the bulldozer unit, the plaintiff has been caused to incur substantial costs in order to remove said damaged bulldozer unit from the job site for analysis, repair evaluation, and ultimate demolition. The plaintiff has been caused to rent at great expense replacement equipment in order to continue with its operation all at its own costs. The plaintiff has been required to expend additional sums to obtain permanent replacement equipment and has lost earnings and profits thereby.

Choice of Law

Illinois choice of law doctrine, of course, applies under familiar *Erie v. Tompkins* principles. *Ingersoll v. Klein*, 46 Ill. 2d 42, 45, 262 N.E.2d 593, 595 (1970), states the Illinois conflicts rule in tort cases: ''The local law of the state where the injury occurred should determine the rights and liabilities of the parties, unless Illinois has a more significant relationship with the occurrence and with the parties, in which case the law of Illinois should apply.'' For that purpose, Illinois courts follow the Restatement (Second) of Conflicts of Law, under Section 145, of which the following contacts are to be evaluated in accordance with their relative importance to the particular issues presented by the lawsuit:

a. the place where the injury occurred
b. the place where the conduct causing the injury occurred
c. the domicile, residence, and nationality, place of incorporation and place of business of the parties
d. the place where the relationship, if any, between the parties is centered.

Effectively the Illinois (and the general) rule is that duplicate prizes are not awarded in case of ties. If the weighting of the several factors is equal, the conventional *lex loci delicti* approach that was once uniformly applied in torts cases prevails.

Here we have (a) a Kentucky accident (b) caused by Illinois conduct (c) where plaintiff is a corporation organized and doing all its business in Kentucky, and defendant is a corporation organized elsewhere, but having its principal place of business in Chicago. Factor (d) really does not apply, because it cannot be said that the single purchase transaction gave rise to a "centered" relationship between the parties. On an unweighted basis, then, the relevant factors balance, and Kentucky law ("where the injury occurred") would apply.

Evaluating the factors "in accordance with their relative importance" to the lawsuit's issues does not lead to a different result. Accordingly, the court concludes that under Illinois conflict-of-law doctrines, the law of Kentucky—where the injury occurred—applies.

Kentucky's Substantive Law

Illinois law clearly supports the position that in actions for either product liability or negligence, a manufacturer's liability is limited to damages for physical injuries and there is no recovery for "economic loss" alone. And it may well be, as defendant asserts (though the court expresses no view on this score), that the Illinois position represents the better reasoned authority and the growing trend on the issue.

But this court is not free to exercise original and independent judgment in this area unless Kentucky courts have left the question entirely open. That is not the case here. Kentucky's Court of Appeals has spoken on this question in *C. D. Herme, Inc. v. R. C. Tway Co.* 294 S.W. 2d 534, 537 (Ky. 1956), when it first extended manufacturers' liability in tort cases beyond the "dangerous instrumentality" doctrine: "Although the *duty* is stated in terms of the foreseeability of *bodily* harm, we think that if the duty has been violated, the mere fact that the actual injury in the particular [case] happens to be to *property* does not relieve the offender from liability." After so stating, the court held that damage to the defective product was itself actionable. The Kentucky court specifically granted relief for the damages to the *product* that controls.

Conclusion

Defendant's motion to strike and dismiss is denied.

CASE QUESTIONS

1. Did the court use the traditional approach and apply the law of the place where the wrong was committed (*lex loci delicti*), or the more flexible approach of significant relationship?
2. What contacts were evaluated by the court in determining which state had a more significant relationship with the occurrence and with the parties?

SUGGESTED READINGS

W. L. PROSSER, LAW OF TORTS §§ 124–25 (4th ed. 1971).
Earle, *Conflict of Laws and the Interest Analysis—An Example for Illinois,* 4 JOHN MARSHALL J. 1 (1972).
Ausubel, *Conflict of Laws Trends—Torts,* 19 DePAUL L. REV. 684 (1970).
Note, *Erosion of Lex Loci Delicti: Toward a More Rational Choice of Tort Law,* 5 U. RICHMOND L. REV. 331 (1971).
Note, *Conflict of Laws—Tort Choice of Law—Lex Loci Delicti and Dissimilarity Doctrine Abandoned and Most Significant Relationship Test Adopted,* 11 ST. MARY L.J. 1009 (1980).

CONTRACT CASES

All states have developed their own conflict-of-laws rules for contractual disputes which differ from the rules that apply to tort cases. In a contractual dispute, depending on the facts involved, the court may apply the law of the place of any of the following: (1) where the action was instituted (*lex fori*), (2) where the contract was made (*lex loci contractus*), (3) where the contract was to be performed (*lex loci solutionis*), (4) which law the parties intended to govern their agreement, and (5) which law has the greatest concern with the event and parties (significant relationship or center of gravity test). A court may choose to follow its own substantive law of contracts and will do so if the application of the foreign law would offend its public policy.

Generally, the law of the state in which the contract was made determines the validity of the contract. This is referred to as the doctrine of *lex loci contractus.* A contract takes place where the last act necessary to complete the contract is done, or, in other words, where the contract first creates a legal obligation. Sometimes the agreement specifies that no contract will come into existence until the completion or happening of a certain event. The place where such last act is done is normally the place where the contract is made.

The place where the contract was made may have little or no connection with the place of performance of the contract. Because the place where the contract is to be performed probably has more connection with the transaction than does the place where the contract was made, a court may choose to apply the law of that state (*lex loci solutionis*). This rule becomes difficult to apply in multistate business dealings in which performance takes place in several states.

Courts often consider the law intended by the parties to be controlling. The parties to the contract may intend that a certain state's law govern the validity of the contract. Their intention is sometimes expressed in the body of the written contract. Insurance companies and other large commercial organizations select favorable state law and insert a provision in the written contract stating that it is applicable in case of dispute. Although most contracts do not state explicitly the law the parties choose to apply, courts may determine the parties' intent by examining the facts surrounding the contract. The state chosen usually has a substantial connection with the contract, but courts have held that no such connection is necessary if the parties intended that that state's law govern.

The law of the state that is most concerned with the event and the parties is often applied by the courts. This is a new approach to contractual conflicts-of-law problems and is called the significant relationship or center of gravity test. All states apply one of the rules discussed above or a combination of all the rules. This often results in confusion, making it impossible to predict the outcome of a case.

Baffin Land Corp. v. Monticello Motor Inn, Inc.
425 P.2d 623
Supreme Court of Washington
March 24, 1967

FINLEY, CHIEF JUSTICE
This action was brought by Baffin Land Corporation, a Delaware corporation, as assignee of Master Video Systems, Inc., to collect delinquent payments under a television rental agreement with an option to purchase made in 1958 with Matthew G. Clark, who was operating what was then known as the Monticello Hotel in Longview, Washington. At the time the contract was made, Mr. Clark, was operating the hotel, now known as the Monticello Motor Inn, Inc., on behalf of the marital community composed of himself and his wife, Eleanor M. Clark. The agreement was signed in Longview, Washington, by Matthew G. Clark and by a salesman of Master Video and forwarded to New York, where it was signed by a vice president of Master Video, a Delaware corporation duly authorized to do business in Washington. Under the provisions of the agreement, a binding contract was not formed until the signature of the vice president was affixed in New York.

Master Video then did the necessary

wiring and installed the television sets in the Monticello Hotel. Monthly rental payments were mailed from Washington to the lessor in New York. Acting under the agreement, Master Video serviced the television sets to a certain extent until the provision of the contract calling for such servicing was deleted by mutual consent.

Subsequently, the Clarks were divorced and the property settlement they had agreed upon was approved in the divorce proceeding. Under the terms of the settlement, certain real and personal assets which had previously been held as community property went to Eleanor M. Clark, and she waived any further interest in the Monticello Hotel or its assets. The agreement also provided that Matthew would indemnify Eleanor and save her harmless from any liability on obligations arising from the operation of the hotel, including costs and attorney fees incurred in any necessary defense by her.

After a trial to the court below, judgment for the plaintiff was entered against Monticello Motor Inn, Inc., and Matthew G. Clark for delinquent rentals of $14,507.40 plus interest and sales tax upon the rental. From the portion of the judgment denying any recovery against Eleanor M. Clark, plaintiff appeals.

The trial court held that the obligations of the contract were governed by the rule of *lex loci contractus*. Since the last act necessary to form a binding contract occurred in New York, and since the contract was therefore made or executed in New York, the trial court held that the obligations of the contract and its effect were determined and governed by the law of New York. The court below further found the law of New York to be such that neither the defendant Eleanor M. Clark nor the former marital community composed of Eleanor M. and Matthew G. Clark has at any time been obligated or liable on the contract, and that the plaintiff has never had any enforceable claim against any property of the defendant Eleanor M. Clark which was formerly the community property of the individual defendants here or against any separate property of Eleanor M. Clark.

The time for adoption of the center of gravity or most significant contacts approach has now come, and we do so by our decision in the instant matter.

The rule of *lex loci contractus* was first applied by this court in *LaSelle v. Woolery*, 14 Wash. 70, 44 P. 115 (1896). The rule of *lex loci contractus*, or the law of the place of contracting, was adopted by the first Restatement of the Law of Conflict of Laws, even though it had never been a majority rule in the United States. The primary virtues of the rule were thought to be simplicity and certainty. The application of the theoretically simple formula to complex phenomena often failed to produce the desired certainty and simplicity. Some practice difficulties which may render its utility dubious can be best demonstrated by a hypothetical.

What if the vice president of Master Video had placed the rental agreement, unsigned, in his briefcase and had left for a business appointment in Florida? Once aloft, he might choose to forego the various pleasures of air travel and make good use of the travel time by perusing the unfinished business in his briefcase. Somewhere en route, he affixes his signature to the Monticello Hotel television rental agreement. Should a court attempt to ascertain the approximate time of the signing during the flight? By interpolating the pilot's log, should the judge conclude that the law of North Carolina applies, since the airspace of the Tar Heel State was the actual scene or *loci* of the execution of the contract? Or should the governing law be the law of the state of destination? Of the state of embarkation?

Is it not more rational and more consistent with standards of equity, fair play, and justice to attempt to ascertain which state had the most significant contacts with the agreement in dispute? The grouping of contacts or center of gravity theory admittedly lacks some of the apparent predictability and certainty of the *lex loci contractus* formula. But again, predictability and certainty are not necessarily the only values which should govern the choice of the applicable law. The place of execution can be given important and possibly controlling effect under the significant contacts approach. However, other factors such as the apparent intention of the parties, the place of performance, and the place under whose law the agreement will be most effective should be accorded appropriate consideration in determining what state's law should govern litigated disputes involving contracts with multistate aspects.

The rule we adopt is more flexible and thus better adapted to deal with the contracts with multistate aspects which are becoming the rule today and make commonplace choice of law problems such as this one. The rule we approve here also gives much more em-

phasis to the desires and expectations of the parties, as the state with the most significant relationship is the state chosen by the parties, if an actual, valid choice is made. Where no choice is made, it is most likely that the parties would expect the law of the state with the most significant contacts to be applied.

We note also that our conclusion as to the change effected by the instant decision is supported by the fact that our state legislature has enacted the Uniform Commercial Code and particularly UCC § 1–105. When this section becomes effective as RCW 62A.1–105 on July 1, 1967, this court would be required to apply the law of the state to which the transaction, if covered by the code, bears an "appropriate relation." We deem this rule to be a departure from *lex loci contractus* and suggestive of the significant relationship approach. See Comment, UCC § 1–105. As a final observation, it is our opinion that applying the law of the state with the most significant relationship to the contract will produce results which are less arbitrary and more just.

The basic rule is that the validity and effect of a contract are governed by the local law of the state which has the most significant relationship to the contract. A general listing of factors which often are significant in regard to a particular contract is found in Section 332b of the Restatement, as modified in November, 1960 (1961):

1. In the absence of an effective choice of law by the parties, consideration will be given to the following factors, among others, in determining

the state with which the contract has its most significant relationship: (a) the place of contracting, (b) the place of negotiation of the contract, (c) the place of performance, (d) the situs of the subject matter of the contract, (e) the domicile, residence, nationality, place of incorporation and place of the business of the parties [and] (f) the place under whose local law the contract will be most effective.

2. If the place of contracting, the place of negotiating the contract, and the place of performance are in the same state, the local law of this state ordinarily determines the validity of the contract, except in the case of usury (see § 334d) and as stated in §§ 346e to 346n.

Since there was no express choice of law determined by the parties in the present instance, we shall apply the above factors to the facts before us. The place of contracting was in New York. The place of negotiation of the contract was at least partially in Washington since both Matthew G. Clark and a salesman for Master Video signed the contract in Longview before mailing it to New York for final acceptance. At least the major portion of the performance of the contract was to, and did, take place in Washington, as it was in Washington that Master Video, among other things, installed the master antenna and amplifier system with an internal distribution network within the hotel, installed numerous television outlets in various rooms so that sets could be moved about, and delivered and connected up the television sets. It was also in Washington that Master

Video performed such repair and maintenance as was accomplished under the contract before it was modified. If there can be said to be a subject matter of the instant contract, it was the television sets which were installed in Washington. Matthew G. Clark was domiciled in and a resident of Washington at the time of contracting, and Master Video, a Delaware corporation, was authorized to and was doing business in Washington.

We come now to the question of what the applicable Washington law is. It is conceded that the agreement, signed by the husband for the benefit of the community business, was initially a community obligation. There is no question but that the former community property now held by respondent Eleanor M. Clark is liable for at least the $588 owing at the time of separation, since it was a community obligation incurred during marriage.

The property settlement with its indemnity agreement did determine, in effect, the character of the obligation as between Matthew and Eleanor Clark, just as the agreement determined the status of the parties' interest in the television sets to be Matthew's separate property. An agreement between spouses, however, cannot determine the nature of the obligation as to, or affect the rights of, creditors holding obligations which have become fully binding before the dissolution of the marital community. Thus the plaintiff in this action is entitled to satisfy its judgment out of any property held by either spouse which was formerly the couple's community property and which is otherwise subject to execution.

The portion of the judgment denying any recovery against Eleanor M. Clark is reversed, and the case is remanded for proceedings consistent with this opinion.

CASE QUESTION

What would the result of the case have been if Matthew and Eleanor Clark's property-settlement agreement had stated that New York law would govern their debt under the television contract?

SUGGESTED READINGS

James, *Effects of the Commerce-Clause Constitutional Limitations on Parties' Intent Choice of Law in the Conflict-of-Laws of Commercial Contracts*, 21 AM. U.L. REV. 543 (1972).

Note, *Enforcement of Forum Selection Provisions in International Commercial Agreements*, 11 COLUM. J. TRANSNAT'L. L. 449 (1972).

Juenger, *Supreme Court Validation of Forum-Selection Clauses*, 19 WAYNE L. REV. 49 (1972).

Note, *Enforceability of "Choice of Forum" Clauses*, 8 CALIF. WESTERN L. REV. 324 (1972).

Kovats, *Inferred Intention on Proper Law*, 121 NEW L.J. 734 (1971).

Full Faith and Credit

Law has no effect, of its own force, outside the sovereignty responsible for its implementation. Since each state in the United States is a distinct sovereignty, the laws of one state have no effect, of their own force, in any other state. A constitutional provision has made state laws effective in other states. Article 4, § 1, of the federal Constitution provides that "full faith and credit shall be given in each state to the public acts, records, and judicial proceedings of every other state." A judgment of a sister state valid on its face must be given full faith and credit, providing that the court had jurisdiction over the parties and over the subject matter of the case, and providing that the judgment is not against the public policy of the forum state.

Public policy is a principle of law holding that no one should be allowed to do what is injurious to the general public or against the public good. A law is contrary to public policy when it violates some conception of good morals, violates some fundamental principle of justice, or is in some way harmful to its people. A foreign law is not against public policy merely because there is no such law in the forum sovereignty or the forum sovereignty law is different.

McCarthy v. McCarthy
276 N.E.2d 891
Appellate Court of Indiana
December 31, 1971

SULLIVAN, PRESIDING JUDGE
This is an appeal from the Vanderburgh Superior Court. The original action was brought by plaintiff-appellee to enforce alimony payments arising out of a foreign divorce decree and to enforce provisions of a settlement agreement.

Plaintiff-appellee and defendant-appellant were residents of Torrington, Connecticut, appellant having been engaged in the practice of medicine in that state. On July 10, 1969, appellee was granted a divorce from her husband, appellant herein, by the superior court for Litchfield County, Connecticut. Pursuant to the divorce decree, appellant was ordered to pay as alimony the sum of $165 per week plus child support. It was further adjudged by that court that if appellant's taxable income should exceed $20,000 in any year, he should pay 25% of the excess to appellee as additional alimony. Following the divorce, appellant moved to Indiana.

On August 6, 1970, appellee filed suit against appellant in the Vanderburgh Superior Court. In her complaint she alleged, among other things, that under the provisions of the Connecticut decree, appellant was in arrears on his alimony payments in the amount of

$1320, including $165 due each week since June 15, 1970. Appellee further alleged that even though notice of default and demand for payment had been made, appellant failed to pay. She alleged in addition that appellant and appellee entered into a binding settlement agreement on May 16, 1969, which appellant has violated by refusing to supply appellee with a copy of his 1969 income tax returns.

Thereafter, appellee moved for summary judgment on the grounds that the pleadings and her accompanying affidavit showed there was no genuine issue of material fact to be litigated. In opposition thereto, appellant's affidavit stated he had at all times conformed to the provisions of the divorce decree and settlement agreement until appellee denied him visitation rights with his children, the latter having been guaranteed to appellant by the terms of said agreement. Appellant stipulated further that only after such breach by appellee did he cease to make alimony payments, but that he did continue to pay child support. Appellant also stated that because Indiana law does not provide for alimony, that provision of the Connecticut decree is not enforceable in Indiana, nor is it entitled to full faith and credit because it is repugnant to the public policy of this state.

In the appellant's supplemental affidavit opposing the motion for summary judgment, he alleged that prior to the execution of the settlement agreement, he had obligated himself to discontinue the practice of medicine in Connecticut and move to Indiana to resume the practice. In this regard, appellant stated that he was threatened by appellee's representative in that if he refused to sign the settlement agreement, he would be enjoined from leaving the state of Connecticut. Appellant argued, therefore, that said agreement was entered into as a result of duress and thus cannot be given effect by this state.

On January 11, 1971, summary judgment was entered for appellee. The trial court held that the Connecticut divorce decree was entitled to full faith and credit, and that the superior court for Litchfield County, Connecticut, had jurisdiction over the appellant. It was then ordered that appellee recover $4950 in delinquent alimony at $165 per week since June 15, 1970, plus future child support and maintenance.

Appellant suggests that to force him to pay alimony is to subject him to involuntary servitude. Appellant argues with great zeal that the so-called women's liberation movement has led to many changes in law, bringing into focus the proposition of complete civil equality for women. Appellant urges that a natural adjunct of such progression is the abolition of alimony. Although Indiana law does not provide for installment alimony, it is nevertheless proper under full faith and credit for this court to enforce an installment alimony decree obtained in another state. If such were not the law of this state, Indiana would become a virtual sanctuary for ex-husbands attempting to avoid the effect of a foreign decree's alimony pro-

visions. We hold then, in keeping with what we consider to be sound public policy, that appellee is entitled to have the installment alimony provision of the Connecticut decree enforced in Indiana under the "full faith and credit" clause of article 4, § 1, of the United States Constitution. To further entertain the manifold questions raised by appellant with regard to the constitutional validity of installment alimony would do no more than to clutter this opinion with subject matter for midnight kitchen discussion.

Appellant argues that genuine issues of material fact existed in this cause, and that therefore, summary judgment in favor of appellee should not have been granted. In support thereof, appellant states that he executed the settlement agreement under duress and that since that agreement was the basis for the Connecticut decree, the Connecticut court lacked proper jurisdiction, that is, that a material issue of fact has been raised whether "full faith and credit" should have been given to the foreign decree since the same was procured by duress. We have no conceptual difficulty with the rationale of appellant's claim inasmuch as the judgment of a foreign court is always open to collateral attack as to the court's jurisdiction. A presumption exists, however, that such court had jurisdiction and accordingly, the rendered judgment or decree is *prima facie* valid. More to the point, we are compelled to agree with appellee that the Connecticut court acquired jurisdiction over the person of appellant by the latter's appearance in that court coupled with his residency in Connecticut at the time of trial. Indeed, such facts not only redound to appellant's detriment, but necessarily render moot the challenge to the jurisdiction of the Connecticut court. We cannot deny ''full faith and credit'' to the Connecticut decree based on appellant's contention that the settlement agreement was obtained by duress thereby poisoning the decree which incorporated it. Such denial would be proper only if the Connecticut court had lacked jurisdiction and the alleged ''duress'' was the sole means of acquiring it. Moreover, the Indiana case law speaks to fraud or duress in the procurement of the jurisdiction itself. It does not contemplate jurisdictional attacks for alleged fraud or duress in the inducement of collateral acts having no connection with a court's power to hear the case before it.

In the alternative, appellant asserts that since the complaint purported to claim relief, not only by virtue of the decree but as well by virtue of the settlement agreement, material issues of fact were presented as to whether or not said agreement was procured by duress, whether the alimony provisions contained therein are enforceable in Indiana, and whether the agreement is entitled to ''full faith and credit'' in this state.

In accordance with the expressly stated intent of the parties herein, the settlement agreement did not ''merge'' into the Connecticut decree, but was ''incorporated'' in the same. Appellant construes this provision of the settlement agreement to mean that absent a merger of the decree and the settlement agreement, the latter is a proper subject for an independent cause of action in Indiana based upon contract. This is a proper statement of the law in Indiana. Conceding *arguendo* that we might reverse on this point, the blatant conflict in appellant's arguments leads to the inescapable conclusion that appellant would not benefit if we were to grant a new trial.

If at this stage of the litigation, we were to hold in favor of Dr. McCarthy upon his contention that his execution of the settlement agreement was induced by duress, he would necessarily lose his case upon retrial. This is so because if appellant were to prevail in this appeal, *a priori* he precludes himself from successfully asserting in a new trial a defense based upon a breach of the very agreement which he has already established as void, that is, appellant claims justification for failing to comply with the alimony provisions of the Connecticut decree because appellee denied visitation rights guaranteed him by the settlement agreement. The law cannot in conscience allow a party to successfully assert the invalidity of a contract ostensibly for the sole purpose of effecting a remand of the cause for new trial at which he must necessarily allege and prove the enforceability of that very contract.

It is the province of this court to dispose of cases whenever possible by granting appropriate relief. In keeping with the spirit of this rule, it is likewise the province of this court to deny inappropriate relief if the particular circumstances warrant. To hold otherwise would permit the sideshow to consume the circus.

Accordingly, we reject appellant's contention as to this issue.

CASE QUESTIONS

1. What was the issue of this case?
2. What constitutional conflicts-of-law rule may be extracted from this case?

SUGGESTED READINGS

Pryles, *Absence of an Appropriate Tribunal or Remedy as a Ground for Denying Enforcement of Sister State Judgments*, 11 WASHBURN L.J. 390 (1972).

Pryles, *Full Faith and Credit: Administrative Determinations*, 24 ALA. L. REV. 87 (1971).

James, *Effects of Federal Due Process of Law and Full Faith and Credit Limitations on a Forum State Using Its Public Policy to Negate Parties' Autonomy in the Validity of Conflict-of-Laws Contracts*, 41 CHI.–KENT L. REV. 1, 147 (1964).

Note, *Full Faith and Credit to Judgments: Law and Reason versus the Restatement Second*, 54 CALIF. L. REV. 282 (1966).

Note, *Recognition of Legislative Interests in Conflicts Cases Arising Under the Full Faith and Credit Clause*, 26 MONTANA L. REV. 80 (1964).

Comity

There is no mandate in international law that requires one nation to give effect to the laws of another country. *Comity* is the recognition that one sovereignty allows to the legislative, executive, or judicial acts of another. Each jurisdiction determines for itself the extent to which comity is applied. Since there is no right to have foreign laws recognized, when one sovereignty recognizes another's laws it is done as a matter of courtesy or respect. Due regard should be given to its international duty and to the interest of those persons under the protection of its laws. A sovereignty is sometimes influenced by whether others accord recognition of its laws. Generally, out of respect, courts will give effect to the laws and judicial decisions of another sovereignty, unless to do so would be repugnant to its public policy or prejudicial to its interests or the interest of its citizens.

Somportex Limited v. Philadelphia Chewing Gum Corporation
453 F.2d 435
United States Court of Appeals, Third Circuit
December 20, 1971

ALDISERT, CIRCUIT JUDGE
Several interesting questions are presented in this appeal from the district court's order granting summary judgment to enforce a default judgment entered by an English court. To resolve them, a complete recitation of the procedural history of this case is necessary.

This case has its genesis in a transaction between appellant, Philadelphia Chewing Gum Corporation, and Somportex Limited, a British corporation, which was to merchandise appellant's wares in Great Britain under the trade name "Tarzan Bubble Gum." According to the facts as alleged by appellant, there was a proposal which involved the participation of Brewster Leeds and Co., Inc., and M. S. International, Inc., third-party defendants in the court below. Brewster made certain arrangements with Somportex to furnish gum manufactured by Philadelphia; M. S. International, as agent for the licensor of the trade name "Tarzan," was to furnish the African name to the American gum to be sold in England. For reasons not relevant to our limited inquiry, the transaction never reached fruition.

Somportex filed an action against Philadelphia for breach of contract in the Queen's Bench Division of the High Court of England. Notice of the issuance of a writ of summons was served, in accordance with the rules and with the leave of the High Court, upon Philadelphia at its registered ad-

dress in Havertown, Pennsylvania, on May 15, 1967. The extraterritorial service was based on the English version of long-arm statutes utilized by many American states. Philadelphia then consulted a firm of English solicitors, who, by letter of July 14, 1967, advised its Pennsylvania lawyers:

I have arranged with the Solicitors for Somportex Limited that they will let me have a copy of their affidavit and exhibits to that affidavit which supported their application to serve out of the jurisdiction. Subject to the contents of the affidavit, and any further information that can be provided by Philadelphia Chewing Gum Corporation after we have had the opportunity of seeing the affidavit, it may be possible to make an application to the court for an order setting the writ aside. But for such an application to be successful we will have to show that on the facts the matter does not fall within the provision of the long-arm statute.

In the meantime we will enter a conditional appearance to the writ on behalf of Philadelphia Chewing Gum Corporation in order to preserve the status quo.

On August 9, 1967, the English solicitors entered a conditional appearance to the writ and filed a motion to set aside the writ of summons. At a hearing before a master on November 13, 1967, the solicitors appeared and disclosed that Philadelphia had elected not to proceed with the summons or to contest the jurisdiction of the English court, but instead intended to obtain leave of court to withdraw appearance of counsel. The master then dismissed Philadelphia's summons to set aside plaintiff's writ of summons. Four days later, the solicitors sought to withdraw their appearance as counsel for Philadelphia, contending that it was a conditional appearance only. On November 27, 1967, after a master granted the motion, Somportex appealed. The appeal was denied after hearing before a single judge, but the court of appeal, reversing the decision of the master, held that the appearance was unconditional and that the submission to the jurisdiction by Philadelphia was, therefore, effective. But the court let stand the original order which was made by the master on November 13 dismissing the application to set aside. The writ therefore will stand. On the other hand, if the American company would wish to appeal from the order of November 13, I see no reason why the time should not be extended, and they can argue that matter out at a later stage if they should so wish.

Thereafter, Philadelphia made a calculated decision: it decided to do nothing. It neither asked for an extension of time nor attempted in any way to proceed with an appeal from the master's order dismissing its application to set aside the writ. Instead, it directed its English solicitors to withdraw from the case. There being no appeal, the master's order became final.

Somportex then filed a statement of claim which was duly served in accordance with English court rules. In addition, by separate letter, it informed Philadelphia of the significance and effect of the pleading, the procedural posture of the case, and its intended course of action.

Philadelphia persisted in its course of inaction; it failed to file a defense. Somportex obtained a default judgment against it in the Queen's Bench Division of the High Court of Justice in England for the sum of £39,562.10.10 (approximately $94,000). The award reflected some $45,000 for loss of profit, $46,000 for loss of good will, and $2500 for costs, including attorneys' fees.

Thereafter, Somportex filed a diversity action in the court below, seeking to enforce the foreign judgment, and attached to the complaint a certified transcript of the English proceeding. The district court granted plaintiff's motion for summary judgment.

Appellant presents a cluster of contentions supporting its major thesis that we should not extend hospitality to the English judgment. First, it contends, and we agree, that because our jurisdiction is based solely on diversity, the law to be applied is the law of the state, in this case, Pennsylvania law. Pennsylvania distinguishes between judgments obtained in the courts of her sister states, which are entitled to full faith and credit, and those of foreign courts, which are subject to principles of comity.

Comity is a recognition which one nation extends within its own territory to the legislative, executive, or judicial acts of another. It is not a rule of law, but one of practice, convenience, and expediency. Although more than mere courtesy and accommodation, comity does not achieve the force of an imperative or obligation. Rather, it is a nation's expression of understanding which demonstrates due regard both to international duty and convenience and to the rights of persons protected by its own laws. Comity should be withheld only when its acceptance would be contrary or prejudicial to the interest of the nation called upon to give it effect.

When an action is brought in a court of this country by a citizen of a foreign country against one of our own citizens and the foreign judgment appears to have been rendered by a competent court, having jurisdiction of the cause and of the parties and upon due allegations and proofs, the opportunity to defend against them, and its proceedings are according to the course of a civilized jurisprudence, and are stated in a clear and formal record, the judgment is *prima facie* evidence, at least, of the truth of the matter adjudged. It should be held conclusive upon the merits tried in the foreign court, unless some special ground is shown for impeaching the judgment, as by showing that it was affected by fraud or prejudice, or that by the principles of international law, and by the comity of our own country, it should not be given full credit and effect.

Appellant's contention that the district court failed to make an independent examination of the factual and legal basis of the jurisdiction of the English court at once argues too much and says too little. The reality is that the court did examine the legal basis of asserted jurisdiction and decided the issue adversely to appellant.

Indeed, we do not believe it was necessary for the court below to reach the question of whether the factual complex of the contractual dispute permitted extraterritorial service under the English long-arm statute. In its opinion denying leave of defense counsel to withdraw, the court of appeal specifically gave Philadelphia the opportunity to have the factual issue tested before the courts; moreover, Philadelphia was allocated additional time to do just that. Lord Denning said, "They can argue that matter out at a later stage if they should so wish." Three months went by with no activity forthcoming. Then, as described by the district court, "during this three-month period, defendant changed its strategy and, not wishing to do anything which might result in its submitting to the English court's jurisdiction, decided to withdraw its appearance altogether." Under these circumstances, we hold that defendant cannot choose its forum to test the factual basis of jurisdiction. It was given, and it waived, the opportunity of making the adequate presentation in the English court.

Additionally, appellant attacks the English practice wherein a conditional appearance attacking jurisdiction may, by court decision, be converted into an unconditional one. It cannot effectively argue that this practice constitutes "some special ground for impeaching the judgment," as to render the English judgment unwelcome in Pennsylvania under principles of international law and comity because it was obtained by procedures contrary or prejudicial to the host state. The English practice in this respect is identical to that set forth in both the federal and Pennsylvania rules of civil procedure. Rule 12 has abolished for the federal courts the age-old distinction between general and special appearances. Similarly, a conditional appearance no longer exists in Pennsylvania. A challenge to jurisdiction must be asserted there by a preliminary objection raising a question of jurisdiction.

Thus, we will not disturb the English court's adjudication. That the English judgment was obtained by appellant's default instead of through an adversary proceeding does not dilute its efficacy. In the absence of fraud or collusion, a default judgment is as conclusive an adjudication between the parties as when rendered after answer and complete contest in the open courtroom.

English law permits recovery, as compensatory damages in breach of contract, of items reflecting loss of good will and costs, including attorneys' fees. These two items formed substantial portions of the English judgment. Because they are not recoverable under Pennsylvania law, appellant would have the foreign judgment declared unenforceable because it constitutes an action on the foreign claim which could not have been maintained because it was contrary to the public policy of the forum. We are satisfied with the district court's disposition of this argument:

The court finds that while Pennsylvania may not agree that these elements should be included in damages for breach of contract, the variance with Pennsylvania law is not such that the enforcement tends clearly to injure the public health, the public morals, the public confidence in the purity of the administration of the law, or to undermine that sense of security for individual rights, whether of personal liberty or of private property, which any citizen ought to feel, is against public policy.

For the reasons heretofore rehearsed, we will not disturb the English court's adjudication of jurisdiction; we have deemed as irrelevant the default nature of the judgment; we have concluded that the English compensatory damage items do not offend Pennsylvania public policy; and we hold that the English procedure comports with our standards of due process.

We are not persuaded that appellant met its burden of showing that the British decree is so palpably tainted by fraud or prejudice as to outrage our sense of justice, or that the process of the foreign tribunal was invoked to achieve a result contrary to our laws of public policy or to circumvent our laws or public policy.

The judgment of the district court will be affirmed.

CASE QUESTIONS

1. Is it likely that there will ever be a "full faith and credit" clause applying to all nations of the world?
2. What effect should be given to a foreign judgment when it comes up for recognition in the courts of another country? Should it make any difference if the foreign forum had applied the other country's laws? Suppose the foreign judgment was handed down under the foreign forum's own law

in an effort to promote a racist policy of that government. Should that judgment be enforceable in the United States?

SUGGESTED READINGS

Comment, *Reciprocal Recognition of Foreign Country Money Judgments: The Canada-United States Example*, 45 FORDHAM L. REV. 1456 (1977).

Carl, *Proposed Legislation: Uniform Foreign Country Judgments Recognition Act*, 40 TEX. B.J. 40 (1977).

von Mehren and Patterson, *Recognition and Enforcement of Foreign Country Judgments in the United States*, 6 LAW & POL. INT'L BUS. 37 (1974).

Chapter Questions

1. Define the following terms:
   a. alimony
   b. *amicus curiae*
   c. comity
   d. common law
   e. conflict of laws
   f. consortium
   g. *dictum*
   h. foreign law
   i. forum
   j. full faith and credit
   k. guardian
   l. holding
   m. *lex fori*
   n. *lex loci*
   o. sovereignty
   p. *stare decisis*
   q. ward

2. On May 20, Evans crashed into a train owned and operated by the Pennsylvania Railroad Co. at its crossing in Nassau, Sussex County. As a matter of law, the court found that the "Nassau crossing is extremely hazardous." On December 1 of that same year, Edna Wyatt and George Wyatt ran into a Pennsylvania Railroad train at the same crossing while George was driving them home from a party. Does the doctrine of *stare decisis* require that the court in *Wyatt* accept the conclusion announced in the *Evans* case?
   Wyatt v. Pennsylvania Railroad Co., 158 F. Supp. 502 (D. Del. 1958)

3. Constable Dunn received a radio report that Arthur and Spencer Parker had left a beer garden in Cheatham County, Tennessee, without paying for their beer, a possible misdemeanor. When the Parkers' car passed Dunn's cruiser at high speed, Dunn switched on his siren

and began chasing them. As they raced into Davidson County, Dunn fired his gun several times at the fleeing car. The bullets punctured the Parker car's tires, overturning the vehicle and killing Spencer Parker. According to Tennessee law, a police officer has no right to use deadly force to stop a fleeing misdemeanant, but the question arose whether the constable's surety was liable on his bond. The Tennessee Supreme Court has ruled several times that a surety was not liable to an injured party when the damage was done under mere color of office. In this situation, since the constable committed an act that he was not permitted to do (shooting at Parker's car), the surety would not be liable for the damages because the act was done under mere color of office. However, since the last ruling of the supreme court on the subject, the Tennessee legislature passed a law holding sureties liable even when the act was done under mere color of office. The case is before an appellate court after being dismissed in trial court. Must the appellate court follow the supreme court rulings as controlling precedents, or should it follow the recent statute?
State v. Dunn, 282 S. W.2d 203 (Tenn. 1943)

4. While en route to jury duty, Mrs. Evans sustained a personal injury as a result of carelessness on the part of the county commissioners in permitting the concrete steps at the El Paso County Courthouse to deteriorate. The lower court dismissed the complaint under the doctrine of governmental immunity. Upon appeal, the Supreme Court of Colorado in its opinion dated March 22, 1971, decided to abolish governmental immunity for that state. The courts stated, "Except as to the parties in this proceeding the ruling here shall be prospective only and shall be effective only as to causes of action arising after June 30, 1972." Why would a court make its decision effective as a precedent some 15 months after the date of its decision?
Evans v. Board of County Commissioners, 174 Colo. 97, 482 P.2d 968 (1971)

5. Mr. S. P. Whitney, a West Virginia contractor, was under contract with the state of West Virginia to construct state route 2 near East Steubenville, just across the border from Steubenville, Ohio. Since the area was very hilly, Whitney used high explosives, such as dynamite and nitroglycerin, to clear the way for the road. One particularly large blast damaged a storeroom of the Steubenville Plate and Window Glass Co., located across the border in Ohio. The damage was extensive and most of the stored glass was broken and unusable. Keeping in mind that the blasting was done in West Virginia and the damage occurred in Ohio, which state's law will govern the action brought in a West Virginia court by Steubenville Plate Glass against Whitney?
Dallas v. Whitney, 118 W. Va. 106 (1936)

6. ABC, Inc., entered into a contract with XYZ, Inc., whereby ABC was to build a building for XYZ in Detroit, Michigan, at the price of $1 million. ABC was incorporated in Ohio with its principal place of business in Chicago, Illinois. XYZ is a Delaware corporation with its home office in New York. The contract was negotiated primarily in Chicago but became effective when it was signed at XYZ's home office. There was a dispute concerning the agreement, and XYZ sued ABC in a federal district court in Ohio. Which state law would govern the dispute if the court follows (1) the *lex fori* approach, (2) the *lex loci contractus* approach, or (3) the *lex loci solutionis* approach?

7. Mr. and Mrs. Barzda bought a motel located in Georgia from William Stagina. Thereafter, they sought a transfer to themselves of Stagina's franchise to operate as a Quality Courts Motel. The franchise agreement had been signed by Stagina in Florida and provided that Florida law should be applied to govern interpretation of the contract. When complications developed regarding the transfer of the franchise, the Barzdas sued Quality Courts Motel, Inc., to force transfer. Under Florida law, the Barzdas had no standing to sue, being merely incidental beneficiaries of the franchise agreement between Stagina and Quality Courts Motel, Inc. However, under Georgia law, the Barzdas had standing and could compel transfer of the franchise. Should the court in Georgia apply its own law or Florida law to settle the dispute between Quality Courts and the Barzdas?

   Barzda v. Quality Courts Motel, Inc., 386 F.2d 417 (5th Cir. 1967)

8. Charles Overcash and his wife Nora moved from Missouri to Kansas so that Charles could work for the Yellow Cab Co. in Kansas. The contract for employment was signed in Kansas, but much of the work done by Overcash was in Missouri. Charles suffered injuries in the regular course of his employment which led to his death. His widow employed counsel and filed a claim under Kansas Workmen's Compensation Law. A stipulation was entered into by the widow and Yellow Cab to pay the maximum amount available under Kansas law. Before the final hearing, Mrs. Overcash, after consulting a Missouri lawyer, decided to pursue her claim under the Missouri Workmen's Compensation Act, which allowed significantly higher awards. Mrs. Overcash appeared at the final Kansas hearing and through her Missouri counsel asked that the stipulation be withdrawn. This motion was denied and the award entered according to the Kansas stipulation. Meanwhile, Yellow Cab filed a suit in federal court asking the court to enjoin the Missouri action to avoid multiplicity of suits. Does full faith and credit require that the previous Kansas award be given precedence over a Missouri Workmen's Compensation award, and that the Missouri proceedings be en-

joined? Note that the Kansas award is the equivalent of a court judgment.

Yellow Cab Transit v. Overcash, 133 F.2d 228 (8th Cir. 1942)

9. Mr. and Mrs. Stewart had been married for five years and were residents of the state of Wyoming until their divorce two years ago. Mr. Stewart initiated divorce proceedings after the couple had become estranged and won a decree of absolute divorce from his wife. The divorce decree of the Wyoming court awarded custody of the children to their mother. After the divorce became final, Mrs. Stewart took the children and moved to Buffalo, New York. Mr. Stewart came to New York a month ago and obtained a write of *habeas corpus*, asking for the custody of his children. In his petition, Mr. Stewart alleged that his former wife was incapable of properly raising the children. Consider the nature of the decree, the relief prayed for by Mr. Stewart, and the issues of public policy involved. Must the New York court accord full faith and credit to the Wyoming decree awarding custody of the children to the mother, or may it make an independent inquiry into the facts?

Ex parte Stewart, 137 N.Y. Supp. 202, 77 Misc. 524 (1912)

10. Thome, a resident of the state of Oregon, brought an action in superior court in California charging that Macken, while in the state of Oregon, "did alienate and destroy the affections of plaintiff's wife, and did entice and abduct her from said plaintiff, thereby depriving him of the assistance, comfort, and society of his wife to his damage in the sum of $25,000." Macken defended on the ground that California law had abolished the cause of action for alienation of affections. Under the doctrine of comity, must the California court entertain an action, abolished by statute in California, but permitted in Oregon where the cause of action originally arose?

Thome v. Macken, 136 P.2d 116 (Cal. 1943)

V Judicial Remedies

Equitable Remedies

Judicial remedies are the relief granted by the court once a person has established a substantive right through judicial procedure. The most common judicial remedies include (1) the court's awarding money damages to compensate for an injury, (2) a court's requiring someone to do or refrain from doing something, in the form of an injunction, (3) a court's attempt to restore a person to a previous position to prevent unjust enrichment, which is called restitution, (4) a court's determination of the parties' rights in the form of a declaratory judgment, and (5) a court's granting reformation of a written instrument so that it reflects the real agreement of the parties.

In American jurisprudence, the remedies that courts award in civil cases are classified either as *equitable remedies* or as *common-law remedies*. An equitable remedy is a remedy that would be handled by a court of equity and a common-law remedy by a common-law court before the merger of equity and common-law courts. Today, most courts in the United States are empowered to grant both equitable and legal relief as required to achieve justice.

Common-law remedies are generally limited to the court's determination of some legal right and the awarding of money damages. *Equitable remedies* generally consist of the court's command directing a person to do (or refrain from doing) something.

An *injunction* is an order directing the defendant to act or refrain from acting in a specified way. An order compelling one to do an act is called a *mandatory* injunction, whereas one prohibiting an act is a *prohibitory* injunction. An injunction is very powerful, in that it may be enforced by the

Judicial Remedies

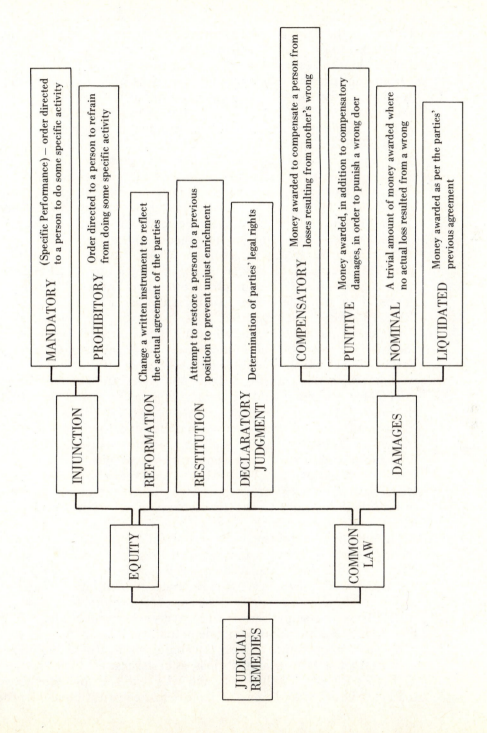

contempt power of a court. Thus a defendant may be fined, sent to jail, or deprived of the right to litigate issues if the person disobeys an injunction. This order must be obeyed until it is reversed, even if it is issued erroneously or the court lacks jurisdiction.

Injunctions may be divided into three classes: (1) permanent, (2) preliminary or interlocutory, and (3) temporary restraining orders. A permanent injunction is a decree issued after a full opportunity to present evidence. It is permanent only in the sense that it is supposed to be a final solution to a dispute. It may still be modified or dissolved later. A preliminary or interlocutory injunction is granted as an emergency measure before a full hearing is held. There must be notice to the defendant and a hearing, usually informal. This remedy is generally limited to situations in which there is a serious need to preserve the status quo until the parties' rights have finally been decided. Thus a preliminary injunction continues only until a further order of the court is issued.

The temporary restraining order, known as a TRO, is an *ex parte* injunction. This means that it is granted without notice to the defendant. The trial judge has heard only the plaintiff's side of the case. Because of the potential for abuse here, there are certain procedures to protect a defendant. A TRO may not be granted unless irreparable harm would result and there is no time for notice and a hearing. There must be clear evidence on the merits of the case. The court should look at any damage to defendant that would be noncompensable in money if plaintiff's relief is later shown to be improper. This must be balanced with plaintiff's harm if the TRO is not granted. Factors should weigh more heavily against the plaintiff, since there is no notice to defendant.

There are certain classes of cases that are not considered proper subject matter for injunctions. In general, an injunction is not issued to stop a criminal prosecution or to prevent crimes. However, this law has been modified in recent years by regulatory statutes or civil-rights statutes. Usually, injunctions are not proper in defamation cases, since this would intrude on the defendant's constitutional right of free speech and would be considered prior restraint.

The remedy of restitution is in some situations an equitable remedy and in other cases a common-law remedy. *Restitution* means restoration, either in money or in the recovery of a specific thing. The purpose of restitution is to prevent unjust enrichment, which means that a person should not be allowed to profit or be enriched inequitably at another's expense. Thus a person is permitted recovery when another has received a benefit and retention of it would be unjust.

If restoration involves money, the amount is determined by the defendant's gain, not by the plaintiff's loss, as in the case of money damages. So if *D* takes *P*'s car, worth $4000, and sells it to someone else above the market price at $8000, *D* may be liable to make restitution to *P* for the full amount of $8000. *P* never had $8000, only a car worth half as much, but is still entitled to the total amount. If there was cash in the glove compartment, *P* would be entitled to recover that also.

When someone seeks a declaratory judgment, the court declares what that person's rights are under the circumstances. The court determines rights and obligations of parties, but does not actually order anything to be done. This is a statutory remedy and the object is to prevent future injury. The court determines what the law *is*, or the constitutionality or the meaning of the law. For example, if a legislative body passes a statute making your business activity illegal, you could continue to operate the business and be arrested. Or you could possibly seek a declaratory judgment asking a court to declare that the statute is unconstitutional. Even though relief under declaratory judgment statutes did not exist at old common law, some courts consider it to be a legal remedy and others consider it an equitable remedy.

The equitable remedy of reformation is granted when a written agreement fails to express accurately the parties' agreement because of mistake, fraud, or the drafter's ambiguous language. The object of reformation is to rectify or reform a written instrument in order that it may express the real agreement or intention of the parties. It is granted when parties come to an understanding, but a person in reducing the agreement to writing fails to accurately express the understanding through mistake or fraud.

Development

The distinction between equity and common law is a historical one. Equity in the United States is that portion of remedial justice that was formerly administered in England by the court of chancery. English equity was a system of justice administered by a tribunal apart from the common-law courts. The common-law system of justice in England was deficient in that its procedural requirements were rigid and highly technical. These requirements confined the courts to redressing wrongs usually by just awarding money damages to an injured party.

In situations in which a common-law remedy either did not exist or was inadequate to redress the wrong, the king referred the matter to the Lord High Chancellor. Chancellors were high-ranking clergy of the church and advisers to the king. When a person came to a chancellor with an unusual situation for which there was no remedy at common law, the chancellor was given power by the king to grant relief. This practice became institutionalized to the point where the chancellor, presiding over a court of chancery, issued decrees on his own authority. The court of chancery, or equity court, came into being to provide a forum for granting relief in accordance with broad principles of right and justice in cases in which restrictive technicalities of the common-law system prevented it.

For centuries, common law and equity were administered in England by two separate sets of courts, each applying its own system of jurisprudence and following its own system of procedure. Each one was an entirely separate system of courts that administered justice with its own judicial rules and remedies. Equity furnished a remedy only when the common-law procedure was deficient or the remedy at common law was inadequate. A case in equity involves questions of discretion, or judgment, or possibly principles of justice and conscience rather than rigid legal rules. Much of traditional equity is based on an analysis of concepts such as adequacy, practicality, clean hands, estoppel, and hardship. The underlying concepts of law and equity have been retained in the United States, although the formalism that historically distinguished the two has largely disappeared.

Much equity doctrine was established, of which some still is used today. For example, the practical enforceability of the remedy was taken into consideration in granting equitable relief, since the chancellor did not want enforcement to be too burdensome. Today, before a court commands someone to do something or to refrain from certain action, it examines the practical enforceability of the remedy. For instance, specific performance of an employment contract is usually not granted as a remedy because the employee could just do a poor job and make enforcement of the decree burdensome. In such a situation, if money damages are not adequate as a remedy, the court enjoins the employee from performing for any other employer.

One of the principal deficiencies of the common-law system is that it generally awarded only money damages as relief to an injured party. Since equity granted relief only when the common-law system's remedy was inadequate, equitable relief was obtainable when damages were not capable of rectifying the injustice. Even today in our legal system, equitable remedies are granted only when the common-law remedies are inadequate.

Severt v. Beckley Coals, Inc.
153 W. Va. 600, 170 S.E.2d 577
Supreme Court of Appeals of West Virginia
July 15, 1969

HAYMOND, PRESIDING JUDGE
On this appeal the defendant, Beckley Coals, Inc., a corporation, is seeking reversal of a judgment in favor of the plaintiffs, Wiley Severt and Edna Severt, husband and wife, for $7000 for damages to real estate owned by them, and separate judgments in favor of the plaintiff Wiley Severt for $2000 for personal injury, of the plaintiff Edna Severt for $2,000 for personal injury, and of the plaintiff Suzanne Severt, who was

formerly an infant but is now an adult, for $1000 for personal injury, in a civil action in the circuit court of Wyoming County, West Virginia. The plaintiffs cross-assign as error the refusal of the circuit court to grant them injunctive relief to prevent the defendant from operating its coal mining facility near the residence of the plaintiffs Wiley Severt and Edna Severt, in the rural community of Pierpoint, in Wyoming County, West Virginia, and to award temporary damages to those plaintiffs. The circuit court rendered the foregoing judgments upon the verdicts of the jury; the circuit court overruled the motions of the defendant to set aside the foregoing judgments and to grant the defendant a new trial and also overruled the motion of the plaintiffs for injunctive relief.

This appeal was granted upon the application of the defendant.

In their complaint, the plaintiffs seek recovery of damages for injury to real estate and personal injuries caused by the negligence of the defendant and by a nuisance maintained by it or, in the alternative, for injunctive relief to enjoin the operation of the coal mining facility of the defendant and an award of temporary damages resulting from such operation.

There is little if any dispute in the material facts, and the questions presented for decision are questions of law.

The plaintiffs Wiley Severt and Edna Severt own jointly lots 67, 68, and 69 in the small community of Pierpoint, in Slab Pork District, Wyoming County, West Virginia. They acquired lots 67 and 68 in 1948 and improved them with a six-room dwelling house which they have occupied as a residence. Some-

time later they purchased lot 69. When they constructed their home, and until 1965, there were no coal, rail, or other industrial operations within a quarter of a mile of the Pierpoint community. There were several small and two large mining operations within a range of a quarter of a mile and two miles from the home of the plaintiffs. The plaintiffs and several witnesses in their behalf testified that none of those operations produced or cast or deposited dust upon their property or other property in the Pierpoint community. Several witnesses in behalf of the defendant, however, testified that these operations caused the presence of some dust, though less than that produced by the mining operation of the defendant.

The defendant in 1965 began the operation of its mine at a distance of approximately 60 feet from the property line of the plaintiffs and within 120 feet of their home, and installed an exhaust fan, a crusher, and a belt carrier, and trucks to transport coal, all of which are in constant operation from approximately 6 o'clock in the morning until 2 o'clock in the morning of the following day and that such operation continues for six days during each week. These facilities cast and deposit large quantities of black coal dust in and upon the yard and porch, the exterior walls and roof, and all parts of the interior of their home, covering the furniture, clothing, linens, food, and other contents of the home, and the person of the plaintiffs, and causing them to clean the property and their person oftener than usual and almost continually. They produce constant loud and disturbing noise, which disrupts the rest and sleep and disturbs the peace and comfort of the plaintiffs. The dust has destroyed the paint on the exterior of the dwelling, covers the porch and the yard, destroys vegetation, and prevents the usual and ordinary use of the yard and the porch of the home. The evidence that the mining operation of the defendant produces, casts, and deposits large quantities of dust in and upon the property of the plaintiffs and upon their person and causes continuous loud noise which disturbs the peace and comfort of the plaintiffs and disrupts their sleep and rest is not controverted. The only evidence in behalf of the defendants on that point relates to the amount or the quantity of the dust, and such evidence was that the amount or the quantity of such dust was less than that testified to by the plaintiffs and the witnesses in their behalf.

On the question of the alleged negligence of the defendant in the location and operation of its mining facility, there is evidence in behalf of the plaintiffs that the fan could have been otherwise located and placed at a greater distance from the property of the plaintiffs. But there is also evidence in behalf of the defendant that the fan was placed at the only available location for installation and effective use in connection with its operation. There is also evidence that the defendant operates its mining facility according to approved and generally acceptable mining standards and that it is not negligent in the operation of its facility.

The plaintiff Wiley Severt testified that the operation of the mining facility by the defendant depreciated the value of his residence from approximately $15,000 before to less than $5000 after the defendant began its operation. He testified that he could not give away his property after the defendant started to operate its mining facility. A real estate appraiser, a witness in behalf of the plaintiffs, testified that the market value of the property before the operation of the facility was $13,400 and afterwards was $6400. There was also evidence, admitted over the objection of the defendant, that its employees, after the institution of this action, committed various acts which caused damage to the property and disturbed the peace and comfort of the plaintiffs. The plaintiffs introduced, over objection, evidence to show the effects of such acts. Such evidence included samples showing discoloration caused by the dust, profane utterances by some employees of the defendant, and the use as a toilet facility of portions of the yard of the plaintiffs near their residence.

The plaintiffs seek an injunction to prohibit the further operation by the defendant of the coal mining facility and an award of temporary damages for the injuries that have occurred prior to the issuance of such injunction. They contend that under the evidence adduced upon the trial of this action they are entitled to such injunction, and they cross-assign as error the action of the circuit court in denying them the injunctive relief which they seek.

This contention of the plaintiff is devoid of merit.

In the absence of a statute providing an absolute right to injunctive relief, such relief is not a matter of right but its grant or refusal usually rests in the sound discretion of the court to be exercised in harmony with well-established equitable principles. The granting or refusal of an injunction, whether mandatory or preventive, calls for the exercise of sound judicial discretion in view of all the circumstances of the particular case; regard being had to the nature of the controversy, the object for which the injunction is being sought, and the comparative hardship or convenience to the respective parties involved in the award or denial of the writ.

It clearly appears from the evidence disclosed by the record that the plaintiffs have an adequate remedy at law for the recovery of damages to compensate them fully for the injuries and damages caused by the defendant. The principle is firmly established that equity is without jurisdiction to grant relief by injunction where there is a full, complete and adequate remedy at law. This court has repeatedly and uniformly held in many cases that equity does not have jurisdiction of a case in which the plaintiff has a full, complete, and adequate remedy at law, unless some peculiar feature of the case comes within the province of a court of equity.

Here the plaintiffs have a full, complete, and adequate remedy as indicated by their recovery of substantial damages in the trial of this action. There is no peculiar feature in this proceeding which comes within the province of a court of equity.

The defendant contends that the operation of its mining facility is temporary instead of permanent in duration and that the recoverable coal will be completely mined within an estimated period of one-and-one-half to two years from the date of the trial in September 1967. It appears, however, from the evidence that the original estimate of the period within which the recoverable coal would be completely mined was four or five years from the commencement of the operation which occurred in October 1965. Two years after that date in September 1967, the estimate was a period of one-and-one-half to two years if the operation continued without trouble, interruption, or delays which could not be definitely anticipated. In short, the remaining period of the operation required to recover all of the mineable coal is of indefinite duration and cannot now be fixed or determined.

The controlling question to be determined on this appeal is whether the construction and operation of the mining facility of the defendant are permanent or temporary in character and whether the injury to the real estate of the plaintiffs Wiley Severt and Edna Severt caused by the operation and maintenance of the facility is permanent or temporary in character.

As to the determination whether, in a particular case, damages to real estate are permanent or temporary, this court has said that the nature of damages to real estate, whether temporary or permanent, is determined by the character of the nuisance to which the land is subjected and not by the quantity of the resultant damages.

Where the cause of injury is in its nature permanent, and a recovery for such injury would confer a license on the defendant to continue it, the entire damages may be recovered in a single action. But where the cause of injury is in the nature of a nuisance, and not permanent in character, but such that it may be supposed that the defendant would remove it rather than suffer at once entire damages, which it might inflict if permanent, then the entire damages, so as to include future damages, cannot be recovered in a single action. But actions may be maintained from time to time as long as the cause of the injury continues.

The general rule in determining the amount of damages for injury to real property in a case of this kind is to allow the difference between the market value of the plaintiff's premises before the injury happened and the market value immediately after the injury, taking into account only the damage which had resulted from the defendant's acts.

It is clear from the evidence that the coal mining facility, whether or not constructed or operated negligently or properly or maintained as a nuisance, is a permanent structure. Though the estimate by the defendant is that all the coal will be removed within a period of approximately two years, such coal mining facility is a permanent operation. It will continue for an indefinite period and until all the mineable coal is removed, and the period required for such removal cannot now be fixed or determined. The operation of the facility is continuous and uninterrupted, and is not intermittent, occasional, or recurrent. In consequence, the injury which the construction and operation of the coal mining facility of the defendant caused to the real estate of its owners, the plaintiffs, Wiley Severt and Edna Severt, is a permanent injury for which they are entitled to recover entire damages, past, present and future, in a single action. The measure of such damages is the diminution in the market value of the real estate caused by the construction and maintenance of such facility.

The judgment of the circuit court in denying the plaintiffs the injunctive relief which they seek in this action and the judgments rendered by the court in favor of the plaintiffs and against the defendant, being free from prejudicial error, are affirmed.

Affirmed

CASE QUESTIONS

1. Why did the court deny the plaintiffs' claim for injunctive relief?
2. How did the court characterize the nature of the plaintiffs' injuries? What did the court look to as determinative of the characterization of the injuries?
3. What was the measure of damages that the court used in computing the plaintiffs' monetary award?
4. What would have been the plaintiffs' recovery had the court determined that the plaintiffs' damages were temporary?

SUGGESTED READINGS

Chafee, *Progress of the Law, 1919–1920, Equitable Relief Against Torts*, 34 HARV. L. REV. 388 (1921).
RESTATEMENT OF TORTS § 936 (1939).
H. L. MCCLINTOCK, EQUITY § 30 (2d ed. 1948).
Weinberg, *New Meaning of Equity*, 28 J. LEGAL ED. 532 (1977).
Black, *Brief for Resurrection of Equity Jurisprudence*, 60 MICH. B. J. 381 (1981).

Court of Conscience

In equity's early period, chancellors were almost always members of the clergy attempting to attain justice between the parties to a dispute. A court of equity is considered to be a court of conscience in which natural justice takes priority over precedent. Its decisions are based on moral rights and natural justice. Since equity has had such a concern for high moral standards, a chancellor would decline relief when a plaintiff had been involved in some wrongdoing in connection with the dispute. For instance, equity does not enforce a contract clause that is too unfair or one-sided. Such a clause would be declared to be *unconscionable*. To enforce it by granting equitable remedies would shock the conscience of the court.

Campbell Soup Company v. Wentz
172 F.2d 80
United States Court of Appeals,
Third Circuit
December 23, 1948

GOODRICH, CIRCUIT JUDGE
These are appeals from judgments of the district court denying equitable relief to the buyer under a contract for the sale of carrots.

The transactions which raise the issues may be briefly summarized. On June 21, 1947, Campbell Soup Company (Campbell), a New Jersey corporation, entered into a written contract with George B. Wentz and Harry T. Wentz, who are Pennsylvania farmers, for delivery by the Wentzes to Campbell of *all* the Chantenay red-cored carrots to be grown on fifteen acres of the Wentz farm during the 1947 season. The contract provides for delivery of the carrots at the Campbell plant in Camden, New Jersey. The prices specified in the contract ranged from $23 to $30 per ton according to the time of delivery. The contract price for January 1948 was $30 a ton.

The Wentzes harvested approximately 100 tons of carrots from the 15 acres covered by the contract. Early in January 1948, they told a Campbell representative that they would not deliver their carrots at the contract price. The market price at that time was at least $90 per ton, and Chantenay red-cored carrots were virtually unobtainable.

On January 9, 1948, Campbell, suspecting that defendant was selling its "contract carrots," refused to purchase any more, and instituted these suits against the Wentz brothers to enjoin further sale of the contract carrots to others, and to compel specific performance of the contract. The trial court denied equitable relief. We agree with the result reached, but on a different ground from that relied upon by the district court. A party may have specific performance of a contract for the sale of chattels if the legal remedy is inadequate. Inadequacy of the legal remedy is necessarily a matter to be determined by an examination of the facts in each particular instance.

We think that on the question of adequacy of the legal remedy, the case is one appropriate for specific performance. It was expressly found that at the time of the trial it was "virtually impossible to obtain Chantenay carrots in the open market." This Chantenay carrot is one which the plaintiff uses in large quantities, furnishing the seed to the growers with whom it makes contracts. It was not claimed that in nutritive value it is any better than other types of carrots. Its blunt shape makes it easier to handle in processing, and its color and texture differ from other varieties. The color is brighter than other carrots. It appears that the plaintiff uses carrots in 15 of its 21 soups. It also appeared that it uses these Chantenay carrots diced in some of them and that the appearance is uniform. The preservation of uniformity in appearance in a food article marketed throughout the country and sold under the manufacturer's name is a matter of considerable commercial significance and one which is properly considered in determining whether a substitute ingredient is just as good as the original.

The trial court concluded that the plaintiff had failed to establish that the carrots, "judged by objective standards," are unique goods. This we think is not a pure fact conclusion like a finding that Chantenay carrots are of uniform color. It is either a conclusion of law or of mixed fact and law and we are bound to exercise our independent judgment upon it. That the test for specific performance is not necessarily "objective" is shown by the many cases in which equity has given it to enforce contracts for articles—family heirlooms and the like—the value of which was personal to the plaintiff.

Judged by the general standards applicable to determining the adequacy of the legal remedy, we think that on this point the case is a proper one for equitable relief. There is considerable authority, old and new, showing liberality in the granting of an equitable remedy. We see no reason why a court should be reluctant to grant specific relief when it can be given without supervision of the court or other time-consuming processes against one who has deliberately broken his agreement. Here the goods of the special type contracted for were unavailable on the open market, the plaintiff had contracted for them long ahead in anticipation of its needs, and had built up a general reputation for its products as part of which reputation uniform appearance was important. We think if this were all that was involved in the case, specific performance should have been granted.

The reason that we shall affirm instead of reversing with an order for specific performance is found in the contract itself. We think it is too hard a bargain and too one-sided an agreement to entitle the plaintiff to relief in a court of conscience. For each individual grower, the agreement is made by filling in names and quantity and price on a printed form furnished by the buyer. This form has quite obviously been drawn by skillful draftsmen with the buyer's interests in mind.

Paragraph 2 provides for the manner of delivery. Carrots are to have their stalks cut off and be in clean sanitary bags or other containers approved by Campbell. This paragraph concludes with a statement that Campbell's determination of conformance with specifications shall be conclusive.

The defendants attack this provision as unconscionable. We do not think that it is, standing by itself. We think that the provision is comparable to the promise to perform to the satisfaction of another and that Campbell would be held liable if it refused carrots which did in fact conform to the specifications.

The next paragraph allows Campbell to refuse carrots in excess of twelve tons to the acre. The next contains a covenant by the grower that he will not sell carrots to anyone else (except the carrots rejected by Campbell) nor will he permit anyone else to grow carrots on his land. Paragraph 10 provides liquidated damages to the extent of $50 per acre for any breach by the grower. There is no provision for liquidated or any other damages for breach of contract by Campbell.

The provision of the contract which we think is the hardest is paragraph 9.[1] It will be noted that Campbell is excused from accepting carrots under certain circumstances. But even under such circumstances, the grower, while he cannot say Campbell is liable for failure to take the carrots, is not permitted to sell them elsewhere unless Campbell agrees. This is the kind of provision which the late Francis H. Bohlen would call "carrying a good joke too far." What the grower may do with his product under the circumstances set out is not clear. He has covenanted not to store it anywhere except on his own farm and also not to sell to anybody else.

We are not suggesting that the contract is illegal. Nor are we suggesting

---

[1] "Grower shall not be obligated to deliver any Carrots which he is unable to harvest or deliver, nor shall Campbell be obligated to receive or pay for any Carrots which it is unable to inspect, grade, receive, handle, use or pack at or ship in processed form from its plants in Camden (1) because of any circumstance beyond the control of Grower or Campbell, as the case may be, or (2) because of any labor disturbance, work stoppage, slow-down, or strike involving any of Campbell's employees. Campbell shall not be liable for any delay in receiving Carrots due to any of the above contingencies. During periods when Campbell is unable to receive Grower's Carrots, Grower may with Campbell's written consent, dispose of his Carrots elsewhere. Grower may not, however, sell or otherwise dispose of any Carrots which he is unable to deliver to Campbell."

any excuse for the grower in this case who has deliberately broken an agreement entered into with Campbell. We do think, however, that a party who has offered and succeeded in getting an agreement as tough as this one is should not come to a chancellor and ask court help in the enforcement of its terms. That equity does not enforce unconscionable bargains is too well established to require elaborate citation.

The plaintiff argues that the provisions of the contract are separable. We agree that they are, but do not think that decisions separating out certain provisions from illegal contracts are in point here. As already said, we do not suggest that this contract is illegal. All we say is that the sum total of its provisions drives too hard a bargain for a court of conscience to assist.

The judgments will be affirmed.

CASE QUESTIONS

1. If the plaintiff had sued for damages, would the result of the suit have been different?
2. Campbell Soup Co. lost this case in its attempt to get equitable relief. May it now sue for money damages?
3. If the contract between Campbell Soup Co. and Wentz were not unconscionable, would specific performance of the contract be an appropriate remedy? What is necessary before specific performance will be granted?
4. Why did the court hold the contract to be unconscionable and therefore unenforceable in equity?

SUGGESTED READINGS

C. D. CALAMARI and J. M. PERILLO, THE LAW OF CONTRACTS § 56 (1970).
Note, 79 HARV. L. REV. 1299 (1966).
Newman, *Hidden Equity: An Analysis of the Moral Content of the Principles of Equity*, 19 HASTINGS L. J. 147 (1967).
Note, *Equitable Relief Against Unconscionable Transactions—A Dissent*, 25 FAC. L. REV. 154 (1967).

A common-law court would enforce a clause considered unconscionable by equity if it were part of a valid, binding agreement. That court would grant the legal relief of money damages for the failure to perform the obligation contained in the clause. Beginning in the 1950s, through legislation, the Uniform Commercial Code and the Uniform Consumer Credit Code made the defense of unconscionability applicable to some common-law cases. Now in addition to equitable cases, the defense is applicable to transactions involving the sale of goods, consumer loans, and leases. It is a defense as to the unfair terms of the contract. Unconscionability is not a ground for damages. Instead, courts may either refuse enforcement or strike or limit the unconscionable terms.

Williams v. Walker-Thomas Furniture Company
350 F.2d 445
United States Court of Appeals
District of Columbia Circuit
August 11, 1965

J. Skelly Wright, Circuit Judge
Appellee, Walker-Thomas Furniture Company, operates a retail furniture store in the District of Columbia. During the period from 1957 to 1962, appellant purchased a number of household items from Walker-Thomas, for which payment was to be made in installments. The terms of each purchase were contained in a printed form contract which set forth the value of the purchased item and purported to lease the item to appellant for a stipulated monthly rent payment. The contract then provided, in substance, that title would remain in Walker-Thomas until the total of all the monthly payments made equaled the stated value of the item, at which time appellants could take title. In the event of a default in the payment of any monthly installment, Walker-Thomas could repossess the item.

The contract further provided that "the amount of each periodical installment payment to be made by (purchaser) to the Company under this present lease shall be inclusive of and not in addition to the amount of each installment payment to be made by (purchaser) under such prior leases, bills or accounts; *and all payments now and hereafter made by (purchaser) shall be credited pro rata on all outstanding leases, bills and accounts* due the Company by (purchaser) at the time each such payment is made." (Emphasis added.) The effect of this rather obscure provision was to keep a balance due on every item purchased until the balance due on all items, whenever purchased, was liquidated. As a result, the debt incurred at the time of purchase of each item was secured by the right to repossess all the items previously purchased by the same purchaser, and each new item purchased automatically became subject to a security interest arising out of the previous dealings.

On April 17, 1962, appellant Williams bought a stereo set of stated value of $514.95. At the time of this purchase, her account showed a balance of $164 still owing from her prior purchases. The total of all the purchases made over the years in question came to $1800. The total payments amounted to $1400. She defaulted shortly thereafter, and appellee sought to replevy[2] all the items purchased since December 1957. The court of

---

[2] An action to have goods returned to the original possessor.—*Ed.*

general sessions granted judgment for appellee. The District of Columbia Court of Appeals affirmed, and we granted appellants' motion for leave to appeal to this court.

Appellant's principal contention, rejected by both the trial and the appellate courts below, is that these contracts, or at least some of them, are unconscionable and, hence, not enforceable. Appellee was aware of appellant's financial position. The reverse side of the stereo contract listed the name of appellant's social worker and her $218 monthly stipend from the government. Nevertheless, with full knowledge that appellant had to feed, clothe, and support both herself and seven children on this amount, appellee sold her a $514 stereo set.

In its opinion, the lower court stated: "We cannot condemn too strongly appellee's conduct. It raises serious questions of sharp practice and irresponsible business dealings. A review of the legislation in the District of Columbia affecting retail sales and the pertinent decisions of the highest court in this jurisdiction disclose, however, no ground upon which this court can declare the contracts in question contrary to public policy."

We do not agree that the court lacked the power to refuse enforcement to contracts found to be unconscionable. Congress has recently enacted the Uniform Commercial Code, which specifically provides that the court may refuse to enforce a contract which it finds to be unconscionable at the time it was made. The enactment of this section, which occurred subsequent to the contracts here in suit, does not mean

that the common law of the District of Columbia was otherwise at the time of enactment, nor does it preclude the court from adopting a similar rule in the exercise of its powers to develop the common law for the District of Columbia. In fact, on the point, we consider the congressional adoption of § 2–302 persuasive authority for following the rationale of the cases from which the section is explicitly derived. Accordingly, we hold that where the element of unconscionability is present at the time a contract is made, the contract should not be enforced.

Unconscionability has generally been recognized to include an absence of meaningful choice on the part of one of the parties together with contract terms which are unreasonably favorable to the other party. Whether a meaningful choice is present in a particular case can only be determined by consideration of all the circumstances surrounding the transaction. In many cases, the meaningfulness of the choice is negated by a gross inequality of bargaining power. The manner in which the contract was entered is also relevant to this consideration. Did each party to the contract, considering his obvious education or lack of it, have a reasonable opportunity to understand the terms of the contract, or were the important terms hidden in a maze of fine print and minimized by deceptive sales practices? Ordinarily, one who signs an agreement without full knowledge of its terms might be held to assume the risk that he has entered a one-sided bargain. But when a party of little bargaining power, and hence little real choice, signs a commercially unreasonable contract with little or no knowledge of its terms, it is hardly likely that his consent, or even an objective manifestation of his consent, was ever given to all the terms. In such a case, the usual rule that the terms of the agreement are not to be questioned should be abandoned, and the court should consider whether the terms of the contract are so unfair that enforcement should be withheld.

In determining reasonableness or fairness, the primary concern must be with the terms of the contract considered in light of the circumstances existing when the contract was made. The test is not simple, nor can it be mechanically applied.

Because the trial court and the appellate court did not feel that enforcement could be refused, no findings were made on the possible unconscionability of the contracts in these cases. Since the record is not sufficient for our deciding the issue as a matter of law, the cases must be remanded to the trial court for further proceedings.

So ordered.

DANAHER, CIRCUIT JUDGE, dissenting

My view is thus summed up by an able court which made no finding that there had actually been sharp practice. Rather the appellant seems to have known precisely where she stood. Many relief clients may well need credit, and certain business establishments take long chances on the sale of items, expecting their pricing policies will afford a degree of protection commensurate with the risk.

I mention such matters only to emphasize the desirability of a cautious approach to any such problem, particularly since the law for so long has allowed parties such great latitude in making their own contracts. I dare say there must annually be thousands upon thousands of installment credit transactions in this jurisdiction, and one can only speculate as to the effect the decision in these cases will have.

I join the District of Columbia Court of Appeals in its disposition of the issues.

CASE QUESTIONS

1. Did it matter that the Uniform Commercial Code was adopted after these contracts were entered into?
2. What type of analysis of the bargaining process and the contract terms did the court undertake?
3. What is the objection of the dissenting opinion?
4. Suppose that the plaintiff is on welfare and buys a freezer for $900 from a salesperson who comes to his home. Total charges come to $1234.80, and plaintiff has paid $619.88 of that. The actual value of the freezer is about $300. Should this contract be considered unconscionable under the UCC?

SUGGESTED READINGS

Rubin, *Unenforceable Contracts: Penalty Clauses and Specific Performance*, 10 J. LEGAL STUDIES 237 (1981).

Muris, *Opportunistic Behavior and the Law of Contracts*, 65 Minn. L. Rev. 521 (1981).

Fletcher, *Review of Unconscionable Transactions*, 8 U. QUEENS L.J. 45 (1973).

Equitable Maxims

Instead of using rules of law in reaching decisions, courts of equity used *equitable maxims*, which are short statements that contain the gist of much equity law. These maxims were developed over the years with no agreement as to the number or order. They are presently being used as guides in the decision-making process in disputes in equity. The following are some of the equitable maxims:

> Equity does not suffer a wrong to be without a remedy.
> Equity regards substance rather than form.
> Equality is equity.
> Equity regards as done that which should be done.
> Equity follows the law.
> Equity acts *in personam* rather than *in rem*.
> He who seeks equity must do equity.
> He who comes into equity must do so with clean hands.
> Delay resulting in a prejudicial change defeats equity (*laches*).

New York Football Giants v. Los Angeles Chargers F. Club
291 F.2d 471
United States Court of Appeals·
Fifth Circuit
June 14, 1961

TUTTLE, CHIEF JUDGE
In the case of *Detroit Football Company v. Robinson*, 186 F.Supp. 933, 934, Judge Wright, of the District Court for the Eastern District of Louisiana, said: "This case is but another round in the sordid fight for football players, a fight which begins before these athletes enter college and follows them through their professional careers. It is a fight characterized by deception, double dealing, campus jumping, secret alumni subsidization, semiprofessionalism and professionalism. It is a fight which has produced as part of its harvest this current rash of contract jumping suits. It is a fight which so conditions the minds and hearts of these athletes that one day they can agree to play football for a stated amount for one group, only to repudiate that agreement the follow-

ing day or whenever a better offer comes along.''

We have read cases cited in Judge Wright's opinion, and we share his disgust at the sordid picture too often presented in this kind of litigation. So much so, in fact, that we conclude that in an appropriate case, the federal equity court, which is the tribunal usually appealed to for a decree of specific performance of injunction, must decline to lend its aid to either party to a transaction that in its inception offends concepts of decency and honest dealing, such as the case before us.

In the fall of 1959, Flowers was an outstanding football player on the University of Mississippi team. His team was to play a postseason game on January 1, 1960, at the Sugar Bowl in New Orleans against a traditional rival, Louisiana State University.

The well-understood rules of the Southeastern Conference (SEC) and the National Collegiate Athletic Association (NCAA) made ineligible from further participation in intercollegiate games any player who had signed a contract to play with a professional team. Flowers wanted above all else to play in the Sugar Bowl game. On a trip to New York City for other purposes, he was invited by the Giants' official Mara on December 1 to come to his office where he was urged to sign a contract to play two seasons, beginning in 1960, with the Giants. He told Mara he wanted to retain his eligibility to play in the Sugar Bowl game.

Following a proposal by Mara, Flowers signed the standard form of contract of the National Football League, and received checks totaling $3500 as a sign-on bonus, and then returned to Mississippi. One of the terms of the contract was that: ''This agreement shall become valid and binding upon each party hereto only when, as, and if it shall be approved by the Commissioner.'' Part of the deceit agreed to between the parties was an agreement that Mara would not submit the contract to the Commissioner until after January 1. Flowers later made some effort by telephone on or about December 5 to withdraw from the contract. Thereafter, the Giants promptly filed the contract with the Commissioner, and he ''approved'' it on December 15. However, at Mara's request, he withheld announcement of his approval until after January 1. On December 29 Flowers had negotiations with the Los Angeles Chargers, as a result of which he was offered a better contract, but which was not formally executed until after the Sugar Bowl game on January 1. He wrote a letter to the Giants on December 29, stating that he was withdrawing from his agreement with them. He returned the uncashed checks for the bonus money. Flowers played in the game, all his fans presumably thinking that he was still an eligible player, thanks to the deception proposed by the Giants and entered into by him.

The trial court held that until the contract was approved by the Commissioner, it was not binding. It held, therefore, that when Mara, contrary to his agreement not to submit the contract to the Commissioner until after January 1, did so, the approval by the Commissioner was not effective to make it binding and that Flowers still had the legal right to cancel until

January 1. The trial court, therefore, entered judgment for both defendants.

Without considering the legal issues on the merits, we affirm the judgment of the trial court. We do so by application of the age-old, but sometimes overlooked, doctrine that ''he who comes into equity must come with clean hands.'' This equitable maxim is far more than a mere banality. It is a self-imposed ordinance that closes the doors of a court of equity to one tainted with inequitableness or bad faith relative to the matter in which he seeks relief, however improper may have been the behavior of defendant. That doctrine is rooted in the historical concept of court of equity as a vehicle for affirmatively enforcing the requirements of conscience and good faith. This presupposes a refusal on its part to be the abettor of iniquity. Thus while equity does not demand that its suitors shall have led blameless lives as to other matters, it does require that they shall have acted fairly and without fraud or deceit as to the controversy in issue.

This maxim necessarily gives wide range to the equity court's use of discretion in refusing to aid the unclean litigant. It is not bound by formula or restrained by any limitation that tends to trammel the free and just exercise of discretion. Accordingly, one's misconduct need not necessarily have been of such a nature as to be punishable as a crime or as to justify legal proceedings of any character. Any willful act concerning the cause of action which rightfully can be said to transgress equitable standards of conduct is sufficient cause for the invocation of the maxim by the chancellor.

Moreover, where a suit in equity concerns the public interest as well as the private interests of the litigants, this doctrine assumes even wider and more significant proportions. For if an equity court properly uses the maxim to withhold its assistance in such a case, it not only prevents a wrongdoer from enjoying the fruits of his transgression but averts an injury to the public. The determination of when the maxim should be applied to bar this type of suit thus becomes of vital significance.

A court of equity acts only when and as conscience commands, and if the conduct of the plaintiff be offensive to the dictates of natural justice, then, whatever may be the rights he possesses and whatever use he may make of them in a court of law, he will be held remedyless in a court of equity.

Here the plaintiff's whole difficulty arises because it admittedly took from Flowers what it claims to be a binding contract, but which it agreed with Flowers that it would, in effect, represent was not in existence in order to deceive others who had a very material and important interest in the subject matter. If there had been a straightforward execution of the document, followed by its filing with the commissioner, none of the legal problems now presented to this court to untangle would exist. We think no party has the right thus to create problems by its devious and deceitful conduct and then approach a court of equity with a plea that the pretended status which it has foisted on the public be ignored and its rights be declared as if it had acted in good faith throughout.

When it became apparent from uncontradicted testimony of Mara that this deceit was practiced in order to bring into being the contract sued upon, the trial court should have dismissed the suit without more on the basis of the clean-hands doctrine.

To the extent that the final judgment of the trial court dismissed the complaint as amended, with costs adjudged against the plaintiff, the said judgment is affirmed. To the extent that the judgment proceeded to a legal determination as to the validity of the contracts between the parties, we conclude that, in the view we take of the equitable principles applicable, these judgments should not have been reached.

As thus modified the judgment is affirmed.

CASE QUESTIONS

1. What is the equitable maxim used here, and how was it violated?
2. What approach or role should the court use in a situation in which both parties have done wrong?
3. Did the court appear to have any personal feelings about this case or its subject matter? Should the court allow this to be evident?

SUGGESTED READINGS

Leighton, *Elements of Equitable Relief*, 2 JOHN MARSHALL J. 230 (1969).
Newman, *Place and Function of Pure Equity in the Structure of Law*, 16 HASTINGS L.J. 401 (1965).
Chafee, *Coming into Equity with Clean Hands*, 47 MICH. L. REV. 877 (1949).
C.A. HUSTON, ENFORCEMENT OF DECREES IN EQUITY 114–35 (1915).
Akehurst, *Equity and General Principles of Law*, 25 INT. & COMP. L.Q. 801 (1976).

Jury Trial

Cases are normally tried before a jury only if the parties have a right to a trial by jury and when one of the parties takes the required steps necessary to assert this right. In cases in equity, the parties have no right to a jury trial. Jury trial was not a part of chancery procedure.

For the most part, trial by jury is a constitutional right. Litigants are guaranteed a jury trial in federal courts by the Seventh Amendment to the United States Constitution, which provides: "In suits at common law, where the value in controversy shall exceed twenty dollars, the right of trial by jury shall be preserved. . . .'' Most state constitutions make similar provisions for a jury in suits at common law. There is no constitutional right to a jury trial in equity cases.

Common law and equitable remedies may be sought in the same action in most American courts. The parties do not give up their right to a trial by jury when legal and equitable issues are joined in the same suit. In this situation, the legal and equitable issues should be separated. The legal issues are determined by the jury, and the equitable issues are for the judge sitting as a chancellor.

State v. Yelsen Land Company
257 S.C. 401, 185 S.E.2d 897
Supreme Court of South Carolina
January 5, 1972

LITTLEJOHN, JUSTICE
This action was commenced by the state of South Carolina to settle a dispute concerning ownership and control of certain tidelands, submerged lands, and waters adjacent to Morris Island in Charleston Harbor. The state seeks to enjoin the defendants from trespassing upon the property involved, and seeks confirmation of title to the land in the state.

By way of answer and counterclaim, defendants assert title to the area in question, and allege that the state has trespassed upon it. They seek judgment confirming title in themselves, and seek monetary damages for wrongful taking, forbidden by the constitution. They also seek attorney fees and an injunction against the state. Their claim of title to the area stems from grants by the state of South Carolina to their predecessors in title.

After the case had been placed on the calendar for a jury trial, and the case reached for trial on the roster, the judge, on his own motion and over the objection of the state, referred all issues for trial to the master in equity for Charleston County. The state duly excepted to this order of reference and has appealed.

The sole question raised on this appeal is whether the judge erred in ordering the issues tried by the master instead of by a jury.

The complaint in this action asserts that ''Plaintiff has no adequate remedy at law and therefore brings this action in equity. . . .'' Defendants Yelsen Land Company, Inc. and Dajon Realty Company likewise assert in their answer and counterclaim that ''Defendants have no adequate remedy at law to prevent further trespass. . . .'' Defendants contend that all parties have alleged this to be a matter in equity, and that a trial by jury has therefore been waived.

The state's assertion that it ''has no adequate remedy at law'' was, perhaps, unfortunate. Obviously, it referred to the injunctive relief sought, which is purely equitable. But the character of an action is not necessarily determined by such recitations in the pleadings. Rather, it is the nature of the issues and the remedies which are sought that is determinative.

A great many actions are of a hybrid

nature. They involve not only issues normally tried by a jury, but also issues normally tried in equity without a jury.

This court noted in *Airfare, Inc., v. Greenville Airport Commission*, 249 S.C. 265, 153 S.E.2d 846 (1967), that

Under our code practice, legal and equitable issues and rights may be asserted in the same complaint, and legal and equitable remedies and relief afforded in the same action. In such event the legal issues are for determination by the jury, and the equitable issues for the judge sitting as a chancellor. The legal and equitable issues should be separated and each tried by the appropriate branch of the court.

Both the state and the defendants seek injunctive relief in this action. An action for such relief is equitable.

But both the state and the defendants assert title to the tidelands here in question. And when an issue of title to real estate is raised, such issue is generally triable by jury.

Bryan v. Freeman, 253 S.C. 50, 168 S.E.2d 793 (1969), was a suit to remove a cloud on and quiet title to land. The complaint alleged that plaintiffs had title to land. Defendants, by answers, asserted paramount title. The issue there was whether the action should have been referred to a master. In holding that the trial court acted properly in refusing to refer the action to a master, we said:

An action to remove a cloud on and quiet title land is one in equity. However, when the defendant's answer raises an issue of paramount title to land, such as would, if established, defeat plaintiff's action, it is the duty of the court to submit to a jury the issue of title as raised by the pleadings.

The facts before us require the same holding as the *Bryan* case. All parties seek equitable relief, and all parties seek relief triable at law. We do not think that the allegation in the complaint that this is an action in equity warrants the conclusion, as argued by defendants, that the plaintiff waived its right to a jury trial. To hold that the state voluntarily relinquished its right to a jury trial of the law issues involved would require a strained construction of the allegation in the complaint. It was the duty of the lower court to submit the law issues to a jury.

Reversed

CASE QUESTIONS

1. What was the common-law part of the case? What was the equity part of the case?
2. Who will decide the equity claims? Who will decide the common-law claims?
3. Suppose a party has a single claim of relief, but demands various remedies, some available at law and some available only in equity. Will the case be tried before a jury?

4. What determined the character of the action in the instant case—the nature of the issues, or the recitations in the pleadings?

SUGGESTED READINGS

Note, *Law or Equity: The Right to Trial by Jury in a Civil Action*, 35 Mo. L. Rev. 43 (1970).

Note, *Right to Trial by Jury: Is It Necessary?* 15 DePaul L. Rev. 398 (1966).

O'Neil, *Law or Equity: The Right to Trial by Jury in a Civil Action*, 27 Mo. B.J. 14 (1971).

C.A. Wright, Law of Federal Courts § 92 (3d ed. 1976).

Mayhall, *Note on Recent Cases Discussing Jury Trials in Cases Combining Legal and Equitable Relief*, 38 Ala. Law. 216 (1977).

Devlin, *Jury Trial of Complex Cases: English Practice at the Time of the Seventh Amendment*, 80 Colum. L. Rev. 43 (1980).

Common-Law Remedies

Common-law remedies are generally limited to the court's determination of some legal right and the award of money damages. There are some exceptions. For example, when parties want the court's opinion concerning their legal rights, without seeking damages or injunctive relief, they seek a declaratory judgment. Both the common-law remedies of ejectment and replevin seek restitution. An *ejectment* occurs when a trespasser secures full possession of the land and the owner brings an action to regain possession. Usually, this involves a title dispute between plaintiff and defendant, and the ejectment action settles this dispute. Not only does the plaintiff receive possession of land but also damages for the unlawful detention of possession. *Replevin* is an action used to recover possession of personal property wrongfully taken. Once the action is brought, the goods are seized from defendant after proper notice has been given.

Usually, a common-law court grants relief in the form of damages, a sum of money awarded as compensation for an injury sustained as the consequence of either a tortious act or a breach of a legal obligation. Damages are classified into (1) compensatory damages, (2) punitive damages, (3) nominal damages, and (4) liquidated damages.

Compensatory Damages

Compensatory damages are awarded to compensate the plaintiff for those pecuniary losses which resulted from the defendant's wrong. These losses may have resulted from either tortious conduct or breach of contract. Future losses are also recoverable. Compensatory damages may be awarded for loss of time or money, bodily pain and suffering, permanent disabilities or disfigurement, injury to reputation, and mental anguish. Recovery is not allowed for consequences that are remote, indirect or speculative.

Damages are usually limited to those reasonably foreseeable by the defendant as a result of the breach. Assume two plaintiffs have a contract to buy some equipment needed in order to open their new business, and a defendant breaches by nondelivery. If the plaintiffs sue for lost profits from the delay in opening because they have to procure alternative goods, they would probably not recover. This is because there is no way defendant could have foreseen this, not knowing that the opening depended on the delivery. Also, future profits are very difficult to measure with any degree of certainty. Damages are not awarded on the basis of conjecture only.

In awarding compensatory damages, the court's objective is to put the plaintiff in the same financial position as existed prior to the commission of the tort; or, in a contract case, in the financial position that would have held had the promise been fulfilled. In the absence of circumstances giving rise to an allowance of punitive damages, the law will not put the injured party in a better position than the person would have been in had the wrong not been done.

A person who is injured must use whatever means are reasonable in order to avoid or minimize damages. This is called the *avoidable harm doctrine*. It prevents recovery for damages that could have been foreseen and avoided by reasonable effort without undue risk, expense, or humiliation. For example, *P* sues to recover the loss of a crop, because *D* removed some rods from *P*'s fence, and as a result, cattle escaped and destroyed the crop. Since *P*, though knowing the rods were missing, did not repair the fence, only the cost of repairing the fence is recoverable, because if it had been repaired, the loss of the crop could have been avoided.

When the defendant's misconduct causes damages, but also operates directly to confer some benefit on the plaintiff, then the plaintiff's damage claim may be diminished by the amount of the benefit conferred. This is called the *benefit rule*. To illustrate, a trespasser digs on plaintiff's land, but the digging works to drain swampy areas and improve the value. The plaintiff may recover for the trespass and any damage it causes, but the defendant gets a credit for the value of the benefit conferred. However, this credit exists only for clear benefits and not for those that are remote and uncertain. Problems occur in deciding what is a benefit and by what standard to measure it.

Compensatory damages may be categorized as either general or special. *General damages* are those that are the natural and necessary result of the wrongful act or omission. *Special damages* are those that are the natural but not the necessary result of the defendant's wrong. The law presumes that certain injuries result from the happening of certain acts. They spring directly from the wrong and are compensable by general damages without having to examine any special circumstances involved in the injury. Special damages are awarded for injuries that arise from special circumstances of the wrong. They are directly traceable to the defendant's breach of an agreement or failure to perform a duty imposed by law by reason of special circumstances or conditions present in the case.

Putting a dollar value on the plaintiff's loss for the purpose of compensation often becomes a difficult task. Since the amount of damages is a factual question and decisions on factual issues do not create precedent, previous case decisions are not binding. The amount of damages is decided by a jury, unless a jury trial has been waived.

Troppi v. Scarf
31 Mich. App. 240, 187 N.W.2d 511
Court of Appeals of Michigan
February 26, 1971

LEVIN, PRESIDING JUDGE
In this case we consider the civil liability of a pharmacist who negligently supplied the wrong drug to a married woman who had ordered an oral contraceptive and, as a consequence, became pregnant and delivered a normal, healthy child.

A summary judgment was entered by the lower court dismissing the complaint of the plaintiffs, John and Dorothy Troppi, on the ground that it does not state a claim upon which relief can be granted.

In August 1964, plaintiffs were the parents of seven children, ranging in age from 6 to 16 years of age. John Troppi was 43 years old, his wife 37.

While pregnant with an eighth child, Mrs. Troppi suffered a miscarriage. She and her husband consulted with their physician and decided to limit the size of their family. The physician prescribed an oral contraceptive, Norinyl,

as the most desirable means of ensuring that Mrs. Troppi would bear no more children. He telephoned the prescription to defendant, Frank H. Scarf, a licensed pharmacist. Instead of filling the prescription, Scarf negligently supplied Mrs. Troppi with a drug called Nardil, a mild tranquilizer.

Believing that the pills she had purchased were contraceptives, Mrs. Troppi took them on a daily basis. In December 1964, Mrs. Troppi became pregnant. She delivered a well-born son on August 12, 1965.

Plaintiffs' complaint alleges four separate items of damage: (1) Mrs. Troppi's lost wages; (2) medical and hospital expenses; (3) the pain and anxiety of pregnancy and childbirth; and (4) the economic costs of rearing the eighth child.

In dismissing the complaint, the judge declared that whatever damage plaintiffs suffered was more than offset by the benefit to them of having a healthy child.

At issue here is simply the extent to which defendant is civilly liable for the consequences of his negligence. In reversing and remanding for trial, we go no further than to apply settled common-law principles.

We begin by noting that the fundamental conditions of tort liability are present here. The defendant's conduct constituted a clear breach of duty. A pharmacist is held to a very high standard of care in filling prescriptions. When he negligently supplies a drug other than the drug requested, he is liable for resulting harm to the purchaser. People trust not merely their health but their lives to the knowledge, care, and prudence of druggists, and in many cases, a slight want of care is liable to prove fatal to someone. It is therefore proper and reasonable that the care required shall be proportioned to the danger involved.

This review of the elements of tort liability points up the extraordinary nature of the trial court's holding that the plaintiffs were entitled to no recovery as a matter of law. We have here a negligent, wrongful act by the defendant, which act proximately caused injury to the plaintiffs.

What we must decide is whether there is justification here for a departure from generally applicable, well-established principles of law. The general rule of damages in an action of tort is that the wrongdoer is liable for all injuries resulting directly from the wrongful acts, whether they could or could not have been foreseen by him, provided the particular damages in respect to which he proceeds are the legal and natural consequences of the wrongful act imputed to the defendant, and are such as, according to common experience and the usual course of events, might reasonably have been an-

ticipated. Remote, contingent, or speculative damages will not be considered in conformity to the general rule above laid down.

Our review has been conducted to determine whether the defendant in this case should be exempted from the consequences of his negligence. We conclude that there is no valid reason why the trier of fact should not be free to assess damages as it would in any other negligence case.

The trial court found that "to allow damages such as claimed here would be in contravention of public policy." Where the state's advocacy of family planning is so vigorous as to include payments for contraceptives as part of the welfare program, public policy cannot be said to disfavor contraception. The notion that public policy may favor contraception for the poor, yet disapprove of it for the more affluent, is unworthy of serious discussion.

Contraceptives are used to prevent the birth of healthy children. To say that for reasons of public policy, contraceptive failure can result in no damage as a matter of law ignores the fact that tens of millions of persons use contraceptives daily to avoid the very result which the defendant would have us say is always a benefit, never a detriment. Those tens of millions of persons, by their conduct, express the sense of the community.

It is arguable that the birth of a healthy child confers so substantial a benefit as to outweigh the expenses of his birth and support. In the great majority of cases, this is no doubt true, else, presumably, people would not choose to multiply so freely. But can we say, as a matter of law, that a healthy child always confers such an overriding benefit?

The so-called benefit rule is pertinent. The restatement declares: "Where the defendant's tortious conduct has caused harm to the plaintiff or to his property and in so doing has conferred upon the plaintiff a special benefit to the interest which was harmed, the value of the benefit conferred is considered in mitigation of damages, where this is equitable." Restatement, Torts, § 920, p. 616.

Thus, if the defendant's tortious conduct conferred a benefit to the same interest which was harmed by his conduct, the dollar value of the benefit is to be subtracted from the dollar value of the injury in arriving at the amount of damages properly awardable.

The trial court evidently believed that application of the benefits rule prevents any recovery for the expenses of rearing an unwanted child. This is unsound. Such a rule would be equivalent to declaring that in every case, as a matter of law, the services and companionship of a child have a dollar equivalent greater than the economic costs of his support, to say nothing of the inhibitions, the restrictions, and the pain and suffering caused by pregnancy and the obligation to rear the child.

There is a growing recognition that the financial "services" which parents can expect from their offspring are largely illusory. As to companionship, cases decided when "loss of companionship" was a compensable item of damage for the wrongful death of a child reveal no tendency on the part of juries to value companionship so highly

as to outweigh expenses in every foreseeable case.

Consider, for example, the case of the unwed college student who becomes pregnant due to a pharmacist's failure to fill properly her prescription for oral contraceptives. Is it not likely that she has suffered far greater damage than the young newlywed who, although her pregnancy arose from the same sort of negligence, had planned the use of contraceptives only temporarily, say, while she and her husband took an extended honeymoon trip? Without the benefits rule, both plaintiffs would be entitled to recover substantially the same damages.

The essential point, of course, is that the trier must have the power to evaluate the benefit according to all the circumstances of the case presented. Family size, family income, age of the parents, and marital status are some, but not all, the factors which the trier must consider in determining the extent to which the birth of a particular child represents a benefit to his parents. That the benefits so conferred and calculated will vary widely from case to case is inevitable.

It has been suggested that parents who seek to recover for the birth of an unwanted child are under a duty to mitigate damages by placing the child for adoption. If the child is "unwanted," why should they object to placing him for adoption, thereby reducing the financial burden on defendant for his maintenance?

However, to impose such a duty upon the injured plaintiff is to ignore the very real difference which our law recognizes between the avoidance of conception and the disposition of the human organism after conception. At the moment of conception, an entirely different set of legal obligations is imposed upon the parents. A living child almost universally gives rise to emotional and spiritual bonds which few parents can bring themselves to break.

Once a child is born, he obviously should be treated with love regardless of whether he was wanted when he was conceived. Many, perhaps most, persons living today are conceptional accidents in the sense that their parents did not desire that a child result from the particular intercourse in which the person was conceived. Nevertheless, when the child is born, most parents accept him with love. That the plaintiffs accepted their eighth child does not change the fact that the birth of another child, seven years younger than the youngest of their previously born children, unbalanced their lifestyle and was not desired by them.

The doctrine which requires a plaintiff to take measures to minimize the financial consequences of a defendant's negligence requires only that reasonable measures be taken. In determining reasonableness, the best interests of the child must be considered.

The defendant does not have the right to insist that the victim of his negligence have the emotional and mental makeup of a woman who is willing to abort or place a child for adoption. If the negligence of a tortfeasor results in conception of a child by a woman whose emotional and mental makeup is inconsistent with aborting or placing the child for adoption, then, under the principle that the tortfeasor takes the injured party as he finds him, the tortfeasor cannot complain that the damages that will be assessed against him are greater than those that would be determined if he had negligently caused the conception of a child by a woman who was willing to abort or place the child for adoption.

While the reasonableness of a plaintiff's efforts to mitigate is ordinarily to be decided by the trier of fact, we are persuaded to rule, as a matter of law, that no mother, wed or unwed, can reasonably be required to abort (even if legal) or place her child for adoption. The plaintiffs are entitled to have the jurors instructed that if they find that negligence of the defendant was a cause in fact of the plaintiffs' injury, they may not, in computing the amount, if any, of the plaintiffs' damages, take into consideration the fact that the plaintiffs might have aborted the child or placed the child for adoption.

Of the four items of damage claimed by plaintiffs, each is capable of reasonable ascertainment. The medical and hospital expenses and Mrs. Troppi's lost wages may be computed with some exactitude. Plaintiff's claimed pain and anxiety, if not capable of precise determination, is a component of damage which triers of fact traditionally have been entrusted to ascertain. As to the costs of rearing the child until his majority, this is a computation which is routinely performed in countless cases.

It should be clear that ascertainment of *gross* damages is a routine task. Whatever uncertainty attends the final award arises from application of the benefits rule, which requires that the trier of fact compute the dollar value of the companionship and services of an unwanted child. Placing a dollar value on these segments may well be more difficult than assessing damages for, say, Mrs. Troppi's lost wages. But difficulty in determining the amount to be subtracted from the gross damages does not justify throwing up our hands and denying recovery altogether.

Michigan law is clear that there need only be a basis for reasonable ascertainment of the amount of the damages. Where the fact of liability is proven, difficulty in determining damages will not bar recovery. But where injury to some degree is found, we do not preclude recovery for lack of precise proof. We do the best we can with what we have. We do not, "in the assessment of damages, require a mathematical precision in situations of injury where, from the very nature of the circumstances, precision is unattainable."

The assessment of damages in this case is properly within the competence of the trier of fact. The element of uncertainty in the net recovery does not render the damages unduly speculative.

Reversed and remanded for trial.

Case Questions

1. What was the lower court's decision?
2. This court sent the case back to the trial court to determine the amount of damages. What items are to be considered in computing damages?
3. Can dollar values easily be placed on the above items?

Suggested Readings

Switzer and Reynolds, *Medical Malpractice Compensation—A Proposal*, 13 Am. Bus. L.J. 65 (1975).

Barrett, *Damages for Wrongful Birth*, 21 Clev. St. L. Rev. 34 (1972).

Restatement (Second) of Torts § 920 (1965).

Note, *Negligence—Damages—Birth of Healthy but Unplanned Child Due to Pharmacist's Negligence Held a Compensable Injury*, 3 Seton Hall L. Rev. 492 (1972).

Weiser, *Proof of Damages: A Defendant's Viewpoint*, 38 Brooklyn L. Rev. 371 (1971).

Note, *Damages for Infant's Pain and Suffering*, 11 Am. Bus. L.J. 83 (1973).

Comment, *Liability for Failure of Birth Control Methods*, 76 Colum. L. Rev. 1187 (1976).

Punitive Damages

Damages awarded in addition to compensatory damages in order to punish defendants for their conduct and to deter others from similar conduct are referred to as *punitive damages*. Punitive damages, also known as *exemplary* damages, are awarded to the plaintiff over and above the compensatory amount, where the wrong done was aggravated by wanton, reckless, malicious, or oppressive conduct on the part of the defendant. The type of malice required for punitive damages includes all acts done with an evil disposition, a wrong and unlawful motive, or the willful doing of an injurious act without a lawful excuse. Any type of negligence, even gross or extreme, is not sufficient to warrant punitive damages. These damages are not imposed as a substitute for criminal punishment, but rather as enlarged damages for a civil wrong. Punitive damages may be awarded in tort actions. These various torts that may recover punitive damages include: copyright and trademark infringement, corporate crimes like antitrust violations, insurers not paying off on their policies, wrongful discharge by employer, libel and slander, wrongful death, trespass, conversion, and securities fraud. Attorneys' fees may also be included in an award of punitive damages. Traditionally, punitive damages have not been awarded in contract cases, even in situations in which there has been a malicious breach. If a breach of contract is accompanied by a malicious tort, exemplary damages will be awarded for the tort.

Ebaugh v. Rabkin
22 Cal. App. 3d 891, 99 Cal. Rptr. 706
California Court of Appeals
January 26, 1972

KANE, ASSOCIATE JUSTICE
Defendants T. Scruggs, M.D., and Permanente Medical Group, a co-partnership ("Permanente"), appeal from a judgment entered on a jury verdict awarding to respondent Elizabeth Ebaugh both compensatory and punitive damages. Defendants R. Rabkin, M.D., and Kaiser Foundation Hospitals also appeal from the judgment but the appeal by those parties has been rendered moot by the entry of a judgment in their favor notwithstanding the ver-

dict, which judgment has become final. Accordingly, the appeal by Rabkin and Kaiser is ordered dismissed.

Respondent, a patient of Dr. Rabkin, was admitted to the Kaiser Foundation Hospital in Walnut Creek on February 6, 1967, and was scheduled for a breast biopsy the next day at 8 A.M. Appellant Scruggs was the treating physician for one Mary Notarmaso who was admitted to the same hospital and was scheduled for gall bladder surgery on the same day and at the same hour as respondent. Both patients were in the same ward and attended by the same nurses. On the operation day, one patient left the ward at 7:35 A.M., the other shortly after, at 7:40 A.M. Somehow a mixup in the charts occurred, as a result of which each patient was subjected to the surgery scheduled for the other. Dr. Scruggs, who was supposed to perform the operation on Mrs. Notarmaso, opened up respondent's abdomen and examined her gall bladder. When this examination revealed a normal gall bladder, Dr. Scruggs inspected the chart and the wrist band of respondent. It was at this point that he discovered the error.

In the meantime, Dr. Rabkin made an incision on Mrs. Notarmaso. He soon discovered that he was not operating on respondent and immediately terminated the procedure. He repaired the wound that he had made and placed a dressing on it. Shortly after, he located respondent and performed the scheduled breast biopsy on her.

The jury returned verdicts awarding respondent $7500 compensatory damages against all defendants and punitive damages in the sums of $10,000 against Dr. Rabkin, $5000 against Dr. Scruggs, $30,000 against Kaiser Foundation Hospitals and $30,000 against Permanente.

Appellants do not challenge the propriety of the award of $7500 for compensatory damages. However, they contend (1) that the issue of punitive damages should not have been submitted to the jury, and (2) that even assuming punitive damages to be a jury issue, the trial court committed prejudicial error in its instructions on this subject. Both contentions are sound.

I. The evidence was insufficient to support a verdict for punitive damages.

Civil Code § 3294 provides that "In an action for the breach of an obligation not arising from contract, where the defendant has been guilty of oppression, fraud, or malice, express or implied, the plaintiff in addition to the actual damages, may recover damages for the sake of example and by way of punishing the defendant." The cases interpreting section 3294 make it clear that in order to warrant the allowance of punitive damages the act complained of must not only be willful in the sense of intentional, but it must also be accompanied by aggravating circumstances, amounting to malice. The malice required implies an act conceived in a spirit of mischief or with criminal indifference toward the obligations owed to others. There must be an intent to vex, annoy, or injure. Mere spite or ill will is not sufficient; and mere negligence, even gross negligence, is not sufficient to justify an award of punitive damages.

The cases also point out that the only form of malice contemplated by Civil Code § 3294, which creates the right to exemplary damages, is malice in fact. Under general definition, malice in fact denotes ill will on the part of the defendant, or his desire to do harm for the mere satisfaction of doing it. In ultimate analysis, malice in fact is malice of evil motive.

In the instant case, there is simply no evidence that any of the appellants were guilty of malice, either "express or implied." On the contrary, the record negates any conclusion that the unauthorized operation on respondent's person took place out of evil motive or criminal indifference by appellants, or with an intent to injure or do harm to respondent for the mere satisfaction of doing it.

Dr. Scruggs's action was admittedly

negligent, amounting to a technical battery. However, the facts disclose that he did not know that he was operating on the wrong person. Thus, due to inadvertence, he was acting under a mistake of fact. Punitive damages are not recoverable where a person, acting in good faith, commits the tort of battery under a mistake of fact.

There is a further error with respect to the award of punitive damages against Permanente, the employer of Dr. Scruggs. It is well settled that while an employer may be held liable for an employee's tort under the doctrine of *respondeat superior*, he is not responsible for punitive damages where he neither directed nor ratified the act. In the case at bar, there is no evidence whatever that any partner or managing agent of Permanente directed, authorized, or subsequently ratified any alleged malicious conduct of any employee with knowledge as to the malicious quality of such act or conduct.

II. The trial court committed prejudicial error on its instructions to the jury on the issue of punitive damages.

The trial court twice instructed the jury in the following language: "You are further instructed, in addition to any actual damages under the second cause of action, if you find that there were any, you may award exemplary damages to the plaintiff in case you should find that the wrongful acts, if any, by the defendants, or any of them, causing such actual damages were committed in a wanton, willful, or reckless manner, or in case you find such acts were committed wantonly, recklessly, and without due regard to the rights of the plaintiff, or, if you find the wrongful acts of the defendants, or any of them, causing such damages were from any bad motive or so recklessly done as to imply a disregard for the obligations and rights of the plaintiff."

The above instruction, couched in the alternative, was prejudicially erroneous because the jury was allowed to award punitive damages thereunder if it found that the wrongful act of appellants was "willful" or "reckless" or "wanton" or "so recklessly done as to imply a disregard for the obligations and rights of the plaintiff." Under this reasoning, punitive damages would be allowable in any case of a willful or reckless act or conduct without the required aggravating circumstances amounting to malice.

Specifically directing the attention of the jury to the subject of punitive damages, the court gave the following instruction: "A master, or employer, may be liable for the willful and malicious acts of a servant within the scope of his employment. It is not necessary that a specific act or failure to act, be authorized as such by the principal to bring it within the scope of the agent's authority. It is within the scope of his authority if it is done while the agent is engaged in the transaction of business which has been assigned to him for attention by his principal, and while the agent is doing any reasonable thing which his contract of employment expressly or impliedly authorizes him to do, and which may reasonably be said to have been contemplated by the contract as necessary, or probably incidental to the employment."

This instruction which is germane only to the issue of *respondeat superior* has no application to the question of an employer's liability for punitive damages. In other words, an employer may be liable for the willful and/or malicious acts of his employee and thereby responsible for compensatory damages. It does not follow *ipso facto*, however, that the employer is also subject to an award of punitive damages.

As we have pointed out, to hold the employer responsible for punitive damages, it must be shown that the employee's malicious acts were done with the knowledge, or under the direction, of the employer or were ratified by him with knowledge of the willful and malicious quality of such acts.

The portion of the judgment awarding plaintiff compensatory damages on the first cause of action is affirmed; the portion of the judgment awarding punitive damages against appellants Scruggs and Permanente on the second cause of action is reversed with directions to grant their motion for judgment notwithstanding the verdict and to enter judgment in their favor accordingly. The appeal of Rabkin and Kaiser is dismissed.

CASE QUESTIONS

1. Should not punitive damages be awarded in this case since the defendants committed gross negligence?
2. What must be present to justify an award of punitive damages?
3. How did the court define "malice in fact"?
4. What public policy is promoted by punitive damages?

SUGGESTED READINGS

Note, *Relationship of Punitive Damages and Compensatory Damages in Tort Actions*, 75 Dick. L. Rev. 585 (1971).

Morris, *Punitive Damages in Personal Injury Cases*, 21 Ohio St. L.J. 216 (1960).

Note, 70 Yale L.J. 1296 (1961).

Long, *Insurance Protection Against Punitive Damages*, 32 Tenn. L. Rev. 573 (1965).

Long, *Punitive Damages; An Unsettled Doctrine*, 25 Drake L. Rev. 870 (1976).

Nominal Damages

Where there has been a breach of an agreement or an invasion of a right, but no evidence of any particular amount of loss, the court awards nominal damages. *Nominal damages* are trivial amounts awarded as a recognition of some breach of a duty owed by the defendant to the plaintiff, where no actual loss resulted or was proved. If a right is breached with loss resulting, the aggrieved person receives a judgment of compensatory damages measured by the loss. If no loss resulted from the breach or no loss is proved, nominal damages are awarded because damages are the only kind of judgment that the common law recognizes. Nominal damages are allowable even though the invasion of the plaintiff's rights result in a benefit. Nominal damages are fixed at some amount in the judge's discretion, such as $1 or $50. They are not to be confused with small compensatory damages, which are awarded where the actual loss was minor.

Nominal damages are awarded to vindicate or establish a legal right, or even if some economic harm has occurred but plaintiff is unable to prove it. For example, you are entitled to exclusive possession of your land. Even though a defendant's trespass caused no economic harm, you may demonstrate your right by recovery of nominal damages.

Cook Industries, Inc., v. Carlson
334 F. Supp. 809
United States District Court, N.D.
Mississippi
December 3, 1971

KEADY, CHIEF JUDGE

In this diversity action, the plaintiffs are Cook Industries, Inc., suing on behalf of its corporate subsidiary, Riverside Industries (Riverside), a business entity engaged in processing cotton and bean seed, refining vegetable oil, and manufacturing agricultural chemicals, and the City of Marks, Mississippi (Marks). The defendants are two sisters, Beverly M. Carlson and Ellen M. Berlin, who are Tennessee citizens owning certain farmlands and subdivision property in and near Marks, Mississippi. The suit was originally brought on December 16, 1969, in the chancery court of Quitman County, Mississippi, in which plaintiffs averred that Riverside as lessee-operator of the industrial property and Marks as its lessor-owner held an easement for water drainage across the adjoining property of defendants and sought an injunction to require the opening of a drainage ditch on the Carlson property as well as damages for defendants' closing the ditch on the previous day. The chancellor immediately and without notice issued the temporary injunction requested.

On January 14, 1970, defendants removed the case to federal court.

By an amended complaint, plaintiffs pled that Marks held an easement grant which defendants executed on May 31, 1961, for a right-of-way through and across an area later known as Morgan Manor Subdivision to construct a drainage ditch and to enlarge and clean out drainage ditches on the described property.

Many basic facts are undisputed. On December 15, 1969, the defendants together with their husbands hired a bulldozer and operator and directed the building of a small dam in an open ditch which drained industrial water from Riverside's plant through defendant's lands. This dam was built on subdivision lots owned by Mrs. Carlson southeast of Riverside's fence line. This abrupt halt to the flow of water soon caused a backup on Riverside's property. Because Riverside's operations required a place to discharge liquid waste and used water, the plant was forced to shut down nine hours until the backwater subsided. An emergency means of drainage was obtained by digging a ditch southerly on Riverside property to an established east-west drain along Roger Road, the water then going east to a point at which the flow re-entered the ditch in controversy on other property of Mrs. Berlin.

The general course of the disputed ditch extended southeasterly across subdivision lots for approximately 1000 feet, or to Roger Road, from which the drainage continued in an open ditch in the same direction for another 1200 feet to Tom Hill Bayou. Tom Hill Bayou flows on a northerly course and empties into Coldwater River.

In the mid-1960s, Marks, in accordance with city-developed plans, was permitted to come upon the subdivision area to cover old ditches, put in underground sewer pipes, adjust remaining ditches, and pave certain streets. The elimination of unnecessary ditches, without doubt, made the ter-

ritory more suitable for subdivision development. As a part of this program, Marks secured from defendants an easement grant which confirmed the historical natural drainage through the open ditch.

In 1966, Marks acquired by purchase Riverside's entire industrial property and made extensive expansions of plant and equipment at a cost of $2,500,000, financed by industrial revenue bonds. These improvements included the installation of a new system of seed crushing and oil refining, which called for the use of a much greater amount of water. Riverside then became the operator of the expanded property, under a long-term lease executed with the city.

The new oil refinery process entailed the commingling of raw materials and chemical substances with large volumes of water supplied by three wells. The oil refinery discharged effluent directly into the open ditch at the rate of approximately 3200 gallons of used water per minute. This volume of discharge never exceeded the ditch banks or overflowed on adjoining property. The effluent, however, contained quantities of oily substances and waste materials mixed with water, which produces an unpleasant odor varying in intensity with weather and operational conditions, and presents an unsightly appearance in pools of discolored water and greasy film alongside ditch banks. Riverside's effluent was the only industrial waste entering the ditch system and, without doubt, caused the stated specific conditions which had not previously existed.

In September 1969, defendants began objecting to Riverside and Marks that the effluent, because of its odor and appearance, was hampering the development of their land for residential purposes. They threatened litigation to abate the offensive condition. A series of letters passed, and certain meetings took place among the parties. Riverside advised defendants that it was planning to install a 20,000-gallon digester tank to reduce the amount of oil content in the effluent. The new filtering process would be in operation by December 19, 1969. Defendants found these proposals unacceptable and, after arranging for newspaper publicity, caused the ditch to be dammed up, as heretofore stated, to get the better attention of Riverside and Marks and force them to take more effective measures.

The expert testimony of defendants' engineers was to the effect that the polluted condition of the ditch was abatable by the installation at Riverside's plant of secondary waste treatment methods which would effectively remove practically all oil content from the water, and also that systems could be devised to reuse the water, although this would entail substantial cost. These experts viewed Riverside's present filtering methods as no more than an inadequate primary system that was only 50% effective, in contrast with secondary waste treatment systems available on the market that are 90% effective in pollution control.

The first issue for decision is whether the defendants had the right to resort to self-help by damming the ditch, assuming that the effluent was a private nuisance under the circumstances disclosed by the evidence. Mississippi recognizes the common-law right of an owner of property to abate a nuisance without resort to legal proceedings, provided he is able to do so without provoking a breach of the peace. There are, however, well-known limitations upon the exercise of this right of summary abatement, and one who summarily abates a nuisance acts at his own peril and assumes all liability for exceeding the right.

Under the foregoing principles, the defendants have surely exceeded the right of summary abatement, for there was neither a necessity for blocking the flow of drainage from Riverside's plant nor was the nuisance abated by their act of damming the ditch. Having inaugurated discussions with Riverside and Marks regarding corrective measures, defendants, if dissatisfied with the progress of those negotiations, had every opportunity to institute legal proceedings, as indeed they more than once threatened. Indeed, defendants admit that blocking the ditch was not to remove an offensive condition but a maneuver to gain publicity and community support for their position and force Riverside and Marks to take more effective action. The law does not countenance this sort of self-help.

We, therefore, hold that the defendants exceeded any right of summary abatement of conditions which they deemed to be a nuisance, and their unlawful act in blocking the drainage ditch renders them liable for the invasion of Riverside's right to the enjoyment of its property.

There remains Riverside's claim for damages of $10,625.98 which it seeks to recover as gross income lost while the refinery was shut down because of flood threat. Certainly, Riverside's shutting down the plant was a reasonable business decision, and its business interruption was held to minimum time because of the efficient way in which Riverside supervised its operation and diverted the discharge elsewhere. Riverside has not sought to establish what the actual outlays or costs incident to the shutdown were or to recover incurred expenses attributable to defendants' act, but demands recovery of the gross operating income that the refinery would have earned during the nine-hour period but for the shutdown.

Riverside has computed "gross income loss" based upon the monetary value of nine hours' production of crude oil, protein meal, and refined oil, less the cost of soybeans and freight-in. No deduction has been made for other expenses saved, such as fuel, chemicals, and other materials used in the manufacturing process, or of unneeded labor during the shutdown. The record is silent on such matters. Thus, an award to Riverside based on gross income, or gross profits, would be more than the actual loss sustained, and the court must reject the claim accordingly. Nor does the court have any data or information from which it may determine the necessary deductions, and thus ascertain the net loss with reasonable certainty and not upon conjecture. Unquestionably, Riverside had records which would throw light upon this inquiry but they were not disclosed to the court, although under the Mississippi rule, the most accurate and reliable evidence available is required to prove anticipated profits. Riverside has thus failed to carry its burden of proving lost profits in accordance with legal requirements even though some loss was likely sustained. Riverside is entitled to recover nominal damages only, which are hereby assessed at $500 because of defendant's invasion of Riverside's rights.

Plaintiffs unquestionably held drainage easements, collectively acquired, by prescription, express grant, and implied grant. These easements did not confer a right for either plaintiff to discharge polluted and contaminated water, which began in 1968 when new manufacturing processes were installed in the oil refinery and caused damage to defendants' property. The offensive odors and appearance thereby produced amount to a private nuisance.

The final issue concerns what the appropriate relief is in view of the determination that plaintiffs are maintaining a private nuisance on defendants' property. The court must consider the propriety of legal damages, equitable relief, or both remedies. While the law allows special or incidental damages in a case of this kind, the defendants, who are nonresidents, were unable to present evidence of legally cognizable special damages. The court is again confronted with allowing only nominal damages, which are hereby assessed in favor of defendants against both plaintiffs in the amount of $350.

CASE QUESTIONS

1. What was the amount of damages awarded by the court? Was the amount nominal?

2. Why are nominal damages rather than actual damages awarded in this case?

3. What were the plaintiffs' and defendants' rights in this case?

4. Should the amount for nominal damages be treated as an entirely relative matter, that is, one that is trivial when compared to the amount involved in the plaintiffs' claim?

5. If the fact of actual loss or damage is shown, but the proof is not sufficient to fix the amount, should nominal damages be allowed?

6. What are the practical functions and effects of nominal damages?

SUGGESTED READINGS

North, *Problem of Damages*, 30 CONVEY. 372 (1966).

J.D. CALAMARI and J.M. PERILLO, LAW OF CONTRACTS § 203 (1970).

Glover, *Plaintiff's Duty to Mitigate Loss*, 121 NEW L.J. 713 (1971).

Liquidated Damages

Parties may agree, in advance, as to the amount to be paid as compensation for loss in the event of a breach of a contract. This stipulated sum contained in an agreement is called *liquidated damages*. If the court determines that the amount stipulated in the agreement is not meant to be an estimate of actual damages, but rather a punishment used to prevent a breach, it deems that sum a penalty and does not enforce it. Traditionally, the court upholds a liquidated-damage clause only when (1) the damages in case of breach are uncertain or difficult to ascertain, (2) the parties have agreed in advance to liquidate the damages, and (3) the amount agreed on is reasonable and not disproportionate to the probable loss. Another form of liquidated damages results when money is deposited to guarantee against future damages.

Theoretically, it is possible for a plaintiff to recover substantial liquidated damages when no actual damage has been suffered at all. In the rare case of this occurring, some courts have rejected the possibility and have required the plaintiff to prove some actual loss before the liquidated damage clause could be triggered.

Niccoli v. Denver Burglar Alarm, Inc.
490 P.2d 304
Colorado Court of Appeals
November 2, 1971

COYTE, JUDGE

This is an appeal by the Denver Burglar Alarm Company, defendant below, from a judgment for $50 entered in favor of the plaintiff. Plaintiff has chosen not to make an appearance on appeal.

The facts are these. The defendant contracted to install a burglar alarm system in plaintiff's place of business. The contract provided that in case the alarm went off, the defendant would immediately dispatch one of its agents to plaintiff's business. The contract further provided:

the Contractor's liability hereunder shall be limited to a fixed sum of $50 or 10% of the annual service charge, whichever is greater, as liquidated damages and not as penalty, and this liability shall be exclusive.

Plaintiff's business was burglarized, and the defendant failed to dispatch an agent to plaintiff's place of business as agreed upon. Plaintiff thereupon sued the defendant both in tort and in contract for damages sustained as a result of the burglary. The defendant generally denied all liability and counterclaimed for $180, this being the amount plaintiff owed on the contract.

Trial was to the court, which found in defendant's favor on its counterclaim. Insofar as plaintiff was concerned, the court dismissed the cause of action based on negligence, but found in plaintiff's favor on the contract theory, since the defendant did fail to abide by its agreement to send an agent to plaintiff's business when the alarm went off. Governed by the liquidated-damages provision of the contract, the court found in plaintiff's favor in the amount of $50.

The error asserted by the defendant is that it is not liable for any damages sustained by plaintiff, either in tort or in contract, because it is not responsible for the losses suffered by the plaintiff.

We disagree with this assertion. There can be no doubt that the defendant breached its contract with the plaintiff when it failed to dispatch an agent to plaintiff's place of business. Ordinarily, when a breach of contract occurs, the party causing the breach is liable to the other party concerned for the damages resulting from the breach. In certain cases where the contract itself sets forth an amount as damages to be recovered in case of a breach, this figure is used in allowing recovery, unless the figure is deemed to be a penalty.

The essential elements necessary for a valid and enforceable liquidated damages clause are: (1) the anticipated damages in case of a breach must be difficult to ascertain, (2) the parties must mutually intend to liquidate them in advance, and (3) the amount stated as liquidated damages must be reasonable and proportionate to the presumed injury occurring as a result of any breach. The intent of the parties is the determining factor in whether or not a sum named in the contract shall be regarded as liquidated damages rather than as a penalty. Such an intent must be found from the wording used, as well as from the attendant facts and circumstances surrounding the particular case.

The facts here leave little doubt but that this contractual provision was intended to operate as a liquidated damages clause rather than as a penalty. The facts meet the requirements set forth since it was extremely difficult to anticipate precisely any potential damages occurring as result of defendant's breach.

Insofar as the intention of the parties

is concerned, we take note of the fact that this was a printed contract supplied by the defendant, and we therefore consider any provisions in the contract strictly in favor of the plaintiff and against the defendant who prepared the instrument. Inasmuch as the defendant prepared the instrument setting $50 for damages in case it failed to perform and then specifically stated that this figure was not to be construed as a penalty but rather as liquidated damages, we hold the defendant must abide by the terms it chose to use and that this figure is a liquidated damages clause and not a penalty.

Judgment affirmed

Case Questions

1. Why would a court recognize and enforce a liquidated-damage clause in a case such as this, in which the defendant clearly failed to abide by its agreement to send an agent to plaintiff's business?
2. What policy reason prevents a court from enforcing a penalty designed to deter a party from breaching a contract and to punish the party in the event the deterrent is ineffective?
3. Suppose that a contract provides for fixed damages in the event of a breach, with an option on the part of the aggrieved party to sue for such actual damages as may be established. Is this a valid liquidated-damage clause?
4. The Uniform Commercial Code § 2–718(1) provides that liquidated damages may be agreed on, "but only at an amount which is reasonable in light of the anticipated or actual harm caused by the breach, the difficulties of proof of loss, and the inconvenience or nonfeasibility of otherwise obtaining an adequate remedy. A term fixing unreasonably large liquidated damages is void as a penalty." How does this change the law?

Suggested Readings

J.D. Calamari and J.M. Perillo, Law of Contracts §§ 234–36 (1970).

Anderson, *Liquidated Damage Problems in Construction Contracts*, 5 Prac. Law. 72 (1959).

MacNeil, *Power of Contract and Agreed Remedies*, 47 Cornell L.Q. 495 (1962).

Uniform Commercial Code § 2–718(1).

C.T. McCormick, Damages (1935).

Comment, *Liquidated Damages: A Comparison of the Common Law and the Uniform Commercial Code*, 45 Fordham 1349 (1977).

Chapter Questions

1. Define the following terms:
   a. compensatory damages
   c. ejectment
   e. fraud
   g. laches
   i. master
   k. natural law
   m. nuisance
   o. remedy
   q. restitution
   s. specific performance
   u. waiver
   b. declaratory judgment
   d. exemplary damages
   f. jurisprudence
   h. liquidated damages
   j. maxim
   l. nominal damages
   n. reformation
   p. replevin
   r. special damages
   t. title

2. Since 1950, Harris-Walsh, Inc., has been engaged in the removal of anthracite coal by strip mining within the limits of the Borough of Dickson City, Pennsylvania. On June 28, 1963, the borough adopted an ordinance requiring that strip-mine operators furnish bond sufficient to reclaim stripped land in all future mining operations. The Dickson City ordinance also provides for certain criminal penalties for violation of the above ordinance. Since Harris-Walsh has been mining the area for many years, it feels it should be able to continue to mine in its old fashion. Can Harris-Walsh invoke the jurisdiction of a court of equity?

   Harris-Walsh, Inc., v. Dickson City, 216 A.2d 329 (Pa. 1966)

3. Pet Ponderosa Memorial Gardens leased 10 acres of land from Memory Gardens to be used as a pet cemetery. This land was adjacent to Memory Gardens' human cemetery. As part of the lease, the pet cemetery was allowed to use all available water each evening for two hours to develop and maintain its landscaping. Then Memory Gardens abruptly cut off the water supply, and as a result, the grass and other plantings died. The pet cemetery tried to renegotiate the lease without success. It found that hiring a water truck to haul in water was too expensive. Other water supplies could not be obtained. The pet cemetery instituted a suit and sought a preliminary injunction. Should this relief be granted?

   Memory Gardens of Las Vegas v. Pet Ponderosa M.G., 492 P.2d 123 (Nev. 1972)

4. For a number of years, a gambling establishment and saloon, called the Sycamore Cafe, was conducted on Central Avenue in Louisville, Kentucky, in an industrial and residential district. The proprietors, the Goose brothers, had been arrested numerous times for gambling, disorderly conduct, malicious assault, and other crimes. Records show that these charges were "filed away," or stooges were employed

to "take the rap." The record of the Goose brothers and the Sycamore Cafe is a sordid one of flagrant violations of the law occurring at all times of the day and night. Can the commonwealth's attorney enjoin the continuation of these activities at the Sycamore Cafe by invoking the jurisdiction of a court of equity for injunctive purposes?

Goose v. Commonwealth, 305 Ky 644, 205 S.W.2d 326 (1947)

5. During the summer of 1961, Harry Kapchuk and other stockholders reorganized the capital structure of Seashore Food Products, Inc., by creating an issue of no-par common stock with voting rights. The Kapchuk group retained 15% of this issue for themselves on the basis of three shares for every dollar of contributed capital. In August 1962, Seashore Food Products became heavily indebted to Seymour Friend and other creditors, some being close affiliates of the corporation. The debts were so large that the corporation faced bankruptcy. Acting as officers of the corporation, the Kapchuk group explained the situation to Friend and the creditors' group, and proposed that bankruptcy could be averted if the creditors would accept corporate stock in payment of their claims against the corporation. This was agreed to, and the transfer of stock to the creditors was made on the basis of one share of stock for every three dollars of corporate debt. Primarily because of the Kapchuk's skillful management, the corporation regained its solvency and began to prosper. In February 1966, Friend and other creditors filed suit, asking that a constructive trust be imposed on the stock acquired by Kapchuk during corporate reorganization because Kapchuk failed to disclose during the 1962 negotiations that he obtained this stock at three shares for one dollar. What equitable doctrine bars such relief to Friend and the creditors' group? Why?

Friend v. Kapchuk, 216 So. 2d 783 (Fla. 1968)

6. The owners of a professional basketball club, the Carolina Cougars, sued to enjoin William Cunningham, a professional basketball player, from performing services as a player for any other basketball club. The trial court denied the relief because the Cougars had unclean hands. The Cougars had contacted Cunningham while he was under contract with the Philadelphia 76ers and agreed to pay him $80,000 for sitting out the 1970–71 season, thereby repudiating the option on his services. Cunningham, while under contract with the 76ers, signed a three-year contract with the Cougars, commencing with the 1971–72 season, which was after the term of his contract with the 76ers. Cunningham refused to perform for the Cougars because he received a higher offer from the 76ers. In your opinion, should the equitable relief sought have been denied under the clean-hands doctrine?

Munchak Corp. v. Cunningham, 457 F.2d 721 (4th Cir. 1972)

7. Archie Sparrow, a cowboy experienced in training horses, met a rancher and fellow rodeo rider, Chip Morris, at a rodeo in Florida. After comparing notes on various rodeos, Morris offered Sparrow a job for 16 weeks working on Morris's ranch in Arkansas. Sparrow accepted, and as compensation, Morris agreed to give Sparrow $400 and a brown horse named Kerro. When Sparrow first came to Morris's ranch, Kerro was practically unbroken. However, Sparrow worked with the horse during his spare time, and by the time his 16 weeks were up, Kerro was well on his way to becoming a first-class riding horse. Morris returned at the end of the 16 weeks and gave Sparrow a check for $400, but refused to deliver the horse. Is Sparrow entitled to specific performance on the contract to deliver the horse? Why or why not?

   Morris v. Sparrow, 287 S.W.2d 583 (Ark. 1956)

8. Mrs. Vacarro, who had two miscarriages, received injections of a hormone to prevent miscarriages throughout the third pregnancy. A child was born with severe birth defects. The child's deformity was the result of the ingestion of the drug Delalutin, manufactured and sold by Squibb Corporation to prevent miscarriages. In a suit against Squibb, should the father, mother, and/or child be allowed recovery for emotional distress?

   Vacarro v. Squibb Corp., 71 A.D.2d 270, 422 N.Y.S.2d 679 (1979)

9. Mrs. Lamm's first husband died on August 3. She employed Shingleton, an undertaker, to conduct the funeral and purchased from him a casket and vault. Shingleton represented the vault as watertight, and warranted that it would protect the body from water for years. On the Wednesday before Thanksgiving, Mrs. Lamm discovered that the vault had risen six inches above the ground during the preceding period of rainy weather. She reported this immediately to Shingleton. On the following Saturday, employees of Shingleton and the cemetery met at the grave to move the vault into a freshly prepared adjoining grave. When the vault was raised it was discovered that mud and water had entered it and the casket was wet. Mrs. Lamm testified that this caused her considerable shock and she became a nervous wreck. She also testified that while the men were discussing getting the mud out of the vault, Shingleton loudly said he was not going to clean it out and "To hell with the whole damned business, it's no concern of mine." This language made Mrs. Lamm so nervous that she could hardly stand. Mrs. Lamm is suing Shingleton and the cemetery for failure to perform their contractual duties in a reasonable and workmanlike manner. Consider the nature of the contract. Can Mrs. Lamm recover for mental anguish as part of her compensatory damages?

   Lamm v. Shingleton, 231 N.C. 10, 55 S.E.2d 810 (1949)

10. In January, Evergreen Amusement Corp. entered into a contract with Milstead for the construction of a drive-in theater on land it had recently purchased. Work was to be completed by June 1 so that Evergreen could operate its theater during the peak summer months. Because unforeseen difficulties arose due to a faulty survey, thousands of dollars of extra fill dirt was needed, and work was not completed until the middle of August. Evergreen refused to pay Milstead for the extra work, and Milstead sued Evergreen for the cost of the extra fill, labor, and other materials. Evergreen counterclaimed for $12,500 profits allegedly lost during the period from June 1 to the middle of August. Evergreen sought to introduce a local drive-in owner and marketing consultant as a witness. The witness was prepared to testify that (1) a market survey showed a need for a drive-in theater in the area; (2) profits for the months in question could be estimated accurately by examining the theater's profits during the corresponding months of its second year of operation; and (3) weather, population, and competition were approximately the same in both years. However, the court refused to hear such testimony and in effect disallowed Evergreen's counterclaim for lost profits. Loss of profits are a well-recognized element of damages. Why did the court refuse to consider the issue?

    Evergreen Amusement Corp. v. Milstead, 112 A.2d 901 (Md. 1955)

11. Kim Capelouto contracted a salmonella infection immediately after her birth at Kaiser Hospital. Salmonella spreads by transmission from the stools of an infected person to the mouth of the recipient. Some neutral medium such as unwashed hands transmitted the disease from another infant to Kim. The infection spread throughout the nursery of the hospital and resulted in the temporary closing of the entire Kaiser maternity unit. Kim's disorder caused her recurrent distress throughout the entire first year of her life. During this period Kim was hospitalized six times. She suffered from projectile vomiting, severe diarrhea, dehydration, cramps, and shock. Intravenous feeding became necessary at times because of the severity of the dehydration. Does Kim have the right to recover damages for pain and suffering on the same basis as an adult?

    Capelouto v. Kaiser Foundation Hospitals, 7 Cal. 3d 889, 500 P.2d 880, 103 Cal. Rptr. 856 (1972).

12. Prisoners sued their jailers for money damages for cruel and unusual punishment by the state prison authorities in violation of their constitutional rights. Included among these practices were the imposition of a bread-and-water diet; arbitrary use of tear gas; taping, chaining, or handcuffing of inmates to cell bars; extended periods of confinement in solitary-confinement cells; placing prisoners naked in a hot, roach-infested cell; and arbitrary removal of good-conduct time,

thereby extending a man's compulsory prison term by months, and in the case of one of the plaintiffs, by years. Is the computation of damages possible?

Landman v. Royster, 354 F. Supp. 1302 (E.D. Va. 1973)

13. Florence Allman and her husband were the owners of a 150-horsepower ski boat which they kept at the Lake of the Ozarks in Missouri. On August 9, Florence decided to go water-skiing and asked Jesse Bird, a fellow skier, to drive the tow boat. They went out on the lake accompanied by Florence's son Johnny. The boat was stopped in the middle of the lake, and Florence jumped into the water and began to adjust her skis. As she was taking up the slack in the towline, Bird suddenly slammed the boat into forward gear and took off, catching Florence's hand and arm in the tangled towline. Johnny shouted for Bird to stop, but Bird kept accelerating. Finally, Johnny's shouts induced Bird to stop the boat. Florence's hand and arm were severely and permanently injured. As Bird knew, it is customary for drivers to take the slack out of the line and signal the skier when they are ready to start. Florence Allman is suing Jesse Bird for her personal injuries. Can she recover punitive damages on the above facts? What legal language characterizes the nature of Bird's action of starting the boat without regard for Florence's safety?

Allman v. Bird, 353 P.2d 216 (Kan. 1960)

14. Elizabeth Younce went for a drive one summer's day with her infant daughter Gloria. When they stopped for a stop sign, their car was struck from the rear by a car driven by Mr. Baker. Mrs. Younce and her daughter sued Baker for personal injuries sustained as a result of the collision. Mr. Baker admitted that his negligence was the proximate cause of the collision, but denied that the plaintiffs suffered injury or damage as a result thereof. The court instructed the jury to find whether the plaintiff suffered any injury as a result of the collision, and, if so, the dollar amount of the damage. The jury returned its verdict of no injuries and no damages. Are the plaintiffs still entitled to nominal damages, since the defendant admitted that he negligently caused the collision?

Younce v. Baker, 9 Ohio App. 2d 259, 224 N.E.2d 144 (1966)

15. On July 17, 1944, the Tally brothers, owners of the Glenn Ranch, a summer resort in the San Bernardino mountains, leased the ranch and its hotel and tourist facilities to Mr. and Mrs. McCarthy. The lease was for ten years, and rental was $10,000 per year. The McCarthys moved in on August 31, 1944, and operated the resort business and paid the rent until October 31, 1950. On November 28, 1950, the Tallys served the McCarthys a notice to pay rent or vacate the

premises. On December 1, 1950, McCarthy notified the Tally brothers that he surrendered the premises. A receiver was appointed, and the Tallys sued the McCarthys for damages. The lease provided, *inter alia*, that if the lessee abandoned the property within 10 years, lessees would be liable to lessors for actual damages plus liquidated damages of $10,000 for injury to the goodwill and trade name of the business. At the time of the breach in November, the Glenn Ranch was closed for the season and no tourists were permitted to occupy the premises. May the Tallys recover the liquidated damages?

McCarthy v. Tally, 297 P.2d 981 (Cal. 1956)

VI Civil Procedure

Proceedings Prior to Trial

Civil procedure is the name given to the sum total of rules, forms, doctrines, and devices that govern the conduct of most noncriminal judicial proceedings. Rules of procedure govern the conduct of the lawsuit. They exist so that substantive law can be implemented. The principal objective of procedural law is to give the parties to a dispute an equal and fair opportunity to present their sides of a case before a nonprejudiced and convenient tribunal. If procedural rules are correctly drafted and effectively implemented, both parties to the dispute should feel that they have been treated fairly. The purpose of this chapter is to provide a general explanation of the procedures that govern a civil suit from the time a litigant decides to sue until final court judgment. The legal system in the United States is composed of 51 different court systems, each with its own procedures. Indispensable to an understanding of these systems is a familiarity with the various stages and terms that are encountered in a civil proceeding.

Hiring a Lawyer

Procedural rules are intended to give each party to a controversy full access to as many facts as possible prior to the beginning of trial. Perry Mason's courtroom antics notwithstanding, real trial lawyers hate surprises. Since the side that is better prepared has a better chance of winning, the procedural rules are geared to promote the fullest possible preparation. Moreover, great latitude in pretrial discovery is likely to lead to a pretrial settlement between the parties, which is viewed as more desirable than an adjudicative settlement.

The period between the event that gives rise to the suit (the triggering event) and the filing of a complaint is known as the *informal discovery* period. The court has neither knowledge of nor interest in the plaintiff's cause of action against the defendant. The court as a passive adjudicator of controversies neither initiates nor encourages litigation. It acts as an arena of last, not first, resort. The court system does nothing until it has been called on by one of the parties through the use of the appropriate procedural mechanisms.

During the period between the triggering event and the filing of a complaint and summons, the parties conduct legal and factual investigations in order to determine their respective positions. The plaintiff contacts an attorney and describes the circumstances that led to the injury. The attorney discusses in general terms the legal alternatives available and usually asks for an opportunity to conduct an independent investigation to assess the value of the claim. This meeting is known as an *exploratory conversation*. At this point, the plaintiff and the attorney are not contractually bound to each other.

After the exploratory conversation and further investigation, the plaintiff meets once again with the attorney to determine which course of action should be taken. The attorney presents an evaluation of the case in terms of the remedies available, the probability of achieving a favorable verdict, and the nature and amount of the award likely to be granted. At this point the plaintiff retains the attorney as a representative in the judicial proceedings that are likely to follow.

Attorney's fees may be determined in several ways. They may charge the client by the hour. They may take a percentage of the damages collected (contingent fee), in which case they receive nothing if the client loses. They may be on a retainer, in which case they are paid a certain sum per year to handle all their clients' legal problems. Or they may charge a flat rate for their services.

When the plaintiff's lawyer has been officially retained, the defendant is so informed. This information puts the defendant on notice that the plaintiff is preparing to seek an adjudicative settlement of the claim. If the defendant has not already retained an attorney, this is the time to do so. The attorneys meet, with or without their clients, to discuss a reasonable settlement. These discussions are referred to as *settlement conferences.* If they prove unsuccessful, the judicial machinery is set in motion.

The role of lawyers in the legal contest is of crucial importance. Since both parties to the litigation are represented by lawyers, the party with the more competent and skillful attorney is likely to be in a better position. Lawyers owe their clients the duty of doing whatever they can to enable them to win their case. However, lawyers must obey their own con-

PROCEEDINGS BEFORE A CIVIL TRIAL

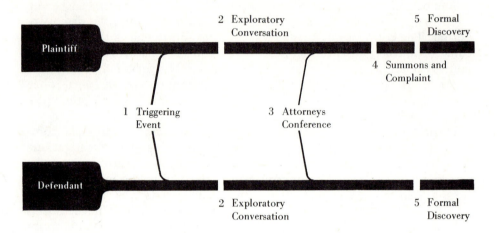

1 Commission of tort, breach of contract, or other event out of which a cause of action may arise.

2 Each party meets with own attorney and relates all facts surrounding triggering event. Attorney tells party whether case has merit and decides whether to handle it. For defendant this meeting may take place after receipt of the summons and complaint.

3 Attorneys exchange letters, talk on phone, or meet in person to define issues of case, determine their clients' chances, and discuss a possible settlement. This can take place at any stage of controversy.

4 Plaintiff files complaint with clerk of courts describing injuries and exact cause of action. Clerk issues a summons and has it delivered, with a copy of complaint, to defendant.

5 Both parties engage in formal discovery in the form of 1) depositions, 2) interrogatories, 3) productions of documents, 4) physical and mental examinations, and 5) requests for admissions. The purpose of discovery is for each party to obtain all information in possession of others and to narrow issues prior to trial. Discovery may begin after filing of complaint, but usually commences after answer is filed and continues until trial.

sciences—not that of their clients. Lawyers' duties must be performed within the law. Clients retain the power to discharge their lawyers at any time.

Fracasse v. Brent
6 Cal. 3d 784, 494 P.2d 9
Supreme Court of California
March 10, 1972

BURKE, ASSOCIATE JUSTICE
In this case we are asked to reconsider the rule of damages which allows an attorney who has been discharged with-

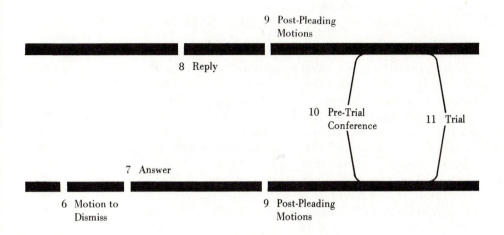

9 Post-Pleading Motions

8 Reply

10 Pre-Trial Conference   11 Trial

7 Answer

6 Motion to Dismiss

9 Post-Pleading Motions

6   Defendant may file a *demurrer*, a *motion to dismiss*, or a *motion for summary judgment* depending on the jurisdiction. With all these motions, defendant claims that plaintiff's complaint fails to state a cause of action. If motion is granted, plaintiff can amend complaint. If not, case is dismissed and defendant wins. If motion is denied, pretrial proceedings continue.

7   Defendant files an answer with clerk and sends copy to plaintiff. The answer includes admissions, denials, and defenses to allegations in complaint. Defendant may also include claims, called counterclaims, arising from the triggering event, against plaintiff.

8   If defendant's answer includes counterclaim, plaintiff files reply which includes admission or denial of allegation in answer.

9   Depending on jurisdiction, parties can make one of two motions following pleadings. If either party files a *motion for a summary judgment* or a *motion for a judgment on the pleadings*, they are claiming that allegations in opponent's pleadings cannot be proved. If motion is granted, the moving party wins. If it is denied, the pretrial proceedings continue.

10   Judge and both attorneys meet to define issues and discuss a possible settlement.

11   Trial of case before a judge and jury.

out cause by his client to recover as damages the full fee specified in the contract of employment, regardless of the reasonable value of his services or the extent of work performed under that contract. For the reasons hereinafter stated, we have concluded that this rule is inconsistent with the strong policy, expressed both judicially and legislatively in favor of the client's ab-

solute right to discharge his attorney at any time, and that the attorney should be limited to a *quantum meruit* recovery for the reasonable value of his services, upon the occurrence of any contingency contemplated by his contract.

Plaintiff George Fracasse is a duly licensed attorney at law, who was retained by defendant Ray Raka Brent to prosecute a claim for personal injuries in her behalf. On or about March 12, 1969, Fracasse and Brent entered into a written contingent fee[1] agreement, under which Brent agreed that Fracasse's compensation would be 33⅓% of any settlement made at least 30 days prior to the original trial date and 40% of any recovery obtained thereafter, whether by settlement or judgment.

Sometime thereafter, but before any recovery had been obtained in the personal injury suit, Brent informed Fracasse that she wished to discharge him and retain another attorney. She did so and, on January 16, 1970, Fracasse filed the instant action, entitled "Complaint for Declaratory Relief." Alleging that his discharge was without cause, and that Brent had breached her contract and had refused to give Fracasse the fee to which he would have been entitled thereunder, Fracasse prayed for a declaration that the contract was valid and that he had a one-third interest in any moneys ultimately recovered in the personal injury action. The trial court held that the complaint did not state a cause of action. This appeal followed.

It is recognized as a part of the ethical rules governing the legal profession that an attorney will not sue a client for a fee except to prevent injustice, imposition, or fraud. See American Bar Association, Canons of Professional Ethics, Canon 14. The relation of attorney and client is one of special confidence and trust, and the dignity and integrity of the legal profession demand that the interests of the client be fully protected. Without public confidence in the members of the legal profession which is dependent upon absolute fairness in the dealings between attorney and client, courts cannot function in the proper administration of justice. And inherent in the relationship between attorney and client is the fact that the client must rely almost entirely upon the good faith of the attorney who alone can make an informed estimate of the value of the client's legal right and of the expense and effort necessary to enforce it. These considerations have given rise to the generally accepted rule that a client may discharge his attorney at any time with or without cause. But that is not enough. The right to discharge is of little value if the client must risk paying the full contract price for services not rendered upon a determination by a court that the discharge was without legal cause. The client may frequently be forced to choose between continuing the employment of an attorney in whom he has lost faith, or risking the payment of double contingent fees equal to the greater portion of any amount eventually recovered.

It has long been recognized in this state that the client's power to discharge an attorney, with or without cause, is absolute. In discussing the unique relationship between attorney and client, this court stated that "The interest of the client in the successful prosecution or defense of the action is superior to that of the attorney, and he has the right to employ such attorney as will in his opinion best subserve his in-

---

[1] A *contingent fee* is an attorney's charge for services that is based on a percentage of the amount recovered for the client. The fee is charged only if there is a recovery.—*Ed.*

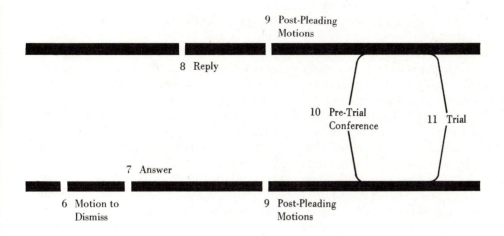

9 Post-Pleading
Motions

8 Reply

10 Pre-Trial
Conference

11 Trial

7 Answer

6 Motion to
Dismiss

9 Post-Pleading
Motions

6   Defendant may file a *demurrer*, a *motion to dismiss*, or a *motion for summary judgment* depending on the jurisdiction. With all these motions, defendant claims that plaintiff's complaint fails to state a cause of action. If motion is granted, plaintiff can amend complaint. If not, case is dismissed and defendant wins. If motion is denied, pretrial proceedings continue.

7   Defendant files an answer with clerk and sends copy to plaintiff. The answer includes admissions, denials, and defenses to allegations in complaint. Defendant may also include claims, called counterclaims, arising from the triggering event, against plaintiff.

8   If defendant's answer includes counterclaim, plaintiff files reply which includes admission or denial of allegation in answer.

9   Depending on jurisdiction, parties can make one of two motions following pleadings. If either party files a *motion for a summary judgment* or a *motion for a judgment on the pleadings*, they are claiming that allegations in opponent's pleadings cannot be proved. If motion is granted, the moving party wins. If it is denied, the pretrial proceedings continue.

10   Judge and both attorneys meet to define issues and discuss a possible settlement.

11   Trial of case before a judge and jury.

out cause by his client to recover as damages the full fee specified in the contract of employment, regardless of the reasonable value of his services or the extent of work performed under that contract. For the reasons hereinafter stated, we have concluded that this rule is inconsistent with the strong policy, expressed both judicially and legislatively in favor of the client's ab-

solute right to discharge his attorney at any time, and that the attorney should be limited to a *quantum meruit* recovery for the reasonable value of his services, upon the occurrence of any contingency contemplated by his contract.

Plaintiff George Fracasse is a duly licensed attorney at law, who was retained by defendant Ray Raka Brent to prosecute a claim for personal injuries in her behalf. On or about March 12, 1969, Fracasse and Brent entered into a written contingent fee[1] agreement, under which Brent agreed that Fracasse's compensation would be 33⅓% of any settlement made at least 30 days prior to the original trial date and 40% of any recovery obtained thereafter, whether by settlement or judgment.

Sometime thereafter, but before any recovery had been obtained in the personal injury suit, Brent informed Fracasse that she wished to discharge him and retain another attorney. She did so and, on January 16, 1970, Fracasse filed the instant action, entitled "Complaint for Declaratory Relief." Alleging that his discharge was without cause, and that Brent had breached her contract and had refused to give Fracasse the fee to which he would have been entitled thereunder, Fracasse prayed for a declaration that the contract was valid and that he had a one-third interest in any moneys ultimately recovered in the personal injury action. The trial court held that the complaint did not state a cause of action. This appeal followed.

It is recognized as a part of the ethical rules governing the legal profession that an attorney will not sue a client for a fee except to prevent injustice, imposition, or fraud. See American Bar Association, Canons of Professional Ethics, Canon 14. The relation of attorney and client is one of special confidence and trust, and the dignity and integrity of the legal profession demand that the interests of the client be fully protected. Without public confidence in the members of the legal profession which is dependent upon absolute fairness in the dealings between attorney and client, courts cannot function in the proper administration of justice. And inherent in the relationship between attorney and client is the fact that the client must rely almost entirely upon the good faith of the attorney who alone can make an informed estimate of the value of the client's legal right and of the expense and effort necessary to enforce it. These considerations have given rise to the generally accepted rule that a client may discharge his attorney at any time with or without cause. But that is not enough. The right to discharge is of little value if the client must risk paying the full contract price for services not rendered upon a determination by a court that the discharge was without legal cause. The client may frequently be forced to choose between continuing the employment of an attorney in whom he has lost faith, or risking the payment of double contingent fees equal to the greater portion of any amount eventually recovered.

It has long been recognized in this state that the client's power to discharge an attorney, with or without cause, is absolute. In discussing the unique relationship between attorney and client, this court stated that "The interest of the client in the successful prosecution or defense of the action is superior to that of the attorney, and he has the right to employ such attorney as will in his opinion best subserve his in-

---

[1] A *contingent fee* is an attorney's charge for services that is based on a percentage of the amount recovered for the client. The fee is charged only if there is a recovery.—*Ed.*

terest. The relation between them is such that the client is justified in seeking to dissolve that relation whenever he ceases to have absolute confidence in either the integrity or the judgment or the capacity of the attorney.... The fact that the attorney has rendered valuable services under his employment, or that the client is indebted to him therefor, or for moneys advanced in the prosecution or defense of the action, does not deprive the client of this right...." *Gage v. Atwater*, 136 Cal. 170, 172, 68 P. 581, 582.

We have concluded that a client should have both the power and the right at any time to discharge his attorney with or without cause. Such a discharge does not constitute a breach of contract for the reason that it is a basic term of the contract, implied by law into it by reason of the special relationship between the contracting parties, that the client may terminate that contract at will. It would be anomalous and unjust to hold the client liable in damages for exercising that basic implied right.

Amicus contends that there will be substantial difficulty in ascertaining the amount of recovery under a *quantum meruit* theory. The same difficulty—if such it be—is also present, however, in cases in which an attorney has been discharged with "cause" and yet such difficulty does not appear to have been insurmountable. Nor do we believe that abandonment of the present rule will lead to a wholesale discharging of attorneys by clients motivated solely by a desire to save attorneys' fees. To the extent that such discharge is followed by the retention of another attorney, the client will in any event be required, out of any recovery, to pay the former attorney for the reasonable value of his services. Such payment, in addition to the fee charged by the second attorney, should certainly operate as a self-limiting factor on the number of attorneys so discharged. To the extent that such discharge occurs "on the courthouse steps," where the client executes a settlement obtained after much work by the attorney, the factors involved in a determination of reasonableness would certainly justify a finding that the entire fee was the reasonable value of the attorney's services.

In short, we find no injustice in a rule awarding a discharged attorney the reasonable value of the services he has rendered up to the time of discharge. In doing so, we preserve the client's right to discharge his attorney without undue restriction, and yet acknowledge the attorney's right to fair compensation for work performed.

We return, therefore, to the question of the timeliness of the action filed by plaintiff. It had been held that a claim based upon unlawful discharge of an attorney retained under a contingent-fee contract did not accrue until the happening of the contingency. The basis for the rule was, of course, the fact that until the happening of the contingency, the amount of damages suffered by the attorney could not be ascertained. Having held herein that an attorney henceforth will be entitled to recover only the reasonable value of his services to the time of discharge, the question arises whether his cause of action has accrued at that time. With respect to contingent-fee contracts, we hold otherwise for two reasons.

First, one of the significant factors in determining the reasonableness of an attorney's fee is "the amount involved and the result obtained." It is apparent that any determination of the "result obtained" is impossible, and any determination of the "amount involved" is, at best, highly speculative, until the matter has finally been resolved. Second, and perhaps more significantly, we believe it would be improper to burden the client with an absolute obligation to pay his former attorney regardless of the outcome of the litigation. The client may and often is very likely to be a person of limited means for whom the contingent fee arrangement offers the only realistic hope of establishing a legal claim. Having determined that he no longer has the trust and confidence in his attorney necessary to sustain that unique relationship, he should not be held to have incurred an absolute obligation to compensate his former attorney. Rather, since the attorney agreed initially to take his chances on recovering any fee whatever, we believe that the fact that the success of the litigation is no longer under his control is insufficient to justify imposing a new and more onerous burden on the client. Hence, we believe that the attorney's action for reasonable compensation accrues only when the contingency stated in the original agreement has occurred—that is, the client has had a recovery by settlement or judgment. It follows that the attorney will be denied compensation in the event such recovery is not obtained.

In summary, we hold that an attorney discharged with or without cause is entitled to recover the reasonable value of his services rendered to the time of discharge. We further hold that the cause of action to recover compensation for services rendered under a contingent-fee contract does not accrue until the occurrence of the stated contingency. In light of these rules, it seems clear that there is no present controversy such as would justify the courts in exercising its discretion to entertain an action for declaratory relief. Whether there might be some circumstances in which a declaratory relief action might properly be brought by an attorney we need not decide. The facts presented in the instant case cannot support such an action.

The judgment of the trial court is affirmed.

SULLIVAN, JUSTICE, dissenting

We are confronted here with two questions: First, whether an attorney at law who has been discharged without cause by his client may bring a declaratory relief action to obtain a determination of his rights under a written contingency fee contract; and second, what may be the extent of his recovery under such circumstances.

The majority hold (1) that the action for declaratory relief is premature because the amount of any possible award cannot be determined before disposition of the client's underlying claim; and (2) that the client's discharge of the attorney without cause does not constitute a breach of the contingency fee contract so as to make the client liable for damages on the contract because he has "both the power and the right at any time to discharge his attorney with or without cause." Neither logic, traditional principles of contract law, nor the weight of precedent supports either holding. The court held that since the attorney's damages could not be assessed until his former client recovered a specific amount, the attorney's action was premature.

Here, plaintiff is not seeking damages for breach, but merely a *declaratory judgment* determining that defendant is *conditionally* liable under the contract and applying the established rule for calculating the amount of liability. The relief sought here by plaintiff does not require the court to predict whether and to what extent defendant will recover in his underlying personal injury suit. Plaintiff prays only for the court's recognition of his contractual right to receive a fixed percentage of any amount eventually recovered by defendant. The fact that no judgment has been rendered furnishes no reason for denying the former equitable relief under the declaratory relief procedure.

The majority, however, do not stop at this point, but, fashioning new rules as to the measure of damages in respect to attorney-client contracts, conclude that the action should be dismissed on this basis also. I cannot accept these new rules which are arrived at only after a wholesale uprooting of settled principles of contract law and an omnibus overturning of precedent. I now turn to this aspect of the case.

I start with an established rule of general contract law long recognized and adhered to by California courts. "One who has been injured by a breach of contract has an election to pursue any of three remedies. He may treat the contract as rescinded and may recover upon a *quantum meruit* so far as he has performed; or he may keep the contract alive, for the benefit of both parties, being at all times ready and able to perform; or, third, he may treat the repudiation as putting an end to the contract for all purposes of performance, and sue for the profits he would have realized if he had not been prevented from performing." This rule applies as to contracts between principal and agent and to contracts for services. Until today there has been nothing in the development of California law which has qualified or restricted the above rule when applied to agreements between an attorney and his client. Although such contracts are subject to the usual precepts governing persons standing in a confidential relationship, no statute, decision, or rule of professional conduct has declared that they are not subject to general contract law. No authority has ever so jettisoned respected contract principles to decree, as do the majority today, that a solemn, valid agreement between attorney and client may be dissolved into thin air at the mere whim of the client.

CASE QUESTIONS

1. What is the difference between contracts between attorneys and their clients and other contracts?
2. List the pros and cons of contingent fees.

3. Should a court uphold a contingent-fee contract between attorney and client that prohibits a settlement by the client?

4. If an attorney's client decides not to prosecute the claim, should the attorney be allowed to continue to prosecute the cause to secure the contingent fee?

5. A criminal defendant is accorded the right to have a court-appointed attorney. Should civil litigants be accorded a similar right to court-appointed counsel? Are prepaid legal services—for example, group insurance coverage for litigation expenses—the solution? Are legal services such as public-defender systems and legal-aid societies the solution?

6. Should an attorney who fits the description of an "ambulance chaser" be disbarred? What if the attorney solicits professional employment by advertising?

SUGGESTED READINGS

Warren, Monahan, and Duhot, *Role of the Lawyer in International Business Transactions*, 58 A.B.A.J. 181 (1972).

Schrader, *Attorney Decision-Maker*, 34 Ky. S.B.J. 37 (1970).

Note, *In Search of the Average Lawyer*, 56 A.B.A.J. 1164 (1970).

Miller, *Justice Report on Complaints Against Lawyers*, 33 Modern L. Rev. 542 (1970).

Teitelbaum, *Advocate's Role in the Legal System*, 6 New Mex. L. Rev. 1 (1975).

Stein, *Legal Services and the Middle Class*, 53 N.D. L. Rev. 573 (1977).

Ticcioni, *Civilizing Civil Procedure*, 31 J. Legal Educ. 152 (1981).

Notifying the Defendant

When it is decided that a suit should be brought, the plaintiff's lawyer files a complaint with the clerk of the appropriate court. The defendant is then served with a summons prepared by the clerk and a copy of the complaint. The purpose of the summons is formal notification that a lawsuit has been initiated against the defendant. The purpose of the complaint is to make the suit a matter of public record and to apprise the defendant of the nature of the claims. A typical summons contains the name of the court, the name of the party bringing the suit, and the lawyer representing that party. It warns that judgment will be rendered against the defendant unless certain action is taken within a stated time.

The summons must be served to the defendant in time for the person to take action in defense. This is a right constitutionally guaranteed by the due-process clause. The summons, sometimes called *process*, is generally served by a process server or sheriff. There are several methods by which process may be served successfully. The most common means is to deliver the summons to the defendant personally. Sometimes the party being sued is not present for personal service, in which case the process server may leave the summons with a reponsible person at the defendant's home. If no one is present at the defendant's residence, it is usually permissible to affix a copy upon the property. A defendant who is not within the court's jurisdiction cannot be personally served, so an agent may be authorized by law or appointed to receive service. Under certain circumstances, process may be served by certified mail or publication in a newspaper. A default judgment for the relief demanded by a plaintiff may be taken against a defendant who has received proper service and fails to do anything.

Summons

UNITED STATES DISTRICT COURT
. . . . DISTRICT . . . .

Civil Action, File No. . . . . . .

. . . . , Plaintiff

v.   } SUMMONS

. . . ., Defendant

To the above-named Defendant:
  You are hereby summoned and required to serve upon . . . ., plaintiff's attorney, whose address is . . . ., an answer to the complaint which is herewith served upon you, within 20 days after service of this summons upon you, exclusive of the day of service. If you fail to do so, judgment by default will be taken against you for the relief demanded in the complaint.

. . . .
Clerk of Court

[Seal of the U.S. District Court]

Dated, ...

Velazquez v. Thompson
451 F.2d 202
United States Court of Appeals
Second Circuit
November 3, 1971

MULLIGAN, CIRCUIT JUDGE
This is an appeal from an order of the United States District Court for the Southern District of New York, dismissing constitutional claims against defendants Thompson, Abrams, Moritt, and Feeley and denying plaintiffs' request for issuance of a preliminary injunction and application for an order determining this action as a class suit. Plaintiffs sought damages and injunctive and declaratory relief to redress the alleged deprivation of rights secured by the Fourteenth Amendment of the Constitution of the United States. We affirm.

The plaintiffs in this case are all New York City apartment dwellers who were summarily evicted, pursuant to article 7 of the New York Real Property Actions and Proceedings Law, for nonpayment of rent. The defendants Thompson, Abrams, Moritt, and Feeley are judges of the Civil Court of the City of New York against whom injunctive relief is sought preventing the prospective entry of summary default judgments and the issuing of warrants of eviction except under specified conditions. The defendant, Herbert Klein, is marshal of the City of New York and Georgio and Karp are process servers. The remaining defendants are the plaintiffs' former landlords and their employees.

We believe that there was no showing that the summary procedures transgressed constitutional guarantees and therefore the claim for damages and declaratory and injunctive relief was properly dismissed.

Summary proceedings for the recovery of real property were first authorized in New York in 1820 and have since been continued as a speedy and effective means for the recovery of realty. Summary eviction procedures exist in virtually every state. Their primary purpose is to enable landlords to regain possession quickly and inexpensively and thereby avoid the plenary action for ejectment and its incident delays which had prompted landlords to short-circuit the judicial process by resort to "self-help."

The plaintiffs have here mounted a constitutional attack on article 7 of the Real Property Actions and Proceedings Law. However, upon analysis, the principal target is § 735 which provides for the manner of service of process in such actions. They contend that this section is violative of the due-process guarantees of the Fourteenth Amendment, both on its face and as it has been applied to them. It is urged that the statutory scheme is, in any event, frustrated by vicious process servers who file fraudulent affidavits of service. "Sewer service" (or the throwing away of papers) is an ignominious practice. It is not limited to summary proceedings for the eviction of tenants but is also employed in suits on installment payment contracts for personal property, permitting repossession and garnishment and providing a fertile field for the fleecing of the poor and the disadvantaged. We believe that the statute (§ 735) clearly complies with due-process requirements and that its recent amendment, as will be developed *infra,* substantially minimizes the opportunity for "sewer service."

The test of the adequacy of notice for due-process purposes is whether it is "reasonably calculated, under all the circumstances, to apprise interested parties of the pendency of the action and afford them an opportunity to present their objections." Since the notice must fit the circumstances, it is "impossible to draw a standard set of specifications as to what is constitutionally adequate notice, to be mechanically applied in every situation." New York has drawn a separate service of process section for this special proceeding which is particularly designed and intended to bring notice home to the tenant. Service of the petition and notice of petition on a natural person (the plaintiffs in this action) is accomplished in one of three ways: (a) personal delivery to the respondent (personal); or (b) delivery to and personally leaving a copy with a person of suitable age and discretion who resides or is employed at the property sought to be recovered, if upon reasonable application admittance can be obtained and such person found (substituted); or (c) if substituted service cannot be accomplished, by affixing a copy upon a conspicuous part of the property sought to be recovered (conspicuous). If either the substituted or conspicuous methods of service are used, a copy of the notice of petition and petition must be mailed to the respondent (by certified or registered mail) within one day after the delivery or affixing.

It is to be noted initially that since this is an action to recover the possession of premises occupied by a person who is resisting removal, his whereabouts are obviously fixed and easily determinable. Thus the usual problem of serving a person whose present residence is unknown, which gives rise to much of the constitutional litigation in this area, is absent. Moreover, this statute specifies that the substituted or conspicuous service be made at the premises sought to be recovered. Appellants' first attack on the statute (§ 735) is that it is constitutionally deficient, since it does not require that a diligent effort be first made to accomplish personal service before permitting substituted or conspicuous service. This is simply frivolous. The general service of process statute in New York, which had required diligent effort to accomplish personal service, was amended in 1970 to eliminate the need for priority of personal service on the recommendation of the Judicial Conference of the state of New York precisely because that requirement was considered to be "the single most important cause of sewer service." The reluctance of process servers to find the person led to the fraudulent affidavit. Appellants' suggestion that this discredited priority device be now engrafted on § 735 and that the section is constitutionally infirm without it is not only without any substance but would exacerbate and not ameliorate a deplorable situation.

Both substituted and conspicuous service are incomplete unless, within one day thereafter, the petition and notice of petition are mailed to the respondent. In the case below, plaintiffs urged that this statutory safeguard was rendered ineffective by reason of perjurious affidavits of mailing. They suggest that there be a registered or certified mailing amendment. This point has evanesced, since the New York legislature has amended § 735 in 1971 to require mailing to the respondent "by registered or certified mail." Prior to the amendment, it was the word of the process server against the word of the respondent. Since this amendment became effective only on September 1, 1971, it is too soon to gauge its effectiveness. However, it is patently designed to minimize "sewer service." If the mailing is questioned and the server is unable to produce postal return receipts, it will no longer be a question of whom to believe.

Thus we hold that § 735 as amended in 1971 is carefully drafted and calculated to apprise tenants of the pendency of the action and is not vulnerable to constitutional attack. Having made every effort to ensure that tenants receive ample notice so as to prevent unintentional defaults, appellants' objection to the post-service procedures of article 7 are not meritorious.

Affirmed

CASE QUESTIONS

1. Why is the law so concerned with proper service of process?
2. What test did the court use to determine the adequacy of the notice?
3. What methods of serving process were provided for by the New York statute?
4. If the circumstances allow a court in the plaintiff's state to assert jurisdiction over an out-of-state defendant, what is the proper method of serving process?

SUGGESTED READINGS

Note, *Manageability of Notice and Damage Calculation in Consumer Class Actions*, 70 MICH. L. REV. 338 (1971).

Farrall, *Delay in Notice of Tort Claim Against a Government Agency*, 20 CLEV. ST. L. REV. 23 (1971).

F. JAMES and G. C. HAZARD, CIVIL PROCEDURE § 1.16 2d ed. (1977).

Note, *Civil Procedure—A Possible Solution to the Problem of "Sewer Service" in Consumer Credit Actions*, 51 N.C. L. REV. 1517 (1973).

Pleadings and Pretrial Motions

The complaint, answer, and reply constitute the *pleadings*. The complaint is prepared by the plaintiff, the answer by the defendant, and the

Complaint

UNITED STATES DISTRICT COURT

. . . . District of . . . .

. . . ., Plaintiffs

v.

Civil Action No. . . . . . .

COMPLAINT

. . . ., Defendant

1. The court has jurisdiction of this matter by virtue of the fact that the plaintiffs, ..., and . . . . . ., are citizens of the State of . . . . . ., and the defendant, ..., is a citizen of the State of . . . . . ., and the amount in controversy, exclusive of costs, exceeds $10,000.

2. This suit is brought pursuant to . . . . . . Statutes Section . . . . . .

3. At all times hereinafter mentioned, plaintiffs were in the exercise of all due care and caution for their own safety and the safety of others.

4. On . . . ., 19. . ., at or about . . P.M., plaintiff, ..., was operating her automobile in a northerly direction along United States Route . . at or about . . . . . . miles north of . . . ., ..., and plaintiff, ... was then and there a passenger of said automobile.

5. On . . . ., 19 . . . at or about . . . P.M., defendant, ... was operating his automobile in a southerly direction along United States Route . . . at or about twenty-five miles north of . . . ., ...

6. On the date and time aforesaid, defendant, ...misconducted himself in the operation of his vehicle in one or more of the following ways:

    a. Improperly failed to give a signal of his intention to make a left turn.

    b. Negligently made an improper left-hand turn, without yielding the right-of-way to traffic coming in the opposite direction.

    c. Negligently failed to yield the right-of-way.

    d. Operating said vehicle on the wrong side of the road.

    e. Negligently failed to keep said vehicle under proper control.

    f. Operated said vehicle in a negligent manner.

    g. Negligently failed to stop said vehicle when danger to plaintiffs was imminent.

7. As a result of one or more of the acts or omissions complained of, the vehicle driven by . . . . was caused violently to come in contact with the vehicle driven by . . . ., thereby injuring both plaintiffs and substantially damaging said vehicle of . . . . as hereinafter set forth.

8. That as a direct and proximate result thereof, plaintiffs . . . . . . and . . . ., suffered painful, severe and permanent injuries, loss of income and have incurred, and will continue to incur expenses for medical attention and further, ... was caused to expend the sum of $. . . . . . to repair the damages to her automobile caused by this accident.

WHEREFORE, plaintiffs, ..., pray for judgment against the defendant, ... in the sum of . . . . . . Dollars ($. . . . .).

. . . .

Attorney for Plaintiffs

Office and P.O. Address . .

. . . .

. . . .

reply by the plaintiff. The pleadings inform the court and the parties of the contentions of each party and aid in the formulation of the issues. The pleadings establish the jurisdiction of the court to adjudicate the controversy, briefly state the facts that gave rise to the plaintiff's claim, state the injury incurred as a result of the defendant's action, and present a demand for relief.

A *complaint*, or declaration, is drafted by the plaintiff's lawyer for the purpose of formally informing the defendant and the court of the basis of the plaintiff's claim. The complaint is served to the defendant with the summons. It is also filed with the clerk of the court. It is a concise statement of the plaintiff's factual contentions constituting the cause of action and a prayer for relief. A *prayer for relief* may consist of a demand that the court award the legal damage of a certain stated sum or any other relief that the plaintiff may seek.

Upon receiving the plaintiff's complaint, the defendant's lawyer analyzes its legal sufficiency. Depending on the jurisdiction, the defendant's lawyer can challenge the legal sufficiency of the complaint by filing a *motion to dismiss* or a *demurrer* with the clerk of courts and having it delivered to the plaintiff. In a motion to dismiss, the defendant says that the suit should not be heard because of a specific deficiency. The deficiency may be lack of jurisdiction, improper service of process, or simply that the complaint fails to state a claim on which relief could be granted.

In a demurrer, the defendant says that even if everything the plaintiff says is true, the plaintiff is not entitled to a legal remedy. When deciding whether to grant the demurrer, the judge assumes that the facts in the complaint are true and determines whether there is any legal basis for granting relief. The assumption that the facts are true is made only for the purpose of determining whether to grant the demurrer. It has no bearing on the trial.

The motions are decided by a judge at a hearing at which the parties argue the legal sufficiency of the complaint. If the judge decides to sustain the motion, the plaintiff may try to amend the complaint. Otherwise the case can be considered lost. If the judge overrules the motion, this does not mean that a judgment is rendered against the defendant. The defendant may then prepare an answer to the complaint before the case goes to trial.

Other pretrial motions are often available to the parties in order to correct the pleadings. A motion to strike scandalous, immaterial, or irrelevant matter from the pleadings and a motion to make a pleading more definite and certain are examples of pretrial motions.

If the complaint survives the motions, the defendant submits an *answer*. The defendant's written answer to the complaint may contain (1) admissions, (2) denials, (3) defenses, and (4) counterclaims. An admission contained in an answer means that there is no need to prove that fact during the trial. A denial creates a factual issue to be proved. Facts contained in the answer that may bar the plaintiff from recovery constitute a defense. When the defendant creates a separate action by seeking relief against the plaintiff, this is referred to as a *counterclaim*. If the defendant has a cause of action against the plaintiff arising out of essentially the same set of events that gave rise to the plaintiff's claim, the defendant must present that claim to the court in response to the plaintiff's claim.

The plaintiff may want to file a reply to the defendant's answer. In a reply, the plaintiff may admit, deny, or defend against the factual allegations contained in the answer.

Answer

UNITED STATES DISTRICT COURT
. . . . DISTRICT . . . .

. . . ., Plaintiffs

v.   Civil Action No. . . . .
                                      ANSWER

. . . ., Defendant

FIRST DEFENSE

The complaint fails to state a claim against defendant upon which relief can be granted.

SECOND DEFENSE

Defendant admits the allegation contained in paragraphs 1, 4, and 5 of the complaint; and denies each and every other allegation contained in the complaint.

THIRD DEFENSE

Plaintiff was guilty of negligence which was a contributing cause of the accident in that plaintiff was negligently operating his automobile at the time that same collided with defendant's automobile.

. . . .
Attorney for Defendant
Office & P. O. Address

. . . .

. . . .

One of two motions (depending on the jurisdiction) may be used to weed out meritless cases at the close of the pleadings and before trial. Either party may make a motion for a summary judgment or a motion for a judgment on the pleadings. The motion for a *summary judgment* is intended to dispose of controversies when the material facts cannot be proved. The motion may be made with documentary proof illustrating that the facts necessary to prove the opposing party's case are not provable or are not true. If the falsity can be demonstrated, the motion is granted and judgment is rendered in favor of the moving party. For example, assume that a complaint accuses the defendant of various counts of negligence in operating a car. However, because the defendant was in jail that day, it could be proved that the defendant could not possibly have committed the acts in question. The defendant in this instance would move for a summary judgment.

A *motion for judgment on the pleadings* questions the legal sufficiency of the pleadings, rather than disputing the facts in the pleadings. The motion for judgment on the pleadings, like the demurrer, raises only issues of law and assumes that the allegations in the pleading of both parties are admitted. Suppose, for example, that a plaintiff accuses a defendant of driving on the wrong side of the street and colliding with the plaintiff's car. The defendant admits driving on the wrong side of the street and colliding with the plaintiff. However, the defendant claims that the street is a one-way street and that plaintiff was going the wrong way. Since both parties agree on the facts, the only issue is whether the street is indeed one way. Consequently, defendant could move for a judgment on the pleadings.

No pretrial motion is granted if there is a genuine issue of fact between the parties, because this would deprive the parties of their right to a trial.

Bear v. Reformed Mennonite Church
462 Pa. 330, 341 A.2d 105
Supreme Court of Pennsylvania
July 7, 1975

O'Brien, Justice
On November 13, 1973, appellant, Robert L. Bear, filed a two-count complaint in equity against appellees, Reformed Mennonite Church, Glenn M. Gross, and J. Henry Fisher, in their capacities as bishops and as individuals. Count one of the complaint was against all the appellees and alleged the appellant was excommunicated from appellee church for his criticisms of the teachings and practices of both the church and its bishops. It was further alleged that the church and bishops, as part of the excommunication, ordered that all members of the church must "shun" appellant in all business and social matters. ("Shunning," as practiced by the church, involves total boycotting of appellant by other members of the church, including his wife and children, under pain that they themselves be excommunicated and shunned.) Ap-

pellant, in his complaint in equity, alleged that because of his being shunned, his business is in collapse since he is unable to hire workers, obtain loans, or market his produce. Moreover, appellant alleged that his family is in collapse because his wife and children do not speak to him or have any social or physical contact with him. Appellant has, therefore, requested the appropriate relief.

In count two of the complaint, appellant alleged that appellee Glenn M. Gross, while a bishop of appellee church, is also the brother of appellant's wife and that he has "advised" or "encouraged" her to "shun and boycott" appellant, resulting in appellant's wife not having any social or physical contact with him.

No responsive pleadings were filed by appellee church or appellees Gross and Fisher, either in their capacity as bishops or individuals. Rather, a two-line preliminary objection, demurring for failure to state a cause of action, was filed. This demurrer was sustained and this appeal followed.[1]

Appellant argues that the court below erred in sustaining appellees' preliminary objection in the nature of a demurrer. We agree.

In *Buchanan v. Brentwood F. S. & L. Assoc.*, 457 Pa. 135, 320 A.2d 117 (1974), this court reiterated the standard for judging a demurrer:

A demurrer admits as true all well-pleaded facts and all inferences reasonably deductible from them, but not any conclusions of law. Only if upon the facts averred, the law says with *certainty* that *no* recovery is permitted, will this court sustain the demurrer. Where a doubt exists as to whether a demurrer should be sustained, this should be resolved in favor of overruling it.

Appellees and the court below took the position that in examining the complaint in the above light, the "free exercise" clause of the First Amendment was a complete defense to both counts of the complaint and thus the granting of appellees' demurrer was proper. We do not agree.

In our opinion, the complaint, in counts one and two, raises issues that the shunning practice of appellee church and the conduct of the individuals may be an excessive interference within areas of "paramount state concern," that is, the maintenance of marriage and family relationships, alienation of affection, and the tortious interference with a business relationship, which the courts of this commonwealth *may* have authority to regulate, even in light of the establishment and free-exercise clauses of the First Amendment.

The United States Supreme Court, in discussing permissible governmental

---

[1] Appellees-defendants filed a preliminary objection pursuant to Pa. R.C.P. No. 1017 (b) (4), 12 P.S. Appendix, alleging a failure to state a cause of action. The applicable procedure is to review the pleadings to which such preliminary objection was filed and determine solely therefrom whether a cause of action was stated. A summary judgment pursuant to Pa. R.C.P. No. 1035 allows consideration of matters outside of the pleading. In the instant matter, we shall treat the order of the court below as sustaining a demurrer for failure to state a cause of action pursuant to Rule 1017 rather than that of granting a summary judgment.

curtailment acts done in furtherance of or pursuant to religious belief, has allowed a certain degree of regulation. In *Sherbert v. Verner*, 374 U.S. 398, 403, 83 S.Ct. 1790, 1793 (1963), the Supreme Court stated:

The Court has rejected challenges under the free-exercise clause to governmental regulation of certain overt acts prompted by religious beliefs or principles, for even when the action is in accord with one's religious convictions, it is not totally free from legislative restrictions. The conduct or actions so regulated have invariably posed some substantial threat to public safety, peace, or order. It is basic that no showing merely of a rational relationship to some colorable state interest would suf-

fice. In this highly sensitive constitutional area, only the gravest abuses, endangering paramount interests, give occasion for permissible limitation.

While the First Amendment may present a complete and valid defense to the allegations of the complaint, in the instant case, appellant has pleaded sufficient facts and created sufficient "doubt" that would entitle him to proceed with his action in order that he may attempt to prove the requisite elements that would entitle him to relief under *Sherbert, supra.*

Decree reversed. Case remanded for proceedings consistent with this opinion. Costs to be borne by appellees.

Case Questions

1. What purposes are the pleadings expected to serve?
2. When can the courts step in to prohibit religious practices? What if the religion handles snakes during ceremonies? What about religions that permit polygamy?

Suggested Readings

Browning, *Glance at Summary Judgment*, 27 Mercer L. Rev. 285 (1975).

F. James and G.C. Hazard, Civil Procedure, §§ 2.1–4.13 2d ed. (1977).

Smyser, *Summary Judgment—Ascertainment of the Genuine Issue*, 16 S.D. L. Rev. 20 (1971).

Note, *Pleading—Pretrial Amendments—Judicial Discretion to Deny Because of Delay*, 37 Mo. L. Rev. 340 (1972).

Rodda, *Ex Parte Matters Relating to the Pleadings*, 41 LAB Bull. 31, 97 (1965).

Bashara, *Elusive Summary Judgment Rule: Sifting Through the Maze*, 1976 Det. Coll. L. Rev. 397.

Other Pretrial Procedures

To prevent surprise at the trial, each party is provided with tools of *discovery* before trial in order to discover the relevant facts concerning the case. Discovery is based on the premise that prior to a civil action each party is entitled to information in the possession of others. The party entitled to win should prevail on the basis of all the information and facts available. Discovery includes the identity and location of persons; the existence and location of documents; known facts; and opinions of experts.

There is a distinction between the right to obtain discovery and the right to use in court the statements or information that are the product of discovery. The restrictions that are made concerning the admissibility in court of the product of discovery will be discussed later in the chapter. The requirements for discovery are: The information sought cannot be privileged, it must be relevant, it cannot be the ''work product'' of an attorney, and good cause must be shown to require a physical or mental examination.

The tools of discovery are depositions, interrogatories to the parties, production of documents, physical and mental examinations, and requests for admissions. An *oral deposition* is a tool by which a witness may be examined under oath outside court before an official of the court. The party wishing the deposition must give notice to the opposing party to the suit so that that person may be present to cross-examine the witness. The questioning of the witness at an oral deposition is thus much the same as it would be in a courtroom. Alternatively, an attorney may prepare a list of questions to be answered by a witness in writing. This is called a *written deposition. Interrogatories to the parties* are similar to written depositions in that both are lists of questions that must be answered in writing and under oath. Interrogatories are simpler, however, and can be submitted only to the parties to the case, not to witnesses. One party to the suit may compel the *production of documents* or things in the possession of the other party for inspection. When the mental or physical condition of a party is at issue, a court may order the party to submit to an examination by a physician. One party may send to the other party a *request for admissions* or denials to certain specified facts or to the genuineness of certain documents. If no reply is made to such a request, the matters are considered admitted for the purpose of the suit. All discovery except for physical examinations can be done without a court order. In case of noncompliance, the discovering party may request a court order to compel compliance. Failure to comply with the court order results in sanctions provided in the discovery statute.

A pretrial conference may be called by the judge in order to discuss the issues of the case. A judge and the two opposing lawyers discuss and evaluate the controversy informally. They consider the simplification and sharpening of the issues, admissions and disclosure of facts, possible amendments to the pleadings, the limitation of the number of witnesses, the possibility of reaching an out-of-court settlement, and any other matters that may aid in the speedy and just disposition of the action.

Securities & Exch. Com'n v. Research Automation Corp.
521 F.2d 585
United States Court of Appeals
Second Circuit
July 23, 1975

MANSFIELD, CIRCUIT JUDGE
The principal issue on this appeal is whether a district judge has the power under Rule 37(d), F.R.Civ.P., to enter a default judgment against a defendant who appears for the taking of his pretrial deposition but, in a willful effort to disrupt and to impede discovery, refuses to be sworn or to testify. We hold that under these circumstances, unless the plaintiff first obtains a court order, directing the defendant to testify, the court lacks the power to impose this severe sanction.

On August 12, 1972, the Securities and Exchange Commission (SEC herein) commenced an action against the defendants in connection with the offer and sale of securities of Research Automation Corporation (RAC herein).

A preliminary injunction was granted by the district court. Following an appeal by the defendants, the SEC decided to drop the § 5 charges, and we remanded the case for findings of fact to the district court, where it remained dormant for several months, pending negotiations for a settlement that never materialized. Thereafter, the SEC noticed the taking of the deposition of defendant Tserpes, president of RAC, for May 20, 1974, at the SEC's

New York regional office, requesting him to bring with him certain documents. Tserpes appeared at the designated time and place, but refused to enter the room where his deposition was to be taken, insisting on seeing William D. Moran, administrator of the SEC's New York regional office, who was engaged in conference on other business at the time. The SEC planned to have the examination of the witnesses conducted by Mark N. Jacobs, a staff attorney. Tserpes finally succeeded in forcing Mr. Moran to leave his other business in order to receive the documents personally before Tserpes would enter the room where his deposition was to be taken, all of which wasted about one and a half hours. Upon entering the room where Jacobs was waiting to depose him, Tserpes proceeded to engage in a course of obstructive conduct that made it impossible for Jacobs to take the deposition. Tserpes' obstructive tactics took the form of his erroneously insisting that certain discussions had not been transcribed by the court reporter, haranguing Jacobs with statements to the effect that Tserpes did not propose to be deposed by Jacobs, whom he distrusted and characterized as a ''liar,'' or by anyone associated with him, and finally by his refusing to be sworn when Jacobs repeatedly asked the reporter to administer the oath. Finding it impossible to proceed, Jacobs adjourned Tserpes' deposition and then attempted unsuccessfully to take the depositions of Martos and Hamos, the other RAC officers. In this effort, he was frustrated by the further disruptive efforts of Tserpes who, appearing *pro se*, proceeded to volunteer statements, interrupt the questioning, answer questions put to the deponents, and attack Jacobs personally. Finally Jacobs was compelled by this conduct to adjourn the depositions entirely.

The SEC responded to Tserpes' conduct by moving in the district court, purportedly pursuant to Rule 37(d), F.R.Civ.P., for an order which would strike the answers of the defendants RAC and Tserpes and enter a default judgment against them. Magistrate Harold J. Raby, to whom the motion was referred, found after a hearing that Tserpes had deliberately engaged in a course of conduct designed to harass the SEC, to obstruct the taking of the depositions, and to sabotage the orderly conduct of the proceedings in the case. With respect to Tserpes' disruption of the depositions of Martos and Hamos, the magistrate further found that Tserpes had "outrageously injected himself into the depositions which the SEC was trying to conduct respecting the other two defendants and in effect, by the process of filibuster made it impossible to depose the other two witnesses."

Accepting Magistrate Raby's recommendations, Judge Ryan granted the SEC's motion, striking the answers of Tserpes and RAC and entering a default judgment against them.

A default judgment granting relief against a defendant for failure to cooperate in pretrial discovery is a harsh sanction, which must be cautiously used lest the resulting grant of relief amount to a deprivation of property without due process. Recognizing the severity of the sanction of a judgment granting affirmative relief by default, we have held that, notwithstanding the elimination of the term *willful* from Rule 37 as a result of the 1970 amendments, the sanction should not be imposed because of negligence, and that the plaintiff must demonstrate that the defendant's failure to comply is due to willfulness, bad faith, or fault and not to be an inability to comply.

The drafters of Rule 37(d) provided that the court might impose the sanctions available under Rule 37(b)(2), which include the entry of a default judgment, when a party "fails (1) to appear before the officer who is to take his deposition, after being served with a proper notice." In recognition of the policy against a grant of relief by default except in a clear case, we believe that the term *appear*, as used in Rule 37(d), must be strictly construed, limiting it to the case where a defendant literally fails to show up for a deposition session. Where a defendant does in fact appear physically for the taking of his deposition but refuses to cooperate by being sworn and by testifying, the proper procedure is first to obtain an order from the court directing him to be sworn and to testify. This serves the purpose of impressing upon the defendant the seriousness of his actions and avoids a default judgment resulting from some misunderstanding on his part. If the defendant then refuses to obey the court's order, Rule 37(b) authorizes the court to impose the drastic sanction of default. Since Tserpes did in fact appear for the taking of his deposition, Rule 37(d) could not properly be invoked in this case to grant a default judgment against him.

The SEC, relying principally on Judge Skelly Wright's decision in *Bourne, Inc. v. Romero*, 23 F.R.D. 292, 296–97 (E.D. La. 1959), argues that Tserpes' mere physical presence did not amount to an ''appearance'' within the meaning of Rule 37(d) when he refused to be sworn or to testify. Although language along these lines may be found in *Bourne*, Judge Wright was dealing with a readily distinguishable situation. There the defendants' refusal to be sworn or to testify and produce documents was in willful defiance of an outstanding *subpoena* issued by the court ordering them to do so, which had been personally served upon them. Thus their conduct clearly constituted contempt of court. The default judgment, moreover, was entered only after the defendants had been afforded several opportunities to comply. No such order has been obtained in the present case.

The other decisions relied upon by the SEC do not support its position that, absent a court order, Rule 37(d) empowers the court to enter a default judgment against a party who appears but refuses to testify. In each case, the party either failed to appear or disobeyed a court order.

The district court's entry of default judgment against RAC, a New York corporation, stands on a different footing. The only purported appearance of RAC in this case has been through its officers, Tserpes, Martos, and Hamos, none of whom is an attorney. It is settled by law that a corporation may not appear in a lawsuit against it except through an attorney and that, where a corporation repeatedly fails to appear by counsel, a default judgment may be entered against it pursuant to Rule 55, F.R.Civ.P., *id.* RAC's officers named as defendants appeared *pro se* in the present case, and it is unclear whether they were aware of this requirement of a corporate party. Furthermore, the district court does not appear to have based its action in granting a default judgment upon Rule 55. For these reasons, although we affirm the entry of a default judgment against RAC, we do so without prejudice to its right to seek to reopen the judgment in the district court upon satisfying the court that its officers were unaware of the requirement and that it will promptly appear through counsel.

For the foregoing reasons we reverse the district court's order granting a default judgment against Tserpes, without prejudice to the SEC's right, upon remand, to seek an order against him pursuant to Rule 37(a). The default judgment against RAC is affirmed, without prejudice to RAC's moving to reopen the judgment upon a proper showing.

CASE QUESTIONS

1. What does dismissing without prejudice mean?
2. Why was the judgment against Tserpes reversed, whereas the judgment against RAC was affirmed?
3. What would enable the SEC to get a default judgment against Tserpes?
4. Why is the court reluctant to impose a default judgment?

SUGGESTED READINGS

Becker, *Modern, Efficient Use of the Bar and Other Parajudicial Personnel in Pretrial of Ordinary Civil Actions*, 53 F.R.D. 160 (1971).

F. JAMES and G.C. HAZARD, CIVIL PROCEDURE §§ 6.1–6.18 (1977).

Schmertz, *Written Depositions Under Federal and State Rules as Cost-effective Discovery at Home and Abroad*, 16 VILL. L. REV. 7 (1970).

Johnston, *Appealability and Reviewability of Discovery Orders*, 53 CHI. B. REC. 210 (1972).

Note, *Patient–Physician Privilege in the Discovery Process*, 17 S.D. L. REV. 188 (1972).

O'Kane and O'Kane, *Taking Depositions Abroad: The Problems Still Remain*, 31 FEDERATION INS. COUN. Q. 343 (1981).

The Trial

Presentation of Evidence

The procedure discussed here applies to jury trials. A jury acts as the conscience of the community. Jurors are selected at random from a fair cross section of the community, usually from a list of registered voters, and summoned to the courthouse for jury duty. After a case has been assigned to a courtroom, the judge calls in a group of prospective jurors, who take their seats in the jury box and are asked questions by the lawyers and the judge. A *voir dire* (literally, to speak the truth) examination is conducted to determine each juror's qualifications for duty under the appropriate statute, and any grounds for a challenge for cause, or information on which to base a peremptory challenge. Securing an impartial jury is the objective of the examination. Attorneys for both sides may make as many challenges for cause as they wish, and it is within the judge's sound discretion to replace a juror for cause. A challenge for cause may be based on prejudice or bias. A juror's relationship, business involvement, or other close connection with one of the parties or attorneys may also be considered cause for replacing a juror. In addition to the challenges for cause, each party is given a limited number of peremptory challenges that may be exercised at will, where no reason for the challenge need be given.

After a jury has been selected and sworn, as described above, then the trial begins with an opening statement given by the plaintiff's attorney. The opening statement is an explanation of the case in general, including the attorney's legal theories and what he intends to prove. The defendant's lawyer may also present an opening statement presenting legal theories of the case and the facts the defense intends to prove.

In order for the plaintiff to win the case, the disputed allegations of the complaint must be proved. This is done by the presentation of evidence.

Proceedings During a Civil Trial

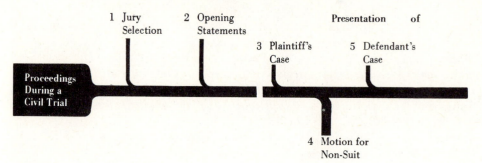

1 Prospective jurors are questioned by attorneys and judge. A prospective juror is dismissed if an attorney successfully makes a challenge for cause or exercises a peremptory challenge.

2 Attorneys explain facts of case in general to judge and jury. Plaintiff's attorney's opening argument usually precedes defendant's.

3 Plaintiff's attorney presents witnesses, documents and other evidence to substantiate allegations in complaint.

4 Defendant's attorney moves for an *involuntary dismissal* if it is felt that plaintiff failed to prove allegations. If judge agrees, motion is granted and plaintiff loses. If judge disagrees, motion is denied and trial continues.

5 Defendant's attorney presents witnesses, documents and other evidence to rebut plaintiff's case.

6 Plaintiff's attorney presents evidence to rebut evidence brought out during presentation of defendant's case.

7 Defendant's attorney presents evidence to rebut any new matters brought out during plaintiff's rebuttal.

8 After both parties rest their case, either or both parties may move for a directed verdict. If judge feels that reasonable persons could not disagree that the moving party should win, judge grants motion. If motion is granted, moving party wins and trial is over. If motion is denied, trial continues.

Witnesses and exhibits are produced by both parties to the suit. If witnesses do not voluntarily appear to testify, they may be ordered by means of a *subpoena* (see p. 258) to appear in court. A *subpoena duces tecum* issued by the court commands a witness to produce a document that is in his possession. If witnesses refuse to appear to testify, or to produce required documents, or if they perform any act that disrupts the judicial proceedings, they may be punished for contempt of court.

There is much variation among courts in the order of production of evidence. Judges have much discretion with respect to this procedure. Normally, a plaintiff's attorney presents the plaintiff's case first. The attorney presents witnesses, documents, and other evidence, and rests his case when he decides that enough evidence has been produced to substantiate the allegations. Defendant's lawyer then presents the defendant's case in the same manner. When the defense is finished, the plaintiff's attorney may introduce additional witnesses and exhibits in rebuttal of the

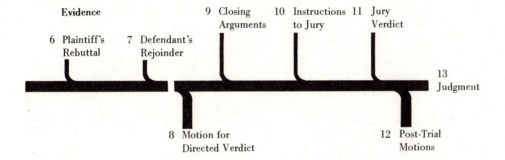

9 Both attorneys sum up evidence for jury. They suggest how the jury should resolve specific disputed items. Plaintiff's attorney argues first, but may reserve time to rebut defendant's attorney's closing argument.

10 Judge explains substantive law to jury, and tells how it should be applied to facts. Both attorneys may suggest specific instructions to judge, but final instructions are left to judge's discretion.

11 After deliberation, jury returns either a general or special verdict or both. A general verdict is simply a declaration of winner and amount of recovery. A special verdict is answer to specific factual questions requested by judge.

12 After jury returns its verdict, either or both parties may move to have verdict set aside by filing a motion for a new trial or a motion for a judgment notwithstanding verdict of jury. If the judge grants the motion, the moving party either wins case or gets a new trial. If judge denies motion, judge renders judgment in accordance with jury verdict.

13 By rendering judgment, judge declares who prevailed at trial and amount of recovery. If losing party does not voluntarily pay prescribed amount, winning party can force payment by obtaining an order of execution.

defense's case. If there are new matters brought out by the rebuttal, the defendant may introduce evidence in rejoinder, limited to answering the new matters.

Both attorneys introduce their own witnesses and question them. This is called *direct examination*. The opposing attorney cross-examines the witnesses after the direct examination is completed. Attorneys may conduct *redirect examinations* of their own witnesses following the cross-examinations. Attorneys generally may not ask their own witnesses leading questions (except for preliminary questions to introduce a witness or questions to a hostile witness). A leading question is one that suggests the answer to the witness. For instance, if an attorney asks, "You've never seen this gun before, have you?" the witness is almost told to answer no. Thus this is a leading question. Leading questions are permissible on cross-examination because they promote the purpose of cross-examination: testing the credibility of witnesses.

Subpoena—For attendance of witness [FRCP 45(a)]

UNITED STATES DISTRICT COURT
FOR THE __1_____ DISTRICT OF __2_____
__3_____ DIVISION

__4_____
            Plaintiff,
                  v   Civil Action, File No. __6__
__5_____
            Defendant.

To: __7_____ *[name and address of witness]*
    You are commanded to appear in the United States District Court for the
__8_____ District of __9_____, at __10_____ in the City of __11_____, State
of __12_____ on the __13_____ day of __14_____, 19_15_ at __16__ o'clock
__17__.m. to testify on behalf of __18_____ in the above pending action.
Dated __19_____, 19_20_.
[Name and address of attorney]

                                                    [Signature and title of clerk]

[Seal]

Farr v. Superior Court
22 Cal. App. 3d 60, 99 Cal. Rptr. 342
California Court of Appeal
December 17, 1971

THOMPSON, ASSOCIATE JUSTICE
This is a petition for writ of review of an order of respondent court adjudging petitioner Farr to be in contempt for failing to answer questions put to him. We conclude that the trial court properly found petitioner to be in contempt of court.

The matter at bench is an outgrowth of the trial of Charles Manson and his codefendants for two sets of multiple murders. The crimes themselves and the ensuing trial were the subjects of much sensational notoriety. Early in the proceedings the superior court entered an Order re Publicity. That order prohibited any attorney, court employee, attache, or witness from releasing for public dissemination the content or nature of any testimony that might be given at trial or any evidence the admissibility of which might have to be determined by the court. The order became effective December 10, 1969, and remained in effect throughout the trial.

On October 5, 1970, during the course of the trial, Stephen R. Kay, one of the deputy district attorneys assigned to the prosecution of the Manson case, obtained a written statement from Mrs. Virginia Graham, a potential witness. The statement recites that Susan Atkins, a codefendant in the murder prosecution, had confessed the crimes to Mrs. Graham in lurid detail and implicated Manson. It states that the defendants planned after the murders to cross the country by bus and in

administrative body, for refusing to disclose the source of any information procured for publication and published in a newspaper. Nor can a radio or television station be so adjudged in contempt for refusing to disclose the source of any information procured for and used for news or news commentary purposes on radio or television.''

Section 1070 read strictly does not include petitioner within the scope of its immunity. At the time of the hearing at which he refused to answer questions, he was not a person described in the section. Petitioner argues that § 1070 must be construed broadly to include within its immunity a person who occupied a described status at the time he acquired the information whose source is sought, although he no longer occupies the status when disclosure is required. He contends that otherwise the underlying purpose of the statute, the encouragement of free flow of information to the public, will be impaired by the reluctance of persons to communicate with reporters because of the possibility of the revelation of their identity if the reporter's status changes. Respondent counters with the argument that Evidence Code § 1070 is considerably less than an all-embracing effort to aid the flow of information by protecting sources. Thus, respondent notes that the section, while immunizing persons connected with newspapers, radio, and television from contempt for failure to reveal a source, does not protect persons connected with magazines, free-lance authors, lecturers, or pamphleteers.

On the narrow facts of the case at bench, we do not reach the issue of construction of Evidence code § 1070 as protecting former members of the newspaper, radio, and television profession from liability to the sanction of contempt. To construe the statute as granting immunity to petitioner, Farr, in the face of the facts here present would be to countenance an unconstitutional interference by the legislative branch with an inherent and vital power of the court to control its own proceedings and officers.

The power of contempt possessed by the courts is inherent in their constitutional status. While the legislature can impose reasonable restrictions upon the exercise of that power or the procedures by which it may be exercised, it cannot declare that certain acts shall not constitute a contempt. Thus, former subdivision 13 of Code of Civil Procedure § 1209 which provided: ''No speech or publication reflecting upon or concerning any court or any officer thereof shall be treated or punished as a contempt of such court unless made in the immediate presence of such court while in session and in such a manner as to actually interfere with its proceedings'' was held unconstitutional by our Supreme Court as an invalid legislative effort to abridge the inherent power of the court.

If Evidence Code § 1070 were to be applied to the matter at bench to immunize petitioner from liability, that application would violate the principle of separation of powers established by our Supreme Court. That application would severely impair the trial court's discharge of a constitutionally compelled duty to control its own officers. The trial court must take reasonable action to protect the defendants in the Manson case from the effects of prejudicial publicity. It performed its duty by issuing the Order re Publicity. By petitioner's own statement, that order was violated by two attorneys of record, of a list of six counsel in the case. Those attorneys were officers of respondent court. By petitioner's own statement, the violations occurred because of his solicitation. Respondent court was both bound and empowered to explore the violations of its order by its own officers.

Without the ability to compel petitioner to reveal which of the six attorney officers of the court leaked the Graham statement to him, the court is without power to discipline the two attorneys who did so, both for their violations of the court order and for their misstatement to the court that they were not the source of the leak. Equally significant is the proposition that petitioner tarred six counsel with the same brush. Unless the court compels him to reveal which two of the six violated their professional obligation, reputations of four officers of the court will remain unjustly impaired.

We thus conclude that Evidence Code § 1070 cannot be applied to shield petitioner from contempt for failure to reveal the names of the two attorneys of record in the Manson trial who furnished him with copies of the Graham statement. A closer question exists with respect to petitioner's refusal to divulge the identity of the third person, possibly not an attorney of record but subject to the Order re Publicity who gave him a copy of the statement. Here the court's power to compel an answer in the face of Evidence Code § 1070 must rest primarily upon the necessity of disclosure as a means of enforcement of its obligation to prevent prejudicial publicity emanating from its attaches or the office of the prosecuting attorney. We conclude here, also, that section 1070 if applied to immunize petitioner from contempt would unconstitutionally interfere with the power and duty of the court. The record is clear that the only persons other than attorneys of record who had access to the Graham statement and who were subject to the Order re Publicity were attaches of the court and members of the district attorney's office. The mandate of the United States Supreme Court that the trial court control prejudicial publicity emanating from such sources can be discharged only if that court can compel disclosure of the origins of such publicity.

The order imposing judgment of contempt is affirmed.

CASE QUESTIONS

1. Should the courts construct a journalist privilege under the aegis of the First Amendment?
2. What public interest would be served by legislation protecting a journalist's confidential sources?

3. What policy rationale underscores the creation of a privilege with regard to certain communications? What public interest would be served by a general limitation of the proliferation of privileges?
4. Can you conceive of an appropriate method for dealing with a situation such as the *Farr* case that would reconcile the interests of privacy and confidentiality with the needs of litigants?

SUGGESTED READINGS

F. JAMES and G.C. HAZARD, CIVIL PROCEDURE, §§ 7.1–7.12 2d ed. (1977).
Lawson, *Experimental Research on the Organization of Persuasive Arguments: An Application to Courtroom Communications*, 1970 L. & SOC. ORDER 579.
Blews and Patterson, *On Trial: Videotape*, 46 FLA. B.J. 159 (1972).
Hill, *Trial Procedure: A Composition Analyzing Some of the Elements*, 36 J. AIR. L. & COM. 497 (1970).
Nelson, *Newsmen's Privilege Against Disclosure of Confidential Sources and Information*, 24 VAND. L. REV. 667 (1971).

Rules of Evidence

There are rules governing the admissibility of evidence that must be followed in the examination of witnesses and in the production of documents. The rules apply both to jury and nonjury trials, although they are applied less strictly in the latter. When evidence has been presented erroneously before a jury, the judge instructs the jury to disregard it. An instruction by the judge explaining to the jury why the particular evidence is not to be considered helps the jurors understand the process and promotes their cooperation. If the prejudice caused by the presentation of the evidence cannot be rectified by such an instruction, the judge orders a mistrial. It is difficult to evaluate the effect that this excluded evidence has on the jurors' decision-making process. Once jurors have heard testimony, they may not be able simply to forget it.

Relevancy is the first requirement for the admissibility of evidence. The evidence must relate to the matter at issue and tend to prove the proposition alleged. Relevancy is sometimes confused with materiality. Immaterial facts are those that are not essential to the right of action. Immaterial evidence may be relevant to a proposition of fact, but if the proposition itself is not relevant to the fact situation under the substantive law, then the evidence should be excluded.

Witnesses, other than experts, must testify to what they have heard or seen, that is, to facts of which they have firsthand knowledge. Their opinions and conclusions are not admissible. Rather, it is the function of the jury as fact-finder to form its own conclusions from the evidence. Where evaluation of a fact situation requires special expertise, a jury may not be competent to form an opinion, and an expert witness may be called to assist the court. For example, doctors are frequently called as expert witnesses in personal-injury cases. The opinions of expert witnesses concerning their specialized knowledge are admissible.

Moran v. Ford Motor Company
476 F.2d 289
United States Court of Appeals
Eighth Circuit
April 20, 1973

LAY, CIRCUIT JUDGE

The plaintiff, Donald E. Moran, appeals from the judgment dismissing his claim for personal injury damages allegedly arising from the defendant Ford Motor Company's breach of warranty and negligence. Plaintiff's injuries were incurred in an automobile accident on July 9, 1967, near Millard, Nebraska, when his car swerved off the road and overturned. Plaintiff claims that Ford Motor Company breached its duty to furnish a car reasonably fit for the purposes intended and was negligent in the design and assembly of the wheel suspension system. After plaintiff presented his case before a jury, the district court granted defendant's motion for a directed verdict, holding that plaintiff had failed to make a submissible case for the jury.

On appeal, plaintiff raises three grounds of error:

1. Whether the trial court erred in directing a verdict for the defendant for the reason that plaintiff failed to offer suffi-

cient evidence to sustain a *prima facie* case;

2. Whether the trial court erred in simultaneously refusing a continuance and forbidding the testimony of Herbert Egerer, an engineer and metallurgist, because his name was not promptly communicated to the defendant in compliance with pretrial orders; and

3. Whether the court properly excluded the expert opinion testimony of Robert Stungis, an automobile repairman.

We find it unnecessary to respond to plaintiff's contentions 1 and 2 because of our reversal based on plaintiff's last contention, that is, the exclusion of the expert testimony of the witness Robert Stungis.

The accident occurred on July 9, 1967, while Moran was driving his 1966 Ford Mustang on a dry, paved highway. He testified that the car began to shimmy, then suddenly it veered left across the road and rolled over. Following the accident, it was discovered that the right front upper ball joint of the car's suspension system was separated. Plaintiff contends that said upper ball joint of the suspension system was defective prior to the accident. Thus he presented considerable evidence at trial to show that although the right side of the front fender collapsed against the right wall of the engine compartment upon impact, the right front wheel and tire were not damaged. Plaintiff's theory is that the wheel had become detached prior to impact, because otherwise the wheel would have been within the wheel well at the time of impact and the tire and wheel would have been damaged.

Plaintiff called as an expert witness Robert Stungis, an owner and operator of a body and fender shop. Stungis had been in the auto repair business for 18 years and had frequently examined wrecked cars. In doing so, he had on many occasions inspected suspension systems to discover what parts were broken or worn, what had caused the damages, and what pressures were exerted that might cause damage. He stated that he was familiar with the function and operation of a ball joint and that from his experience in the auto repair business he was able to recognize visible wear patterns on most automobile metal parts. Although the trial court allowed Stungis to point out wear that was readily observable, the trial judge did not permit him to testify whether the lower ball joint post was worn, whether the ball was set in the socket straight, whether the wear patterns were uniform, whether he could distinguish between a wear-produced condition and one that was produced by an accident, or whether he had an opinion on how the wear occurred. The trial judge believed Stungis was "unquestionably qualified to do repair work," but he was not "qualified metallurgy-wise, or to demonstrate cause."

A witness may be qualified as an expert based on his knowledge, skill, experience, training, or education. The test is whether the witness' training and experience demonstrate a knowledge of the subject matter. And practical experience as well as academic training and credentials may be the basis of qualification. Whether a witness is qualified to testify as an expert is normally within the discretion of the trial court. However, as this court observed in *Twin City Plaza, Inc. v. Century Surety & Insurance Corp.*, 409 F.2d 1195, 1203 (8 Cir. 1969):

If the witness, on the basis of his background skill, possesses extraordinary training to aid laymen in determining facts and if he bases his answer on what he believes to be reasonable scientific or engineering certainty, generally the evidence should be admitted, subject, of course, to the cross-examination of the adversary. The weaker the scientific opinion or the less qualified the expert, the more vigorous will be the cross-examining attack and undoubtedly the less persuasive will be the opinion to the trier of fact.

In the instant case, we believe Stungis possessed sufficient knowledge and practical experience to make him well qualified as an expert witness. The failure to permit his testimony resulted in prejudicial damage to plaintiff's attempt to prove causation. We refuse to speculate, as defendant urges, as to whether plaintiff could have proved a submissible case with Stungis' testimony. To answer this question requires resolution of a hypothetical record not before us. This we have no power to do.

We reverse and remand for a new trial.

CASE QUESTIONS

1. With no requirement that experts be formally certified in some way, what counters the possibility that everyone will claim to be an expert?
2. Why did this court grant a new trial instead of deciding for Moran?

SUGGESTED READINGS

Belli, *Demonstration Evidence: Seeing Is Believing*, 16 TRIAL 70 (1980).
Saltzburg, *Federal Rules of Evidence and the Quality of Practice in Federal Courts*, 27 CLEV. ST. L.R. 173 (1978).
Theis, *Doctor as Witness: Statements for Purposes of Medical Diagnosis or Treatment*, 10 LOYOLA U.L.J. 363 (1979).

The best possible evidence must be presented. This requires that original documents rather than copies be introduced into evidence. Unless it is unobtainable, a writing must be original to be admissible. Even when the original writing is unobtainable, secondary evidence of the contents is admissible only if the unavailability is not the fault of the party seeking to introduce the evidence. In this situation, the best available alternative proof must be presented. For example, a carbon copy of a writing is preferred over oral testimony as to its contents.

Evidence may also be excluded because a privilege exists. The Fifth Amendment provides that persons cannot be compelled to be witnesses against themselves in a criminal matter. Witnesses cannot be forced to give testimony—in or out of court—that could possibly be used to convict them of a crime. Confidential communications between husband and wife are privileged in any judicial proceeding, and testimony of one spouse against the other may be suppressed in a criminal trial because of the privilege. Information given by a patient to a doctor for the purpose of consultation for treatment is privileged. The purpose of the doctor–patient privilege is to promote medical care and improved treatment. It is also consistent with the physician's ethical duty of nondisclosure. All jurisdictions recognize the attorney–client privilege in order to encourage informed legal services. The privilege applies to all communications from a client to a lawyer in the course of professional consultation. In addition, the attorney's work product, including all matters considered to be part of the preparation of a case, are privileged. These privileges may be waived by the witness for whose protection they are intended.

The hearsay evidence rule excludes evidence proceeding not from the personal knowledge of the witness but from the repetition of what was said or written outside court by another person, and which is offered for the purpose of establishing the truth of what was said or written. The person who made the out-of-court statement may have been lying, joking, or speaking carelessly. The witness reporting the statement in court may have a poor memory. This exclusionary rule guarantees the opportunity to cross-examine the person who made the out-of-court statement and prevents highly unreliable evidence from being considered.

There are many exceptions to the rules governing the admissibility of evidence. The *res gestae* (spontaneous exclamations) exception to the hearsay evidence rule allows the admission in court of a spontaneous declaration uttered simultaneously with the occurrence of an act. The basis for the admission is the belief that a statement made instinctively at the time of an event, without the opportunity for formulation of a statement favorable to one's own cause, is likely to be truthful.

Moore v. United States
429 U.S. 20
United States Supreme Court
October 18, 1976

PER CURIAM

John David Moore, Jr., was convicted in a bench trial of possession of heroin with intent to distribute it, in violation of 21 U.S.C. Section 841(a)(1). In an unpublished order, the court of appeals summarily affirmed the judgment of conviction.

In early January 1975, police officers received a tip from an informant that Moore and others were in possession of heroin at "Moore's apartment." The police obtained a search warrant and entered the apartment, where they found Moore lying face down near a coffee table in the living room. Also present in the apartment was a woman who was sitting on a couch in the same room. Bags containing heroin were found both on top of and beneath the coffee table, and they were seized along with various narcotics paraphernalia.

At a consolidated hearing on Moore's motion to suppress evidence and on the merits, the prosecution adduced no admissible evidence showing that Moore was in possession of the heroin in the apartment in which he and the woman were found other than his proximity to the narcotics at the time the warrant was executed. Indeed, one police officer testified that he did not find "any indications of ownership of the apartment." In his closing argument on the merits, however, the prosecutor placed substantial emphasis on the out-of-court declaration of the unidentified informant:

(A) confidential informant came to Detective Uribe and said, "I have information or

I have—through personal observation—known that John David Moore resides at a certain apartment here in El Paso, Texas, and he is in possession of a certain amount of heroin.''

In adjudging Moore guilty, the trial court found that he had been in close proximity to the seized heroin, that he was the tenant of the apartment in question, and that he had, therefore, been in possession of the contraband. In making these findings, the court *expressly* relied on the hearsay declaration of the informant:

Information revealed by the confidential informant and relied upon in the preparation of the affidavit disclosed that John David Moore was the occupant of apartment #60, building #7, Hill Country Apartments, 213 Argonaut, El Paso, Texas.

Defense counsel objected to the court's reliance on hearsay evidence, but the judge refused to amend this finding except to add the phrase ''at the time of the seizure'' to the end of the sentence.

There can be no doubt that the informant's out-of-court declaration that the apartment in question was ''Moore's apartment,'' either as related in the search warrant affidavit or as reiterated in live testimony by the police officers, was hearsay and thus inadmissible in evidence on the issue of Moore's guilt. Introduction of this testimony deprived Moore of the opportunity to cross-examine the informant as to exactly what he meant by ''Moore's apartment,'' and what factual basis, if any, there was for believing that Moore was a tenant or regular resident there.

Moore was similarly deprived of the chance to show that the witness' recollection was erroneous or that he was not credible. The informant's declaration falls within no exception to the hearsay rule recognized in the Federal Rules of Evidence, and reliance on this hearsay statement in determining petitioner's guilt or innocence was error.

Although the only competent evidence of Moore's possession of the narcotics was his proximity to them in an apartment in which another person was also present and of which he was not shown to be the tenant or even a regular resident, the solicitor general now argues that the error in admitting the hearsay evidence was harmless. That is far from clear. Whether or not the evidence of proximity alone, when viewed in the light most favorable to the prosecution, could suffice to prove beyond a reasonable doubt that Moore was in possession of the heroin, the fact is that the trial court did not find Moore guilty on that evidence alone.

The government suggests that Moore's failure to testify or to adduce any evidence showing ''that his presence in the apartment was unrelated to the heroin'' highlights the alleged harmlessness of the error, but this suggestion can carry no weight in view of the elementary proposition that the prosecution bore the burden of proving beyond a reasonable doubt every element of the charged offense.

The judgment of the court of appeals is vacated, and the case is remanded to that court so it may determine whether the wrongful admission of the hearsay evidence was harmless error.

CASE QUESTIONS

1. What is the justification of the hearsay-evidence rule?
2. How might the government have asserted Moore's occupancy of the apartment without using the hearsay evidence?

SUGGESTED READINGS

Note, *Federal Courts and the Catchall Hearsay Exceptions*, 25 WAYNE L. REV. 1361 (1979).

Note, *Theoretical Foundation of the Hearsay Rules*, 93 HARV. L. REV. 1786 (1980).

Waltz, *Present Sense Impression Exception to the Rule Against Hearsay: Origins and Attributes*, 66 IOWA L. REV. 869 (1981).

Trial Motions

If, after the plaintiff's attorney presents plaintiff's case, the defendant's attorney believes that the plaintiff was unable to substantiate the essential allegations adequately, the defendant may make a motion for nonsuit. The judge grants the motion only if a reasonable person could not find in favor of the plaintiff upon considering the evidence most favorable to the plaintiff. If the motion is granted, the case is over and the plaintiff loses.

If the motion for a nonsuit is denied or not made at all, the defendant's lawyer then presents the defendant's case and tries to disprove the plaintiff's evidence or substantiate the defendant's arguments. Witnesses and exhibits are presented, following the same procedure as the plaintiff's— direct examination followed by cross examination. After the defendant rests his case, the plaintiff then may produce evidence to rebut the defendant's evidence.

At the end of the presentation of evidence—but before the issues are submitted to the jury—either party may make a motion for a directed verdict. The motion is granted for the party making the motion if the judge decides that the case is perfectly clear and that reasonable persons could not disagree on the result. If the motion is granted, the moving party wins the dispute without the jury deciding the case. If no motion for a directed verdict is made, or if made and denied, the case is submitted to the jury.

McCullough v. United States

442 F.2d 1011
United States Court of Appeals
Fifth Circuit
May, 7, 1971

INGRAHAM, CIRCUIT JUDGE

This action was commenced by R. F. McCullough (hereinafter taxpayer) for refund of a 100% penalty assessment against him under § 6672[1] of the Internal Revenue Code of 1954, stemming from his failure to pay over the income tax withholding and F.I.C.A. taxes of McCullough Industries, Inc. (hereinafter company), for the periods ending December 31, 1963, March 31, 1964, and June 30, 1964. A counterclaim was filed by the government. The case was tried before a jury. On May 4, 1970, taxpayer moved for a directed verdict and the government filed a cross motion for a directed verdict. Following argument on the motions, the court granted the taxpayer's motion. The court's orders granting a directed verdict for the taxpayer were entered on June 4, 1970, and the government's notice of appeal was timely filed on August 3, 1970.

From the facts developed by the evidence, taxpayer was the son of G. C. McCullough, who was the organizer of the company. When taxpayer returned from military service in 1945, he became associated with the company. He was an original incorporator and, next to his father, the largest stockholder.

He was and continued to be a director of the company from the time of its creation in 1945. He served as treasurer of the company from 1945 to 1956, and since 1956 as its president. He signed checks, contracts on behalf of the company, and notes for corporate loans in substantial amounts. Bylaws adopted in 1956 provided that the chairman of the board, G. C. McCullough, was chief executive officer, and there was evidence that G. C. McCullough was the decision maker.

The issue here in dispute is whether the record contained substantial evidence to support the government's contentions that taxpayer was a responsible person under § 6672 of the Internal Revenue Code of 1954.

On motion for directed verdict, the court should consider all the evidence —not just that evidence which supports the non-mover's case—but in the light of and with all reasonable inferences most favorable to the party opposed to the motion. If the facts and inferences point so strongly and overwhelmingly in favor of one party that the court believes that reasonable men could not arrive at a contrary verdict, granting of the motion is proper. On the other hand, if there is substantial evidence opposed to the motion, that is, evidence of such quality and weight that reasonable and fair-minded men in the exercise of impartial judgment might reach different conclusions, the motion

---

[1] 26 USCA (IRC 1954) § 6672. Failure to collect and pay over tax, or attempt to evade or defeat tax: "Any person required to collect, truthfully account for, and pay over any tax imposed by this title who willfully fails to collect such tax, or truthfully account for and pay over such tax, or willfully attempts in any manner to evade or defeat any such tax or the payment thereof, shall, in addition to other penalties provided by law, be liable to a penalty equal to the total amount of the tax evaded, or not collected, or not accounted for and paid over.''

should be denied, and the case submitted to the jury.

We are firmly of the opinion that the case at bar does not meet the test of motion for directed verdict. The evidence in the case raises inferences on which reasonable and fair-minded men in the exercise of impartial judgment might reach different conclusions. Evidence that taxpayer was an original incorporator and director, a substantial stockholder, treasurer of the company from 1945 to 1956, president of the company since 1956, and president of the company at the time of the acts or omissions complained of is evidence on which reasonable and fair-minded jurors might conclude that taxpayer was a responsible person under § 6672 of the Internal Revenue Code of 1954. It is inconsequential that exclusive control over all corporate affairs was not vested in him.

The case should have been submitted to the jury for consideration upon all the competent evidence before it.

Reversed and remanded for trial by jury.

CASE QUESTIONS

1. What test did the court employ to determine whether a directed verdict should have been granted?
2. What does this case demonstrate about the roles of judge and jury?

SUGGESTED READINGS

F. JAMES and G.C. HAZARD, CIVIL PROCEDURE §§ 7.12–7.13 2d ed. (1977).

Note, *Trial-Motion for Directed Verdict by Both Parties*, 24 ARK. L. REV. 599 (1971).

Note, *Federal Procedure—Rule 41(b)—a Dismissal with Prejudice Is Res Judicata of the Cause of Action and Operates as an Adjudication of the Merits Regardless of Whether the Merits Have Been Reached*, 49 TEXAS L. REV. 372 (1971).

Cooper, *Directions for Directed Verdicts: A Compass for Federal Courts*, 55 MINN. L. REV. 903 (1971).

Jury Verdict

Both lawyers have an opportunity to give oral statements to the jury summarizing their cases. The judge then instructs the members of the jury as to how they should proceed. Although jury deliberations are secret, certain restrictions must still be observed to avoid possible grounds for setting aside the verdict. Among these restrictions are prohibitions on misconduct on the part of the jurors, such as drunkenness; the use of unauthorized evidence, such as secretly visiting the scene of a crime; or noncompliance with instructions, such as a majority determining guilt instead of the jury reaching unanimity.

Post-Trial Motions

After the verdict has been rendered, a party not satisifed with it may move for judgment notwithstanding the verdict, a new trial, and relief from judgment. A motion for judgment notwithstanding the verdict (*judgment n.o.v.*) is granted when the judge decides that reasonable persons could not have reached the verdict that the jury has reached. A *new trial* before another jury may be granted by a judge for a variety of reasons. Excessive or grossly inadequate damages, newly discovered evidence, questionable jury verdict, errors in the production of evidence, and, simply, the interest of justice are some of the reasons for granting a new trial. A motion for *relief from judgment* is granted if the judge finds a clerical error in the judgment, newly discovered evidence, or fraud that induced the judgment.

Pike v. Roe
213 Kan. 389, 516 P.2d 972
Supreme Court of Kansas
December 8, 1973

PRAGER, JUSTICE
This is an action to recover damages for personal injuries suffered in an automobile collision. The plaintiff-appellee, Anthony C. Pike, was awarded a jury verdict in the amount of $50,000. The defendants–appellants, Hayden Roe and the Elder Catering Company, have appealed to this court.

There is no issue as to the liability of the defendants raised on this appeal. The evidence clearly justified a finding that the defendant, Hayden Roe, failed to yield the right of way at the intersection where the collision occurred. The plaintiff Pike was a passenger in the other vehicle.

The defendants' first point on this appeal is that the verdict in the amount of $50,000 is excessive and is not supported by the evidence. The defendants recognize that in order for a judgment to be set aside on the ground of an excessive verdict, it must appear that the amount of the verdict is so grossly excessive as to shock the conscience of the court. At the trial, the evidence disclosed that following the collision the plaintiff Pike, then a minor 16 years of age, was thrown out of the truck and dragged along the street a distance of 50 feet. When the vehicle in which he was riding came to rest, he was pinned between the right front wheel and the curb, having suffered a severe blow to his leg. The whole right side of his face was torn and scratched with deep abrasions. The bottom lobe of his ear was torn loose and his right leg was badly bruised. The plaintiff was taken to the Providence Hospital in Kansas City, Kansas, where x rays were obtained. He was permitted to leave the hospital in a wheelchair about four hours later. He was examined and treated by a number of doctors for a painful condition in his leg for several months. The initial injury occurred in the area of his upper thigh close to the groin. It was described as a blood hematoma with the tearing of tissue and the lymphatic channels in an area known as Scarpa's triangle. The hematoma did not disappear following the injury. As a result, the plaintiff was left with a permanent condition consisting of a doughy mass about the size of a fist in the upper leg area.

The plaintiff was 21 years old at the time of the trial, and his life expectancy was about 49 years. Although his actual medical expenses were only $368.61, he was faced with many years of pain and physical disability and the possibility of additional medical treatment. Under these factual circumstances, we are unable to say that the verdict is shocking to the conscience or wholly beyond reason. In this case, the trial judge heard the evidence, approved the verdict, and refused to grant a new trial on the ground that the verdict was excessive. We should not substitute our judgment for either that of the jury or the trial judge in arriving at an award of damages for the plaintiff.

The defendants' second point is that the trial court abused its discretion in denying the defendants' motion for a new trial on the ground of misconduct of the jury. Their claim of misconduct is based on a number of circumstances which will be briefly noted. The defendants complain that Juror Williamson failed to disclose on *voir dire* a previous accident which she had experienced as a passenger on a bus in 1965, seven years prior to the trial. For this occurrence, she received a settlement of $1750 from the bus company. There was no evidence that Mrs. Williamson mentioned this previous accident in the jury room. She testified that she did not intentionally withhold the information but simply did not think it was that important. Another juror, Mr. Whisman, failed to disclose on *voir dire* that he had calcium deposits on his knees which caused him some pain. Counsel for the defendants asked the entire panel about prior injuries they had suffered. The condition of Whisman's knees was brought about by a disease and not by injury. He merely mentioned his bad knees in the discussion in the jury room. Also, during the days of the trial, Juror Easterwood drove several times through the intersection where the collision occurred. He lives in the same general area of the intersection and customarily drove by it every day. It is clear that he did not stop at the intersection, or take measurements, or try to judge distances. He merely mentioned to the jury that he is familiar with the intersection and customarily drives through it.

The defendants complain that insurance was discussed by the jury. It was apparently brought up when a woman juror suggested that a high verdict would increase their insurance rates. All the jurors who were called to testify declared that insurance was not a factor in their verdict. There was some discussion that insurance was not a proper subject to be taken into consideration. Some brought up the question of how much the plaintiff would have to pay by way of attorney fees out of any recovery. There was no evidence that this matter had any significance in the amount of the verdict. There was some discussion that the young plaintiff might develop cancer in his leg at a later date. The three jurors who discussed the subject at the hearing on the motion for a new trial testified clearly that although the subject was mentioned, it was not a factor in their verdict. The defendants complain that the jurors discussed the possibility of the plaintiff having future medical expenses. We cannot say that this was improper, since defendants' Dr. Williams recommended surgery for removal of the mass from plaintiff's leg if the pain became worse. Finally, the defendants complain that the jury considered a $50,000 verdict in the light of plaintiff's life expectancy of 49 years, which would come to around $2 per day. Juror Whisman testified that this method was used only after the jury had already discussed a $50,000 verdict and they were simply checking on the $50,000 figure.

It appears to us that the trial court was extremely liberal in permitting defendants' counsel on the motion for a new trial to go into matters affecting the way in which the jury arrived at its verdict. Matters similar to those mentioned above quite often arise during the give-and-take conversation in a jury room. If such matters were always a basis for a new trial, few jury verdicts would stand appellate scrutiny in personal-injury cases. The trial court on motion for a new trial and this court on appeal are primarily concerned with whether or not the parties received a fair trial. It is not the misconduct of jurors alone that necessitates a new trial, but misconduct that results in prejudice to a litigant and deprives him of his right to a fair and impartial trial. The refusal or denial of a motion for a new trial for the alleged misconduct of the jury is generally within the sound discretion of the trial court, and unless it appears that this discretion has been abused, refusal to grant a new trial will not be disturbed. The trial court has an opportunity personally to see and hear all the witnesses and is in a position to observe the conduct of and interrelationship existing between litigants, counsel, and jury. It can intuitively sense the atmosphere in which the proceedings are being conducted. The trial court can thus call to its assistance experiences, observations, and occurrences which are denied to us. From the record as a whole, we cannot say that the trial court abused its discretion in refusing to grant the defendants a new trial in this case.

The judgment is affirmed.

CASE QUESTIONS

1. Why should the jury be restricted in using personal experience to persuade fellow jurors?
2. Does granting a new trial because the jury awarded excessive damages infringe the plaintiffs' constitutional right to a jury trial?

3. Does a reduction of the amount of damages by the court as a condition for denying a new trial invade the province of the jury?

4. What factors should govern a court's granting of a new trial when damages are excessive?

5. How much power does a court have in determining whether to grant a new trial because of an error in the amount of recovery or damages?

6. Should a court be empowered to grant a new trial on the ground of the inadequacy of damages?

SUGGESTED READINGS

F. JAMES and G.C. HAZARD, CIVIL PROCEDURE §§7.14–7.22 2d ed. (1977).

Note, *Post-Verdict Motions Under Rule 50: Protecting the Verdict Winner*, 53 MINN. L. REV. 358 (1968).

Note, *Civil Procedure—Judgment Non Obstante Veredicto—The Right to Move to Disregard Jury Findings Is Not Limited to the Party Against Whom the Unsupported Issues Were Found*, 49 TEXAS L. REV. 332 (1971).

Palmer, *Post-Trial Interview of Jurors in the Federal Courts—A Lawyer's Dilemma*, 6 HOUSTON L. REV. 290 (1968).

Boyd, *Current State of Jury Misconduct Claims in Texas Civil Cases*, 21 S. TEX. L.J. 23 (1980).

Judgment and Execution

A *judgment* is made by the judge, based on the finding of the jury. Judgment follows an unsuccessful motion to set aside the verdict. Either party may appeal the decision to an appellate court if dissatisfied with the judgment. In itself the judgment does no more than to state the recovery of the plaintiff against the defendant. The defendant can be punished for contempt of court by a fine, imprisonment, or both for disobeying a judgment to do or to refrain from doing something. If the judgment is for money damages and the defendant does not voluntarily pay the prescribed amount, upon application of the winning party, the court clerk issues an *execution* addressed to the sheriff. The sheriff seizes the defendant's property and sells it to pay for the judgment. In the alternative, the plaintiff may have a lien placed on the defendant's property. The statute authorizing judicial sale includes safeguards to prevent abuse of defendant's rights.

Collum v. DeLoughter
535 S.W. 2d 390
Court of Civil Appeals of Texas
March 16, 1976

CORNELIUS, JUSTICE

This suit was by Jessie DeLoughter to set aside a sale under execution. The writ of execution as issued upon a judgment obtained by S. A. Meazelle against DeLoughter for $870 plus interest, costs, and attorney's fees, all totaling $1840.10. The writ was levied on two lots in the city of Dallas. Tommy Collum, a stranger to the judgment, purchased the lots for $2000 at the sheriff's sale.

The trial court, sitting without a jury, found and concluded that: (1) the property description in the published notice of sale inverted the block designations—that is, the property was described as Lot 3, *Blk. 7183/33* (2007 Chalk Hill) and Lot 2, *Blk. 33/7183* (2015 Chalk Hill) rather than Lot 3, *Blk. 33/7183* and Lot 2, *33/7183* which was the correct description; (2) the notice mailed to DeLoughter was sent by ordinary mail, whereas registered mail was required; (3) the notice was addressed to DeLoughter at an address in Irving where he had not resided for almost a year; (4) DeLoughter was not notified personally of the sale and did not receive the written notice until nine days after the sale; and (5) the sheriff did not give DeLoughter an opportunity to designate property which he desired be levied on first, as required. It was stipulated that the actual market value of the lots was $13,500. Based on these facts and conclusions and the further fact that DeLoughter tendered into court the sum of $2000 as

restitution to Collum, the trial court entered its judgment setting aside the sale and awarding Collum the $2000 together with $350 attorney's fees and all costs.

Collum contends that the facts found by the trial court do not constitute such irregularities as authorize the sale to be avoided. He asserts that the notice required is perfected by mailing alone, and it is not necessary that the mail be registered or that the judgment debtor actually receive the notice. DeLoughter's address was not listed in the telephone directory, and the address used was that shown for him on the tax rolls of the county. The evidence was in conflict as to whether the property description in the notice of sale was sufficient to enable a person of ordinary prudence to locate the property. DeLoughter testified that had he been given an opportunity to point out property to the sheriff, he would have designated the unimproved one of the lots in question, which he contended was of sufficient value to satisfy the judgment.

An execution sale will be set aside upon proof that it was made for a grossly inadequate price and was accompanied by irregularities that tended to contribute to the inadequacy of price.

An inversion of the lot and block numbers in the notice of sale may or may not be an irregularity, depending on the adverse effect, if any, it would have on an ordinary person's ability to locate the property. Here the trial court found such inversion was an irregularity, and there is evidence to support such finding.

The failure to send the notice by registered mail was also an irregularity.

Tex. R.Civ.P. 647 requires the officer making the levy to "give the defendant . . . written notice of such sale, either in person or by *mail. . . ."* But Tex. R.Civ.P. 21a, adopted subsequent to Rule 647, provides that:

Every notice required by *these* rules . . . except as *otherwise expressly provided* in these rules . . . . may be served . . . either in person or by *registered mail. . . .* The provisions hereof relating to the method of service of notice are *cumulative of all other methods of service* prescribed by these rules.

Therefore, the specific language of Rule 21a imposes the requirement of registered mail upon the general provisions for "mail" in Rule 647.

Under the circumstances shown in this record, we have concluded that the addressing of the notice to DeLoughter at the address shown for him on the tax rolls and the fact that he was not notified personally of the sale did not constitute irregularities. But the failure of the officer to make any attempt to give DeLoughter an opportunity to designate property, as required by Tex. R.Civ.P. 637, was an irregularity.

Standing alone, none of these irregularities would be sufficient to justify setting aside the sale, but together with an inadequate price paid for the property, and the trial court's presumed finding that these irregularities were calculated to and did contribute to such inadequacy of price, they are sufficient to avoid the sale.

Moreover, it is settled that inadequacy of price, standing alone, is sufficient to justify a court of equity in setting aside the sale when the judgment debtor makes a prompt offer to make the purchaser whole by returning his investment in the property and paying all costs. There was certainly such an inadequacy of price here as to justify the application of these equitable principles. The market value of the property was stipulated to be $13,500. The price paid was $2000, which was less than 15% of that value. Although Collum contends that he actually paid $4743.04 for the property, since it had $2743.04 in tax liens and assessments against it, the stipulation agreed that the *"actual cash* market value" of the property was $13,500. Whether the encumbrances were considered in arriving at this agreed value is not shown, but when for the purposes of the trial the parties have stipulated that the actual cash market value of property is a certain amount, neither the trial court nor we can go behind that stipulation and speculate that because of other considerations the value is actually less than that stipulated. It is to be presumed that the figure is a net one; that is, that all factors affecting its value have been considered in arriving at the stipulated figure.

The sale was on October 1, 1974. Suit was filed on October 23, 1974. On November 15, 1974, DeLoughter tendered into court the price Collum paid for the property. Such a tender was consistent with the requirements in cases of this kind. The judgment awarded Collum the sum so tendered, together with attorney's fees and his costs. Under these circumstances, equity was done and the judgment should be affirmed.

It is so ordered.

CASE QUESTIONS

1. Should there be a requirement that sheriff's sales be public competitive events?

2. Suppose that a judgment creditor has a judgment against a debtor for $1000, and the debtor owns 100 acres of land worth $200 an acre. Should the sheriff be allowed to sell all 100 acres, giving $1000 to the judgment creditor and $19,000 to the debtor? Suppose that the only property the debtor owned was a car worth $5000. How should the sheriff dispose of the property?

SUGGESTED READINGS

Gordon, *Action on a Judgment Under Appeal*, 84 L.Q. REV. 318 (1968).

Palmer, *Admissibility of Judgments in Subsequent Proceedings*, 3 N.Z.U.L. REV. 142 (1968).

Note, *Confessions of Judgment: The Due Process Defects*, 43 TEMP. L.Q. 279 (1970).

Note, *Federal Rule 60(b): Finality of Civil Judgments v. Self-Correction by District Court of Judicial Error of Law*, 43 NOTRE DAME LAWYER 98 (1967).

Note, *Acceptance of Additur under Protest*, 22 LOYOLA L. REV. 846 (1976).

Hudspeth, *Judgment Liens and Abstracts of Judgment in Texas*, 32 TEX. B.J. 520 (1969).

Dobbs, *Validation of Void Judgments: The Bootstrap Principle*, 53 VA. L. REV. 1003, 1241 (1967).

Note, *Additur and Remittitur in Federal and State Courts: An Anomaly?* 3 CUMBER.-SAM. L. REV. 150 (1972).

Ager, *Problem: The Effect on the Surety of a Judgment Against the Principal Solution: The Due Process Clause*, 36 INS. COUNSEL J. 245 (1969).

Chapter Questions

1. Define the following terms:

a. answer	b. contempt
c. counterclaim	d. default
e. deposition	f. directed verdict
g. discovery	h. execution
i. general verdict	j. hearsay evidence

k. interrogatories   l. issue
m. lien   n. petition
o. pleading   p. prayer
q. pretrial conference   r. privilege
s. process   t. *res gestae*
u. respondent   v. special verdict
w. *subpoena*   x. summary judgment

2. Robert Wilkinson was a resident of California and an officer of the now defunct St. Paul Transportation Co. In June, Wilkinson was served in California with a criminal summons from a Minnesota court for a misdemeanor allegedly committed when Wilkinson was in Minnesota. The arraignment for the misdemeanor charge was scheduled for September 25. Wilkinson flew to Minnesota to attend the arraignment. As he ascended the courthouse steps, a United States marshal approached him and handed him a summons to appear in a civil action brought against him by the Interstate Commerce Commission for activities involving the St. Paul Transportation Co. Consider policy questions arising from Wilkinson's appearance in response to the criminal summons. Was the service of summons and complaint on Wilkinson sufficient to give the Minnesota court jurisdiction in the civil action?

   I.C.C. v. St. Paul Transportation Co., 39 F.R.D. 309 (D.C. Minn. 1966)

3. A car driven by James Murphy struck a boy, Thomas Ball, and injured him. Immediately after the accident, according to Ball's mother, Murphy "told me that he was sorry, that he hoped my son wasn't hurt. He had to call on a customer and was in a bit of a hurry to get home." At trial, Murphy denied telling Ball that he was involved in his employment at the time of the accident. It was shown, however, that part of his normal duties for his employer, Murphy Auto Parts Co., included making calls on customers in his car. Can Ball have the statement admitted in court as a spontaneous exclamation?

   Murphy Auto Parts Co. v. Ball, 249 F. 2d 508 (1957)

4. On June 30, 1961, Trans World Airlines, Inc., filed a complaint against Toolco in federal court alleging that Toolco was guilty of various anti-trust violations arising from the period when Toolco controlled T.W.A.'s management decisions. Jurisdiction over Toolco was properly obtained and plaintiff commenced discovery proceedings. Howard Hughes has at all times been the sole owner of Toolco and the guiding light in all transactions between Toolco and T.W.A. On February 7, 1963, the court ordered a deposition to be taken from Howard Hughes on February 11, 1963, under the Federal Rules of Civil Procedure. Toolco and Hughes advised the court that they had

made a decision not to attend the deposition. Hughes did not attend the deposition, and a default judgment for $145 million was rendered against Hughes and Toolco, including treble damages under the Antitrust Act. Would such a drastic remedy be proper?

T.W.A. v. Hughes Tool Co., 308 F. Supp. 679 (S.D.N.Y. 1969), aff'd, 449 F.2d 51 (2d Cir. 1971)

5. James Duke filed a suit against Pacific Telephone and Telegraph Company and two of its employees for invasion of privacy through unauthorized wiretapping. Duke claimed that defendant's employees installed an interception device on his telephone line without his knowledge or consent for the sole purpose of eavesdropping. Through the use of the bugging devices, defendants acquired information that they communicated to the police department, resulting in his arrest. Although the charges were dismissed, he was discharged from his job. As part of the plaintiff's discovery, oral depositions were taken of the employees. The defendants refused to answer: (1) questions relating to the procedure used in making unauthorized tapes of phone conversations (training of personnel, equipment, authority among employees), (2) questions relating to the deponent's knowledge of the illegality of unauthorized monitoring, (3) questions relating to a possible working relationship between the police and PT&T, and (4) questions relating to the monitoring of telephone conversations of subscribers other than the plaintiff. The defendants claimed that these questions were irrelevant to the litigation and therefore not proper matters for discovery. Do you agree?

Pacific T & T Co. v. Superior Court, 2 Cal.3d 161, 465 P.2d 854, 84 Cal. Rptr. 718 (1970)

6. A doctor testified in a personal-injury case that the plaintiff had become 20% disabled as a result of a back injury. However, during jury deliberations, one of the jurors said that it had been his experience that employers are very reluctant to hire people with a history of back trouble, and that therefore the plaintiff might never get a job at all. Should a juror be permitted to make such statements to fellow jurors during their deliberations?

Texas Employers' Insurance Association v. Price, 336 S.W.2d 304 (Texas 1960)

7. W. R. Reeves filed suit under the Federal Employers Liability Act against his employer, Central of Georgia Railway Co., seeking damages he allegedly suffered when the train on which he was working derailed near Griffin, Georgia. The liability of the defendant railroad was established at trial, and the issue of damages remained to be fixed. Several physicians testified regarding the injuries received by Reeves. Reeves also testified. On the witness stand, he said that an examining physician had told him that he would be unable to work be-

cause of a weakness in his right arm, a dead place on his arm, stiffness in his neck, and nerve trouble in his back. Why did admission of this testimony into evidence constitute reversible error?

Central of Georgia Ry. Co. v. Reeves, 257 So.2d 839 (Ga. 1972)

8. William Cothey was driving west on Brookpark Road at a speed of 25 to 35 miles per hour in a 35-mile-per-hour zone. A truck driven by an employee of the Jones-Lemley Trucking Co. started to turn left across the road into the driveway of the Clifton Concrete Co., and the right front of Cothey's car struck the right side of the Jones-Lemley truck. The point of impact was on Cothey's side of the road, 7 feet north of the double yellow line and 15 feet south of the north curb line and driveway entrance. Cothey is suing Jones-Lemley on a negligence theory for injuries sustained in the collision. Ohio law imposes a duty on a motorist to operate his vehicle as would a reasonably prudent person under the circumstances. At the close of plaintiff's evidence, as summarized above, is Jones-Lemley entitled to a directed verdict that it was not negligent?

Cothey v. Jones-Lemley Trucking Co., 176 Ohio St. 342 (1964)

9. Lemmie Branch sued Ben Bullock for negligence after a metal sign affixed to the front of Bullock's store broke loose and fell on Branch as he walked down the sidewalk. Evidence was introduced, and the lawyers went into their final argument. Before a jury, Branch's attorney argued, "What would I have to pay to inflict a half-inch cut into your skull, to render you unconscious, to put you home in bed for a week, to force you to use a cane or crutches for the balance of your life with your walk affected, with your speech affected, with your handwriting affected? What do you think it's worth? The older you grow, the more precious and sweeter life becomes. How much would you sell me a year of your life for?" Was this argument improper? Why? Is Bullock entitled to a new trial?

Bullock v. Branch, 130 So.2d 74 (Fla. 1961)

10. Smith brought a suit against Bryant for trespassing on her property and for maliciously cutting down growing crops. Bryant's lawyer filed an answer to the complaint, but withdrew from the case on the day set for trial, because of nonpayment of his fee. The judge granted a continuance until the next morning. In the morning following the day her counsel resigned, Bryant defended her case without the assistance of a lawyer, and lost the dispute. Was Bryant's lawyer at liberty to abandon her case? Is Bryant entitled to a new trial?

Smith v. Bryant, 264 N.C. 208, 141 S.E.2d 303 (1965)

11. On December 10, 1962, Rosch obtained a judgment against Kelly in the superior court of Orange County, California. The California Code

permits execution of a judgment only within 10 years after entry of a judgment. If this is not done, the judgment may be enforced only by leave of court, after notice to the judgment debtors, accompanied by an affidavit setting forth the reasons for the failure to proceed earlier. The plaintiff made no attempt to enforce the judgment in California before Kelly moved to Texas in 1970. On February 15, 1974, the plaintiff attempted to execute on the California judgment in Texas. Does the Texas court have to allow execution under the full-faith-and-credit clause?

Rosch v. Kelly, 527 F.2d 871 (5th Cir. 1976)

Criminal Procedure VII

A crime is an offense against a sovereignty. An act is not a crime unless it has been made so by a statute or by common law. In many jurisdictions, there are no common-law crimes. There are no common-law crimes against the United States.

The objective of criminal law is to regulate the conduct of individuals in order to maintain public order. Criminal law provides punishment for those who deviate from the defined social norms, as well as protection for society from the consequences of antisocial behavior. The preservation of the integrity of the community is of paramount importance in determining what conduct is antisocial.

Crimes traditionally have been classified as treason, felonies, and misdemeanors. Whether a crime is considered to be a felony or a misdemeanor depends on the character of the punishment prescribed for it, not on the nature of the act. Offenses punishable by death or by imprisonment in a state penitentiary are *felonies*. All others, including those that are punishable by imprisonment in a county jail, are *misdemeanors*. Less serious misdemeanors are often referred to as *petty offenses*.

Criminal procedure is that area of the law that deals with the judicial process in criminal cases. It is concerned with the administration of criminal justice, from the initial investigation of a crime and the arrest of a suspect through trial, sentence, and release. The goal of criminal justice is to protect society from antisocial activity without sacrificing individual rights, justice, and fair play.

The court umpires the confrontation between the interests of society and the rights of the accused. The judge and jury determine the guilt or innocence of the accused by evaluating facts properly presented in open court. Ideally, the truth emerges from an adversary proceeding conducted

General View of the Criminal Justice System

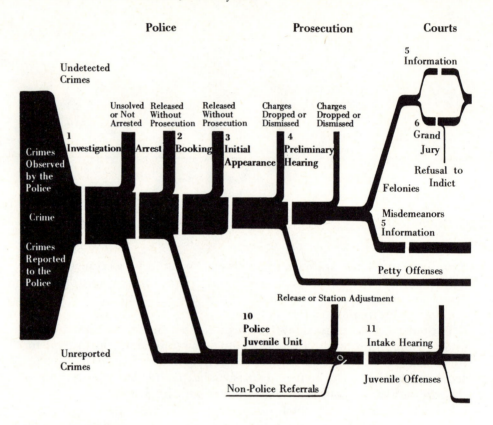

A simple yet comprehensive view of the movement of cases through the criminal justice system. Procedures in individual jurisdictions may vary from pattern shown here. Differing weights of lines indicate relative volumes of cases disposed of at various points in system, but this is only suggestive, since no nationwide data of the sort exists. Source: *The Challenge of Crime in a Free Society*, The President's Commission on Law Enforcement and Administration of Justice (Washington, D.C. 1967).

1 May continue until trial.

2 Administrative record of arrest. First step of which, temporary release on bail, may be available.

3 Before magistrate, commissioner, or justice of peace. Formal notice of charge, advice of rights. Bail set. Summary trials for petty offenses usually conducted here without further processing.

4 Preliminary testing of evidence against defendant. Charge may be reduced. No separate preliminary hearing for misdemeanors in some systems.

5 Charge filed by prosecutor on basis of information submitted by police or citizens. Alternative to grand jury indictment; often used in felonies, almost always in misdemeanors.

Corrections

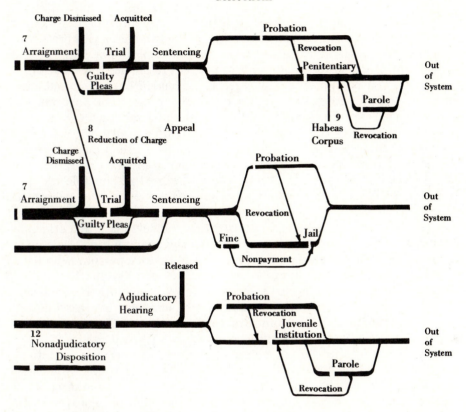

6   Reviews whether Government evidence sufficient to justify trial. Some States have no grand jury system; others seldom use it.

7   Appearance for plea; defendant elects trial by judge or jury (if available); counsel for indigent usually appointed here in felonies. Often not at all in other cases.

8   Charge may be reduced at any time prior to trial in return for plea of guilty or for other reasons.

9   Challenge on constitutional grounds to legality of detention. May be sought at any point in process.

10   Police often hold informal hearings, dismiss or adjust many cases without further processing.

11   Probation officer decides desirability of further court action.

12   Welfare agency, social services, counseling, medical care, etc. for cases where adjudicatory handling not needed.

in a manner consistent with constitutional guarantees. The due-process guarantee of the Fifth and Fourteenth Amendments requires reasonable notice of the charges and an adequate opportunity to defend oneself at a fair hearing before a competent and impartial tribunal. The guarantee applies whether the crime charged is a felony or misdemeanor.

It is a fundamental principle of criminal procedure that one is presumed to be innocent until proved guilty beyond a reasonable doubt. The purpose of this principle is not to protect the guilty, but to prevent the conviction of one who may be innocent. The prosecution has the burden of producing evidence and proving guilt beyond a reasonable doubt. The presumption of innocence is not specifically guaranteed by the Constitution, yet it has remained unchallenged by the courts of the United States.

One of the knottiest problems that bothers the criminal justice system is whether a person who is thought to have lacked mental capacity at the time of the commission of a crime should be held responsible for that crime. The 1982 verdict in the trial of John Hinckley for the attempted assassination of President Reagan made this issue a subject for national concern. The so-called M'Naghten rule (that the defendant in a criminal trial was "too mentally unbalanced to know right from wrong") seems in the last few decades to have been extended to include persons who have either a mental disease or a temporary mental defect. Psychiatrists called on to testify at a criminal trial seldom agree with each other's analyses, yet psychiatric testimony often results in light sentences being meted out to persons who have clearly committed heinous crimes. There appears to be a disproportion between a crime and society's response to it.

The integrity of the judicial system must prevail. Thus criminals must occasionally be freed when their constitutional guarantees have been abrogated at some step in the criminal justice process. The guarantees that deal with criminal procedure are defined primarily in the Fourth, Fifth, Sixth, Eighth, and Fourteenth Amendments to the Constitution. They are delineated in general language, the practical meaning of which is interpreted by the courts. In the 1960s, the trend of the Supreme Court was an expansive one, tending to increase the scope of the rights of persons accused of crimes.

QUESTIONS ON THE CHART

1. The chart on pages 284–285 shows the criminal justice system as a continuum. Can the system be more accurately characterized as a disharmony?
2. As illustrated by the chart, does the criminal justice system seem replete with discretion? If so, why does it?

Proceedings Prior to Trial

Custodial Interrogation

In order to perform the function of gathering information concerning crimes, police officers conduct investigations. Part of the criminal investigation procedure involves the questioning of suspects with the aim of obtaining confessions and disclosures of crimes. The conduct of the police must not be offensive to the common decency of civilized society, nor may it violate any constitutional right. Any inhumane treatment by a law-enforcement officer violates an accused's right of due process, regardless of whether the party is considered to be in custody.

The privilege against self-incrimination applies to questioning outside the courtroom as well as at the trial. Any statement made during police investigation must be made voluntarily. A torture chamber may not replace the witness stand and its procedural safeguards. A pretrial confession is never admissible during the trial if it was not given voluntarily. Requiring that statements be the product of free and rational choice helps prevent convictions based on unreliable evidence.

An accused has a constitutional right to the assistance of counsel, which is guaranteed by the due-process clause. The right applies to in-custody interrogation and to pretrial proceedings, as well as during the trial. Except for very minor criminal charges, an indigent is entitled to be represented by court-appointed counsel.

In addition to the requirement that a statement be voluntary, the Supreme Court, in the case of *Miranda v. Arizona*, 384 U.S. 436 (1966), required that certain warnings be made in a custodial interrogation. The Court held that persons being interrogated in custody must first be informed in clear and unequivocal language that (1) they have the right to remain silent, (2) anything said can and will be used against them in court, (3) they have the right to consult with a lawyer and to have a lawyer with them during the interrogation, and (4) they have the right to an appointed lawyer to represent them if they are indigent. The failure to make these warnings violates the accused's Fifth Amendment privilege against self-incrimination.

The protections afforded by the *Miranda* warnings may be waived in certain circumstances. The standard to be used is whether defendants in fact knowingly and voluntarily waived their rights. For the waiver to be effective, the court must be able to find an intelligent and understanding rejection.

South Dakota v. Long
465 F.2d 65
United States Court of Appeals
Eighth Circuit
August 24, 1972

Ross, Circuit Judge

The state of South Dakota has appealed from a judgment entered by the United States District Court, 336 F. Supp. 1360, granting writs of *habeas corpus* to Hale, Long, and Tisdale on the grounds that their confessions were illegally obtained. We affirm the judgment as to Long, but reverse as to Hale and Tisdale.

On March 11, 1968, the cabin of Forrest A. Koos, located in Spearfish Canyon near Spearfish, South Dakota, was broken into. A portable television and other personal property were taken. The next day, the sheriff of Lawrence County, Richard McGrath, investigated the break-in and observed tire tracks of a compact car, together with footprints which appeared to be made by "football or track shoes" near the scene. Based on another lead, the sheriff advised acquaintances in the canyon to be on the lookout for a red Volkswagen with Iowa plates, county number 77.

The following day, March 13, Bell, a part-time deputy who ran a filling station near the canyon, called the sheriff and told him that he had just filled the gas tank of a red Volkswagen, with 77 county Iowa plates, that the car contained three youths, and that it was heading into the canyon. The sheriff radioed two of his deputies in the canyon to intercept the car and bring the boys into Spearfish so that he could talk to them. Long, Tisdale, and another youth named Johnson were in Long's Volkswagen when it was stopped. Long testified that after they were stopped, a deputy said, "We want to look in your car." When asked, "What for?" the deputy replied, "Because the sheriff wants us to search it." After the search, the three were told the sheriff wanted to talk to them, and they followed the deputies to the Spearfish Police Department. The car was again searched with Long's "consent," but the youths were not advised of their rights.

Because Long had to have his wrestling-team picture taken at that time, the sheriff had Deputy Palmer, who was in plainclothes, accompany him. The sheriff testified that he did not know why he failed to allow Long to go alone. Meanwhile, the sheriff accompanied Tisdale to the college which all the defendants attended, and, with Tisdale's permission, searched his dormitory room. No warnings were given Tisdale at that time, but no incriminating statements were made. Upon Long's return, with the deputy, from the picture-taking session, the sheriff, with Long's permission, searched his room. In it he found a raincoat of the type taken from another cabin and some soccer shoes that had been wet. At that time the sheriff was certain Long was a "suspect." Then, the sheriff and Deputy Palmer sat down with Long in his room and talked for 30 to 45 minutes. The door was closed, although people kept opening it and looking in.

The sheriff used a fatherlike approach and gained Long's friendship. As the sheriff acknowledged, he developed a "mutual trusting relationship" which continued throughout the remaining prearrest transactions. When Long decided to admit his part in the break-in, he was told by the sheriff that he did not have to say anything and that he had a right to an attorney. Deputy Palmer testified that the sheriff told Long, ''You don't have to tell me a thing, and anything you tell me I'd have to use against you.'' However, it is undisputed that the sheriff did not advise Long of his right to have an attorney appointed if indigent, or that he had a right to stop talking any time he wished.

Long testified that he did not reveal the identity of the other individuals involved in the break-in at that first interrogation because he wanted to talk it over with them first. Long also testified that the sheriff told him: ''We know a few things you don't think we know. We have a card up our sleeves.'' At the conclusion of the meeting, the sheriff told Long to bring the others involved, together with the stolen goods, to his office in Deadwood the following day. The sheriff and Deputy Palmer then left.

All three defendants went to the sheriff's office the following afternoon, March 14, on their own volition, with the stolen TV and other articles. The sheriff did not advise them of their rights at this time. Long claims he asked the sheriff if they should call an attorney, but that the sheriff replied, ''Boys, I just can't tell you.'' The sheriff could not remember saying that or whether Long asked the question. Long further claims it appeared to the three defendants that things would be worse for them if they refused to make the statements, and that it would be better for them if they threw themselves on the mercy of the sheriff and the court.

After talking to the defendants, the sheriff handed each of them a statement form, at the top of which was a list of their rights and an acknowledgment, which each defendant signed, that those rights had been explained to them. Below this explanation of their rights and signature, the defendants wrote out their statements themselves as the sheriff had told them to do. The sheriff testified that he did not know whether they read the top of the forms or not. Long admitted that he read the rights listed at the top of the form, but claimed he did not understand the legal consequences of those warnings. Although the statements were signed at the top, after the warnings, they were not signed at the end. After writing out their statements, the three defendants returned to the college.

At the trial, Mr. Hoggatt, the state's attorney, examined the sheriff as to the contents of the statements. The court overruled objections thereto, stating that the statements were being used only as memoranda to refresh the witness's recollection. The judge also found the statements to have been made by compulsion of conscience rather than any coercion on the part of Sheriff McGrath. All three defendants testified and admitted their part in the burglary, but only after the sheriff had been permitted to testify concerning the confessions obtained from them.

Prior to a determination of whether the warnings given were adequate, we must determine whether there existed a custodial interrogation as contemplated by *Miranda v. Arizona*, 384 U.S. 436, 444 (1966). By ''custodial interrogation,'' we mean questioning initiated by law-enforcement officers after a person has been taken into custody or otherwise deprived of his freedom of action in any significant way. The Court, in *Miranda*, did not note that all the cases involved there shared a salient feature—incommunicado interrogation of individuals in police-dominated atmosphere, resulting in self-incriminating statements without full warnings of constitutional rights.

The Supreme Court has held, of course, that a custodial situation need not be strictly limited to a police station. On the other hand, a general on-the-scene or other noncoercive questioning conducted in the course of routine investigation is not encompassed by *Miranda*. With this in mind, we now examine the two occasions during which the damaging admissions were elicited.

Long was the only one who made admissions at the dormitory. Although Tisdale had been questioned, he admitted nothing at this time. The chain of events leading up to Long's admission in his dormitory room was as follows: Long's car was stopped and searched in the canyon. He was told that the sheriff wanted to talk to the occupants and that they were to follow the deputies to Spearfish. At the Spearfish Police Station, the car was again searched, this time by the sheriff. The sheriff had Deputy Palmer remain with Long while he went to have his picture taken and then accompany him back to his room. Upon their return to the dormitory, the sheriff asked Long if he could search the room. The sheriff admitted that at least by the time he saw the raincoat and the shoes he felt Long was a "suspect." The sheriff and Deputy Palmer then sat down with Long in

his room, with the door closed, and talked. Thus, from the time they were stopped in the canyon until the admissions were made later in the room, Long was continuously accompanied by or in the presence of the sheriff or one of his deputies or both. This certainly was a significant deprivation of Long's freedom of action. He could have reasonably believed that he was in custody, particularly when the sheriff insisted on a deputy accompanying him to have his picture taken.

Because of this custodial setting, Long should have been afforded a complete and meaningful statement of his constitutional rights. At most, Long was told he didn't have to say anything and that he could have a lawyer. This was a once-stated offering without further admonishment that he could stop talking at any time, that he had the right to have counsel present, and that he could have a court-appointed counsel if he could not afford to retain counsel.

It is the substance of the warnings, not the form, that is important. The warnings given must be complete and meaningful to the accused. The warnings were inadequate where the accused, although advised he had the right to an attorney, was not advised that he had the right to the presence of an attorney and that, if he could not afford one, a lawyer could be appointed to represent him *prior to any questioning*.

A warning that the indigent may have counsel appointed need not be given to a person who is known to have an attorney or is known to have ample funds to secure one.

In this case, the state argues that no prejudice resulted because the defendants were all able to retain counsel. But that is an *ex post facto* determination that does not justify the failure to advise the defendants of their rights if indigent. Here, Long, a college student, could not necessarily have been expected to have adequate funds for retention of counsel. More importantly, although we do not know his or his family's financial situation, Long may not at the time have known whether he was capable of retaining an attorney, or whether it was advantageous to try, especially since he was not fully apprised of the seriousness or consequences of the charge. We conclude, therefore, that the federal trial court was correct in its determination that the statement given by Long was the result of in-custody interrogation without adequate warnings as prescribed by *Miranda*, and that the admissions made by Long to the sheriff in his dormitory room should not have been received in evidence at the trial.

When the sheriff left the defendants' dormitory rooms, any custody there may have been terminated. Whatever psychological force compelled the defendants to go to the sheriff's office with the stolen articles the next day was not the type of coercion contemplated in *Miranda*. Because the defendants arrived at the sheriff's office voluntarily, and, according to Long's testimony, were not guarded or told they could not leave, they were not in custody. Warnings required by *Miranda* are, of course, inapplicable to noncustodial interrogations. For this reason, we conclude that these statements were not elicited under constitutionally impermissible circumstances, and the sheriff was properly allowed to testify as to the confessions of Hale and Tisdale.

The judgment is affirmed as to Long. The judgment as to Hale and Tisdale is reversed, with directions to enter judgment dismissing their petitions.

CASE QUESTIONS

1. Hale's and Tisdale's statements were held admissible in spite of the fact that their statements were made at the police station and there was some question as to whether the *Miranda* warnings were given to them. Long's statement was held inadmissible, even though he made it in his dormitory room. Why was Long's statement not admissible? Why were the statements by Hale and Tisdale admissible?

2. Assume that Hale and Tisdale were not free to leave the sheriff's office at the time they made their statements, that they were not given the *Miranda* warnings, and that they voluntarily made statements. Would their statements be admissible?

3. How did the court determine that the statements by Hale and Tisdale were voluntarily given?

SUGGESTED READINGS

Friendly, *The Fifth Amendment Tomorrow: The Case for Constitutional Change*, 37 CIN. L. REV. 671 (1968).

L.W. LEVY, ORIGINS OF THE FIFTH AMENDMENT—THE RIGHT AGAINST SELF-INCRIMINATION (1968).

Driver, *Confessions and the Social Psychology of Coercion*, 82 HARV. L. REV. 42 (1968).

Branson, *When Is a Confession Not a Confession?* 12 CRIM. L.Q. 133 (1970).

Vogel, *Duress: An Affirmative Defense to Criminal Prosecution*, 29 JAG. J. 85 (1976).

Note, *Criminal Procedure—Miranda Interrogations—Interrogation Defined as Express Questioning or Its Functional Equivalent*, 85 DICK. L. REV. 361 (1981).

Lineups

The police conduct lineups before witnesses for the purpose of identifying a suspect. When formal charges are pending, an accused may not be put in a lineup before witnesses for identification unless the accused and accused's counsel have been notified in advance. The lineup may not be conducted unless counsel is present. These procedures are required by the right of confrontation and the right to counsel contained in the Sixth Amendment. If identification in a lineup without counsel when formal charges are pending were permissible, counsel would be deprived of the right to effectively attack the identifying witnesses' credibility.

Arrest

An arrest occurs when an officer takes someone into custody for the purpose of holding the person to answer a criminal charge. The arrest must be effected in a reasonable manner. The force employed must be in proportion to the circumstances and conduct of the party being arrested. The arresting officer is justified in the use of only that force believed necessary to accomplish the arrest and to protect the officer and others.

An arrest for the commission of a crime may be made with or without a warrant. Most arrests are made without a warrant and are authorized if an officer of the law has reasonable grounds or probable cause to believe that the arrestee has committed or is committing a crime. The officer does not have to be an eyewitness to the crime, so long as there is probable cause, the well-grounded belief that the party being arrested has committed an offense.

If an arrest is made with a warrant, a police officer files a written complaint under oath with a judge, alleging that a person has committed a crime. If the judge issues a warrant for the arrest of the accused, the police officer makes the arrest by serving the warrant. Following the arrest, the accused is taken to a police station or jail for booking and the recording of charges.

An arrest warrant is an order issued by a court commanding the arresting officer to take an individual into custody and to bring the person before the court to answer criminal charges. The Fourth Amendment of the Constitution provides that ''no warrants shall issue, but upon probable cause, supported by oath or affirmation.'' Before the court will issue a warrant, a written complaint containing the name of the accused, or a description of the accused, must be filed. The complaint must be supported by affidavits and contain a description of the offense and the surrounding circumstances. A warrant is then issued if the magistrate of the court decides that the evidence supports the belief that probable cause exists that a crime has been committed.

When the complaining party does not have firsthand information and relies on hearsay, the court issues the warrant if there is substantial basis for crediting it.

Michigan v. DeFillippo
443 U.S. 31
United States Supreme Court
June 25, 1979

Mr. Chief Justice Burger
The question presented by this case is whether an arrest made in good-faith reliance on an ordinance, which at the time had not been declared unconstitutional, is valid regardless of a subsequent judicial determination of its unconstitutionality. We decide that the arrest is valid.

At approximately 10 P.M. on September 14, 1976, Detroit police officers on duty in a patrol car received a radio call to investigate two persons reportedly appearing to be intoxicated in an alley. When they arrived at the alley, they found respondent and a young woman. The woman was in the process of lowering her slacks. One of the officers asked what they were doing, and the woman replied that she was about to relieve herself. The officer then asked respondent for identification. Respondent asserted that he was Sergeant Mash, of the Detroit Police Department. He also purported to give his badge number, but the officer was unable to hear it. When respondent again was asked for identification, he changed his answer and said either that he worked for or that he knew Sergeant Mash. Respondent did not appear to be intoxicated.

Section 39–1–52.3 of the Code of the City of Detroit provides that a police officer may stop and question an individual if he has reasonable cause to believe that the individual's behavior warrants further investigation for criminal activity. It should be unlawful for any person stopped pursuant thereto to refuse to identify himself and produce evidence of his identity.

When he failed to identify himself, respondent was taken into custody for violation of § 39–1–52.3. He was searched by one of the officers, who found a package of marijuana in one of respondent's shirt pockets, and a tinfoil packet secreted inside a cigarette package in the other. The tinfoil packet subsequently was opened at the station. An analysis established that it contained phencyclidine, another controlled substance.

Respondent was charged with possession of the controlled substance phencyclidine. At the preliminary examination, he moved to suppress the evidence obtained in the search following the arrest. The trial court denied the motion. The Michigan Court of Appeals allowed an interlocutory appeal and reversed. It held that the Detroit ordinance, § 39–1–52.3, was unconstitutionally vague, and concluded that since respondent had been arrested pursuant to that ordinance, both the arrest and the search were invalid. The Michigan Supreme Court denied leave to appeal. We granted *certiorari*.

Respondent was not charged with or tried for violation of the Detroit ordinance. The state contends that because of the violation of the ordinance, that is, refusal to identify himself, which respondent committed in the presence of the officers, respondent was subject to a valid arrest. The search that followed being incidental to that arrest,

the state argues that it was equally valid, and that the drugs found should not have been suppressed. Respondent contends that since the ordinance which he was arrested for violating has been found unconstitutionally vague on its face, the arrest and search were invalid as violative of his rights under the Fourth and Fourteenth Amendments. Accordingly, he contends the drugs found in the search were correctly suppressed.

It is not disputed that the Constitution permits an officer to arrest a suspect without a warrant if there is probable cause to believe that the suspect has committed or is committing an offense. The validity of the arrest does not depend on whether the suspect actually committed a crime. The mere fact that the suspect is later acquitted of the offense for which he is arrested is irrelevant to the validity of the arrest. We have made clear that the kinds and degree of proof and the procedural requirements necessary for a conviction are not prerequisites to a valid arrest.

When the officer arrested respondent, he had abundant probable cause to believe that respondent's conduct violated the terms of the ordinance. The ordinance provides that a person commits an offense if (a) an officer has reasonable cause to believe that a given behavior warrants further investigation, (b) the officer stops him, and (c) the suspect refuses to identify himself. The offense is then complete.

Respondent's presence with a woman in the circumstances described in an alley at 10 P.M. was clearly, in the words of the ordinance, "behavior . . . warrant(ing) further investigation." Respondent's inconsistent and evasive responses to the officer's request that he identify himself, stating first that he was Sergeant Mash of the Detroit Police Department and then that he worked for or knew Sergeant Mash, constituted a refusal by respondent to identify himself as the ordinance required. Assuming, *arguendo*, that a person may not constitutionally be required to answer questions put by an officer in some circumstances, the false identification violated the plain language of the Detroit ordinance.

The remaining question, then, is whether, in these circumstances, it can be said that the officer lacked probable cause to believe that the conduct he observed and the words spoken constituted a violation of law simply because he should have known the ordinance was invalid and would be judicially declared unconstitutional. The answer is clearly negative.

This Court repeatedly has explained that "probable cause" to justify an arrest means facts and circumstances within the officer's knowledge that are sufficient to warrant a prudent person, or one of reasonable caution, to believe in the circumstances shown, that the suspect has committed, is committing, or is about to commit an offense.

On this record there was abundant probable cause to satisfy the constitutional prerequisite for an arrest. At that time, of course, there was no controlling precedent that this ordinance was or was not constitutional, and hence the conduct observed violated a presumptively valid ordinance. A prudent officer, in the course of determining whether respondent had committed an offense under all the circumstances shown by this record, should not have

been required to anticipate that a court would later hold the ordinance unconstitutional.

Police are charged to enforce laws until and unless they are declared unconstitutional. The enactment of a law forecloses speculation by enforcement officers concerning its constitutionality—with the possible exception of a law so grossly and flagrantly unconstitutional that any person of reasonable prudence would be bound to see its flaws. Society would be ill served if its police officers took it upon themselves to determine which laws are and which are not constitutionally entitled to enforcement.

Once respondent refused to identify himself as the presumptively valid ordinance required, the officer had probable cause to believe respondent was committing an offense in his presence, and Michigan's general arrest statute authorized the arrest of respondent, independent of the ordinance. The search which followed was valid because it was incidental to that arrest. The ordinance is relevant to the validity of the arrest and search only as it pertains to the "facts and circumstances" that we hold constituted probable cause for arrest.

The subsequently determined invalidity of the Detroit ordinance on vagueness grounds does not undermine the validity of the arrest made for violation of that ordinance, and the evidence discovered in the search of respondent should not have been suppressed. Accordingly, the case is remanded for further proceedings not inconsistent with this opinion.

Reversed and remanded

CASE QUESTIONS

1. What were the state's arguments for using the drug evidence? How did respondent answer these arguments?
2. What is the Court's definition of *probable cause*?
3. When the court was determining the validity of the arrest and search, why did it not matter that the ordinance had been declared unconstitutional?

SUGGESTED READINGS

Note, *Criminal Law—Sixth Amendment—Photographing Nonaccused Suspects and the Right to Counsel at Photographic Identifications*, 7 WAKE FOREST L. REV. 333 (1971).
Cook, *Probable Cause to Arrest*, 24 VAND. L. REV. 317 (1971).
Note, *Right to Resist an Unlawful Arrest*, 31 LA. L. REV. 120 (1970).
Cook, *Varieties of Detention and the Fourth Amendment*, 23 ALA. L. REV. 287 (1971).
Note, *Use of Deadly Force in the Arrest Process*, 31 LA. L. REV. 131 (1970).

Searches and Seizures

Examinations of one's person or premises are conducted by officers of the law in order to find stolen property or other evidence of guilt to be used by the prosecutor in a criminal action. The officer conducting the search must execute it in a reasonable manner. It must be conducted with common sense and in a civilized manner and must not be offensive to one's sense of justice. With some exceptions, discussed below, a warrant must be obtained by an officer before making a search.

The Fourth Amendment provides that: "no warrants shall issue, but upon probable cause . . . and particularly describing the place to be searched, and the persons or things to be seized." A search warrant will be issued by the court upon the establishment of probable cause. As in the case of an arrest warrant, probable cause is determined by the magistrate from a written complaint supported by oath or affirmation, filed by one who has personal knowledge or reliable information concerning items to be seized. If a warrant is not specific and not sufficiently descriptive, it is invalid and unconstitutional as an exploratory or general warrant. The officer conducting the search cannot go outside the limits set by the warrant. With the exception of some jurisdictions that allow "no-knock"

Search warrant [FRCrP 41(c)]

SEARCH WARRANT

To __1_____ *[specify official or officials authorized to execute warrant]:*

　　Affidavit having been made before me by __2_____ *[affiant]* that he has reason to believe that on the __3_____ [person of *or* premises known as] __4_____ *[state name of suspect or specify exact address, including apartment or room number, if any, and give description of premises],* in the City of __5_____, State of __6_____, in the __7_____ District of __8_____, there is now being concealed certain property, namely, __9_____ *[specify, such as:* certain dies, hubs, molds and plates, fitted and intended to be used for the manufacture of counterfeit coins of the United States, in violation of __10_____ *(cite statute)],* and as I am satisfied that there is probable cause to believe that the property so described is being concealed on the __11_____ [person *or* premises] above __12_____ [named *or* described], and that grounds for issuance of a search warrant exist,

　　You are hereby commanded to search within __13_____ [ten] days from this date the __14_____ [person *or* place] named for the property specified, serving this warrant and making the search __15_____ [in the daytime *or* at any time in the day or night], and if the property be found there to seize it, leaving a copy of this warrant and a receipt for the property taken, and prepare a written inventory of the property seized, and promptly return this warrant and bring the property before me, as required by law.

Dated __16_____, 19__17__.

　　　　　　　　　　　　　　　　　　　　　　[Signature and title]

---

warrants, the officer must give notice of the search before entering by force. All items seized are to be delivered to the judge issuing the warrant.

　　A person may legally permit a law-enforcement officer to perform a search without a warrant or to extend the area of the search beyond that which is authorized by a warrant. In order for the consent to be legally effective, the party giving the permission must be fully aware of the nature of the search and the legal implications. Consent is a waiver of one's Fourth Amendment rights.

　　A police officer may conduct a limited search incidental to an arrest without first obtaining a search warrant. The exception is necessary to secure the safety of the police officer and the custody of the suspect being arrested. The search also enables the officer to gather the fruits of the crime and prevent the destruction of the evidence. The search incidental to an arrest is limited to the person of the arrestee and the surrounding area under the arrestee's immediate control.

New York v. Belton
101 S.Ct. 2860
United States Supreme Court
July 1, 1981

MR. JUSTICE STEWART

When the occupant of an automobile is subjected to a lawful custodial arrest, does the constitutionally permissible scope of a search incident to his arrest include the passenger compartment of the automobile in which he was riding? That is the question at issue in the present case, and we decide that it does.

On April 9, 1978, Trooper Douglas Nicot, a New York State policeman driving an unmarked car on the New York Thruway, was passed by another automobile traveling at an excessive rate of speed. Nicot gave chase, overtook the speeding vehicle, and ordered its driver to pull it over to the side of the road and stop. There were four men in the car, one of whom was Roger Belton, the respondent in this case. The policeman asked to see the driver's license and automobile registration, and discovered that none of the men owned the vehicle or was related to its owner. Meanwhile, the policeman had smelled burnt marijuana and had seen on the floor of the car an envelope marked "Supergold" that he associated with marijuana. He therefore directed the men to get out of the car, and placed them under arrest for the unlawful possession of marijuana. He patted down each of the men and "split them up into four separate areas of the Thruway at this time so they would not be in physical touching area of each other." He then picked up the envelope marked "Supergold" and found that it contained marijuana. After giving the arrestees the warnings required by *Miranda v. Arizona*, the state policeman searched each one of them. He then searched the passenger compartment of the car. On the back seat, he found a black leather jacket belonging to Belton. He unzipped one of the pockets of the jacket and discovered cocaine. Placing the jacket in his automobile, he drove the four arrestees to a nearby police station.

Belton was subsequently indicted for criminal possession of a controlled substance. In the trial court, he moved that the cocaine the trooper had seized from the jacket pocket be suppressed. The court denied the motion. Belton then pleaded guilty to a lesser included offense, but preserved his claim that the cocaine had been seized in violation of the Fourth and Fourteenth Amendments. The Appellate Division of the New York Supreme Court upheld the constitutionality of the search and seizure, reasoning that "once defendant was validly arrested for possession of marijuana, the officer was justified in searching the immediate area for other contraband." 68 App. Div. 2d 198, 201.

The New York Court of Appeals reversed, holding that "a warrantless search of the zippered pockets of an unaccessible jacket may not be upheld as a search incident to a lawful arrest where there is no longer any danger that the arrestee or a confederate might gain access to the article." 50 NY 2d 447, 449. We granted *certiorari* to consider the constitutionally permissible scope of a search in circumstances such as these.

It is a first principle of Fourth Amendment jurisprudence that the police may not conduct a search unless they first convince a neutral magistrate that there is probable cause to do so. This Court has recognized, however, that "the exigencies of the situation" may sometimes make exemption from the warrant requirement "imperative." A lawful custodial arrest creates a situation that justifies the contemporaneous search without a warrant of the person arrested and of the immediately surrounding area. Such searches have long been considered valid because of the need to remove any weapons that the arrestee might seek to use in order to resist arrest or effect his escape and the need to prevent the concealment or destruction of evidence. The scope of a search must be strictly tied to and justified by the circumstances that rendered its initiation permissible.

Although the principle that limits a search incident to a lawful custodial arrest may be stated clearly enough, courts have discovered the principle difficult to apply in specific cases. The protection of the Fourth and Fourteenth Amendments can be realized only if the police are acting under a set of rules which, in most instances, make it possible to reach a correct determination beforehand as to whether an invasion of privacy is justified in the interest of law enforcement.

So it was that, in *United States v. Robinson*, 414 U.S. 218, the Court hewed to a straightforward rule, easily applied and predictably enforced: "In the case of a lawful custodial arrest, a full search of the person is not only an exception to the warrant requirement, but it is also a 'reasonable' search under that amendment." In so holding, the Court rejected the suggestion "that there must be litigated in each case the

issue of whether or not there was present one of the reasons supporting the authority for a search of the person incident to a lawful arrest."

But no straightforward rule has emerged from the litigated cases respecting the question inolved here— the question of the proper scope of a search of the interior of an automobile incident to a lawful custodial arrest of its occupants. The difficulty courts have had is reflected in the conflicting views of the New York judges who dealt with the problem in the present case.

When a person cannot know how a court will apply a settled principle to a recurring factual situation, that person cannot know the scope of his constitutional protection, nor can a policeman know the scope of his authority. While a search incident to an arrest may not stray beyond the area within the immediate control of the arrestee, courts have found no workable definition of "the area within the immediate control of the arrestee" when that area arguably includes the interior of an automobile and the arrestee is its recent occupant. Our reading of the cases suggests the generalization that articles inside the relatively narrow compass of the passenger compartment of an automobile are in fact generally, even if not inevitably, within the area into which an arrestee might reach in order to grab a weapon or evidentiary item.

It follows from this conclusion that the police may also examine the contents of any containers found within the passenger compartment, for if the passenger compartment is within reach of the arrestee, so also will containers in it be within his reach. Such a container may, of course, be searched whether it is open or closed, since the justification for the search is not that the arrestee has no privacy interest in the container, but that the lawful custodial arrest justifies the infringement of any privacy interest the arrestee may have.

It is true, of course, that these containers will sometimes be such that they could hold neither a weapon nor evidence of the criminal conduct for which the suspect was arrested. However, in *United States v. Robinson, supra*, the Court rejected the argument that such a container—there a "crumpled-up cigarette package"—located during a search of Robinson incident to his arrest could not be searched. The authority to search the person incident to a lawful custodial arrest, while based on the need to disarm and to discover evidence, does not depend on what a court may later decide was the probability in a particular arrest situation that weapons or evidence would in fact be found on the person of the suspect. A custodial arrest of a suspect based on probable cause is a reasonable intrusion under the Fourth Amendment. That intrusion being lawful, a search incident to the arrest requires no additional justification.

It is not questioned that the respondent was the subject of a lawful custodial arrest on a charge of possessing marijuana. The search of the respondent's jacket followed immediately upon that arrest. The jacket was located inside the passenger compartment of the car in which the respondent had been a passenger just before he was arrested. The jacket was thus within the area which we have concluded was "within the arrestee's immediate con-

trol." The search of the jacket, therefore, was a search incident to a lawful custodial arrest, and it did not violate the Fourth and Fourteenth Amendments. Accordingly, the judgment is reversed.

It is so ordered.

JUSTICE BRENNAN, with whom JUSTICE MARSHALL joins, dissenting

It has long been a fundamental principle of Fourth Amendment analysis that exceptions to the warrant requirement are to be narrowly construed.

As the facts of this case make clear, the Court today substantially expands the permissible scope of searches incident to arrest by permitting police officers to search areas and containers the arrestee could not possibly reach at the time of arrest. These facts demonstrate that at the time Belton and his three companions were placed under custodial arrest—which was *after* they had been removed from the car, patted down, and separated—none of them could have reached the jackets that had been left on the back seat of the car.

The Court for the first time grants police officers authority to conduct a warrantless area search under circumstances where there is no chance that the arrestee might gain possession of a weapon or destructible evidence. Under the approach taken today, the result would presumably be the same even if Officer Nicot had handcuffed Belton and his companions in the patrol car before placing them under arrest, and even if his search had extended to locked luggage or other inaccessible containers located in the back seat of the car.

CASE QUESTIONS

1. Why did this court allow the warrantless search?
2. Suppose that these officers were acting on information from a reliable informant that a particular person was selling narcotics kept in the trunk of his car. The police officers stopped the car and arrested the person, then opened the trunk and found a closed paper bag, which they opened. In the bag was a white powder (later discovered to be heroin). The officers also found and opened a zippered leather pouch in which there was a large sum of cash. Would the warrantless search be proper under the Fourth Amendment?

SUGGESTED READINGS

Note, *Warrantless Searches and Seizures of Automobiles*, 87 HARV. L. REV. 835 (1974).

W.E. RINGEL, SEARCHES AND SEIZURES, ARRESTS AND CONFESSIONS (1972).

Clark, *Some Notes on the Continuing Life of the Fourth Amendment*, 5 AM. J. CRIM. L. 275 (1977).

Knuckles, *Warrantless Automobile Searches, When Are They Constitutionally Permissible?*, 65 ILL. B.J. 532 (1977).

Note, *Warrantless Automobile Searches and Telephonic Search Warrants: Should the "Automobile Exception" Be Redrawn?* 7 HASTINGS CONST. L.Q. 1031 (1980).

Preliminary Hearing and Grand Jury

In order to weed out groundless or unsupported criminal charges before trial, a preliminary hearing is conducted or a grand jury is convened. The preliminary hearing or grand jury proceedings may result in saving both the accused and the state the time and trouble of a criminal trial. Innocent parties may be protected from the harassment of a trial when there is no reason to believe they committed a crime.

A person who is arrested is entitled to be brought promptly before a magistrate in an informal *preliminary hearing*. The magistrate examines the facts superficially to determine whether there is a strong enough case to hold the arrestee for further proceedings. The prosecution presents evidence before the magistrate, without a jury, in order to determine if there is probable cause. The accused has a right to be present at the preliminary hearing and present evidence. If there is no chance of conviction because of lack of evidence, the magistrate dismisses the charges.

Indictment [FRCrP 7(c)]

UNITED STATES DISTRICT COURT
FOR THE __1_____ DISTRICT OF __2_____
__3_____ DIVISION

United States of America,
Plaintiff,

v

__4_____)
Defendant.

Crim. No. __5__

(__6__—USC § __7_____

INDICTMENT

The grand jury charges:

On or about the __8_____ day of __9_____, 19__10__, in the __11_____
District of __12_____, __13_____ *[defendant]* __14_____ *[state essential facts
constituting offense charged]*, in violation of __15_____ USC § __16_____.

Dated __17_____, 19__18__.

A True Bill.

[Signature],
Foreman

__19_____,
United States Attorney.

A *grand jury*, composed of people selected at random from the list of registered voters, is charged with the duty of determining whether a person should be brought to trial. The grand jury decides whether there is reason to believe an accused has committed an offense, not whether the person is guilty or innocent. The decision is based on the evidence heard during the course of a secret criminal investigation attended by representatives of the state and witnesses. The grand jury has the right to *subpoena* witnesses and documents for their investigation. The accused has no right to be present at the proceedings. A grand jury returns an indictment if it believes that the evidence warrants a conviction. An *indictment* is an accusation in writing by a grand jury to the court against one who is believed to have committed a crime.

For prosecutions involving crimes against the United States, the Fifth Amendment provides that all prosecution for infamous crimes must be commenced by a grand jury indictment. An *infamous crime* is an offense carrying a term of imprisonment in excess of one year. A prosecutor's decision to bring charges for an infamous crime is effective only if the grand jury decides to issue an indictment. Virtually all states provide for a preliminary hearing for charges involving a felony. Approximately half of the states require a grand jury indictment.

Arraignment

An arraignment follows a grand jury indictment or the judge's finding of probable cause at a preliminary hearing. At *arraignments*, accused persons are advised of the formal charges against them. They are asked whether they understand the charges and whether they have an attorney. The court appoints counsel if the accused cannot afford an attorney. The Sixth Amendment states that the accused "be informed of the nature and cause of the accusation." This requires that the description of the charges be sufficiently clear so that the defendant may be able to enter an intelligent plea. A trial date is set at the arraignment. Defendants and their counsel must be given adequate opportunity to prepare for trial.

The defendant is called upon to enter a plea at the arraignment. This plea may be guilty, *nolo contendere*, or not guilty. The plea of *guilty* is entered in the greatest majority of situations; it is simply a confession of guilt. The plea of *nolo contendere* is the same as a guilty plea, except that it cannot be used later against the accused as an admission. It is a confession only for the purposes of the criminal prosecution and does not bind the defendant in a civil suit for the same wrong. When the defendant pleads *not guilty*, the prosecution has the burden of proving guilt beyond a reasonable doubt at the trial.

Plea bargaining is the process in which the accused agrees to enter a plea of guilty, often to a lesser offense, in exchange for a promise by the prosecuting attorney to recommend either a relatively light sentence or a dismissal of part of the charges. The judge does not have to accept the prosecutor's recommendations. Judges as well as prosecutors engage in plea bargaining with defendants.

Bail

The judge sets bail to ensure the defendant's attendance in court and obedience to the court's orders and judgment. When the accused deposits the amount of bail set by the judge with a clerk of the court, the accused may be released from jail. When a defendant's family and friends do not have enough money to post bail, they may see a bail bondsman who, for a fee, deposits a bond with the clerk of the court so that the accused may be set free.

The Eighth Amendment states that "excessive bail shall not be required." Bail that is set at a figure higher than an amount reasonably calculated to provide assurance that the accused will show up for trial is considered excessive. A judge may decide to release accused persons on their own recognizance if there is good reason to believe that the defendants will show up even if no bail is posted. Bail for traffic law offenses is, generally, a fine. It is employed for purposes of punishment and judicial convenience rather than to ensure that the trial process will take place. Because of the hardship and unfairness of bail, statutes are being passed to establish alternatives to it.

United States v. Cowper
349 F. Supp. 560
United States District Court, N.D. Ohio
October 12, 1972

LAMBROS, DISTRICT JUDGE

The accused, Wallace Cowper, came before this court requesting a reduction of the $100,000 surety bond previously set by the United States magistrate on the charge of bank larceny. Although the accused did not claim to be indigent, he was unable to post a bond in this amount. The court, therefore, ordered a bond reduction investigation by the probation department.

The case presents significant questions as to the application of the Bail Reform Act of 1966 (the "act"). The major issue is whether pretrial release conditions should be used to encourage the release of persons before trial or, instead, should be utilized to retain certain persons in jail before trial in order to accomplish other goals.

It is the opinion of this court that the act requires the release of an accused on the least restrictive alternative conditions that will provide reasonable assurance that the accused will appear in court. Furthermore, the court finds that, in applying that principle, it must consider more than the extreme alternatives of unsupervised release and jail and must permit monetary conditions to be met by the use of the deposit plan.

The doctrine that the federal courts are obligated to release those accused of noncapital offenses under the least restrictive alternative conditions which will provide reasonable assurance that the accused will appear in court is founded on the Eighth Amendment and presumption of innocence. From the passage of the Judiciary Act of 1789 to the present Federal Rules of Criminal Procedure, federal law has unequivocally provided that a person arrested for a noncapital offense shall be admitted to bail. Unless this right to bail before trial is preserved, the presumption of innocence, secured only after centuries of struggle, would lose its meaning. The right to release before trial is conditioned upon the accused's giving adequate assurance that he will stand trial and submit to sentence if found guilty. Bail set at a figure higher than an amount reasonably calculated to fulfill this purpose is "excessive" under the Eighth Amendment. The Bail Reform Act in 1966 re-emphasized that the purpose of any restrictions on release was to assure the presence of the accused at trial.

In applying the law of pretrial release to this case, the court finds that the following two questions predominate: First, may the court set pretrial release conditions to ensure that the accused remains in jail when it determines that unsupervised release will not reasonably assure the appearance of the accused at trial? Second, is the requirement of surety bond consistent with the court's statutory obligation to choose the least restrictive alternative conditions?

The framers of the Bail Reform Act intended not only to re-emphasize the principle of release as of right but also to destroy the concept that everyone not completely released prior to trial must be kept in maximum security conditions. In fact, the statute itself lists a number of alternatives between total release and surety bond, including release into the custody of a third person, requirement that a person report, daytime release, and restrictions on travel.[1] The thrust of the statute is that the court and counsel should use conditions of release in a flexible manner, varying them to fit individual needs.

The failure of the courts to use the conditions flexibly has resulted in massive overdetention. The President's commission estimated that less than a third of those detained on a nationwide basis actually needed jail detention. Other studies concur that the majority of those now held in jail detention prior to trial could be accommodated by release into the custody of others or the imposition of certain conditions upon release.

In this case, the $100,000 surety bond represents a refusal to use the flex-ible provisions of the act to effectuate release. It represents, in fact, the use of pretrial conditions to assure that the accused is held in jail prior to trial. It is apparent that in this instance, as in many others familiar to all of us, the statement of the astronomical numbers is not meant to be literally significant. It is a mildly cynical but wholly undeceptive fiction, meaning to everyone ''no bail.'' There is, on the evidence adduced, no possibility that the defendant will achieve release by posting bond in anything like the amount which has been set.

Because the denial of release conflicts with the act, the motion to modify the bond to conditions which can reasonably be met must be granted.

Although monetary conditions of release are to be used as a last resort under the Bail Reform Act, the court may find the imposition of such monetary conditions useful in a case involving a nonindigent defendant. In such a situation, there is some question whether and when the courts should use the deposit plan or the surety bond method of monetary bail.

Under the deposit plan, the accused may obtain release by executing a promise to pay the full amount of the bond and by depositing with the registry of the court an amount equal to not more (but less if the court so provides)

---

[1] The statute lists the following alternatives between total release and surety bond: ''(1) place the person in the custody of a designated person or organization agreeing to supervise him; (2) place restrictions on the travel, association, or place of abode of the person during the period of release; (3) require the execution of an appearance bond in a specified amount and the deposit in the registry of the court, in cash or other security as directed, of a sum not to exceed 10% of the amount of the bond, such deposit to be returned upon the performance of the conditions of release; ... (5) impose any other condition deemed reasonably necessary to assure appearance as required, including a condition requiring that the person return to custody after specified hours.''

than 10% of the amount of the bond. While the 10% is roughly equivalent to the fee required for a similar bond to a bail bondsman, the difference under the deposit plan is that the money deposited with the court is returned to the accused when he appears for trial.

Studies comparing the deposit plan with the surety bond have been conducted in Illinois. There, the use of the deposit plan resulted in greater numbers of persons released prior to trial with no increase in the number of persons not appearing for trial.

The senate subcommittee drafting the Bail Reform Act was familiar with this study of the surety bond and intended to abolish the bail bondsman through a preference for the use of the deposit plan when monetary release conditions were set.

A comparison of the advantages and disadvantages of the surety bond and the deposit plan shows that the use of the deposit plan is preferable. The commonly stated advantage of the surety bond is that the bondsman has a financial incentive to make sure that the accused appears. However, recent studies have discredited this view. First, the bondsman does not always have a financial incentive to produce the accused for trial. When, for example, he has obtained collateral for the entire amount of the bond in addition to the fee for posting the bond, he does not risk financial loss if the accused fails to appear. Second, investigations of bail bondsmen's activities have indicated that bail bondsmen seldom make efforts to assure the appearance of their clients. Furthermore, a report by the judicial council for the District of Columbia indicates that bail bondsmen

are unwilling to undertake any third-party custodial functions.

As for the effect on the accused, there is no indication that the surety bond presents a greater monetary incentive to appear than the deposit plan, especially where no collateral is required for the surety bond. Under the surety bond system, the accused pays a nonreturnable fee of about 10% of the amount of the bond. In contrast, the money placed in the registry of the court under the deposit plan is returnable if the accused abides by the conditions of release.

Finally, while bondsmen have little constructive value in assuring the appearance of the accused persons, they have a highly destructive value. A significant disadvantage of the surety bond system is that it takes pretrial release out of the control of the courts and puts the release decision in the hands of private individuals who are not accountable to the public for the release of poor risks. In addition, the court cannot ignore the literature describing the illicit activity which stems from the control and extortion powers of the bail bondsman. Furthermore, it cannot tolerate the needless overdetention of persons whose bonds are not posted because the bond is too small to make the trip to post it profitable or because of other reasons unrelated to assuring appearance.

In summary, the court is unable to justify the use of the surety bond as a better method than the deposit plan to assure court appearance. Therefore, it must rule that, when monetary conditions are used, the accused shall be permitted to meet the monetary conditions under the provisions of the deposit plan.

We have discussed above that the $100,000 surety bond violated the act by denying release and by requiring the unjustifiable bondsman's fee. In modifying the conditions of release, the court considered those factors listed in this act. The act provides:

In determining which conditions of release will reasonably assure appearance, the judicial officer shall, on the basis of available information, take into account the nature and circumstances of the offense charged, the weight of the evidence against the accused, the accused's family ties, employment, financial resources, character and mental condition, the length of his residence in the community, his record of convictions, and his record of appearance at court proceedings or of flight to avoid prosecution or failure to appear at court proceedings.

The facts provided by the probation department and presented at the hearing in this case showed that the accused had steady employment as a policeman in this community and that his family resided here. There was no record that he had previously fled or even that he had been convicted of a nontraffic offense. The only significant indication that he had incentive to flee was the government's allegation that roughly $300,000 stolen in the crime charged has not been recovered.

In light of these factors and of the fact that the accused was not indigent, this court imposed the following nonmonetary and monetary conditions:

1. The accused shall report personally to the probation department once each week.
2. The accused shall not travel except within Lake County, Ohio, and Cuyahoga County, Ohio.
3. The accused shall execute an appearance bond of $50,000 and shall make a cash deposit of $5000 in the registry of the court, such deposit to be returned upon performance of release conditions.
4. The accused shall be advised of the penalties for nonappearance.

The Bail Reform Act requires the courts to re-examine pretrial release practices. In no other field of law is the conflict between reality and legal theory more pronounced. While adhering in theory to the constitutional principle that a person should not be punished until he has been found guilty in a court of law, the courts in this nation have acquiesced to the fact that more than a third of those persons incarcerated on any given day have not been found guilty and that pretrial detainees are jailed in far worse conditions than those convicted of crimes.

In making these rulings, the court is cognizant of the necessity for the prompt administration of criminal justice and, where appropriate, for the imposition of punishment after valid criminal convictions. At the same time, the court must use care to avoid constitutional transgressions. On this basis, it is time to sound the death knell for the bail bondsman, lest the constitutional right of reasonable bail and the presumption of innocence become luxuries for the affluent.

The court, therefore, grants the defense motion for a modification of pretrial release and imposes those conditions listed above.

It is so ordered.

CASE QUESTIONS

1. The court in *Cowper* stated that bail set at a figure higher than an amount calculated to assure the defendant's court appearance is excessive. Suppose a defendant does not have any money. Is the setting of any amount excessive?

2. The District of Columbia Crime Control Bill provides a form of preventive detention. Under this act, a defendant may be detained up to 60 days without a trial before the Federal Bail Reform Act is applicable. Can this scheme pass constitutional requirements? What does *Cowper* suggest would be the constitutional problems? Make an argument for preventive detention.

SUGGESTED READINGS

Hruska, *Preventive Detention: The Constitution and the Congress*, 3 CREIGHTON L. REV. 36 (1969).

Mitchell, *Bail Reform and the Constitutionality of Pretrial Detention*, 55 VA. L. REV. 1223 (1969).

Hickey, *Preventive Detention and the Crime of Being Dangerous*, 58 GEO. L.J. 287 (1969).

Ervin, *Preventive Detention—A Step Backward for Criminal Justice*, 6 HARV. CIV. RIGHTS-CIV. LIB. L. REV. 291 (1971).

Murphy, *State Control of the Operation of Professional Bail Bondsmen*, 36 U. CIN. L. REV. 375 (1967).

Foote, *The Coming Constitutional Crisis in Bail*, 113 U. Pa. L. Rev. 1125 (1965).

D.J. FREED and P.M. WALD, BAIL IN THE UNITED STATES (1964).

Sweet, *Bail or Jail*, 19 RECORDS OF N.Y.C.B.A. 11 (1964).

Right to a Speedy Trial

The Sixth Amendment states: "the accused shall enjoy the right to a speedy . . . trial." This provision is interpreted as meaning that the trial should take place as soon as possible without depriving the parties of a reasonable period of time for preparation. The purposes of the right to a speedy trial, applicable to both the state and federal courts, are (1) to protect an accused from prolonged imprisonment prior to trial, (2) to prevent long delay that could impair the defense of an accused person through the

loss of evidence, and (3) to prevent or minimize public suspicion and anx
iety connected with an accused who is yet untried.

The right to speedy trial attaches when the prosecution begins, either by
indictment or by the actual restraints imposed by arrest. How much time
must elapse to result in an unconstitutional delay varies with the circumstances. The accused has the burden of showing that the delay was
the fault of the state and that it resulted in prejudice.

United States v. Bishton
463 F.2d 887
United States Court of Appeals
District of Columbia Circuit
April 17, 1972

PER CURIAM
Appellant was found guilty of soliciting, and of accepting, a bribe in violation of 18 U.S.C. § 201 (g) (1970), fined
$2000, and given a suspended sentence
of 6 to 18 months. His principal claim
on appeal presents the recurring problem of the right to a speedy trial.

On January 17, 1969, appellant, then
division chief of the District of Columbia Sewer Operations Division, allegedly approached one Glen Carrico,
an employee of the division, and asked
for a payment of $400 in return for ap-
pellant's approving Carrico's promotion to a higher job. Although Carrico
refused, he was in fact promoted on
February 23, 1969. Nevertheless, appellant continued to make demands
and threats for payment, until Carrico
finally alerted the FBI and the Metropolitan Police. The police arranged
for Carrico to give appellant $100 in
marked bills at work on the morning of
April 24, and the transaction was to be

both recorded by a device attached to
Carrico and observed by police officers
nearby. When the payment took place
as planned, the police promptly arrested appellant and advised him of his
rights, whereupon appellant handed
the money to the police and said, "This
is gratitude for you. I paid $400 out of
my own pocket to get Glen this promotion." Appellant then expressed concern over the effect the incident would
have on his wife if it were reported in
the papers.

Appellant was initially charged by information in the District of Columbia
Court of General Sessions (now the
superior court) under 22 D.C. Code §
702, which provides in pertinent part:

Every person who . . . receives . . . any
money . . . from any person for . . . procuring . . . any . . . promotion in office from
the commissioners of the District of Columbia, or from any officer under them . . .
shall be deemed guilty of a misdemeanor.

The case was called to trial on July 26,
1969, but was dismissed on the grounds
that the commissioners of the District
of Columbia had been abolished in the
reorganization of the district in 1967,

and thus the information failed to charge a crime. The government appealed to the District of Columbia Court of Appeals, which affirmed on April 13, 1970. *United States v. Bishton*, 264 A.2d 139. Three months later, on July 22, 1970, appellant was indicted by a federal grand jury for the same offense under the federal statute. On September 15, 1970, and again immediately before trial, appellant moved to dismiss for lack of speedy trial. The motion was denied on both occasions, and the case was tried on January 4–5, 1971, some 20 months after his arrest.

While fundamental to our notions of criminal justice, the right to speedy trial has proved to be one of the most difficult constitutional protections to apply to the circumstances of particular cases. The Supreme Court has recognized that the right is necessarily relative, requiring a balance between the interest of the public in bringing criminals to justice and the interest of the citizen in being free from oppressive and vexatious delay. In each case, therefore, courts must carefully examine the totality of circumstances surrounding the delay and must consider the length of the delay; reasons for the delay; diligence of prosecutor, court, and defense counsel; and reasonable possibility of prejudice from the delay. Weighing these factors in this case, we conclude that appellant's right to speedy trial was not unacceptably abridged.

The first three months after appellant's arrest were spent in preparation for trial, and there is no indication that appellant ever desired or sought expediation at that time. During the following eight months, the case was pending in the District of Columbia Court of Appeals, and thus beyond the power of the prosecutor to expedite. Courts, of course, are not excluded from the obligation to give defendants a speedy trial. But the function of appellate courts necessarily casts the delay attendant upon their deliberations in a somewhat different light, and the time spent on appeals is not generally included for purposes of calculating the period of delay in prosecution. The right of the government to appeal decisions in the defendant's favor before jeopardy attaches is designed to protect the interest of society in lawfully prosecuting criminal offenders, and, while such an appeal is not at the defendant's instance, the fact that he is legally, albeit conditionally, a free man minimizes the oppressiveness of the attendant delay.

We do not intimate that the delay caused by appeals by the government may never constitute denial of a defendant's right to speedy trial. Whenever the government's action at any stage of the proceeding indicates bad faith, neglect, or a purpose to secure delay itself or some other procedural advantage, the resulting delay is not justified. Thus, in *Petition of Provoo*, 17 F.R.D. 183 (D. Md. 1955), *aff'd per curiam*, 350 U.S. 857, the court dismissed a case brought to trial 4½ years after the indictment and 9 to 12 years after the alleged offenses:

The serious delay in this case was caused by the deliberate act of the government in bringing the case in New York in the first place, when the government must have known that venue in New York was at best doubtful, and took the chance of the supposed advantage to the government of proceeding in New York. Where the government chooses to proceed in a certain district of doubtful venue, when venue in another case is clear, the government must be held responsible for the effects of its election.

While appellant would characterize as similarly unjustifiable the government's initial decision to prosecute in the court of general sessions under the D.C. Code rather than in the federal court under the U.S. Code, and its decision to appeal the dismissal in the former court rather than immediately to seek a federal indictment, we do not agree that these decisions reflected arbitrary, negligent, or purposefully oppressive behavior on the part of the government. The District of Columbia Court of Appeals itself recognized that the flaw it found in the indictment was highly technical. Thus, unlike the court in *Petition of Provoo, supra,* we cannot say that the government's decision to proceed in the court of general sessions was "at best doubtful," or that it "must have known" that it would not prevail on appeal.

The federal indictment was brought three months later. While the record supplies no explanation for this delay, it is significant that during this time appellant was a free man against whom no prosecution was pending. The Supreme Court has recently held that the right to speedy trial attaches when a prosecution has begun, either by indictment or by the actual restraints imposed by arrest. Even before arrest or indictment, of course, a defendant may claim the right to be free from purposeful or oppressive delays in instituting the prosecution that tend to deprive him of a fair trial. In the circumstances of this case, however, there is no indication that this lapse of three months had such an effect.

Following the federal indictment, the case proceeded with reasonable alacrity, and the record suggests that the delays that did occur were at the instance, or with the acquiescence, of appellant. For example, on the very eve of trial, appellant's counsel introduced a motion to dismiss based on an entirely new theory of law. The government strenuously objected to any delay in the proceedings that consideration of this last-minute motion would entail:

The Court: We set this case two months ahead so that everybody could be ready to go, and now to hit me with a last-minute motion that has nothing but the effect of delay doesn't make me very happy. I am ready to throw the case over unless you are ready to go forward.

Assistant U.S. Attorney: We are ready to go forward, your Honor. . . .

Appellant's Counsel: Your Honor, I feel very bad about the delay, but I don't think I can withdraw the motion.

The foregoing analysis of the delays in this case reflects no neglect, indifference, or lack of reasonable diligence on the part of the government. Turning then to appellant's claim of prejudice, we note that (1) at all times he was free on bond, (2) he has never claimed the unavailability of any witness as a result of the delay, (3) his preparation for the first trial in 1969 diminished the likelihood that his ability or the ability of his witnesses to recall the critical facts had irreparably faded, and (4) the case against him, in light of his remarks to the arresting officers, was strong. We have intimated that when the delay in prosecution exceeds 12 months, prejudice to the defendant is presumed and need not be affirmatively shown. But even the prejudice which is presumed to inhere in all cases where the delay is particularly long must be weighed against the other considerations we have mentioned. If this were a case where the delays could not be explained or justified by the government, or where the defendant's ability to present a defense was demonstrably affected, or where the government's case on the merits was close, then the balance between the interest of the public and the protection of the individual might be different. Here, however, the balance is otherwise.

Affirmed

CASE QUESTIONS

1. According to the *Bishton* opinion, what factors do the courts consider in determining whether a defendant has been deprived of the right to a speedy trial?
2. In what way are the due-process clauses of the Fifth and Fourteenth Amendments applicable to the argument that a defendant has been denied a speedy trial?
3. Besides the defendant's interest in obtaining a speedy resolution of charges, is there a public interest in the right to a speedy trial?

SUGGESTED READINGS

Note, *The Right to a Speedy Criminal Trial*, 57 COLUM. L. REV. 846 (1957).

Note, *Justice Overdue—Speedy Trial for the Potential Defendant*, 5 STAN. L. REV. 95 (1952).

Note, *Dismissal of the Indictment as a Remedy for Denial of the Right to a Speedy Trial*, 64 YALE L.J. 1208 (1955).

Note, *Convict's Right to a Speedy Trial*, 61 J. CRIM. L. 352 (1970).

Note, *Criminal Law—Speedy Trial—The Three Term Rule*, 73 W. VA. L. REV. 184 (1971).

Province, *Defendant's Dilemma: Valid Charge or Speedy Trial*, 6 CRIM. L. BULL. 421 (1970).

Note, *Criminal Law: Crowded Dockets No Longer Justify Denial of Speedy Trial*, 23 U. FLA. L. REV. 603 (1971).

The Trial

Rules of Evidence

The chronological sequence during a criminal trial is much the same as in a civil trial. Rules concerning the admissibility of evidence are also similar with one significant exception: the *exclusionary rule*. This rule provides that evidence obtained in violation of the Constitution is inadmissible in a criminal trial. The rule excludes all evidence secured by police in violation of recognized constitutional restrictions. Because of this rule, many of the pretrial proceedings have more practical significance in the criminal process than the trial itself.

Evidence obtained by officers in violation of the Fourth Amendment prohibition of unreasonable searches, statements obtained from the accused after accused has been denied the assistance of counsel, and lineup identification obtained in violation of the accused's Sixth Amendment right have been held to be inadmissible by reason of the exclusionary rule under certain circumstances. Evidence obtained through pretrial procedures that are in violation of the due-process clause or self-incrimination clause are likewise inadmissible.

Trial by Jury

The Sixth Amendment helps to ensure a fair trial for accused persons. It gives them the right to receive notice of the charges against them and to have their guilt or innocence decided at a trial by jury. They have a right to a public trial and to representation by counsel. They may present witnesses and evidence and cross-examine witnesses against them.

Accused persons have a constitutional right to have their guilt or innocence decided by a jury composed of people representing a cross section of their community. This right does not extend to offenses traditionally characterized as petty offenses. If a defendant pleads guilty, the case is tried before a judge without a jury, since no question of fact exists for a jury to decide. The jury is to be free of bias and prejudice. Since jurors are representatives of the community, they are often compassionate and understanding, whereas a judge might be more inclined to severity. The jury right is a safeguard against arbitrary and high-handed action of judges.

Unless a jury trial is waived, the jury is selected at the beginning of the trial. The number of jurors ranges from four to twelve, depending on what is provided by state law. A unanimous decision is not required for conviction in all states. Twelve jurors are required in federal criminal courts and a unanimous decision is necessary for a conviction. If a jury cannot agree on a verdict, it is referred to as a *hung jury* and the judge dismisses the jury. In this situation, the prosecutor may retry the defendant before a new jury.

Fair and Public Trial

It is essential for a fair criminal trial that accused persons have the right to be confronted by their accusers. This protects them from being convicted by testimony given in their absence without the opportunity of cross examination. The fact-finder should reach a decision after seeing and hearing the testimony of the accuser and the accused in an adversary proceeding. The defendant has a right to a public trial. The purpose of this constitutional right is to prevent courts from becoming instruments of persecution through secret action. The right is not unlimited. It is subject to the judge's power and duty to preserve order and decorum in the courtroom. Judges possess broad powers in conducting a trial. They may limit the number of spectators in order to prevent overcrowding or to prevent disturbances. And they have the power to regulate activities outside the courtroom when they threaten the process of justice. Judges have the power to find persons in contempt of court for acts that hinder or obstruct the court in the administration of justice.

Gannett Co. v. DePasquale
443 U.S. 368
United States Supreme Court
July 2, 1979

Mr. Justice Stewart
The question presented in this case is whether members of the public have an independent constitutional right to insist on access to a pretrial judicial proceeding, even though the accused, the prosecutor, and the trial judge all have agreed to the closure of that proceeding in order to assure a fair trial.

Wayne Clapp, aged 42 and residing at Henrietta, a Rochester, N.Y., suburb, disappeared in July 1976. He was last seen on July 16 when, with two male companions, he went out on his boat to fish in Seneca Lake, about 40 miles from Rochester. The two companions returned in the boat the same day and drove away in Clapp's pickup truck. Clapp was not with them. When he failed to return home by July 19, his family reported his absence to the police. An examination of the boat, laced with bullet holes, seemed to indicate that Clapp had met a violent death aboard it. Police then began an intensive search for the two men. They also began lake-dragging operations in an attempt to locate Clapp's body.

The petitioner, Gannett Co., Inc., publishes two Rochester newspapers, the morning *Democrat and Chronicle* and the evening *Times-Union.* On July 20, each paper carried its first story about Clapp's disappearance. Each reported the few details that were then known and stated that the police were theorizing that Clapp had been shot on his boat and his body dumped overboard. Each stated that the body was missing. The *Times-Union* mentioned the names of respondents Greathouse and Jones and said that Greathouse "was identified as one of the two companions who accompanied Clapp Friday" on the boat, that the two were aged 16 and 21, respectively, and that the police were seeking the two men and Greathouse's wife, also 16. Accompanying the evening story was a 1959 photograph of Clapp. The report also contained an appeal from the state police for assistance.

Michigan police apprehended Greathouse, Jones, and the woman on July 21. This came about when an interstate bulletin describing Clapp's truck led to their discovery in Jackson County, Mich., by police who observed the truck parked at a local motel. The petitioner's two Rochester papers on July 22 reported the details of the capture. The stories also stated that Seneca County police theorized that Clapp was shot with his own pistol, robbed, and his body thrown into Seneca Lake.

The *Democrat and Chronicle* carried another story on the morning of July 24. It stated that Greathouse had led the Michigan police to the spot where he had buried a .357 magnum revolver belonging to Clapp and that the gun was being returned to New York with the three suspects.

Greathouse, Jones, and the woman were indicted by a Seneca County grand jury on August 2. Both the *Democrat and Chronicle* and the *Times-Union* on August 3 reported the filing of the indictments. Each story stated that the murder charges specified that the two men had shot Clapp with his own gun, had weighted his body with anchors and tossed it into the lake, and then had made off with Clapp's credit card, gun, and truck.

On August 6, each paper carried a story reporting the details of the arraignments of Greathouse and Jones the day before. The papers stated that both men had pleaded not guilty to all charges. The stories noted that defense attorneys had been given 90 days in which to file pretrial motions.

During this 90-day period, Greathouse and Jones moved to suppress statements made to the police. The ground they asserted was that those statements had been given involuntarily. They also sought to suppress physical evidence seized as fruits of the allegedly involuntary confessions. The primary physical evidence they sought to suppress was the gun to which, as petitioner's newspaper had reported, Greathouse had led the Michigan police.

The motions to suppress came on before Judge DePasquale on November 4. At this hearing, defense attorneys argued that the unabated build-up of adverse publicity had jeopardized the ability of the defendants to receive a fair trial. They thus requested that the public and the press be excluded from the hearing. The district attorney did not oppose the motion. Although Carol Ritter, a reporter employed by the petitioner, was present in the courtroom, no objection was made at the time of the closure motion. The trial judge granted the motion.

The next day, however, Ritter wrote a letter to the trial judge asserting a "right to cover this hearing," and requesting that "we . . . be given access to the transcript." The judge responded later the same day. He stated that the suppression hearing had concluded and that any decision on immediate release of the transcript had been reversed. The petitioner then moved the court to set aside its exclusionary order.

The trial judge scheduled a hearing on this motion for November 16 after allowing the parties to file briefs. After finding on the record that an open suppression hearing would pose a "reasonable probability of prejudice to these defendants," the judge ruled that the interest of the press and the public was outweighed in this case by the defendants' right to a fair trial. The judge thus refused to vacate his exclusion order or grant the petitioner immediate access to a transcript of the pretrial hearing.

The following day, an original proceeding challenging the closure orders on First, Sixth, and Fourteenth Amendment grounds, was commenced in the Supreme Court of the State of New York, Appellate Division. That court held that the exclusionary orders transgressed the public's vital interest in open judicial proceedings and further constituted an unlawful prior restraint in violation of the First and Fourteenth Amendments. It accordingly vacated the trial court's orders.

On appeal, the New York Court of Appeals noted that under state law "criminal trials are presumptively open to the public, including the press," but held that this presumption was overcome in this case because of the danger posed to the defendants' ability to receive a fair trial. Thus, the court of appeals upheld the exclusion of the press and the public from the pretrial proceeding. Because of the significance of the constitutional questions involved, we granted *certiorari.*

This Court has long recognized that adverse publicity can endanger the ability of a defendant to receive a fair trial. To safeguard the due-process rights of the accused, a trial judge has an affirmative constitutional duty to minimize the effects of prejudicial pretrial publicity. And because of the Constitution's pervasive concern for these due-process rights, a trial judge may surely take protective measures even when they are not strictly and inescapably necessary.

Publicity concerning pretrial suppression hearings such as the one involved in the present case poses special risks of unfairness. The whole purpose of such hearings is to screen out unreliable or illegally obtained evidence and ensure that this evidence does not become known to the jury. Publicity concerning the proceedings at a pretrial hearing, however, could influence public opinion against a defendant and inform potential jurors of inculpatory information wholly inadmissible at the actual trial.

The Sixth Amendment surrounds a criminal trial with guarantees such as the rights to notice, confrontation, and compulsory process that have as their overriding purpose the protection of the accused from prosecutorial and judicial abuses. Among the guarantees that the Amendment provides to a person charged with the commission of a criminal offense, and to him alone, is the "right to a speedy and public trial, by an impartial jury." The Constitution nowhere mentions any right of access to a criminal trial on the part of the public; its guarantee, like the others enumerated, is personal to the accused.

Our cases have uniformly recognized the public trial guarantee as one created for the benefit of the defendant. The right to a public trial has always been recognized as a safeguard against any attempt to employ our courts as instruments of persecution.

In *Estes v. Texas*, 381 US 532 (1965), this Court held that a defendant was deprived of his right to due process of law under the Fourteenth Amendment by the televising and broadcasting of his trial. In rejecting the claim that the media representatives had a constitutional right to televise the trial, the Court stated that "the purpose of the requirement of a public trial was to guarantee that the accused would be fairly dealt with and not unjustly condemned."

The *Estes* case recognized that the constitutional guarantee of a public trial is for the benefit of the defendant. There is not the slightest suggestion in the case that there is any correlative right of members of the public to insist upon a public trial.

While the Sixth Amendment guarantees to a defendant in a criminal case the right to a public trial, it does not guarantee the right to compel a private trial. But the issue here is not whether the defendant can compel a private trial. Rather, the issue is whether members of the public have an enforceable right to a public trial that can be asserted independently of the parties in the litigation.

There can be no blinking the fact that there is a strong societal interest in public trials. But there is a strong societal interest in other constitutional guarantees extended to the accused as well. The public, for example, has a definite and concrete interest in seeing that justice is swiftly and fairly administered. Similarly, the public has an interest in having a criminal case heard by a jury, an interest distinct from the defendant's interest in being tried by a jury of his peers.

Recognition of an independent public interest in the enforcement of Sixth Amendment guarantees is a far cry, however, from the creation of a constitutional right on the part of the public. In an adversary system of criminal justice, the public interest in the administration of justice is protected by the participants in the litigation.

There is no question that the Sixth Amendment permits and even presumes open trials as a norm. But the issue here is whether the Constitution *requires* that a pretrial proceeding such as this one be opened to the public, even though the participants in the litigation agree that it should be closed to protect the defendants' right to a fair trial. The history on which the petitioner relies totally fails to demonstrate that the framers of the Sixth Amendment intended to create a constitutional right in strangers to attend a pretrial proceeding, when all that they actually did was to confer on the accused an explicit right to demand a public trial. In conspicuous contrast with some of the early state constitutions that provided for a public right to open civil and criminal trials, the Sixth Amendment confers the right to a public trial only on a defendant and only in a criminal case.

For these reasons, we hold that members of the public have no constitutional right under the Sixth and Fourteenth Amendments to attend criminal trials.

The petitioner also argues that members of the press and the public have a right of access to the pretrial hearing by reason of the First and Fourteenth Amendments.

Several factors lead to the conclusion that the actions of the trial judge here were consistent with any right of access the petitioner may have had under the First and Fourteenth Amendments. First, none of the spectators present in the courtroom, including the reporter employed by the petitioner, objected when the defendants made the closure motion. Despite this failure to make a contemporaneous objection, counsel for the petitioner was given an opportunity to be heard at a proceeding where he was allowed to voice the petitioner's objections to closure of the pretrial hearing. At this proceeding, which took place after the filing of briefs, the trial court balanced the "constitutional rights of the press and the public" against the "defendants' right to a fair trial." The trial judge concluded after making this appraisal that the press and the public could be excluded from the suppression hearing and could be denied immediate access to a transcript, because an open proceeding would pose a "reasonable probability of prejudice

to these defendants." Thus, the trial court found that the representatives of the press did have a right of access of constitutional dimension, but held, under the circumstances of this case, that this right was outweighed by the defendants' right to a fair trial. In short, the closure decision was based on an assessment of the competing societal interests involved rather than on any determination that First Amendment freedoms were not implicated.

Furthermore, any denial of access in this case was not absolute but only temporary. Once the danger of prejudice had dissipated, a transcript of the suppression hearing was made available. The press and the public then had a full opportunity to scrutinize the suppression hearing. Unlike the case of an absolute ban on access, therefore, the press here had the opportunity to inform the public of the details of the pretrial hearing accurately and completely. Under these circumstances, any First and Fourteenth Amendment right of the petitioner to attend a criminal trial was not violated.

We are asked to hold that the Constitution itself gave the petitioner an affirmative right of access to this pretrial proceeding, even though all the participants in the litigation agreed that it should be closed to protect the fair-trial rights of the defendants.

For all the reasons discussed in this opinion, we hold that the Constitution provides no such right. Accordingly, the judgment of the New York Court of Appeals is affirmed.

CASE QUESTIONS

1. What approach did the Court use to decide this case, and what were the competing interests involved?
2. What is the purpose of the right to a public trial?
3. What if a defendant complains of being denied a fair trial because jurors learned from news accounts that defendant had prior felony convictions and even learned certain facts concerning the present case? Should defendant be released?

SUGGESTED READINGS

Taylor, *Crime Reporting and Publicity of Criminal Proceedings*, 66 COLUM. L. REV. 34 (1966).

Dowd, *Symposium on a Free Press and a Fair Trial*, 11 VILL. L. REV. 677 (1966).

Note, *"Free Press—Fair Trial" Revisited: Defendant-Centered Remedies as a Publicity Policy*, 33 U. CHI. L. REV. 512 (1966).

Note, *Criminal Law—The Binding and Gagging of Unwilling Defendants*, 38 TENN. L. REV. 440 (1971).

Note, *Constitutional Law—Sixth Amendment Confrontation Clause— Right of Defendant to be Present at Criminal Trial*, 59 KY. L.J. 489 (1970–71).

Note, *First Amendment—Constitutional Right of Access to Criminal Trials*, 71 J. CRIM. L. 547 (1980).

Prosecution

The sovereignty has the duty of prosecuting those who commit crimes; its attorney for this purpose is the prosecutor. The prosecutor, who performs the function of trial lawyer for the sovereignty, has extensive resources for purposes of investigation and preparation. The prosecutor is not at liberty to distort or misuse this information, and must disclose information tending to relieve the accused of guilt. Any conduct of a prosecutor or judge that hinders the fairness of a trial to the extent that the outcome is adversely affected violates the defendant's right to due process. The efforts of the prosecutor and the court should be directed toward fairness and justice.

State v. Farrell
61 N.J. 99, 293 A.2d 176
Supreme Court of New Jersey
July 7, 1972

PROCTOR, JUDGE
Defendant Farrell was convicted by a jury of robbery while armed, and sentenced to a 14–15-year term for the robbery and a consecutive 4–5-year term for being armed. The conviction was sustained by the appellate division, and we granted certification upon defendant's petition.

At the trial, the only evidence linking the defendant with the robbery was the testimony of Harold Lutz, who had pleaded guilty to the same indictment but had not yet been sentenced. He said that while armed he robbed the cashier of a drive-in theater, taking about $200. He further testified that the defendant suggested the robbery, provided the gun, drove him to and from the scene of the crime, and split the money with him.

The primary contention on this appeal is that the prosecutor made improper remarks during summation which prejudiced the defendant. We agree.

It is error for a trial judge to permit a prosecutor in summing up to comment on facts not shown or reasonably inferable from the evidence in the case. During his summation the prosecutor made the following remarks: "Farrell knew that Lutz had something to testify about. *Farrell knows it today and remember what he tried to do with the young kid when he was on the stand yesterday? While he was on the stand yesterday, did you look in the back of the courtroom and see those characters seated right in the back trying to intimidate that kid during his entire testimony? If they were interested in the case, and only one of them testified, where are they today? There is no Harold William Lutz here today to intimidate, but there was yesterday. Those four characters sat there during the whole trial and during Mr. Lutz's entire testimony and stared him down and intimidated him. If Mr. Lutz seemed scared, I think we can all understand why he was scared.*" Other than this statement, there was nothing in the record to indicate that the four men even existed.[1] These comments were the equivalent of testimony by the prosecutor that the defendant had procured the presence of these men for the purpose of intimidating a state witness and therefore was a party in an attempt to obstruct justice. They also had the tendency to enhance Lutz's believability in that he testified despite a foreboding atmosphere.

It is also error to permit the prosecutor to declare his personal belief of a defendant's guilt in such a manner that the jury may understand that belief to be based on something which the prosecutor knows outside the evidence. The prosecutor included the following in his summation: "Ladies and gentlemen of the jury, a lot of times during this case you have heard objections and

---

[1] If such spectators existed and behaved as the prosecutor alleged, the proper procedure to follow, as defense counsel pointed out at trial, would be to bring the matter to the court's attention.

I have seemed overzealous. Please do not hold that against me because I have a strong feeling about this case. *There is no question in my mind as to what happened on that night, and I have the responsibility*, not only to myself, but to my office and to each and every one of you seated in this jury and to each and every person that resides in this county and to each and every person who lives in this state; *because a brutal crime was committed on that date and there is no question in my mind that Mr. Farrell had something to do with that crime.* So, if I have seemed to be overzealous, please don't hold that against me because as I have said, *I feel very strongly about this case.* If I seem youthful, please don't hold that against me. Please don't feel that I have no experience with people because although I may be youthful, during my tenure as assistant prosecutor, I have had an opportunity to try many, many cases. *I have tried at least 50 cases, not counting those that ended up in a plea, and I have seen many, many people and I can say now, that I don't think I have ever felt stronger about a case than I do about this one.* Now, ladies and gentlemen of the jury, that's why I say to you *that I feel about this case like I have never felt before. There are very few cases where I have felt like I feel now.* I want to see justice done and I want to see this man convicted of a crime that he committed.''

We are convinced such comments tended to create the impression that aside from the evidence presented to the jury, the prosecutor had personal knowledge of the defendant's guilt. We are not discussing a situation where the prosecutor argues that the jury should

be persuaded that the state's evidence was credible. Here the prosecutor went beyond an argumentative evaluation of the state's proof and sought to add to that proof some special expertise that he claimed in this area. After all, the simple question was whether Lutz was a believable witness. In this light, the statements made by the prosecutor which we quoted above went beyond any discussion of the inherent worth of Lutz's testimony and sought to add strength to that testimony on the basis of the prosecutor's comparison of this case with others he had tried.

We think it clear the prosecutor in his summation disregarded the guidelines set forth in our cases. It is apparent from the number of instances recently brought to our attention that improper comments by prosecutors are becoming much too prevalent. We remind prosecutors again, we hope for the last time, of their function in the role of state's attorneys. Canon 5 of the Canons of Professional Ethics sets forth this function: ''The primary duty of a lawyer engaged in public prosecution is not to convict, but to see that justice is done.''

The prosecuting attorney is the representative not of an ordinary party to a controversy, but of a sovereignty whose obligation to govern impartially is as compelling as its obligation to govern at all; and whose interest, therefore, in a criminal prosecution is not that it shall win a case, but that justice shall be done. As such, he is in a peculiar and very definite sense the servant of the law, the twofold aim of which is that guilt shall not escape or innocence suffer. He may prosecute with earnestness and vigor—indeed, he should do so.

But, while he may strike hard blows, he is not at liberty to strike foul ones. It is as much his duty to refrain from improper methods calculated to produce a wrongful conviction as it is to use every legitimate means to bring about a just one.

It is fair to say that the average jury, in a greater or less degree, has confidence that these obligations, which so plainly rest upon the prosecuting attorney, will be faithfully observed. Consequently, improper suggestions, insinuations, and especially, assertions of personal knowledge are apt to carry much weight against the accused when they should properly carry none.

It was error to permit the prosecutor's remarks referred to above to remain, and we are convinced the remarks were prejudicial to the defendant's rights. The state's case consisted entirely of the testimony of an alleged accomplice, Lutz, who had pleaded guilty to the offense but had not yet been sentenced at the time of the trial. There is no doubt in our minds that reference by the prosecutor to things not in the record which had the tendency to bolster Lutz's credibility and to show that Farrell attempted to obstruct justice was harmful to the defendant. What is a juror who did not notice the supposed spectators or the alleged intimidation of Lutz to think? Because the prosecutor represents the government and people of the state, it is reasonable to say that jurors have confidence that he will fairly fulfill his duty to see that justice is done whether by conviction of the guilty or acquittal of the innocent. His comments in summation, whether proper or improper, carry with them the authority of all he represents. It is unlikely a juror will believe a prosecutor would intentionally mislead him. Rather, he will probably accept the statement that Lutz had been threatened and that he testified truthfully in the face of that threat, and the implication that Farrell attempted to obstruct justice. The witness's credibility so bolstered and the alleged wrongful conduct of the defendant and his friends in the courtroom so emphasized, it is not much of a step for a juror to take to vote for a conviction.

Statements by the prosecutor of his personal belief, aside from the evidence about defendant's guilt, are also likely to have a damaging impact. Where those statements are repeatedly made, as in this case, the damage is compounded. The prosecutor here in effect told the jury he knew that Lutz was telling the truth and that Farrell was guilty, not on the basis of what was in the record but rather through his own expert evaluation of this case as compared with others he had tried. The jury was then put in a position where to acquit the defendant they had to believe the prosecutor was either exaggerating or fabricating. We do not think any juror can be expected to believe the prosecutor would do so, and thus we cannot say the defendant was not prejudiced by the prosecutor's comments as to this private belief.

We hold the prosecutor's remarks referred to above were improper and prejudicial.

The judgment of the appellate division is reversed and the case is remanded for a new trial.

CASE QUESTIONS

1. The prosecutor in *Farrell* stated that he felt strongly about the case against Farrell, and that he wanted a conviction. Suppose that Farrell had been indicted for an offense that the prosecutor had repeatedly failed to prosecute in the past. Should the defendant be allowed to raise the previous pattern of nonenforcement on a motion to dismiss?

2. Suppose that, during the course of a criminal trial, the defense attorney knows of, or has possession of, evidence that would clearly convict the defendant. What is the ethical course of action?

SUGGESTED READINGS

Alschuler, *Courtroom Misconduct by Prosecutors and Trial Judges*, 50 TEXAS L. REV. 629 (1972).

Abrams, *Internal Policy: Guiding the Exercise of Prosecutorial Discretion*, 19 U.C.L.A. L. REV. 1 (1971).

Younger, *Changing Role of the District Attorney*, 45 LAB BULL. 455 (1970).

Newman, *Prosecutor and Defender Reform: Reorganization to Increase Effectiveness*, 44 CONN. B.J. 567 (1970).

McIntyre and Lippman, *Prosecutors and Early Disposition of Felony Cases*, 56 A.B.A.J. 1154 (1970).

Uviller, *Virtuous Prosecutor in Quest of an Ethical Standard: Guidance from the ABA*, 71 MICH. L. REV. 1145–68 (1973).

Underwood, *Thumb on the Scales of Justice: Burdens of Persuasion in Criminal Cases*, 86 YALE L.J. 1299 (1977).

Sentencing

Following jury conviction or a guilty plea, judges decide the punishment based on broad legislative guidelines. In reaching their decisions, judges may consider unsworn or out-of-court information relative to the circumstances of the crime and to the convicted person's life. Judges may spend days hearing testimony during a criminal trial, yet spend very little time deciding on a sentence. Sentences are based on such statutory guidelines as, "from five years to life," or "not more than twenty-five years." Judges' decisions may range from the maximum allowed by law to a suspended sentence, depending on the crime, the defendant's prior record, or any other matters they may consider relevant. Judges' power is unchecked and there is almost no right of review of their decisions. Parties found guilty may challenge the constitutionality of their sentences. They may argue that a sentence is "cruel and unusual" in violation of the Eighth Amendment, or that it violates the equal-protection clause of the Fourteenth Amendment.

Appeal and Habeas Corpus

A criminal conviction is always reviewable by a higher court. At common law the defendant is the only party entitled to an appeal in a criminal case. The sovereignty has no common-law right of appeal. In some jurisdictions, statutes allow the state to appeal in limited instances. However, any statute that allowed a reversal of a verdict of acquittal would be unconstitutional, prohibited by the double-jeopardy clause of the *Fifth Amendment* and by the due-process clause. Statutes generally allow the state only a review of the pretrial rulings on questions of law, or an appeal from a judgment of acquittal for the sole purpose of clarifying the law.

The writ of *habeas corpus* is used to question the legality of the detention of a prisoner. *Habeas corpus* is Latin for "you have the body," and the sole function of the writ is to release petitioners from unlawful imprisonment. If petitioners are able to show in a full hearing that there is no legal authority to hold them, the courts must discharge them from custody. The writ is granted when prisoners are able to show through arguments that their incarceration is in violation of their legal rights. There is no limit to the number of petitions for a writ of *habeas corpus* allowed to one who is incarcerated. However, very few *habeas corpus* proceedings are successful.

Tate v. Short
401 U.S. 395
United States Supreme Court
March 2, 1971

MR. JUSTICE BRENNAN
Petitioner accumulated fines of $425 on nine convictions for traffic offenses. He was unable to pay the fines because of indigency, and the Corporation Court of Houston committed him to the municipal prison farm according to the provisions of a state statute and municipal ordinance which required that he remain there a sufficient time to satisfy the fines at the rate of $5 for each day. This required that he serve 85 days at the prison farm. After 21 days in custody, petitioner was released on bond when he applied to the county criminal court of Harris County for a writ of *habeas corpus*. He alleged that: "Because I am too poor, I am, therefore, unable to pay the accumulated fine of

LaReau v. MacDougall
473 F.2d 974
United States Court of Appeals
Second Circuit
December 15, 1972

TIMBERS, CIRCUIT JUDGE

This appeal presents again questions which are being raised with increasing frequency by state prisoners with respect to alleged unconstitutional conduct by state prison officials. The issues are raised here in the context of alleged violations of a state prisoner's First and Eighth Amendment rights in connection with his confinement in a strip cell at the Connecticut state prison.

Appellant LaReau, presently an inmate of the Connecticut Correctional Institution at Somers, Connecticut, appeals from a judgment for defendants entered on May 25, 1971, after a four-day trial on the merits in the District Court for the District of Connecticut. The judgment dismissed LaReau's action brought under the Civil Rights Act, seeking equitable relief and $50,000 damages for alleged violations of his rights under the First Amendment (free exercise of religion clause) and the Eighth Amendment (cruel and unusual punishment clause), as well as other alleged constitutional violations not raised on appeal. After trial, Judge Clarie filed a well-reasoned opinion setting forth detailed findings of fact and conclusions of law, which we affirm in all respects except as indicated below. In short, we affirm on the First Amendment claim and reverse and remand on the Eighth Amendment claim.

Appellant's Eighth Amendment claim is that a disciplinary measure imposed upon him while imprisoned at the Connecticut Correctional Institution at Somers, namely, his confinement in a so-called strip cell, constituted cruel and unusual punishment.

The facts are as follows. On February 3, 1970, correctional officers found in LaReau's possession certain contraband items, including what was variously described by witnesses as "a rope fashioned from parts of a towel" or towels or "a string made from the edges of bed sheets." Because LaReau at that time was in punitive segregation, these items were contraband under prison regulations. A disciplinary proceeding followed on February 5. LaReau was ordered confined in a strip cell for an "indefinite period." He in fact served five days in the strip cell, from February 6 to February 11. He contends that the strip cell in which he was confined is *per se* unconstitutional or, alternatively, that it was grossly excessive punishment for his violation. We hold, under the circumstances of this case, that his confinement in the strip cell violated his Eighth Amendment rights.

The strip cell was described by witnesses at the trial as follows. Its dimensions are 6 feet wide, 10 feet deep and 8 feet high, approximately the same size as other cells in the prison. The cell has an outer door made of solid steel and an inner door made of steel bars, with a space of 2 feet between the two doors. The outer door has a 2-square-foot window at eye level which can be covered by a metal plate. Prison officials testified that the window usually is not closed unless the prisoner creates a disturbance. The walls and floor of the cell are cement. The walls have no windows. There is a 100-watt light outside the cell which shines through a hole at the rear of the cell and can be turned on and off only by the guard. Judge Clarie found that this light was turned on for LaReau only at meal times and when he was allowed to write. Thus it appears that LaReau for substantial periods of time was in almost total darkness when the light was off and the window in the door was closed. He was also in total silence, since the walls and door did not permit transmission of sound.

The cell contained no sink, water fountain, or commode. The only facility for disposing of human waste was a device called a "Chinese toilet." It was merely a hole in the floor in the corner of the cell covered with a grate. It was flushed with water by a manually controlled valve operated from *outside* the cell.

A prisoner confined to a strip cell apparently is permitted to have a toothbrush and toothpaste upon request. It is normal practice for the prisoner to receive three meals per day. A glass of water is given at least twice daily. A mattress is provided between 3 P.M. and 8 A.M. and blankets are supplied when the room temperature so requires.

The prisoner is not allowed to have reading materials (they would be useless in the darkness anyway), except a Bible upon request. He is given no opportunity to exercise. He has no one to talk to or communicate with in any way except that he is permitted to write. A prisoner can be confined in such a cell for a maximum of eight days, but that period can be extended upon approval by the commissioner of corrections.

The cruel and unusual punishment clause does not forbid all excessive or severe penalties. Nor does it give constitutional dimension to the theories of penologists on what is the most appropriate disposition of an offender. The language of the clause is ill-suited to the performance of such a task. It condemns only that punishment which is "barbarous" or "shocking to the conscience." And the "conscience" the clause is concerned with is the collective conscience of our society, not the conscience of judges or prison officials as individuals.

Courts must be particularly careful not to intercede needlessly on behalf of an inmate engaged in a dispute with prison administrators. The Eighth Amendment should not be used to divest prison authorities of the administrative discretion necessary to maintain order and discipline in penal institutions. Unless a prisoner is exemplarily punished for violating a prison regulation, he and other prisoners will not be deterred from committing further offenses. And the determination of what punishment is effective and fair considering the nature of the offense and the character of the offender ordinarily should be left to the informed judgment of prison authorities. But prison officials, no less than sentencing judges, are bound by the strictures of the Eighth Amendment. Disciplinary measures that violate civilized standards of human decency are proscribed.

We hold that the conditions to which LaReau was subjected in the strip cell fall below the irreducible minimum of decency required by the Eighth Amendment. Enforced isolation and boredom are permissible methods of discipline, although they might not remain so if extended over a long period of time. But the conditions here went beyond mere coerced stagnation. We cannot approve of threatening an inmate's sanity and severing his contacts with reality by placing him in a dark cell almost continuously day and night. Nor can we find any justification for denying a man the ability to maintain his personal cleanliness. What is most offensive to this court was the use of the "Chinese toilet." Causing a man to live, eat, and perhaps sleep in close confines with his own human waste is too debasing and degrading to be permitted. The indecent conditions that existed in this Somers prison strip cell seriously threatened the physical and mental soundness of its unfortunate occupant. In order to preserve the human dignity of inmates and the standards of humanity embraced by our society, we cannot sanction such punishment.

Since the district court did not reach the issue of what relief should be granted, we remand with directions that the district court frame an appropriate injunction and that it determine what damages, if any, should be awarded. Our remand is not to be construed as any expression of opinion on our part, one way or the other, on the issue of damages.

Appellant's First Amendment claim is that he was denied his constitutional right to free exercise of religion during the periods he was held in various segregation units.

A prisoner confined to any segregation unit at the Somers prison, whether it be administrative segregation, punitive segregation, maximum punitive, or the strip cell, is not permitted to visit the prison chapel. Catholic mass is performed in the chapel only, with the exception of an occasional service performed in the segregation unit. An inmate in segregation therefore normally cannot attend mass. The Catholic chaplain, however, does make himself available to administer the sacraments—penance and holy communion—in the segregated unit itself. Chaplain Stanley, the Catholic chaplain at Somers, testified that LaReau never requested his services in the segregation unit, but continually demanded access to the chapel. The chaplain also testified that he had taken care of LaReau's spiritual needs adequately and "to the best of his ability."

Segregated prisoners are not permitted to attend mass in the chapel, according to the testimony of prison officials, because to allow them to do so would be to invite trouble. Most of these inmates are disciplinary problems, and many of them are would-be leaders of mass prison disruption. LaReau, for example, was a compulsive letter writer and had been involved in several major disputes, including a widespread hunger strike. To allow him to attend Sunday mass along with the general prison population, according to the prison authorities, would facilitate a major incident by providing the inmates with a rebellious leader.

Sherbert v. Verner, 374 U.S. 398 (1963), firmly established that the First Amendment guarantees to every person the right to participate in acts and practices that are an integral part of his religious faith. *Sherbert* also announced that a balancing principle should be employed to determine whether the free-exercise clause has been infringed by a secular regulation: The state can deny a person participation in religious exercises if the state regulation has an important objective and the restraint on religious liberty is reasonably adapted to achieving that objective.

Attendance at Sunday mass clearly is a fundamental practice in the Catholic religion. We hold, however, that the prison authorities at Somers have denied segregated prisoners attendance at mass for a substantial reason. They have made a reasonable judgment, one which we are not inclined to disturb, that unruly prisoners should not be given the opportunity to instigate trouble with the general inmate population. Such a hazard can be avoided only by denying these prisoners access to the chapel for Sunday mass. Judge Clarie found, and the record supports the finding, that La Reau is a potential instigator of large-scale disorder. We therefore affirm the judgment of the court below on the First Amendment claim.

Affirmed in part; reversed and remanded in part.

CASE QUESTIONS

1. Should the Eighth Amendment's prohibition against cruel and unusual punishment be invoked to prevent mentally cruel punishments?
2. One school of thought among criminologists is that prisons should be rehabilitative. Do you believe inmates should be accorded a "right to rehabilitation"? Can you think of any examples in which the inmate may desire a right to be free from rehabilitation?

SUGGESTED READINGS

R.L. GOLDFARB and L.R. SINGER, AFTER CONVICTION (1973).

PRACTICING LAW INSTITUTE, PRISONERS' RIGHTS (Vols. I & II) (1972).

Singer, *Prison Conditions: An Unconstitutional Roadblock to Rehabilitation*, 20 CATH. U. L. REV. 365 (1971).

Cole, *The Constitutional Status of Solitary Confinement*, 57 CORNELL L. REV. 476 (1972).

Mann, *Prison Discipline and the Eighth Amendment—Out of the Quagmire*, 1 AM. J. CRIM. L. 4 (1972).

Hirschkop and Millemann, *The Unconstitutionality of Prison Life*, 55 VA. L. REV. 795 (1969).

Symposium: Prisons and Prisoners, 23 HASTINGS L.J. 995 (1972).

Note, *Prison Discipline and the Eighth Amendment: A Psychological Perspective*, 43 CIN. L. REV. 101 (1974).

Jensen and Giegold, *Finding Jobs for Ex-Offenders: A Study of Employers' Attitudes*, 14 AM. BUS. L.J. 195 (1976).

Chapter Questions

1. Define the following terms:

   a. arraign   b. arrest
   c. bail   d. felony
   e. grand jury   f. *habeas corpus*
   g. indictment   h. larceny
   i. magistrate   j. misdemeanor
   k. *nolo contendere*   l. pardon
   m. parole   n. probable cause
   o. prosecutor   p. recognizance
   q. surety   r. warrant
   s. writ

2. Viven Harris was charged on two counts of selling heroin to an under-cover police officer. At trial, Harris admitted knowing the undercover police officer, but denied that he had made one of the sales charged, and claimed that the contents of the two bags delivered to the officer was baking powder, not heroin. On cross examination, the prosecution questioned Harris concerning statements he had made immediately following arrest that partially contradicted his direct testimony. Harris responded that he could not remember any of the questions or answers of the police interrogation recited by the prosecutor. Although Harris did not claim that the statements made to the police were coerced or involuntary, the prosecution conceded that the statements were inadmissible in its case-in-chief because of the absence of the *Miranda* warnings. The trial judge instructed the jury that the statements could be used only in determining the defendant's credibility. Was it proper to admit the statements for purposes of discrediting Harris's testimony?
   Harris v. New York, 401 U.S. 222 (1971)

3. Mr. Beckwith, a taxpayer, made certain statements to Internal Revenue agents. These statements were made during the course of a noncustodial interview in a criminal tax investigation. The interview was conducted in Beckwith's home after he voluntarily allowed the agents to enter. Beckwith was later tried for criminal tax fraud and—although he had not been given *Miranda* warnings before making the statements—they were admitted and used against him. What would be the court's reasoning in permitting these incriminating statements to be used?
   Beckwith v. United States, 425 U.S. 341 (1976)

4. Defendant Butler moved to suppress evidence of his incriminating statements at his trial. These statements were made to a federal agent

during custodial interrogation without counsel present. The agent testified that Butler had been advised of his rights at the time of his arrest and then taken to a local FBI office for interrogation. Butler had an eleventh-grade education. He was given an advice-of-rights form, which he read, and he stated that he understood his rights. However, Butler refused to sign a waiver provision at the bottom. After being told that he need not talk or sign anything, Butler stated that he would talk, but not sign anything. He said nothing when advised of his right to counsel. He never requested counsel or attempted to terminate the questioning. Did Butler effectively waive his rights under *Miranda?*

North Carolina v. Butler, 441 U.S. 369 (1979)

5. Roosevelt Harris was convicted of possessing non-tax-paid liquor in violation of federal law. The federal tax investigator's affidavit supporting the search warrant, the execution of which resulted in the discovery of the illicit liquor, stated that: (1) Harris had a reputation with the investigator for over four years as being a trafficker in non-tax-paid distilled spirits. (2) During that time the local constable had located illicit whiskey in an abandoned house under Harris's control. (3) On the date of the affidavit, the affiant (tax investigator) had received sworn oral information from a person whom the affiant found to be a prudent person, and who feared for his life should his name be revealed, that the informant had purchased illicit whiskey from the residence described. Is the affidavit sufficient to establish probable cause for issuing a search warrant?

United States v. Harris, 403 U.S. 573 (1971)

6. An experienced federal narcotics agent was told by an informer, whose information the agent had always found to be accurate and reliable, that James Draper, who the agent did not know but who was described by the informer, was peddling narcotics, had gone to Chicago to obtain a supply, and would return on a certain train on a certain day or on the day after. The agent met the train, easily recognized Draper from the informer's description, and arrested him, without a warrant, searched him, and seized narcotics and a hypodermic syringe found in his possession. Can these items be admitted into evidence against Draper at trial?

Draper v. United States, 358 U.S. 307 (1959)

7. Police officers, armed with an arrest warrant but not a search warrant, were admitted to Chimel's home by his wife. They waited until Chimel arrived and served him with the warrant. Although he denied the officers' request to "look around," they conducted a search of the

entire house ''as incident to the lawful arrest.'' Are items taken from Chimel's home admissible at trial?

Chimel v. California, 395 U.S. 752 (1969)

8. Murphy voluntarily came to the stationhouse in connection with the strangulation death of his wife. At that time he had not been arrested, although there was probable cause to believe that he had committed the murder. Shortly after Murphy's arrival at the stationhouse (where he was met by retained counsel), the police noticed a dark spot on his finger. Suspecting that the spot might be dried blood and knowing the evidence of strangulation is often found under the assailant's fingernails, the police asked him if they could take a sample of scrapings from his fingernails. He refused. Under protest and without a warrant, the police proceeded to take the samples, which turned out to contain traces of skin and blood cells, and fabric from the victim's nightgown. This incriminating evidence was admitted at his trial, which ended in a conviction. Murphy appealed the conviction, claiming that the fingernail scrapings were the product of a search prohibited by the Fourth Amendment. Is this a valid argument?

Cupp v. Murphy, 412 U.S. 291 (1973)

9. A complaint charges the defendant with breaking and entering. The defendant has an honorable discharge from the Army, a family living in the community, and is unemployed. It appears that drug addiction was a motivation. What must the judge consider in determining bail under the Federal Bail Reform Act?

10. An Illinois statute provides that accused persons can secure pretrial release: (1) on personal recognizance; (2) by execution of a bail bond, with a deposit of 10% of the bail, all but 10% of which (amounting to 1% of the bail) is returned on performance of the bond conditions; and (3) by execution of a bail bond, secured by a full-amount deposit in cash, authorized securities, or certain real estate, all of which is returned on performance of the bond conditions. John Schilb, charged with two traffic offenses, secured pretrial release after depositing 10% of the bail fixed. He was convicted of one offense and acquitted of the other. After he paid his fine, all but 1% of the bail (amounting to $7.50) was refunded. In a class action, he challenged the Illinois system on due-process and equal-protection grounds, claiming that the 1% retention charge is imposed on only one segment of the class gaining pretrial release, and on the poor, but not the rich; and that its imposition on an accused-found-innocent constitutes a court cost against the nonguilty. Do his arguments have merit?

Schilb v. Kuebel, 404 U.S. 357 (1971)

11. Defendant's trial on a North Carolina criminal trespass indictment ended with a declaration of a mistrial when the jury failed to reach a verdict. After the case had been postponed for two terms the defendant filed a motion in which he petitioned the court to ascertain when the state intended to bring him to trial. While this motion was being considered, the state's prosecutor moved for permission to take a *"nolle prosequi* with leave," a procedural device whereby the accused is discharged from custody but remains subject to prosecution at any time in the future at the discretion of the prosecutor. Would entry of the *nolle prosequi* order violate the defendant's right to a speedy trial?
    Klopfer v. North Carolina, 386 U.S. 213 (1967)

12. Florida law provides for a six-person jury in noncapital cases. Defendant Williams, charged with robbery, makes a pretrial motion to impanel a twelve-person jury instead of a six-person jury, claiming that a six-person jury violates his Sixth Amendment right to a "trial by jury." Rule on the motion.
    Williams v. Florida, 399 U.S. 78 (1970)

13. Somerville was indicted for theft on March 19, 1965. His case was called for trial in November of that year, and a jury was impaneled and sworn. On the following day, the prosecuting attorney realized that the indictment was deficient because it did not allege that Somerville intended to deprive the owner of his property permanently. The Illinois Constitution prohibits amendment of indictments except for formal errors. The trial court decided that it was useless to proceed with the trial and granted the state's motion for a mistrial. Somerville was reindicted, tried, and found guilty. Was this double jeopardy?
    Illinois v. Somerville, 410 U.S. 458 (1973)

14. William Allen was indicted by an Illinois grand jury for armed robbery, a crime carrying a sentence of up to 30 years in prison. At the pretrial stage, Allen refused court-appointed counsel and insisted on conducting his own defense. When it was time to examine prospective jurors, Allen asked insulting and repetitive questions. After a warning by the trial judge, Allen used vile language in addressing the judge and repeatedly berated the jury. When Allen tore up the file of his advisory counsel and threw it on the courtroom floor, the trial judge ordered Allen removed from the courtroom. Periodically Allen was returned to the courtroom, only to resume his obscene outbursts. The Sixth Amendment to the Constitution provides that the accused has a right to be present at trial and confront the accusers. Did the trial judge violate Allen's rights by removing him from the courtroom? What alternative sanctions were available?
    Illinois v. Allen, 397 U.S. 337 (1970)

15. Defendant's wife was bludgeoned to death. From the outset, officials focused suspicion on the defendant, who was arrested and charged with murder. During the entire pretrial period, virulent and incriminating publicity about the defendant and the murder made the case notorious, and the news media frequently aired charges besides those for which the defendant w•s tried. During the trial, news reporters were allowed to take over almost the entire courtroom. The movement of the reporters in the courtroom caused frequent confusion and disrupted the trial. Before the jurors began deliberations, they were not sequestered and had access to all news media. The petitioner filed a *habeas corpus* petition, contending that he did not receive a fair trial. What result?
    Sheppard v. Maxwell, 384 U.S. 333 (1966)

16. A California statute makes it a misdemeanor punishable by imprisonment for any person ''to be addicted to the use of narcotics.'' Thus the statute makes the ''status'' of narcotic addiction a criminal offense for which offenders may be prosecuted at any time before they reform, even though they have never used or possessed any narcotics within the state and have not been guilty of any antisocial behavior there. If someone has been sentenced to prison under this statute, what issue should be raised on appeal?
    Robinson v. California, 370 U.S. 660 (1962)

17. Willie Francis was convicted of murder in a state court and sentenced to be electrocuted. A warrant for his execution was duly issued. He was prepared for electrocution, placed in the electric chair, and subjected to a shock that was intended to cause his death but failed to do so, presumably because of some mechanical difficulty. He was removed from the chair and returned to prison. Another warrant for his execution at a later date was issued. Was this a violation of the cruel and unusual clause?
    Louisiana ex rel. Francis v. Resweber, 329 U.S. 459 (1947)

VIII Legislation

Members of society require uniformly operating rules of conduct in order to maintain social harmony. The judicial branch of the government creates rules of law through case decisions. The legislative branch, which is responsible for more substantial changes, creates law by enacting statutes. An examination of legislation reveals the problems and moods of the nation. Legislatures write history through the legislative process. There have been legislative reactions to almost all political, social, and business problems that have faced society. Laws have been passed in response to wars, depressions, civil-rights problems, crime, and concern for cities and the environment. Checks and balances have been built into the system in order to prevent overreaction by the legislature and to promote wise and timely legislation.

The process of enacting statutes is lengthy and complex. At the federal level, it is a procedure that involves 535 persons in the House and Senate who represent the interests of their constituents, themselves, and the country. A proposed bill may encounter numerous obstacles. Mere approval by the legislative bodies does not ensure passage, for at both federal and state levels, the executive branch has the power to veto a bill. Another check on legislation can come once a bill becomes law. At that point, the constitutionality of the legislative act may be challenged in court.

It makes no difference which body a bill is introduced in, since a statute must be approved by both houses of the legislature. However, the legislative process varies slightly between the Senate and House. If differences exist between the House and Senate versions of a bill, a joint conference committee meets to reconcile the conflicts and draft a compromise bill.

After a bill has been approved by both houses and certain formalities have been completed, it must be approved and signed by the President

338

of the United States to become effective. If the President vetoes a bill—which rarely occurs—it does not become law unless the veto is overridden by a two-thirds vote of both houses.

Defeat of a bill is far more common than passage. More than 95% of all legislation introduced is defeated at some point. Still, much legislation *is* signed into law each year. Legislative death can result at any stage of the process, and from many sources. For legislation to be successful in passing, assignment to the proper committee is crucial. However, committees can be cruel. They may refuse to hold hearings. They may alter a bill completely. Or they may kill it outright. If a proposed statute survives the committee stage, the House Rules Committee or the Senate majority leaders determine the bill's destiny. Once a bill reaches the floor of the House or Senate, irrelevant proposals—known as *riders*—may be added to it. Or drastic amendments can so alter it that it is defeated. The possibilities are almost endless. Refer to the flowchart on page 390.

The need for certainty and uniformity in the laws among the states is reflected in federal legislation and uniform state laws. A great degree of uniformity has been accomplished among the states on a number of matters. An important example is the Uniform Commercial Code. With increased interstate business operations, business firms pressured for uniform laws dealing with commercial transactions among states. Judges, law professors, and leading members of the bar drafted the Uniform Commercial Code for adoption by the individual states. The U.C.C. was first adopted by the Pennsylvania legislature in 1953, and is now the law throughout the states. The U.C.C. covers sales, commercial paper, bank collection processes, letters of credit, bulk transfers, warehouse receipts, bills of lading, other documents of title, investment securities, and secured transactions.

Power to Legislate

Federal Government

Legislative power is the power to establish rules of law for the government and regulation of the people. The people are the source of all legislative authority. The federal Constitution enumerates the powers granted by the people to the federal government. The United States government is based on delegated and enumerated powers. It cannot exercise any authority that is not granted to it by the Constitution, either expressly or impliedly. Whenever the federal government's right to exercise authority is in question, recourse must be made to the Constitution to determine the government's authority, either in express words or by implication. The powers that the Constitution delegates to the U.S. government are comprehensive and complete. They are without limitations other than those in the Constitution.

Article I, § 8, of the Constitution is an important source of federal regulatory laws. The power to tax and regulate interstate commerce are just two of these expressly delegated powers. The Constitution declares in article I, § 8, clause 18, that Congress is specifically empowered to enact all laws necessary and proper to carry into effect the powers expressly granted to it. This legislative authority has been broadly exercised. Yet any legislation enacted under this provision has had a basis in the enumerated powers of article I, § 8. State powers have been restricted by the necessary-and-proper clause, especially in the area of commerce.

Constitutional amendments are also sources of congressional legislative authority. For example, the Fourteenth, Nineteenth and Twenty-third Amendments are such sources. Congress may also delegate its legislative power. This is the source of regulatory agencies' power to establish rules in selected fields.

United States Postal Serv. v. Brennan
574 F.2d 712
United States Court of Appeals
Second Circuit
April 13, 1978

MULLIGAN, CIRCUIT JUDGE
The facts underlying this litigation are undisputed. Patricia H. Brennan and J. Paul Brennan, doing business under the name of P. H. Brennan Hand Delivery Service (the Brennans), have conducted since March 1976 in downtown Rochester, New York, a service delivering for compensation letters and small- to medium-size parcels. They guarantee same-day delivery in Rochester for all materials picked up from customers before 12 o'clock noon at a rate which is less than that charged by the United States Postal Service (USPS). On February 23, 1977, USPS brought a Civil action in the U.S. District Court seeking permanent injunctive relief prohibiting the Brennans from continued violations of the private express statutes which proscribe the private carriage and delivery of "letters." The Brennans filed an answer which in substance admitted the material facts alleged in the complaint, but as a defense urged that the private express statutes were unconstitutional. The U.S. district judge found that the defendant's contentions were without merit and granted the government's motion for summary judgment. The Brennans appealed.

Under the private express statutes, Congress has granted the United States a monopoly on the conveyance of "letters or packets" and has precluded competition by private express. Appellants' primary position is that the Constitution did not grant exclusive power to Congress to operate a postal system and that the private express statutes are not "necessary and proper" to execute the constitutional power to establish post offices and post roads.

The Constitution does not expressly give Congress "the sole and exclusive right and power" to establish and regulate the carriage of mail, as did the Articles of Confederation. However, the postal power, like all other enumerated powers of Congress, is complete in itself, may be exercised to its utmost extent, and acknowledges no limitations, other than those that are prescribed in the Constitution. Moreover, the Constitution grants Congress the power to enact all laws it deems necessary and proper to execute its power to establish post offices. The congressional choice, as expressed in the private express statutes, was to retain in the United States an exclusive and monopolistic authority over the delivery of letters. The question is whether that determination was "necessary and proper."

The scope of the necessary-and-proper clause was indelibly sketched in *McCulloch v. Maryland*, 4 Wheat. 316, 4 L.Ed. 579 (1819), where Chief Justice Marshall gave a broad interpretation to that clause in upholding congressional action under the commerce clause:

We admit, as all must admit, that the powers of the government are limited, and that its limits are not to be transcended. But we think the sound construction of the Constitution must allow to the national legislature that discretion, with respect to the means by which the powers it confers are to be carried into execution, which will enable that body to perform the high duties assigned to it, in the manner most beneficial to the people. Let the end be legitimate, let it be within the scope of the Constitution, and all means which are appropriate, which are plainly adapted to that end, which are not prohibited, but consistent with the letter and spirit of the Constitution, are constitutional.

There is nothing novel or unprecedented in the governmental monopoly. Congress certainly could have determined that something less than a federal monopoly would allow the continuance of an effective postal system. However, the wisdom of the choice is not the question for the court; we may only pass on Congress' power to make it.

The constitutionality of the postal monopoly has been challenged rarely and never successfully. If private agencies can be established, the income of the government may be so reduced that economy might demand a discontinuance of the system. Thus the business which it is the right and duty of the government to conduct for the interest of all, and on such terms that all may avail themselves of it with advantage, may be handed over to individuals or corporations who will conduct it with the sole view of making money, and who may find it for their profit to exclude localities or classes from the benefit of the service.

The most recent opinion in point is *United States v. Black*, 569 F.2d 1111 (10th Cir. 1978). In *Black* the defendants operated a private express conveying letters between the cities of Pittsburgh and Frontenac in the state of Kansas. The court held that the postal monopoly was constitutional because it was a valid exercise by Congress of the power granted it by art. I, § 8. This case is indistinguishable from the present appeal.

We conclude that the postal power,

in conjunction with the necessary-and-proper clause, authorizes Congress to exercise its power to the utmost extent. The monopoly which Congress created is an appropriate and plainly adapted means of providing postal service beneficial to the citizenry at large. Consequently, the private express statutes are constitutional.

Appellants' remaining constitutional arguments are even less persuasive. They rely on the Tenth Amendment, which provides: "The powers not delegated to the United States by the Constitution, nor prohibited by it to the states, are reserved to the states respectively, or to the people." However, the postal power is a delegated power and, as we have found under the necessary-and-proper clause, in determining to occupy the field exclusively in the conveyance of letters, Congress was not exceeding its powers. Since we have decided the creation of a postal monopoly is a proper exercise of power, the Tenth Amendment argument adds nothing of substance to the constitutional issue here, particularly since no threat to state sovereignty is involved.

Finally, the appellants also claim that since the postal monopoly encompasses only letter mail and permits private competition in the delivery of non–letter mail (for example, fourth-class mail parcels), there is a violation of their Fifth Amendment equal protection rights. No authority at all is cited that supports this proposition. As the Supreme Court has often stated, "A classification 'must be reasonable, not arbitrary, and must rest on some ground of difference having a fair and substantial relation to the object of the legislation, so that *all persons similarly circumstanced shall be treated alike.'"* *Johnson v. Robinson*, 415 U.S. 361 (1974). But here the classification is not directed against persons; rather it is based on types of mail. Obviously, the distinction between types of mail is not invidious. No fundamental rights are involved. The reason for the classification is obvious and rational. The carriage of letters in selected areas is highly profitable compared to the carriage of bulky materials. This permits a subsidy of sorts to those services which inevitably lose money.

We conclude that the appellants have utterly failed to establish the unconstitutionality of the private express statutes on any basis. While American citizens may properly complain about the cost or inefficiency of mail service, this hardly raises a matter of constitutional proportions. It is a matter for the Congress and not the courts.

Judgment affirmed

CASE QUESTIONS

1. How does the relationship between constitutional provisions and statutory law affect a court's initial point of inquiry?
2. What are the limitations on the enumerated powers of Congress? Does the Tenth Amendment limit them?
3. Have the private express statutes denied the Brennans a right to earn a livelihood?

SUGGESTED READINGS

Brodie, *A Question of Enumerated Powers: Constitutional Issues Surrounding Federal Ownership of the Public Lands*, 12 PAC. L.J. 693 (1981).

Kennedy, *Time to Re-examine the 'Legislative Function' of Congress*, 66 A.B.A.J. 730 (1980).

Prygoski, *Supreme Court Review of Congressional Action in the Federalism Area*, 18 DUQUESNE L. REV. 197 (1980).

State Government

The authority that resides in every sovereignty to pass laws for its internal regulation and government is called *police power*. It is the power inherent in the state to pass reasonable laws necessary to preserve the public health, safety, morals, and welfare. Police power of the states is not a grant derived from a written constitution; the federal Constitution assumes the pre-existence of the police power. The Tenth Amendment to the federal Constitution reserves to the states any power not delegated to the federal government. It exists without any reservation in the Constitution, although the federal and state constitutions set limits in the exercise of this power.

The basis of the police power is the state's obligation to protect its citizens and provide for the safety and order of society. This yields a broad, comprehensive authority. The defining of criminal action and the regulating of trades and professions are examples of this vast scope of power. A mandatory precondition to the exercise of police power is the existence of an ascertainable public need for a particular statute, and the statute must bear a real and substantial relation to the end that is sought. The possession and enjoyment of all rights may be limited under the police power, provided that it is reasonably exercised.

Limitations on the police power have never been drawn with exactness or determined by a general formula. The power may not be exercised for private purposes or for the exclusive benefit of a few. Its scope has been declared to be greater in emergency situations. Otherwise its exercise must be in the public interest, must be reasonable, and may not be repugnant to the rights implied or secured in the Constitution.

Powers delegated by the federal government and individual state constitutions also serve as a basis for state legislation. Any activity solely attributable to the sovereignty of the state may not be restrained by Congress.

Metromedia, Inc. v. City of San Diego
23 Cal. 3d 848, 610 P.2d 407
Supreme Court of California
April 14, 1980

TOBRINER, JUSTICE

The city of San Diego enacted an ordinance which bans all off-site advertising billboards and requires the removal of existing billboards following expiration of an amortization period. Plaintiffs, owners of billboards affected by the ordinance, sued to enjoin its enforcement. Upon motion for summary judgment, the superior court adjudged the ordinance unconstitutional, and issued the injunction as prayed.

We reject the superior court's conclusion that the ordinance exceeded the city's authority under the police power. We hold that the achievement of the purposes recited in the ordinance—eliminating traffic hazards and improving the appearance of the city—represent proper objectives for the exercise of the city's police power, and that the present ordinance bears a reasonable relationship to those objectives.

The present case concerns the constitutionality of San Diego ordinance no. 10795. The ordinance prohibits all off-site "outdoor advertising display signs." Off-site signs are defined as those which do not identify a use, facility, or service located on the premises or a product which is produced, sold, or manufactured on the premises. All existing signs which do not conform to the requirements of the ordinance must be removed following expiration of an amortization period, ranging from 90 days to 4 years, depending on the location and depreciated value of the sign.

Plaintiffs, Metromedia, Inc., and Pa-

cific Outdoor Advertising Co., Inc., are engaged in the outdoor advertising business and own a substantial number of off-site billboards subject to removal under ordinance no. 10795.

The San Diego ordinance, as we shall explain, represents a proper application of municipal authority over zoning and land use for the purpose of promoting the public safety and welfare. The ordinance recites the purposes for which it was enacted, including the elimination of traffic hazards brought about by distracting advertising displays and the improvement of the appearance of the city. Since these goals are proper objectives for the exercise of the city's police power, the city council, asserting its legislative judgment, could reasonably believe the instant ordinance would further those objectives.

We hold as a matter of law that an ordinance which eliminates billboards designed to be viewed from streets and highways reasonably relates to traffic safety. Billboards are intended to, and undoubtedly do, divert a driver's attention from the roadway. Whether this distracting effect contributes to traffic accidents invokes an issue of continuing controversy. But as the New York Court of Appeals pointed out, "mere disagreement" as to "whether billboards or other advertising devices . . . constitute a traffic hazard . . . may not cast doubt on the statute's validity. Matters such as these are reserved for legislative judgment, and the legislative determination, here expressly announced, will not be disturbed unless manifestly unreasonable." [*New York State Thruway Auth. v. Ashley Motor Ct.* (1961) N.Y.2d 151, 218 N.Y.S.2d 640, 176 N.E.2d 566.] Many other decisions have upheld billboard ordinances on the ground that such ordinances reasonably relate to traffic safety; we cannot find it manifestly unreasonable for the San Diego City Council to reach the same conclusion.

We further hold that even if, as plaintiffs maintain, the principal purpose of the ordinance is not to promote traffic safety but to improve the appearance of the community, such a purpose falls within the city's authority under the police power. Because this state relies on its scenery to attract tourists and commerce, aesthetic considerations assume economic value. Consequently, any distinction between aesthetic and economic grounds as a justification for billboard regulation must fail. Today, economic and aesthetic considerations together constitute the nearly inseparable warp and woof of the fabric upon which the modern city must design its future.

If the San Diego ordinance reasonably relates to the public safety and welfare, it should logically follow that the ordinance represents a valid exercise of the police power. Plaintiffs contend, however, that the police power is subject to an additional limiting doctrine: that regardless of the reasonableness of the act in relation to the public health, safety, morals, and welfare, the police power can never be employed to prohibit completely a business not found to be a public nuisance.

The distinction between prohibition and regulation in this case is one of words and not substance. "Every regulation necessarily speaks as a prohibition." [*Goldblatt v. Hempstead* (1962) 369 U.S. 590.] In the present case, for example, plaintiffs describe the ordinance as a prohibition of off-site advertising, while the city describes it as a regulation of advertising, one which limits advertising to on-site signs. Surely the validity of the ordinance does not depend on the court's choice between such verbal formulas.

Rather than strive to develop a logical distinction between "regulation" and "prohibition," and to find themselves embroiled in language rather than fact, courts of other jurisdictions in recent decisions have held that a community can entirely prohibit off-site advertising.

Plaintiffs stress that most of the cases upholding a community ban on billboards or other commercial uses have involved small, predominantly residential towns or rural localities. Recently, however, the Massachusetts Supreme Judicial Court upheld an ordinance similar to the one at issue here involving a total prohibition of billboards in a densely populated town with a sizable business and industrial district. (*John Donnelly & Sons, Inc. v. Outdoor Advertising Bd.* (1975) 369 Mass. 206, 339 N.E.2d 709.) The court there stated that "We believe that it is within the scope of the police power for the town to decide that its total living area should be improved so as to be more attractive to both its residents and visitors. Whether an area is urban, suburban, or rural should not be determinative of whether the residents are entitled to preserve and enhance their environment. Urban residents are not immune to ugliness."

Nor do we perceive how we could rationally establish a rule that a city's police power diminishes as its population grows, and that once it reaches some unspecified size, it no longer has the power to prohibit billboards. San Diego, for example, has already prohibited billboards within 97% of its limits—a region which in area and population far surpasses most California cities. Plaintiffs claim that a ban covering 97% of the city is a "regulation," while the extension of that ban to the remaining 3% of the city is a "prohibition," but such sophistry is a mere play on words.

Thus the validity of ordinance no. 10795 under the police power does not turn on its regulatory or prohibitory character, nor on the size of the city which enacted it, but solely on whether it reasonably relates to the public safety and welfare. As we have explained, the ordinance recites that it was enacted to eliminate traffic hazards, improve the appearance of the community, and thereby protect property values. The asserted goals are proper objectives under the police power, and plaintiffs have failed to prove that the ordinance lacks a reasonable relationship to the achievement of those goals. We conclude that the summary judgment cannot be sustained on the ground that the ordinance exceeds the city's authority under the police power.

To hold that a city cannot prohibit off-site commercial billboards for the purpose of protecting and preserving the beauty of the environment is to succumb to a bleak materialism. We conclude with the pungent words of Ogden Nash:

I think that I shall never see
A billboard lovely as a tree.
Indeed, unless the billboards fall,
I'll never see a tree at all.

The judgment is reversed.

CLARK, JUSTICE, dissenting.
While recognizing that aesthetic beauty and traffic safety are legitimate police power objectives, the majority fail to show these interests outweigh First Amendment rights of plaintiffs, advertisers, and the viewing public. The conflict between police powers on the one hand and First Amendment rights on the other must seek compromise, allowing government to reasonably regulate the time, place, and manner in which First Amendment rights may be exercised. To be constitutionally reasonable, regulation of time, place, or manner must be written narrowly and explicitly, in furtherance of a legitimate police power purpose.

CASE QUESTIONS

1. When the exercise of police power is challenged, who has the burden of proof as to the question of its reasonableness?
2. If the state uses its police power to regulate fundamental rights guaranteed by the Constitution, what is the reasonableness test used to determine its validity?
3. What would be some of San Diego's economic considerations for enacting the billboard ordinance?

SUGGESTED READINGS

Bufford, *Beyond the Eye of the Beholder: A New Majority of Jurisdictions Authorize Aesthetic Regulation*, 48 U.M.K.C. L. REV. 125 (1980).

Duker, *Mr. Justice Rufus W. Peckham: The Police Power and the Individual in a Changing World*, BRIGHAM YOUNG UNIVERSITY L. REV. 47 (1980).

Romero, *The State and Federal Quandary over Billboard Controls*, 19 NATURAL RESOURCES JOURNAL 711 (1979).

Sax, *Takings, Private Property and Public Rights*, 81 YALE L.J. 149 (1971).

Tosney, *Health Care Regulation in California: Constitutional?* 11 PACIFIC L.J. 895 (1980).

Federal Supremacy

The Constitution divides powers between the federal government and the states. Certain powers are delegated to the federal government alone. Others are reserved to the states. Still others are exercised concurrently by both. The Tenth Amendment to the Constitution specifies that the "powers not delegated to the United States by the Constitution . . . are reserved to the states . . . or to the people." Unlike the federal power, which is granted, the state already has its power, unless expressly or implicitly denied by the state or federal constitutions. Each state has the power to govern its own affairs, except where the Constitution has withdrawn that power.

The powers of both the federal and state governments are to be exercised so as not to interfere with each other's exercise of power. Whenever there is a conflict, state laws must yield to federal acts to the extent of the conflict. This is the requirement of the supremacy clause in article VI of the Constitution.

Under the supremacy clause, Congress can enact legislation that may supersede state authority and pre-empt state regulations. The pre-emption doctrine is based on the supremacy clause. Hence state laws that frustrate or are contrary to congressional objectives in a specific area are invalid. When one considers state law, one takes into account the nature of the subject matter, any vital national interests that may be involved, or perhaps the need for uniformity between state and federal laws, and the expressed or implied intent of Congress. It is necessary to determine whether Congress has sought to occupy a particular field to the exclusion of the states. All interests, both state and federal, must be examined.

DeCanas v. Bica
424 U.S. 351
United States Supreme Court
February 25, 1976

MR. JUSTICE BRENNAN

California Labor Code § 2805(a) provides that "No employer shall knowingly employ an alien who is not entitled to lawful residence in the United States if such employment would have an adverse effect on lawful resident workers." The question presented in this case is whether § 2805(a) is unconstitutional, either because it is an attempt to regulate immigration and naturalization or because it is preempted under the supremacy clause, art. VI, clause 2 of the Constitution, by the Immigration and Nationality Act, 8 U.S.C. § 1101 *et seq.* (INA), the comprehensive federal statutory scheme for regulation of immigration and naturalization.

Petitioners, who are immigrant migrant farmworkers, brought this action pursuant to § 2805(c) against respondent farm-labor contractors in California Superior Court. The complaint alleged that respondents had refused petitioners continued employment due to a surplus of labor resulting from respondents' knowing employment, in violation of § 2805(a), of aliens not lawfully admitted to residence in the United States. Petitioners sought reinstatement and a permanent injunction against respondents' wilful employment of illegal aliens. The Superior Court, in an unreported opinion, dismissed the complaint, holding "that Labor Code 2805 is unconstitutional ... [because] [i]t encroaches upon, and interferes with, a comprehensive regulatory scheme enacted by Congress in the exercise of its exclusive power over immigration. . . ." The California Court of Appeal, Second Appellate District, affirmed, 40 Cal. App.3d 976, 115 Cal. Rptr. 444 (1974). The court of appeal held that § 2805(a) is an attempt to regulate the conditions for admission of foreign nationals, and therefore unconstitutional because, "in the area of immigration and naturalization, congressional power is exclusive." *Id.* at 979, 115 Cal. Rptr., at 446. The court of appeal further indicated that state regulatory power over this subject matter was foreclosed when Congress, "as an incident of national sovereignty," enacted the INA as a comprehensive scheme governing all aspects of immigration and naturalization, including the employment of aliens, and "specifically and intentionally declined to add sanctions on employers to its control mechanism." *Ibid.* The Supreme Court of California denied review. We granted *certiorari* and we reverse.

Power to regulate immigration is unquestionably exclusively a federal power. But this Court has never held that every state enactment which in any way deals with aliens is a regulation of immigration and thus *per se* pre-empted by this constitutional power, whether latent or exercised. In this case, California has sought to strengthen its economy by adopting federal standards in imposing criminal sanctions against state employers who knowingly employ aliens who have no federal right to employment within the country. Even if such local regulation has some purely speculative and indirect impact on immigration, it does not thereby become a constitutionally proscribed regulation of immigration that Congress itself would be powerless to authorize or approve. Thus, absent congressional action, § 2805 would not be an invalid state incursion on federal power.

Even when the Constitution does not itself commit exclusive power to regulate a particular field to the federal government, there are situations in which state regulation, although harmonious with federal regulation, must nevertheless be invalidated under the supremacy clause. As we stated in *Florida Lime & Avocado Growers, Inc., v. Paul*, 373 U.S. 132 (1963):

Federal regulation . . . should not be deemed pre-emptive of state regulatory power in the absence of persuasive reasons—either that the nature of the regulated subject matter permits no other conclusion, or that Congress has unmistakably so ordained.

In this case, we cannot conclude that pre-emption is required either because "the nature of the subject matter [regulation of employment of illegal aliens] permits no other conclusion," or because "Congress has unmistakably so ordained" that result.

States possess broad authority under their police powers to regulate the employment relationship to protect workers within the state. Child-labor laws, minimum and other wage laws, laws affecting occupational health and safety, and workmen's compensation laws are only a few examples. California's attempt in § 2805(a) to prohibit the knowing employment by California employers of persons not entitled to lawful residence in the United States, let alone to work here, is certainly within the mainstream of such police power regulation. Employment of illegal aliens in times of high unemployment deprives citizens and legally admitted aliens of jobs. Acceptance by illegal aliens of jobs on substandard terms as to wages and working conditions can seriously depress wage scales and working conditions of citizens and legally admitted aliens. Employment of illegal aliens under such conditions can diminish the effectiveness of labor unions. These local problems are particularly acute in California in light of the significant influx into that state of illegal aliens from neighboring Mexico. In attempting to protect California's fiscal interests and lawfully resident labor force from the deleterious effects on its economy resulting from the employment of illegal aliens, § 2805(a) focuses directly upon these essentially local problems and is tailored to combat effectively the perceived evils.

Of course, even state regulation designed to protect vital state interests must give way to paramount federal legislation. But we will not presume that Congress, in enacting the INA, intended to oust state authority to regulate the employment relationship covered by § 2805(a) in a manner consistent with pertinent federal laws. Only a demonstration that complete ouster of state power—including state power to promulgate laws not in conflict with federal laws—was "the clear and manifest purpose of Congress" would justify that conclusion. An independent review does not reveal any specific indication in either the wording or the legislative history of the INA that Congress intended to preclude even harmonious state regulation touching on aliens in general, or the employment of illegal aliens in particular.

Finally, rather than evidence that Congress has unmistakably ordained exclusivity of federal regulation in this field, there is evidence in the form of the 1974 amendments to the Farm Labor Contractor Registration Act, 7 U.S.C. § 2041 *et seq.*, that Congress intends that states may, to the extent consistent with federal law, regulate the employment of illegal aliens. Section 2044(b) authorizes revocation of the certificate of registration of any farm labor contractor found to have employed "an alien not lawfully admitted for permanent residence, or who has not been authorized by the Attorney General to accept employment." Section 2045 prohibits farm labor contractors from employing "an alien not lawfully admitted for permanent residence or who has not been authorized

by the Attorney General to accept employment." Of particular significance to our inquiry is the provision that "this chapter and the provisions contained herein are *intended to supplement state action* and compliance with this chapter shall not excuse anyone from compliance with *appropriate state law and regulation*." *Id.*, § 2051 (emphasis supplied). Although concerned only with agricultural employment, the Farm Labor Contractor Registration Act is thus persuasive evidence that the INA should not be taken as legislation by Congress expressing its judgment to have uniform federal regulations in matters affecting employment of illegal aliens and therefore barring state legislation such as § 2805(a).

The judgment of the court of appeal is reversed, and the case is remanded for further proceedings not inconsistent with this opinion.

Reversed and remanded

CASE QUESTIONS

1. The superior court and the California Court of Appeal held the California Labor Code 2805 unconstitutional. Why?
2. Legal writers have said that by occupying a field, Congress had excluded from it all state legislation. After studying the Supreme Court decision in *DeCanas v. Bica*, do you feel that this is a valid formula?

SUGGESTED READINGS

Benke, *Doctrine of Preemption and the Illegal Alien: A Case of State Regulation and a Uniform Preemption Theory*, 13 SAN DIEGO L. REV. 166 (1975).

Burchell, *Federal Supremacy in the Regulation of Commerce*, 43 ICC
    PRAC. J. 72 (1975).
Franklin, *Applicability of Federal Antitrust Laws to State and Municipal
    Action: A Case Against the Current Approach*, 16 HOUSTON L. REV.
    903 (1979).
Meek, *Nuclear Powers and State Radiation Protective Measures: The
    Importance of Preemption*, 10 ENVIRONMENTAL LAW 1 (1979).
Note, *Immigration—a State May Prohibit the Employment of Illegal
    Aliens*, 9 VAND. J. TRANS. 907 (1976).

Constitutionality of Statutes

The power to declare legislative acts unconstitutional is the province and
the duty of the judiciary, even though there is no express constitutional
grant of the power. It is generally presumed that all statutes are constitutional and that a statute will not be invalidated unless the party
challenging it clearly shows that it is offensive to either a state or federal
constitution. An act of the legislature is declared invalid only if it is
clearly incompatible with a constitutional provision.

The right and power of the courts to declare whether the legislature has
exceeded the constitutional limitations is one of the highest functions of
the judiciary. The Supreme Court declared in *Marbury v. Madison*, 5 U.S.
(1 Cranch) 137 (1803) that the judicial branch has the power to declare an
act of the legislature void if it conflicts with the Constitution. The issue of
the supremacy of the federal Constitution and the right of individuals to
claim protection thereunder whenever they were aggrieved by application
of a contrary statute was decided in *Marbury*. Chief Justice John Marshall
wrote the opinion for the Court, stating in part:

> The question, whether an act, repugnant to the Constitution, can
> become the law of the land, is a question deeply interesting to the
> United States; but, happily, not of an intricacy proportioned to its in-
> terest. It seems only necessary to recognize certain principles, supposed
> to have been long and well established, to decide it.
>
> That the people have an original right to establish, for their future
> government, such principles as, in their opinion, shall most conduce to
> their own happiness, is the basis on which the whole American fabric
> has been erected. The exercise of this original right is a very great exer-
> tion; nor can it, nor ought it, to be frequently repeated. The principles,
> therefore, so established, are deemed fundamental. And as the authority
> from which they proceed is supreme, and can seldom act, they are
> designated to be permanent.

. . . It is a proposition too plain to be contested, that the Constitution controls any legislative act repugnant to it; or that the legislature may alter the Constitution by an ordinary act.

Between these alternatives there is no middle ground. The Constitution is either a superior paramount law, unchangeable by ordinary means, or it is on a level with ordinary legislative acts, and, like other acts, is alterable when the legislature shall please to alter it.

If the former part of the alternative be true, then a legislative act, contrary to the Constitution, is not law; if the latter part be true, then written constitutions are absurd attempts, on the part of people, to limit a power, in its own nature illimitable.

. . .

It is, emphatically, the province and duty of the judicial department to say what the law is. Those who apply the rule to particular cases must of necessity expound and interpret that rule. If two laws conflict with each other, the courts must decide on the operation of each.

So, if a law be in opposition to the Constitution; if both the law and the Constitution apply to a particular case, so that the court must either decide that case, conformable to the law, disregarding the Constitution, or conformable to the Constitution, disregarding the law; the court must determine which of the conflicting rules governs the case. This is of the very essence of judicial duty.

If, then, the courts are to regard the Constitution—and the Constitution is superior to any ordinary act of the legislature—the Constitution, and not such ordinary act, must govern the case to which they both apply.

Ex Post Facto *Laws*

Article 1, § 9, of the federal Constitution prohibits Congress from enacting *ex post facto* laws or bills of attainder. The state legislatures are likewise prohibited by article 1, § 10.

An *ex post facto* law is a law that makes criminal acts that were not criminal at the time they were committed. Statutes that make a crime greater than when committed, impose greater punishment, or make proof of guilt easier have also been held to be unconstitutional *ex post facto* laws. Laws are unconstitutional when they alter the definition of a penal offense or its consequence to persons who commit that offense, to their disadvantage. An accused is deprived of a substantial right provided by the law that was in force at the time of the commission of the offense.

The *ex post facto* clause is a restriction on legislative power and does not apply to the judicial function. The doctrine applies exclusively to criminal or penal statutes. The impact of *ex post facto* may not be avoided by disguising criminal punishment in a civil form. When a law imposes punishment for certain activity of the past and future, even though it is void for the punishment of past activity, it is valid insofar as the law acts prospectively. A law is not *ex post facto* if it "mitigates the rigor" of the law or is a re-enactment of the law in force at the time of the crime or activity involved.

In determining whether a legislative act unconstitutionally imposes punishment for past activity, one examines the intent of the legislature. The objective of the legislature in enacting the law is always determined in order to decide whether an act punishes when it imposes a disqualification on the happening of a past event. The principle governing the inquiry is whether the aim of the legislature was to punish an individual for past activity, or whether a restriction on a person is merely incident to a valid regulation of a present situation, such as the appropriate qualifications for a profession.

A constitutionally prohibited bill of attainder involves the singling out of an individual or group for punishment. Bills of attainder are acts of a legislature that apply either to named individuals or to easily ascertainable members of a group in such a way as to impose punishment on them without a trial. For example, an act of Congress that made it a crime for a member of the Communist party to serve as an officer of a labor union was held unconstitutional as a bill of attainder. (*United States v. Brown*, 381 U.S. 437 [1965])

Hiss v. Hampton
338 F. Supp. 1141
United States District Court
District of Columbia
March 3, 1972

Robb, Circuit Judge

Plaintiff, Alger Hiss, former employee of the federal government, applied for an annuity under the Civil Service Retirement Act. His application was denied by the Civil Service Comission on the ground that payment to him was prohibited by certain provisions of 5 U.S.C. §§ 8311–8322, commonly known as the "Hiss Act." The plaintiff challenges that denial.

The plaintiff seeks a declaration that the Hiss Act is unconstitutional on its face and as applied to him; or in the alternative, that it is not applicable to him. The complaint prays further for an order enjoining the defendants from applying the act to the plaintiff and requiring the defendants to make all past-due annuity payments to the plaintiff.

The defendants admit that the plaintiff is an "annuitant" or individual generally qualified for annuity benefits under 5 U.S.C. §§ 8331–8348. The defendants assert, however, that the provisions of the Hiss Act forbid payment of these benefits to the plaintiff, and that the act is constitutional and applies to the plaintiff.

The material facts are not in dispute and the action is before us on cross motions for summary judgment.

Alger Hiss entered the federal service October 1, 1929, and thereafter was employed by the government in various capacities. On January 15, 1947, he resigned from his last federal position, which was with the Department of State. His total federal service for retirement purposes is approximately 15 years. On November 11, 1966, his 62nd birthday, he met the age and service requirements for a civil service retirement annuity at the rate of $61 per month.

On January 27, 1967, Hiss filed a claim for his annuity. By letter dated April 24, 1967, the director of the Civil Service Commission's Bureau of Retirement and Insurance notified Hiss that he was barred from receiving a retirement annuity by section 1(a)(3)(B) of Public Law 87–299, approved September 26, 1961 (the Hiss Act). The section of the act to which the director referred is now codified as part of 5 U.S.C. § 8312 and provides that:

A. An individual, or his survivor or beneficiary, may not be paid annuity or retired pay on the basis of the service of the individual which is creditable toward the annuity or retired pay, subject to the exceptions in § 8311(2) and (3) of this title, if the individual—
1. was convicted before, on, or after September 1, 1954, of an offense named by subsection B of this section, to the extent provided by that subsection;

. . .

B. The following are the offenses to which subsection A of this section applies if the individual was convicted before, on, or after September 1, 1954:

3. Perjury committed under the statutes of the United States or the District of Columbia—

. . .

b. in falsely testifying before a federal grand jury, court of the United States, or court-martial with respect to his service as an employee in connection with a matter involving or relating to an interference with or endangerment of, or involving or relating to a plan or attempt to interfere with or endanger the national security or defense of the United States. . . .

The director informed Hiss that the basis of his ruling was:

The commission has information to the effect that you were indicted by the grand jury impaneled and sworn in the United States District Court for the Southern District of New York on December 15, 1948 for violation of title 18, § 1621, of the United States Code [perjury]. This indictment was a result of your testimony before the aforesaid grand jury investigating possible violations of espionage laws of the United States and other criminal statutes. In addition, the commission has information that you were convicted of the aforesaid perjury violation on January 21, 1950, and were sentenced to five years' imprisonment on January 25, 1950. (Copies of certified court records attached.)

The director's letter of April 24, 1967, informed Hiss that he was entitled to a refund of his retirement contributions. He was further informed that he had a right to submit an answer and to request a hearing before a final decision was made. Hiss waived a hearing and submitted his case to a hearing examiner on a stipulated record. On June 26, 1968, the examiner issued a decision sustaining the denial of Hiss's claim for an annuity. On appeal, the Civil Service Commission on October 22, 1968, sustained the examiner by adopting his findings, conclusions, and decisions as its own. Having thus exhausted his administrative remedies, Hiss commenced this suit. He has not requested or received a refund of his contributions to the annuity fund, which would amount to approximately $3556, exclusive of interest.

The Constitution, art. I, § 9, clause 3, provides that "No bill of attainder or *ex post facto* law shall be passed." In many cases, beginning with *Calder v. Bull*, 3 U.S. (3 Dall.) 386, 390 (1798), the Supreme Court has defined an *ex post facto* law as invalid if its purpose and effect are to punish for past conduct and not to regulate a profession, calling, or present situation.

We think the disabilities imposed on the plaintiff by the Hiss Act are punitive and not regulatory. Hiss was not a federal employee at the time the act was passed, and we do not understand how the conduct of federal employees could be regulated or their moral standards elevated by imposing a financial penalty for prior conduct on a man who was not a federal employee or likely ever again to become a federal employee. Retroactive punishment of former employees for their past misdoings has no reasonable bearing on regulation of the conduct of those presently employed. The proper function of regulation is to guide and control present and future conduct, not to penalize former employees for acts done long ago.

Our conclusion that the statute, as applied retroactively to plaintiff, is penal rather than regulatory, is supported by the legislative history of the Hiss Act. Although courts should not strike down "an otherwise constitutional statute on the basis of an alleged illicit legislative motive," the intent or purpose of Congress may determine whether a particular law is penal or regulatory. Therefore it is appropriate that we now consider the "objective manifestations of congressional purpose" in enacting the Hiss Act.

There is substantial evidence in the "objective manifestations of congressional purpose" that the primary target of the act was Alger Hiss, and not general regulation of the federal service.

We take notice that the trial and conviction of Alger Hiss received widespread attention. This attention was renewed when it was realized, at the time Hiss was about to be released from prison in 1954, that despite his conviction he would be eligible to receive federal annuity payments upon reaching the age of 62. As a result 10 bills were introduced in the House. The original bill was enacted in 1954, and a minor amendment was added in 1956. Further amendments were proposed in 1959 and 1960 and were enacted in 1961. In 1966 the statute was codified in Title 5 of the United States Code, 5. U.S.C. §§ 8311–8322. House and Senate committee reports on the proposed statute and on proposed amendments were published in 1954, 1959, 1960, and 1961. Committee hearings on the proposed legislation were held in each of those years except 1960. Floor debate took place in each year.

We mention a few of the many objective manifestations which we think fairly evidence the congressional purpose.

On June 22, 1954, the House Committee on Post Office and Civil Service held a hearing on the 10 bills which had been introduced. The testimony of the supporters of the bills made it plain that their target was Alger Hiss. Thus, Representative Clardy stated that "I am not opposed to the adoption of a bill that is general, but I put in my bill the name of Alger Hiss because at this moment he is the one outstanding character that ought to be treated in the way the bill suggests. I recognize the fact that a general bill would raise a lot of questions that have probably not yet arisen, and there would be protracted debate and the bill perhaps would never get through, but I do not think any member of Congress would have the hardihood to vote against a bill denying privileges to Alger Hiss, the traitor." (1954 *House Hearing*, at 16.) A member of the committee expressed the opinion that if a "general bill" were passed it "could be called the Alger Hiss bill, and probably would be." (1954 *House Hearing*, at 19.) Indeed, the proposed legislation focused so sharply on Alger Hiss that before the hearings began, the committee invited him to submit a statement or to designate a representative to appear in his behalf. He declined the invitation. (See 1954 *House Hearing*, at 14–15.)

The 1961 amendments furnish additional support for our conclusion that the retroactive application of the act to the plaintiff is penal and cannot be sustained as regulation of the government service. As we have noted, the premise of the amendments was that the act imposed penalties or punishments, which in some cases were unjust. Moreover, § 2 of the act as amended restored annuities to all "nontreasonous" criminals who had been denied benefits under the 1954 statute. Thus the right to receive annuities was restored to former government employees who had been convicted of such offenses as bribery, fraud, embezzlement, rape, and murder. The restoration to grace of such offenders makes it difficult for us to accept the government's contention that the retroactive condemnation of Hiss is incident to a regulation calculated to cleanse the government service. As applied to Hiss, the act does not regulate, it punishes.

The question before us is not whether Hiss is a good or bad man, nor is it whether we would grant him an annuity if we had unfettered discretion in the matter. The question is simply whether the Constitution permits Congress to deprive him of his annuity by retroactive penal legislation. We conclude that it does not. We hold that, as applied retroactively to the plaintiff, the challenged statute is penal, cannot be sustained as regulation, and is invalid as an *ex post facto* law prohibited by the Constitution.

In accordance with this opinion, the plaintiff's motion for summary judgment will be granted.

CASE QUESTIONS

1. Was the Hiss Act a criminal statute?
2. Judicial decisions often involve the imposition of punishment for past misconduct. Is the *ex post facto* clause applicable to judicial decisions?

SUGGESTED READINGS

Fikso, *Legal Method—Deciding the Retroactive Effect of Overruling Decisions*, 55 WASHINGTON L. REV. 833 (1980).

Lehman and McClatchey, *Prospectivity Doctrine: Which Way Out of the Morass?* 29 JAG 65 (1976).

Note, *Ex Post Facto Limitations on Legislative Power*, 73 MICH. L. REV. 1491 (1975).

Note, *Retroactivity of Criminal Procedure Decisions*, 55 IOWA L. REV. 1309 (1970).

Obligation of Contracts

People's right to contract is recognized as a basic right under the due-process clause of the Fourteenth Amendment. Article 1, § 10, of the Constitution states: "No state shall . . . pass any . . . law impairing the obligation of contracts." Similar provisions are found in the various state constitutions. All valid contractual agreements are protected from destruction or impairment by subsequent acts of legislatures. Note that there are no constitutional provisions limiting the powers of Congress in this area. It has been held that the same protection is afforded congressional acts by the due-process clause of the Fifth Amendment to the Constitution, which forbids deprivation of property without due process of law.

The constitutional contract clause contained in art. 1, § 10, limits the power of the states to modify their own contracts as well as to regulate those between private individuals. Although the clause appears literally to proscribe all impairment or change, the prohibition is not absolute. The finding that there has been an impairment is merely a preliminary step by a court in resolving the more difficult question as to whether that impairment is permitted under the Constitution. An impairment is considered to be constitutional if it is reasonable and necessary to serve an important public purpose. The legislation must not be arbitrary or capricious. The government should have broad power to adopt necessary regulatory legislation without being concerned that private contracts will be impaired.

Allied Structural Steel Co. v. Spannaus
438 U.S. 234
United States Supreme Court
June 28, 1978

MR. JUSTICE STEWART
The issue in this case is whether the application of Minnesota's Private Pension Benefits Protection Act to the appellant violates the contract clause of the U.S. Constitution.

In 1974 appellant, Allied Structural Steel Co., a corporation with its principal place of business in Illinois, maintained an office in Minnesota with 30 employees. The company's general pension plan was adopted in 1963 and qualified as a single-employer plan under section 401 of the Internal Revenue Code.

On April 9, 1974, Minnesota enacted the Private Pension Benefits Protection Act. Under the act, a private employer of 100 employees or more—at least one of whom was a Minnesota resident—who provided pension benefits under a plan meeting the qualifications of section 401 of the Internal Revenue Code, was subject to a "pension funding charge" if he either terminated the plan or closed a Minnesota office. Although the company had only 30 employees in Minnesota, it was subject to the act because it had over 100 employees altogether. The charge was assessed if the pension funds were not sufficient to cover full pensions for all employees who had worked at least 10 years.

During the summer of 1974, the company began closing its Minnesota office. On July 31, it discharged 11 of its 30 Minnesota employees, and the following month it notified the Minnesota Commissioner of Labor and Industry, as required by the act, that it was terminating an office in the state. At least 9 of the discharged employees did not have any vested pension rights under the company's plan, but had worked for the company for 10 years or more and thus qualified as pension obligees of the company under the law that Minnesota had enacted a few months earlier. On August 18, the state notified the company that it owed a pension funding charge of approximately $185,000 under the provisions of the Private Pension Benefits Protection Act.

The company brought suit in a federal district court asking for injunctive and declaratory relief. The three-judge court upheld the constitutional validity of the act as applied to the company, and an appeal was brought to this Court.

The language of the contract clause appears unambiguously absolute: "No state shall . . . pass any . . . law impairing the obligation of contracts." (U.S. Const., art. I, § 10.) The clause is not, however, the Draconian provision that its words might seem to imply. Literalism in the construction of the contract clause would make it destructive of the public interest by depriving the state of its prerogative of self-protection. If the contract clause is to retain any meaning at all, however, it must be understood to impose *some* limits on the power of a state to abridge existing contractual relationships, even in the exercise of its otherwise legitimate police power.

The first inquiry must be whether the state law has, in fact, operated as a substantial impairment of a contractual relationship. The severity of the impairment measures the height of the hurdle the state legislation must clear. Minimal alteration of contractual obligations may end the inquiry at its first stage. Severe impairment, on the other hand, will push the inquiry to a careful examination of the nature and purpose of the state legislation.

Here, the company's contracts of employment with its employees included as a fringe benefit, or additional form of compensation, the pension plan. The company's maximum obligation was to set aside each year an amount based on the plan's requirements for vesting. The plan satisfied the current federal income tax code and was subject to no other legislative requirements. And, of course, the company was free to amend or terminate the pension plan at any time. The company thus had no reason to anticipate that its employees' pension rights could become vested except in accordance with the terms of the plan. It relied heavily, and reasonably, on this legitimate contractual expectation in calculating its annual contributions to the pension fund.

The effect of Minnesota's Private Pension Benefits Protection Act on this contractual obligation was severe. Thus a basic term of the pension contract—one on which the company had relied for 10 years—was substantially modified. The result was that although the company's past contributions were adequate when made, they were not adequate when computed under the 10-year statutory vesting requirement. The act thus forced a current recalculation of the past 10 years' contributions based on the new, unanticipated 10-year vesting requirement.

Not only did the state law thus retroactively modify the compensation that the company had agreed to pay its employees from 1963 to 1974, but it did so by changing the company's obligations in an area where the element of reliance was vital—the funding of a pension plan.

Moreover, the retroactive state-imposed vesting requirement was applied only to those employers who terminated their pension plans or who, like the company, closed their Minnesota offices. The company was thus forced to make all the retroactive changes in its contractual obligations at one time. By simply proceeding to close its office in Minnesota, a move that had been planned before the passage of the act, the company was assessed an immediate pension funding charge of approximately $185,000.

Thus, the statute in question here nullifies express terms of the company's contractual obligations and imposes a completely unexpected liability in potentially disabling amounts. There is not even any provision for gradual applicability or grace periods. Yet there is no showing in the record before us that this severe disruption of contractual expectations was necessary to meet an important general social problem. The presumption favoring legislative judgment as to the necessity and reasonableness of a particular measure simply cannot stand in this case.

The only indication of legislative intent in the record before us is to be found in a statement in the district court's opinion: "It seems clear that the problem of plant closure and pension plan termination was brought to the attention of the Minnesota legislature when the Minneapolis-Moline Division of White Motor Corporation closed one of its Minnesota plants and attempted to terminate its pension plan."

But whether or not the legislation was aimed largely at a single employer, it clearly has an extremely narrow focus. It applies only to private employers who have at least 100 employees, at least one of whom works in Minnesota, and who have established voluntary private pension plans, qualified under § 401 of the Internal Revenue Code. And it applies only when such an employer closes his Minnesota office or terminates his pension plan. Thus, this law can hardly be characterized as one enacted to protect a broad societal interest rather than a narrow class.

Entering a field it had never before sought to regulate, the Minnesota legislature grossly distorted the company's existing contractual relationships with its employees by superimposing retroactive obligations on the company substantially beyond the terms of its employment contracts. And that burden was imposed on the company only because it closed its office in the state.

This Minnesota law simply does not possess the attributes of those state laws that in the past have survived challenge under the contract clause of the Constitution. The law was not even purportedly enacted to deal with a broad, generalized economic or social problem. It did not operate in an area already subject to state regulation at the time the company's contractual obligations were originally undertaken, but invaded an area never before subject to regulation by the state. It did not effect simply a temporary alteration of the contractual relationships of those within its coverage, but worked a severe, permanent, and immediate change in those relationships—irrevocably and retroactively. And its narrow aim was leveled, not at every Minnesota employer, not even at every Minnesota employer who left the state, but only at those who had in the past been sufficiently enlightened as voluntarily to agree to establish pension plans for their employees.

We do hold that if the contract clause means anything at all, it means that Minnesota could not constitutionally do what it tried to do to the company in this case.

The judgment of the district court is reversed.

MR. JUSTICE BRENNAN, with whom MR. JUSTICE WHITE and MR. JUSTICE MARSHALL join, dissenting

In cases involving state legislation affecting private contracts, this Court's decisions over the past half century, consistent with both the constitutional text and its original understanding, have interpreted the contract clause as prohibiting state legislative acts which, "with studied indifference to the interests of the contracting party or to his appropriate protection," effectively diminished or nullified the obligation due him under the terms of a contract. But the contract clause has not, during this period, been applied to state legislation that, while creating new duties, in nowise diminished the efficacy of any contractual obligation owed the constitutional claimant.

Today's decision greatly expands the reach of the clause. The Minnesota Private Pension Benefits Protection Act does not abrogate or dilute any obligation due a party to a private contract. Rather, like all positive social legislation, the act imposes new, additional obligations on a particular class of persons. In my view, any constitutional infirmity in the law must therefore derive, not from the contract clause, but from the due-process clause of the Fourteenth Amendment. I perceive nothing in the act that works a denial of due process and therefore I dissent.

CASE QUESTIONS

1. What reasoning did the Court use in reaching its decision?
2. May a state justify impairment of a contract on the basis of its police power?

SUGGESTED READINGS

Dewey, *Freedom to Contract: Is It Still Relevant?* 31 OHIO ST. L.J. 724 (1970).

Note, *The Contract Clause: Revived or Revised?* 33 UNIV. OF MIAMI L. REV. 667 (1979).

Peterson, *The Contract Clause: The Use of a Strict Standard of Review for State Legislation that Impairs Private Contracts—Allied Structural Steel Co. v. Spannaus,* 28 DE PAUL L. REV. 503 (1979).

Note, *Impairment of Contract—Retroactive Application of Statute Is an Unconstitutional Impairment of a Road Construction Contract—State v. Chadbourne,* 8 FLA. ST. U. L. REV. 549 (1980).

Equal Protection

The Fourteenth Amendment to the Constitution reads ''No state shall . . . deny to any person within its jurisdiction the equal protection of the laws.'' Even though the purpose of the equal-protection clause was to secure to black people the enjoyment of freedom, its protection is extended to all persons. It guarantees only equal laws, not necessarily equal results from the laws. It prohibits any state legislation that has the effect of denying to any race, class, or individual the equal protection of the law. Any legal restriction that curtails the civil rights of a single group is immediately subject to strict scrutiny and can be justified only by a "compelling" state interest. The boundaries of the protection afforded by the equal-protection clause have not been precisely defined. This clause simply means that differences—whether due to color, race, or sex—do not justify discriminatory treatment and that all persons shall enjoy equal protection of the laws.

Wengler v. Druggists Mut. Ins. Co.
446 U.S. 142
United States Supreme Court
April 22, 1980

Mr. Justice White
This case challenges under the equal-protection clause of the Fourteenth Amendment a provision of the Missouri workers' compensation laws, Mo. Ann. Stat. § 287.240, which is claimed to involve an invalid gender-based discrimination.

The facts are not in dispute. On February 11, 1977, Ruth Wengler, wife of appellant Paul J. Wengler, died in a work-related accident in the parking lot of her employer, appellee Dicus Prescription Drugs, Inc. Appellant filed a claim for death benefits under Mo. Ann. Stat. § 287.240, under which a widower is not entitled to death benefits unless he either is mentally or physically incapacitated from wage earning or proves actual dependence on his wife's earnings. In contrast, a widow qualifies for death benefits without having to prove actual dependence on her husband's earnings.

Appellant stipulated that he was neither incapacitated nor dependent on his wife's earnings, but argued that, owing to its disparate treatment of similarly situated widows and widowers, section 287.240 violated the equal-

protection clause of the U.S. Constitution. The claim was administratively denied, but the circuit court of Madison County reversed, holding that section 287.240 violated the equal-protection clause because the statutory restriction on a widower's recovery of death benefits did not also apply to a surviving wife. Dicus and its insurer, appellee Druggists Mutual Insurance Company, were ordered to pay death benefits to appellant in the appropriate amount.

The Missouri Supreme Court reversed the circuit court's decision. The equal-protection challenge to section 287.240 failed because "the substantive difference in the economic standing of working men and women justifies the advantage that section 287.240 administratively gives to a widow." *Wengler v. Druggists Mutual Ins. Co.,* 583 S.W.2d 162, 168 (Mo. 1979).

Because the decision of the supreme court of Missouri conflicted with our precedents, we now reverse.

The Missouri law indisputably mandates gender-based discrimination. Although the Missouri Supreme Court was of the view that the law favored, rather than disfavored, women, it is apparent that the statute discriminates against both men and women. The provision discriminates against a woman covered by the Missouri workers' compensation system since, in the case of her death, benefits are payable to her spouse only if he is mentally or physically incapacitated or was to some extent dependent on her. Under these tests, Mrs. Wengler's spouse was entitled to no benefits. If Mr. Wengler had died, however, Mrs. Wengler would have been conclusively presumed to be dependent and would have been paid the statutory amount for life or until she remarried, even though she may not in fact have been dependent on Mr. Wengler. The benefits, therefore, that the working woman can expect to be paid to her spouse in the case of her work-related death are less than those payable to the spouse of the deceased male wage earner.

The Missouri law also discriminates against men who survive their employed wives dying in work-related accidents. To receive benefits, the surviving male spouse must prove his incapacity or dependency. The widow of a deceased wage earner, in contrast, is presumed dependent and is guaranteed a weekly benefit for life or until remarriage.

Our precedents require that gender-based discriminations must serve important governmental objectives and that the discriminatory means employed must be substantially related to the achievement of those objectives.

Providing for needy spouses is surely an important governmental objective, and the Missouri statute effects that goal by paying benefits to all surviving female spouses and to all surviving male spouses who prove their dependency. But the question remains whether the discriminatory means employed—discrimination against women wage earners and surviving male spouses—itself substantially serves the statutory end. The only justification offered by the state court or appellees for not treating males and females alike, whether viewed as wage earners or survivors of wage earners, is the assertion that most women are dependent on male wage earners and that it is more efficient to presume dependency in the case of women than to engage in case-to-case determination, whereas individualized inquiries in the postulated few cases in which men might be dependent are not prohibitively costly.

The burden, however, is on those defending the discrimination to make out the claimed justification, and this burden is not carried simply by noting that in 1925 the state legislature thought widows to be more in need of prompt help than men or that today the substantive difference in the economic standing of working men and women justifies the advantage given to widows. The bare assertion of this argument falls far short of justifying gender-based discrimination on the grounds of administrative convenience. Yet neither the court below nor appellees in this Court essay any persuasive demonstration as to what the economic consequences to the state or to the beneficiaries might be.

We think, then, that the claimed justification of administrative convenience fails, just as it has in our prior cases. It may be that there are levels of administrative convenience that will justify discriminations that are subject to heightened scrutiny under the equal-protection clause, but the requisite showing has not been made here by the mere claim that it would be inconvenient to individualize determinations about widows as well as widowers.

Thus we conclude that the Supreme

Court of Missouri erred in upholding the constitutional validity of section 287.240. Accordingly, we reverse the decision of the Supreme Court of Missouri and remand the case to that court for further proceedings not inconsistent with this opinion.

CASE QUESTIONS

1. Are all legislative acts that are discriminatory unconstitutional under the equal-protection clause?
2. Who bears the burden of defending an alleged discriminatory statute?
3. The courts apply the equal-protection clause of the Fourteenth Amendment to gender-based discrimination. Why do some persons see a need for an equal-rights amendment?

SUGGESTED READINGS

Abrams, *The Effects of Invalidating a Law on the Grounds of Equal Protection*, 8 HASTINGS CONST. L.Q. 29 (1980).

Dixon, *Supreme Court and Equality: Legislative Classifications, Desegregation and Reverse Discrimination*, 62 CORNELL L. REV. 494 (1977).

Ginsberg, *Gender and the Constitution*, 44 CIN. L. REV. 1 (1975).

Mirabile, *Rape Laws, Equal Protection, and Privacy Rights*, 54 TULANE L. REV. 456 (1980).

Treiman, *Equal Protection and Fundamental Rights—A Judicial Shell Game*, 15 TULSA L.J. 183 (1980).

Note, *Gender-Based Classifications in Alimony Statutes Violate Equal Protection Clause*, 54 TULANE L. REV. 500 (1980).

Right of Privacy

The Constitution affords protection against many types of intrusions by the government into our private matters and personal lives. The right of privacy is the right to be left alone. There is, however, no specific provision in the federal Constitution guaranteeing such a right. The courts do recognize that a right of personal privacy does exist under the Constitution, but the concept and the zones of privacy remain largely undefined. The basis of this privilege is found in the due-process guarantees of life, liberty, and property in the Fourth and Fifth Amendments, and in the First, Ninth, and Fourteenth Amendments.

The government's invasion of the right of personal privacy may happen in several ways. The Fourth Amendment specifically protects people from government intrusion and surveillance of their private affairs. People have the right to be free from governmental compulsion in their beliefs, expressions, and actions. This protection is guaranteed primarily by the First Amendment. The right of a person not to have private affairs made public by the government seems to be the least-defined zone of privacy. Our traditional informational privacy is being threatened with the increase of both governmental and private data-gathering activities.

As is the case with other constitutional guarantees, the right of privacy is not absolute and is subject to limitations. At some point, the government's interest in protecting society becomes dominant. In order for a legislative enactment to be constitutional, it must be narrowly drafted to express only the legitimate governmental interest at stake.

Whalen v. Roe
429 U.S. 589
United States Supreme Court
February 22, 1977

MR. JUSTICE STEVENS
The constitutional question presented is whether the state of New York may record, in a centralized computer file, the names and addresses of all persons who have obtained, pursuant to a doctor's prescription, certain drugs for which there is both a lawful and an unlawful market.

The district court enjoined enforcement of the portions of the New York State Controlled Substances Act of 1972 which require such recording on the ground that they violate appellees' constitutionally protected rights of privacy. We now reverse.

Many drugs have both legitimate and illegitimate uses. In response to a concern that such drugs were being diverted into unlawful channels, in 1970 the New York Legislature created a special commission to evaluate the state's drug-control laws. The commission found the existing laws deficient in several respects. There was no effective way to prevent the use of stolen or revised prescriptions, to prevent unscrupulous pharmacists from repeatedly refilling prescriptions, to prevent users from obtaining prescriptions from more than one doctor, or to prevent doctors from overprescribing, either by authorizing an excessive amount in one prescription or by giving one patient multiple prescriptions. In drafting new legislation to correct such defects, the commission consulted with enforcement officials in California and Illinois, where central reporting systems were being used effectively.

The new New York statute classified potentially harmful drugs in five schedules. Drugs, such as heroin, which are highly abused and have no recognized medical use, are in Schedule I; they cannot be prescribed. Schedules II through V include drugs which have a progressively lower potential for abuse but also have a recognized medical use. Our concern is limited to Schedule II, which includes the most dangerous of the legitimate drugs.

With an exception for emergencies, the act requires that all prescriptions for Schedule II drugs be prepared by the physician in triplicate on an official form. The completed form identifies the prescribing physician, the dispensing pharmacy, the drug and dosage, and the name, address, and age of the patient. One copy of the form is retained by the physician, the second by the pharmacist, and the third is forwarded to the New York State Department of Health in Albany. A prescription made on an official form may not exceed a 30-day supply, and may not be refilled.

The district court found that about 100,000 Schedule II prescription forms are delivered to a receiving room at the Department of Health in Albany each month. They are sorted, coded, and logged and then taken to another room where the data on the forms is recorded on magnetic tapes for processing by a computer. Thereafter, the forms are returned to the receiving room to be retained in a vault for a five-year period and then destroyed as required by the statute. The receiving room is surrounded by a locked wire fence and protected by an alarm system. The computer tapes containing the prescription data are kept in a locked cabinet. When the tapes are used, the computer is run "off-line," which means that no terminal outside of the computer room can read or record any information. Public disclosure of the identity of pa-

tients is expressly prohibited by the statute and by a Department of Health regulation. Willful violation of these prohibitions is a crime punishable by up to one year in prison and a $2000 fine. At the time of trial there were 17 Department of Health employees with access to the files. In addition, there were 24 investigators with authority to investigate cases of overdispensing which might be identified by the computer. Twenty months after the effective date of the act, the computerized data had been used in only two investigations involving alleged overuse by specific patients.

The district court held "that the doctor–patient relationship is one of the zones of privacy accorded constitutional protection"; that the patient-identification provisions of the act invaded this zone with a "needlessly broad sweep," and enjoined enforcement of the provisions of the act which deal with the reporting of patients' names and addresses.

I. The district court found that the state had been unable to demonstrate the necessity for the patient-identification requirement on the basis of its experience during the first 20 months of administration of the new statute. State legislation which has some effect on individual liberty or privacy may not be held unconstitutional simply because a court finds it unnecessary, in whole or in part. For we have frequently recognized that individual states have broad latitude in experimenting with possible solutions to problems of vital local concern.

The New York statute challenged in this case represents a considered attempt to deal with such a problem. It is manifestly the product of an orderly and rational legislative decision. It was recommended by a specially appointed commission which held extensive hearings on the proposed legislation, and drew on experience with similar programs in other states. There surely was nothing unreasonable in the assumption that the patient-identification requirement might aid in the enforcement of laws designed to minimize the misuse of dangerous drugs. For the requirement could reasonably be expected to have a deterrent effect on potential violators as well as to aid in the detection or investigation of specific instances of apparent abuse. At the very least, it would seem clear that the state's vital interest in controlling the distribution of dangerous drugs would support a decision to experiment with new techniques for control. For if an experiment fails—if in this case experience teaches that the patient-identification requirement results in the foolish expenditure of funds to acquire a mountain of useless information—the legislative process remains available to terminate the unwise experiment. It follows that the legislature's enactment of the patient-identification requirement was a reasonable exercise of New York's broad police powers. The district court's finding that the necessity for the requirement had not been proved is not, therefore, a sufficient reason for holding the statutory requirement unconstitutional.

II. Appellees contend that the statute invades a constitutionally protected "zone of privacy." The cases sometimes characterized as protecting "privacy" have in fact involved at least two different kinds of interest. One is the individual interest in avoiding disclosure of personal matters, and another is the interest in independence in making certain kinds of important decisions. Appellees argue that both of these interests are impaired by this statute. The mere existence in readily available form of the information about patients' use of Schedule II drugs creates a genuine concern that the information will become publicly known and that it will adversely affect their reputations. This concern makes some patients reluctant to use, and some doctors reluctant to prescribe, such drugs even when their use is medically indicated. It follows, they argue, that the making of decisions about matters vital to the care of their health is inevitably affected by the statute. Thus, the statute threatens to impair both their interest in the nondisclosure of private information and also their interest in making important decisions independently.

We are persuaded, however, that the New York program does not, on its face, pose a sufficiently grievous threat to either interest to establish a constitutional violation.

Public disclosure of patient information can come about in three ways. Health department employees may violate the statute by failing, either deliberately or negligently, to maintain proper security. A patient or a doctor may be accused of a violation and the stored data may be offered in evidence in a judicial proceeding. Or, thirdly, a doctor, a pharmacist, or the patient may voluntarily reveal information on a prescription form.

The third possibility existed under the prior law and is entirely unrelated to the existence of the computerized data bank. Neither of the other two possibilities provides a proper ground for attacking the statute as invalid on its face. There is no support in the record, or in the experience of the two states that New York has emulated, for an assumption that the security provisions of the statute will be administered improperly. And the remote possibility that judicial supervision of the evidentiary use of particular items of stored information will provide inadequate protection against unwarranted disclosures is surely not a sufficient reason for invalidating the entire patient-identification program.

Even without public disclosure, it is, of course, true that private information must be disclosed to the authorized employees of the New York Department of Health. Such disclosures, however, are not significantly different from those that were required under the prior law. Nor are they meaningfully distinguishable from a host of other unpleasant invasions of privacy that are associated with many facets of health care. Unquestionably, some individuals' concerns for their own privacy may lead them to avoid or to postpone needed medical attention. Nevertheless, disclosures of private medical information to doctors, to hospital personnel, to insurance companies, and to public health agencies are often an essential part of modern medical practice, even when the disclosure may reflect unfavorably on the character of the patient. Requiring such disclosures

to representatives of the state having responsibility for the health of the community does not automatically amount to an impermissible invasion of privacy.

Appellees also argue, however, that even if unwarranted disclosures do not actually occur, the knowledge that the information is readily available in a computerized file creates a genuine concern that causes some persons to decline needed medication. The record supports the conclusion that some use of Schedule II drugs has been discouraged by that concern. It is also clear, however, that about 100,000 prescriptions for such drugs were being filled each month prior to the entry of the district court's injunction. Clearly, therefore, the statute did not deprive the public of access to the drugs.

Nor can it be said that any individual has been deprived of the right to decide independently, with the advice of his physician, to acquire and to use needed medication. Although the state no doubt could prohibit entirely the use of particular Schedule II drugs, it has not done so. This case is therefore unlike those in which the Court held that a total prohibition of certain conduct was an impermissible deprivation of liberty. Nor does the state require access to these drugs to be conditioned on the consent of any state official or other third party. Within dosage limits which appellees do not challenge, the decision to prescribe, or to use, is left entirely to the physician and the patient.

We hold that neither the immediate nor the threatened impact of the patient-identification requirements in the New York State Controlled Substances Act of 1972 on either the reputation or the independence of patients for whom Schedule II drugs are medically indicated is sufficient to constitute an invasion of any right or liberty protected by the Fourteenth Amendment.

III. The appellee doctors argue separately that the statute impairs their right to practice medicine free of unwarranted state interference. If the doctors' claim has any reference to the impact of the 1972 statute on their own procedures, it is clearly frivolous. For even the prior statute required the doctor to prepare a written prescription identifying the name and address of the patient and the dosage of the prescribed drug. To the extent that their claim has reference to the possibility that the patients' concern about disclosure may induce them to refuse needed medication, the doctors' claim is derivative from, and therefore no stronger than, the patients'. Our rejection of their claim therefore disposes of the doctors' as well.

IV. A final word about issues we have not decided. We are not unaware of the threat to privacy implicit in the accumulation of vast amounts of personal information in computerized data banks or other massive government files. The collection of taxes, the distribution of welfare and Social Security benefits, the supervision of public health, the direction of our armed forces, and the enforcement of the criminal laws, all require the orderly preservation of great quantities of information, much of which is personal in character and potentially embarrassing or harmful if disclosed. The right to collect and use such data for public purposes is typically accompanied by a concomitant statutory or regulatory duty to avoid unwarranted disclosures. Recognizing that, in some circumstances, that duty arguably has its roots in the Constitution, nevertheless New York's statutory scheme, and its implementing administrative procedures, evidence a proper concern with, and protection of, the individual's interest in privacy. We therefore need not, and do not, decide any question which might be presented by the unwarranted disclosure of accumulated private data—whether intentional or unintentional—or by a system that did not contain comparable security provisions. We simply hold that this record does not establish an invasion of any right or liberty protected by the Fourteenth Amendment.

Reversed

CASE QUESTIONS

1. In many situations a person's physical and mental ills and the nature of the medication taken are among the most sensitive information. Why did the Court consider the governmental gathering of such personal information to be *not* an unconstitutional invasion of privacy?

2. Twenty months after the effective date of the New York State Controlled Substances Act of 1972, the computerized data had been used in

only two investigations involving alleged overuse by specific patients. Did the Court consider this history of the act important in rendering its decision?

3. Publication of what kinds of data are not protected under the right of privacy?

SUGGESTED READINGS

Boyer, *Computerized Medical Records and the Right to Privacy*, 25 BUFFALO L. REV. 37 (1975).

Gavison, *Privacy and the Limits of Law*, 89 YALE L.J. 421 (1980).

Humphrey, *The Right of Privacy: A Renewed Challenge to Laws Regulating Private Consensual Behavior*, 25 WAYNE L. REV. 1067 (1979).

Miller, *Computers, Data Banks and Individual Privacy*, 4 COLUM. HUMAN RIGHTS L. REV. 1 (1972).

Reinert, *Federal Protection of Employment Record Privacy*, 18 HARV. J. ON LEGIS. 207 (1981).

Smith, *Constitutional Privacy in Psychotherapy*, 49 GEO. WASH. L. REV. 1 (1980).

Statutory Construction

To declare what the law shall be is a legislative power; to declare what the law *is* is a judicial power. The courts are the appropriate body for construing acts of the legislature. Since courts decide only real controversies and not abstract or moot questions, a court does not construe statutory provisions unless required for the resolution of a case before it. A statute is open to construction only when the language used in the act is ambiguous and requires interpretation. Where the statutory language conveys a clear and definite meaning, there is no occasion to use rules of statutory interpretation.

Courts have developed rules of statutory construction to determine the meaning of legislative acts. In the interpretation of statutes, the legislative will is the all-important and controlling factor. The sole object of all rules for interpreting statutes is to discover the legislative intent; every other rule of construction is secondary.

It is the duty of the judiciary in construing criminal statutes to determine whether particular conduct falls within the intended prohibition of the statute. Criminal statutes are enforced by the court if worded so that they clearly convey the nature of the proscribed behavior. Legislation must be appropriately tailored to meet its objectives. Therefore it cannot be arbitrary, unreasonable, or capricious. A court holds a statute void for vagueness if it does not give a person of ordinary intelligence fair notice that some contemplated conduct is forbidden by the act. The enforcement of a vague statute would encourage arbitrary and erratic arrests and convictions.

Papachristou v. Jacksonville
405 U.S. 156
United States Supreme Court
February 24, 1972

MR. JUSTICE DOUGLAS
This case involves eight defendants who were convicted in a Florida municipal court of violating a Jacksonville, Florida, vagrancy ordinance.[1] Their convictions were affirmed by the Florida Circuit Court in a consolidated appeal, and their petition for *certiorari* was denied by the district court of appeal. The case is here on a petition for *certiorari*, which we granted. For reasons which will appear, we reverse.

At issue are five consolidated cases. Margaret Papachristou, Betty Calloway, Eugene Eddie Melton, and Leonard Johnson were all arrested early on a Sunday morning, and charged with vagrancy—"prowling by auto."

Jimmy Lee Smith and Milton Henry were charged with vagrancy—"vagabonds."

Henry Edward Heath and a codefendant were arrested for vagrancy—"loitering" and "common thief."

Thomas Owen Campbell was charged with vagrancy—"common thief."

Hugh Brown was charged with vagrancy—"disorderly loitering on street" and "disorderly conduct—resisting arrest with violence."

The facts are stipulated. Papachristou and Calloway are white females. Melton and Johnson are black males. Papachristou was enrolled in a job-training program sponsored by the State Employment Service at Florida Junior College in Jacksonville. Calloway was a typing and shorthand teacher at a state mental institution located near Jacksonville. She was the owner of the automobile in which the four defendants were arrested. Melton was a Viet-

---

[1] Jacksonville Ordinance Code, § 26–57, provided at the time of these arrests and convictions as follows: "Rogues and vagabonds, or dissolute persons who go about begging, common gamblers, persons who use juggling or unlawful games or plays, common drunkards, common night walkers, thieves, pilferers or pickpockets, traders in stolen property, lewd, wanton and lascivious persons, keepers of gambling places, common railers and brawlers, persons wandering or strolling from place to place without any lawful purpose or object, habitual loafers, disorderly persons, persons neglecting all lawful business and habitually spending their time by frequenting houses of ill fame, gaming houses, or places where alcoholic beverages are sold or served, persons able to work but habitually living upon the earnings of their wives or minor children shall be deemed vagrants, and upon conviction in the municipal court shall be punished as provided for class D offenses." Class D offenses at the time of these arrests and convictions were punishable by 90 days imprisonment, $500 fine, or both.

nam war veteran who had been released from the Navy after nine months in a veterans' hospital. On the date of his arrest, he was a part-time computer helper while attending college as a full-time student in Jacksonville. Johnson was a tow-motor operator in a grocery chain warehouse and was a lifelong resident of Jacksonville.

At the time of their arrest, the four of them were riding in Calloway's car on the main thoroughfare in Jacksonville. They had left a restaurant owned by Johnson's uncle where they had eaten and were on their way to a nightclub. The arresting officers denied that the racial mixture in the car played any part in the decision to make the arrest. The arrest, they said, was made because the defendants had stopped near a used-car lot which had been broken into several times. There was, however, no evidence of any breaking and entering on the night in question.

Of these four charged with "prowling by auto," none had been previously arrested except Papachristou, who had once been convicted of a municipal offense.

Jimmy Lee Smith and Milton Henry (who is not a petitioner) were arrested between 9 and 10 A.M. on a weekday in downtown Jacksonville, while waiting for a friend who was to lend them a car so they could apply for a job at a produce company. Smith was a part-time produce worker and part-time organizer for a Negro political group. He had a common-law wife and three children supported by him and his wife. He had been arrested several times but convicted only once. Smith's companion, Henry, was an 18 year-old high school student with no previous record of arrest.

This morning it was cold, and Smith had no jacket, so they went briefly into a dry cleaning shop to wait, but left when requested to do so. They thereafter walked back and forth two or three times over a two-block stretch looking for their friend. The store owners, who apparently were wary of Smith and his companion, summoned two police officers who searched the men and found neither had a weapon. But they were arrested because the officers said they had no identification and because the officers did not believe their story.

Heath and a codefendant were arrested for "loitering" and for "common thief." Both were residents of Jacksonville, Heath having lived there all his life and being employed at an automobile and body shop. Heath had previously been arrested but his codefendant had no arrest record. Heath and his companion were arrested when they drove up to a residence shared by Heath's girlfriend and some other girls. Some police officers were already there in the process of arresting another man. When Heath and his companion started backing out of the driveway, the officers signaled to them to stop and asked them to get out of the car, which they did. Thereupon they and the automobile were searched. Although no contraband or incriminating evidence was found, they were both arrested, Heath being charged with being a "common thief" because he was reputed to be a thief. The codefendant was charged with "loitering" because he was standing in the driveway, an act which the officers admitted was done only at their command.

Campbell was arrested as he reached his home very early one morning and was charged with "common thief." He was stopped by officers because he was traveling at a high rate of speed, yet no speeding charge was placed against him.

Brown was arrested when he was observed leaving a downtown Jacksonville hotel by a police officer seated in a cruiser. The police testified he was reputed to be a thief, narcotics pusher, and generally opprobrious character. The officer called Brown over to the car, intending at that time to arrest him unless he had a good explanation for being on the street. Brown walked over to the police cruiser, as commanded, and the officer began to search him, apparently preparatory to placing him in the car. In the process of the search, he came on two small packets which were later found to contain heroin. When the officer touched the pocket where the packets were, Brown began to resist. He was charged with "disorderly loitering on the street" and "disorderly conduct—resisting arrest with violence." While he was also charged with a narcotics violation, that charge was *nolled*.

Jacksonville's ordinance and Florida's statute were "derived from early English law," and employ "archaic language" in their definitions of vagrants. The history is an oftentold tale. The breakup of feudal estates in England led to labor shortages which in turn resulted in the Statutes of Laborers, designed to stabilize the labor force by prohibiting increases in wages and prohibiting the movement of workers from their home areas in search of improved conditions. Later vagrancy laws became criminal aspects of the poor laws. The series of laws passed in England on the subject became increasingly severe. But the theory of the Eliza-bethan poor laws no longer fits the facts. The conditions which spawned these laws may be gone, but the archaic classifications remain.

This ordinance is void-for-vagueness, both in the sense that it "fails to give a person of ordinary intelligence fair notice that his contemplated conduct is forbidden by the statute," and because it encourages arbitrary and erratic arrests and convictions.

Living under a rule of law entails various suppositions, one of which is that "all persons are entitled to be informed as to what the state commands or forbids." *Lanzetta v. New Jersey*, 306 U.S. 451.

The Jacksonville ordinance makes criminal activities which by modern standards are normally innocent. "Night walking" is one. Florida construes the ordinance not to make criminal one night's wandering, *Johnson v. State, supra*, only the "habitual" wanderer or as the ordinance describes it "common night walkers." We know, however, from experience that sleepless people often walk at night, perhaps hopeful that sleep-inducing relaxation will result. Luis Munoz-Marin, former governor of Puerto Rico, commented once that "loafing" was a national virtue in his commonwealth and that it should be encouraged. It is, however, a crime in Jacksonville.

This aspect of the vagrancy ordinance before us is suggested by what this Court said in 1875 about a broad criminal statute enacted by Congress: "It would certainly be dangerous if the legislature could set a net large enough to catch all possible offenders, and leave it to the courts to step inside and say who could be rightfully detained, and who should be set at large." While that was a federal case, the due-process implications are equally applicable to the states and to this vagrancy ordinance. Here the net case is large, not to give the courts the power to pick and choose but to increase the arsenal of the police.

Where the list of crimes is so all-inclusive and generalized as the one in this ordinance, those convicted may be punished for no more than vindicating affronts to police authority. The common ground which brings such a motley assortment of human troubles before the magistrates in vagrancy-type proceedings is the procedural laxity which permits conviction for almost any kind of conduct and the existence of the house of correction as an easy and convenient dumping ground for problems that appear to have no other immediate solution.

Another aspect of the ordinance's vagueness appears when we focus not on the lack of notice given a potential offender, but on the effect of the unfettered discretion it places in the hands of the Jacksonville police. Such crimes, though long common in Russia, are not compatible with our constitutional system. We allow our police to make arrests only on "probable cause," a Fourth and Fourteenth Amendment standard applicable to the states as well as to the federal government. Arresting a person on suspicion, like arresting a person for investigation, is foreign to our system, even when the arrest is for past criminality. Future criminality, however, is the common justification for the presence of vagrancy statutes. Florida has indeed construed her vagrancy statute as a necessary regulation to deter vagabondage and prevent crimes.

A direction by a legislature to the police to arrest all "suspicious persons" would not pass constitutional muster. A vagrancy prosecution may be merely the cloak for a conviction which could not be obtained on the real but undisclosed grounds for the arrest.

Those generally implicated by the imprecise terms of the ordinance—poor people, noncomformists, dissenters, idlers—may be required to comport themselves according to the lifestyle deemed appropriate by the Jacksonville police and the courts. Where, as here, there are no standards governing the exercise of the discretion granted by the ordinance, the scheme permits and encourages an arbitrary and discriminatory enforcement of the law. It furnishes a convenient tool for harsh and discriminatory enforcement by prosecuting officials, against particular groups deemed to merit their displeasure. It results in a regime in which the poor and the unpopular are permitted to stand on a public sidewalk . . . only at the whim of any police officer. Under this ordinance, if some carefree type of fellow is satisfied to work just so much, and no more, as will pay for one square meal, some wine, and a flophouse daily, but a court thinks this kind of living subhuman, the fellow can be forced to raise his sights or go to jail as a vagrant.

A presumption that people who might walk or loaf or loiter or stroll or frequent houses where liquor is sold, or who are supported by their wives or who look suspicious to the police are to become future criminals is too precarious for a rule of law. The implicit presumption in these generalized vagrancy standards—that crime is being nipped in the bud—is too extravagant to deserve extended treatment. Of course, vagrancy statutes are useful to the police. Of course, they are nets making easy the roundup of so-called undesirables. But the rule of law implies equality and justice in its application. Vagrancy laws of the Jacksonville type teach that the scales of justice are so tipped that evenhanded administration of the law is not possible. The rule of law, evenly applied to minorities as well as majorities, to the poor as well as the rich, is the great mucilage that holds society together.

The Jacksonville ordinance cannot be squared with our constitutional standards and is plainly unconstitutional.

Reversed

CASE QUESTIONS

1. On what basis was the ordinance found void for vagueness?
2. If a statute is on its face repugnant to the due-process clause on account of vagueness, should specification of the details of the offense validate it?
3. Should the standard of certainty in statutes be higher for criminal statutes than those depending primarily on civil sanctions for enforcement?
4. Should a criminal statute be rendered unconstitutional by the fact that its application may be uncertain in exceptional cases?

SUGGESTED READINGS

Bennion, *The Science of Interpretation,* 130 NEW L.J. 493 (1980).

Evans, *Void for Vagueness—Judicial Response to Allegedly Vague Statutes —State v. Zvanich,* 56 WASH. L. REV. 131 (1980).

Note, *Reconciliation of Conflicting Void-for-Vagueness Theories Applied by the Supreme Court,* 9 HOUS. L. REV. 82 (1971).

Note, *Vagueness and Overbreadth in University Regulations,* 2 TEX. TECH. L. REV. 255 (1971).

Roybal, *Void for Vagueness: State Statutes Proscribing Conduct Only for a Juvenile,* 1 PEPPERDINE L. REV. 1 (1973).

Penal Statutes

Penal statutes impose punishment for offenses committed against the state. They include all statutes that command or prohibit certain acts and establish penalties for their violation. Penal statutes are enacted for the benefit of the public. They should receive a fair and reasonable construction. The words used should be given the meaning commonly attributed to them. Criminal statutes are to be strictly construed, and doubts are to be resolved in favor of the accused. *Strict construction* means that the statute should not be enlarged by implication beyond the fair meaning of the language used. However, the statute should not be construed so as to defeat the obvious intention of the legislature.

Knott v. Rawlings
250 Iowa 892, 96 N.W.2d 900
Supreme Court of Iowa
June 9, 1959

GARRETT, JUSTICE
Original proceeding to determine legality of action of the district court, in overruling defendant's motion to dismiss indictment charging defendant with having committed lascivious acts with one 16 years of age.

The petitioner was charged by indictment with having committed lascivious acts with one "who was 16 years of age, in violation of section 725.2 of the 1958 Code of Iowa." The material part of said section is as follows: "725.2. Lascivious acts with children: Any person over 18 years of age who shall willfully commit any lewd, immoral, or lascivious act in the presence, or upon or with the body or any part or member thereof, of a child of the age of 16 years, or under, with the intent of arousing, appealing to, or gratifying the lusts or passions or sexual desires of such person, or of such child, . . . shall be punished. . . ."

It was alleged the crime was committed on or about August 12, 1958, and it was shown the child involved was born February 9, 1942, so that he was 16 years, 6 months, and 3 days old at the time in question. The indictment was attacked by demurrer which was overruled. The defendant then filed in

two counts his plea to the jurisdiction and motion to dismiss which likewise were overruled. Upon proper application, a writ of *certiorari* issued from this court on January 13, 1959, and return thereto was filed.

The respondent's brief and argument states, "As set out by the petitioner, the sole question before the court is the interpretation of the phrase, 'of a child of the age of 16 years, or under.'" This calls for an answer to the following question: Is one who is 16 years, 6 months, and 3 days old "a child of the age of 16 years, or under," within the contemplation of § 725.2 of the 1958 Code, I.C.A.? We have no hesitancy in answering this question in the negative. The learned trial court, in his well-considered opinion, set out what he believed to be sound reasons sustaining his contrary view and cited supporting authorities. We prefer, however, to follow the majority rule which seems to us to be supported not only by the better authority but also by the better reasoning.

A child is 1 year old on the 1st anniversary of his birth and is 16 years old on the 16th anniversary. Before the 16th anniversary, he is under the age of 16 years and after that anniversary, he is over the age of 16. Sixteen years is an exact and definite period of time. It does not mean or include 16 years and 6 months. We should be realistic and not read something into the statute which is not there and which clearly was not intended to be there. This is a criminal statute and cannot be added to by statutory construction.

"Of the age of 16 years" must be construed to mean just what it says, that is, 16 years and not 16 years, 6 months, and 3 days. If, speaking in terms of money, one were to say, "The fee or charge will be $15 or under," there would be no possibility of misunderstanding. To say that 16 years and 6 months means the same as 16 years is to play loosely with words which have a definite meaning. It has been suggested that when one is asked to state his age he gives only the age at the last anniversary of his birth and does not add the additional months and days which a completely correct statement would require. This is cited as indicating it is commonly accepted that one is 16 until his 17th birthday anniversary. All such arguments are unsound. When the legislature wrote "16 years" into the statute it intended the words to be construed according to their ordinary meaning. It is contended that when the legislature used the words "a child of the age of 16 years, or under," it intended such words to mean "a child under 17 years of age." That contention is answered by the fact that it chose the words "16 years, or under" in preference to the words "under 17 years," which it would have used had it intended what the state maintains it intended.

Section 698.1, Code 1958, I.C.A. provides, ". . . if any person carnally know and abuse any female child under the age of 16 years, or if any person over the age of 25 years carnally know and abuse any female under the age of 17 years, he shall be imprisoned. . . ." Suppose a man 25 years and 6 months of age were charged under this statute with an attack upon a female under the age of 17. Would the state excuse him on the ground that he is only 25 years of age until the day he becomes 26?

"Words and phrases shall be construed according to the context and the approved usage of the language." Sec. 4.1(2), 1958 Code, I.C.A. It is the settled rule in this state that criminal statutes are to be strictly construed and doubts, if any, are to be resolved in favor of the accused. Such statutes may not be extended by implication to include an offense not clearly within the fair scope of the language used. "It is a fundamental rule . . . that no one may be required . . . to speculate as to the meaning of penal statutes."

The legislative intent is the all-important and controlling factor in the interpretation of statutes. "Since the intention of the legislature, embodied in a statute, is the law, the fundamental rule of construction, to which all other rules are subordinate, is that the court shall, by all aids available, ascertain and give effect, unless it is in conflict with the constitutional provisions, or is inconsistent with the organic law of the state, to the intention or purpose of the legislature as expressed in the statute." We cannot bring ourselves to believe that when the legislature said "of the age of 16 years, or under" it meant and intended to say "of the age of 16 years, or under, or over up to 1 additional year."

The courts of other states have had occasion to decide the question here involved. We would not be justified in taking the time or space to quote extensively from them. To show the trend of opinion a few quotations will suffice. A case in point and often cited as *Gibson v. People*, 44 Colo. 600, 99 P. 333, 334. The act there reviewed was one relating to delinquent children in which it was said:

Section 1 of the delinquent children law says that the act shall apply only to children *sixteen (16) years of age or under*. The words "delinquent child" shall include any child sixteen (16) years of age or under such age who violates any law, etc. Any child *sixteen (16) years of age or under such age* may, therefore, become a delinquent child or a juvenile delinquent person. The attorney general contends that these italicized words include children during their entire sixteenth year and up to the seventeenth anniversary of their birth, while defendant maintains that it excludes children who have passed beyond the first day of their sixteenth year. . . . It is obvious that the general assembly intended to fix some limit to the age of children affected by the statute—a point of time beyond which they no longer are amenable to its provisions. In one sense a child is sixteen years of age until it is seventeen; so also it is sixteen when it is eighteen; but, in the true sense, it is sixteen and over whenever it has passed beyond the first day of the sixteenth anniversary of its birth. Had it been the intention to include children up to the time they reach their seventeenth birthday, the general assembly would naturally have said "children under seventeen years of age." But, when only those "sixteen (16) years of age or under" were mentioned, it obviously meant what it said, namely, children "sixteen (16) years of age, or under," not "sixteen years of age and over." A child is sixteen years of age on the sixteenth anniversary of his birth, and thereafter is over sixteen years of age. The alleged delinquent juvenile being sixteen years and four months old at the time defendant is said to have contributed to his delinquency was "sixteen years and over," not "sixteen years, or under," hence was not a juvenile delinquent person within the meaning of the statute.

The respondent cites *Watson v. Loyal Union Life Association*, 143 Okla. 4, 286 P. 888, and *Wilson v. Mid-Continent Life Ins. Co.*, 159 Okla. 191, 14 P.2d 945, as bearing directly on the interpretation of the phrase "of a child of the age of 16 years, or under." These cases involve insurance contracts and are subject to somewhat different rules of construction. The insurer having written the contract, it must be given a construction most favorable to the insured. We do not consider these cases as being in point, since private contracts and criminal statutes are subject to different rules of construction.

Writ sustained

CASE QUESTIONS

1. What is a penal statute? Articulate a test for determining whether a statute is a penal statute.
2. What policy reasons exist for the rule that penal statutes are to be strictly construed? In what kinds of situations should the rule be relaxed?

3. Should the rule of strict construction of penal statutes mean that they should be given the narrowest meaning that the statute will allow? What limitations, if any, should be placed on the rule?

4. If the following provisions were included as part of a general provision of a state's penal code, what effect would they have on the rule of strict construction of penal statutes?

a. ''The articles of this code cannot be extended by analogy so as to create crimes not provided for herein. However, in order to promote justice and to effect the objects of the law, all of its provisions shall be given a genuine construction according to the fair import of their words, taken in their usual sense, in connection with the context, and with reference to the purposes of the provision.''

b. ''All general provisions, terms, phrases, and expressions used in any statute shall be liberally construed in order that the true intent and meaning of the legislature may be fully carried out.''

c. ''The rule of the common law that statutes in derogation thereto are to be strictly construed, has no application to these applied laws. Their provisions and all proceedings under them are to be liberally construed, with a view to effecting their objects and promoting justice.''

SUGGESTED READINGS

Casper, *Guardians of the Constitution*, 53 S. CAL. L. REV. 773 (1980).

Dickerson, *Statutory Interpretation: A Peek into the Mind and Will of a Legislature*, 50 IND. L.J. 206 (1975).

Goldberg, *Reflections on the Role of the Supreme Court in the Pursuit of Equal Justice*, 7 N. KY. L. REV. 1 (1980).

Hill, *Court Curbing, Court Reversals and Judicial Review, The Supreme Court Versus Congress*, 14 LAW AND SOCIETY REV. 309 (1980).

Taylor, *Limits of Judicial Creativity*, 63 IOWA L. REV. 1 (1977).

Note, *Construction and Misconstruction—ORS 12.030*, Kenner v. Schmidt, 49 ORE. L. REV. 337 (1970).

The *Wilson* case cited in the last paragraph of the court opinion of the *Knott* case was not used as precedent because the case involved the construction of a contract rather than a criminal statute. Contracts and criminal statutes are subject to different rules of construction. The *Wilson* case was a suit brought by a beneficiary against Mid-Continent Life Insurance Company to recover money under an automobile accident policy. The insured was accidentally killed when he was 65 years and 8 months old. The insurance policy provided, ''The insurance under this policy shall not cover any person under the age of 18 years nor over the age of 65 years. . . .'' The court allowed the beneficiary to recover, holding that one is not over the age of 65 years until one has reached the 66th birthday, and fractions of a year should not be considered. The court stated that provisions of an insurance policy should be given their ordinary and generally accepted meaning. If a policy of insurance is susceptible to two constructions, the one that is most favorable to the insured is adopted.

Limits on Construction

A literal interpretation of statutory language can lead to unreasonable, unjust, or even absurd consequences. In such a case, a court is justified in adopting a construction that sustains the validity of the legislative act, rather than one that defeats it.

Courts do not have legislative authority and should avoid ''judicial legislation.'' To depart from the meaning expressed by the words of the statute so as to alter it is not construction—it is legislative alteration. A statute should not be construed more broadly or given greater effect than its terms require. Nothing should be read into a statute that was not intended by the legislature, as manifested in the statute itself.

Statutes are to be read in the light of conditions at the time of their enactment. A new meaning should not be given to the words of an old statute because of changed conditions. Sometimes, however, the scope of a statute may appear to include conduct that did not exist when the statute was enacted—for example, certain activity related to technological progress. Such a case does not preclude the application of the statute thereto.

United States v. Standard Oil Company
384 U.S. 224
United States Supreme Court
May 23, 1966

Mr. Justice Douglas
An indictment in the United States District Court for the Middle District of Florida charged an oil company with violating § 13 of the Rivers and Harbors Act by discharging into a navigable river ''refuse matter'' consisting of 100-octane aviation gasoline. The district court dismissed the indictment on the ground that the statutory phrase ''refuse matter'' does not include commercially valuable oil.

The question presented for decision is whether the statutory ban on depositing ''any refuse matter of any kind or description'' in a navigable water covers the discharge of commercially valuable aviation gasoline.

Section 13 of the Rivers and Harbors Act provides:

It shall not be lawful to throw, discharge, or deposit . . . any refuse matter of any

kind or description whatever other than
that flowing from streets and sewers
and passing therefrom in a liquid state,
into any navigable water of the United
States. . . .

The indictment charged appellee, Standard Oil (Kentucky), with violating § 13 by allowing to be discharged into the St. Johns River "refuse matter" consisting of 100-octane aviation gasoline. Appellee moved to dismiss the indictment, and, for the purposes of the motion, the parties entered into a stipulation of fact. It states that the gasoline was commercially valuable and that it was discharged into the St. Johns only because a shut-off valve at dockside had been "accidentally" left open.

The district court dismissed the indictment because it was of the view that the statutory phrase "refuse matter" does not include commercially valuable oil.

This case comes to us at a time in the nation's history when there is greater concern than ever over pollution—one of the main threats to our free-flowing rivers and to our lakes as well. The crisis that we face in this respect would not, of course, warrant us in manufacturing offenses where Congress has not acted nor in stretching statutory language in a criminal field to meet strange conditions. But whatever may be said of the rule of strict construction, it cannot provide a substitute for common sense, precedent, and legislative history. We cannot construe § 13 of the Rivers and Harbors Act in a vacuum.

The statutory words are "any refuse matter of any kind or description." We said in *United States v. Republic Steel Corp.*, 362 U.S. 482, 491, that the history of this provision and of related legislation dealing with our free-flowing rivers "forbids a narrow, cramped reading" of § 13. The district court recognized that if this were waste oil it would be "refuse matter" within the meaning of § 13 but concluded that it was not within the statute because it was "valuable" oil. This is "a narrow, cramped reading" of § 13 in partial defeat of its purpose.

Oil is oil, and whether usable or not by industrial standards, it has the same deleterious effect on waterways. In either case, its presence in our rivers and harbors is both a menace to navigation and a pollutant. This seems to be the administrative construction of § 13, the solicitor general advising us that it is the basis of prosecution in approximately one-third of the oil pollution cases reported to the Department of Justice by the Office of the Chief of Engineers.

Section 13 codified pre-existing statutes:

An 1886 act (24 Stat. 329) made it unlawful to empty "any ballast, stone, slate, gravel, earth, slack, rubbish, wreck, filth, slabs, edgings, sawdust, slag, or cinders, or other refuse or millwaste of any kind into New York Harbor"—which plainly includes valuable predischarge material.

An 1888 act (25 Stat. 209) "to prevent obstructive and injurious deposits" within the harbor of New York and adjacent waters banned the discharge of "refuse, dirt, ashes, cinders, mud, sand, dredgings, sludge, acid, or any other matter of any kind, other than that flowing from streets, sewers, and passing therefrom in a liquid state"—which also plainly includes valuable predischarge material.

The 1890 act (26 Stat. 453) made unlawful emptying into navigable waters "any ballast, stone, slate, gravel, earth, rubbish, wreck, filth, slabs, edgings, sawdust, slag, cinders, ashes, refuse, or other waste of any kind . . . which shall tend to impede or obstruct navigation." Here also valuable predischarge materials were included.

The 1894 act (28 Stat. 363) prohibited deposits in harbors and rivers for which Congress had appropriated money for improvements, of "ballast, refuse, dirt, ashes, cinders, mud, sand, dredgings, sludge, acid, or any other matter of any kind other than that flowing from streets and sewers and passing therefrom in a liquid state." This act also included valuable predischarge material.

The acts of 1886 and 1888, then, dealt specifically with the New York Harbor; the scope of the latter was considerably broader, covering as it did the deposit of "any other matter of any kind." The acts of 1890 and 1894 paralleled the earlier enactments, pertaining to New York, applying their terms to waterways throughout the nation.

The 1899 act now before us was no more than an attempt to consolidate these prior acts into one. It was indeed stated by the sponsor in the Senate to be "in accord with the statutes now in existence, only scattered . . . from the beginning of the statutes down through to the end" (32 Cong. Rec. 2296), and reflecting merely "[v]ery slight changes to remove ambiguities." *Id.*, p. 2297.

From an examination of these statutes, several points are clear. First, the 1894 act and its antecedent, the 1888 act applicable to the New York Harbor, drew on their face no distinction between valuable and valueless substances. Second, of the enumerated substances, some may well have had commercial or industrial value prior to discharge into the covered waterways. To be more specific, ashes and acids were banned whether or not they had any remaining commercial or industrial value. Third, these acts applied not only to the enumerated substances but also to the discharge of "any other matter of any kind." Since the enumerated substances included those with a predischarge value, the rule of *ejusdem generis* does not require limiting this latter category to substances lacking a predischarge value. Fourth, the coverage of these acts was not diminished by the codification of 1899. The use of the term *refuse* in the codification serves in the place of the lengthy list of enumerated substances found in the earlier acts and the catchall provision found in the act of 1890. The legislative history demonstrates without contradiction that Congress intended to codify without substantive changes the earlier acts.

The philosophy of those antecedent laws seems to us to be clearly embodied in the present law. It is plain from its legislative history that the "serious injury" to our watercourses sought to be remedied was caused in part by obstacles that impeded navigation and in part by pollution—"the discharge of sawmill waste into streams" and the injury of channels by "deposits of ballast, steamboat ashes, oysters, and rubbish from passing vessels." The list is obviously not an exhaustive list of pollutants. The words of the act are broad and inclusive: "any refuse matter of any kind or description whatever.'' Only one exception is stated: ''other than that flowing from streets and sewers and passing therefrom in a liquid state, into any navigable water of the United States.'' More comprehensive language would be difficult to select. The word *refuse* does not stand alone; the ''refuse'' banned is ''of any kind or description whatever,'' apart from the one exception noted. And for the reasons already stated, the meaning we must give the term *refuse* must reflect the present codification's statutory antecedents.

The court of appeals in *United States v. Ballard Oil Co.* held that causing good oil to spill into a watercourse violated § 13. The word *refuse* in that setting, said the court, ''is satisfied by anything which has become waste, however useful it may earlier have been.'' *Id.*, p. 371. There is nothing more deserving of the label *refuse* than oil spilled into a river.

That seems to us to be the common sense of the matter. The word *refuse* includes all foreign substances and pollutants apart from those ''flowing from streets and sewers and passing therefrom in a liquid state'' into the watercourse.

Reversed

MR. JUSTICE HARLAN, with whom MR. JUSTICE BLACK and MR. JUSTICE STEWART join, dissenting
Had the majority in judging this case been content to confine itself to applying relevant rules of law and to leave policies affecting the proper conservation of the nation's rivers to be dealt with by the Congress, I think that to-day's decision in this criminal case would have eventuated differently. The best that can be said for the government's case is that the reach of the provision of § 13 of the Rivers and Harbors Act of 1899, under which this indictment is laid, is uncertain. This calls into play the traditional rule that penal statutes are to be strictly construed. In my opinion, application of that rule requires a dismissal of the indictment.

Section 13 forbids the deposit of all kinds of ''refuse matter'' into navigable rivers ''other than that flowing from streets and sewers and passing therefrom in a liquid state.'' As the Court notes, this 1899 act was part of a codification of prior statutes. This revamping was not discussed at any length on the floor of either house of Congress; the Senate was informed only that the provisions were merely a codification of existing law, without changes in substance. Section 13 was in fact based on two very similar prior statutes.

Whatever might be said about how properly to interpret the 1890 and, more especially, the 1894 statutes, it is the 1899 act that has been on the books for the last 67 years, and its purposes and language must guide the determination of this case. To the extent that there were some differences in scope between the 1890 and 1894 acts, these were necessarily resolved in the 1899 codification, which, while embodying the essential thrust of both prior statutes, appears from its plain language to have favored the more restrictive coverage of the 1890 act. Moreover, it is questionable to what extent the Court's speculation as to the meaning of a phrase in one of the prior statutes is relevant at all when the language of the present statute, which is penal in nature, is in itself explicit and unambiguous.

It is of course true, as the Court observes, that "oil is oil," and that the accidental spillage of valuable oil may have substantially the same "deleterious effect on waterways" as the wholesale depositing of waste oil. But the relevant inquiry is not the admittedly important concerns of pollution control, but Congress's purpose in enacting this act, and that appears quite plainly to be a desire to halt through the imposition of criminal penalties the depositing of obstructing refuse matter in rivers and harbors.

The Court's construction eschews the everyday meaning of *refuse matter* —waste, rubbish, trash, debris, garbage, see Webster's *New International Dictionary*, 3d ed.—and adopts instead an approach that either reads *refuse* out of the act altogether, or gives to it a tortured meaning. The Court declares, at the point, that "The word *refuse* includes all foreign substances and pollutants apart from those 'flowing from streets and sewers and passing therefrom in a liquid state' into the watercourse." Thus, dropping anything but pure water into a river would appear to be a federal misdemeanor. At the same time, the Court also appears to endorse the Second Circuit's somewhat narrower view that *refuse matter* refers to any material, however valuable, which becomes unsalvageable when introduced into the water. On this latter approach, the imposition of criminal penalties would in effect depend in each instance on a prospective estimate of salvage costs. Such strained definitions of a phrase that is clear as a matter of ordinary English hardly commend themselves and at the very least raise serious doubts as to the intended reach of § 13.

Given these doubts as to the proper construction of "refuse matter" in § 13, we must reckon with a traditional canon that a penal statute will be narrowly construed. The reasons underlying this maxim are various. It appears likely that the rule was originally adopted in order to spare people from the effects of exceedingly harsh penalties. Even though this rationale might be thought to have force were the defendant a natural person, I cannot say that it is particularly compelling in this instance where the maximum penalty to which Standard Oil might be subject is a fine of $2500.

A more important contemporary purpose of the notion of strict construction is to give notice of what the law is, in order to guide people in their everyday activities. Again, however, it is difficult to justify a narrow reading of § 13 on this basis. The spilling of oil of any type into rivers is not something one would be likely to do whether or not it is legally proscribed by a federal statute. A broad construction would hardly raise dangers of penalizing people who have been innocently pouring valuable oil into navigable waters.

There is, however, a further reason for applying a seemingly straightforward statute in a straightforward way. In *McBoyle v. United States*, 283 U.S. 25, this Court held that a statute making it a federal crime to move a stolen "motor vehicle" in interstate commerce did not apply to a stolen airplane. That too was a case in which precise clarity was not required in order to give due warning of the line between permissible and wrongful conduct, for there could not have been any question but that stealing aircraft was unlawful. Nevertheless, Mr. Justice Holmes declared that "Although it is not likely that a criminal will carefully consider the text of the law before he murders or steals, it is reasonable that a fair warning should be given to the world in language that the common world will understand, of what the law intends to do if a certain line is passed." The policy thus expressed is based primarily on a notion of fair play: in a civilized state, the least that can be expected of government is that it express its rules in language all can reasonably be expected to understand. Moreover, this requirement of clear expression is essential in a practical sense to confine the discretion of prosecuting authorities, particularly important under a statute such as § 13 which imposes criminal penalties with a minimum, if any, *scienter* requirement.

In an area in which state or local law has traditionally regulated primary activity, there is good reason to restrict federal penal legislation within the confines of its langauge. If the federal government finds that there is sufficient obstruction or pollution of navigable waters caused by the introduction of commercial oil or other nonrefuse material, it is an easy matter to enact appropriate regulatory or penal legislation.

To conclude that this attempted prosecution cannot stand is not to be oblivious to the importance of preserving the beauties and utility of the country's rivers. It is simply to take the statute as we find it. I would affirm the judgment of the district court.

CASE QUESTIONS

1. Does a court invade the province of the legislature when it extends or restricts the application of a statute in reliance on its notions as to its spirit?
2. To what extent does the doctrine that a statute should be construed so as to have effect in conformity with its spirit reflect a theory of semantics?
3. What should be the limits within which the courts will apply a statute to objects or situations outside the customary or normal meaning of its application?

SUGGESTED READINGS

Berger, *The Scope of Judicial Review: A Continuing Dialogue*, 31 S.C. L. REV. 171 (1980).

Bice, *Studying the Court of Justice: What Message for Federal Jurisdiction?* 53 S. Cal. L. Rev. 527 (1980).

Downs, *Judges, Law-Making and the Constitution: A Response to Professor White*, 63 Judicature 444 (1980).

Satter, *Changing Roles of Courts and Legislatures*, 85 Case and Com. 18 (1980).

Note, *Construction and Misconstruction—ORS 12.030*, Kenner v. Schmidt, 49 Ore. L. Rev. 337 (1970).

Note, *Interpretation of Statute*, 117 New L.J. 939 (1967).

Chapter Questions

1. Define the following terms:
   a. bill of attainder
   b. citizen
   c. equal protection
   d. *ex post facto*
   e. legislature
   f. naturalization
   g. ordinance
   h. police power
   i. presumption

2. Mrs. Dial was the wife of a soldier attached to a tank battalion of the U.S. Army and resided with her husband on a military base in Germany. Because of the death of one of their children, she was tried along with her husband before a military court for unpremeditated murder. Since she was a civilian, Mrs. Dial challenged the jurisdiction of the military court by motion, but her motion was denied and she was convicted on a guilty plea. While she was in prison in West Virginia, her mother filed a petition for *habeas corpus*, alleging that the military trial deprived her daughter of her rights to trial by jury and indictment. The government has for many years exercised military jurisdiction over dependent civilian spouses at military bases overseas. The government claims that the power of military courts over civilian dependents is a necessary and proper incident to the congressional power to make rules for the government and regulation of land and naval forces. Since Mrs. Dial was not actually a member of the armed forces, can she properly be subject to the military court's jurisdiction under the necessary-and-proper clause?
   Kinsella v. Singleton, 361 U.S. 234 (1960)

3. In 1961, Congress expanded the coverage of the Fair Labor Standards Act to include employees of state hospitals and institutions of higher education. The new law extended minimum wage and other protection to employees of certain "enterprises" affecting interstate commerce, including hospitals and schools. The 1961 law also modified

the act's definition of *employer* to include states and their political subdivisions. Maryland and 26 other states and one school district brought suit to enjoin the operation of the law as it affected state hospitals and schools, alleging that the federal government was interfering with the states' sovereign governmental powers. May Congress under the commerce power invade the states' governmental or proprietary interests?

Maryland v. Wirtz, 392 U.S. 183 (1968)

4. The city of Oberlin passed a fair-housing ordinance designed to prohibit racial discrimination in the sale or rental of real estate within city limits. The ordinance forbade discrimination because of race, creed, or color in the sale or lease of real property by the owner, through the terms of sale, by the agent or broker, or by a lending institution. A taxpayer, Mr. Porter, attacked the constitutionality of the ordinance, alleging that it deprived individuals of their property and contract rights. May such an ordinance passed under the police power abridge constitutionally guaranteed property rights and contract rights?

Porter v. Oberlin, 3 Ohio App. 2d 158, 209 N.E.2d 629 (1964)

5. As a result of several highly publicized anticrime hearings of the U.S. Congress and the legislatures of New York and New Jersey, the New York and New Jersey legislatures passed the Waterfront Commission Act, which imposed strict government supervision of waterfront activities. Section 8 of the act provided that no person could legally solicit dues on behalf of a waterfront labor organization if any officer of that organization was a convicted felon who had not received either a pardon or a certificate of good conduct. George DeVeau was an officer of Local 1346, Longshoremen's Union. The union was informed by the local prosecutor that he would prosecute any person attempting to collect dues because DeVeau had been convicted of a felony some 30 years earlier. Was section 8 of the Waterfront Commission Act as applied to DeVeau void as a bill of attainder or an *ex post facto* law?

DeVeau v. Braisted, 363 U.S. 144 (1960)

6. An airplane owned by Gaseteria, Inc., crashed into a television tower located in Hudson County, New Jersey, causing extensive damage to the tower and to many surrounding homes and businesses. A New Jersey law provides in part, "The owner of every aircraft which is operated over the land or waters of this state is absolutely liable for injuries to persons or property on the land or water beneath, caused by ascent, descent, or flight of the aircraft . . . unless the injury is caused in whole or in part by the negligence of the person injured or the

owner or bailee of property injured.'' The local property owners bring an action for damages, and Gaseteria defends on the ground that the New Jersey law is an unconstitutional exercise of police power which deprives owners of their airplanes without due process of law. May the New Jersey legislature under the police power enact a law imposing liability on a party without requiring proof of fault?

Adler's Quality Bakery, Inc., v. Gaseteria, Inc., 32 N.J. 55, 159 A.2d 97 (1960)

7. Employees of a large discount department store were convicted of making sales on a Sunday in violation of the Maryland Sunday closing laws. On appeal, they argued that the legislation violated the equal-protection clause because it excepts the retail sale of certain products, such as tobacco, food, and gasoline. Other statutes provide for additional exceptions, such as amusements, including games of chance. Do you think the Maryland statutes are unconstitutional under the equal-protection clause?

   McGowan v. Maryland, 366 U.S. 420 (1961)

8. Both parents filed a petition seeking to be the administrator of their deceased minor son's estate. An Idaho probate court, without attempting to determine the relative capability of the competing applicants, ordered that the letters of administration be issued to the father. The decision was based on the probate code which provides that males must be preferred to females when persons of equal entitlement seek to administer an estate. What argument should the mother make on appeal?

   Reed v. Reed, 404 U.S. 71 (1971)

9. The executive director and medical director of the Planned Parenthood League of Connecticut were arrested for violating the Connecticut birth-control law. The statute provided, ''Any person who uses any drug, medicinal article, or instrument for the purpose of preventing conception shall be fined. . . .'' It further provided, ''Any person who assists, abets, counsels, causes, hires, or commands another to commit any offense may be prosecuted and punished as if he were the principal offender.'' What constitutional argument should the directors use in defending themselves?

   Griswold v. State of Connecticut, 381 U.S. 479 (1965)

10. On March 14, 1960, two black college students took seats in the restaurant department of Eckerd's Drug Store in Columbia, South Carolina, and waited to be served. No one spoke to them or asked to take their orders. An employee put up a ''no trespassing'' sign and asked the students to leave, but they continued to sit. The store manager called the police, who arrested the students under the local

trespass statute. The statute defines the prohibited conduct as "entry upon the lands of another . . . after notice from the owner or tenant prohibiting such entry." The two students were convicted under the trespass statute. Is the statute void for vagueness? Is their conviction subject to other constitutional infirmities?

Bouie v. Columbia, 378 U.S. 347 (1964)

11. Mr. Sorensen was sterile and Mrs. Sorensen wanted a child. Mr. Sorensen agreed to artificial insemination of his wife. They signed an agreement requesting a physician to inseminate the wife with the sperm of a white male. Under no circumstances were the parties to demand the name of the donor. Mrs. Sorensen had a child and named Mr. Sorensen as the father on the birth certificate. Four years later, the Sorensens got a divorce, at which time she wanted no support for the child. Later when she became ill and could not work, she applied for public assistance. Aid was granted, but the district attorney demanded support from Mr. Sorensen, who paid nothing. Mr. Sorensen was criminally prosecuted for violating § 270 of the penal code, which reads: "A father of either a legitimate or illegitimate minor child who willfully omits without lawful excuse to furnish necessary clothing, food, shelter, or medical attendance or other remedial care for his child is guilty of a misdemeanor . . ." Is Mr. Sorensen the "father" of the child within the meaning of the penal code?

People v. Sorensen, 68 C.2d 280, 66 Cal. Rptr. 7, 437 P.2d 495 (1968)

12. Ignatius Lanzetta was arrested under a New Jersey law that provides: "Any person not engaged in any lawful occupation, known to be a member of any gang consisting of two or more persons, who has been convicted at least three times of being a disorderly person, or who has been convicted of any crime in this or in any other state, is declared to be a gangster." Violations of the statute are punishable by a $10,000 fine or imprisonment for up to 20 years. Lanzetta was convicted of being a gangster under this statute and on his appeal attacks the statute as being violative of due process. What due-process concept does this statute violate? Why?

Lanzetta v. New Jersey, 306 U.S. 451 (1939)

13. An Ohio State highway patrolman arrested Joseph Williamson on March 6 for driving while intoxicated. The officer asked Williamson to allow him to take a sample of blood, urine, or breath to determine alcohol content under Ohio's implied consent law. Williamson refused and was advised by the patrolman that such refusal could mean that his driver's license could be suspended for six months by the Bureau of Motor Vehicles. Ten days later, Williamson appeared in court and pleaded guilty to driving while intoxicated. He was sen-

tenced to three days in jail and his driver's license was suspended for 30 days. The Bureau of Motor Vehicles received notice of Williamson's refusal to submit to the alcohol test and suspended his driver's license for six months. May the bureau suspend Williamson's license for six months, despite the fact that he pleaded guilty to driving while intoxicated and was sentenced in criminal court?

Appeal of Williamson, 246 N.E.2d 618 (Ohio 1969)

Overview of Federal Legislative Process

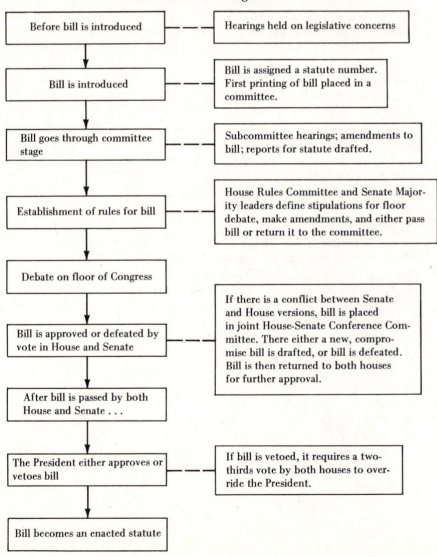

Before bill is introduced	Hearings held on legislative concerns
Bill is introduced	Bill is assigned a statute number. First printing of bill placed in a committee.
Bill goes through committee stage	Subcommittee hearings; amendments to bill; reports for statute drafted.
Establishment of rules for bill	House Rules Committee and Senate Majority leaders define stipulations for floor debate, make amendments, and either pass bill or return it to the committee.
Debate on floor of Congress	
Bill is approved or defeated by vote in House and Senate	If there is a conflict between Senate and House versions, bill is placed in joint House-Senate Conference Committee. There either a new, compromise bill is drafted, or bill is defeated. Bill is then returned to both houses for further approval.
After bill is passed by both House and Senate . . .	
The President either approves or vetoes bill	If bill is vetoed, it requires a two-thirds vote by both houses to override the President.
Bill becomes an enacted statute	

The Administrative Process   IX

The Function of Administrative Agencies

The most striking development in the U.S. government in the twentieth century has been the multiplication of administrative agencies and the extension of their power and activities. Today, numerous local, state, and federal administrative agencies have a tremendous impact on our governmental system. Citizens and businesses are affected more by the administrative process than by the judicial process. The following are examples of areas of everyday life subject to the regulatory power of agencies: rates for insurance, telephone, gas, electric, and other utilities; rates and schedules of buses, airlines, and railroads; programming of television and radio; labor practices of employers and unions; pollution of water and air; wholesomeness of food and drugs; zoning of neighborhoods; and supplemental income received by the unemployed and retired.

The operations of businesses and industry, as well as professions and institutions, are becoming more regulated. For example, agencies monitor business in order to prevent the use of unfair methods of competition and deceptive practices. As previously mentioned, rates that businesses charge are often regulated. Many businesses and professionals are not permitted to function without being licensed. In fact, the operation of such industries as broadcasting are almost completely dependent on the regulatory power of an agency.

Administrative agencies are authorities of the government, other than the executive, legislative, or judicial branches, created for the purpose of administering particular legislation. They are sometimes called commissions, bureaus, authorities, offices, corporations, departments, administrations, and divisions. They may be created by legislative, or enabling,

Example of Federal Administrative Agency: Its Structure and Function [1]

FEDERAL MARITIME COMMISSION

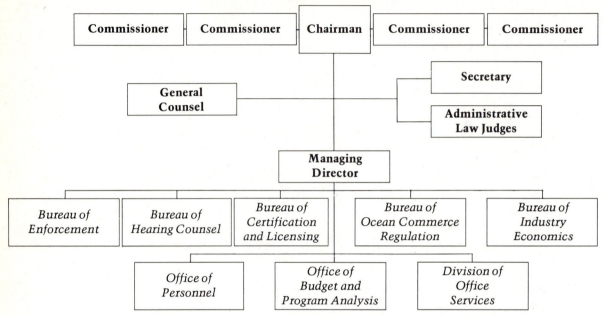

The Federal Maritime Commission regulates the waterborne foreign and domestic offshore commerce of the United States, assures that United States international trade is open to all nations on fair and equitable terms, and guards against unauthorized monopoly in the waterborne commerce of the United States. This is accomplished through maintaining surveillance over steamship conferences and common carriers by water; assuring that only the rates on file with the Commission are charged; approving agreements between persons subject to the Shipping Act; guaranteeing equal treatment to shippers and carriers by terminal operators, freight forwarders, and other persons subject to the shipping statutes; and ensuring that adequate levels of financial responsibility are maintained for indemnification of passengers or oil and hazardous substance spill cleanup.

The Federal Maritime Commission was established by Reorganization Plan 7, effective August 12, 1961. It is an independent agency which administers the functions and discharges the regulatory authorities under the following statutes: Shipping Act, 1916; Merchant Marine Act, 1920; Intercoastal Shipping Act, 1933; Merchant Marine Act, 1936; and certain provisions of the act of November 6, 1966 (80 Stat. 1356; 46 U.S.C. 362), the Federal Water Pollution Control Act, as amended by the Clean Water Act of 1977 (91 Stat. 1566), the Trans-Alaska Pipeline Authorization Act (87 Stat. 584), and the Outer Continental Shelf Lands Act Amendments of 1978 (92 Stat. 670; 43 U.S.C. 1815).

Functions and Activities

Agreements

The Commission approves or disapproves agreements filed by common carriers, including conference agreements, interconference agreements, and cooperative working agreements between common carriers, terminal operators, freight forwarders, and other persons subject to the shipping laws, and reviews activities under approved agreements for compliance with the provisions of law and the rules, orders, and regulations of the Commission.

Practices

The Commission regulates the practices of common carriers by water and other persons engaged in the foreign and domestic offshore commerce of the United States, and conferences

---

[1] Reprinted from *United States Government Manual 1979–1980*, published by Office of the Federal Register, National Archives and Records Service.

of such common carriers in accordance with the requirements of the shipping statutes and the rules, orders, and regulations of the Commission.

Tariffs

The Commission accepts or rejects tariff filings of domestic offshore carriers and common carriers engaged in the foreign commerce of the United States, or conferences of such carriers, in accordance with the requirements of the shipping statutes and the Commission's rules and regulations. In the domestic offshore trade, the Commission has the authority to set maximum or minimum rates or suspend rates. It approves or disapproves Special Permission applications submitted by domestic offshore carriers and carriers in the foreign commerce, or conferences of such carriers, for relief from the statutory and/or Commission tariff requirements.

Licenses

The Commission issues or denies the issuance of licenses to persons, partnerships, corporations, or associations desiring to engage in ocean freight forwarding activities.

Passenger Indemnity

The Commission administers the passenger indemnity provisions of the act of November 6, 1966, issues or denies the issuance of certificates of financial responsibility of shipowners and operators to pay judgments for personal injury or death and to refund fares in the event of nonperformance of voyages.

Water Pollution

The Commission administers the vessel certification provisions of section 311 (p)(1) of the Federal Water Pollution Control Act, as amended by the Clean Water Act of 1977 (91 Stat. 1566), section 204(c) of the Trans-Alaska Pipeline Authorization Act (87 Stat. 584), and section 305(a)(1) of the Outer Continental Shelf Lands Act Amendments of 1978 (92 Stat. 670) with respect to evidence of financial responsibility required from operators of vessels which may be subjected to liability for damages and removal of oil and hazardous substances discharged into United States waters.

Informal Complaints

The Commission reviews and determines the validity of alleged or suspected violations of the shipping statutes and rules and regulations of the Commission by common carriers by water in the domestic offshore and the foreign commerce of the United States, terminal operators, freight forwarders, and other persons subject to the provisions of the shipping statutes. After investigation, it concludes such complaints by administrative action, formal proceedings, referral to the Department of Justice, or by achieving voluntary agreement between the parties.

Formal Adjudicatory Procedure

The Commission conducts formal investigations and hearings on its own motion and adjudicates formal complaints pursuant to the Administrative Procedure Act.

Rulemaking

The Commission promulgates rules and regulations to interpret, enforce, and assure compliance with shipping and other statutes of common carriers by water and other persons subject to the statutes.

Investigation, Audit, and Financial and Economic Analyses

The Commission prescribes and administers programs to assure compliance with the provisions of the shipping statutes of all persons subject thereto, including without limitation those for: the submission of regular and special reports, information, and data; the conduct of a plan for the field investigation and audit of activities and practices of common carriers by water in the domestic offshore trade and the foreign commerce of the United States, conferences of such carriers, terminal operators, freight forwarders, and other persons subject to the shipping statutes; and rate and related financial analysis studies, economic studies, and the preparation of reports reflecting the various trade areas, the extent and nature of competition, commodities carried, and future commodity trends.

International Affairs

The Commission, in conjunction with the Department of State, conducts activities to effect the elimination of discriminatory practices on the part of foreign governments against United States–flag shipping.

acts, by executive orders authorized by statutes, or by constitutional provisions. The powers and functions of an agency are generally contained in the instrument that created it. Courts require that the instrument creating the agency contain intelligible standards or guidelines for the agency to consult in effectuating the power delegated to it.

Agencies affect the rights of private parties and businesses by exercising powers of investigation, rule making, enforcement, and adjudication. This combination of functions does not conflict with the doctrine of the *separation of powers*, the constitutional principle that the legislative, executive, and judicial functions of government should not exist in the same person or groups of persons. Even though a wide range of powers are delegated to an agency by the enabling act, there are checks on its activities. The creator of an agency, which is generally the legislature, retains the power to destroy it or alter the rules governing it. The judiciary retains the power of final review of the determinations of administrative agencies. There is a right to judicial review of the agency's findings, but this right is, as a practical matter, very limited.

Thygesen v. Callahan
74 Ill.2d 404
385 N.E.2d 699
Supreme Court of Illinois
January 26, 1979

Thomas J. Moran, Justice
Currency exchange owners and operators brought action challenging the constitutionality of the Currency Exchange Act provision authorizing directors of financial institutions to formulate and issue schedules of maximum rates chargeable for check cashing and writing of money orders by currency exchanges.

Section 19.3 of the act, which became effective on October 1, 1977, provides:

The director (of financial institutions) shall, by rules adopted in accordance with the Illinois Administrative Procedure Act, formulate and issue, within 120 days from the effective date of this amendatory act, schedules of maximum rates which can be charged for check cashing and writing of money orders by community currency exchanges and ambulatory currency exchanges. Such rates may vary according to such circumstances and conditions as the director determines to be appropriate. The schedule so established may be modified by the director from time to time by the same procedure. Any currency exchange may charge lower fees than those of the applicable maximum fee schedule after filing with the director a schedule of the fees it proposes to use.

The rate schedules in effect for any currency exchange shall be prominently displayed on the premises of such currency exchanges in such fashion as shall be required by the director.

Plaintiffs each own and operate one of the approximately 613 licensed community currency exchanges in Illinois.

Prior to the enactment of the section, the rates which plaintiffs and all other currency exchange licensees could charge for cashing checks and writing money orders were not regulated in any manner by the director of financial institutions (defendant), by the Currency Exchange Act, or by any other statute. Consequently, plaintiffs had set their rates in open competition with other currency exchanges, banks, savings and loan associations, food stores, drugstores, and other establishments offering similar services. Plaintiffs question neither the right of the legislature to set maximum rates nor its decision to delegate to defendant the power to set maximum rates. Rather, plaintiffs direct our attention to the failure of the legislature to provide any intelligible standards or guidelines for defendant to consult in effectuating the statutory mandate to set maximum rates. The total absence of standards or guidelines, plaintiffs assert, renders the section invalid as an unconstitutional delegation of legislative power. Ill. Const. 1970, art. IV, § 1.

Though courts and commentators have exhaustively discussed the varied and evolving aspects of the delegation of legislative power, no meaningful consensus has been reached regarding the need for standards or guidelines to validate legislative delegation. For this court's most recent and comprehensive pronouncement on the delegation of power to administrative agencies, we refer to *Stofer v. Motor Vehicle Casualty Co.* (1977), 68 Ill. 2d 361, 12 Ill. Dec. 168, 369 N.E. 2d 875. In *Stofer*, the court reaffirmed its adherence to the guiding principle that intelligible standards or guidelines must accompany legislative delegations of power. Intelligible standards help guide the administrative agency in the application of the statutes involved and, thereby, safeguard against the unwarranted or unintended extension of legislative delegation. They tend to ensure that the legislature does not abdicate to the agency the legislature's primary responsibility to determine, from among the policy alternatives, those objectives the legislation is meant to achieve. Moreover, intelligible standards are indispensable to a meaningful judicial review of any action ultimately taken by the administrative agency.

The *Stofer* court declared that a legislative delegation is valid if it sufficiently identifies:

1. The persons and *activities* potentially subject to regulations;
2. the *harm* sought to be prevented; and
3. the general *means* intended to be available to the administrator to prevent the identified harm. (Emphasis in original.)

In *Stofer*, the legislature had delegated to the director of insurance the power to promulgate a standard policy as a means of ensuring uniformity in the insurance of identical risks. The legislation clearly satisfied the first prong of the test by specifying that the regulation was to apply to fire and lightning insurance issued in Illinois. As to the second prong, the court noted that the legislature had articulated its intention to prevent a chaotic proliferation of disparate fire insurance policies. In discussing the general means intended to be available to the director to prevent the identified harm (the third prong), the court cautioned:

(H)ad the legislature left the director completely free to promulgate a "reasonable" uniform fire insurance policy, we would have serious doubts as to the constitutionality of such uncabined discretion. We find, however, that the legislature has provided substantial additional standards defining the harm sought to be prevented and thereby limit(ed) the director's discretion.

Here, as in *Stofer*, the legislature clearly satisfied the first prong of the test. Those subject to regulation under § 19.3 of the Currency Exchange Act are community and ambulatory currency exchanges, and the regulation is limited to the activities of cashing checks and issuing money orders. In contrast to *Stofer*, the legislature made no attempt to identify the "harm sought to be prevented" in delegating to defendant the power to set maximum rates and did not sufficiently identify the "means . . . intended to be available . . . to prevent the identified harm." Section 19.3 is devoid of any reference to the harm to be remedied. The Currency Exchange Act contains no other provision that indicates, explicitly or implicitly, general purposes which the legislature might have intended to foster with respect to setting rates for cashing checks and issuing money orders.

The legislature's failure to convey, within the act, the harm that it sought to remedy by the setting of maximum rates, is compounded by its failure to set forth any meaningful standards to guide defendant in setting the maximum rates. The only provision cited by defendant which in any way guides defendant's discretion in setting maximum rates is an omnibus provision which states:

The director may make and enforce such reasonable, relevant regulations, directions, orders, decisions, and findings as may be necessary for the execution and enforcement of this act and the purposes sought to be attained herein.

We find that the only statutory limitation on defendant's discretion in establishing maximum rates is that the rates be reasonable. Where the legislature has not only failed to provide any additional standards to guide defendant's discretion, but has failed to communicate to defendant the harm it intended to prevent, it is clear that the legislature has unlawfully delegated its power to set such maximum rates.

We hold § 19.3 of the Currency Exchange Act unconstitutional; therefore, the judgment of the circuit court is reversed.

Judgment reversed

CASE QUESTIONS

1. What is the role of the enabling act in administrative law?
2. What standards or guidelines should the legislature have provided in delegating its authority so that the Currency Exchange Act would be constitutional?

3. Is an administrative agency a distinct branch of government?
4. Are administrative agencies legitimate, or does the concept and logic of the separation-of-powers doctrine nullify them?

SUGGESTED READINGS

Parker, *The Historical Basis of Administrative Law: Separation of Powers and Judicial Supremacy*, 12 RUTGERS L. REV. 449 (1958).
K.C. DAVIS, ADMINISTRATIVE LAW TEXT, §§ 1.01–1.08, 3.01–3.08 (3d ed. 1972).
Rotunda, *Combination of Functions in Administrative Actions: An Examination of European Alternatives*, 40 FORDHAM L. REV. 101 (1971).
Williams, *Fifty Years of the Law of the Federal Administrative Agencies— and Beyond*, 29 FED. B. J. 267 (1970).
Schwartz, *Administrative Law: The Third Century*, 29 AD. L. REV. 291 (1977).
Sirico, *Agencies in Conflict: Overlapping Agencies and the Legitimacy of the Administrative Process*, 33 VAND. L. REV. 101 (1980).

Investigative Power

The investigative power is conferred on practically all administrative agencies. In order for the agency to perform adequately its rulemaking and adjudicative functions, the administrative power of investigation must be fully effective. Agencies cannot operate without access to facts for intelligent regulation and adjudication. As regulation has expanded and intensified, the agencies' quest for facts has gained momentum. Some agencies are created primarily to perform the fact-finding or investigative function.

Statutes commonly grant an agency the power to use several methods to carry out its fact-finding functions. Requiring reports from regulated businesses, conducting inspections, and using judicially enforced subpoenas are methods of accomplishing the information-gathering task. The production of records and the questioning of witnesses under oath are effective investigative devices.

The power to investigate is one of the functions that distinguishes agencies from courts. This power is usually exercised in order to properly perform another primary function. Like any other power or function of the government, it must be exercised so as to not violate constitutionally protected rights.

See v. Seattle
387 U.S. 541
United States Supreme Court
June 5, 1967

MR. JUSTICE WHITE

Appellant seeks reversal of his conviction for refusing to permit a representative of the city of Seattle Fire Department to enter and inspect appellant's locked commercial warehouse without a warrant and without probable cause to believe that a violation of any municipal ordinance existed therein. The inspection was conducted as part of a routine, periodic citywide canvass to obtain compliance with Seattle's Fire Code. After he refused the inspector access, appellant was arrested and charged with violating § 8.01.050 of the code:

Inspection of Building and Premises: It shall be the duty of the fire chief to inspect and he may enter all buildings and premises, except the interiors of dwellings, as often as may be necessary for the purpose of ascertaining and causing to be corrected any conditions liable to cause fire, or any violations of the provisions of this Title, and of any other ordinance concerning fire hazards.

Appellant was convicted and given a suspended fine of $100 despite his claim that § 8.01.050, if interpreted to authorize this warrantless inspection of his warehouse, would violate his rights under the Fourth and Fourteenth Amendments. We noted probable jurisdiction and set this case for argument with *Camara v. Municipal Court*, 385 U.S. 808. We find the principles enunciated in the *Camara* opinion applicable here, and therefore we reverse.

In *Camara*, we held that the Fourth Amendment bars prosecution of a person who has refused to permit a warrantless code-enforcement inspection of his personal residence. The only question which this case presents is whether *Camara* applies to similar inspections of commercial structures which are not used as private residences. The Supreme Court of Washington, in affirming appellant's conviction, suggested that this Court "has applied different standards of reasonableness to searches of dwellings than to places of business," citing *Davis v. United States*, 328 U.S. 582. The Washington court held, and appellee here argues, that § 8.01.050, which excludes "the interiors of dwellings," establishes a reasonable scheme for the warrantless inspection of commercial premises pursuant to the Seattle Fire Code.

In *Go-Bart Importing Co. v. United States*, 282 U.S. 344, this Court refused to uphold otherwise unreasonable criminal investigative searches merely because commercial rather than residential premises were the object of the police intrusions. Likewise, we see no justification for so relaxing Fourth Amendment safeguards where the official inspection is intended to aid enforcement of laws prescribing minimum physical standards for commercial premises. As we explained in *Camara*, a search of private houses is presumptively unreasonable if conducted without a warrant. The businessman, like the occupant of a residence, has a constitutional right to go about his business free from unreasonable official entries upon his private commercial property. The businessman, too, has that right placed in jeopardy if the decision to enter and inspect for violation of regulatory laws can be made and enforced by the inspector in the field without official authority evidenced by a warrant.

As government regulation of business enterprise has mushroomed in recent years, the need for effective investigative techniques to achieve the aims of such regulation has been the subject of substantial comment and legislation. Official entry upon commercial property is a technique commonly adopted by administrative agencies at all levels of government to enforce a variety of regulatory laws; thus, entry may permit inspection of the structure in which a business is housed, as in this case, or inspection of business products, or a perusal of financial books and records. This Court has not had occasion to consider the Fourth Amendment's relation to this broad range of investigations. However, we have dealt with the Fourth Amendment issues raised by another common investigative technique, the administrative *subpoena* of corporate books and records. We find strong support in these *subpoena* cases for our conclusion that warrants are a necessary and a tolerable limitation on the right to enter upon and inspect commercial premises.

It is now settled that, when an administrative agency *subpoenas* corporate books or records, the Fourth Amendment requires that the *subpoena* be sufficiently limited in scope, relevant in purpose, and specific in direction so that compliance will not be unreasonably burdensome. The agency has the right to conduct all reasonable inspections of such documents which are contemplated by statute, but it must delimit the confines of a search by designating the needed documents in a formal *subpoena*. In addition, while the demand to inspect may be issued by the agency, in the form of an administrative *subpoena*, it may not be made and enforced by the inspector in the field, and the *subpoenaed* party may obtain judicial review of the reasonableness of the demand prior to suffering penalties for refusing to comply.

It is these rather minimal limitations on administrative action which we think are constitutionally required in the case of investigative entry upon commercial establishments. The agency's particular demand for access will of course be measured, in terms of probable cause to issue a warrant, against a flexible standard of reasonableness that takes into account the public need for effective enforcement of the particular regulation involved. But the decision to enter and inspect will not be the product of the unreviewed discretion of the enforcement officer in the field. Given the analogous investigative functions performed by the administrative *subpoena* and the demand for entry, we find untenable the proposition that the *subpoena*, which has been termed a ''constructive'' search, is subject to Fourth Amendment limitations which do not apply to actual searches and inspections of commercial premises.

We therefore conclude that administrative entry, without consent, upon the portions of commercial premises which are not open to the public may only be compelled through prosecution or physical force within the framework of a warrant procedure. We do not in any way imply that business premises may not reasonably be inspected in many more situations than private homes, nor do we question such accepted regulatory techniques as licensing programs which require inspections prior to operating a business or marketing a product. Any constitutional challenge to such programs can only be resolved, as many have been in the past, on a case-by-case basis under the general Fourth Amendment standard of reasonableness. We hold only that the basic component of a reasonable search under the Fourth Amendment—that it not be enforced without a suitable warrant procedure—is applicable in this context, as in others, to business as well as to residential premises. Therefore, appellant may not be prosecuted for exercising his constitutional right to insist that the fire inspector obtain a warrant authorizing entry upon appellant's locked warehouse.

Reversed

CASE QUESTIONS

1. Does the warrant procedure required by this case really place an increased burden on the officers and provide increased protection to the private party?
2. Would the best way to protect privacy be to give notice to the private party of the officer's application for a warrant and to allow a hearing before the magistrate on the question of issuance of the warrant?
3. Based on the *See* case, when may there be a constitutional administrative entry, without consent, upon the portions of commercial premises which are not open to the public?
4. Are there more situations in which constitutionally permissible administrative inspections can be made of business premises than of private homes?

SUGGESTED READINGS

Note, *The Fourth Amendment and Housing Inspections*, 77 YALE L.J. 521 (1968).

Burditt, *What to Do When the F.D.A. Inspector Arrives*, 8 LAW NOTES 33 (1972).

Greenberg, *Balance of Interests Theory and the Fourth Amendment: A Selective Analysis of Supreme Court Action Since* Camara *and* See 61 CALIF. L. REV. 1011 (1973).

K.C. DAVIS, ADMINISTRATIVE LAW TEXT, §§ 3.01–3.08 (3d ed. 1972).
Bartelstone, *Administrative Searches and the Implied Consent Doctrine:*
   Beyond the Fourth Amendment, 43 BROOKLYN L. REV. 91 (1976).
Slatery, *Constitutional Law—Fourth Amendment: Warrant Requirement*
   for OSHA Inspections, 46 TENN. L. REV. 446 (1979).

Rulemaking Power

Rulemaking is legislation on the administrative level, within the confines of the enabling statute. Rulemaking is often referred to as the quasi-legislative function of administrative agencies. It consists of the power to make, alter, or repeal rules and regulations. Administrative rules are promulgated pursuant to specific delegatory provisions in the governing statutes. The statutes set the general standards, authorize the agencies to determine the content of the regulations, and provide general sanctions for noncompliance with the rules. The power of the administrative agencies to promulgate regulations having the force of law covers a vast range of business and governmental functions.

The Federal Administrative Procedure Act was enacted in 1946 by a unanimous vote of both houses of Congress. It applies to the federal administrative agencies. The goals of the APA were to improve and strengthen the administrative process and preserve the basic limits on judicial review. The APA requires general notice of proposed rulemaking to be published in the *Federal Register.* This notice gives interested parties a right to participate in the rule-making process by submitting written data or arguments. The opportunity for oral presentation may or may not be granted by the agency. Publication of a substantive rule in the *Federal Register* is required not less than 30 days before its effective date. Most states have similar legislation.

Chip Steak Company v. Hardin
332 F. Supp. 1084
United States District Court, N.D.
California
October 20, 1971

SWEIGERT, DISTRICT JUDGE
This action, brought for declaratory and injunctive relief, is before the court on plaintiffs' and defendants' cross motions for summary judgment.

Plaintiffs Chip Steak Co. and Western Meat Packers Association bring this action against Clifford Hardin, Secretary of Agriculture; J. C. Leighty, director, Technical Service Division, Consumer and Marketing Service, United States Department of Agriculture (U.S.D.A.); and M. E. Christopherson, director, Western District Meat Inspection, San Francisco, California.

Plaintiffs allege in their first amended

complaint that the Technical Service Division, Consumer and Marketing Service of U.S.D.A. prohibits the use of certain food preservatives, specifically calcium sorbate, sodium sorbate, potassium sorbate, and sorbic acid, in the manufacturing and processing of certain meat food products, by its practice of *not* approving labels which declare the presence of said preservatives; that said practice is contrary to the provisions of the Wholesome Meat Act; that no scientific basis exists for prohibiting the use of these preservatives; that plaintiffs desire to use these chemical preservatives in their products and that continued enforcement of the above practice threatens great and irreparable damage to plaintiff's property rights.

On the basis of the above allegations, plaintiffs seek in their amended complaint a declaratory judgment "that an administrative practice of the United States Department of Agriculture is invalid in that it is contrary to the procedures of the Wholesome Meat Act of 1967"; an injunction against the enforcement of said administrative practice; and an order directing U.S.D.A. to comply with statutory rulemaking procedures.

Defendants deny the existence of the practice as alleged by plaintiffs but admit that U.S.D.A. is continuing to disapprove labels which declare that chemical preservatives are present such as to cause the product to be adulterated or misbranded.

U.S.D.A. has adopted a regulation pursuant to the Federal Meat Inspection Act of 1907, as amended by the Wholesome Meat Act of 1967, which provides as follows:

d. No substance may be used in or on any product if it conceals damage or inferiority or makes the product appear to be better or of greater value than it is.
    Therefore:

. . .

2. Sorbic acid, calcium sorbate, sodium sorbate, and other salts of sorbic acid may not be used in cooked sausage or any other product. . . .

Plaintiffs allege that the prohibited additives have been safely used in the past; that plaintiffs desire to use these additives in their products; and that to prohibit these additives would cause plaintiffs irreparable harm. We will assume that, if plaintiffs endeavor to market products bearing or containing the additives prohibited by the regulation, the products will be deemed "adulterated" by the Secretary of Agriculture and that plaintiffs may be subject to adverse publicity, defense of condemnation charges, and possible fines.

Plaintiffs first contend that the Secretary of Agriculture, in promulgating the above regulation under the Federal Meat Inspection Act, was required by law to follow the same formalized rulemaking procedures as are made applicable to the Secretary of Health, Education and Welfare under the Food, Drug and Cosmetic Act, that is, oral public hearings if requested by interested parties. The record indicates that plaintiffs demanded an oral hearing in the instant rulemaking but that no such oral hearing was held.

Since there are no rulemaking requirements in the Meat Inspection Act, as amended, plaintiffs base their contention on the principle that the Federal Meat Inspection Act and the Food, Drug and Cosmetic Act must be read together when they deal with the same subject matter, that is, food additives.

If Congress had intended that the Secretary of Agriculture's rulemaking functions under the Federal Meat Inspection Act were to be bound by the procedures governing the Secretary of Health, Education and Welfare under the Food, Drug and Cosmetic Act, it would have expressly so provided. Plaintiffs have cited no provision in the Federal Meat Inspection Act, wherein the procedural requirements of the Food, Drug and Cosmetic Act are made applicable to the Secretary of Agriculture. Absent such a provision, rulemaking procedures would be governed by the Administrative Procedure Act.

Plaintiffs contend that they are entitled to a public oral hearing under the Administrative Procedure Act. Plaintiffs are in error. The act merely provides that, after having given notice of proposed rulemaking, the agency must give "interested parties an opportunity to participate in the rulemaking through submission of written data, views, or arguments with or without opportunity for oral presentation." In the discretion of the Secretary of Agriculture, opportunity to submit written comments or materials sufficiently met the hearing requirement of the act. The administrative record of the rulemaking proceedings here in question indicates that plaintiffs were given the opportunity to submit such written data and views as provided by the act and that they in fact did so.

Plaintiffs next contend that the Secretary of Agriculture, in promulgating regulations on the use of food additives in meat products is bound by 21 C.F.R. 121.101, a regulation promulgated by the Secretary of Health, Education and Welfare pursuant to the Food, Drug and Cosmetic Act, 21 U.S.C. § 301 *et seq.*, permitting the use of certain food additives set forth in a list of substances characterized as "generally recognized as safe," among them calcium sorbate, potassium sorbate, sodium sorbate, and sorbic acid.

It is clear, however, that Congress, in amending the Federal Meat Inspection Act of 1907, 34 Stat. 1260 by enacting the Wholesome Meat Act of 1967, Pub. L. 90–201, 81 Stat. 584, 21 U.S.C. § 601 *et seq.* (Supp. 1971), intended to vest the Secretary of Agriculture with the power to pass regulations prohibiting or restricting the use of food additives *in meat products* notwithstanding the designation of such additives as "generally recognized as safe" in regulations promulgated by the Secretary of Health, Education and Welfare under the Food, Drug and Cosmetic Act.

The legislative history of the Federal Meat Inspection Act indicates that Congress intended to "allow the Secretary of Agriculture to impose *more stringent restrictions . . . for food additives . . .* in or on meat products subject to the new act than are imposed by the Secretary of Health, Education and Welfare under the Federal Food, Drug and Cosmetic Act." [*U.S. Code Cong. & Admin. News*, 90th Cong., 1st Sess., vol. 2 at p. 2195 (1967).]

Further, an act of September 6, 1958, Pub. L. 85–929, 72 Stat. 1789, amending the Food, Drug and Cosmetic Act to empower the Secretary of Health, Education and Welfare to promulgate regulations on food additives, expressly provides in section 7 as follows:

Nothing in this act (Federal Food, Drug and Cosmetic Act) shall be construed to exempt any meat or meat food product or any person from any requirement imposed by or pursuant to the . . . Meat Inspection Act of March 4, 1907, 34 Stat. 1260, as amended and extended (21 U.S.C. § 71 and the following).

Plaintiffs finally contend that there exists no rational basis for the regulation. The regulation was promulgated by the Secretary of Agriculture pursuant to the authority granted in the proviso which provides that products will be considered to be adulterated if they contain food additives which are prohibited by regulations of the Secretary of Agriculture and Federal Meat Inspection Act. This act provides that a meat product shall be considered "adulterated" if damage or inferiority has been concealed in any manner or if any substance has been added to it to make it appear better or of greater value than it actually is.

The prohibition of sorbates in the challenged regulation is expressly based on the ground that sorbates and sorbic acid are additives which conceal inferiority and damage and make the product appear better than it actually is.

The Secretary of Agriculture in promulgating the regulation made a finding to that effect in the following stated "considerations":

Mold and bacterial slime develop on the surface of cooked sausages and similar products held for long periods under good refrigeration or for shorter periods at higher temperatures. The appearance of mold and other surface growth serves to alert consumers to the condition of the product. Sorbates are most effective moldicides and bactericides for products with high acidity, that is, a pH of 5 or below. These chemicals are not effective in products such as cooked sausages since their pH ranges from 5.9 to 6.2. The presence of sorbates in subsurface sausage tissues results in changes in bacterial flora of the products. Sorbates have been demonstrated to inhibit selectively the development of aerobic bacteria and "simultaneously permit the luxuriant growth of clostridium perfringes and clostidium botulinum, which are organisms associated with serious health hazards. The use of sorbates for such products therefore conceals damage and inferiority because of bacterial action, and makes the products appear better and of greater value than they are in view of their decomposing condition."

These considerations are supported by materials set forth in the documentary record of the rulemaking proceedings, specifically by the memorandum of Ralph W. Johnson, head, microbiology group, Laboratory Branch Technical Services Division, U.S.D.A., dated July 31, 1970, and by a number of publications authorized by experts in the fields of microbacteriology and food science.

On the basis of the above record and in view of the fact that the regulation in question presents questions of a technical nature which are properly within the expertise of the administrative agency, this court concludes that there was rational basis for the regulation.

From the affidavits of Vaughn and York, submitted by plaintiffs, and the affidavits of Johnson, submitted by defendants, as well as the documentary record of the rulemaking proceedings, it appears that there is no genuine issue as to the following material fact, that is, that sorbic acid and sorbates prevent the growth of mold and other surface growths in meat products, such as cooked sausages, while not inhibiting certain bacterial subsurface spoilage and thus make meat products appear better than they actually are, thereby misleading the consumer.

It follows, therefore, that, even assuming there could be dispute about the secretary's second ground for his regulation, the undisputed first ground would alone constitute a rational basis for 9 C.F.R. 318.7(d)(2).

Having found that the regulation is both procedurally and substantively valid, this court is of the opinion that U.S.D.A. is authorized to disapprove labels which declare the presence of the prohibited additives because the use of the prohibited additives would render the product "adulterated" within the meaning of the Federal Meat Inspection Act.

The Federal Meat Inspection Act charges U.S.D.A. with the responsibility of ascertaining that products to which the official inspection legend is affixed are not "adulterated." The disapproval of labels bearing additives which would render the product "adulterated" is, therefore, a lawful exercise of the functions of U.S.D.A.

For the reasons above set forth, it is ordered that plaintiffs' motion for summary judgment is denied; and defendants' motion for summary judgment granted, insofar as it seeks a declaratory judgment that the regulation is a valid and enforceable regulation of the Secretary of Agriculture and that the practice of disapproving labels as admitted by defendants is a lawful exercise of its functions under the Federal Meat Inspection Act.

Case Questions

1. What two agencies regulate meat products?
2. Administrative rule-making procedure has been acclaimed as "one of the greatest inventions of modern government." Why is this so?

Suggested Readings

Peck, *The Atrophied Rulemaking Powers of the National Labor Relations Board*, 70 Yale L.J. 729 (1961).

K.C. Davis, Discretionary Justice (1969).

K.C. Davis, Administrative Law Text, §§ 6.01–6.10 (3d ed. 1972).

Fuchs, *Development and Diversification in Administrative Rule Making*, 72 Nw. U. L. Rev. 83 (1977).

Seyffer, *Due Process in FTC Rulemaking*, 1979 Ariz. St. L.J. 543 (1979).

Adjudicatory Power

It is important to distinguish between adjudication and rulemaking, since there are important procedural differences between these functions. The *adjudicatory function* of administrative agencies involves the decision or determination of the rights, duties, and obligations of a specific person or persons. Adjudicatory hearings—sometimes called quasi-judicial hearings or adversary hearings—resemble a court's decision-making process.

The type of power being exercised by an administrative agency determines the character of appropriate proceedings. When an agency's action involves the rule-making function, it is not necessary to make use of judicial procedures. When, however, an agency is making a binding determination or adjudication which directly affects the legal rights of an individual or individuals, it must use the procedures that have traditionally been associated with the judicial process.

An agency employee may conclude from an investigation that an agency regulation has been violated. Before sanctions can be imposed, the alleged violator is entitled to an administrative hearing. The procedure followed by an agency in a hearing may be prescribed by the statute that created it, by rules created by the agency itself, or by administrative procedure statutes. The Administrative Procedure Act provides the rules for federal agencies. Many states have passed statutes similar to the APA to govern their state agencies. An agency must follow the prescribed procedure, as well as observe the due-process requirements of the Fifth and Fourteenth Amendments, or their actions will not be upheld in a court of law.

Although no particular form of proceeding is required, an administrative agency may not deprive one of life, liberty, or property through the exercise of its adjudicatory power without notice and a fair and open hearing before an impartial and competent tribunal. The Administrative Procedure Act requires that the notice set forth (1) the time, place, and nature of the hearing, (2) the legal authority and jurisdiction under which the hearing is to be held, and (3) the matters of fact and law asserted. Parties affected by the agency action must be given the opportunity to confront any adverse witness and present oral and written evidence on their own behalf. An agency may confine cross-examination to the essentials, thus avoiding discursive and repetitive questioning common to courtroom-type cross-examinations.

The hearing is conducted by an administrative law judge, whose function is similar to that of a judge presiding over a trial. However, administrative law judges perceive their function as that of implementing and administering a legislative purpose. Their judicial attitude is that of an executive wanting to get the job done, rather than of a person impartially deciding between two litigants. In fact, it is the duty of an agency to keep its decisions abreast of changing conditions, yet within the enabling statute.

Administrative law judges are also empowered to make findings of fact and to recommend a decision. The recommendation is sent to the board of final review in the administrative agency. The board retains the power to adopt, alter, or reverse the recommendation.

Adams v. Marshall
212 Kan. 595, 512 P.2d 365
Supreme Court of Kansas
July 14, 1973

FONTRON, JUSTICE

This is a *mandamus* action brought by William F. Adams, a member of the Leavenworth Police Department, to compel the defendants, who constitute the Civil Service Commission of Leavenworth, Kansas, to follow certain due-process procedures at a scheduled hearing of his appeal to that body. The district court issued an *ex parte* alternative order at the time the action was filed, and that order was later made permanent after a hearing had been held. We shall refer to the parties as Adams or plaintiff, on the one hand, and the commission or defendants, on the other.

There is no substantial dispute of fact. On December 1, 1971, Police Chief Alfred H. Pickles, by letter, suspended Adams from the police force for a period of two weeks without pay. On receipt of the communication, Adams filed a notice of appeal with Pickles, who thereupon confirmed his order of suspension. The appeal from Pickles was heard by the city manager who threw out one charge, found Adams guilty of two charges, and reduced the period of suspension to eight days, again without pay. From the city manager's order, Adams took an appeal to the Civil Service Commission, which scheduled a hearing for January 24, 1972, at 7 P.M.

Before the appointed hour arrived, and following conferences between counsel on both sides, the commission laid down a set of four ground rules which were anathema to the plaintiff and his counsel. Two of the controversial rules were subsequently settled to everyone's satisfaction, but two remained, namely, that the witnesses appearing at the hearing could not be examined or cross-examined and that the hearing would be closed to the public and particularly to members of the press.

At approximately 3:20 P.M. of the day on which the appeal was scheduled to be heard, the present action was commenced. An alternative order was issued by the court directing the commission to permit examination and cross-examination of all witnesses and to admit the public, including accredited members of the press, at all stages of the proceedings, except during its deliberations, or else to show cause to the contrary.

The alternative order was not served on the defendants immediately, but only after they had convened for the hearing and after a lengthy preliminary argument had been presented by plaintiff's counsel which resulted in the commission revising its rules to permit five minutes' cross-examination of each witness. When served with the alternative order, the defendants peremptorily adjourned the hearing without further ado. Subsequently, the commission filed a motion to quash, and a hearing on the alternative order was held before the district court on February 4, 1972. Following the hearing, and on February 24, 1972, the court found (1) that the defendants were acting in a quasi-judicial capacity, (2) that counsel should be permitted to conduct such examination of witnesses as was required for a full disclosure of the facts and that the commission should refrain from imposing arbitrary time limits upon examination or cross-examination of witnesses, (3) that the hearing should be open to the public and accredited members of the press except during deliberations, and (4) that other issues raised in plaintiff's motion had been settled. Final judgment was entered in conformity with these findings. As we have said, the defendants have appealed from the judgment.

The commission's argument covered in the briefs relates to the nature of the hearing conducted by the commission and the requirements of due process with respect thereto. Section 1–517 of the 1972 Code of Leavenworth, Kansas, said code being a compilation of city ordinances, provides as follows:

Rules Governing Removal, Suspensions; appeals: An employee may be removed only for such cause as will promote the efficiency of the service. The employee must receive written notice of such action fifteen (15) days before the effective date of removal, specifying the charges preferred against him.

A supervisor has the authority to suspend a subordinate for neglect of duty, disobedience of orders, or for such other reasons demanding prompt action.

An employee may be placed on annual leave, if available, and or leave without pay as appropriate. Within twenty-four

(24) hours, the supervisor will be required to advise the employee the reason for his action in sufficient detail to clearly relate the cause and actions taken. Original of such letter will be presented to the employee.

An employee may submit to the supervisor a written reply to the charges brought against him within twenty-four (24) hours. Unless an extension of time is requested and granted, the original will be sent to the supervisor. The supervisor will consider the employee's reply in arriving at a decision. The employee will receive a written decision by the supervisor. The employee will have the right to appeal the action taken against him by the supervisor to the city manager. The city manager will review the actions taken and shall make a decision which shall be presented to the employee in writing. *The employee may appeal the city manager's decision to the Civil Service Commission. The commissioners shall have the power to enforce the attendance at hearings of employees involved, call witnesses, have access to security files and administer oaths of truthfulness. The commission will conduct a thorough investigation of the facts in the case, actions taken, and conformance to the rules and regulations of the merit system.* The decision of the commissioners will be decided by the majority vote of those in attendance and will be final. The employee will be notified in writing of the decision of the Board of Commissioners. Copies of charges, employee replies, and related correspondence will be sent to the secretary of the commission.

It is within the context of the foregoing ordinance that we examine the due-process questions raised on appeal. The trial court was correct in its finding that the members of the commission were acting in a quasi-judicial capacity in hearing the Adams appeal. *Quasi-judicial* is a term applied to administrative boards or officers empowered to investigate facts, weigh evidence, draw conclusions as a basis for official actions, and exercise discretion of judicial nature.

Where an administrative body acts in a quasi-judicial capacity, the requirements of due process will attach to the proceedings held before it. The constitutional guarantee of due process of law applies to, and must be observed in, administrative as well as judicial proceedings, particularly where such proceedings are specifically classified as judicial or quasi-judicial in nature, or where the legislature is deemed to have intended the due-process safeguard to apply. Procedure embodying due-process requirements is essential not only to the legal validity of the administrative regulation, but also to the maintenance of public confidence in the value and soundness of this important governmental process.

Two ground rules laid down by the commission in this case are said by the plaintiff to violate basic due-process demands: (1) the right to examine and cross-examine witnesses and (2) the right to an open or public hearing. We are inclined to agree.

The right to the cross-examination of witnesses in quasi-judicial or adjudicatory proceedings is one of fundamental importance and is generally, if not universally, recognized as an important requirement of due process. In speaking of due process requirements, the United States Supreme Court, in *Int. Com. Comm. v. Louis. & Nash. R. R.*, 227 U.S. 88, 93, said: "All parties must be fully apprised of the evidence submitted or to be considered, and must be given opportunity to cross-examine witnesses, to inspect documents, and to offer evidence in explanation or rebuttal. In no other way can a party maintain its rights or make its defense. In no other way can it test the sufficiency of the facts to support the finding."

Although the commission eventually modified its stand on cross-examination, we do not view its concession as satisfying due-process requirements. In the first place, the commission did not relent so far as direct examination of witnesses was concerned. Of equal, if not greater importance, was its arbitrary, before-the-fact time limitation imposed on the cross-examination of witnesses.

We have said many times that the extent of cross-examination lies largely within the sound judicial discretion of the court. However, cross-examination may not be unduly curtailed in testing the soundness of a witness's testimony, nor may it be so limited and circumscribed as to preclude a full disclosure of the facts. No administrative body, no matter how prescient its members, can foretell in advance of hearing the extent to which the testimony of witnesses may be limited without impinging upon the pursuit of truth. The five-minute limitation which the commission, before trial, placed on the cross-examination of all witnesses was in our opinion an impermissible restriction on due process.

Passing to the question of public trial, we believe it may generally be said that proceedings of a judicial nature held behind closed doors and shielded from public scrutiny have long been repugnant to our system of justice. The concept that trials and judicatory hearings be open to the public gaze is inherent in our idea of due process. This view was voiced many years ago by the United States Supreme Court in *Morgan v. United States*, 304 U.S. 1, in the following words:

The vast expansion of this field of administrative regulation in response to the pressure of social needs is made possible under our system by adherence to the basic principles that the legislature shall appropriately determine the standards of administrative action, and that in administrative proceedings of a quasi-judicial character, the liberty and property of the citizen shall be protected by the rudimentary requirements of fair play. These demand ''a fair and open hearing,'' essential alike to the legal validity of the administrative regulation and to the maintenance of public confidence in the value and soundness of this important governmental process. Such a hearing has been described as an inexorable safeguard.

Even though, as sometimes said, the power to remove or suspend from an office or position is administrative rather than judicial, it is none the less to be exercised in a judicial manner. If the administrative body, such as a local board, has been clothed with quasi-judicial functions, there must be a hearing of the character of an informal trial in accordance with the provisions of the controlling law.

The trial must be fair. Requirements of substantial justice must be observed. The officer or tribunal hearing the charges is bound to a reasonably strict observance of all legal requirements and the fundamentals of a fair and impartial trial.

The theme of fairness threads its way through the notice, hearing, and right-of-appeal provisions of civil service laws relating to the discipline of public servants. A proceeding in the nature of a judicial investigation is contemplated. The commission is bound to a reasonably strict observance of all legal requirements and the fundamentals of a fair and impartial trial. The elements of fairness and impartiality must appear in the conduct of the hearing itself and in the deliberations and decision that follow. Due process must be followed.

Reference is made in the commission's brief to private and informal procedures followed by the Veterans Administration, although neither the alleged procedures nor V.A. regulations are shown by the record. We are not disposed to dissect or construe undisclosed regulations of a federal agency. We deal with a quasi-judicial hearing conducted by a civil service commission under explicit provisions of a municipal ordinance, concerning which we are constrained to hold that due-process requirements are applicable.

We conclude that the judgment entered by the trial court was correct, and the same is hereby affirmed.

CASE QUESTION

What were the two ground rules imposed by the Civil Service Commission that the court found to have violated due process? Why did the court decide that these ground rules violated due process?

Suggested Readings

K.C. Davis, Administrative Law Text, §§ 8.01–8.13 (3d ed. 1972).

Tomlinson, *Discovery in Agency Adjudication*, 1971 Duke L.J. 89.

Gellhorn, *Rules of Evidence and Official Notice in Formal Administrative Hearings*, 1971 Duke L.J. 1.

Gellhorn and Robinson, *Summary Judgment in Administrative Adjudication*, 84 Harv. L. Rev. 612 (1971).

Gellhorn and Robinson, *Perspectives on Administrative Law*, 75 Colum. L. Rev. 771 (1975).

Carrow, *Administrative Justice Comes of Age*, 60 A. B. A. J. 1396 (1974).

Pops, *Judicialization of Federal Administrative Law Judges: Implications for Policymaking*, 81 W. Va. L. Rev. 169 (1979).

In theory, the decision of the administrative law judge is thoroughly reviewed before the agency's board of final review adopts it as its opinion. In reality, however, the review may be something less than thorough. Because of a board's heavy workload, the review may be delegated to members of its staff. Board members may never even read the administrative law judge's opinion. Failure of a board to personally review the decision has been challenged as a lack of due process for the defendant. The courts recognize the tremendous workload of the administrative agencies and sometimes permit delegation of review to the staff. They require only that the board understand the decision adopted by the agency.

KFC National Management Corp. v. NLRB
497 F.2d 298
United States Court of Appeals
Second Circuit
May 8, 1974

J. Joseph Smith, Circuit Judge
KFC National Management Corp., ordered by the National Labor Relations Board to bargain with a union certified as representative of its employees, petitions for review of the order, and the board cross-petitions for enforcement.

This petition for review of an unfair labor practice decision raises the troublesome question of delegation of authority in administrative decision making. The genesis of the petition was a representation election contested by the employer, KFC, on grounds of prounion activity of supervisory employees. The NLRB regional director, to whom KFC protested, conducted an *ex parte* investigation into the company's claims and concluded that they had "no merit" and that therefore the union should be certified as the duly-elected bargaining representative.

Dissatisfied with both the director's findings and his failure to conduct an adversary hearing, KFC petitioned the board for review. On September 7, 1972—approximately two weeks after the petition was filed—KFC's counsel received a brief telegram informing him that the request had been denied "as it raises no substantial issues warranting review." The telegram was signed, "By direction of the Board." A further petition for reconsideration was similarly telegraphically denied, "as lacking in merit"—again "By direction of the Board."

The company challenged the denials of review and reconsideration on the grounds that the "board" had in fact been composed of but one board member and two staff assistants.

The board responded with an affidavit from its executive secretary stating:

Member Jenkins was personally present and Chairman Miller and Member Fanning were each represented by an attorney assistant employed on his respective staff who has been authorized to cast a vote for him at the said agenda. The vote at the agenda was unanimous to deny review.

From its own argument—both written and oral—we have further learned that the authorizations referred to were quite general in nature. In the normal course of events, board members seldom discuss individual cases with their assistants prior to these voting sessions. There is, apparently, a one-day period between the votes and the filing of decisions, but there is no evidence that the members normally review the votes cast by their staff assistants. The board has represented—and we have no reason to doubt—that particularly difficult or significant cases receive the individual attention of the members either before or after their votes are cast

by their proxies. But there is no suggestion that such was the case here. Indeed it is the board's position that this case —like the vast majority of review petitions—was so routine that it was well suited to this general delegation approach.

The question then is whether this virtually complete delegation comports with the requirements of the National Labor Relations Act and of administrative due process in general.

We believe that the authors of Taft-Hartley were only prepared to permit the staff assistants to aid the members who were themselves to be responsible for the board's actions. For example, while the allocation of the board's administrative, prosecutorial, and adjudicative functions is well discussed in the Taft-Hartley conference report, there is no suggestion that the board members could or should delegate their "quasi-judicial" function to their staff assistants beyond that of reviewing transcripts or preparing draft opinions.

Here, of course, the staff assistants of two members did far more and, more importantly, they did so without guidance from the members themselves. They did not merely assist the members; they acted in their stead. In view of the rather clear congressional distrust of staff assistants—who are, of course, neither appointed by the President nor approved by the Senate, as are the board members—we cannot say that Congress intended, or would have approved, the general proxies issued here. We hold, therefore, that the "board's" votes in this case fail to satisfy the two-member quorum and three-member panel requirements of the act.

The courts have adopted the principle that those legally responsible for a decision must in fact make it, but that their method of doing so—their thought processes, their reliance on their staffs—is largely beyond judicial scrutiny.

This court and many others have consistently upheld the use of hearing examiners in developing evidence and forming preliminary decisions, the reliance on staff assistants for recommendations and draft opinions, and a variety of other procedures designed to apprise those legally responsible for administrative decisions with the critical issues and evidence in a case and to record their individual determinations. Concomitantly, the courts have consistently refused to issue *subpoenas* for the work product of such decision-making processes. Staff memos, expert reports, preliminary drafts, the oral testimony of the decision makers as to the basis for their opinions—all have been held to be beyond the purview of the contesting parties and the reviewing courts.

But even as the courts have upheld these various practices, they have developed the corollary principle that once there has been a *prima facie* demonstration of impropriety, the courts will inquire into the administrative process in order to ensure that the decision making was informed, unbiased, and personal. Here, of course, the relevant facts have largely been admitted. The boards' counsel conceded at oral argument that there was no claim of proof that the individual members whose votes were cast by the assistants ever considered this case. Indeed the board further admitted—and Professor Murphy's account suggests—that such individual consideration of routine cases is the exception rather than the rule.

We deny enforcement and remand for consideration of petitioner's request for board review of the regional director's representation decision.

CASE QUESTION

How could the members of the board have utilized their staffs so as to give KFC administrative due process?

SUGGESTED READINGS

DAVIS, ADMINISTRATIVE LAW TEXT, § 11.07 (3d ed. 1972).

Thomforde, *Controlling Administrative Sanctions*, 74 MICH. L. REV. 709 (1976).

Freedman, *Crisis and Legitimacy in the Administrative Process*, 27 STAN. L. REV. 1041 (1975).

Note, *Improper Delegation of Decision-making Responsibility within the NLRB*, 1974 WASH. U. L. Q. 778 (1974).

Judicial Review

Judicial review is a relatively minor aspect of administrative law because only a small proportion of administrative determinations are reviewed by the courts. The number of administrative adjudications is too great to allow court review in more than a small percentage of the cases decided by agencies. The expense of obtaining judicial review often discourages potential appeals.

The problems of judicial review of the action of any particular agency must be analyzed by critical attention to the governing statutes, the specific circumstances of the agency, and the parties dealing with it. The respective roles of courts and administrative agencies in our governmental system are questioned when courts review agency decisions. Courts and administrative agencies are not competitors or rivals in the task of safeguarding the public interest, but are collaborative governmental instruments for realizing public purpose.

Courts and agencies may be considered as coordinate instrumentalities of justice. The attitude of a court toward the sharing of this joint responsibility has an important effect in determining the extent of its practice of self-restraint. Unless exceptional circumstances exist, courts are reluctant to interfere with the operation of a program administered by an agency. As the courts' respect of the administrative process increases, judicial self-restraint increases.

Timing of Review

Parties must address their complaints to administrative tribunals and explore every possibility for obtaining relief through administrative channels ("exhaust their administrative remedies") before appealing to the courts. The courts recognize the power of the administrative agencies and will generally not interrupt an agency's procedure until it has issued a final decision. Administrative action that is not final cannot be judicially attacked because where the administrative power has not been finally exercised, no irreparable harm has occurred—the controversy is not ripe.

The courts, however, will hear a case before a final agency decision if the aggrieved party can prove that failure to interrupt the administrative process would be unfair. To determine the extent of fairness, the court will consider (1) the possibility of injury if the case is not heard, (2) the degree of doubt of the agency's jurisdiction, and (3) the requirement of the agency's specialized knowledge.

The requirements of exhaustion of administrative remedies and ripeness are concerned with the timing of judicial review of administrative action; but the two requirements are not the same. Finality and exhaustion focus on whether the administrative position being challenged has crystallized and is, in fact, an institutional decision. Ripeness asks whether the issues presented are appropriate for judicial resolution. Although each doctrine has a separate and distinct aim, they frequently overlap.

Haddon Township Board of Ed. v. New Jersey Dept. of Ed.
476 F.Supp. 681
United States District Court, D. New Jersey
July 18, 1979

BROTMAN, DISTRICT JUDGE
This is an action by three local school boards to compel the U.S. Department of Agriculture and the New Jersey Department of Education to reimburse their schools under the National School Lunch Act for nutritionally adequate lunches provided by the schools, but consumed by the students at their homes. Defendants contend they cannot subsidize the schools, because the act allows reimbursement only for lunches consumed on school grounds.

Plaintiffs are three local boards of education. Each district is obligated under N.J. Stat. 18A:33-4 to provide lunch to all children enrolled in its district. To comply with this mandate, plaintiff districts provide certain students with take-home bag lunches which may not be consumed on school premises but are taken by the students to their homes during a specified lunch period. The Haddon District began its take-home program in February 1977, and was in fact reimbursed by the Department of Education for seven months.

Under the National School Lunch Act, 42 U.S.C. Sec. 1751 *et seq.*, federal financial assistance is given to states to help schools defray the costs of serving lunches to school pupils. States participating in the program enter into written agreements with the U.S. Department of Agriculture (USDA), and match each federal dollar with three state dollars. The states are funded by a formula which depends, in part, on the number of schoolchildren provided lunches. The combined funds are distributed by the states to local school boards.

While each plaintiff entered into agreements with the New Jersey Department of Education, which administers the School Lunch Act for the state, the department has refused to reimburse the districts. It has also asked the Haddon Township Board to repay the state funds paid to the board for lunches served between February and October 1977.

The department's refusal to fund these districts is based on the USDA's position that take-home lunches do not qualify for subsidy under the Lunch Act. Apparently the department believes USDA will not match funds paid by the state for such lunches.

By letter dated August 12, 1977, Lewis B. Straus, the administrator of the Food and Nutrition Service, the USDA agency administering the Lunch Act, requested a legal opinion on the

Riverton program from USDA general counsel. On December 7, 1977, John A. Harris, assistant general counsel, sent Straus a two-page opinion letter, briefly analyzing the legal issue and concluding, "In our opinion, there is no authority in the National School Lunch Act for payment of claims for reimbursement for take-home lunches." This letter was forwarded to the USDA regional office on December 21, and apparently was then brought to the attention of state officials.

Plaintiffs have sued the USDA, state Department of Education and the agencies' respective officers for monetary declaratory and injunctive relief. Plaintiffs ask the court to hold that the School Lunch Act does not require in-school consumption of meals, that the two agencies cannot so require, and accordingly, to order the state to reimburse the plaintiffs for meals previously served and those which will be served in the future.

The federal defendants contend that this case is not ripe for judicial review, and should therefore be dismissed without consideration of the substantive issues. They argue that the general counsel's letter is simply an advisory opinion by a subordinate agency official, and that USDA never sought reimbursement from the state for those lunches which the state initially paid the Haddon school board, nor otherwise specifically refused to fund take-home lunches.

The criteria for determining ripeness were established in the case of *Abbott Laboratories v. Gardner*, 387 U.S. 136 (1967). The reviewing court must examine "the fitness of the issues for judicial decision and the hardship to

the parties of withholding court consideration." The fitness criterion encompasses two inquiries: whether the case presents a crystallized legal question suitable for judicial resolution, and whether the ruling is a "final agency action" within the meaning of section 10(c) of the APA, 5 U.S.C. § 704.

The issues here are certainly fit for judicial decision. The primary questions involve statutory interpretation of the School Lunch Act and the APA. Here the general counsel, once familiar with the simple factual premise of the Riverton program, based his decision entirely on the statute and its regulations.

The court also believes that USDA's letter constituted final agency action. The finality concept was further refined by the Supreme Court in the case *Port of Boston Marine Terminal Association v. Rederiaktiebolaget Transatlantic*, 400 U.S. 62 (1970). The Court stated that "the relevant considerations . . . are whether the process of administrative decision making has reached a stage where judicial review will not disrupt the orderly process of adjudication and whether rights or obligations have been determined or legal consequences will flow from the action."

There is no contention that a court determination now will disrupt the federal administrative process; indeed USDA concedes that plaintiffs have no avenue of review of the general counsel's determination. While the federal government has not made any specific denial of reimbursements to the state under the act as a consequence of its determination, as long as the state continues to deny reimbursement to the school boards based on the USDA opinion letter, the question of federal funding of take-home lunches will never be directly faced by the Department of Agriculture. The agency did, in theory, match the state monies paid to Haddon Township for the first seven months of its program, but there is nothing in the record to indicate that USDA knew that its monies were used in that way.

The general counsel's opinion letter, however, was directly addressed to the situation at Riverton. Although USDA has never specifically threatened to deny federal monies or take any other sanction against New Jersey if it were to pay for take-home lunches, federal officials are aware, if only because of this litigation, that New Jersey is following the federal agency's interpretation of the law and has refused reimbursement for take-home lunches. The court concludes that the rights of plaintiffs have effectively been determined by the opinion letter; legal consequences may not flow directly from the USDA ruling, but the indirect result is certain.

The informal nature of the letter opinion does not preclude the required finality. In *National Automatic Laundry and Cleaning Council v. Schultz*, 443 F.2d 689 (D.C. Cir. 1971), the court held that an opinion stated in a letter of the agency administrator presented a ruling ripe for review. It was noted that the agency decision was neither based on a hypothetical situation nor subject to certain reconsideration. Similarly, here the USDA ruling was based on the existence of the Riverton program, and as was indicated previously, there is not further review of the letter within the agency. The major decision in this circuit, holding a ruling unripe, *West*

Penn Power Co. v. Train, 522 F.2d 302 (3rd Cir. 1975), cert. *denied*, 426 U.S. 947 (1976), can be distinguished on this basis. In *West Penn*, the court of appeals found that a notice of violation of environmental standards was not final agency action because it only preceded enforcement procedures, which were at the discretion of the agency administrator.

The court also finds a letter from the USDA general counsel sufficiently authoritative to be final agency action. In *National Automatic Laundry*, the court found that a letter from the administrator of the Wage and Hour Division of the Department of Labor constituted a final ruling. In the case here, the administrator of the Food and Nutrition Service did not issue the letter, rather, he specifically requested a ruling from the Office of General Counsel for the entire department. The response is signed by an assistant general counsel, and not the general counsel. However, the government has indicated the letter will not be reviewed within the department and that the agency stands by its conclusion. Therefore, the letter must be taken as sufficiently authoritative for judicial review.

The general counsel's ruling has the requisite finality, and the legal conclusion therein is quite fit for judicial review. The ruling also meets the second major criterion of *Abbott Laboratories*, as denial of judicial review would work a hardship on all plaintiffs. The three plaintiffs have no other legal redress as long as the state chooses to follow the USDA's ruling. They must either forego state and federal money by continuing the take-home program, or take the costly step of building facilities to adhere to what they believe to be an incorrect policy. The impact of the USDA ruling is "direct and immediate"; compliance is expensive and noncompliance engenders serious penalties.

The Supreme Court's ripeness cri-

teria are fully satisfied here. [The decision of the Department of Agriculture was upheld by the court and the plaintiffs' complaint was dismissed. The discussion of the interpretation of the National School Lunch Act is omitted.]

CASE QUESTIONS

1. Why must an administrative agency's order be final?
2. Why did the opinion letter present a crystallized legal question suitable for judicial review?
3. Can the doctrine of exhaustion of administrative remedies be carried beyond practical bounds? Suppose the available administrative remedies are inadequate?

SUGGESTED READINGS

Berger, *Exhaustion of Administrative Remedies*, 48 YALE L.J. 981 (1939).

K.C. DAVIS, ADMINISTRATIVE LAW TEXT, §§ 20.01–21.08 (3d ed. 1972).

J.J. JAFFE, JUDICIAL CONTROL OF ADMINISTRATIVE ACTION, 395–450 (Student ed. 1965).

Vining, *Direct Judicial Review and the Doctrine of Ripeness in Administrative Law*, 69 MICH. L. REV. 1443 (1971).

McNeil, *Pre-enforcement Review of Administrative Agency Action: Developments in the Ripeness Doctrine*, 53 NOTRE DAME LAW. 346 (1977).

Recognition of Administrative Competence

Courts should interfere as little as possible with the determinations of administrative agencies, for such determinations are made by tribunals of experts. Courts will uphold administrative findings if they are satisfied that the agency examined the issues and reached its decision within the appropriate standards.

It is impossible for the reviewing court to consider more than the highlights of the questions actually argued before an administrative agency. The fact situations may be complex and technical, and the time available for argument short; courts rely on the agency's expertise. Recognition of the agency's competence is exemplified by the fact that when a court holds an original determination invalid, it usually remands the case for further consideration by the agency, rather than making its own final decision.

Greater Boston Television Corporation v. FCC
444 F.2d 841
United States Court of Appeals
District of Columbia Circuit
November 13, 1970

LEVENTHAL, CIRCUIT JUDGE
This appeal marks the culmination of a struggle to determine the licensee to operate a television station on channel 5 in Boston.

The Federal Communications Commission previously made a limited award to WHDH, Inc., and that company has been operating the station, WHDH, under temporary authorization. In the decision now under appeal, the commission, after an extensive comparative hearing, approved the application of Boston Broadcasters, Inc. (BBI), and denied the mutually exclusive applications of WHDH, Inc., Charles River Civic Television, Inc., and Greater Boston Television Corp. (II). 16 F.C.C.2d 1 (January 22, 1969). We affirm the decision of the commission.

The consolidated comparative proceeding began in May 1964, and there was full presentation by WHDH and the other three applicants. On August 10, 1966, Hearing Examiner Herbert Sharfman issued an exhaustive initial decision, in favor of granting the renewal by WHDH. In the bulk of his conclusions, related to a comparison of the applicants, the hearing examiner took account of the evidence pertaining to the various criteria laid down in the Policy Statement on Comparative Broadcast Hearings, 1 F.C.C.2d 393 (July 28, 1965): past performance, diversity of ownership, integration of ownership and management, and program proposals. In determining the weight he felt appropriate under the circumstances of the case, the examiner placed primary emphasis on the actual operating record of WHDH under the temporary authorizations of the preceding nine years.

On January 22, 1969, the commission reversed the hearing examiner's decision, and entered an order denying the application of WHDH and granting that of BBI, 16 F.C.C.2d 1. Its decision reviewed the comparative merits of the applications.

Past Performance of WHDH: The commission's decision stated that the principles of the 1965 policy statement would be applied to the proceeding. Specifically it invoked the provision of its 1965 policy statement that an applicant's past record was to be given an affirmative preference only if it were outside the bounds of average performance. It read the examiner's findings of fact as showing that the record of WHDH-TV was "favorable" on the whole—except for its failure to editorialize—but concluded that it was only within the bounds of average performance, and "does not demonstrate unusual attention to the public's needs or interests."

Diversification of Media of Mass Communications: WHDH's ownership by the *Herald-Traveler* resulted in an adverse factor on the diversification criterion. The commission stated that the desirability of maximizing the diffusion of control of the media of mass communications in Boston was highlighted by the incident wherein the *Herald-Traveler* prematurely published a preliminary draft of the report of the Massachusetts Crime Commission without also simultaneously publicizing the report over the broadcast station. It was brought out at the hearing that such a news broadcast would have impaired the story's "scoop" value for the *Herald-Traveler.*

The commission further referred to the contention of WHDH that since it had never editorialized there existed a factor that minimized the charge of concentration of control. The commission disagreed, stating that licensees have an obligation to devote reasonable broadcast time to controversial programs, and the failure to editorialize, if anything, demonstrated the wisdom of the commission's policy for diversification of control of media of mass communications. On the factor of diversification, it concluded by awarding a substantial preference to both BBI and Charles River as against WHDH and giving BBI a slight edge over Charles River (which also operates an FM station in Waltham, Massachusetts, devoted to serious music).

Integration of Ownership with Management: The commission affirmed the examiner's conclusion that the applica-tions of both Charles River and BBI reflect an integration—which in FCC parlance means integration of ownership with management—of substantially greater degree than WHDH, whose integration is small. It restated its view that the public interest is furthered through participation in operation by proprietors, as increasing the likelihood of greater sensitivity to an area's changing needs and programming to serve these needs.

As between Charles River and BBI, the commission found that BBI rated a significant preference on integration (six of BBI's stockholders propose to serve as full-time management, two of whom have had significant television experience, as opposed to only one Charles River participating owner, whose experience was limited to radio).

Proposed Program Service: The commission agreed that both BBI and Charles River proposed generally well-balanced program schedules, and concluded that neither proposal demonstrated such a substantial difference as to constitute a "superior devotion to public service."

Other Factors: The commission assessed a demerit against WHDH because of a failure to obtain the approval of the commission on the transfer of *de facto* control when Choate was selected as president following the death of his predecessor, and when his death was followed by the accession of Akerson. However, since there was no attempt at misrepresentation or concealment, it was concluded that the circumstances did not reflect so adversely on character qualifications as to warrant the absolute disqualification of WHDH.

The Commission's Vote: The commission voted to grant the application of BBI. Its decision was written by Commissioner Bartley, who was joined by Commissioner Wadsworth. Three commissioners did not participate in the decision (Hyde, Cox, and Rex Lee). Commissioner Johnson concurred, with a statement indicating his strong opposition to the application of WHDH, and noting that this was supported not only by diversity of media, but also by the "healthy" result of having at least one network-affiliated VHF television station that is independently and locally owned. "I feel no passion," he remarked, about the choice between BBI and Charles River. He stated that while normally he would not participate in a case that essentially involved a reconsideration of matters that arose before he became a member of the FCC, "in this instance, however, my participation is necessary to constitute a working majority for decision. Accordingly I concur in today's decision." Commissioner Robert Lee dissented, voting to grant the application of WHDH, and abstaining from any choice as between BBI and Charles River.

We have given particular consideration to the commission's procedures, findings, and reasons, in this case, in order to assure ourselves that the decision on appeal was established by administrative law doctrine. Our alertness was also prompted in this case by the circumstance first that the agency rejected the result reached by its hearing examiner, and further, that it was manifestly in a state of flux and evolution of its approach to the kind of issue presented by this proceeding.

Approaching this case as we have

with full awareness of and responsiveness to the court's "supervisory" function in review of agency decision, it may be appropriate to take note of the salient aspects of that review. It begins at the threshold, with enforcement of the requirement of reasonable procedure, and with fair notice and opportunity to the parties to present their case. It continues into examination of the evidence and agency's findings of facts, for the court must be satisfied that the agency's evidentiary fact findings are supported by substantial evidence, and provide rational support for the agency's inferences of ultimate fact. Full allowance must be given not only for the opportunity of the agency, or at least its examiners, to observe the demeanor of the witnesses, but also for the reality that agency matters typically involve a kind of expertise— sometimes technical in a scientific sense, sometimes more a matter of specialization in kinds of regulatory programs. Expert discretion is secured, not crippled, by the requirements for substantial evidence, findings, and reasoned analysis. Expertise is strengthened in its proper role as the servant of government when it is denied the opportunity to "become a monster which rules with no practical limits on its discretion." A court does not depart from its proper function when it undertakes a study of the record, even as to the evidence on technical and specialized matters, for this enables the court to penetrate to the underlying decisions of the agency, to satisfy itself that the agency has exercised a reasoned discretion, with reasons that do not deviate from or ignore the ascertainable legislative intent. "The deference owed to an expert tribunal cannot be allowed to slip into a judicial inertia.''

Assuming consistency with law and the legislative mandate, the agency has latitude not merely to find facts and make judgments, but also to select the policies deemed in the public interest. The function of the court is to assure that the agency has given reasoned consideration to all the material facts and issues. This calls for insistence that the agency articulate with reasonable clarity its reasons for decision, and identify the significance of the crucial facts, a course that tends to assure that the agency's policies effectuate general standards, applied without unreasonable discrimination. As for the particular subject of comparative hearings, the findings must cover all the substantial differences between the applicants and the ultimate conclusion must be based on a composite consideration of the findings as to each applicant.

Its supervisory function calls on the court to intervene not merely in case of procedural inadequacies, or bypassing of the mandate in the legislative charter, but more broadly if the court becomes aware, especially from a combination of danger signals, that the agency has not really taken a ''hard look'' at the salient problems, and has not genuinely engaged in reasoned decision making. If the agency has not shirked this fundamental task, however, the court exercises restraint and affirms the agency's action, even though the court would on its own account have made different findings or adopted different standards. Nor will the court upset a decision because of errors that are not material, there being room for the doctrine of harmless error.

If satisfied that the agency has taken a hard look at the issues with the use of reasons and standards, the court will uphold its findings, though of less than ideal clarity, if the agency's path may reasonably be discerned, though of course the court must not be left to guess as to the agency's findings or reasons.

The process thus combines judicial supervision with a salutary principle of judicial restraint, an awareness that agencies and courts together constitute a ''partnership'' in furtherance of the public interest, and are ''collaborative instrumentalities of justice.'' The court is in a real sense part of the total administrative process, and not a hostile stranger to the office of first instance. This collaborative spirit does not undercut, it rather underlines the court's rigorous insistence on the need for conjunction of articulated standards and reflective findings, in furtherance of evenhanded application of law, rather than impermissible whim, improper influence, or misplaced zeal. Reasoned decision promotes results in the public interest by requiring the agency to focus on the values served by its decision, and hence releasing the clutch of unconscious preference and irrelevant prejudice. It furthers the broad public interest of enabling the public to repose confidence in the process as well as the judgments of its decision makers.

The net result of our study and reflection in this case is our conclusion that the record findings and opinions before us, while not without problems, reveal in essence that the commission has been diligent to take a hard look at the problem areas, and to set forth with clarity grounds of reasoned decision which we think permissible.

It merits interjection that the shape of the agency's disposition was aided in no small measure by the initial decision of the hearing examiner, and the examiner's careful and indeed exhaustive review of the evidence and issues, and comparisons of the applicants in regard to each of the pertinent criteria. It does not decry the significance and value of the examiner's efforts that the commission disagreed with his decision and with several of his conclusions; indeed, it attests to his care that his decision was useful although the conclusion was reversed.

The examiner's decision is part of the record, and the record must be considered as a whole in order to see whether the result is supported by substantial evidence. The agency's departures from the examiner's findings are vulnerable if they fail to reflect attentive consideration to the examiner's decision. Yet in the last analysis, it is the agency's function, not the examiner's, to make the findings of fact and select the ultimate decision, and where there is substantial evidence supporting each result, it is the agency's choice that governs. Here, the commission accepted the examiner's findings and conclusions to a substantial degree; and when it did not, the commission made clear not only its awareness of what the examiner had concluded, but also its reasons for taking a different course.

Affirmed

CASE QUESTION

Is the function of judicial review of administrative action to ensure the correctness of the administrative decision?

SUGGESTED READINGS

K.C. Davis, ADMINISTRATIVE LAW TEXT, § 23.08 (3d ed. 1972).

Jaffe, *Administrative Finality on Judicial Review*, 2 Pub. CONTRACT L.J. 115 (1968).

Kaufman, *Judicial Review of Agency Action: A Judge's Unburdening*, 45 N.Y.U.L. REV. 201 (1970).

Forkosch, *Credibility Gap in Judicial Review of Administrative Determinations*, 18 CLEV.-MAR. L. REV. 257 (1969).

Note, 56 GEO. L.J. 1023 (1968).

Note, *The Authority of Administrative Agencies to Consider the Constitutionality of Statutes*, 90 HARV. L. REV. 1682 (1977).

Scope of Review

The courts have established general standards as to the scope of review. These standards relate to the nature of the issues—whether questions of law or questions of fact are involved in the appeal. Questions of law are for the ultimate determination by the court; questions of fact will be considered only to a very limited extent.

Final decisions on questions of law must be reserved for the courts because the power of final decision on judicial matters involving private rights cannot constitutionally be taken from the courts. This does not mean that the courts will review every issue of law involved in an administrative determination. When a court does not review a question of law, it is not denying the power to do so; it is simply reluctant to exercise this power.

Courts will not reverse an agency's finding of fact unless (1) the action exceeded the agency's granted power, (2) procedural due process was lacking, or (3) there was lack of substantial evidence on the record as a whole to support its finding. If the agency acts fairly and reasonably with the grant of power constitutionally conferred, its orders are not open to judicial review.

American Beauty Homes Corp. v. Planning and Zoning Commission
379 S.W.2d 450
Court of Appeals of Kentucky
June 26, 1964

CLAY, JUDGE

This is a zoning case which raises a very important question of administrative appeal procedure. Appellant, the owner of a tract of land in Jefferson County, sought to have the zoning classification changed from a one-family residential district to a D-1 commercial district. The zoning commission denied the request. The circuit court, on a trial *de novo* under KRS 100.057(2), upheld the ruling of the commission.

The property involved is a two-and-one-half-acre tract of land located in Jefferson County. There are but a few residences already built in the im-

mediate vicinity but it is in the middle of an area originally zoned residential. About one-half mile in a southwesterly direction from the property is a commercial zone.

Appellant proposes to use its property for a community shopping center. Neighboring property owners raised no objection to the zoning reclassification. The trial court found it would be a community advantage; that the property generally in this immediate area would not be adversely affected; and that it would not result in substantial detriment to others. However, the court decided these considerations were outweighed by others.

In support of the commission's ruling, there was evidence appellant's tract was more suitable for residential use than commercial development; that the particular location did not fit with the planned development of community shopping centers in Jefferson County; that there was an ample sufficiency of additional property in the general area zoned commercial; that there were no peculiar characteristics of this tract that would prevent its development for residential purposes; and that this was a clear case of spot zoning. There was no evidence of substantial change in the character of the neighborhood which would justify special treatment of this particular tract.

The chancellor, relying principally upon *Hodge v. Luckett*, Ky., 357 S.W.2d 303, upheld the integrity of the original zoning plan in adjudging that the decision of the commission was neither arbitrary nor unreasonable and that there was no tenable basis for reclassifying this property. The chancellor's opinion understandably indicates some uncertainty as to the court's role in deciding the issues on a *de novo* hearing. We will subsequently in this opinion dispose of this difficulty.

Appellant first contends the trial court improperly required it to introduce evidence first, thereby imposing upon it the burden of proof. It may be observed the court's order related only to the *order* of proof, not the burden. The court has discretion in this matter, and we find neither abuse of discretion nor prejudice.

The question of the *burden of proof* has impelled us to re-examine comprehensively our administrative appeal procedure and former decisions. This reappraisal has convinced us that one phase of the procedure provided by KRS 100.057 not only is impractical and unworkable, but is unconstitutional.

Section (2) of KRS 100.057 provides that "Hearings in the circuit court shall be *de novo . . .*" *The root of the trouble is that this statute undertakes to impose on the court a nonjudicial administrative function.* It thereby violates the Kentucky Constitution which provides for the separation of powers.

In order that the independence of the three distinct departments of government be preserved, it is a fundamental principle that the legislature cannot invade the province of the judiciary. It cannot take away judicial power. Nor may it impose upon the judiciary nonjudicial duties. In short, the legislature can neither reduce nor enlarge the scope of the judicial function.

The duties or functions which the legislature may not transfer to the judiciary have been characterized as either legislative or executive. That many of these may be delegated to administrative agencies has long been acknowledged. Their descriptive classification is not, however, the significant point. The vice lies in the fact that the duties or functions sought to be conferred upon the courts lie beyond the scope of judicial power.

If the legislature cannot impose upon the courts the administrative duty or function of making an initial discretionary decision, it cannot do so by the fiction of an appeal which requires the court to adjudicate upon administrative rather than judicial considerations.

In a recent opinion of the Alabama Supreme Court, this precise question was carefully examined. *Ball v. Jones*, 272 Ala. 305, 132 So. 2d 120. The statute involved was similar to KRS 100.057, and prescribed a *de novo* trial in the circuit court upon an appeal by an aggrieved person from a decision, order, or act of the legislative body of a city on the subject of zoning. The opinion points out that zoning is a legislative matter and the legislature could not delegate to or confer upon the courts this function. Since authorizing the circuit court on appeal to try the matter *de novo* has this effect, the act was held unconstitutional as imposing upon the court a nonjudicial function.

We accept as sound the reasoning of this opinion on the general principle involved. Let us examine its application to the present case.

The subject matter of this controversy is a proposed adjustment to a master zoning plan. It is clear under our statutes that the Planning and Zoning Commission, when acting on a proposed adjustment, performs the identical legislative function involved in promulgating the master zoning plan. KRS 100.055 is entitled in part "Delegation to commission of power to approve adjustments; controlling factors." Section (2) of this statute provides that the commission shall be guided and governed by the purposes and provisions of certain zoning statutes (enumerating them) and shall be "particularly in accordance with" the purposes and provisions of other statutes (enumerating them), ". . . to the end that said master plan, or part or parts thereof, as the case may be, as so adjusted shall accomplish a coordinated and harmonious development of the incorporated and unincorporated area of the entire county."

Here obviously is a delegation of legislative power to an administrative agency (whether characterized as a part of the legislative or executive branch of the government) to be exercised in conformity with a legislative policy and in a discretionary manner in the light of prevailing local conditions. It calls for policy decisions by a body with specialized training and experience in this field. In no sense does the commission perform a judicial function.

The legislature has undertaken to confer upon the judiciary the identical duties and powers of the commission. This is accomplished by requiring a *de novo* trial on appeal to the circuit court. KRS 100.057 (2). The futility of the initial proceedings is obvious when we recognize that all the steps taken before the commission are nullified by taking an appeal. The detailed administrative process is a mockery.

If a court is required to try out independently the propriety of an adjustment in a zoning plan, then the court is simply substituted for the commission in determining and applying legislative policy to local conditions which require the expertise of an administrative agency. The legislature cannot, by directing a method of appeal procedure, impose upon the courts administrative duties to carry out its policies by discretionary decisions.[1] We therefore conclude that KRS 100.057, to the extent it requires a *de novo* trial in the circuit court upon an appeal from an act or

---

[1] If the legislature creates a *cause of action*, it may designate a court rather than an administrative agency to decide a question of *liability* in the first instance. For example, the legislature could probably require the courts to entertain initially such claims as those now presented to the Workmen's Compensation Board or the Board of Claims. It steps over the line, however, when it imposes on the court the duty of making policy decisions in the administrative field.

decision of the Planning and Zoning Commission, is unconstitutional and void. We think the *de novo* provision of KRS 100.057 is clearly severable from the rest of this statute.

An appeal from any action or decision of a Planning and Zoning Commission in cities of the first class and counties containing such cities was authorized as an integral part of zoning procedure. Since we have decided that a trial *de novo* does not constitute a proper judicial review of this administrative action, our remaining question concerns the scope of review under KRS 100.057 with the *de novo* feature eliminated.

Section (1) of this statute provides that the circuit court shall have jurisdiction "to hear and determine all questions and issues properly brought before it on such appeal." As we shall show, this provision sufficiently encompasses the essential elements of adequate review.

Basically, judicial review of administrative action is concerned with the question of *arbitrariness*. On this ground, the courts will assume jurisdiction even in the absence of statutory authorization of an appeal. There is an inherent right of appeal from orders of administrative agencies where constitutional rights are involved.

Obviously, within the scope of a proper review, the court may determine whether the agency acted in excess of its statutory powers. Such action would be arbitrary. In the interest of fairness, a party to be affected by an administrative order is entitled to procedural due process. Administrative proceedings affecting a party's rights which did not afford an opportunity to be heard could likewise be classified as arbitrary. Unless action taken by an administrative agency is supported by substantial evidence, it is arbitrary.

The above three grounds of judicial review—(1) action in excess of granted powers, (2) lack of procedural due process, and (3) lack of substantial evidentiary support—effectually delineate its necessary and permissible scope. It is possible that other apparently unrelated matters of law may be considered. Judicial review of legal questions cannot be impaired by the legislature. In the final analysis, all of these issues may be reduced to the ultimate question of whether the action taken by the administrative agency was arbitrary. As a general rule, the yardstick of fairness is sufficiently broad to measure the validity of administrative action.

The uncorrelated legislative attempts to designate specific considerations controlling the scope of judicial review are aimed in the proper general direction, but the fact of the matter is that they have not materially affected or changed the pattern of review. This is so because the scope of review is basically founded upon the independent exercise of judicial power, and limitations imposed by the legislature will not prevail if they fail to protect the legal rights of a complaining party. As we have heretofore indicated, the courts can and will safeguard those rights when questions of law properly present the ultimate issue of arbitrary action on the part of the administrative agency.

To return to our recent point of departure, we reaffirm that the legislature in enacting KRS 100.057 intended to grant a procedural right of direct appeal in a case such as the one before us. Since we have determined that the legislature could not convert judicial review into the making of an administrative decision, the appellant is limited to those issues which may properly be brought to the court for review. As we have indicated, those issues are confined to questions of law which are encompassed in the question: "Was the administrative decision arbitrary?"

There is one minor problem of procedure in properly presenting this question to the circuit court on appeal. The record made before the zoning commission is of course important and KRS 100.057 makes no specific provision for bringing up that record. No new or additional evidence would be admissible on appeal except to determine what state of facts the commission acted on, or possibly to establish the violation of some legal right with respect to a matter not in issue in proceedings before the commission.

The only claim of arbitrariness in this proceeding could be that there was not substantial evidence to support the ruling of the zoning commission. Our recitation of the evidence in support of this order, appearing in the first part of this opinion, makes it clear that this re-

quirement was amply fulfilled. There was a presumption in favor of the original zoning plan. The evidence for the appellant showed no more than convenience to it and neighboring property owners in the immediate area if a change of classification were made. On the other hand, the maintenance of the original plan was shown to be in the best public interest from the standpoint of the entire zoned area.

We conclude that regardless of whether an administrative agency is promulgating an original zoning plan or allowing adjustments or exceptions to it, if it has been designated to carry out a legislative policy by the exercise of discretionary judgment in a specialized field, it is performing a nonjudicial function. The legislature may not delegate to or impose upon the judiciary such an administrative decision or require a court to substitute its independent judgment on the facts for that of an administrative agency of another branch of government to which the right of decision has been duly delegated. Therefore, this opinion governs appeals taken under KRS 100.085.

CASE QUESTION

What was the reason for the court's holding in *American Beauty?*

SUGGESTED READINGS

K.C. DAVIS, ADMINISTRATIVE LAW TEXT, §§ 16.01–16.10, 29.01–29.10 (3d ed. 1972).

J.J. JAFFE, JUDICIAL CONTROL OF ADMINISTRATIVE ACTIONS, 546–618 (Student ed. 1965).

Brown, *Fact and Law in Judicial Review*, 56 Harv. L. Rev. 899 (1943).

Stern, *Review of Findings of Administrators, Judges and Juries: A Comparative Analysis*, 58 Harv. L. Rev. 70 (1944).

Waas, *Administrative Appeal*, 51 Fla. B.J. 276 (1977).

Hahn, *Perfecting the Partnership: Structuring the Judicial Control of Administrative Determinations of Questions of Law*, 31 Vand. L. Rev. 91 (1978).

Chapter Questions

1. Define the following terms:

a. adjudication	b. Administrative Procedure Act
c. burden of proof	d. cross examination
e. *de novo*	f. delegate
g. direct examination	h. discretion
i. final decision	j. hearing
k. license	l. notice
m. quasi	n. record
o. substantial evidence	p. zoning

2. Community Antenna Television (CATV) systems receive television broadcast signals, amplify them, and transmit them by wire to their subscribers' receivers. CATV did not exist when the Communications Act of 1934 was enacted. In the early stages of CATV development, the Federal Communications Commission, which derives its authority to regulate broadcasting from the Communications Act, took the position that it had no power to regulate CATV. The provisions of the act are explicitly applicable to "all interstate and foreign communications by wire or radio. . . ." The commission is required to endeavor to "make available to all the people of the United States a rapid, efficient, nationwide, and worldwide wire and radio communication service. . . ." In 1959 and 1966, the commission sought legislation from the Congress that would have explicitly authorized it to regulate CATV. Congress refused, stating that the question of whether or not the FCC had the authority to regulate CATV under the present law was for the courts to decide. Meanwhile, the CATV industry was growing rapidly. In 1960, the FCC gradually began to assert its authority to regulate, eventually issuing detailed rules. Pursuant to these rules, it issued an order restricting expansion of a particular CATV service. The court of appeals held that FCC lacked authority under the Communications Act of 1934 to issue such an order. Was the court of appeals correct? Why or why not?

   United States v. Southwestern Cable Co., 392 U.S. 157 (1968)

3. New York's Aid to Families with Dependent Children (AFDC) program, stressing "close contact" with beneficiaries, requires home visits by caseworkers as a condition for assistance "in order that any treatment or service tending to restore [beneficiaries] to a condition of self-support and to relieve their distress may be rendered and . . . that assistance or care may be given only in such amount and as long as necessary." Visitation with a beneficiary, who is the primary source of information to welfare authorities about eligibility for assistance, is not permitted outside working hours, and forcible entry and snooping are prohibited. The appellee was a beneficiary under the AFDC program. Although she had received several days advance notice, she refused to permit a caseworker to visit her home. Following a hearing and advice that assistance would consequently be terminated, she brought suit for injunctive and declaratory relief, contending that home visitation is a search and, when not consented to or supported by a warrant based on probable cause, would violate her Fourth and Fourteenth Amendment rights. The district court upheld the appellee's constitutional claim. Was the district court correct? Why or why not?

   Wyman v. James, 400 U.S. 309 (1971)

4. Columbia East, Inc., the owner of 34.3 acres of farm land, wanted the zoning changed in order to develop a mobile home park. The board of zoning appeals granted a preliminary approval of the application for a special exception to develop a mobile home park in the area zoned as agricultural. Final approval by the board of zoning appeals could only be granted after the plans and specifications for the development of the proposed trailer court had been completed and approved by the appropriate agencies. Neighboring landowners filed a suit in court challenging the board's preliminary approval, claiming the decision was made without adequate provision for sewage treatment. What should the court decide?

   Downing v. Board of Zoning Appeals, 274 N.E.2d 542 (Ind. 1971)

5. The Occupational Safety and Health Act (OSHA or act) empowers agents of the Secretary of Labor to search the work area of any employment facility within the act's jurisdiction. No search warrant or other process is expressly required under the act. An OSHA inspector entered the customer service area of Barlows, Inc., an electrical and plumbing installation business, and stated that he wished to conduct a search of the working areas of the business. The president and general manager, Mr. Barlow, asked the inspector whether he had received any complaints about the working conditions and whether he had a search warrant. The inspector answered both questions in the negative. The inspector was denied entry into the working areas.

Marshall, Secretary of Labor, argued that warrantless inspections to enforce OSHA regulations are reasonable within the meaning of the Fourth Amendment, and relied on the act, which authorizes inspection of business premises without a warrant. Should the court accept Marshall's argument?

Marshall v. Barlow's, Inc., 436 U.S. 307 (1978)

6. The city of Denver was authorized by its charter to make local improvements and to assess the cost upon the property specifically benefited. However, there first had to be notice by publication, and any interested person's comments were required to be heard. Then the City Council had to approve. After completion of a project, the total cost of the improvement had to be published, and the share of the cost for each piece of land determined. Objections had to be heard by the City Council before it could pass an ordinance assessing the cost of the improvement. Following this procedure an improvement was made. The complainants filed objections, challenging the creation of the assessment district, the method of carrying out the improvement, and the final assessments against each piece of property. However, the City Council adopted a resolution that "no complaint or objection had been filed or made against the apportionment of said assessment . . . but the complaints and objections filed deny wholly the right of the city to assess any district or portion of the assessable property of the city of Denver." Therefore, the council enacted an ordinance approving the proposed assessments. Was there a violation of complainants' rights of due process of law? Why or why not?

Londoner v. Denver, 210 U.S. 373 (1908)

7. The owner of real estate in Denver brought a suit to enjoin the State Board of Equalization, the Colorado Tax Commission, and the assessor of Denver from effecting a 40% increase in the state tax valuation of all taxable property in Denver. The plaintiff claimed that he was given no opportunity to be heard, and that his property would therefore be taken without due process of law, contrary to the Fourteenth Amendment of the Constitution. The Supreme Court of Colorado sustained the order of the board and directed the suit to be dismissed. Compare the tax proposal with the subject matter of the procedure in question 6. What are the differences? Was the Colorado Supreme Court correct?

Bi-Metallic Investment Co. v. State Board of Equalization, 239 U.S. 441 (1915)

8. Under the United States Community Health Centers Act, the Secretary of the Department of Health, Education and Welfare was empowered to award monetary grants to health centers that complied with federal regulations. Temple University received funds under the

act and was therefore required to meet the federal regulations. In addition, the Pennsylvania Department of Public Welfare and the County Mental Health and Retardation Board were charged with responsibility of administering county health programs. In 1970, the Temple University Mental Health Center was required to cut back services and impose strict security measures because of campus riots. Members of the surrounding community brought suit against Temple University, charging that the center was not providing required services and that members of the community were deprived of access to the facility. What should the court's decision be?

North Philadelphia Community Board v. Temple University, 330 F.Supp. 1107 (1971)

9. In proceedings arising out of alleged violations of the price discrimination provisions of the Clayton Act, as amended by the Robinson-Patman Act, two courts of appeals reached opposite conclusions. The issue was whether it is within the authority of a court of appeals to postpone the operation of a valid cease-and-desist order of the Federal Trade Commission against a single firm until similar orders have been entered against that firm's competitors. The Eighth Circuit affirmed the commission's order against Moog Industries. Moog had moved to hold the entry of judgment in abeyance, on the ground that it would suffer serious financial loss if prohibited from engaging in pricing practices open to its competitors. In another case, C. E. Niehoff & Co. had requested the commission to hold the order in abeyance on the ground that it would have to go out of business if compelled to sell at a uniform price while its competitors were not under a similar restraint; the commission had denied this request. On review, the Seventh Circuit directed that the cease-and-desist order should take effect ''at such time as the United States Court of Appeals for the Seventh Circuit may direct, *sua sponte*, or upon motion of the Federal Trade Commission.'' What is involved in determining and correcting price discriminations? Is this an area requiring special agency expertise? Which court of appeals was correct?

Moog Industries, Inc., v. FTC, 355 U.S. 411 (1958)

10. A contractor, engaged in construction work for the Navy on the Island of Guam, maintained a recreation center for its employees. The center adjoined a channel that was so dangerous that swimming was forbidden and signs to that effect were erected. One afternoon, an employee was drowned when he attempted to swim the channel in order to rescue two men in distress. Under the Longshoremen's and Harbor Worker's Compensation Act, extended to this employee by the Defense Bases Act, the deputy commissioner found as a ''fact'' that the employee's death arose out of and in the course of his employment, and awarded a death benefit to his mother. A petition

by the contractor to set aside the award was denied by the district court on the ground that "there is substantial evidence . . . to sustain the compensation order." On appeal, the court of appeals reversed, concluding: "The lethal currents were not a part of the recreational facilities supplied by the employer, and the swimming in them for the rescue of the unknown men was not recreation. It was an act entirely disconnected from any use for which the recreational camp was provided and not in the course of employment." Which court was correct? Why?

O'Leary v. Brown-Pacific-Maxon, Inc., 340 U.S. 504 (1951)

X Government Regulation of Business

A discussion of the American legal system would not be complete without examining the legal relationship between government and business. Congress and state legislatures have passed many laws regulating business activity, and have established administrative agencies to constantly monitor and enforce the laws. Both state and federal administrative agencies, within the confines of the granting statute, have the power to make additional regulations that have the force of law. This chapter is designed to acquaint you with just some of the major attempts by the federal government to regulate business activity. Antitrust regulation, employment regulation, and consumer-protection legislation are among the more important attempts by Congress to curb unjust business practices.

Antitrust Regulation

The basis of the economic system in the United States is free competition. Free competition (1) permits the laws of supply and demand to determine the prices of goods and services and (2) provides incentives for innovations, technological advancement, and increased efficiency. In an effort to increase profits, business leaders have tried to decrease competition by creating monopolistic combinations. Early state laws attempting to deal with this problem were largely ineffective, due to the fact that monopolies were a problem of national scope. Recognizing the detrimental impact of such combinations on the economy and the need for federal regulation,

Congress has passed laws prohibiting a variety of monopolistic activities. The Sherman Act of 1890, the Clayton Act of 1914, and the Federal Trade Commission Act of 1914 are the core of the *antitrust laws.*

Monopolistic activities may be *horizontal*—that is, a company or group of companies may control all the supplies of a particular item. For example, a utility company is a monopoly. Monopolistic activities may also be *vertical.* That is, a business firm controls a product after the product leaves the company, or overly controls each step of its production, distribution, and sale. An example of a vertical monopoly is a manufacturer who requires a distributor to sell its product at a fixed price. Both kinds of monopolistic activity—horizontal and vertical—are outlawed by the Sherman Act and the acts following.

The Sherman Act

The *Sherman act*, enacted in 1890 by Congress, using its power to regulate interstate commerce, was a response to the ruthless monopolistic practices that characterized the post–Civil War marketplace. The act was passed to preserve and promote free competition within the American economy. It prohibits conduct that restrains trade and attempts to monopolize.

Section 1 of the Sherman Act declares that contracts, combinations, and conspiracies in restraint of trade are illegal. Section 2 is directed against monopoly attempts. Thus the Sherman Act prohibits most activity that restrains trade. Violation of the act is a felony, although when the act was originally passed, a violation was only a misdemeanor.

Four sanctions may be imposed on violators of the Sherman Act. First, because a violation is a felony, individuals may be fined up to $100,000 and imprisoned up to three years. Corporations may be fined up to $1 million. Second, injunctions may be granted to prevent further violations. Third—and perhaps most important—a victim of monopolistic activity may recover triple damages. Rather than simply compensating the victim for the harm done, these punitive damages may be imposed so that the victim recovers three times the amount of the actual injury. Fourth, the government may seize property that is transported across state lines. This sanction, however, has rarely been used.

Two major problems emerged from the relatively simple language of the Sherman Act. One: A victim, in order to recover damages, had to actually prove the harm resulted from the monopolistic activities. This meant that monopolistic activities could be stopped only after they had taken some toll. Furthermore, such injury was often difficult to show. This problem was partially remedied by the passage of the Clayton act, which we shall discuss later. The other major problem that emerged was that the

Sherman act prohibited nearly all activity that resulted in restraint of trade. However, almost *all* business contracts result in *some* restraint of trade. And the Constitution protects the rights of individuals to freely contract. The language of the Sherman act is thus too inclusive. A conflict ensued from these opposing considerations, and the courts have resolved this conflict by interpreting the act more narrowly than it was written.

Because the broad language of the Sherman act had to be narrowly interpreted, the courts developed a standard for judging when a contract violated the act and when it did not: *the rule of reason.* Only contracts that *unreasonably* restrain trade are considered to be illegal. A court must determine not only that the contract violates the literal language of the Sherman Act, but also that the contract in that particular instance unreasonably restricts the flow of trade. However, certain business practices that seriously restrict competition are deemed to be illegal *per se.* These business practices are considered so blatantly monopolistic in nearly every case as to render unnecessary any inquiry into the particular harm of a given case. Acts that are illegal *per se* are actually a subset of acts that violate the rule of reason. Such acts are simply presumed to be unreasonable, and no further examination is needed to determine their unreasonableness. Among the practices generally deemed to be illegal *per se* are some agreements to control production, to fix prices, to divide markets, and to allocate customers.

Continental T.V., Inc., v. GTE Sylvania, Inc.
433 U.S. 36
United States Supreme Court
June 23, 1977

MR. JUSTICE POWELL
In an attempt to improve its market position by attracting more aggressive and competent retailers, respondent manufacturer of television sets limited the number of retail franchises granted for any given area and required each franchisee to sell respondent's products only from the location or locations at which it was franchised. Petitioner Continental, one of respondent's franchised retailers, claimed that respondent had violated § 1 of the Sherman Act by entering into and enforcing franchise agreements that prohibited the sale of respondent's products other than from specified locations. The district court rejected respondent's requested jury instruction that the location restriction was illegal only if it unreasonably restrained or suppressed competition. Instead, relying on *United States v. Arnold, Schwinn & Co.,* 388 U.S. 365 (1967), the district court instructed the jury that it was a *per se* violation of § 1 if respondent entered into a contract, combination, or conspiracy with one or more of its retailers, pursuant to which it attempted to restrict the locations from which the retailers resold the merchandise they had purchased from respon-

dent. The jury found that the location restriction violated § 1, and treble damages were assessed against respondent. Concluding that *Schwinn* was distinguishable, the court of appeals reversed, holding that respondent's location restriction had less potential for competitive harm than the restrictions invalidated in *Schwinn*, and thus should be judged under the "rule of reason."

Franchise agreements between manufacturers and retailers frequently include provisions barring the retailers from selling franchised products from locations other than those specified in the agreements. This case represents important questions concerning the appropriate antitrust analysis of these restrictions under § 1 of the Sherman Act. We granted Continental's petition for *certiorari* to resolve these important questions of antitrust law.

We turn first to Continental's contention that Sylvania's restriction on retail locations is a *per se* violation of § 1 of the Sherman Act as interpreted in *Schwinn*. In *Schwinn*, the Court proceeded to articulate the following *per se* rule of illegality for vertical restrictions: "Under the Sherman Act, it is unreasonable . . . for a manufacturer to seek to restrict and confine areas or persons with whom an article may be traded after the manufacturer has parted with dominion over it." But the Court expressly stated that the rule of reason governs when "the manufacturer retains title, dominion, and risk with respect to the product, and the position and function of the dealer in question are, in fact, indistinguishable from those of an agent or salesman of the manufacturer."

In the present case, it is undisputed that title to the television sets passed from Sylvania to Continental. Thus, the *Schwinn per se* rule applies. As the court of appeals conceded, the language of *Schwinn* is clearly broad enough to apply to the present case. Unlike the court of appeals, however, we are unable to find a principled basis for distinguishing *Schwinn* from the case now before us.

Both Schwinn and Sylvania sought to reduce but not to eliminate competition among their respective retailers through the adoption of a franchise system. These restrictions allowed Schwinn and Sylvania to regulate the amount of competition among their retailers by preventing a franchisee from selling franchised products from outlets other than the one covered by the franchise agreement. In *Schwinn*, the Court expressly held that this restriction was impermissible under the broad principle stated there. In intent and competitive impact, the retail-customer restriction in *Schwinn* is indistinguishable from the location restriction in the present case.

Sylvania argues that if *Schwinn* cannot be distinguished, it should be reconsidered. We are convinced that the need for clarification of the law in this area justifies reconsideration. *Schwinn* itself was an abrupt and largely unexplained departure from *White Motor Co. v. United States*, 372 U.S. 253 (1963), where only four years earlier the Court had refused to endorse a *per se* rule for vertical restrictions.

The traditional framework of analysis under § 1 of the Sherman Act is familiar and does not require extended discussion. Section 1 prohibits "every contract, combination ..., or conspiracy, in restraint of trade or commerce." Since the early years of this century a judicial gloss on this statutory language has established the "rule of reason" as the prevailing standard of analysis. Under this rule, the factfinder weighs all of the circumstances of a case in deciding whether a restrictive practice should be prohibited as imposing an unreasonable restraint on competition. *Per se* rules of illegality are appropriate only when they relate to conduct that is manifestly anticompetitive. As the Court explained in *Northern Pacific R. R. Co. v. United States*, 356 U.S. 1 (1958), "there are certain agreements or practices which because of their pernicious effect on competition and lack of any redeeming virtue are conclusively presumed to be unreasonable and therefore illegal, without elaborate inquiry as to the precise harm they have caused or the business excuse for their use."

The market impact of vertical restrictions is complex because of their potential for a simultaneous reduction of intrabrand competition and stimulation of interbrand competition. Significantly, the Court in *Schwinn* did not distinguish among the challenged restrictions on the basis of their individual potential for intrabrand harm or interbrand benefit. The pivotal factor was the passage of title: All restrictions were held to be *per se* illegal where title had passed, and all were evaluated and sustained under the rule of reason where it had not. The location restriction at issue here would be subject to the same pattern of analysis under *Schwinn.*

It appears that this distinction between sale and nonsale transactions resulted from the Court's effort to accommodate the perceived intrabrand harm and interbrand benefit of vertical restrictions. The *per se* rule for sale transactions reflected the view that vertical restrictions are "so obviously destructive" of intrabrand competition that their use would "open the door to exclusivity of outlets and limitation of territory further than prudence permits." Conversely, the continued adherence to the traditional rule of reason for nonsale transactions reflected the view that the restrictions have too great a potential for the promotion of interbrand competition to justify complete prohibition. The Court's opinion provides no analytical support for these contrasting positions. Nor is there even an assertion in the opinion that the competitive impact of vertical restrictions is significantly affected by the form of the transaction. Nonsale transactions appear to be excluded from the *per se* rule, not because of a greater danger of intrabrand harm or a greater promise of interbrand benefit, but rather because of the Court's unexplained belief that a complete *per se* prohibition would be too "inflexible."

Vertical restrictions reduce intrabrand competition by limiting the number of sellers of a particular product competing for the business of a given group of buyers. Location restrictions have this effect because of practical constraints on the effective marketing area of retail outlets. Although intrabrand competition may be reduced, the ability of retailers to exploit the resulting market may be limited both by the ability of consumers to travel to other franchised locations and, perhaps more importantly, to purchase the competing products of other manufacturers. None of these key variables, however, is affected by the form of the transaction by which a manufacturer conveys his products to the retailers.

Vertical restrictions promote interbrand competition by allowing the manufacturer to achieve certain efficiencies in the distribution of his products. These "redeeming virtues" are implicit in every decision sustaining vertical restrictions under the rule of reason. Economists have identified a number of ways in which manufacturers can use such restrictions to compete more effectively against other manufacturers. For example, new manufacturers and manufacturers entering new markets can use the restrictions in order to induce competent and aggressive retailers to make the kind of investment of capital and labor that is often required in the distribution of products unknown to the consumer. Established manufacturers can use them to induce retailers to engage in promotional activities or to provide service and repair facilities necessary to the efficient marketing of their products. Service and repair are vital for many products, such as automobiles and major household appliances. The availability and quality of such services affect a manufacturer's goodwill and the competitiveness of his product.

We conclude that the distinction drawn in *Schwinn* between sale and nonsale transactions is not sufficient to justify the application of a *per se* rule in one situation and a rule of reason in the other. The question remains whether the *per se* rule stated in *Schwinn* should be expanded to include nonsale transactions or abandoned in favor of a return to the rule of reason. We have found no persuasive support for expanding the *per se* rule.

We revert to the standard articulated in *Northern Pacific R.R. Co.*, and reiterated in *White Motor*, for determining whether vertical restrictions must be "conclusively presumed to be unreasonable and therefore illegal without elaborate inquiry as to the precise harm they have caused or the business excuse for their use." Such restrictions, in varying forms, are widely used in our free market economy. As indicated above, there is substantial scholarly and judicial authority supporting their economic utility. There is relatively little authority to the contrary. Certainly, there has been no showing in this case, either generally or with respect to Sylvania's agreements, that vertical restrictions have or are likely to have a pernicious effect on competition or that they lack any redeeming virtue. Accordingly, we conclude that the *per se* rule stated in *Schwinn* must be overruled. In so holding, we do not foreclose the possibility that particular applications of vertical restrictions might justify *per se* prohibition under *Northern Pacific R.R. Co.* But we do make clear that departure from the rule of reason standard must be based on demonstrable economic effect rather than—as in *Schwinn*—on formalistic line drawing.

In sum, we conclude that the appropriate decision is to return to the rule of reason that governed vertical restrictions prior to *Schwinn*. When anticompetitive effects are shown to result from particular vertical restrictions, they can be adequately policed under

the rule of reason, the standard traditionally applied for the majority of anticompetitive practices challenged under
§ 1 of the Act. Accordingly, the decision
of the Court of Appeals is
    Affirmed.

CASE QUESTIONS

1. Why was Sylvania's business practice considered a vertical monopolistic act?
2. Did the Court find that Sylvania's practice of geographically restricting
its franchises had an illegal monopolistic effect on the market?
3. In the paragraph that begins, "Vertical restrictions promote interbrand
competition," the Court explains why some vertical restrictions are
proper. When the Court makes such statements, is it relying simply on its
own notions of business practices?

SUGGESTED READINGS

15 U.S.C., §§ 1–7 (1970).
L.A. SULLIVAN, ANTITRUST, §§ 1–4, 40–48, 53–59, 63–72 (1977).
Baker, *Antitrust in the Sunshine*, 21 ST. LOUIS U. L.J. 347 (1977).
Note, 88 HARV. L. REV. 1021 (1975).
Note, 42 FORD. L. REV. 909 (1974).
Kamerschen, *Antitrust Goes to the Dogs*, 15 AM. BUS. L.J. 249 (1977).
Note, *Criticism of the Post-Sylvania Decisions and a Proposal to Make
    the Rule of Reason Reasonable Again*, 1980 UTAH L. REV. 795.
McDavid, *Failing Companies and the Antitrust Laws*, 14 U. MICH. J. L.
    REF. 229 (1981).

The Clayton Act

The continued market concentration of large companies after the passage
of the Sherman act indicated a need to strengthen the antitrust laws.
Moreover, some critics believed that because the act is overly general, the
courts have had difficulty in applying the law, and business leaders have
had difficulty in planning their activities.

This dissatisfaction with the Sherman act resulted in the passage of the
Clayton act in 1914. The Clayton act was intended to strengthen the antitrust laws and to prohibit *specific* monopolistic practices in their incipiency. The act prohibits mergers and other specific activities that *may*
lessen competition. An actual decrease in competition need not have oc-

curred for a violation of the Clayton act to exist. However, the Clayton act is not quite as broad in power and scope as the Sherman act. The Sherman act applies to all transactions that *affect* interstate commerce, whereas the Clayton act applies only to transactions *in* interstate commerce. Another difference between these acts is that the Clayton act contains almost no criminal provisions. Therefore the burden of proof is less stringent under this act than under the Sherman act.

PRICE DISCRIMINATION

One of the specific activities that is outlawed by the Clayton act, under § 2 of that act, is price discrimination. *Price discrimination* exists when supplier A sells the same product to customer B at a higher price than to customer C. As a result, customer B cannot compete with customer C. However, the Clayton act was so riddled with exceptions to this general rule that the act was ineffective in stopping most price discrimination. Some violations of price-discrimination laws became criminal acts. Under the Robinson-Patman act, a company can bring suit if it has been injured by price discrimination. The court terminates the discriminatory practice and awards civil damages to the plaintiff unless the defendant can show that the price differential was due to (1) actual cost savings because of a quantity order, (2) changing conditions affecting the marketability of the goods, or (3) a good-faith effort to meet the lower prices of competitors. These defenses and other exceptions in some cases undermine the effectiveness of the law against price discrimination, whereas in other areas, the act overly protects small business from price discrimination and actually results in less price competition. For example, some price discounts based on buying in large quantities are illegal. Overall, there is much dissatisfaction with the Robinson-Patman act.

FTC v. Borden Company
383 U.S. 637
United States Supreme Court
March 23, 1966

MR. JUSTICE WHITE
The Borden Company, respondent here, produces and sells evaporated milk under the Borden name, a nationally advertised brand. At the same time, Borden packs and markets evaporated milk under various private brands owned by its customers. This milk is physically and chemically identical with the milk it distributes under its own brand, but is sold at both the wholesale and retail level at prices regularly below those obtained for the Borden brand milk. The Federal Trade Commission found the milk sold under the Borden and the private labels to be of like grade and quality as required

for the applicability of § 2(a) of the Robinson-Patman act, held the price differential to be discriminatory within the meaning of the section, ascertained the requisite effect on commerce, rejected Borden's claim of cost justification, and consequently issued a cease-and-desist order. The court of appeals set aside the commission's order on the sole ground that as a matter of law, the customer-label milk was not of the same grade and quality as the milk sold under the Borden brand. Because of the importance of this issue, which bears on the reach and coverage of the Robinson-Patman act, we granted *certiorari*. We now reverse the decision of the court of appeals and remand the case to that court for the determination of the remaining issues raised by respondent Borden in that court.

The position of Borden and of the court of appeals is that the determination of like grade and quality, which is a threshold finding essential to the applicability of § 2(a), may not be based solely on the physical properties of the products without regard to the brand names they bear and the relative public acceptance these brands enjoy— "consideration should be given to all commercially significant distinctions which affect market value, whether they be physical or promotional." Here, because the milk bearing the Borden brand regularly sold at a higher price than did the milk with a buyer's label, the court considered the products to be "commercially" different and hence of different "grade" for the purposes of § 2(a), even though they were physically identical and of equal quality. Although a mere difference in brand would not in itself demonstrate a difference in grade, decided consumer

preference for one brand over another, reflected in the willingness to pay a higher price for the well-known brand, was, in the view of the court of appeals, sufficient to differentiate chemically identical products and to place the price differential beyond the reach of § 2(a).

We reject this construction of § 2(a), as did both the examiner and the commission in this case. The commission's view is that labels do not differentiate products for the purpose of determining grade or quality, even though the one label may have more customer appeal and command a higher price in the marketplace from a substantial segment of the public.

The commission's construction of the statute also appears to us to further the purpose and policy of the Robinson-Patman act. Subject to specified exceptions and defenses, § 2(a) proscribes unequal treatment of different customers in comparable transactions, but only if there is the requisite effect on competition, actual or potential. But if the transactions are deemed to involve goods of disparate grade or quality, the section has no application at all, and the commission never reaches either the issue of discrimination or that of anticompetitive impact. We doubt that Congress intended to foreclose these inquiries in situations where a single seller markets the identical product under several different brands, whether his own, his customers', or both. Such transactions are too laden with potential discrimination and adverse competitive effect to be excluded from the reach of § 2(a) by permitting a difference in grade to be established by the label alone or by the label and its consumer appeal.

If two products, physically identical but differently branded, are to be deemed of different grade because the seller regularly and successfully markets some quantity of both at different prices, the seller could, as far as § 2(a) is concerned, make either product available to some customers and deny it to others, however discriminatory this might be and however damaging to competition. Those who were offered only one of the two products would be barred from competing for those customers who want or might buy the other. The retailer who was permitted to buy and sell only the more expensive brand would have no chance to sell to those who always buy the cheaper product, or to convince others, by experience or otherwise, of the fact which he and all other dealers already know— that the cheaper product is actually identical with that carrying the more expensive label.

The seller, to escape the act, would have only to succeed in selling some unspecified amount of each product to some unspecified portion of his customers, however large or small the price differential might be. The seller's pricing and branding policy, by being successful, would apparently validate itself by creating a difference in "grade" and thus taking itself beyond the purview of the act.

Our holding neither ignores the economic realities of the marketplace nor denies that some labels will command a higher price than others, at least from some portion of the public. But it does mean that "the economic factors inherent in brand names and national advertising should not be considered in the jurisdictional inquiry under the statutory 'like grade and quality' test." Report of the Attorney General's National Committee to Study the Antitrust Laws 158 (1955). And it does mean that transactions like those involved in this case may be examined by the commission under § 2(a). The commission will determine, subject to judicial review, whether the differential under attack is discriminatory within the meaning of the act, whether competition may be injured, and whether the differential is cost-justified or is defensible as a good-faith effort to meet the price of a competitor. "Tangible consumer preferences between branded and unbranded commodities should receive due legal recognition in the more flexible 'injury' and 'cost justification' provisions of the statute." *Id.*, at 159. This, we think, is precisely what Congress intended.

The judgment of the court of appeals is reversed, and the case is remanded for further proceedings consistent with this opinion.

Reversed and remanded

CASE QUESTIONS

1. Did the Court find an actual violation of section 2 in this case?
2. Why should only the physical properties of a product be examined to see whether a possible violation of section 2 of the act occurred?
3. Do you believe that advertising a product substantially changes that product, so that different prices can be charged for advertised products

than for identical unadvertised products? What weight should be given to a consumer's peace of mind regarding the quality of an advertised product?

Suggested Readings

L.A. Sullivan, Antitrust, §§ 130–141, 217–225 (1977).

F.M. Rowe, Price Discrimination Under the Robinson-Patman Act (1962).

Kirkpatrick, *Antitrust Enforcement in the 70's*, 30 Cath. U. L. Rev. 431 (1981).

Clanton, *Antitrust Realities and Directions*, 62 Chi. B. Rec. 230 (1981).

Fischer, *Geographic Markets Under the Microscope: The Proximity Theory Fails a Test*, 98 Banking L.J. 463 (1981).

Another specific act that was made illegal under section 3 of the Clayton act relates to *tying contracts.* In a tying arrangement, a commodity is sold only on the condition that the buyer purchase another product or service as well. These activities are generally illegal *per se.*

Interlocking directorates are also illegal, under section 8 of the Clayton Act. A person cannot serve on the board of directors of different corporations if the corporations are substantial businesses and they compete against each other, or *should* compete against each other, in the marketplace.

Monopolistic Activity

Section 7 of the Clayton act prohibits mergers and other acquisitions that may lessen competition. To determine whether a party has violated the Clayton act, a court must first decide whether the defendant actively sought some power over a relevant market. The relevant market consists of a product market (the line of commerce) as well as a geographic market (the section of the country). Then the court decides whether the power acquired is enough to control price or competition in the market. The scope of the power is determined by calculating the percent of the market held by the defendant. If the court finds that the power to control price or competition exists in the relevant market, the guilty party may be subject to both civil and criminal sanctions.

The courts have found numerous practices monopolistic under the

Clayton act. Among these practices are holding companies, interlocking directorates, informal agreements, and mergers.

Boyertown Burial Casket Co. v. Amedco, Inc.
407 F.Supp. 811
United States District Court, E. D. Pennsylvania
January 31, 1976

TROUTMAN, DISTRICT JUDGE

This matter comes before the court on the motion of Boyertown Burial Casket Company for a preliminary injunction to restrain a tender offer to Boyertown shareholders made by the defendant, Amedco, Inc., on December 22, 1975.

Boyertown alleges that defendant's "offer to purchase outstanding shares of common stock" of plaintiff may result, if successful, in a violation of § 7 of the Clayton act, since the effect of Amedco's control of plaintiff would be to substantially lessen competition, or tend to create a monopoly in the burial casket industry, in which there is a nationwide trend toward economic concentration.

The Clayton Act, § 7, prohibits a corporation engaged in commerce from acquiring:

. . . directly or indirectly, the whole or any part of the stock . . . of another corporation engaged also in commerce, where in any line of commerce in any section of the country, the effect of such acquisition may be substantially to lessen competition or tend to create a monopoly.

Prior to granting preliminary relief enjoining a threatened violation of § 7 of the Clayton act, we are required in this circuit to apply the following criteria, as stated in *Allis-Chalmers Mfg. Co. v. White Consolidated Industries, Inc.*, 414 F.2d 506, 510, 511 (3d Cir. 1969), cert. denied 396 U.S. 1009 (1970).

Recognizing that preliminary relief is a serious remedy, and because application for such relief, particularly in a complex case, is often based on a record less comprehensive than that which a full adjudication would yield, the courts have required that a plaintiff show a reasonable chance of ultimately prevailing on the merits. In an action by a private party, the plaintiff must also show that it will suffer irreparable injury unless relief is granted.

A plaintiff need not prove that an industry has become heavily concentrated in order to show an antitrust violation, since § 7 is intended to check the trend toward concentration in its incipiency. *United States v. Von's Grocery Co.*, 384 U.S. 270 (1966). Accordingly, in a preliminary hearing, plaintiff need only show a reasonable probability of ultimately proving that the effect of a merger between two corporations engaged in any relevant line of commerce in any section of the country may be to substantially lessen competition or tend to create a monopoly. On the basis of the evidence adduced at the preliminary hearing, we conclude that plaintiff met this burden.

As to the relevant line of commerce, sufficient evidence was introduced to show that the relevant industry is the manufacture and sale of burial caskets. This industry includes firms which manufacture completed caskets for sale to funeral directors, companies which produce incomplete shells or casket parts, and jobbers or finishers who add hardware, interiors and finish to incomplete units and sell the completed caskets to funeral directors.

As to the relevant geographical market, the following standard was set in *United States v. Philadelphia National Bank*, 374 U.S. 321 (1963):

The proper question to be asked in this case is not where the parties to the merger do business or even where they compete, but where, within the area of competitive overlap, the effect of the merger on competition will be direct and immediate. . . . This depends upon "the geographical structure of supplier-customer relations."

The nation as a whole, a regional area consisting of several states, or a more localized area may comprise the relevant geographical market for the purposes of § 7.

Plaintiff adduced sufficient evidence of two relevant geographic markets— areas of competitive overlap between Amedco and Boyertown—the nation as a whole and the Los Angeles–Long Beach Standard Metropolitan Statistical Area.

Finally, the plaintiff was not required to prove with mathematical precision that the effect of the acquisition will be to substantially lessen competition.

Rather, Boyertown's burden was to show with reasonable probability of ultimate success on the merits that the effect of the takeover may be to substantially lessen competition in the relevant sections of the country. As stated in *United States v. Von's Grocery, supra*:

By using these terms in § 7 which look not merely to the actual present effect of a merger, but instead to its effect on future competition, Congress sought to preserve competition among many small businesses by arresting a trend toward concentration in its incipiency before that trend developed to the point that a market was left in the grip of a few big companies. Thus, where concentration is gaining momentum in a market, we must be alert to carry out Congress' intent to protect competition against ever-increasing concentration through mergers. 384 U.S. at 277.

The evidence showed a marked trend toward concentration in the burial casket industry, a trend which has accelerated since 1972 when Chief Judge Lord enjoined permanently a threatened takeover of plaintiff by Walco National on the ground that the acquisition would violate § 7 of the Clayton act. The threatened takeover by Amedco would further accelerate this concentration, and we conclude that plaintiff has shown a reasonable likelihood of ultimately proving a violation of § 7.

CASE QUESTIONS

1. Did Boyertown have to show exactly what effect a purchase by Amedco would have on the market?

2. What was the relevant product market (line of commerce)?

3. What was the relevant geographic market over which Amedco would gain control?

4. Why was the Clayton act passed? That is, why should Congress or the courts be concerned if a company gains control of a certain market?

Suggested Readings

15 U.S.C., §§ 12–27 (1970).

L.A. Sullivan, Antitrust, § 12–21 (1977).

Note, 41 Mo. L. Rev. 268 (1976).

Note, 24 Drake L. Rev. 223 (1974).

Note, 44 U. Cin. L. Rev. 844 (1975).

Williams, *Corporate Mergers and the Antitrust Laws*, 26 Mercer L. Rev. 963 (1975).

Kintner and Selinger, *Section 7 of the Clayton Act: A Survey of Enforcement Options and Opportunities*, 29 Emory L.J. 681 (1980).

The Federal Trade Commission Act

The Federal Trade Commission act, also enacted in 1914 along with the Clayton act, created the Federal Trade Commission, which is empowered to bring civil and criminal actions in federal court against violators of the antitrust laws. Individuals are also permitted to bring civil actions against violators to recover treble damages caused by their monopolistic activities.

The FTC's major purpose is to prevent monopolistic activities from occurring. However, besides enforcing the antitrust laws, it also enforces its own broad provision against "unfair methods of competition." The FTC's powers are vast. They touch nearly every aspect of buying and selling, as well as any act attendant to buying and selling. The FTC controls truth in advertising and truth in lending as well. Many acts—such as the Export Trade act, the Landham Trademark act, and the Fair Packaging and Labeling act—are handled by the FTC.

Many industries—such as insurance, banking, public utilities, and radio and television broadcasting—are not covered by the antitrust laws. These excepted industries are ones in which monopolization is required, either economically (electric utilities, for example) or physically (the limited number of communication channels, for example), hence rendering competition unsuitable for the protection of the public interest. These industries are normally more heavily regulated than those subject to the antitrust laws. The government relies on direct regulation rather than competition to protect the public from the business practices of the excepted industries.

Employment Regulation

Historically, employers could hire anyone they wished, pay any amount they wanted, and fire any employee without reason. Government regulation of employment came early in the Industrial Revolution with laws restricting the number of hours women and children could work. Since then, Congress has systematically imposed more and more restrictions on employers. Today employers must comply with wage and hour regulations, write pension plans in compliance with federal specifications, provide safe working conditions and workers' compensation insurance, and bargain in good faith with a duly elected union.

National Labor Relations Act

Prior to the passage of the National Labor Relations Act (the Wagner act) in 1935, employers were allowed to pursue almost any business tactic that served to inhibit or destroy the collective bargaining power of employees. Companies used tactics ranging from lockouts (withholding work from employees) to court injunctions that prohibited employees from picketing. Clearly, employers had the upper hand over employees. Although some legislation was passed to protect the rights of employees, the first major act that dealt comprehensively with employer–employee relations was the Wagner act. The act helped equalize the bargaining positions of companies and laborers by outlawing employer practices that constituted "unfair labor practices." It affirmatively stated the right of a union to exist and the rights of employees to associate with and bargain collectively through a union without interference from the employer. Thus employees were given the power to legally engage in concerted activities.

The Wagner act also established the National Labor Relations Board. The NLRB has two major functions. First, it oversees union elections and certifies the union that is elected to represent the employees. Second, it hears and settles charges of unfair labor practices committed by either employers or unions.

The NLRB has broad discretionary powers to remedy any unfair labor practice. It may order reinstatement of an employee who was wrongfully fired, and may award back pay and commensurate seniority for that employee. It may issue a cease-and-desist order to an employer who engages in unfair labor practices. It may order a union and employer to bargain.

Because of the wide powers of the NLRB and the powers suddenly vested in unions under the Wagner act, union activity flourished. However, unions developed an edge over employers in bargaining strength. The Wagner act delineated illegal *employer* practices, but not illegal *union* activities. Therefore the Labor–Management Relations act of 1947 (the Taft–Hartley act) was enacted to further balance the power between unions and employers. Union activities such as coercion of employees to get them to join a union, forcing an employer to pay for work that is not performed (*featherbedding*), and secondary boycotts became illegal. *Secondary boycotts* exist when coercive pressure is exerted on customers to make them refrain from patronizing an unfavored business. Employees were given the right to refuse to join a union. The First Amendment rights of free speech of employers were finally protected, allowing them to disseminate probusiness literature. (This was illegal under the Wagner act.) The NLRB was partly divested of its broad power so that it no longer oversaw every phase of a charge of unfair labor practice from beginning to end. In so doing, the Taft–Hartley act established the position of general counsel to the board. The general counsel has final authority to oversee investigation of charges and prosecution of complaints, in addition to the power to obtain court orders to enforce decisions. The board retains the power to adjudicate disputes. Decisions of the NLRB are appealable to the United States court of appeals.

For practical reasons, the NLRB does not choose to investigate every charge brought before it, but limits its own jurisdiction to hear only the larger disputes and disputes in certain settings, such as those of nonprofit hospitals and private universities. Other disputes are overseen by appropriate state agencies and are decided in state courts.

The Wagner act and the Taft–Hartley act were followed by a third: the Labor–Management Reporting and Disclosure act of 1959 (the Landrum–Griffin act). This act is smaller in scope than the Wagner and Taft–Hartley acts. It was enacted primarily to eliminate widespread union corruption and to set out the rights of individual employees. It more completely eliminates the practice of secondary boycotts that were allowed under the Taft–Hartley act. It also sets forth in detail the way that every union is to be administratively governed.

Generally, Congress passed these three major acts to equalize the bargaining positions of unions and employers and to outlaw activities of a coercive or violent nature, while preserving the peaceful but effective activities engaged in by unions and employers.

Continental Insurance Co. v. NLRB
495 F.2d 44
United States Court of Appeals
Second Circuit
April 9, 1974

MANSFIELD, CIRCUIT JUDGE
Continental Insurance Company, Underwriters Adjusting Company, and Underwriters Adjusting Company of Illinois (the Company herein) have petitioned us to review and set aside an order of the National Labor Relations Board (the Board herein) issued against the Company on July 11, 1973, directing it (1) to cease its refusal to bargain collectively in good faith with the American Communications Association, Communications Trade Division, International Brotherhood of Teamsters, Chauffeurs, Warehousemen and Helpers of America (the Union herein) as the certified bargaining representative for certain Company employees located in two certified bargaining units and (2) to take affirmative action to carry out its bargaining duties under the act. The Board has filed a cross-application for enforcement of its order. The sole issue before us is whether there is substantial evidence in the record to support the Board's findings. We find that there is and accordingly deny the Company's petition and grant the enforcement requested by the board.

On March 6, 1968, following elections conducted by the Board, the Union was certified as the bargaining representative for claims adjustors, examiners, and investigators employed by the Company in two bargaining units, its New York City branch and a branch in Newark, New Jersey. Despite the passage of almost six (6) years since the certification of the Union as the exclusive bargaining agent, no agreement has been reached by the parties.

The lion's share of the six-year delay arises from the parties' inability to reach agreement, despite some 27 bargaining sessions held during the period from December 1969 to June 22, 1971. During the course of these negotiations, the Union on June 9, 1970, filed charges with the Board alleging that the Company had failed to bargain in good faith. This led to the Board's issuance of a consolidated complaint to which the Company filed an answer amounting to a general denial. Hearings were held before Administrative Law Judge Herbert Silberman during the period from March 3, 1972 to July 25, 1972, culminating in his issuance of detailed findings and conclusions on December 13, 1972. He found that "the Company conducted its negotiations with no desire or intention of reaching any agreement with the Union," a conclusion based on a detailed analysis of the evidence. It revealed that the Company had prolonged negotiations unduly by various delaying tactics, including unreasonable fragmenting of bargaining sessions, captious questioning of the Union's proposals, and presentation of Company proposals that were unnecessarily complicated, outside the scope of mandatory collective bargaining, or patently unfair and unreasonable.

In a decision and order entered on July 11, 1973, the Board, affirming *in toto* the administrative law judge's findings and conclusions, adopted his recommended order.

The Board's findings must, of course, be upheld if they are supported by substantial evidence on the record as a whole. At the outset, we summarize those basic principles by which we are governed in reviewing a charge of bad-faith bargaining.

The duty imposed on the parties to bargain collectively does not obligate a party to make concessions or yield a position fairly maintained. On the other hand, the parties are obligated to do more than merely go through the formalities of negotiation. There must be a serious intent to adjust differences and to reach an acceptable common ground. To conduct negotiations as a kind of charade or sham, all the while intending to avoid reaching an agreement, would of course violate § 8(a)(5) and amount to bad-faith bargaining. Sophisticated pretense in the form of apparent bargaining, sometimes referred to as "shadow boxing" or "surface bargaining," will not satisfy a party's duty under the act. Where years pass without an agreement being reached, the conduct of the parties must be scrutinized carefully, especially when experience discloses that collective-bargaining agreements are usually reached in a fraction of that time.

The problem, therefore, in resolving a charge of bad-faith bargaining, is to ascertain the state of mind of the party charged, insofar as it bears on that party's negotiations. Since it would be extraordinary for a party directly to admit a bad-faith intention, his motive must of necessity be ascertained from circumstantial evidence. Certain specific conduct, such as the Company's unilateral changing of working conditions during bargaining, may constitute *per se* violations of the duty to bargain in good faith, since they in effect constitute "a refusal to negotiate in fact." Absent such evidence, however, the determination of intent must be founded on the party's overall conduct and on the totality of the circumstances, as distinguished from the individual pieces forming part of the mosaic. Specific conduct, while it may not, standing alone, amount to a *per se* failure to bargain in good faith, may when considered with all of the other evidence support an inference of bad faith.

At the outset of negotiations, which were delayed for more than one and one-half years by the Company's pursuit of an appeal from the Board's bargaining unit determinations, the Company refused to bargain jointly for its two units certified by the Board, even though the Company was represented by one spokesman for both units, Frederick T. Shea, Esq., the Union's proposals for both were virtually identical, and joint negotiations would minimize delay without in any way affecting the Company's right to bargain separately for each unit. Instead, the Company insisted on wasteful, duplicative sessions with respect to each unit, which necessitated repetitious discussion of identical terms and unnecessarily prolonged the bargaining process. From this evidence, the Board was entitled to infer that the Company's objective was to delay and frustrate the bargaining process.

Another example of the Company's bad faith is found in the terms of its wage-increase proposals, which were less than the increases given to its employees the previous year and which made no provision for retroactivity. Furthermore, the Company proposed in effect to bargain individually with respect to each separate employee by granting increases in such amounts and at such times as it deemed appropriate for the employee. Hand in hand with these foot-dragging proposals, the Company sought to undermine the Union's position as the bargaining representative of the employees by continually refusing the Union's proposal that it put into effect the Company's suggested increases without prejudice to further bargaining on the subject, following which the Company put the increases into effect with an announcement to the employees blaming the Union for the delay.

The Board's application for enforcement of its order is granted and the Company's petition for review is denied.

CASE QUESTIONS

1. When did the duty to bargain with the union arise?
2. Continental did negotiate with the union, didn't it? How did it commit an unfair labor practice?
3. What is the policy behind forcing an employer to bargain collectively with employees?

SUGGESTED READINGS

Magruder, *A Half-Century of Legal Influence upon the Development of Collective Bargaining*, 50 HARV. L. REV. 1071 (1937).

H. MILLIS AND E. BROWN, FROM THE WAGNER ACT TO TAFT–HARTLEY (1950).

M.D. FORKOSCH, A TREATISE ON LABOR LAW, §§ 285–290 (2d ed. 1965).

Twomey, *Health Care Institutions under the National Labor Relations Act*, 15 AM. BUS. L.J. 225 (1977).

Marshall, *The Future of the American Labor Movement: The Role of Federal Law*, 57 CHI.-KENT. L. REV. 521 (1981).

Modjeska, *Decisions of the Supreme Court, 1979–80—Labor Relations and Employment Discrimination Law*, 4 INDUS. REL. L.J. 1 (1980).

Truesdale, *Recent Trends at the NLRB and in the Courts*, 32 LAB. L.J. 131 (1981).

Equal Employment Opportunity

The Civil Rights act of 1964, also known as Title VII, was passed by Congress to eliminate discrimination in employment, where such discrimination is based on race, color, national origin, sex, or religion. These out-lawed areas of discrimination are called *protected classes*. These protected classes are not all equally broad in scope. What may constitute illegal racial discrimination may not constitute illegal sex discrimination. Although an employer may not justify discrimination based on race or color for any reason, an employer *may* discriminate for or against someone on the basis of that person's national origin, sex, or religion, if the par-ticular protected class is a *bona fide occupational qualification (bfoq)* for the job. Examples of bfoq's are actors and actresses, French chefs for French restaurants, and Lutheran ministers for Lutheran churches.

Religion differs from the other classes in other ways as well. An employer need only make a reasonable accommodation to an employee's religious needs. For example, an employer must give an employee days off to observe religious holidays if the employee can reasonably make the time up without unfairly affecting other employees' work schedules.

In any case of discrimination, the aggrieved person must establish a *prima facie* case of discrimination. An employer discriminates illegally in one of two ways. The employer may deliberately intend to discriminate against an employee or prospective employee. This kind of discrimination is called *disparate-treatment discrimination*, since an employer treats dif-ferent groups of employees differently. For example, in the past, many companies refused to consider blacks for all but the lower-skilled and lower-paying jobs. Classified want ads often separated jobs on racial and sexual lines. This sort of intentional discrimination was instantly out-lawed by Title VII, and such discrimination has been almost completely eradicated. Proof that an employer intentionally discriminated against an employee or prospective employee constitutes a case of discrimination.

However, more subtle forms of discrimination also exist: The em-ployer's intention to discriminate may be hidden behind an ostensibly neutral reason. Or an intent to discriminate may not exist at all, but a company's employment practices unnecessarily discriminate in fact. This kind of discrimination is called *disparate-impact discrimination*, since only the *impact* of an employer's discriminatory practices are examined, without regard to motive or intent. In order to eliminate this kind of discrimination, the victim of discrimination may show that an employer's work force does not reasonably match the relevant work force of the surrounding area. Under the disparate-impact theory, policies or practices that discriminate—even if apparently neutral—are subject to close scrutiny and evaluation. Companies may be forced to examine their discriminatory practices and either justify them by showing that the com-pany had no choice but to act as it did, or change its practices so that discrimination does not occur.

A victim of discrimination is entitled to receive back pay (what the vic-tim would have earned if hired or promoted at the appropriate time, minus actual earnings) and attorney's fees. The victim may also be hired, reinstated, promoted, or given advanced seniority, as appropriate.

Albemarle Paper Co. v. Moody
422 U.S. 405
United States Supreme Court
June 25, 1975

MR. JUSTICE STEWART

These consolidated cases raise two important questions under Title VII of the Civil Rights act of 1964. First: When employees or applicants for employment have lost the opportunity to earn wages because an employer has engaged in an unlawful discriminatory employment practice, what standards should a federal district court follow in deciding whether to award or deny back pay? Second: What must an employer show to establish that pre-employment tests that are racially discriminatory in effect, though not in intent, are sufficiently "job-related" to survive challenge under Title VII?

The respondents—plaintiffs in the district court—are a certified class of present and former Negro employees at a paper mill in Roanoke Rapids, North Carolina: the petitioners—defendants in the district court—are the plant's owner, the Albemarle Paper Co., and the plant employees' labor union. The respondents brought a class action asking permanent injunctive relief against "any policy, practice, custom, or usage" at the plant that violated Title VII, and a demand for back pay.

The major issues were the plant's seniority system, its program of employment testing, and the question of back pay. The court found that the peti-

tioners had "strictly segregated" the plant's departmental "lines of progression" prior to January 1, 1964, reserving the higher-paying and more skilled lines for whites. The "racial identifiability" of whole lines of progression persisted until 1968, when the lines were reorganized under a new collective-bargaining agreement. The court found, however, that this reorganization left Negro employees "'locked' in the lower-paying job classifications." The formerly "Negro" lines of progression had been merely tacked on to the bottom of the formerly "white" lines, and promotions, demotions, and layoffs continued to be governed—where skills were "relatively equal"—by a system of "job seniority." Because of the plant's previous history of overt segregation, only whites had seniority in the higher job categories. Accordingly, the court ordered the petitioners to implement a system of "plant-wide" seniority.

The court refused, however, to award back pay to the plaintiff class for losses suffered under the job seniority program. The court explained: "In the instant case there was no evidence of bad-faith noncompliance with the act."

The court also refused to enjoin or limit Albemarle's testing program. Albemarle had required applicants for employment in the skilled lines of progression to have a high school diploma and to pass two tests, the Revised Beta Examination, allegedly a measure of nonverbal intelligence, and the Wonderlic Personnel Test (available in alternative Forms A and B), allegedly a measure of verbal facility. After this Court's decision in *Griggs v. Duke Power Co.*, 401 U.S. 424 (1971), Albemarle engaged an industrial psychologist to study the job-relatedness of its testing program. His study compared the test scores of current employees with supervisorial judgments of their competence in ten job groupings selected from the middle or top of the plant's skilled lines of progression. The study showed a statistically significant correlation with supervisorial ratings in three job groupings for the Beta Test, in seven job groupings for either Form A or Form B of the Wonderlic Test, and in two job groupings for the required battery of both the Beta and the Wonderlic Tests. The respondents' experts challenged the reliability of these studies, but the court concluded: "The personnel tests administered at the plant have undergone validation studies and have been proved to be job-related. The defendants have carried the burden of proof in proving that these tests are 'necessary for the safe and efficient operation of the business' and are, therefore, permitted by the act. However, the high-school-education requirement used in conjunction with the testing requirements is unlawful in that the personnel tests alone are adequate to measure the mental ability and reading skills required for the job classifications."

The petitioners did not seek review of the court's judgment, but the respondents appealed the denial of a back-pay award and the refusal to enjoin or limit

Albemarle's use of pre-employment tests. A divided court of appeals for the fourth circuit reversed the judgment of the district court, ruling that back pay should have been awarded and that use of the tests should have been enjoined, 474 F.2d 134 (1973). As for back pay, the court of appeals held that an award could not be denied merely because the employer had not acted in "bad faith."

As for the pre-employment tests, the court of appeals held that it was error "to approve a validation study done without job analysis, to allow Albemarle to require tests for six lines of progression where there has been no validation study at all, and to allow Albemarle to require a person to pass two tests for entrance into seven lines of progression when only one of those tests was validated for that line of progression."

We granted *certiorari* because of an evident circuit conflict as to the standards governing awards of back pay and as to the showing required to establish the job-relatedness of pre-employment tests.

The district court's decision must be measured against the purposes which inform Title VII. As the Court observed in *Griggs v. Duke Power Co.*, 401 U.S., at 429–430, the primary objective was a prophylactic one: "It was to achieve equality of employment opportunities and remove barriers that have operated in the past to favor an identifiable group of white employees over other employees." Back pay has an obvious connection with this purpose. If employers faced only the prospect of an injunctive order, they would have little incentive to shun practices of dubious legality. It is the reasonably certain prospect of a back pay award that provides the spur or catalyst which causes employers and unions to self-examine and to self-evaluate their employment practices and to endeavor to eliminate, so far as possible, the last vestiges of an unfortunate and ignominious page in this country's history.

It is also the purpose of Title VII to make persons whole for injuries suffered on account of unlawful employment discrimination. And where a legal injury is of an economic character, the general rule is that when a wrong has been done and the law gives a remedy, the compensation shall be equal to the injury. The latter is the standard by which the former is to be measured. The injured party is to be placed, as near as may be, in the situation he would have occupied if the wrong had not been committed.

It follows that, given a finding of unlawful discrimination, back pay should be denied only for reasons which, if applied generally, would not frustrate the central statutory purposes of eradicating discrimination throughout the economy and making persons whole for injuries suffered through past discrimination.

The district court's stated grounds for denying back pay in this case must be tested against these standards. The first ground was that Albemarle's breach of Title VII had not been in bad faith. This is not a sufficient reason for denying back pay. Where an employer *has* shown bad faith—he can make no claims whatsoever on the chancellor's conscience. But, under Title VII, the mere absence of bad faith simply opens the door to equity. It does not depress the scales in the employer's favor. If back pay were awardable only upon a showing of bad faith, the remedy would become a punishment for moral turpitude, rather than a compensation for workers' injuries. This would read the "make whole" purpose right out of Title VII, for a worker's injury is no less real simply because his employer did not inflict it in bad faith. Title VII is not concerned with the employer's "good intent or absence of discriminatory intent" for "Congress directed the thrust of the act to the *consequences* of employment practices, not simply the motivation." *Griggs v. Duke Power Co.*, 401 U.S., at 432.

In *Griggs v. Duke Power Co.*, 401 U.S. 424, this Court unanimously held that Title VII forbids the use of employment tests that are discriminatory in effect unless the employer meets "the burden of showing that any given requirement (has) . . . a manifest relationship to the employment in question." This burden arises, of course, only after the complaining party or class has made out a *prima facie* case of discrimination, that is, has shown that the tests in question select applicants for hire or promotion in a racial pattern significantly different from that of the pool of applicants. If an employer does then meet the burden of proving that its tests are job related, it remains open to the complaining party to show that other tests or selection devices, without a similarly undesirable racial effect, would also serve the employer's legitimate interest in "efficient and trustworthy workmanship." Such a showing would be evidence that the employer was using its tests merely as a "pretext" for discrimination. In the present case, however, we are concerned only with the question whether Albemarle has shown its tests to be job-related.

The concept of job-relatedness takes on meaning from the facts of the *Griggs* case. A power company in North Carolina had reserved its skilled jobs for whites prior to 1965. Thereafter, the company allowed Negro workers to transfer to skilled jobs, but all transferees—white and Negro—were required to attain national median scores on two tests. "Neither was directed or intended to measure the ability to learn to perform a particular job or category of jobs. Both were adopted without meaningful study of their relationship to job-performance ability. Rather, a vice president of the company testified, the requirements were instituted on the company's judgment that they generally would improve the overall quality of the work force." The Court took note of "the inadequacy of broad and general testing devices as well as the infirmity of using diplomas or degrees as fixed measures of capability," and concluded: "Nothing in the act precludes the use of testing or measuring procedures; obviously they are useful. What Congress has forbidden is giving these devices and mechanisms controlling force unless they are demonstrably a reasonable measure of job performance. . . . What Congress has commanded is that any tests used must measure the person for the job and not the person in the abstract."

The EEOC has issued guidelines for employers seeking to determine, through professional validation studies, whether their employment tests are job-related.

The message of these guidelines is the same as that of the *Griggs* case—that discriminatory tests are impermissible unless shown, by professionally acceptable methods, to be "predictive of or significantly correlated with important elements of work behavior which comprise or are relevant to the job or jobs for which candidates are being evaluated."

Measured against the guidelines, Albemarle's validation study is materially defective in several respects:

(1) Even if it had been otherwise adequate, the study would not have validated the Beta and Wonderlic test battery for all the skilled lines of progression for which the two tests are, apparently, now required. The study showed significant correlations for the Beta Exam in only three of the eight lines. Though the Wonderlic Test's Form A and Form B are in theory identical and interchangeable measures of verbal facility, significant correlations for one form but not for the other were obtained in four job groupings. In two job groupings, neither form showed a significant correlation. Within some of the lines of progression, one form was found acceptable for some job groupings but not for others. Even if the study were otherwise reliable, this odd patchwork of results would not entitle Albemarle to impose its testing program under the guidelines.

(2) The study compared test scores with subjective supervisorial rankings. While they allow the use of supervisorial rankings in test validation, the

guidelines quite plainly contemplate that the rankings will be elicited with far more care than was demonstrated here. Albemarle's supervisors were asked to rank employees by a standard that was extremely vague and fatally open to divergent interpretations. There is no way of knowing precisely what criteria of job performance the supervisors were considering, whether each of the supervisors was considering the same criteria, or whether, indeed, any of the supervisors actually applied a focused and stable body of criteria of any kind. There is, in short, simply no way to determine whether the criteria *actually* considered were sufficiently related to the company's legitimate interest in job-specific ability to justify a testing system with a racially discriminatory impact.

(3) The company's study focused, in most cases, on job groups near the top of the various lines of progression. The fact that the best of those employees working near the top of a line of progression score well on a test does not necessarily mean that that test, or some particular cutoff score on the test, is a permissible measure of the minimal qualifications of new workers entering lower-level jobs. The issues take on special importance in a case such as this one, where incumbent employees are permitted to work at even high-level jobs without passsing the company's test battery.

(4) Albemarle's validation study dealt only with job-experienced, white workers; but the tests themselves are given to new job applicants, who are younger, largely inexperienced, and in many instances nonwhite. The Standards of the American Psychological Association state that it is "essential" that "the validity of a test should be determined on subjects who are at the age or in the same educational or vocational situation as the persons for whom the test is recommended in practice."

For all these reasons, we agree with the court of appeals that the district court erred in concluding that Albemarle had proved the job-relatedness of its testing program and that the respondents were consequently not entitled to equitable relief.

Accordingly, the judgment is vacated, and these cases are remanded to the district court for proceedings consistent with this opinion.

It is so ordered.

CASE QUESTIONS

1. Under what conditions may an employer continue to use employment tests?
2. Why is the requirement of a high school diploma not allowed to be used to screen applicants?
3. What does the Court say were the objectives of Congress in granting back pay to victims of discrimination?

Suggested Readings

Finkle, *Voluntary Affirmative Action Under Title VII: Standards of Permissibility*, 28 U.C.L.A. L. Rev. 291 (1980).
Note, *Employment Discrimination—Plaintiff's Prima Facie Case and Rebuttal in Disparate Impact Case*, 54 Tul. L. Rev. 1187 (1980).
Note, *Teamsters and Seniority Systems*, 42 Albany L. Rev. 279 (1978).
Schatzki, *United Steel Workers of America v. Weber: An Exercise in Understandable Indecision*, 56 Wash. L. Rev. 51 (1980).

An employer charged with discrimination may state that no illegal discrimination occurred, either because the company applied its neutral policies in a nondiscriminatory fashion that simply adversely affected the aggrieved person, or because the employer simply was not interested in hiring or promoting a particular individual, regardless of that person's race, color, national origin, sex, or religion.

Employers may use other explanations for discriminatory practices. The differences among the protected classes become important. Very few employer justifications can adequately explain racial discrimination, although if the company has instituted a reasonable affirmative-action program, the courts often leave that employer alone. However, the bfoq defense is used extensively in sex-discrimination cases. For example, airlines tried without success to justify their policies of hiring only females for flight attendants by stating that females are better suited for the job. Justifications based on stereotyped classifications of men and women are rarely considered valid.

Other laws may cloud sex-discrimination issues even further. Many states enacted "protective" laws treating women more favorably than men. For example, they required that women have frequent rest breaks, or they excluded women from jobs involving the lifting of heavy objects. Where such laws conflict with the Civil Rights act, they are invalidated, partly because they often prevent women from being considered for many jobs, and partly because employers use such laws to justify paying women less than men for similar jobs. Provisions in union contracts that discriminate are also struck down where they conflict with the act.

The Civil Rights act of 1964 also created the Equal Employment Opportunity Commission (EEOC). This agency handles all disputes under Title VII. Aggrieved persons must report their problems to the EEOC and must usually wait six months before they can directly sue an employer. The EEOC may help arbitrate a conciliatory agreement between employer and employee. It may also find that the employer illegally discriminated against an employee. Any decision by the EEOC may be contested and tried in a U.S. district court *de novo*. This means that the action is tried without regard to the EEOC's findings of discrimination or lack of it. The EEOC is also empowered to investigate employment situations on its own, to issue extensive guidelines for employment practices, and to require affirmative-action programs to be implemented. Generally, affirmative-action programs mandate preferential treatment for recruitment of minorities and women, and training programs for the disadvantaged. However, mandatory quota systems are considered to constitute illegal *reverse discrimination*.

In the past, two major civil-rights acts were passed to alleviate discrimination: the Civil Rights act of 1866 and the Civil Rights act of 1871. These concern racial discrimination only; they are still used today.

Other acts also protect people from unfair discrimination. One is the Equal Pay act of 1963, which specifically relates to the issue of equal pay for equal work without regard to gender. Another is the Age Discrimination in Employment act of 1967, which protects persons between the ages of 40 and 70 from employment discrimination based on age. Another is the Rehabilitation act of 1973, which protects handicapped people from discrimination when large government contracts are involved. In addition, many acts have been passed to protect Native Americans, some of which entitle them to preferential treatment for employment on or near a reservation.

Beyond these acts, constitutional requirements of equal protection and the right to privacy have supported actions against discrimination in employment. The right to privacy is often used by homosexuals to avoid unfair discrimination against them. The states have enacted their own antidiscrimination laws as well.

Chatman v. United States Steel Corp.
425 F. Supp. 753
United States District Court, N. D. California
January 24, 1977

RENFREW, DISTRICT JUDGE
This is an action for employment discrimination brought by Richard C. Chatman (Chatman) a black employee at United States Steel Corporation's Pittsburg Works, located in Pittsburg, California. Defendants are United States Steel Corporation (U.S. Steel, or Company) and United Steelworkers of America, AFL–CIO, and its Local 1440 (Union).

Plaintiff alleges violations of Title VII of the Civil Rights Act of 1964. He seeks broad-based systemic declaratory and injunctive relief as well as back pay, punitive damages, attorneys' fees, and costs.

Asserting that plaintiff's claims "are founded on garden-variety grievances having nothing to do with race," defendants moved for summary judgment on September 9, 1976. In essence, defendants argue that all of the allegedly discriminatory acts complained of by Chatman resulted from the application of neutral rules and regulations equally applicable to employees of other races.

In his complaint of June 16, 1975, Chatman alleges that he was discriminated against because of his race on a number of occasions. Chatman first claims to have been discriminated against on the basis of race on June 22, 1973, when he was assigned two or three graveyard shifts in a row.

Defendants contend that this incident resulted from the application of a neutral policy in force throughout the plant. In support, defendants offer the affidavit of Personnel Superintendent Robert A. Benson who states that Chatman was assigned to the first of two successive graveyard shifts as part of his normal shift rotation. On the date in question, Chatman was employed as a "piler," a job which is one step below that of basement attendant on the relevant line of progression. When an employee with greater seniority than Chatman returned from vacation, he displaced the least senior basement attendant, who in turn displaced Chatman, the least senior piler. Chatman was consequently "bumped back" to the position of tractor operator on a crew which had just rotated onto the graveyard shift.

The rule that a returning employee at one job level displaces the least senior employee at the level immediately below is employed throughout U.S. Steel's Pittsburg Works to minimize the number of displacements required in a move-down situation. According to affiant Benson, this policy, which occasionally results in successive assign-

ments to the same shift, is applied evenhandedly to all employees regardless of race.

In opposition to defendants' motion for summary judgment, plaintiff has produced no fact tending to controvert the explanation contained in the Benson affidavit.

Chatman claims to have been discriminated against on the basis of race when bids posted on October 9, 1974, for vacancies to be filled at a later date were canceled after the bidding.

According to Robert Benson's affidavit of September 8, 1976, bids for two of the positions were canceled because the vacancies no longer existed. Ten nonblack bidders were also adversely affected by the cancellation. Moreover, the bids would doubtless have been awarded to some among the many bidders with earlier plant continuous-service dates than Chatman, had they not been canceled. None of these facts has been controverted by plaintiff, hence no disputed issue remains for trial.

Chatman claims to have been discriminated against on the basis of race in November 1974, when he bid for the position of attendant at the nine-crew level. Although he was posted as having received the bid, the plant failed to go to the nine-crew level of operation, and the bid was voided.

According to facts contained in Robert Benson's affidavit and nowhere contradicted by plaintiff, the nine-crew level was never reached because of adverse economic conditions. Consequently, all successful bidders at the nine-crew level had their bids voided, in conformance with established plant procedure. As plaintiff Chatman conceded in deposition testimony, employees of all races were affected by the cancellation.

Chatman claims to have been discriminated against on the basis of race because, in November 1974, he was not permitted to move to temporary openings on another line. At that time, Chatman was working as a piler on number 3 line, and the number 3 line was shearing.

According to affiant Benson, Chatman was not permitted to move up to temporary openings on other lines for one reason. Under established move-up policy in force throughout the Ferrostan Department, the piler assigned to the number 3 line must perform the piling function if the number 3 line is shearing, as it was on the dates in question. This policy resulted from a Company–Union agreement worked out in 1968 and subsequently updated in 1972. According to information contained in the Benson affidavit, pilers of all races have lost move-ups due to its application. Plaintiff Chatman has produced nothing in opposition to defendant's motion suggesting that, on the dates in question, move-ups were denied him because of his race, rather than his position.

Chatman claims to have been discriminated against on the basis of race because he was given a safety violation warning on November 12, 1974. That Chatman committed the safety violation is not itself in dispute. In deposition testimony, Chatman admitted that he failed to wear his hard hat and wristlets on the date in question. Moreover, Chatman conceded that he had no reason to believe he had received more safety warnings than employees of other races.

According to information contained in Robert Benson's affidavit and nowhere contradicted by plaintiff, safety warnings are issued on a nondiscriminatory basis to all employees who commit infractions. Company records show that during 1974, blacks employed in Chatman's own seniority unit received safety citations with approximately the same statistical frequency as white and Spanish-surnamed employees. The court finds no indication that Chatman received a citation on November 12, 1974, because of his race.

Chatman claims to have been discriminated against on the basis of race on November 29, 1974, when a vacancy sought by Chatman was not put up for bid. In this instance, Harrison, a finisher on Chatman's crew, felt ill and went on sick leave following a vacation.

According to affiant Benson, the entire crew moved up according to seniority level on this occasion, each vacancy being filled by the most senior employee in the position immediately below. Thus, although the Harrison vacancy was not put up for bid, each employee progressed upward in the promotional sequence according to plant continuous service date, as was proper in such a situation. Company records show that on this occasion, Chatman actually moved up to the position to which he claims he was entitled, namely that of electrolytic attendant.

Chatman claims to have been discriminated against on the basis of race because of the manner in which incentive rates were applied to him in January 1975, when he was working as a tractor driver. Instead of separately evaluating the performance of each individual driver for purposes of determining whether incentive pay was merited, the performance of all drivers was evaluated together.

According to affidavits submitted by defendants, all tractor drivers were treated in the manner described by Chatman regardless of racial background. Chatman himself admitted as much in deposition testimony. The basis upon which Chatman rests his claim of race discrimination is, in this instance, obscure.

Chatman claims to have been discriminated against on the basis of race in February 1975, when he was paid as a laborer although scheduled as a tractor/laborer. According to defendants' affidavits, tractor/laborers do not always perform tractor service and are paid according to the work actually performed. In this instance, company records show that Chatman in fact worked and was paid as a tractor operator. Chatman stated that he didn't know what wage he had received. In sum, no evidence has been adduced which tends to show that Chatman received a lower wage on this occasion than that to which he was entitled.

Chatman claims to have been discriminated against on the basis of race on February 22, 1975, when an operator on his line was at the doctor's and the entire crew worked short-handed, instead of each employee moving up along the promotional ladder temporarily. Clearly, all employees in Chat-man's crew, whatever their race, were adversely affected by the foreman's decision to work short-handed. Moreover, affiant Benson testified that the foreman could not have required the crew to work short-handed without the concurrence of all affected employees.

With respect to each of his numerous allegations, the Court concludes that Chatman has failed to demonstrate a causal nexus between his race and the treatment he received from defendants. In order to state an actionable claim of discrimination, it is essential that plaintiff show that he has been treated differently than other employees because of his race. If he has been treated no differently than employees of other races, however unfair he regards the treatment and whatever claim he might have under a collective bargaining agreement, he has no claim of discrimination.

In support of their motion for summary judgment, defendants have produced affidavit testimony demonstrating that in each instance cited by Chatman, the treatment received resulted from an evenhanded application of neutral principles applicable to all employees regardless of race. Chatman has failed to rebut the material facts contained in defendants' affidavits. Inasmuch as no material issue remains in dispute, the Court concludes that summary judgment is an entirely appropriate vehicle for disposing of Chatman's claims at this juncture.

CASE QUESTIONS

1. Mr. Chatman was a member of a minority race and was denied a series of privileges. Isn't this a discriminatory effect?

2. What if all pilers were black and the policy preventing moving up to temporary openings forced them to stay at their present position? Would Chatman have an action against U.S. Steel? Would he have an action against the union for agreeing to the move-up policy?
3. Could Chatman have attacked the seniority system as perpetuating past discriminatory practices?

SUGGESTED READINGS

B.L. SCHLEI AND P. GROSSMAN, EMPLOYMENT DISCRIMINATION LAW, Chaps. 3, 17 (1976).
Note, 28 OKLA. L. REV. 109 (1975).
Note, 1975 WIS. L. REV. 791 (1975).
Rains, *Title VII v. Seniority Based Layoffs: A Question of Who Goes First*, 4 HOFSTRA L. REV. 49 (1975).
Craft, *Equal Opportunity and Seniority: Trends and Manpower Implications*, 26 LAB. L.J. 750 (1975).

Occupational Safety and Health

Because the common law provided an employee injured on the job with little recourse against an employer (due to the availability of the assumption of the risk and contributory-negligence defenses and the fellow-servant doctrine to the employer), there was little incentive for employers to try to reduce employment-related injuries. As manufacturing processes became more complex, the number of industrial injuries increased. Eventually, industrial accidents were resulting in more than 14,000 deaths and two million disabling injuries a year. Also, it has been estimated that a new potentially toxic chemical is introduced into industry every 20 minutes.

Today, state workers' compensation laws have modified the common law and enable the injured employee to recover. Unfortunately, these laws only compensate the injured employee and have failed to substantially reduce the number of injuries. State legislatures were reluctant, despite the severity of the problem, to pass stringent safety regulations, fearing that industry would relocate in other states that did not impose such safety regulations. Congress recognized the need for federal regulation. Through the exercise of its power to regulate interstate commerce, it passed the Occupational Safety and Health act in 1970 to provide safe and healthful working conditions for all employees.

The act established the National Institute of Occupational Safety and

Health to conduct research in the area of employee health and safety. The Occupational Safety and Health Administration (OSHA) was also created to set and enforce standards under the act.

An employee who suspects that there is a safety violation at a place of work can contact the local OSHA office. An OSHA inspector makes an unannounced inspection during reasonable hours and issues appropriate citations. Citations may be civil or criminal. OSHA may impose civil fines up to $10,000 for each willful and repeated violation, $1000 for less serious violations, and $1000 for each day a violation goes uncorrected. An employer may contest the citation at a hearing before an administrative law judge. The administrative law judge's decision is appealable to the Occupational Safety and Health Review Commission, whose decision is appealable to the U.S. court of appeals.

Criminal sanctions provided are fines up to $10,000 and imprisonment for six months for willful violations of standards resulting in the death of an employee, or for knowingly falsifying documents required to be kept. These sanctions may be doubled for repeat offenses. Criminal cases are tried in federal court. As yet, OSHA has pursued criminal sanctions in only four cases.

In addition to civil and criminal sanctions, injunctions may be issued to stop dangerous working conditions from continuing.

OSHA was the first major piece of legislation designed to prevent injuries of employees and to ensure safe and healthful working conditions. Although the necessity for legislation such as OSHA is clear, the agency has been the subject of great criticism. It has been argued that OSHA has focused on issuing large numbers of safety regulations, many of which are unnecessary, wasteful, and difficult to comply with, while at the same time ignoring more serious safety hazards and nearly all health hazards. OSHA is presently trying to reverse this situation.

Whirlpool Corp. v. Marshall
445 U.S. 1
United States Supreme Court
February 26, 1980

JUSTICE STEWART

The Occupational Safety and Health Act of 1970 (Act) prohibits an employer from discharging or discriminating against any employee who exercises ''any right afforded by'' the Act. The Secretary of Labor (Secretary) has prom- ulgated a regulation providing that, among the rights that the Act so protects, is the right of an employee to choose not to perform his assigned task because of a reasonable apprehension of death or serious injury, coupled with a reasonable belief that no less drastic alternative is available. The question presented in the case before us is whether this regulation is consistent with the Act.

The petitioner company maintains a

manufacturing plant in Marion, Ohio, for the production of household appliances. Overhead conveyors transport appliance components throughout the plant. To protect employees from objects that occasionally fall from these conveyors, the petitioner has installed a horizontal wire mesh guard screen approximately 20 feet above the plant floor. This mesh screen is welded to angle-iron frames suspended from the building's structural-steel skeleton.

Maintenance employees of the petitioner spend several hours each week removing objects from the screen, replacing paper spread on the screen to catch grease drippings from the material on the conveyors, and performing occasional maintenance work on the conveyors themselves. To perform these duties, maintenance employees usually are able to stand on the iron frames, but sometimes find it necessary to step onto the steel mesh screen itself. In 1973 the company began to install heavier wire in the screen because its safety had been drawn into question.

On June 28, 1974, a maintenance employee fell to his death through the guard screen in an area where the newer, stronger mesh had not yet been installed. Following this incident, the petitioner effectuated some repairs and issued an order strictly forbidding maintenance employees from stepping on either the screens or the angle-iron supporting structure. An alternative but somewhat more cumbersome and less satisfactory method was developed for removing objects from the screen. This procedure required employees to stand on power-raised mobile platforms and use hooks to recover the material.

On July 7, 1974, two of the peti-tioner's maintenance employees, Virgil Deemer and Thomas Cornwell, met with the plant maintenance superintendent to voice their concern about the safety of the screen. The superintendent disagreed with their view, but permitted the two men to inspect the screen with their foreman and to point out dangerous areas needing repair. Unsatisfied with the petitioner's response to the results of this inspection, Deemer and Cornwell met on July 9 with the plant safety director. At that meeting, they requested the name, address, and telephone number of a representative of the local office of the Occupational Safety and Health Administration (OSHA). The safety director furnished the men with the information they requested.

The next day, Deemer and Cornwell reported for the night shift at 10:45 P.M. Their foreman, after himself walking on some of the angle-iron frames, directed the two men to perform their usual maintenance duties on a section of the old screen. Claiming that the screen was unsafe, they refused to carry out this directive. The foreman then sent them to the personnel office, where they were ordered to punch out without working or being paid for the remaining six hours of the shift. The two men subsequently received written reprimands, which were placed in their employment files.

A little over a month later, the Secretary of Labor filed suit in the U.S. district court alleging that the petitioner's actions against Deemer and Cornwell constituted discrimination in violation of § 11(c)(1) of the Act.

The district court found that the regulation in question justified Deemer's and Cornwell's refusals to obey their foreman's order on July 10, 1974. The district court nevertheless denied relief, holding that the Secretary's regulation was inconsistent with the Act and therefore invalid.

The Court of Appeals for the Sixth Circuit reversed the district court's judgment. Finding ample support in the record for the district court's factual determination that the actions of Deemer and Cornwell had been justified under the Secretary's regulation, the appellate court disagreed with the district court's conclusion that the regulation is invalid because the decision of the court of appeals in this case conflicts with those of two other courts of appeals on the important question in issue. That question, as stated at the outset of this opinion, is whether the Secretary's regulation authorizing employee "self-help" in some circumstances, 29 CFR § 1977.12(b)(2), is permissible under the Act.

The Act itself creates an express mechanism for protecting workers from employment conditions believed to pose an emergent threat of death or serious injury. Upon receipt of an employee inspection request stating reasonable grounds to believe that an imminent danger is present in a work place, OSHA must conduct an inspection. 29 U.S.C. § 657(f)(1). In the event this inspection reveals work-place conditions or practices that "could reasonably be expected to cause death or serious physical harm immediately or before the imminence of such danger can be eliminated through the enforcement procedures otherwise provided by" the Act, 29 U.S.C. § 662(a), the OSHA inspector must inform the af-

fected employees and the employer of the danger and notify them that he is recommending to the Secretary that injunctive relief be sought. 29 U.S.C. § 662(c). At this juncture, the Secretary can petition a federal court to restrain the conditions or practices giving rise to the imminent danger. By means of a temporary restraining order or preliminary injunction, the court may then require the employer to avoid, correct, or remove the danger or to prohibit employees from working in the area. 29 U.S.C. § 662(a).

To ensure that this process functions effectively, the Act expressly accords to every employee several rights, the exercise of which may not subject him to discharge or discrimination. An employee is given the right to inform OSHA of an imminently dangerous work-place condition or practice and request that OSHA inspect that condition or practice. 29 U.S.C. § 657(f)(1). He is given a limited right to assist the OSHA inspector in inspecting the work place, 29 U.S.C. §§ 657(a)(2), (e) and (f)(2), and the right to aid a court in determining whether or not a risk of imminent danger in fact exists. See 29 U.S.C. § 660(c)(1). Finally, an affected employee is given the right to bring an action to compel the Secretary to seek injunctive relief if he believes the Secretary has wrongfully declined to do so. 29 U.S.C. § 662(d).

In the light of this detailed statutory scheme, the Secretary is obviously correct when he acknowledges in his regulation that "as a general matter, there is no right afforded by the Act which would entitle employees to walk off the job because of potential unsafe conditions at the work place."

As this case illustrates, however, circumstances may sometimes exist in which the employee justifiably believes that the express statutory arrangement does not sufficiently protect him from death or serious injury. Such circumstances will probably not often occur, but such a situation may arise when (1) the employee is ordered by his employer to work under conditions that the employee reasonably believes pose an imminent risk of death or serious bodily injury, and (2) the employee has reason to believe that there is not sufficient time or opportunity either to seek effective redress from his employer or to apprise OSHA of the danger.

Nothing in the Act suggests that those few employees who have to face this dilemma must rely exclusively on the remedies expressly set forth in the Act at the risk of their own safety. But nothing in the Act explicitly provides otherwise. Against this background of legislative silence, the Secretary has exercised his rule-making power under 29 U.S.C. § 657(g)(2) and has determined that, when an employee in good faith finds himself in such a predicament, he may refuse to expose himself to the dangerous condition without being subjected to "subsequent discrimination" by the employer.

Our inquiry is informed by an awareness that the regulation is entitled to deference unless it can be said not to be a reasoned and supportable interpretation of the Act.

The regulation clearly conforms to the fundamental objective of the Act— to prevent occupational deaths and serious injuries. The Act, in its preamble, declares that its purpose and policy is "to assure so far as possible every working man and woman in the nation safe and healthful working conditions and to *preserve* our human resources . . ." 29 U.S.C. § 651(b).

To accomplish this basic purpose, the legislation's remedial orientation is prophylactic in nature. The Act does not wait for an employee to die or become injured. It authorizes the promulgation of health and safety standards and the issuance of citations in the hope that these will act to prevent deaths or injuries from ever occurring. It would seem anomalous to construe an act so directed and constructed as prohibiting an employee, with no other reasonable alternative, the freedom to withdraw from a work-place environment that he reasonably believes is highly dangerous.

Moreover, the Secretary's regulation can be viewed as an appropriate aid to the full effectuation of the Act's general-duty clause. That clause provides that "each employer . . . shall furnish to each of his employees employment and a place of employment which are free from recognized hazards that are causing or are likely to cause death or serious harm to his employees." 29 U.S.C. § 654(a)(1). As the legislative history of this provision reflects, it was intended itself to deter the occurrence of occupational deaths and serious injuries by placing on employers a mandatory obligation independent of the specific health and safety standards to be promulgated by the Secretary. Since OSHA inspectors cannot be present around the clock in every work place, the Secretary's regulation ensures that employees will in all circumstances enjoy the rights afforded them by the general-duty clause.

For these reasons we conclude that 29 CFR § 1977.12(b)(2) was promulgated by the Secretary in the valid exercise of his authority under the Act.

Accordingly, the judgment of the court of appeals is affirmed.

It is so ordered.

CASE QUESTIONS

1. Why did the U.S. Supreme Court believe that the regulation was a reasoned and supportable interpretation of the Occupational Safety and Health Act?
2. Are there any constitutional problems that might arise because of a statute that authorizes surprise inspections of businesses?

SUGGESTED READINGS

29 U.S.C., §§ 651–678 (1970).
Steiger, *OSHA: Four Years Later*, 25 Lab. L.J. 723 (1974).
Metzenbaum, *Occupational Safety and Health Act: A Promise That Failed*, 8 Akron L. Rev. 416 (1975).
Miller, *Occupational Safety: Real Costs, Real Benefits*, 17 Trial 47 (1981).
Drapkin, *Right to Refuse Hazardous Work After Whirlpool*, 4 Indus. Rel. L.J. 29 (1980).

Consumer Legislation

The common law offered little recourse against the seller to the buyer of a shoddy product. The law assumed that both parties had equal bargaining abilities, reflected by the maxim, "let the buyer beware." As products became more complex, buyers became less able to protect their interests. Today, numerous state and federal agencies seek to ensure that consumers are not subjected to such business practices as unfair advertising or unsafe products. Consumer credit legislation is another area of consumer law that has developed in recent years because of the increase in credit transactions. Since few laws governed such transactions, Congress passed many acts to define the rights of consumer–debtors and business creditors.

Unfair Advertising Practices

The Federal Trade Commission act of 1914 established the Federal Trade Commission to enforce the existing antitrust laws. The 1938 amendments to the act proscribed all ''unfair or deceptive acts or practices in commerce.'' These amendments expanded the FTC's authority to protect consumers as well as businesses from unfair trade practices.

The major impact of the 1938 amendments for consumers has been in the area of deceptive advertising. An advertiser does not have to intentionally deceive nor does a consumer have to be deceived for the FTC to find a trade practice unfair. All the FTC must show is that the advertisement had the capacity or tendency to deceive. Examples of practices found to be unfair are ''bait and switch'' advertising, in which the public is ''baited'' to come to the store by an item advertised at a very low price, only to have the salesperson attempt to ''switch'' the customer's preference to another, higher-priced item—for example, by telling the customer that the first item is sold out. Other examples of unfair advertising are firms saying that a consumer has won a free gift, and firms misrepresenting the nature, performance, or composition of a product. Statements that are literally correct but nevertheless misleading are unfair. When a seller should make statements to indicate the nature of a product, silence may also be considered a deceptive advertising practice.

Anyone can ask the FTC to investigate a suspected unfair trade practice. If the FTC examiner finds a trade practice unfair, the guilty party is asked to discontinue it. Usually, consent orders to stop the offending advertising are agreed on between the examiner and the advertiser. If no agreement can be reached, the advertiser may challenge the examiner's decision at a hearing before an administrative law judge. If the administrative law judge finds a trade practice unfair, a cease-and-desist order is issued. The FTC may also order corrective advertising, such as requiring a mouthwash company to state that its product does not reduce the likelihood of catching colds. The rationale behind requiring corrective advertising is that former misleading advertising is believed to leave its mark after the advertising ceases, and corrective action is needed to dispel the former advertisements' misleading statements. These orders may be appealed to the FTC commissioners, whose decision can be appealed to the U.S. court of appeals. Failure to comply with an order or to file an appeal within the specified time may result in a civil penalty. The FTC may also order payment by the advertiser to consumers who were hurt by a violation.

In addition to investigating particular instances of unfair advertising, the FTC may issue industrywide orders against certain forms of advertising as well.

Resort Car Rental System v. FTC
518 F.2d 962
United States Court of Appeals
Ninth Circuit
April 14, 1975

PER CURIAM

Petitioners request a review of the Federal Trade Commission's cease-and-desist order of July 31, 1973. The FTC ordered petitioner to stop using the name "Dollar-A-Day." It is contended that the order was not supported by substantial evidence on the record and that it exceeded the scope of the Federal Trade Commission's authority to prescribe remedial measures.

We review the evidence to determine whether it was sufficient to reasonably support the commission's conclusions. The Federal Trade Commission's judgment is entitled to great deference here because deceptive advertising cases necessarily require "inference and pragmatic judgment."

Petitioners' challenge to the evidence is concentrated on hearsay questions regarding the testimony of two consumer witnesses and documents on which their testimony was partially based.

Detailed scrutiny of the hearsay problems raised is unnecessary here because substantial evidence exists even if the disputed testimony and documents are stricken from the record. The Federal Trade Commission has the expertise to determine whether advertisements have the capacity to deceive or mislead the public. Consumer testimony, although sometimes helpful, is not essential. The commission could have arrived at the same conclusions regarding the deceptive nature of petitioners' advertising without its consumer witnesses, whose testimony merely supported the inferences which can logically be drawn by scrutinizing the advertising alone. The "Dollar-A-Day" slogan carries strong psychological appeal. Its connotations are obvious. The design of the form contracts used by petitioners tended to continue the deception initiated by the slogan.

Contrary to petitioners' assertions, the public is not under any duty to make reasonable inquiry into the truth of advertising. The Federal Trade Act is violated if it induces the first contract through deception, even if the buyer later becomes fully informed before entering the contract. Advertising capable of being interpreted in a misleading way should be construed against the advertiser. Neither actual damage to the public nor actual deception need be shown.

Petitioners further complain that the commission's order exceeded its lawful authority to proscribe unlawful trade practices. They argue that excision of the trade name "Dollar-A-Day" destroyed the valuable good will vested in that slogan when less drastic means could have achieved the desired end.

The Federal Trade Commission has broad discretion to fashion orders appropriate to prevent unfair trade practices. That was not abused here. The order was reasonably related to its goals. As the order stated, "[t]he trade name, 'Dollar-A-Day' by its nature has a decisive connotation for which any qualifying language would result in a contradiction in terms."

Affirmed and ordered enforced.

CASE QUESTIONS

1. The FTC did not produce anyone who claimed to have been injured by defendants' name. Why did the FTC want the defendant to stop using it?
2. Are there any constitutional issues involved in trying to prevent deceptive advertising?

SUGGESTED READINGS

15 U.S.C., §§ 41, 44, 45, 52–58 (1970).

Thompson, *Government Regulation of Advertising: Killing the Consumer in Order to Save Him*, 8 ANTITRUST L. E. ECON. REV. 81 (1976).

Cornfeld, *A New Approach to an Old Remedy: Corrective Advertising and the Federal Trade Commission*, 61 IOWA L. REV. 693 (1976).

Reed, *Psychological Impact of TV Advertising and the Need for FTC Regulation*, 13 AM. BUS. L.J. 171 (1975).

Orlans, *FTC Regulation of OTC Drug and Cosmetics Advertising*, 36 F. D. COSM. L.J. 100 (1981).

Craswell, *Identification of Unfair Acts and Practices by the Federal Trade Commission*, 1981 WIS. L. REV. 107.

Unsafe Products

The National Commission on Product Safety found in 1970 that 20 million Americans are injured each year in incidents involving consumer products. Of these, 30,000 are killed, 110,000 are permanently disabled, and 2 million must take off at least one day of work. In 1972, because of these findings, which reflect a need for improved safety of products, the Consumer Product Safety Act was passed.

Other consumer-protection laws had previously been enacted by Congress to enhance the safety of particular products. One of the first effective consumer-safety laws was the Food, Drug and Cosmetic Act passed in 1938. The Food and Drug Administration was established to administer the provisions of this act. The FDA is empowered to conduct tests and issue regulations concerning the effects of food, drugs, and cosmetics. The FDA can prevent the sale of products that may prove harmful to consumers.

Since 1938, Congress has passed many statutes dealing with the safety of particular products, such as the Federal Hazardous Substances act, the Poison Prevention Packaging act, the Flammable Fabrics act, the Household Refrigerator Safety act, and the Child Protection and Toy Safety act.

These acts were enforced by either the Department of Health, Education and Welfare, the Commerce Department, or the Federal Trade Commission. The five acts were made a part of the Consumer Product Safety act, and are at present enforced under this act. The CPSA further protects consumers from unreasonable risk of injury or death caused by most other products around the house.

The CPSA has three major purposes: (1) to promote research and investigation into the causes and prevention of product-related deaths, illnesses, and injuries; (2) to help consumers evaluate the comparative safety of products; and (3) to develop uniform safety standards for consumer products and to minimize conflicts between state and local regulations. This act covers all products consumers are likely to use. Items excluded from the CPSA are motor vehicles, food, drugs, cosmetics, medical devices, aircraft, boats, poisons, tobacco, firearms, meat, poultry, and eggs. These items are controlled by other acts.

The Consumer Product Safety Commission, created by the CPSA, has the power to set industry-wide safety standards for any product under its control, to ban any product that does not meet minimum safety standards, to require labels (especially warning labels) to be placed on products, and to demand safety certifications. In addition, the CPSC requires extensive and detailed records to be kept by manufacturers and distributors of consumer products. Failure to keep records, to manufacture and distribute products properly, to replace or repair defective products or refund some or all of the purchase price, or to notify the commission of any information a company has that indicates a product may be defective, can incur civil and, in some cases, criminal penalties. The commission may impose fines on corporations that do not comply with its rules, it may seize banned merchandise, and it may sue businesses in violation of the act.

One of the most interesting creations of this act is the Injury Information Clearinghouse, a storehouse of all information relating to product-caused injuries. One part of this clearinghouse is the National Electronic Injury Survey System (NEISS). This system consists of a central computer tied to more than 100 hospital emergency rooms around the country. Information regarding all product-related injuries treated in the emergency rooms is fed into the computer to create a current log of such injuries. At this time, the most hazardous products governed by the CPSA are bicycles and bicycle equipment.

Yet, for all of the CPSC's wide-reaching powers, including the affirmative duties set forth for manufacturers and distributors, this agency is small, and has a relatively low budget. Thus it has been fairly ineffectual at enforcing those of its rules that are not complied with voluntarily. The commission depends largely on cooperation and voluntary action on the part of manufacturers, distributors, and sellers. The CPSC has also been slow in creating industry-wide rules. At present, the commission has a large backlog of complaints before it. Even so, industry complains that the commission's broad power goes too far in regulating business, that it costs huge sums of money to comply with the CPSA, and that the costs are eventually borne by consumers.

GTE Sylvania Incorporated v. Consumer Product Safety Com'n
404 F.Supp. 352
United States District Court, D. Delaware
October 23, 1973

LATCHUM, CHIEF JUDGE
In these 13 separate actions, each plaintiff, a manufacturer of television receivers, seeks a preliminary injunction restraining the Consumer Product Safety Commission (Commission), its members, and its officers from disseminating certain information to the public which the plaintiffs contend is privileged, confidential, misleading, and inaccurate.

Congress, in 1972, enacted the Consumer Product Safety Act (the Act) in order to "establish comprehensive and effective regulation over the safety of unreasonably hazardous consumer products." To implement and administer this legislative policy, the Act established the Commission as an independent regulatory agency. Shortly after its creation, the commission became concerned about the safety of television sets. During the spring and summer of 1974, the Commission sought and obtained television-related accident data from television manufacturers. Upon receipt of such information, the data was consolidated and a computer printout was prepared which

listed the alleged accidents separately. On March 28, 1975, the commission decided to release to the public the bulk of the television-related accident material in its possession which it had gathered from the plaintiffs.

Subsequently, each of the 13 plaintiffs brought a suit against the Commission for an injunction prohibiting the public dissemination of the information obtained from each on the ground that such information was privileged, confidential, misleading, and inaccurate.

Standards of reliability and accuracy for the data sought by the Commission were indicated on sample data forms accompanying the *subpoenas* sent to the manufacturers: "The purported information in this form is based upon such reports as are available but in many cases will be incomplete, unverified, and even incorrect." The Commission sought unverified information intentionally because it wanted to obtain as large a data base as possible.

The requirement that manufacturers submit reports of dubious validity apparently reflected the Commission's concern that limiting the *subpoenas* to only verified reports would result in a data base which would be too small for proper analysis. Also, it was thought that trends indicating design inadequacies of a particular manufacturer might appear. However, the Commission never attempted to distinguish the verified reports from the unverified reports. Indeed, of the more than 7600 tabulated reports, the Commission investigated less than 100 of them.

It appears that an accident which would have been television-related in one view could feasibly be perceived by another as not being television-related. That the Commission was well aware of the confusion and its consequences is clearly reflected in an internal memorandum which reads in part:

It should be noted that some manufacturers appear to have submitted accident reports pertaining to fire and shock incidents only. Whereas other manufacturers have submitted incident reports on television tube implosions, carrying handle failures, instability of television stands, and so on, as well as incident reports on fire and shock.

Moreover, although some manufacturers did not comply fully with the *subpoena*, the Commission never made any effort to compel the appropriate response because it had made ''a technical judgment that sufficient information [had been] collectively submitted by the 16 manufacturers to significantly facilitate the Commission's regulatory development activities for television receivers.''

Finally, the Commission's disclaimer accompanying the release to the public of the data submitted by manufacturers who are not parties to these actions focused on another critical source of inaccuracy: ''The television accident statistics being released to you may be misleading because some television manufacturers were more conscientious than others in maintaining television accident files.''

Notwithstanding this melange of inaccuracies, the Commission reached a final decision on March 28, 1975, to release to the public the television-related accident data and the computer printout compiled from the information obtained from the plaintiffs.

Before preliminary injunctive relief may be granted, plaintiffs must show (1) a reasonable probability of eventual success on the merits and (2) that they will suffer irreparable harm *pendente lite* if relief is not granted, and furthermore, the Court must consider (3) the impact of its decision on other interested persons and (4) the public interest.

It is not necessary that the moving party's right to a final decision after trial be wholly without doubt; rather, the burden is on the party seeking relief to make a *prima facie* case showing a reasonable probability that it will prevail on the merits.

Congressional interest in securing manufacturers' cooperation and establishing a harmonious but effective relationship between the manufacturers and the Commission is reflected in 15 U.S.C. § 2055(b)(1), which provides in pertinent part:

The Commission shall take reasonable steps to assure, prior to its public disclosure thereof, [1] that information from which the identity of such manufacturer or private labeler may be readily ascertained is accurate, and [2] that such disclosure is fair in the circumstances, and

[3] reasonably related to effectuating the purposes of [the Act].

Thus, before the Commission may release information to the public, a three-step analysis must be satisfied. Failure to comply with any one of the standards means that disclosure would be improper.

First, the Commission is charged with the duty of taking "reasonable steps to assure," before disclosure, the accuracy of information from which the identity of the manufacturer can be readily ascertained. An affirmative obligation to "take reasonable steps to assure" that information which it releases is accurate has been imposed on the Commission.

The Commission strenuously argues that its method fulfilled the statutory mandate of taking reasonable steps for assuring accuracy, but it is difficult to accept this contention on review of the Commission's data-gathering activities. The company that submitted only accurate reports would not have complied with the requirements of the *subpoena* because production of all reports—verified or unverified—was ordered by the Commission. One is at a loss to understand how demanding submission of inaccurate data constitutes a reasonable step in assuring the accuracy of information which it will eventually disclose.

Second, before release of the television-related accident data can be permitted, disclosure must be "fair in the circumstances." Fairness obviously is a concept that eludes precise definition. Because of the Commission's decision to *subpoena* unverified reports, the ambiguity of the *subpoena*, the failure of

the Commission to seek compliance by all manufacturers, and the differing quality of record keeping, it is conceded that a comparison of the accident data to determine the relative safety of the various manufacturers' products would be improvident and misleading.

Although fairness is difficult to define, it is even more difficult to determine how disclosure of this information would be "fair in the circumstances."

Third, it must be determined whether disclosure is "reasonably related to effectuating the purposes of [the Act]." Only one reason for disclosure was set forth in the contemporaneous Cull Memorandum upon which the Commission relied in deciding to release the information: "The release of the accident data would assist consumers to better evaluate the safety of televisions." One of the purposes of the Act is "to assist consumers in evaluating the comparative safety of consumer products." 15 U.S.C. § 2051(b)(2). Therefore, if it were possible to use this information to contrast the safety records of the various manufacturers, disclosure would be reasonably related to achieving the goals of the Act. However, it is clear that the materials which the Commission proposes to disclose cannot aid consumers in determining which television manufacturer has the safest product, and therefore would not be "reasonably related to effectuating the purpose of [the Act]."

Accordingly, plaintiffs have convinced the Court that they have a reasonable probability of success in showing that the Commission failed to "take reasonable steps to assure" that the accident information would be accurate, and that disclosure would not be "fair in the circumstances" and would not be "reasonably related to effectuating the purpose" of the Act.

The information which the Commission proposes to release would not normally have been made public by the plaintiffs, and it appears that the data would appropriately be deemed confidential. The planned disclosures would undoubtedly harm the plaintiffs by giving their competitors access to sensitive information.

It is difficult to perceive how the public interest would be harmed by enjoining the disclosure of information of dubious accuracy.

Accordingly, the Court finds that it is appropriate to preliminarily enjoin the disclosure to the public of the accident data and the computer printout.

CASE QUESTIONS

1. What exactly were the television manufacturers trying to achieve in this action?
2. What did the CPSC hope to achieve by releasing the accident statistics to the public?

SUGGESTED READINGS

Note, *The Consumer Product Safety Act: A Federal Commitment to Product Safety*, 48 ST. JOHN L. REV. 126 (1973).

Note, *Consumer Product Safety Act*, 5 LOY. U.L.J. 447 (1974).

Kircher, *Consumer Product Safety Act: Its Implications*, 45 PENN. B.A.Q. 122 (1974).

W.L. PROSSER, LAW OF TORTS 631 (4th ed. 1971).

Givens, *Product Safety Standard-Making Powers Under the Consumer Product Safety Act*, 18 ANTITRUST BULL., 243 (1973).

LaMacchia, *The Consumer Product Safety Act: Risk Classification and Product Liability*, 8 IND. L. REV. 846 (1975).

Consumer Credit

Purchases made on credit or by loans have increased phenomenally in recent years. Credit purchasing by individuals is new to this century, and unpaid consumer debt has jumped from $21.5 billion at the end of 1950 to more than $306 billion by mid-1980. The first multi-use credit cards, BankAmericard and Master Charge (now Visa and MasterCard) sprang into existence only in 1959. Little state or federal law existed to handle the new problems that emerged from these credit transactions. Businesses that regularly extended credit to individuals were subject to few legal restraints. Business practices like charging unduly high interest, failing to disclose interest rates and other credit charges, and mailing unsolicited credit cards to potential users were common practice. Under the then-existing law, consumers were helpless to counteract these practices. As a result, in 1968, Congress passed the Consumer Credit Protection Act. The CCPA was designed to promote the disclosure of credit terms, and generally to establish the rights and responsibilities of both creditors and consumers. It is much more protective of the consumer than the existing common law. The CCPA is enforced and controlled by nine federal agencies. However, the FTC assumes principal responsibility for enforcement of these laws.

Under the CCPA, many early credit-card and loan practices became illegal. Issuers of credit cards can no longer mail unsolicited cards. The question of which duties devolved on the merchant who accepts a credit-card charge and which duties devolved on the card-issuing bank were clarified. For example, under the CCPA, a bank may not withdraw funds from a cardholder's savings or checking accounts to cover a credit-card charge without authorization from the cardholder. Also, under the CCPA, a cardholder's liability for unauthorized charges is limited to $50 in most cases.

One major problem not resolved by the CCPA is whether a cardholder may stop payment on a charge when the goods purchased have proved defective. Some states have passed legislation addressing this problem. At present, it appears that under federal law, a bank cardholder may refuse to pay off a card balance if the dispute involves a purchase over $50. Charges less than $50 are treated as cash transactions which the cardholder must pay.

The CCPA is extremely lengthy and complex. It is better known under its various subsections. Title I of the CCPA is known as the Truth in Lending act. In 1970, the Fair Credit Reporting act was added, as was the Equal Credit Opportunity act in 1974. The Fair Debt Collection Practices act was added to the CCPA in 1977. These major acts and other provisions of the CCPA comprise the body of law relating to consumer-credit transactions in effect today.

The Truth in Lending act is designed primarily to regulate the disclosure of terms and conditions of household purchases or purchases to be used for agricultural purposes that will be paid in five or more installments. The act also regulates common real-estate transactions in the same way. The purpose of the act is to enable the consumer to do informed comparison shopping of credit terms. Before the passage of this act, many creditors did not disclose any interest rates, finance charges, or other charges. Creditors who disclosed the rates did so in a variety of ways as well. The consumer had virtually no way to compare different rates. Under the Truth in Lending act, creditors must disclose information about interest rates and other finance charges in a highly regulated and uniform manner. Although the disclosure requirements differ depending on the type of credit arrangement, all disclosures must be made clearly, conspicuously, and in a meaningful sequence. A knowing and willful violation of the disclosure requirements of the Truth in Lending act may result in a criminal penalty of not more than $5000 or imprisonment for not more than one year, or both. However, the most effective and most commonly used method of enforcing this act is through private suit. Violation of a disclosure requirement by a creditor results in a minimum $100 fine up to a maximum $1000 fine. This fine is in addition to attorney's fees and actual damages suffered by the individual consumer.

Because of the length and complexity of the Truth in Lending act, the Truth in Lending Simplification and Reform act was signed into law in 1980, effective in 1982. Extensions of credit primarily for agricultural purposes will now be exempt from the Truth in Lending act. This change was made because the Truth in Lending act was originally designed to handle only consumer purchases, not purchases made mainly for business purposes. Further, requirements for disclosure by creditors were simplified. Model disclosure forms for creditors to follow are available under this act.

The Fair Credit Reporting act of 1970, Title VI of the CCPA, is designed to ensure that consumers are treated fairly by credit-reporting agencies. Prior to the enactment of this provision, agencies that investigated individuals to provide companies with credit, insurance, employment, or other consumer reports were subject to few restraints. Individuals not only had no right to know the contents of the report, but businesses had no duty to disclose the fact that a report even existed. Hence many individuals were denied credit, employment, or other benefits without knowing that an investigation had been made. These reports also contained few guarantees of accuracy. Consumers now have the right to find out the contents of any adverse report relied on by a business, and the name of the agency that compiled the report. Consumers may also correct the report or include their own explanation of facts contained in the report. Investigating agencies must follow "reasonable procedures" in compiling the report.

A consumer may recover actual damages from a business that violates this act, and punitive damages where violations are willful. Criminal sanctions may be imposed by the appropriate federal agency against those who knowingly and willfully obtain information under false pretenses.

The Equal Credit Opportunity act of 1974 is designed to eradicate discrimination in the granting of credit when the decision to grant it or refuse it is based on an individual's sex, marital status, race, color, age, religion, national origin, or receipt of public assistance. The major effect of this act has been to eliminate sex discrimination. Under the ECOA, a married woman can now obtain credit in her own name. A prospective creditor may not inquire about an individual's marital status, childbearing plans, the spouse or former spouse of the individual, or other similar criteria. Questions regarding alimony and child support are proper only if the applicant will rely on those sums to repay the obligation.

Because the ECOA is modeled after the Equal Employment Opportunity Act, if appears that facially neutral practices that have the effect of discriminating against a protected class are also prohibited. As yet, little case law has emerged to mark the boundaries of the ECOA in this area.

The ECOA requires creditors to notify consumers of any decision about the extension or denial of credit, along with the creditor's reasons or a statement indicating that the individual is entitled to know the reasons. An individual may bring suit against a creditor for noncompliance with the ECOA to recover actual and punitive damages. In addition, the appropriate agency may enjoin violations of the ECOA.

Besides the existing federal law, two bodies of law were drafted to offer guidelines to state legislatures regarding credit transactions. One of these statutes is the Uniform Consumer Credit Code. The UCCC contains many provisions to clearly delineate the rights and responsibilities of merchants, creditors, and debtors. The UCCC prohibits unconscionable terms in credit-card agreements, and specifically prohibits many common provisions in such agreements, such as requirements that consumers pay attorneys' fees. The UCCC also requires three months' advance notice for any increase in finance or other charges. The UCCC is, however, extremely lengthy and cumbersome. Further, overall it is much more favorable to businesses than to consumers, and actually does away with some common-law remedies available to consumers. In part because of these reasons, the UCCC has been enacted in only a few states, and was substantially modified before enactment in those states.

The other proposed statute, the Model Consumer Credit act, is much more pro-consumer than the UCCC. To date, it has not been passed into law in any state.

Warren v. Credithrift of America, Inc.
599 F.2d 829
United States Court of Appeals
Seventh Circuit
June 14, 1979

KIRKLAND, SENIOR DISTRICT JUDGE
The issues before us are: (1) whether a creditor's failure to disclose on the loan statement the amount of credit the debtor will have for actual use violates the Truth in Lending Act (the Act) and Regulation Z and (2) whether the disclosures required on the loan statement by the Act and Regulation Z are made by this creditor in meaningful se-

quence. We decide for the creditor. We hold that no liability may be imposed on a creditor who complies in good faith with the requirements of Regulation Z, notwithstanding that creditor's failure to comply with a disclosure of loan proceeds required by the Act. We also hold that the disclosures made by this creditor are made in meaningful sequence. Accordingly, we affirm the judgment of the district court for the defendant.

The essential facts are that on February 16, 1977, defendant extended consumer credit to plaintiff in the form of a loan for her personal use. In connection with the extension of credit, defendants prepared a loan statement which purported to make all the disclosures required by the Act and Regulation Z. Plaintiff alleges that defendant violated § 1639(a) of the Act and Regulation Z by failing to disclose the actual amount of credit to be extended to plaintiff and failing to make other required disclosures in meaningful sequence.

Specifically, plaintiff alleges that the amount-financed figure does not reveal the amount actually to be paid to her because the amount-financed figure includes insurance charges which are to be deducted from the amount of money actually paid to plaintiff. Plaintiff also asserts that the individual insurance charges are not in reasonable proximity to the amount financed, thus obscuring the fact that they are component parts of the latter figure. Plaintiff claims that these are logically related terms which should be grouped together in order to satisfy the meaningful-sequence requirement.

In *Basham v. Finance America Cor-*

poration, 583 F. 2d 918 (7th Cir. 1978), this court considered an issue identical to one presented by this case, that is, whether a creditor's failure to disclose the actual proceeds of a loan on the loan statement constitutes a violaton of § 1639(a). This court's opinion that that case held that good-faith compliance with the provisions of Regulation Z is sufficient to preclude liability on the part of lenders for noncompliance with § 1639(a)(1) of the Act.

Section 226.8(d)(1) of Regulation Z requires disclosure of: ''The amount of credit, . . . which will be paid to the customer or for his account or to another person on his behalf, including all charges, individually itemized, which are included in the amount of credit extended but which are not part of the finance charge, using the term *amount financed.''* This court recognized in *Basham* that this provision of Regulation Z merely required the disclosures spelled out in §§ 1639(a)(2) and (a)(3) of the Act.

Although lenders who rely on Regulation Z may not be technically not in compliance with § 1639(a)(1) of the Act, such lenders are protected from liability by § 1640(f), which provides: ''No provision of this section or sections 1611 of this title imposing any liability shall apply to any act done or omitted in good faith in conformity with any rule, regulation, or interpretation thereof by the board or in conformity with any interpretation or approval by an official or employee of the Federal Reserve System duly authorized by the board to issue such interpretations or approvals under such procedures as the board may prescribe therefore, notwithstanding that after such act or omission has occurred, such rule, regulation, interpretation, or approval is amended, rescinded, or determined by judicial or other authority to be invalid for any reason.'' Thus, no civil liability may be imposed on defendants who act in good-faith conformity with Regulation Z, notwithstanding a failure to comply with the disclosure required by § 1639(a)(1).

Plaintiff also claims that defendant failed to make the required disclosures on the loan statement in meaningful sequence, as required by § 226.6(a) of Regulation Z.

Specifically, plaintiff objects to the horizontal nature of the disclosures. Plaintiff contends that logically related terms are not grouped together, and as a result the statement is less than clear. Plaintiff argues that an alternative format would be more meaningful and would promote greater understanding of the transaction.

This court's decision in *Basham* addresses the precise issues raised by plaintiff with respect to what constitutes ''meaningful sequence'' in a disclosure statement. In *Basham*, this court held that ''the requirements of meaningful sequence cannot be applied mechanically or rigidly.'' The key components of ''meaningful sequence'' are reasonable proximity and comprehensibility.

The forms employed by defendant satisfy these requirements. Although the disclosures are horizontal in nature, the arrangement of terms chosen by defendant is both logical and comprehensible.

Plaintiff argues that there are certain sequences of disclosure which naturally promote the clarity envisioned by the Act and Regulation Z, and that defendant's disclosures are designed to inhibit understanding of the transaction. Disclosures in the agreement or contract are permissible as long as they are clear and conspicuous, and in meaningful sequence. It would seem that there are a multitude of ways by which the creditor could meet these requirements of the regulation. However, the regulation does not prescribe precisely how this is to be accomplished. Therefore it falls on the creditor to be able to support his belief that his disclosures meet the requirements of the regulation.

Defendant argues that the placement of figures in the disclosure statement in issue is no less meaningful because plaintiff suggests an alternative sequence. Although the form in question may not provide disclosure in a sequence that optimizes clarity, we conclude that defendant has provided plaintiff with a disclosure statement that is sufficiently understandable to meet the requirements of Regulation Z.

The judgment appealed from is affirmed.

CASE QUESTION

In this case, the defendant withheld part of the amount loaned, as insurance that the debt would be repaid in the event plaintiff was unable to repay the obligation, yet included the sum as part of the amount financed. Isn't this a deceptive and misleading practice?

SUGGESTED READINGS

Peeler, *Fair Credit Reporting Act: Due Process for Consumers*, 17 TRIAL 30 (1981).
Replansky and Kaffman, *Truth in Lending Simplification and Reform Act of 1980: A New Deal for the Creditor*, 13 U.C.C. L.J. 200 (1981).
BARKLEY CLARK, THE LAW OF BANK DEPOSITS, COLLECTIONS AND CREDIT CARDS, Chap. 9 (1981).

Chapter Questions

1. Define the following terms:
   a. antitrust act(s)
   b. civil action
   c. Civil Rights act of 1964
   d. Clayton act of 1914
   e. collective bargaining
   f. Federal Trade Commission act of 1914
   g. Food, Drug and Cosmetic act of 1938
   h. holding company
   i. merger
   j. monopoly
   k. pension
   l. price discrimination
   m. Robinson-Patman act of 1936
   n. sanctions
   o. secondary boycotts
   p. Sherman act of 1890
   q. Taft-Hartley act of 1947

2. Prior to 1957, Clorox Chemical Co. had almost 50% of the liquid bleach market. In that year, Clorox was purchased by Procter and Gamble, Inc., the leading manufacturer of soaps, detergents, and cleansers. Procter and Gamble does extensive advertising and, as a result, receives discounts from the media. The FTC challenged the acquisition of Clorox. They claimed that it tended to lessen competition because Clorox could now advertise at lesser cost than the other liquid-bleach manufacturers and obtain a greater share of the market. Procter and Gamble said that the FTC's reasoning was pure conjecture. Should the acquisition be allowed?
   FTC v. Procter and Gamble Co., 386 U.S. 568 (1966)

3. The Times-Picayune Publishing Co. published a morning and an evening newspaper in New Orleans. The only competition was an

evening newspaper. Times-Picayune refused to sell ads in one paper without an identical ad in its other paper. The Justice Department claimed that the practice violated the Sherman act as an unreasonable restraint of trade. Was Times-Picayune guilty of any wrongdoing?
Times-Picayune Publishing Co. v. U.S., 345 U.S. 594 (1953)

4. Parke, Davis & Co., which makes and markets nationally some 600 pharmaceutical products, listed suggested minimum resale prices in its wholesalers' and retailers' catalogs. Several retail drugstores in the D.C. area did not observe the suggested prices and sold Parke, Davis products substantially below the minimum retail prices. Parke, Davis told them that if they continued to do so, it would refuse to deal with them. It also informed wholesalers in the area that it would refuse to deal with them if they sold its products to offending retailers. The government brought a suit claiming a violation of the Sherman act. The U.S. district court found no violation of the act because Parke, Davis actions were merely a refusal to have business relations with retailers who disregarded its price policy. The U.S. Supreme Court reversed the district court. Why? Explain.
United States v. Parke, Davis & Co., 362 U.S. 29 (1960)

5. The dominant sellers of corrugated containers, a product for which demand is inelastic, enter into an agreement to furnish information to each other on request as to the most recent price change. This agreement is to exchange price information. It is not an agreement to adhere to a price schedule. Each company, on receiving a request, furnishes the information with the expectation that it will receive reciprocal information when it wants it. Is this agreement in violation of the Sherman act?
See United States v. Container Corp. of America, 393 U.S. 333 (1969)

6. Shreveport Macaroni Manufacturing Co. produced and sold macaroni to various retail food stores in the South. Childs Big Chain and J. Weingarten, large Southern grocery-chain stores, were two of Shreveport's major customers. Shreveport gave these two customers an advertising allowance based on sales in Louisiana. The FTC said that since the advertising allowance was not offered to all of Shreveport's customers, it was illegal price discrimination. Shreveport claimed that since it was located in Louisiana and the allowance was based on sales in Louisiana, it was not in interstate commerce and the federal antitrust laws did not apply. Can the FTC stop the allowance?
Shreveport Macaroni Mfg. Co. v. FTC, 321 F.2d 404 (1963)

7. In 1968, the Oil, Chemical and Atomic Workers Union tried to organize the employees of Fibers International Corp. The organizing effort included distribution of a leaflet listing 95 employees who sup-

ported the union. Fearing reprisals from the company, some of these people renounced their support of the union. Among those who withdrew support was Luis Cruz. On January 28, 1969, Ruben de Jesus, who was a chief union organizer, confronted Cruz in the company parking lot. De Jesus grabbed Cruz, used obscene language, and threatened to injure Cruz if he saw him at work. De Jesus was fired the next day because of the incident in the parking lot. The NLRB investigated the dismissal. They found that de Jesus had been fired for his union activities and ordered him reinstated. Should the court of appeals enforce the board's order?

NLRB v. Fibers International Corp., 439 F.2d 1311 (1971)

8. Hardison, an employee of TWA, observed his sabbath on Saturday. When he sought and obtained a promotion, his new job required him to work on Saturdays. He refused. TWA tried to find an employee who would swap jobs with Hardison, but found none. The only other alternatives were to grant Hardison special seniority in violation of his union's collective-bargaining agreement to enable him to avoid working Saturdays, or to allow Hardison to work only four days a week. TWA did neither and fired Hardison instead. Has TWA violated the Civil Rights act of 1964 by failing to reasonably accommodate Hardison's religious observances?

Trans World Airlines Inc. v. Hardison, 432 U.S. 63 (1977)

9. Alabama imposed a minimum height requirement of 5'2" and minimum weight requirement of 120 pounds for its prison guards. Alabama further excluded women from "contact positions" in the state penal system, thus barring women from 75% of the available jobs. One woman, Rawlinson, who weighed less than 120 pounds, brought an action claiming sex discrimination (1) because 41% of the female population was excluded from consideration for the job because of the height and weight requirements, whereas only 1% of all men was so excluded, and (2) women were barred outright from "contact positions" without proof that sex is a bfoq for those positions. Is Rawlinson entitled to be considered for the job?

Dothard v. Rawlinson, 433 U.S. 321 (1977)

10. The A & P grocery chain solicited offers from various companies to buy milk to be sold under A & P's private label. Borden responded with a high offer. A & P told Borden that its offer was too high and solicited offers from other companies. Borden, in order to help its longstanding account with A & P, submitted a bid that was lower than any competitors, and this bid was accepted. The FTC charged A & P with knowingly inducing or receiving price discrimination from Borden. A & P claimed that Borden's offer had been made to meet competition.

Has A & P established a valid defense to a charge of price discrimination?

Great Atlantic & Pacific Tea Co., Inc., v. FTC, 440 U.S. 69 (1979)

11. Colgate Palmolive Co. had conducted lab tests proving that Rapid Shave shaving cream softened sandpaper to the point that the sand could be shaved off. They ran a television advertisement that purportedly demonstrated their laboratory tests. In actuality, the advertisement showed sand being scraped off a piece of plexiglass. The FTC found the ad deceptive and ordered it discontinued. Should the FTC's order be upheld in the courts?

FTC v. Colgate Palmolive Co., 380 U.S. 374 (1965)

12. Credit Bureau Services, Inc. (CBS), prepared a consumer report on Josephine Colletti. She was in arrears with her account with a furniture store, allegedly because she was dissatisfied with the quality of the furniture. The furniture store reported her indebtedness to CBS. She paid off some of this indebtedness, but these payments remained unknown to CBS. She was turned down for a loan on the basis of the report. Colletti sued CBS for furnishing false, inaccurate, and incomplete information and for failing to use reasonable procedures to ensure the accuracy of the report under the Fair Credit Reporting act. Does Colletti have a valid cause of action against CBS?

Colletti v. Credit Bureau Services, Inc. 644 F. 2d 1148 (1981)

The Law of Torts   XI

A *tort* is a civil wrong other than a breach of contract for which courts provide a remedy in the form of an action for damages. The law of torts seeks to provide reimbursement to members of society who suffer losses because of the dangerous or unreasonable conduct of others. Tort law establishes standards of conduct that all members of society must meet. A remedy is provided when there is a breach of the standard of conduct or duty imposed by law. A *tortious act* is a breach of that standard; it is a wrongful act. It is the commission or omission of an act that causes another to receive some injury for which the law provides relief. The essential elements for recovery for a tortious act are the existence of a duty, and conduct that breaches that duty producing an injury. If the conduct also breaches a duty to society, the tortious act may also be a criminal act.

Social injustices are the primary target of the law of torts. The law is not static, and limits with respect to its development have not been set. New torts are being recognized where none previously existed. In cases of first impression, courts may create new causes of action to remedy the injustice. The argument that the claim is novel does not prevent a court from granting relief when it becomes clear that the law should protect the plaintiff's rights.

Included in the classification of torts are such civil wrongs as failure to exercise reasonable care, intentional interference with one's person, reputation, or property, and liability without fault, which is recognized in some circumstances. These wrongs are unrelated to one another and have little in common, except that they all involve antisocial behavior for which the law provides compensation for injuries or that in some other way refer to a behavior pattern that the law does not condone.

Negligence

Negligence is the failure of one owing a duty to another to do what a reasonable and prudent person would ordinarily have done under the circumstances. It is the unintentional failure to live up to the community's ideal of reasonable care; it is not based on moral fault. Negligent conduct involves an unreasonable risk of harm to those who are within the zone of foreseeable danger. Absence of *intent* to inflict injury is a distinguishing characteristic of negligence. Legal liability for negligence results when an injury is attributable to imprudence with no design to do harm. The fact that defendants may have suffered losses of their own through their negligent acts does not render them any less liable for plaintiffs' injuries.

Negligence cannot be reduced to a set of definite rules. The infinite variety of possible situations makes the determination of an exact set of rules for conduct impossible. A vague standard of conduct is the best the law can provide. Conduct that might be considered prudent in one situation may be deemed negligent in another, depending on the circumstances. The person's physical attributes, mental capacity, age, and knowledge, the person to whom the duty was owed, and the situation at the time may be considered in determining whether negligence exists. Negligence is the failure to exercise the degree of care demanded by the particular circumstances existing at the time of the act. If the defendant could not reasonably foresee any injury as the result of a certain conduct, there is no negligence and no liability. *The Second Restatement of Torts*, § 291, states the test in this way: "Where an act is one which a reasonable man would recognize as involving a risk of harm to another, the risk is unreasonable and the act is negligent if the risk is of such magnitude as to outweigh what the law regards as the utility of the act or of the particular manner in which it is done."

The elements necessary for a cause of action for the tort of negligence are (1) a duty or standard of care recognized by law, (2) a breach of the duty or failure to exercise the requisite care, and (3) the occurrence of harm proximately caused by the breach of duty. No cause of action in negligence is recognized in the absence of any of these elements. The law recognizes a duty or obligation to conform to a certain standard of conduct for the protection of others against unreasonable risk of harm. If the person fails to conform to the required standard, and that failure causes damage or loss, the injured party has a cause of action for negligence.

The plaintiff has the burden of proving, through the presentation of evidence, that the defendant was negligent. Unless the evidence is such that it can reasonably lead to but one conclusion, negligence is primarily a question of fact for the jury. A jury must decide whether the defendant acted as a reasonably prudent person would have under the circumstances—that is, a person having the same information, experience, mental capacity, physique, and professional skill.

Children are not held to the same objective, reasonable-person standard as adults are. A child must conform merely to the conduct of a reasonable person of like age, intelligence, and experience under like circumstances. This is a subjective standard and holds a less intelligent child to what a similarly unintelligent child would do. The adult standard differs in that it makes no allowance for a person less intelligent than the average.

In addition, if a person has a higher degree of knowledge, skill, or experience than a reasonable person, then that individual is charged with using that higher level, and so would be liable for using the skill of only an ordinary reasonable person. Since this issue of superior knowledge occurs mostly with professionals, such as doctors, lawyers, engineers, and so on, the standard used is that skill commonly possessed by members of the profession in good standing. Negligence in this area usually may be shown only by the use of expert testimony. This is a difficult burden for plaintiffs to carry, as professionals are often unwilling to testify against each other.

Crockett v. Crothers
264 Md. 222, 285 A.2d 612
Court of Appeals of Maryland
January 17, 1972

HAMMOND, CHIEF JUDGE
This tripartite appellate confrontation is between householders (plaintiffs and appellees) into whose home came water under pressure after a water main was broken by a contractor, Cullen (a defendant found liable, but not an appellant), while constructing a sewerage system for the town of North East according to plans and specifications which did not reveal that water main, prepared by an engineer, Crockett (a defendant, also found liable, and the appellant), under a contract with the Cecil County Metropolitan Commission.

The jury answered yes to both parts of an issue that read:

A. Was the engineer, Mr. Crockett, negligent in not showing the ruptured water line on the plans he drew up?

B. If yes, was his negligence a proximate cause of the damages?

Crockett argues feelingly that he should have prevailed below as a matter of law, on his motion for a directed verdict or on his motion for judgment n.o.v. because there was no evidence (a) of the standard of care an engineer such as he should have followed, (b) that he failed to exercise the requisite care, or (c) that his failure, assuming it to have been shown, was a proximate cause of the harm that occurred. He makes the subsidiary contentions that the trial court failed to properly instruct the jury as to the standard of care to be exercised and whether that standard was met; that the issue submitted to the jury was prejudicially simple, and that the trial court wrongly entered judgment for Cullen on the cross claim of Crockett for indemnity.

Even as all of us fail to see ourselves as others see us, the image appellants often have of their cause and their contentions is not the image the reviewing court sees. That is true here. We find no merit in any of Crockett's claims and will affirm the judgment he appealed from.

In an action against a professional man for malpractice, the plaintiff bears the burden of overcoming the presumption that due skill and care were used. There may be instances, however, in which the negligence is so gross or that which was done so obviously improper or unskillful as to obviate the need for probative testimony as to the applicable standard of care. Generally there must be produced expert testimony from which the trier of fact can determine the standard of skill and care ordinarily exercised by a professional man of the kind involved in the geographical area involved and that the defendant failed to gratify these standards.

There was the requisite testimony in the present case, largely from Crockett himself. Other testimony had shown that in digging a sewer line, the contractor follows the engineer's plans both as to direction and as to grade, and that the water main that the contractor broke was not on the plans prepared by Crockett, although his aim and general practice were to find and show on the plans all obstructions in the path of the line. Crockett testified that normal practice in preparing plans was to utilize aerial photographs supplemented by a field survey (but no physical subsurface investigation) so as to determine all that could be seen, including first-floor and basement elevations of houses. He said:

We talk to all the utilities that conceivably have utilities in the area, such as the Conowingo Power Company, AT&T, the telephone company, the town if they have water and/or sewerage plants. *We exhaust all possibilities.* We talk to the State Roads Commission, because they own the streets, some of the streets, that go through the town. Sometimes their plans show underground obstructions or surface obstructions that may not show up in an aerial photograph or normal field survey.

We do a fairly thorough job of researching, the purpose for which is as a guide to the contractor. We feel that the more we can show him, the lower he will bid the job.

Q: Are the things you just described the things that are ordinarily done by engineers in preparing plans?

A: Yes, sir. This is very normal practice.

It was shown that Crockett knew that several years earlier Whitman Requardt & Associates, well-known and long-established engineers, had prepared plans for water and sewer lines for the town of North East and that these plans showed the water main that was broken. Crockett said that he, apparently in preparing earlier plans, had seen drawings showing wells near the area involved and that the pipe that was broken apparently had carried water from the wells. Crockett did not inquire of the town of North East as to whether it had plans showing the subsurface pipes in the area. The town had parts of the Whitman Requardt plans. Mayor Johnson, who doubled as at least its *de facto* water engineer, knew that a man named Jones had the rest of these plans, because after the breaking of the pipe he went to Jones "because I was asking about elevations," and saw the part of the Whitman Requardt plans that showed the mischief-causing water main.

We think the jury legitimately and fairly could have found that Crockett did not "exhaust all (reasonable) possibilities" of discovering that the water main was where it was, as the applicable normal and customary standard of care required him to do, and that if he had inquired of Whitman Requardt or the town of North East, the reasonable probability was that the water pipe would have been discovered by him and put on his plans. Therefore, his failure to go further in his investigations and plan preparations than he did could reasonably have been found to be negligence that was a proximate cause of the harms sued on.

The appellant's contention of error in the instructions is premised on the fact that the case turns on whether he was guilty of "professional negligence." In such instance, it is incumbent upon the trial judge "to give more than a general charge [and] address himself to the issue in the case." Judge Mackey charged the jury that the Crothers must prove each element of their cause of action, one facet of which was Crockett's failure to use due care, and said that this

> is the failure to exercise that degree of care that an ordinary and reasonably prudent and careful person would exercise under similar circumstances. And of course, more specifically in this case, it would be the failure to exercise that degree of care that a careful and prudent engineer would exercise under similar circumstances.

In response to counsel's exceptions, the trial court expanded its instructions, saying:

> Mr. Crockett has a duty to perform, which duty is that which any careful and prudent engineer in the Cecil County area or the tri-state area here would perform under like circumstances.

The issue before the jury was simple and uncomplicated, and the instructions fairly and adequately covered it.

Crockett argues further that "the issue presented to the jury did not fairly state the question of the violation of the standard of care." In the light of the testimony and the charge, we think the decisive question to be answered by the jury was precisely that which was presented: "Was Crockett negligent in not showing the ruptured water line on the plans he drew up?"

Judgments affirmed, with costs.

CASE QUESTIONS

1. Why did the court require a higher standard of conduct for Crockett than it would for the average citizen?

2. What are some other examples of professional people for whom the standard of conduct is higher than it would be for a lay person?
3. Why is licensing a common requirement that many professional people must meet?

SUGGESTED READINGS

McCoid, *The Care Required of Medical Practitioners*, 12 VAND. L. REV. 549 (1959).
T.J. ROADY AND W.R. ANDERSON, PROFESSIONAL NEGLIGENCE (1960).
W.L. PROSSER, LAW OF TORTS, §§ 28–35 (4th ed. 1971).
Martin, *Medical Malpractice*, 33 INS. COUNSEL J. 269 (1966).
Note, *Standard of Care for Medical Practitioners—Abandonment of the Locality Rule*, 60 KY. L.J. 209 (1971).

Duty of Care

There can be no actionable negligence when there is no legal duty. The duty of exercising care to protect another may be imposed by legislative acts or by judicial decisions. Common-law duty is found by courts where the kind of relationship that exists between the two parties to a dispute requires the legal recognition of a duty of care. Legislative acts may also prescribe standards of conduct required of a reasonable person. It may be argued that a reasonable person would obey statutes. One who does not is not acting as a reasonable person and therefore must be negligent. Statutes include traffic laws, ordinances, regulations of administrative bodies, and any legislative acts.

Some penal statutes set standards and others do not, depending on the intent of the legislature. Plaintiffs must establish that they are within the limited class of individuals intended to be protected by the legislature. In addition, the harm suffered must be of the kind that the statute was intended to prevent. Often the class of persons intended to be protected may be very broad. For example, regulations requiring the labeling of certain poisons are for the protection of anyone who may come in contact with the bottle. Many of the traffic laws are meant to protect other persons on the highway. Once it is decided that a statute is applicable, most courts hold that an unexcused violation is conclusive as to the issue of negligence. In other words, it is negligence *per se* and the issue of negligence does not go to the jury. Some courts hold that the violation of such a statute is only evidence of negligence, which the jury may accept or reject as it sees fit.

Common law provides that one should guard against that which a reasonably prudent person would anticipate as likely to injure another. Damages for an injury are not recoverable if it was not foreseen or could not have been foreseen or anticipated. It is not necessary that one anticipate the precise injury sustained. It is usually enough to have foreseen that the negligent act would probably result in injury of some kind.

Courts do not ignore the common practices of individuals in society in determining the duty or whether due care was exercised in a particular situation. The scope of the duty of care which a person owes depends on the relationship of the parties. A greater duty of care is owed to those who are unable to care for themselves than those who are capable of doing so. Those persons who lack mental capacity, the young, and the inexperienced are entitled to a degree of care proportionate to their incapacity to care for themselves.

As a general rule, the law does not impose the duty to aid or protect another. Even though a person may feel a moral or humanitarian obligation to assist in the preservation of the person or property of another, the law generally does not impose a duty to do so. There is no legal duty to go to the rescue of another who is in peril or to protect another from an act of violence or criminal assault. However, a duty is imposed where there is a special relationship between the parties. Parents must go to the aid of their children and employers must render protection to their employees. If one puts another in peril, that person must render aid. A person can assume a duty through contract where the duty would not otherwise exist. Persons seeing another in distress have no obligation to be Good Samaritans, but if they choose to do so they incur the duty of exercising ordinary care. Some states have changed this common-law duty by passing Good Samaritan statutes that state that those administering emergency care are liable only if the acts performed constitute willful or wanton misconduct.

Weirum v. RKO General, Inc.
123 Cal. Rptr. 468, 539 P.2d 36
Supreme Court of California
August 21, 1975

MOSK, JUSTICE

A rock radio station with an extensive teen-age audience conducted a contest which rewarded the first contestant to locate a peripatetic disk jockey. Two minors driving in separate automobiles attempted to follow the disc jockey's automobile to its next stop. In the course of their pursuit, one of the minors negligently forced a car off the highway, killing its sole occupant. In a suit filed by the surviving wife and children of the decedent, the jury rendered a verdict against the radio station. We now must determine whether the station owed decedent a duty of due care.

The facts are not disputed. Radio station KHJ is a successful Los Angeles broadcaster with a large teen-age following. In order to attract an even larger portion of the available audience and thus increase advertising revenue, KHJ inaugurated in July of 1970 a promotion entitled "The Super Summer Spectacular." Among the programs included in the "spectacular" was a contest broadcast on July 16, 1970, the date of the accident.

On that day, Donald Steele Revert, known professionally as "The Real Don Steele," a KHJ disc jockey and television personality, traveled in a conspicuous red automobile to a number of locations in the Los Angeles metropolitan area. Periodically, he apprised KHJ of his whereabouts and his intended destination, and the station broadcast the information to its listeners. The first person to physically locate Steele and fulfill a specified condition received a cash prize. In addition, the winning contestant participated in a brief interview on the air with "The Real Don Steele."

In Van Nuys, 17-year-old Robert Sentner was listening to KHJ in his car while searching for "The Real Don Steele." Upon hearing that "The Real Don Steele" was proceeding to Canoga Park, he immediately drove to that vicinity. Meanwhile, in Northridge, 19-year-old Marsha Baime heard and responded to the same information. Both of them arrived at the Holiday Theater in Canoga Park to find that someone had already claimed the prize. Without knowledge of the other, each decided to follow the Steele vehicle to its next stop and thus be the first to arrive when the next contest ques-

tion or condition was announced.

For the next few miles, the Sentner and Baime cars jockeyed for position closest to the Steele vehicle, reaching speeds up to 80 miles an hour. The Steele vehicle left the freeway at the Westlake off ramp. Either Baime or Sentner, in attempting to follow, forced decedent's car onto the center divider, where it overturned. Baime stopped to report the accident. Sentner, after pausing momentarily to relate the tragedy to a passing peace officer, continued to pursue Steele, successfully located him, and collected a cash prize.

Decedent's wife and children brought an action for wrongful death against Sentner, Baime, RKO General, Inc., as owner of KHJ, and the maker of decedent's car. Sentner settled prior to the commencement of trial for the limits of his insurance policy. The jury returned a verdict against Baime and KHJ in the amount of $300,000 and found in favor of the manufacturer of decedent's car. KHJ appeals from the judgment. Baime did not appeal.

The primary question for our determination is whether defendant owed a duty to decedent arising out of its broadcast of the giveaway contest. Any number of considerations may justify the imposition of duty in particular circumstances, including the guidance of history, our continually refined concepts of morals and justice, the convenience of the rule, and social judgment as to where the loss should fall. While the question whether one owes a duty to another must be decided on a case-by-case basis, every case is governed by the rule of general application that all persons are required to use ordinary care to prevent others from being injured as the result of their conduct. Foreseeability of the risk is a primary consideration in establishing the element of duty. The verdict in plaintiffs' favor here necessarily embraced a finding that decedent was exposed to a foreseeable risk of harm.

We conclude that the record amply supports the finding of foreseeability. These tragic events unfolded in the middle of a Los Angeles summer, a time when young people were free from the constraints of school and responsive to relief from vacation tedium. Seeking to attract new listeners, KHJ devised an "exciting" promotion. Money and a small measure of momentary notoriety awaited the swiftest response. It was foreseeable that defendant's youthful listeners, finding the prize had eluded them at one location, would race to arrive first at the next site and in their haste would disregard the demands of highway safety.

Indeed, "The Real Don Steele" testified that he had in the past noticed vehicles following him from location to location. He was further aware that the same contestants sometimes appeared at consecutive stops. This knowledge is not rendered irrelevant, as defendant suggests, by the absence of any prior injury. Such an argument confuses foreseeability with hindsight, and amounts to a contention that the injuries of the first victim are not compensable. The mere fact that a particular kind of accident has not happened before does not show that such accident is one which might not reasonably have been anticipated. Thus, the fortuitous absence of prior injury does not justify relieving defendant from responsibility for the foreseeable consequences of its acts.

It is of no consequence that the harm to decedent was inflicted by third parties acting negligently. Defendant invokes the maxim that an actor is entitled to assume that others will not act negligently. This concept is valid, however, only to the extent that the intervening conduct was not to be anticipated. If the likelihood that a third person may react in a particular manner is a hazard which makes the actor negligent, such reaction whether innocent or negligent does not prevent the actor from being liable for the harm caused thereby. Here, reckless conduct by youthful contestants, stimulated by defendant's broadcast, constituted the hazard to which decedent was exposed.

It is true, of course, that virtually every act involves some conceivable danger. Liability is imposed only if the risk of harm resulting from the act is deemed unreasonable—that is, if the gravity and likelihood of the danger outweigh the utility of the conduct involved.

We need not belabor the grave danger inherent in the contest broadcast by defendant. The risk of a high-speed automobile chase is the risk of death or serious injury. Obviously, neither the entertainment afforded by the contest nor its commercial rewards can justify the creation of such a grave risk. Defendant could have accomplished its objectives of entertaining its listeners and increasing advertising revenues by adopting a contest format which would have avoided danger to the motoring public.

We are not persuaded that the imposition of a duty here will lead to unwarranted extensions of liability. Defendant is fearful that entrepreneurs will henceforth be burdened with an avalanche of obligations: an athletic department will owe a duty to an ardent sports fan injured while hastening to purchase one of a limited number of tickets; a department store will be liable to injuries incurred in response to a "while-they-last" sale. This argument, however, suffers from a myopic view of the facts presented here. The giveaway contest was no commonplace invitation to an attraction available on a limited basis. It was a competitive scramble in which the thrill of the chase to be the one and only victor was intensified by the live broadcasts which accompanied the pursuit. In the assertedly analogous situations described by defendant, any haste involved in the purchase of the commodity is an incidental and unavoidable result of the scarcity of the commodity itself. In such situations, there is no attempt, as here, to generate a competitive pursuit on public streets, accelerated by repeated importuning by radio to be the very first to arrive at a particular destination. Manifestly, the

"spectacular" bears little resemblance to daily commercial activities.

Defendant urges that it owed no duty of care to decedent—absent a special relationship, an actor is under no duty to control the conduct of third parties. This doctrine is rooted in the common-law distinction between action and inaction, or misfeasance and nonfeasance. Misfeasance exists when the defendant is responsible for making the plaintiff's position worse, that is, defendant has created a risk. Conversely, nonfeasance is found when the defendant has failed to aid plaintiff through beneficial intervention. Liability for nonfeasance is largely limited to those circumstances in which some special relationship can be established. If, on the other hand, the act complained of is one of misfeasance, the question of duty is governed by the standards of ordinary care discussed above. In this dispute, liability is not predicated on defendant's failure to intervene for the benefit of decedent but rather on its creation of an unreasonable risk of harm to him.

CASE QUESTIONS

1. Was the exact injury, or result of the contest, foreseeable in this case?
2. Assume that a business entered a float in a commercial parade, and as the float traveled down the street, employees threw candy to the crowd. Children running to collect the candy injured a spectator. Would the injury be foreseeable on the part of the business?
3. Assume that a department store advertises portable television sets at a very low price. There is a limited number to be sold "while they last" after the doors open on a specified day. A customer interested in buying a television set runs over another customer. On the basis of *Weirum*, would the department store have a duty?

SUGGESTED READINGS

Note, *Origin of the Modern Standard of Due Care in Negligence*, 1976 WASH. U.L.Q. 447.

Gravells, *"Duty Situations" and Policy Considerations—The Need for Business Sense*, 35 CAMB. L.J. 225 (1976).

Gerber, *Foreseeable Damages and the Good Samaritan*, 48 AUST. L.J. 463 (1974).

Lantry, *Expanding Legal Duty: The Recovery of Damages for Mental Anguish by Those Observing Tortious Activity*, 19 AM. BUS. L.J. (1981).

The ordinary principles of negligence do not govern occupiers' liability to those entering their premises. Occupiers of land owe a lesser duty to persons who are visiting their premises than they do to persons they come into contact with elsewhere. The lesser duty is determined primarily by the common-law classification of the visitors as invitees, licensees, or trespassers. This status classification system determines the duty owed by the land occupier or possessor. The duty the possessor owes to trespassers and licensees is less than the duty the possessor owes to the general public under the ordinary principles of negligence. The special rules regarding liability of the possessor of land are due to historical considerations stemming from the high regard for land in traditional English thought. The dominance and prestige of the landowning class in England existed during the formative period of the rules governing the possessor's liability. In this setting, in the eighteenth and nineteenth centuries, the rules limiting landowners' liability and establishing landowners in uniquely privileged positions were created. Owners of land were considered to be sovereigns within their own boundaries and privileged to do what they pleased within their domains. The unrestricted use of land was favored over human welfare. The rigid classification system that arose remains as part of the American common law. However, England, which nurtured the common-law rules, has rejected these distinctions.

An invitee is either a *public invitee* or a *business visitor*. A public invitee enters upon land as a member of the public for the purpose for which the land is held open to the public. A business visitor is upon land for a purpose directly or indirectly connected with business dealings with the possessor of the land. Those who are classified as invitees are given the greatest protection by the courts. A landowner owes the invitee a duty to exercise ordinary care under the usual principles of negligence liability. This preferred status applies only to the area of invitation.

One who is privileged to enter or remain upon land by virtue of the possessor's implied or express consent is a *licensee*. Licensees must ordinarily accept the premises as they find them and look out for their own welfare. The reason for this principle is that land occupiers cannot be expected to exercise a higher degree of care for licensees than they would for themselves. Social guests, who may be cordially invited or even strongly urged to come, are generally categorized as licensees, rather than invitees. An explanation often given is that since social guests are considered additional members of the host's family, precautions and preparation of the premises for their reception cannot be expected. A possessor of land generally owes the licensee only the duty to refrain from willful or wanton misconduct. Because of the hardship sometimes resulting from this rule, courts have developed some exceptions. With respect to active operations, the possessor of land is subject to liability to licensees for injury caused by failure to exercise reasonable care for their safety. What might constitute activities dangerous to licensees depends on the court's interpretation. Knowledge of the nature of the activities normally precludes recovery by the licensee. Generally, the possessor of land is under a duty to give warning of known dangers.

A *trespasser* is one who enters and remains on the land of another without the possessor's expressed or implied consent. Licensees or invitees may become trespassers when they venture into an area where they are not invited or expected to venture, or if they remain on the premises for longer than necessary. The general rule is that possessors of land are not liable to trespassers for physical harm caused by their failure either to exercise reasonable care to make their land safe for their reception or to carry on their activities so as not to endanger them. The only duty that is owed to a trespasser by an occupier of land is to refrain from willful or wanton conduct, unless the situation falls within one of the following exceptions: A duty of reasonable care is owed to an adult trespasser whose presence has been discovered, or who habitually intrudes on a limited area. Reasonable care is also owed to the child trespasser whose presence is foreseeable.

There is some question of the legal and moral justification of a rule that varies the legal protection of a person's life and limb according to whether the person has come upon the land of another without permission, or with permission but without a business purpose, or for a business purpose. Abrogation of the common-law distinction of invitee, licensee, and trespasser means discarding the law developed and applied by the courts over a period of many years. Courts have been reluctant to abandon the land occupier's preferred position set forth by history and precedent. A few courts have replaced the common-law distinction with ordinary principles of negligence to govern occupiers' liability to those entering their premises.

dard has been that as a licensee a plaintiff must take the premises as he finds them, and that the owner thereof is liable only if he is found to have committed affirmative acts of negligence or if a trap existed or there was concealed danger not likely to be discovered. There is only a duty to warn of known dangerous defects which the defendant should know or suspect that the licensee will not discover himself after a reasonable inspection of the premises.

Your third option is that if he was there for the business of the Ice Caves Mountain, that is—and the third option, there are two ways that he could have been there under the business of Ice Caves Mountain. One is that he was there as a patron; he had a season pass and he was entitled—if you believe that he had a season pass, he could have been up there as an observer under the season pass which entitled him to the use of the roadways, or he could have been a rescuer helping in the rescue of Mr. Shawcross, which is the business of Ice Caves Mountain. That is, if somebody gets trapped in a crevice on Ice Caves Mountain, getting him out of there is the business of Ice Caves Mountain. Anybody who is there in assisting in that rescue is doing it for the business of Ice Caves Mountain, and in those two circumstances, whether he was legally there as a patron of Ice Caves Mountain or as a rescuer, then the duty owed to him is a little bit more than for the other two. Then the duty is to act—then the duty is to keep the premises in a reasonably safe condition so as to prevent anybody lawfully on the premises from becoming injured. They were under a duty to exercise reasonable care to keep the premises in a reasonably safe condition for the use of a person such as the plaintiff coming on the premises.

Based on the charge as given, the jury

returned a verdict for plaintiff, on the issue of liability, and made an apportionment whereby 60% of the verdict was to be borne by defendant Miller and 40% by defendant Ice Caves Mountain. Both defendants appealed from the judgment of liability and apportionment. The appellate division unanimously affirmed.

As the trial court explained, under one view of the facts, it was possible for the jury to have labeled plaintiff a trespasser when he entered without permission and against the wishes of Ms. Ballentine, a licensee when seen but not ejected by Mr. Grau, the "boss," in the parking lot, and an invitee when assisting in the rescue. This being so, it remains a curiosity of the law that the duty owed to plaintiff on exit may have been many times greater than that owed him on his entrance, though he and the premises all the while remained the same.

Rather than to demand continued attempts to fit a plaintiff into one of the three rigid categories, the court pauses instead to reflect, to reconsider the necessity for such classification, and to state today that the distinctions need no longer be made. The distinctions which the common law draws between licensee and invitee were inherited from a culture deeply rooted to the land, a culture which traced many of its standards to a heritage of feudalism.

New York courts have observed the growing number of well-reasoned decisions abandoning the common-law distinctions and adopting the simple rule of reasonable care under the circumstances. We have not, until today, abandoned the classifications entirely and announced our adherence to the single standard of reasonable care under the circumstances whereby foreseeability shall be a measure of liability. This standard of reasonable care should be no different than that applied in the usual negligence action.

Application of the single rule in the instant case exemplified its good sense, for the duty of keeping the roads of Ice Caves Mountain in repair should not vary with the status of the person who uses them but, rather, with the foreseeability of their use and the possibility of injury resulting therefrom. While the likelihood of a plaintiff's presence had been an implicit consideration in the determination of status and the duty commensurate therewith, it now becomes a primary independent factor in determining foreseeability, and the duty of the owner or occupier will vary with the likelihood of plaintiff's presence at the particular time and place of the injury. While status is no longer determinative, considerations of who plaintiff is and what his purpose is upon the land are factors which, if known, may be included in arriving at what would be reasonable care under the circumstances.

Of course, before it becomes appropriate for the jury to consider all such questions, the court, as it would in the usual negligence action, must make the threshold determination as to whether the plaintiff, by introducing adequate evidence on each element, has made out a case sufficient in law to support a favorable jury verdict. Only in those cases where there arises a real question as to the landowner's negligence should the jury be permitted to proceed. In all others, where proof of any essential element falls short, the case should go no further. While the rigid status classifications are to be dispensed with, the function of the court and the standard of proof remain the same.

A new trial is ordered in supreme court, Kings County, on the issue of liability against the defendant Ice Caves Mountain, Inc. wherein the standard enunciated today should be applied.

CASE QUESTIONS

1. What uniform standard did the court choose to apply? How does that standard differ in application from the entrant's status test?
2. Briefly state the new rule of law with respect to the duties of landowners and entrants, according to this case.

SUGGESTED READINGS

James, *Tort Liability of Occupiers of Land: Duties Owed to Licensees and Invitees*, 63 YALE L.J. 605 (1954).

Prosser, *Business Visitors and Invitees*, 26 MINN. L. REV. 573 (1942).

W.L. PROSSER, LAW OF TORTS, § 62 (4th ed. 1971).

Note, *Courts' Abandonment of the Common Law Classification of Tres-passer, Licensee and Invitee*, 10 Am. Bus. L.J. 284 (1973).

Proximate Cause

For the plaintiff to support a cause of action, there must be a reasonable connection between the negligent act of the defendant and the damage suffered by the plaintiff. In tort law, this connection is called *proximate cause*. It is a limitation the law has set for the extent of responsibility for the consequences of a person's conduct.

Proximate cause should be distinguished from causation in fact. *Causation in fact* means that the injuries were the actual or factual result of the defendant's actions. The plaintiff must prove this in addition to proximate cause. The majority of courts use a "but for" test to measure defendant's conduct. The test may be stated as: Had the defendant not so conducted himself, the plaintiff's injuries would not have resulted.

This test is an extremely broad one and could have far-reaching results. For example, in a nighttime automobile accident, the fact that one of the drivers worked late at the office would be a cause. If he hadn't, he wouldn't have been at the location of the accident. Therefore justice demands that some boundary be set for the consequences of an act; thus the function of proximate cause.

To illustrate further, a driver drives his car carelessly and hits another car loaded with dynamite, which explodes. Ten blocks away, a nurse carrying a baby is startled by the explosion and drops the infant. It is doubtful if any court would hold the driver liable to the infant, even though the driver was negligent and was the cause in fact of the injury. There is no liability because the injured person is so far removed that it would be unfair to hold the driver liable. In other words, the driving is not the proximate cause of the injury.

It is also possible to have more than one cause for a single injury. If each alone would have been sufficient to cause the harm without the other, then liability is possible. There may also be joint tortfeasors of a single injury. Each possible tortfeasor's actions must be examined to see if the acts were so closely related to the damage that they are the proximate cause.

Every event has many contributing causes, even though some may be very remote. The law must place the responsibility for the event on someone. If the defendant's conduct was a substantial factor in causing the plaintiff's injury, the defendant is not relieved from liability merely because other causes have contributed to the result. The question before the court in a negligence case is whether the conduct has been so significant and important a cause that the defendant should be legally responsible.

Magarian v. Bessoni
160 Conn. 442, 280 A.2d 357
Supreme Court of Connecticut
February 23, 1971

ALCORN, CHIEF JUSTICE
The plaintiff was a tenant in an apartment house which was owned by the defendant. The tenancy was under a written lease in which the defendant undertook to make repairs. The plaintiff brought this action to recover damages for torn cartilage in his left knee which he suffered in a fall at the exterior entrance door to his apartment. The jury rendered a verdict for the plaintiff which the defendant moved to set aside, and the court's denial of the motion to set aside the verdict is the determinative issue on this appeal by the defendant.

It is the plaintiff's claim that his fall was caused because a device which he described as a "door check" on the outer storm door of the apartment was broken and a "safety chain" was lacking. The decisive issue is whether the broken door check or the lack of a safety chain, or both, was the proximate cause of the fall. The negligent act complained of was the defendant's failure to provide a door check that functioned properly, and a safety chain.

The case falls "within the principles of proximate causation that if an accident resulting in an injury would have happened whether or not a particular circumstance was present, that circumstance will not be considered to be a cause of the accident, and that circumstances involved in an occurrence may have so inconsequential an effect in its production that the law will

disregard them." The burden rested on the plaintiff to establish that his injury was caused by the claimed negligence of the defendant and to "remove this issue from the realm of surmise, guess, conjecture, and speculation."

Considering the evidence in the light most favorable to the plaintiff, the jury could have found the following facts to have been established. The plaintiff rented his apartment in August 1964, and, on two or three occasions in November and December of that year, he notified the defendant's property manager that the front storm door was defective in that the plunger tube of the door check "which was designed to prevent the door from being opened out too far was disconnected, broken, and not operating properly so that the door could just randomly swing open and close without any control on it, and, second, there was no safety chain installed on the door also to prevent the door swinging out to 180 degrees." Thereafter, the defendant did nothing to correct the condition complained of. At about 7:30 P.M. on January 16, 1965, the plaintiff started to leave his apartment. The day had been a stormy one, it had been snowing, and the wind was blowing with high velocity. The plaintiff opened the inside wooden front door and then started to open the aluminum storm door which was hung so as to swing outward from the building. When he had opened the storm door about a foot, it was caught by the wind and opened violently 180 degrees until it was flattened against the building. The plaintiff was thrown off balance and fell, twisting his knee.

There was no evidence before the

jury other than that already quoted to describe what sort of a device the plaintiff was referring to as a "door check." There was no evidence concerning the function which the door check was intended to serve or what effect it would have when the door was blown by the wind. The only evidence was that the door check "was designed to prevent the door from being opened out too far." There was no evidence concerning the purpose to be served by the safety chain except that it was "to prevent the door swinging out to 180 degrees." The jury could only speculate as to what effect either the door check or the safety chain would have had under the prevailing wind conditions even if they had been installed and were in good working condition. The evidence before the jury was only that the plaintiff was thrown off balance when a wind of high velocity struck the door when the plaintiff had opened it about a foot.

In the absence of some evidence from which the jury could reasonably have concluded that the presence of a properly functioning door check or safety chain would have furnished a safeguard against the force of the high wind velocity with which the plaintiff was confronted, the absence of either device could not properly be found to be a proximate cause of the plaintiff's injury.

The existence of the proximate cause of an injury is determined by looking from the injury to the negligent act complained of for the necessary causal connection. If a defendant's negligence was a substantial factor in causing the plaintiff's injury, the defendant would not be relieved from liability for the injury even though another force concurred to produce it. The plaintiff, in effect, asked the jury to infer that the absence of a properly functioning door check, or a safety chain, or both, was the proximate cause of his fall. While inferences may be drawn from circumstantial evidence, the plaintiff was bound to remove the issue of proximate cause from the realm of speculation by establishing facts which afforded a logical and reasonable basis for the inference which he claimed. This the plaintiff failed to do.

There is error, the judgment is set aside, and the case is remanded with direction to grant the motion to set the verdict aside.

CASE QUESTIONS

1. Suppose that the plaintiff's attorney had introduced evidence concerning the functions that the door check and safety chain were intended to serve and the effect they would have when the door was blown by the wind. Do you think that this additional evidence would have established that the landlord's negligence in failing to keep the door check in good repair was the proximate cause of the tenant's injury? What else would the tenant's attorney have to show?

2. What test did the court use in determining whether the failure of the defendant to maintain the door check and safety chain in proper working order was the proximate cause of the tenant's injury?

SUGGESTED READINGS

W.L. PROSSER, LAW OF TORTS, §§ 41–42 (4th ed. 1971).
Morris, *On the Teaching of Legal Cause*, 39 COLUM. L. REV. 1087 (1939).
RESTATEMENT (SECOND) OF TORTS, § 433.
James and Perry, *Legal Cause*, 60 YALE L.J. 761, 802–3 (1951).
Cole, *Windfall and Probability: A Study of "Cause" in Negligence Law*, 52 CALIF. L. REV. 459 (1964).
Simon, *Proximate Cause in Insurance*, 10 AM. BUS. L.J. 33 (1972).

Defenses

CONTRIBUTORY NEGLIGENCE AND ASSUMPTION OF RISK

Even after a plaintiff has proved that a defendant was negligent, and that the negligence was the proximate cause of his injury, the defendant may prevent recovery by proving a defense. Contributory negligence and assumption of risk are two defenses in negligence cases. Although these defenses are closely associated and frequently overlap, they are distinct defenses based on different legal theories. Contributory negligence is based on carelessness, whereas the essence of assumption of risk is venturousness.

Contributory negligence is a defense that prevents recovery for negligence if the injured persons by their own negligence proximately contributed to their injuries. Even though the defendants were negligent, the plaintiffs are denied recovery because they were also negligent. If the plaintiffs are guilty of undue risk of harm to themselves, they are barred from recovery in their own suits, by reason of negligence. The burden of proving contributory negligence is on the defendant. The doctrine of contributory negligence places the burden of the entire loss on one party, even though both are responsible. The plaintiff is held to the same standard of care as the defendant, that is, that of a reasonable person under like circumstances.

To illustrate, D_1 is driving his car and P is his passenger. Both are injured in a collision with D_2's car. If both cars were driven negligently, D_1 could not recover from D_2 because his own negligence contributed to his own injuries. Yet P could recover from both D_1 and D_2, since they were both joint tortfeasors in causing P's injuries.

The defense of *assumption of risk* exists when the plaintiffs actually had knowledge of the risk and made the free choice of exposing themselves to it. Assumption of risk may be express or implied. The plaintiffs may have expressly given their consent in advance to relieve the defendants of an obligation of conduct toward them. As a result of this consent, defendants are relieved of a legal duty to plaintiffs, and no recovery is allowed against defendants for their negligence. In cases of implied assumption of risk, plaintiffs voluntarily entered into some relation with the defendants, knowing that the defendants would not protect them against the risk. The plaintiffs impliedly consented to take their chances concerning the defendants' negligence.

For example, David Smith is dangerously setting off fireworks near a public street. Pamela Jones watches at close range, even though she is aware of the danger. If she is injured, she has impliedly assumed the risk and therefore cannot recover.

Hildebrand v. Minyard
16 Ariz. App. 583, 494 P.2d 1328
Court of Appeals of Arizona
March 23, 1972

HOWARD, JUDGE
Appellant, plaintiff below, appeals from an adverse jury verdict. The issue in this case revolves around the trial court's giving of an instruction on assumption of risk which appellant claims was unwarranted by the evidence.

Plaintiff's decedent, George Hildebrand, was killed on January 8, 1968, while working on a Michigan loader that he had parked between two buildings within the Herseth Packing Company yard. The decedent was crushed by the left front wheel of the loader as the result of the loader being struck by a tractor which was pulling two trailers filled with fertilizer. It was being driven by appellee defendant George W. Minyard in the course and scope of his employment by the appellee defendant Green Thumb Fertilizer and Spreading Company, Inc.

The facts viewed in the light most favorable to the giving of an assumption of risk instruction are as follows: Decedent, George Hildebrand, was called to the Herseth Packing Company on January 8, 1968, to repair a steam steering ramp on a Michigan bucket loader owned by Herseth. Hildebrand arrived at approximately 3:30 P.M. and parked his pickup north of a shed. At the time he arrived, the loader was located elsewhere in the Herseth yard. A Herseth employee was dispatched to drive the loader to the general vicinity of the shed. Mr. Hildebrand then personally drove the loader to a position where it partially intruded into a driving area within the yard.

After having positioned the loader, Mr. Hildebrand was told by Mr. Kline of the Herseth Packing Company that he was parked in a roadway and that he ought to park the vehicle in another location. However, both Mr. Hildebrand and Mr. Kline believed that there was still room for vehicles to get by. Mr. Hildebrand remarked that "... he was only going to be there a little while," and while he was there, several vehicles, including trucks and cattle trailers, passed around the loader without any difficulty. The loader measured 18 feet in length by 7 feet in width, was over 6 feet high, and was painted yellow. While Hildebrand and another man by the name of Kimball were working on the loader, appellee George Minyard, driving a tractor pulling two trailers loaded with fertilizer, in attempting to negotiate a turn, ran into the loader causing a wheel from the loader to crush Hildebrand. Minyard claimed that he could not see the loader because it was in a shadow and his vision was obscured by the sun. There is some evidence that just prior to the accident, Hildebrand was facing in the direction from which Minyard was coming.

This is another one of those cases demonstrating the failure to understand the difference between contributory negligence and assumption of risk and the failure to appreciate the very limited nature of the defense of assumption of risk.

There are two types of assumption of risk, express assumption of risk and implied assumption of risk. In an express assumption of risk situation, the plaintiff expressly agrees in advance that the defendant is under no obligation to care for him and shall not be liable for the consequences of conduct which would otherwise be negligent. An example of an express assumption of risk is the free railway pass case, wherein, in consideration of a free pass on the railroad, the passenger assumes all risk of personal injury and loss or damage to his property.

Express assumption of risk is covered in *Restatement (Second) of Torts*, § 496(b) (1965), which states:

A plaintiff who by contract or otherwise expressly agrees to accept a risk of harm arising from the defendant's negligent or reckless conduct cannot recover for such harm, unless the agreement is invalid as contrary to public policy.

Implied assumption of risk is epitomized by *Restatement (Second) of Torts*, § 496(c) (1965):

A plaintiff who fully understands a risk of harm to himself or his things caused by the defendant's conduct or by the condition of the defendant's land or chattels, and who nevertheless voluntarily chooses to enter or remain, or to permit his things to enter or to remain within the area of that risk, under circumstances that manifest his willingness to accept it, is not entitled to recover for harm within that risk.

Implied assumption of risk requires the presence of the following elements:

1. There must be a risk of harm to plaintiff caused by defendant's conduct or by the condition of the defendant's land or chattels.
2. Plaintiff must have actual knowledge of

the particular risk and appreciate its magnitude.

3. The plaintiff must voluntarily choose to enter or remain within the area of the risk under circumstances that manifest his willingness to accept that particular risk.

As with express assumption of risk, the touchstone of implied assumption of risk is "consent." Contributory negligence arises when the plaintiff fails to exercise due care. Assumption of risk arises regardless of the due care used. It is based, fundamentally, on consent. Contributory negligence is not. In the implied assumption of risk situation, the consent is manifested by the plaintiff's actions after he has been informed of the nature and magnitude of the specific danger involved. Therefore, when the plaintiff voluntarily enters into some relationship with the defendant, with knowledge that the defendant will not protect him against the risk, he may then be regarded as tacitly or impliedly consenting to the negligence, and agreeing to take a chance. Thus he may accept employment, knowing that he is expected to work with a dangerous horse; or ride in a car with knowledge that the brakes are defective and the driver incompetent; or he may enter a baseball park, sit in an unscreened seat, and thus consent that the players proceed with the game without taking any precautions to protect him from being hit by the ball. The result is that the defendant is simply relieved of the duty which would otherwise exist.

The plaintiff likewise impliedly assumes the risk when he is aware of a risk *already created* by the negligence of the defendant and proceeds to encounter it, as where he has been supplied with a chattel which he knows to be unsafe, and proceeds to use it after he has discovered the danger. If this is voluntary choice, it may be found that he has accepted the situation, and consented to relieve the defendant of his duty.

Putting it into its simplest terms, applying the law to the facts in this case, the question is this: "Did the deceased by his actions impliedly consent that appellee Minyard could run into the loader and that he, the deceased, was willing to take his chances and agreed to relieve Minyard from any duty of due care that Minyard may have owed to him?" Our search of the record has failed to disclose such consent and has further failed to disclose that the deceased had actual knowledge of the specific danger. Although one may assume the risk of the negligence of another if he is fully informed of such negligence, one is not, under the doctrine of assumption of risk, bound to anticipate the negligent conduct of others.

The failure to fully appreciate and comprehend the consequences of one's acts is not properly a matter of assumption of risk, but, rather, a matter of contributory negligence.

The standard to be applied is a subjective one, of what the particular plaintiff in fact sees, knows, understands, and appreciates. All the evidence in this case clearly shows that the deceased thought there was room for vehicles to safely get by. In fact, several did pass through without incident prior to the accident. At most, deceased may have failed to fully appreciate the consequence of his conduct. This could constitute contributory negligence and not assumption of risk.

Reversed and remanded for new trial.

CASE QUESTIONS

1. "In any case in which the plaintiff voluntarily encounters a known danger, he necessarily consents to negligence of the defendant which creates it." Is this statement true with regard to the defense of assumption of risk? Is it true of contributory negligence?
2. Is the standard to be applied to the defense of implied assumption of risk an objective one? How would you express that standard in a way similar to the way the court stated it in this case?
3. What is the basic difference between the defenses of assumption of risk and contributory negligence?

SUGGESTED READINGS

W.L. Prosser, Law of Torts, §§ 65, 68 (4th ed. 1971).

Green, *Assumed Risk as a Defense*, 22 La. L. Rev. 77 (1961).

James, *Assumption of Risk: Unhappy Reincarnation*, 78 Yale L.J. 185 (1968).

Wade, *The Place of Assumption of Risk in the Law of Negligence*, 22 La. L. Rev. 5 (1961).

Note, *Assumption of Risk—Whether a Licensed Driver Accompanying a Person in Possession of a Learner's Permit Should Be Held to Assume the Risk of the Latter's Inexperience*, 72 Dick. L. R. 663 (1968).

COMPARATIVE NEGLIGENCE

When contributory negligence is used, the entire loss is placed on one party even when both are negligent. For this reason, most states now determine the amount of damage by comparing the negligence of the plaintiff with that of the defendant. Under the doctrine of *comparative negligence*, a negligent plaintiff may be able to recover a portion of the cost of an injury. In the same situation, contributory negligence would bar any recovery.

In negligence cases, comparative negligence divides the damages between the parties by reducing the plaintiff's damages in proportion to the extent of that person's contributory fault. The trier of fact in a case assigns a percentage of the total fault to the plaintiff. Although treated somewhat differently under various forms of the doctrine, in general, the plaintiff's total damages are then reduced by that percentage. For example, a plaintiff who was considered to be 40% at fault by the trier of fact would recover $1200 if the total damages were determined to be $2000.

Alvis v. Ribar
85 Ill. 2d 1, 421 N.E. 2d 886
Supreme Court of Illinois
April 17, 1981

MORAN, JUSTICE

This appeal presents a question which arises solely from the pleadings. The plaintiff's complaint included a count based on the doctrine of comparative negligence, which count was dismissed by the trial court on motion by the defendants. Plaintiff asks this court to abolish the doctrine of contributory negligence and to adopt in its place the doctrine of comparative negligence as the law in Illinois.

In *Alvis v. Ribar*, a motor vehicle operated by defendant Ribar skidded out of control and collided with a metal barrel which anchored an official intersection stop sign. The sign had been temporarily placed at the intersection while construction work on the intersecting road was being done by the defendant contractor, Milburn Brothers, Inc., under the supervision of defendant Cook County. Plaintiff Alvis, who was a passenger in defendant Ribar's vehicle, sustained injuries as a result of the collision. He filed a multicount personal-injury complaint, seeking damages from all three defendants.

Generally, under the doctrine of contributory negligence, a plaintiff is barred from recovering compensation for his injuries if his negligence contributed to the accident. The origin of the doctrine can be traced to the case of *Butterfield v. Forrester* (1809). The doctrine was swiftly adopted in American jurisprudence. Legal scholars attribute the swift and universal acceptance of the doctrine to newly formed industry's need for protection "against the ravages which might have been wrought by oversympathetic juries." All the cases have one common basis, and that is found in the old law maxim that "no man shall take advantage of his own wrong or negligence" in his prosecution or defense against another.

In 1910, Mississippi became the first state to adopt a comparative-negligence statute applicable to negligence cases generally. The statute adopted the "pure" form of comparative negligence under which each responsible party would pay for the injuries sustained according to the relative percentage of his fault. Another form of comparative negligence was enacted by Wisconsin in 1931. This "modified" form allowed a negligent plaintiff to recover for his injuries only if his negligence was "not as great as that of the defendant."

Today, a total of 36 states have

adopted comparative negligence. The following is a list of states: Alaska, Arkansas, California, Colorado, Connecticut, Florida, Georgia, Hawaii, Idaho, Kansas, Louisiana, Maine, Massachusetts, Michigan, Minnesota, Mississippi, Montana, Nebraska, Nevada, New Hampshire, New Jersey, New Mexico, New York, North Dakota, Oklahoma, Oregon, Pennsylvania, Rhode Island, South Dakota, Texas, Utah, Vermont, Washington, West Virginia, Wisconsin, and Wyoming.

Twenty-three states have adopted the Wisconsin "modified" approach. Ten states have adopted the Mississippi "pure" comparative-negligence approach. Two states, Nebraska and South Dakota, have a system that allows the plaintiff to recover only if his negligence is "slight" and that of defendant's is "gross." Georgia has its own unique system. It is important to note that 29 of these 36 states have adopted comparative negligence in the last 12 years. In England, the birthplace of *Butterfield v. Forrester*, the concept of contributory negligence was long ago abandoned and replaced by a system of comparative negligence.

The contributory-negligence defense has been subject to attack because of its failure to apportion damages according to the fault of the parties. Under a comparative-negligence standard, the parties are allowed to recover the proportion of damages not attributable to their own fault. The basic logic and fairness of such apportionment is difficult to dispute. We believe that the concept of comparative negligence, which produces a more just and socially desirable distribution of loss, is demanded by today's society.

Defendants contend that the apportionment of relative fault by a jury cannot be scientifically done, as such precise measurement is impossible. The simple and obvious answer to this contention is that in 36 jurisdictions of the United States, such apportionment is being accomplished by juries. We agree that guidelines can assist a jury in making apportionment decisions and view the necessary subtle calculations no more difficult or sophisticated for jury determination than others in a jury's purview, such as compensation for pain and suffering. Although it is admitted that percentage allocations of fault are only approximations, the results are far superior to the all-or-nothing results of the contributory-negligence rule. Small imperfections can be disregarded, small inequities tolerated, if the final result is generally satisfactory.

Defendants claim that the change to comparative negligence will cause administrative difficulties due to an increase in claims, a decrease in settlements, and a resulting overcrowded docket. An Arkansas study showed that, there, the adoption of comparative negligence prompted no drastic change in court burden, and that the change increased potential litigation but promoted more pretrial settlements. The report concluded that concern over court congestion should not be a factor in a state's decision to adopt comparative negligence.

Congestion in the courts cannot justify a legal rule that produces unjust results in litigation simply to encourage speedy out-of-court accommodations.

Defendants claim that the adoption

of comparative negligence would escalate insurance rates to an unbearable level. This has not been found to be the case. Effects, in fact, have been found to be minimal.

The *amicus curiae* brief submitted by the Illinois defense counsel suggests that, under the contributory-negligence rule, the jury has sufficient flexibility to do substantial justice and that this flexibility negates the necessity for the adoption of comparative negligence. In essence, the Illinois defense counsel alludes to the oft-observed phenomenon that, once inside the jury room, juries often ignore the harshness of the contributory-negligence rule and, instead, dole out justice by a common-sense approach according to the relative culpability of the litigants. We agree that such may be the case and, in fact, find the proclivity of juries to ignore the law to be a compelling reason for the abolition of that law. There is something inherently wrong with a rule of law so repulsive to a jury's common sense of justice that veniremen feel compelled to ignore the law.

There remains the question of the form of comparative negligence to be adopted. Under a ''pure'' form, the plaintiff's damages are simply reduced by the percentage of fault attributable to him. Under a ''modified'' form, a negligent plaintiff may recover so long as the percentage of his fault does not exceed 50% of the total.

Defendants argue that should this court decide to adopt comparative negligence, the modified approach should be selected. They point to the basic unfairness of the ''pure'' system by example: A plaintiff who is 90% negligent has suffered $100,000 in damages. Defendants here point out the basic unfairness of requiring the 10%-negligent defendant to pay $10,000 to a plaintiff who was 90% at fault. The liability of a defendant should not depend on what damages he sustained, but should be determined by the relationship of his fault to the ultimate damages. In a suit under a ''pure'' form of comparative negligence, in which the defendant counterclaims for his own damages, each party must bear the burden of the percentage of damages of all parties in direct proportion to his fault. In the example above, the 90%-negligent plaintiff will bear 90% of his own damages as well as 90% of defendant's. On the other hand, the 10%-negligent defendant will be made to bear 10% of his own damages as well as 10% of plaintiff's. Neither party is unjustly enriched. Neither party escapes liability resulting from his negligent acts or omissions. It is difficult to see unfairness in such a distribution of liability.

The ''pure'' form of comparative negligence is the only system which truly apportions damages according to the relative fault of the parties, and thus achieves total justice. The 50% system simply shifts the lottery aspect of the contributory-negligence rule to a different ground. There is no better justification for allowing a defendant who is 49% at fault to completely escape liability than there is to allow a defendant who is 99% at fault under the old rule to escape liability.

For the reasons stated, we hereby abolish the common-law doctrine of contributory negligence and adopt in its place the doctrine of comparative negligence in its pure form. The judgments of the appellate court and circuit courts are reversed, and the causes are remanded to the respective circuit courts for further proceedings in accordance with the views expressed herein.

Reversed and remanded

UNDERWOOD, JUSTICE, dissenting
While I do not totally disagree with the proposition that modification of our heretofore existing contributory-negligence rule is desirable, I am not at all certain that the pure form of comparative negligence is the preferred substitute. If it is, it seems odd that of the 36 states which have adopted some form of comparative negligence, approximately two-thirds have chosen a modified form. And while the majority says that the pure form "achieves total justice," the fact that this form permits a grossly negligent but severely injured plaintiff to recover substantial damages from a slightly negligent defendant with only minor injuries certainly represents a radical departure from the concept of individual responsibility which has heretofore underlain our system of tort law. Despite the assertion by the majority that the pure form produces a utopian form of justice, most of the states adopting a comparative-negligence rule have preferred to deny recovery to one whose own negligence was the principal cause of his injuries.

CASE QUESTIONS

1. List and explain the pros and cons of comparative negligence in comparison with contributory negligence.
2. This case was reversed and sent back to the trial court to determine the outcome on the basis of the pure form of comparative negligence. Assume that it is decided on remand that the total damages of the plaintiff were $1000 and he was charged with 50% of the total negligence. How much would the plaintiff recover? Would your answer be the same whether the contributory-negligence system or the comparative-negligence-up-to-50% system were used?
3. Why did the court decide to adopt comparative negligence and abolish contributory negligence?
4. What are the two types of comparative negligence, and why did the court adopt the form that it did?
5. Is such a decision on negligence as the Illinois court made one for the judiciary or for the legislature?

SUGGESTED READINGS

Note, *Comparative Negligence*, 49 WASH. L. REV. 705 (1974).
Schwartz, *Comparative Negligence: Oiling the System*, 11 TRIAL 58 (1975).

Timby, *Comparative Negligence*, 48 PENN. B. A. Q. 219 (1977).
Kionka, *Comparative Negligence Comes to Illinois*, 70 ILL. B. J. 16 (1981).

Imputed Negligence

By reason of some relationship existing between two parties, one may be held liable for the negligence of another. This is referred to as *imputed negligence*, or vicarious liability. People are always responsible for their own acts.

Imputed negligence results when one person (agent) acts for or represents another (principal) by the latter's authority and to accomplish the latter's ends. A common example is the liability of employers for the torts that employees commit in the scope of their employment. In order to hold one person liable for the negligent act of another, one must prove that a principal–agent or employer–employee relationship existed, and the act must be done in the course or scope of employment.

One should take a liberal view of the scope-of-employment concept, since the basis for vicarious liability is the desire to include in operational costs the inevitable losses to third persons incident to carrying on an enterprise, and thus distribute the burden among those benefited by the enterprise. Generally, an employee would not be within the scope of employment (a) if the employee is en route to or from home, (b) if the employee is on a frolic of his own, (c) if the acts are prohibited by the employer, or (d) if the act is an unauthorized delegation by the employer.

One is not accountable for the negligent act of an independent contractor. *Independent contractors* are those who contract to do work according to their own methods and are not subject to the control of employers except with respect to the results. It is considered to be the independent contractor's own enterprise, since the employer has no right of control over the manner in which the work is done. The right of control of the mode of doing the work contracted for is the main consideration in determining whether one employed is an independent contractor or an agent. However, there are certain exceptions to this nonliability. An employer who is negligent in hiring a contractor or who assigns a nondelegable duty may be liable.

Dumas v. Lloyd
6 Ill. App. 3d 1026, 286 N.E.2d 566
Appellate Court of Illinois
June 9, 1972

ENGLISH, JUSTICE
This action was brought by plaintiff, William Dumas, to recover damages for personal injuries allegedly caused by the negligence of defendants, Clarence Shaefer, Norman Oil Company, Inc., and William H. Frazier. At the close of plaintiff's case at trial, verdicts were directed in favor of Norman Oil and

Shaefer, and it is from the judgments entered thereon that plaintiff has appealed. It appears that the case as to defendant Frazier was abandoned in the trial court.

Defendant Norman Oil Company owns and supplies gasoline stations in the Chicago area, one of which is located at 143 S. California Avenue, Chicago. In September 1962, defendant Shaefer was hired by Dale Norman, an officer of Norman Oil Company, to operate that service station on behalf of Norman Oil. He was not given a written contract by the company, nor did he hold a license to operate the station or give Norman Oil money or security for the operation. Shaefer did not own anything at the station and was not permitted to sell any products other than those supplied by Norman Oil. He received a commission of four cents for each gallon of gasoline sold at the station, and each day he banked the receipts after deducting his commission, and sent copies of the deposit slips to Norman Oil.

Shaefer was empowered to hire other people to help him with work at the station but, in practice, did not hire anyone without telling Dale Norman. Defendant Frazier was one of those hired, and his employment continued at the times pertinent to this case. Each person hired by Shaefer was paid out of his own commissions.

The operating license for the service station was in the name of John Norman, president of Norman Oil Company. Each month, Norman Oil paid the rent on the property, the electric bills, and sales tax on all products sold at the station. All of the equipment, such as the gas pumps, air compressor, underground tanks, and signs, including one which said "Norman Oil Products," were owned by Norman Oil, and all products sold there were furnished and delivered to the station by the company, usually through Dale Norman. Either he or John Norman would visit the station once or twice a week and would instruct Shaefer as to keeping the station clean.

The company supplied all sales books and had its name on all books and records used at the station. Shaefer had no control over the price set for gasoline, that being determined by Norman Oil. Nor could Shaefer draw on the bank account which was in the name of the company.

On various occasions, Shaefer, in the presence of Dale Norman, accepted and held various items as security for products sold when the customer could not pay the full amount. On December 18 or 19, 1963, Shaefer took a revolver from a customer as security for a payment of $3.00 for gasoline. The gun had a belt wrapped around it which Shaefer did not remove, but he placed the gun with the belt in a desk drawer at the station. The desk had only one drawer and it was unlocked. He never unwrapped the belt and never looked to see if the gun was loaded.

The station was located in a rough neighborhood, and almost every day at 3:30 or 4:00 P.M., a small group of friends, including plaintiff, would meet at the station and sit in the room where the desk was located, to laugh and joke and have a good time. They usually stayed there until Frazier was off work at 9:00 or 9:30 P.M.

On December 19, 1963, Preston Evans, a friend of both plaintiff and

Frazier, saw Frazier in the gas station with the gun which had been taken from the desk drawer. He was playing with the revolver by spinning it on his finger. Evans said to Frazier, "You are going to shoot someone if you don't quit playing," and Frazier replied, "There are no bullets in it." When he got through playing with the gun, Frazier put it back in the scabbard in the drawer.

The next day, plaintiff came to the gas station about 3:30 P.M. to visit Frazier and to have a grease job and oil change on his car, but it turned out to be too cold to do the grease job. He and Frazier had been pretty good friends for about five years and Frazier had been driving plaintiff's car all summer. About 5:30, while both men were in the station, along with several others, a man entered and asked Frazier to help him charge the battery in his car. Frazier said he couldn't do it right away and when the man asked how long he would have to wait, Frazier refused to do it and talked to the man in rough language. Plaintiff said he would help, and left the station and got the car started.

When plaintiff returned, Frazier asked him how much the man had paid for plaintiff's help. Plaintiff replied that the man was his friend and he had charged him nothing.

Plaintiff, in a joking manner, "told Frazier if he talked to me like he did to that old man, I would cut his throat off, and I did like this with my keys [indicating], and I walked out the door." As he went out, Frazier, also laughing, turned to a friend and said, "Watch me scare Red" [plaintiff]. He opened the drawer, took out the gun, and said,

"Red, I'm going to shoot you," and shot him. Whereupon, Frazier immediately said, "Damn, look what I done did," and ran to help plaintiff, saying, "Man, I am sorry." They brought plaintiff back into the station, where Frazier called the police and told them he had accidentally shot a man.

Plaintiff suffered severe and permanent injuries and brought an action to recover damages based on defendants' alleged negligence.

Plaintiff declared that, since he had proved a case of agency between Norman Oil and Shaefer, the trial court erred in directing a verdict in favor of either Norman Oil or Shaefer because the latter's negligence is a question of fact for the jury.

Norman Oil makes three points: (1) that Shaefer was not its agent but an independent contractor; (2) that plaintiff's own misconduct bars recovery; and (3) that even if Shaefer were an agent and Frazier a subagent, Frazier's actions were outside the scope of his employment and do not subject Shaefer or Norman Oil to liability under the doctrine of *respondeat superior*.

Of primary consideration in the determination of whether a person is acting as an independent contractor or as an agent or employee is the degree and character of control exercised over the work being done. When one undertakes to produce a given result without being in any way controlled as to the method used, he is considered an independent contractor and not an employee. But the relationship of principal and agent exists if the principal has the right or the duty to supervise and control, and also the right to terminate the relationship at any time. The test is in the right to control and is not dependent upon its exercise. The general rule of liability is that a principal is liable for the negligent act of his agent, but not for those of an independent contractor.

We believe that the evidence as introduced by plaintiff did establish that Shaefer was acting as Norman's agent in the operation of the service station and was not an independent contractor. Although the day-to-day operating procedures were managed by Shaefer, his authority was limited by the interest of the owner whose representative frequently visited the premises and laid down for Shaefer certain rules as to buying and distribution methods. Norman owned all of the equipment used by Shaefer and set the prices for all the products sold. Signs, records, and accounts were in the name of Norman Oil, and Shaefer was powerless to change them. Furthermore, on January 5, 1965, without prior notice to Shaefer, the owners closed the station and terminated their relationship with Shaefer effective at that time. We realize, of course, that at this point in the trial, Norman Oil had had no opportunity or need to introduce any countervailing evidence on this point in view of the court's directed verdict in its favor.

However, even though a principal-agent relationship between Shaefer and Norman Oil could have been found to

exist, a principal cannot be made liable through the doctrine of *respondeat superior* when the actions of his agent in no way constitute negligence. Plaintiff contends that Frazier could not have discharged the gun were it not for the careless and negligent manner in which Shaefer permitted the loaded gun to remain at ready access in the desk drawer. Yet, the uncontroverted testimony of both Shaefer and Frazier discloses that Shaefer did not know if the gun was loaded, and Frazier definitely thought it was not. We believe Shaefer acted reasonably when he allowed the belt to remain wrapped around the pistol and its case and placed it in a drawer which, although unlocked, was out of sight from those persons who might enter the station. Under all the circumstances of this case, for a gas station attendant to keep a gun, whether loaded or not, in a desk of his service station, is, in our opinion, ordinary care as a matter of law. We also believe that the negligent or reckless act of Frazier was clearly not of a character which could be attributed to his employer. For both these reasons, therefore, we conclude that the trial judge acted properly in directing verdicts in favor of defendants Norman Oil and Shaefer. The judgments entered thereon are affirmed.

Affirmed

CASE QUESTIONS

1. Do you agree with the result the court reached in this case? Was there a duty of ordinary care on the part of Shaefer to examine the gun to see whether it was loaded before placing it in the drawer?

2. The court says that a principal cannot be made liable through the doctrine of *respondeat superior* when the actions of his agent in no way constitute negligence. In light of your answer to question 1, could it be argued that Norman Oil Company should be liable for the actions of agent Shaefer, despite the court's decision to the contrary?

3. In determining whether a relationship of principal and agent exists, would you consider the exercise of control by the principal to be the most important factor? Why or why not?

Suggested Readings

W.L. Prosser, Law of Torts, §§ 69–74 (4th ed. 1971).
Ferson, *Bases for Master's Liability and for Principal's Liability to Third Persons*, 4 Vand. L. Rev. 260 (1951).
James, *Vicarious Liability*, 28 Tulane L. Rev. 161 (1954).

No-Fault Liability Statutes

The greatest number of civil cases in the United States are tort actions, and automobile collision suits account for most of these tort claims. With the widespread dissatisfaction with the delay and expense in the litigation of traffic-accident cases, the desire for an alternative to negligence litigation has been sought. Several states have passed no-fault liability statutes in an attempt to correct the injustices and inadequacies of the fault system in automobile-accident cases. The first such statute was passed by Massachusetts, and became effective on January 1, 1971.

Under a no-fault liability statute, parties sustaining damages from automobile accidents are compensated by their own insurance companies rather than by the parties whose negligence caused the accidents, or by those parties' insurers. The goal of the statutes is to reduce the cost of automobile insurance. This is primarily accomplished by saving litigation costs, including attorneys' fees, and by allowing little or no recovery for pain and suffering resulting from an automobile accident.

Intentional Torts

Unlike negligence, which is based on the failure to use reasonable care, *intentional torts* are based on willful misconduct or intentional wrong. The intent with which tort liability for intentional torts is concerned is not necessarily a hostile intent or a desire to do serious harm. The law finds intent when a reasonable person would believe that a particular result was substantially certain to follow. The knowledge and appreciation of a risk, short of substantial certainty, is not the equivalent of intent.

Invasion of Privacy

The law recognizes one's right to be free from unwarranted publicity and, in general, the right to be let alone. If one person invades the right of another to withhold self and property from public scrutiny, the invading party can be held liable in tort for invasion of the right of privacy. A suit for invasion of privacy may involve unwarranted publicity which places the plaintiff in a false light, or intrudes into the plaintiff's private life, or discloses embarrassing private facts, or uses the plaintiff's name or likeness for the defendant's gain. Generally, the motives of the defendant are unimportant.

The standard used to measure any of the types of invasion of privacy is that the effect must be highly offensive to a reasonable person. For example, if a frustrated creditor puts up a notice in a store window stating that a named debtor owes money, this is an invasion of the debtor's privacy. When there is disclosure or intrusion into one's private life, the details involved must be truly private.

The technological developments in information storage and communications have subjected the intimacies of the private lives of everyone to exploitation. The law protects individuals against this type of encroachment. However, certain individuals' right of privacy must yield to the paramount rights of society. A party who has become a public figure has waived this right, and society has a right to information of legitimate public interest.

Defamation

Civil liability for the intentional tort of *defamation* results from the act of injuring one's character, fame, or reputation by false and malicious statements. Defamation is based on the policy that people should be able to enjoy their good name free of malicious and defamatory attacks. A publication is defamatory if it tends to lower a person in others' esteem. Language that is merely annoying cannot be defamatory. Generally, the truth of the statement is a complete defense in a suit for defamation, because true statements are not considered to be malicious.

Libel and slander are both forms of defamation. *Libel* is defamation expressed by print, writing, signs, or pictures. *Slander* involves spoken words. Slanderous words must be spoken in the presence of someone other than the person slandered.

Although invasion of privacy and defamation are similar, they are distinct intentional torts. The same publication may involve both invasion of privacy and defamation, and both may be included in the plaintiff's complaint. The basic difference between a right to privacy and a right to freedom from defamation is that the former is concerned with one's peace of mind, while the latter is concerned with one's reputation or character. Truth is a defense for defamation but not for invasion of privacy.

Infliction of Mental Distress

A person has a cause of action for mental distress when the conduct of the defendant is serious in nature and results in anguish of the mind. The conduct must exceed all bounds usually tolerated by society. Recovery is allowed only in situations involving extreme misconduct. For example, telling a wife the made-up story that her husband shot himself in the head could be serious enough to cause mental distress.

Mental worry, distress, grief, and mortification are proper elements of mental suffering for which an injured person can recover. Recovery is not available for mere annoyance, disappointment, or hurt feelings. For example, the mere disappointment of a grandfather because his grandchildren were prevented from visiting him on account of delay in the transmission of a telegram would not amount to mental distress.

Early cases used to allow recovery for mental distress only when it was accompanied by some other tort, such as assault, battery, or false imprisonment. The difficulty of proving that mental anguish existed and placing a dollar amount on such injury are among the reasons why the courts did not recognize the tort earlier. Money damages have been awarded for pain and suffering, which are just as difficult to assess. In comparatively recent years, there has been a general admission that the infliction of mental distress should serve as a basis for recovery apart from any other tort. Today, the infliction of mental distress is generally considered to be an intentional tort, standing alone.

Signal Oil & Gas Company v. Conway
126 Ga. App. 711, 191 S.E.2d 624
Court of Appeals of Georgia
June 19, 1972

EBERHARDT, JUDGE
Mrs. Betty Conway brought suit against Signal Oil & Gas Company in three counts seeking damages because of a letter that Signal Oil had written to her employer, E. I. Du Pont de Nemours Company.

Mrs. Conway's husband had obtained a credit card from Signal Oil &

Gas Company and had used it in making purchases of gasoline. He was regularly employed as a truck driver and dispatcher. He had other credit cards with American Oil Company, Humble Oil, and Sinclair. Mrs. Conway had charge cards with Master Charge and with the Citizens & Southern bank. The family finances were handled by Mrs. Conway, who ran the only bank checking account and used it for the payment of bills, including the account of Signal Oil & Gas, until December 1970, when she informed her husband (but not Signal Oil & Gas) that she would not make further payments on that account. Thereafter the account became delinquent in the sum of $210.22.

Mrs. Conway was employed by Du Pont as a clerk, typist, teletype operator, and the like. She had worked there for some 14 years and was earning $608 per month.

On March 11, 1971, Signal Oil & Gas directed a letter to the personnel director at Du Pont relative to Mrs. Conway, Account No. 097–23–263, balance $210.22, seeking assistance in getting the account paid. The letter read:

We understand that the above subject is employed by you. If we are correct, we would appreciate your assistance.

Our customer has incurred charges totaling the above amount through the use of our gasoline credit card. Although numerous letters and statements have been sent to subject, they have not resulted in payment of the account. The above charges date back to the December billing.

We realize that you cannot intercede as a collection agency for us. However, we feel

that you will be as anxious as we are to help this individual avoid any costly collection action. Therefore, we would appreciate your interviewing our customer to determine why payment has not been received.

Any information or help you can give us will be greatly appreciated. A business reply envelope is enclosed.

Du Pont's personnel director discussed the letter with her, and she informed him that the account with Signal Oil & Gas was not hers, but that of her husband, that the credit card was in the name of her husband, and that she owed Signal Oil & Gas nothing. She also discussed it with the manager and obtained a copy of the letter through him. Two other people at Du Pont told her that they knew about the letter.

Plaintiff asserted that she had never made purchases from Signal Oil & Gas on the credit card and that that the letter which it had directed to her employer had greatly upset her and made her nervous and subject to headaches.

In her first count, plaintiff seeks recovery for wounded feelings and the disturbance of her peace and happiness, alleging that the letter had defamed her character and reputation and had subjected her to public hatred, contempt, and ridicule.

In her second count, she seeks recovery for the wrongful interference with her employment, alleging that the letter would be a permanent record in her personnel file and that it was an unwarranted invasion and intrusion into the realm of her employment.

In the third count, she seeks recovery for libel, alleging that the letter amounted to an accusation that she had obtained gasoline on credit and had not paid therefor and that the accusation was false and was transmitted to other parties.

Defendant moved for summary judgment as to all counts, supporting the motion with the deposition of the plaintiff and the pleadings. From a denial of the motion defendant appeals.

Plaintiff does not designate the letter as libel in the first count, but she does assert that by it, defendant has defamed her character and reputation and has subjected her to public ridicule, hatred, and contempt. This language comes from Code § 105–701, defining libel, and thus we must examine the letter and the circumstances to determine whether it is libelous.

We conclude that it is not. Certainly there is nothing in the letter that makes it libel *per se*. It does not charge that the plaintiff has committed a crime, that she has committed any debasing act which may exclude her from society, or make any derogatory and defamatory statement against her in reference to her trade or profession.

The question, then, is whether the letter may be libelous *per quod*, that is to say, whether the extrinsic facts developed by the pleadings and the deposition are such that it can be held as a matter of law that plaintiff's reputation and character were or were not damaged thereby. To maintain an action for libel, the matter published must either be libelous *per se*, or it must be so stated that it may reasonably be construed, by innuendo at least, to be libelous.

A creditor has the right to ask his debtor to pay what he owes, without being subject to an action for libel. He may direct a letter to the debtor's employer, seeking assistance in getting the debtor to pay without being subjected to an action for libel.

Does the fact that the credit card was in the name of plaintiff's husband, and that he may have made all purchases represented by the account, require a different result here? We think not. By plaintiff's own admission in her deposition, she had been making payment of the account to Signal Oil & Gas from the checking account through which she handled the family finances, and when she decided to cease doing so, she told her husband that she would not make further payments to it—but she did not notify Signal Oil & Gas. The reasonable inference to be drawn from these facts was that plaintiff, who was handling the family finances, had either purchased gasoline on her husband's credit card, or that she had assumed the payment of the account. Having received prior payments from her, the company might reasonably expect to receive further payments from her. It had received no notice from her or otherwise that the practice had been discontinued, other than the failure to receive payment. In this circumstance, it was wholly reasonable that the company make inquiry to the employer of the party from whom it had been receiving payment and thus either get the arrearages paid up or get information as to why the account was not being paid.

The letter contains no imputation of insolvency. It did not seek to alter her credit status; indeed, she was not then seeking any extension of credit and the information in the letter was neither used nor intended to be used to impair her credit standing.

This situation is easily distinguishable from that in *Southeast Bankcard Association v. Woodruff*, 124 Ga. App. 478, 184 S.E.2d 191, where the information concerning the debtor was sent out to many hundreds of merchants who were using the Master Charge credit card system in extending credit to holders of the cards, and consisted of a listing of his name under a column headed "Most Wanted." We held this sufficiently to implicate that the debtor had wrongfully used the card or his credit in such a manner that it could not be held as a matter of law to be free of libel.

We can see no difference between situations where the debtor contended the charge that a debt was owing was false because it had been paid, or because the merchandise had been faulty, and the present situation where it is contended that the charge was false because the merchandise had been purchased by her husband and not by her. In either event, there is simply a contention by the debtor that the debt was not owed by him. Particularly is this true under the facts here.

The most that plaintiff claims under this count is that she had been annoyed and has been nervous and upset and subject to headaches. That is not enough to make a libel of the letter. Mere annoyance or loss of peace of mind, or even physical illness caused by the alleged defamation is not enough to make it so. In *Mell v. Edge*, 68 Ga. App. 314(3), 22 S.E.2d 738, the charge

that a letter concerning an indebtedness written to a congressman, who was in position to cause plaintiff to lose his civil service employment, had caused him to become "worried, ill, and temporarily crazy and lost 26 days from service" was held to give rise to no action for libel.

As to count 1, defendant was entitled to the grant of a summary judgment.

The second count, in our view, is a charge of wrongful invasion of plaintiff's right of privacy in the area of her employment relationship with Du Pont. As stated above, a creditor has a right to direct a letter to the debtor's employer, seeking assistance in getting the debtor to pay.

For the reasons stated in our discussion of count 1, no actionable libel is alleged in count 3 of the complaint, and since it does not, the charge that the feelings, peace, and happiness of the plaintiff have been disturbed adds nothing to it.

Defendant was entitled to a summary judgment as to all counts.

Judgment reversed.

Evans, Judge, dissenting.

Signal Oil Company wrote to the employer of Mrs. Betty Conway, advising that she owed $210.22 as a balance on a gasoline account, because of her use of a gasoline credit card, and stated that it had sent her numerous letters and statements but without results. Her employer was requested to assist Signal Oil and to interview Mrs. Conway to learn why she had not paid the account. The contents of the letter were completely false, and Signal Oil knew they were false. It wrote the letter with the design and intent to interfere with her employment, and her employment was thereby interfered with. Signal Oil's purpose was to intimidate Mrs. Conway and to deliberately defame her character and reputation and subject her to public hatred, contempt, and ridicule.

If the majority opinion is correct, if indeed plaintiff is completely without remedy for such a flagrant and unwarranted violation of her rights, it is a great pity, and our laws are greatly in need of revision. The Georgia Code provides that ''for every wrong there shall be a remedy.'' Code § 3–105. What is Mrs. Conway's remedy here? Surely the law of Georgia will not sanction the defendant's conduct in seeking to intimidate this woman by *falsely accusing her* of owing money (which she did not owe) and failing to pay attention to the many statements and requests for payment (which had not even been sent to her) and in effect telling her employer that she was a dead-beat, for the purpose of extorting money from her and thus unjustly enriching the defendant corporation at her expense.

But libel is much more comprehensive and all-inclusive. Recovery for libel may be had for any false written charge against another which tends to *injure his reputation, and exposes him to public hatred, or contempt, or ridicule.* Code § 105–701. The word *public* means any member of the public, other than the plaintiff; and a letter written to another person meets the definition of *public*.

Despite the clear distinction between *libel* and *slander*, many of the cases on *libel* reach over into the *slander* statute and attempt to measure *libel* by such statute, such as whether the article makes a charge as to one's ''trade, office, or profession, calculated to injure him therein,'' which words are peculiarly and solely applicable to the statute on *slander*. See *Davis v. General Finance etc. Corp.*, 80 Ga. App. 708 (1), 57 S.E.2d 225. We repeat that slander and libel should not be confused or mixed together.

The majority opinion argues that it was a ''reasonable inference'' that Mrs. Conway had purchased gasoline on her husband's credit card or she had assumed payment of the account. But a wife is not liable for her husband's debt, and Signal Oil had no right to assume she would become liable therefor unless she had notified it to that effect. The majority argues that ''having received prior payments from her, the company might reasonably expect to receive further payments from her''— but that is not what Signal Oil told her employer; it falsely told the employer that *Mrs. Conway owed it*, falsely told that she had been notified about the account and paid no attention to its many demands.

The majority argues that it was ''wholly reasonable'' that the company make inquiry to the employer of the party from whom it had been receiving payment. Being ''wholly reasonable'' is not equivalent to piercing the allegations of a complaint in a motion for summary judgment by a defendant. Further, the company did not content itself with making inquiry; it communicated a falsehood to the effect that she *owed* the money and *refused to pay* or give any attention to its many demands (all of which was false).

I, therefore, dissent and would affirm the trial court in overruling the motion for summary judgment. I am authorized to state that Judges PANNELL and DEEN join in this dissent.[1]

CASE QUESTIONS

1. What is the heart of the dispute between the majority and dissenting opinions? Why is the determination of their quarrelsome issue so important with respect to an action for libel?
2. What rule will this court now apply in future cases dealing with invasion-of-privacy suits by debtors against their creditors for letters regarding unpaid bills sent to the debtors' employers? See *Mann v. King*, 127 Ga. App. 39, 192 S.E.2d 400 (1972).

SUGGESTED READINGS

W.L. PROSSER, LAW OF TORTS, §§ 111, 112, 117 (4th ed. 1971).
Eldredge, *The Spurious Rule of Libel Per Quod*, 79 HARV. L. REV. 733 (1966).
RESTATEMENT OF TORTS, § 568, Comment L.
Leflar, *Legal Remedies for Defamation*, 6 ARK. L. REV. 423 (1952).
Warren and Brandeis, *The Right to Privacy*, 4 HARV. L. REV. 193 (1890).
Kalven, *Privacy in Tort Law—Were Warren and Brandeis Wrong?* 31 LAW & CONTEMPT. PROB. 326 (1966).
Prosser, *Privacy*, 48 CALIF. L. REV. 383 (1960).
Wade, *Defamation and the Right to Privacy*, 15 VAND. L. REV. 1093 (1962).

Assault

Civil liability for assault results from an act—other than the utterance of words—that puts another in apprehension of immediate and harmful contact. Liability for assault results, even if the purpose of inflicting injury is abandoned, as long as the actor placed another in a state of apprehension. Usually mere words do not constitute an assault, no matter how threaten-

---

[1] The Supreme Court of Georgia reversed the decision reached by the majority of this court and agreed with the dissenting opinion (*Conway v. Signal Oil & Gas Company*, 194 S.E.2d 909).—*Ed.*

ing or abusive the words may be. *Assault* is an attempt to inflict injury on another person when there is the opportunity of doing so.

Battery

An unpermitted, unprivileged, intentional contact with another's person is defined as *battery*. It is not essential that the plaintiff be conscious of the contact at the time it occurs. Either assault or battery may occur without the other, but usually they both result from the same occurrence. As a result of an assault and battery—as well as other intentional torts—the injured party may bring a civil suit for damages and have a criminal prosecution brought for the same act. Both criminal and civil actions are available, and a choice need not be made. The two actions are independent of each other; the outcome of one does not determine the result of the other.

Battery includes contact that is actually harmful or is merely offensive. The standard used to determine offensiveness is not whether a particular plaintiff is offended, but whether an ordinary person who is not unusually sensitive in the matter of dignity is offended.

Estate of Berthiaume v. Pratt, M.D.
365 A.2d 792
Supreme Judicial Court of Maine
November 10, 1976

POMEROY, JUSTICE
The appellant, as administratrix, based her claim of right to damages on an alleged invasion of her late husband's "right to privacy" and on an alleged assault and battery of him. At the close of the evidence produced at trial, a justice of the superior court granted defendant's motion for a directed verdict. Appellant's seasonable appeal brings the case to this court.

The appellee is a physician and surgeon practicing in Waterville, Maine. It was established at trial without contradiction that the deceased, Henry Berthiaume, was suffering from a cancer of his larynx. Appellee, an otolaryngologist, had treated him twice surgically. A laryngectomy was performed; and later, because of a tumor which had appeared in his neck, a radical neck dissection on one side was done. No complaint is made with respect to the surgical interventions.

During the period appellee was serving Mr. Berthiaume as a surgeon, many photographs of Berthiaume had been taken by appellee or under his direction. The jury was told that the sole use to which these photographs were to be put was to make the medical record for the appellee's use.

Although at no time did the appellee receive any written consent for taking of photographs from Berthiaume or any members of his family, it was appellee's testimony that Berthiaume had always consented to having such photographs made.

At all times material hereto, Mr. Berthiaume was the patient of a physician other than the appellee. Such other physician had referred the patient to appellee for surgery. On September 2, 1970, appellee saw the patient for the last time for the purpose of treatment or diagnosis. The incident which gave rise to this lawsuit occurred on September 23, 1970. It was also on that day Mr. Berthiaume died.

Although appellee disputed the evidence appellant produced at trial in many material respects, the jury could have concluded from the evidence that shortly before Mr. Berthiaume died on the 23rd, the appellee and a nurse appeared in his hospital room. In the presence of Mrs. Berthiaume and a visitor of the patient in the next bed, either Dr. Pratt or the nurse, at his direction, raised the dying Mr. Berthiaume's head and placed some blue operating room toweling under his head and beside him on the bed. The appellee testified that this blue toweling was placed there for the purpose of obtaining a color contrast for the photographs which he proposed to take. He then proceeded to take several photographs of Mr. Berthiaume.

The jury could have concluded from the testimony that Mr. Berthiaume protested the taking of pictures by raising a clenched fist and moving his head in an attempt to remove his head from the camera's range. The appellee himself testified that before taking the pictures, he had been told by Mrs. Berthiaume when he talked with her in the corridor before entering the room that she "didn't think that Henry wanted his picture taken."

It is the raising of the deceased's head in order to put the operating room towels under and around him that appellant claims was an assault and battery. It is the taking of the pictures of the dying Mr. Berthiaume that appellant claims constituted the actionable invasion of Mr. Berthiaume's right to privacy.

The law of privacy addresses the invasion of four distinct interests of the individual. Each of the four different interests, taken as a whole, represent an individual's right "to be let alone." These four kinds of invasion are: (1) intrusion upon the plaintiff's physical and mental solitude or seclusion; (2) public disclosure of private facts; (3) publicity which places the plaintiff in a false light in the public eye; and (4) appropriation for the defendant's benefit or advantage of the plaintiff's name or likeness.

As it has appeared in the cases thus far decided, it is not one tort, but a complex of four. To date the law of privacy comprises four distinct kinds of invasion of four different interests of the plaintiff, which are tied together by the common name, but otherwise have almost nothing in common except that each represents an interference with the right of the plaintiff "to be let alone." (W. Prosser, *Law of Torts*, 804 [4th ed. 1971]).

Taking them in order—intrusion, disclosure, false light, and appropriation—the first and second require the invasion of something secret, secluded, or private pertaining to the plaintiff; the third and fourth do not. The second and third depend upon publicity, while the first does not, nor does the fourth, although it usually involves it. The third requires falsity or fiction; the other three do not. The fourth involves a use for the defendant's advantage, which is not true of the rest. (*Id.*, at 814.)

All cases so far decided on the point agree that the plaintiff need not plead or prove special damages. Punitive damages can be awarded on the same basis as in other torts where a wrongful motive or state of mind appears but not in cases where the defendant has acted innocently as, for example, in the mistaken but good-faith belief that the plaintiff has given his consent.

In this case, we are concerned only with a claimed intrusion upon the plaintiff's intestate's physical and mental solitude or seclusion. The jury had a right to conclude from the evidence that plaintiff's intestate was dying. It could have concluded he desired not to be photographed in his hospital bed in such condition and that he manifested such desire by his physical motions. The jury should have been instructed, if it found these facts, that the taking of pictures without decedent's consent or over his objection was an invasion of his legally protected right to privacy, which invasion was an actionable tort for which money damages could be recovered.

Instead, a directed verdict for the defendant was entered, obviously premised on the presiding justice's announced incorrect conclusion that the taking of pictures without consent did not constitute an invasion of privacy and the further erroneous conclusion that no tort was committed in the absence of ''proof they [the photographs] were published.''

Another claimed basis for appellant's assertion that a right to recover damages was demonstrated by the evidence is the allegations in her complaint sounding in the tort of assault and battery. The presiding justice announced as his conclusion that consent to a battery is implied from the existence of a physician–patient relationship.

There is nothing to suggest that the appellee's visit to plaintiff's intestate's room on the day of the alleged invasion of privacy was for any purpose relating to the *treatment* of the patient. Appellee acknowledges that his sole purpose in going to the Berthiaume hospital room and the taking of pictures was to conclude the making of a photographic record to complete appellee's record of the case. From the evidence, then, it is apparent that the jury had a right to conclude that the physician–patient relationship once existing between Dr. Pratt and Henry Berthiaume, the deceased, had terminated.

As to the claimed assault and battery, on the state of the evidence, the jury should have been permitted to consider the evidence and return a verdict in accordance with its fact-finding. It should have been instructed that consent to a touching of the body of a patient may be implied from the patient's consent to enter into a physician–patient relationship whenever such touching is reasonably necessary for the diagnosis and treatment of the patient's ailments while the physician–patient relationship continues. Quite obviously also, there would be no actionable assault and battery if the touching was expressly consented to. Absent express consent by the patient or one authorized to give consent on the patient's behalf, or absent consent implied from the circumstances, including the physician–patient relationship, the touching of the patient in the manner described by the evidence in this case would constitute assault and battery if it was part of an undertaking which, in legal effect, was an invasion of plaintiff's intestate's "right to be let alone."

We recognize the benefit to the science of medicine which comes from the making of photographs of the treatment and of medical abnormalities found in patients. The court also recognizes that an individual has the right to decide whether that which is his shall be given to the public and not only to restrict and limit but also to withhold absolutely his talents, property, or other subjects of the right of privacy from all dissemination.

Because there were unresolved, disputed questions of fact, which, if decided by the fact-finder in favor of the plaintiff, would have justified a verdict for the plaintiff, it was reversible error to have directed a verdict for the defendant.

New trial ordered.

Case Questions

1. Battery is unpermitted, unprivileged, intentional contact with another's person. In a physician–patient relationship, how does physician receive consent to touch the body of a patient?
2. Could there have been a battery if Dr. Pratt used rubber gloves in handling Mr. Berthiaume's head in preparation for the pictures? Could there have been a battery if Dr. Pratt raised Mr. Berthiaume's head by cranking the hospital bed?
3. Could there have been an assault if Mr. Berthiaume was unconscious at the time Dr. Pratt raised his head and placed the blue operating-room towel under his head?
4. Are plaintiffs able to recover anything in suits for battery if they are unable to prove any actual physical injury?

Suggested Readings

Note, *Respondeat Superior and the Intentional Tort: A Short Discourse on How to Make Assault and Battery a Part of the Job*, 45 U. Cin. L. Rev. 235 (1976).

Elliott, *Frightening a Person into Injuring Himself*, 1974 Crim. L.Rev. 15.

Skegg, *"Informed Consent" to Medical Procedures*, 15 Med. Sci. & L. 124 (1975).

Interference with Contract Relations

A *contract* is an agreement between two or more persons that is enforceable by law. A right obtained by a party to the contract is something of value. A cause of action is appropriate when someone interferes with such a right. If one of the contracting parties interferes with its performance, the other party's action is a contract action for breach of the agreement. An intentional tort takes place when a noncontracting party or third person wrongfully interferes with the contract relations.

In order to maintain an action against a third person for interference, it must be proved that the defendant maliciously and substantially interfered with the performance of a valid and enforceable contract. The motive or purpose of the party interfering with the contract is an important factor in determining liability. The tort of *interference* includes all intentional invasion of contract relations, including any act injuring a person or destroying property that interferes with the performance of a contract. For example, an intentional tort takes place when someone wrongfully prevents an employee from working for an employer or prevents a tenant from paying rent to the landlord.

Conversion

Any unauthorized act that deprives an owner of possession of his tangible personal property is *conversion*. There may be liability for the intentional tort of conversion even when the defendant acted innocently, if there was an unauthorized exercise of the right of ownership over another's personal property. For example, *D*, an auctioneer, receives a valuable painting from *X*, reasonably believing that *X* owns it. *D* sells the painting for *X*, but it turns out that *P* owns the painting. *D* is liable to *P* for conversion, even though the mistake is honest and reasonable.

Conversion may be accomplished in a number of ways. If a defendant refuses to return goods to the owner or destroys or alters the goods, conversion results. Even a use of the chattel may suffice. If you lend your car to a dealer to sell and the dealer drives the car once on business for a few miles, it would probably not be conversion. But if the dealer drives it for 2000 miles, that amounts to conversion.

Courts consider several factors in determining whether defendant's interference with plaintiff's property is sufficient to require defendant to pay its entire value. These factors include dominion, good faith, harm, and inconvenience. Since conversion is considered a forced sale, the defendant must pay the full value, not merely the amount of the actual harm.

Trespass

The intentional tort of *trespass* includes every unauthorized entry upon the land of another and any offense or transgression that damages another's personal property. Entry upon someone's land may be in person or by causing or permitting a thing to cross the boundary of the premises.

Trespass includes any physical entry upon the surface of the land of another, such as walking on it, flooding it with water, or throwing an object upon it.

The interest of the law in protecting exclusive possession of land is not limited to the surface of real property. It extends below the surface as well. The extent of landowners' air rights above their land and their rights below the surface is still in the process of determination. Overhanging structures, telephone wires, and shooting across land have been held to be violations of owners' rights to the air space above their land. Trespass may also be to personal property, but most of the interference with the possession of personal property would be considered conversion.

Indiana & Michigan Elec. Co. v. Stevenson
363 N.E.2d 1254
Court of Appeals of Indiana
June 15, 1977

LOWDERMILK, JUDGE
Defendant-appellant, Indiana & Michigan Electric Company (IMEC), appeals from the adverse judgments of the trial court entered upon jury verdicts which awarded plaintiffs-appellees, Joe and Lloyd Collins (Collins), compensatory damages of $120 and punitive damages of $60,000, and which awarded plaintiff-appellee, Jack Stevenson (Stevenson), compensatory damages of $300 and punitive damages of $50,000. These two cases were consolidated for purposes of this appeal.

The facts necessary for our disposition of this appeal are as follows: IMEC is a public utility engaged in the generation and transmission of electric energy. IMEC has the power of eminent domain.[1]

In October 1974, IMEC was examin-

ing and surveying land in Clay County, Indiana, in preparation for the construction of its proposed Breed-Tipton-Pipe-Creed 765,000-volt electrical transmission facility.

The Collins and Stevenson were residents and landowners in Clay County whose property IMEC wished to survey.

When IMEC's survey crew reached the Collins' land, they found corn 10 to 12 feet high in the line of sight of their survey routes. IMEC ran what are known as centerlines from a tripod when conducting its surveys. Inasmuch as the Collins' corn was in its line of sight for approximately 1800 feet of the survey route, IMEC cut the corn without first obtaining the Collins' permission.

On Stevenson's land, there was a woods consisting of brush, saplings, trees, and dense foliage along approximately 1100 feet of IMEC's survey route. In order to obtain what it believed to be an accurate line of sight and tower elevations, IMEC cut approx-

---

[1] *Eminent domain* is the power to take private property for public use.—*Ed.*

imately 23 saplings and trees without Stevenson's permission.

IMEC contends that as an incident to its right to enter and survey property prior to it being condemned, it has the right to cut minimal quantities of crops or timber in order to produce an accurate survey. The Collins and Stevenson contend that such conduct on the part of IMEC would allow an unconstitutional "taking" of their property.

We are thus faced with the unenviable task of reconciling two important and oftentimes competing interests. On the one hand, we have the interest of the landowner to be secure in the ownership and possession of his property; on the other hand, we have the interest of society as a whole who in our technologically advanced civilization have become accustomed at the mere flick of a switch to be provided with a valuable source of energy—electricity.

We must now proceed with the difficult task of balancing these two important interests.

In the first instance, our legislature by vesting the right of eminent domain in specific entities has recognized that the desires of the individual landowner(s) to the undisturbed enjoyment of his property must succumb to the practical needs of society as a whole. Further, our legislature has provided that any entity preparing to exercise its statutory right of eminent domain has the further right to enter, examine, and survey the property about to be condemned. It is the generally accepted rule that a public utility's mere entry upon land for the purposes of examination and survey pursuant to a statutory grant of authority does not *ipso facto*

amount to a *taking* of property in the constitutional sense for which compensation must be assessed and tendered before the entry and survey are made. We fully adhere to this rule. Properly exercised the precondemnation survey can serve the interests of both landowner and public utility. The landowner will have only so much of his land condemned as is needed for the particular utility purpose involved; and, the utility will not be forced to engage in the wasteful expenditure of the ratepayer's money by blindly purchasing a "pig in a poke."

However, a public utility's right to enter private property for the purpose of examination and survey confers no license to engage in a course of destruction of crops, timber, and so on.

Having recognized the competing interests involved and the two extremes of the spectrum, our focal point becomes narrowed to this question, "When do acts by a public utility—when conducting an examination and survey of property prior to condemning that property—amount to a *taking* of private property?"

Before private property is "taken" in a constitutional sense, there must be a *substantial interference* with the owner's use and enjoyment of the specific property allegedly taken. Whether the interference is substantial is a factual question which must be resolved in each case by the trier of fact.

IMEC contends that by not allowing utilities to cut a minimum number of trees, crops, and so on, needed to effectuate accurate surveys, it will become in essence impossible to conduct surveys, and without surveys, there can be no eminent domain. It is argued that any entry upon a person's property will result in some damage. IMEC posits the extreme example of blades of grass being trampled under the feet of the survey crew.

We do not accept the total picture of oblivion which IMEC paints for utilities in such broad strokes for two reasons. First, there was expert testimony presented at trial from which reasonable men could find that methods of surveying through cornfields and timber were available which would not result in the destruction of corn and trees. For example, the experts posited offset surveying and surveying from platformed elevations as practical alternatives to cutting. The costs in money and time in adopting these techniques must yield at this point to the paramount interests of the landowner. Secondly, the law does not concern itself with trifling injuries. Such an injury as posited by IMEC could not properly be considered a substantial interference with the owner's use and enjoyment of his property. In the same vein would be the case of a utility driving survey stakes into land. The land could not properly be considered substantially interfered with and thereby taken.

We think it important to emphasize that a taking in the constitutional sense is a relative term and that not all *damage* to property amounts to a *taking* of that property. For example, to cut a tree down at its base would be a taking of that tree. However, reasonable men might well find that to cut a limb or branch from a tree does not amount to a taking of the tree, the reason being that the owner's use and enjoyment of the

tree would not be substantially interfered with.

In the case at bar, reasonable men could have found that IMEC's cutting of a strip of corn 1800 feet long and 4 to 8 feet wide substantially interfered with the Collins' free use and enjoyment of their corn. Likewise, IMEC's cutting of approximately 23 saplings and trees on Stevenson's property was a substantial interference with his free use and enjoyment of his saplings and trees.

IMEC contends that the evidence was insufficient to merit an award of punitive damages in either case.

IMEC's unconstitutional taking of private property revoked its statutory grant of authority to enter private property for the purposes of examination and survey and thereby relegated IMEC to the status of a trespasser. It is settled that an award of punitive damages is proper in a trespass action upon a showing of fraud, malice, or oppressive conduct. As noted above, there was evidence that there were alternative means of surveying available which would have resulted in slight, if any, damage to corn or trees. The jury could have reasonably inferred that IMEC had knowledge of these alternative methods of surveying property, but elected not to use them because of the additional time and expense involved; hence, IMEC's actions exhibited a heedless disregard for the property rights of landowners.

Therefore, it is the opinion of this court that there was sufficient evidence to merit an award of punitive damages in both cases.

Judgment affirmed.

CASE QUESTIONS

1. What were the competing interests that faced the court in the decision of this case?
2. When did Indiana & Michigan Electric Company become trespassers on the plaintiffs' property?

SUGGESTED READINGS

Note, *Constitutional Law—First Amendment—Shopping Center Owner May Use State Trespass Statutes to Prohibit Speech Within His Shopping Center*, 8 ST. MARY'S L.J. 366 (1976).

Weaver, *Forgiving Our Trespassers*, 124 NEW L.J. 92 (1974).

Thweatt, *Defendant Broke Our Pipe Line*, 6 NAT. RESOURCES LAW 249 (1973).

Malicious Prosecution

Civil liability may result from malicious prosecution, based on the instituting of a judicial proceeding in malice, without probable cause to believe that it can succeed, and which finally ends in failure. A civil suit for the tort of malicious prosecution may result from either a criminal prosecution or a civil suit, as long as the proceeding was instituted maliciously, without probable cause, and with a decision favorable to the defendant. The threat of bringing suit is not enough. A proceeding must actually have been started, and must end in favor of the one who brings the action for malicious prosecution.

In a criminal case, the prosecutor is absolutely immune from malicious prosecution suits, even if it is shown the prosecutor acted in bad faith. Plea bargaining does not suffice to meet the favorable-decision criterion.

False Imprisonment

The unlawful detention of persons, whereby they are deprived of their personal liberty against their will, is false imprisonment. The detention need not be in a jail. Confinement for any length of time may take place in a mental institution, hospital, restaurant, hotel room, automobile, parking lot, office, and so forth. The restraint of liberty must be against one's will and without authority. Most courts have held that plaintiffs must be aware of their confinement while suffering it, or if not, then they must suffer some type of actual harm.

Jacques v. Sears, Roebuck & Co.
30 N.Y.2d 466, 285 N.E.2d 871
Court of Appeals of New York
June 8, 1972

BREITEL, JUDGE

Section 218 of the General Business Law gives a retail merchant a defense in an action for false arrest and imprisonment for its detention of a suspected shoplifter if reasonable. The issue is whether the merchant's defense extends to the arrest outside its store and to the continuing custody, including that by the police, of one who left the store with unpaid-for merchandise.

The jury response to the interrogatory that plaintiff was detained for a reasonable time and that there were reasonable grounds for detaining him gives the merchant a complete defense under the statute. The ensuing custody in the hands of the police was based on at least the same reasonable grounds and is not distinguishable from the preceding period of detention.

On May 7, 1966, plaintiff Jacques, a self-employed carpenter with only three fingers on one hand, entered a Sears, Roebuck store in Syracuse to purchase business supplies. He picked up 19 reflectorized letters and numbers worth ten cents apiece and put them in his pants pocket. He then selected a mailbox and had two extra keys made. He paid for the mailbox and keys, but not for the letters. He also bought a bulletin board, chalk, an eraser, and a pencil sharpener. He left the store without paying for the letters still in his pocket. At the time, he had over $600 in cash and a $400 check in his wallet.

Mr. Varisco, an individual defendant and a Sears security officer, had observed plaintiff put the letters in his pocket and leave the store without paying. As plaintiff approached his automobile in the store parking lot, Varisco stopped him and told him he was under arrest. Varisco took him back to the security office. There plaintiff filled out a questionnaire in which he admitted having taken the letters without paying. He said he wished then to pay for the letters; that he was "sorry about the whole thing"; and that he "would never do anything like this again."

Sears' security officers called the Syracuse police, who arrived about 20 minutes after the detention began. With the security officers accompanying them, the police took plaintiff to police headquarters, booked him, and later released him on bail. Two days later, plaintiff appeared before the police court and stated that he was guilty of petit larceny. The court, however, refused to take a plea and advised him to get a lawyer. Later, the charge of petit larceny was dismissed on motion of an assistant district attorney because of lack of proof of intent.

In this action for damages, the jury was charged that if the detention by Sears was reasonable, no damages could be awarded from the time plaintiff was taken into custody until the time when he was turned over to police officers. In answer to an interrogatory submitted by the court, the jury found that plaintiff was "detained for a reasonable time at Sears, Roebuck & Co., and that there were reasonable grounds to detain him."

Section 218 of the General Business

Law, enacted in 1960, provides merchants a defense in various types of actions, including actions for false arrest: "Defense of lawful detention. In any action for false arrest, false imprisonment, unlawful detention, defamation of character, assault, trespass, or invasion of civil rights, brought by any person by reason of having been detained on or in the immediate vicinity of the premises of a retail mercantile establishment for the purpose of investigation or questioning as to the ownership of any merchandise, it shall be a defense to such action that the person was detained in a reasonable manner and for not more than a reasonable time to permit such investigation or questioning by a peace officer or by the owner of the retail mercantile establishment, his authorized employee, or agent, and that such peace officer, owner, employee, or agent had reasonable grounds to believe that the person so detained was committing or attempting to commit larceny on such premises of such merchandise." As used in this section, "reasonable grounds" shall include, but not be limited to, knowledge that a person has concealed possession of unpurchased merchandise of a retail mercantile establishment, and a "reasonable time" shall mean the time necessary to permit the person detained to make a statement or to refuse to make a statement, and the time necessary to examine employees and records of the mercantile establishment relative to the ownership of the merchandise. The section has been interpreted to make "reasonable detention" a defense in an action against a merchant for false ar-

rest, thus wiping out plaintiff's asserted distinction between "arrest" and "detention."

The legislative history indicates a purpose to protect merchants from false arrest suits even where the criminal actions are eventually dismissed. The governor's memorandum stated in part: "The sponsors of this measure urge that it will reduce such costs by helping to overcome the extreme reluctance with which merchants now attempt to interfere with or apprehend shoplifters. This reluctance is apparently caused by the vulnerability of merchants to suits for false arrest in the event of dismissal of the criminal case against a shoplifter."

Antishoplifting statutes in other states with provisions similar to section 218 have been interpreted to provide merchants with immunity from civil liability for false arrest where there were reasonable grounds for the arrest, but no criminal conviction resulted.

In this case, there was overwhelming evidence supporting the finding of reasonable detention, from the initial arrest to the arrival of the police. Plaintiff admitted immediately upon being stopped or arrested in the parking lot that he had taken Sears' goods and carried them out of the store in his pocket without paying for them. He repeated the admission in his own handwriting when he filled out the written questionnaire in the security office. At no time did he offer any exculpatory explanation. Then, two days later, he confessed guilt before a judge of the police court.

It makes no difference that, subjectively, plaintiff may not have had the requisite intent to commit a crime. Thus, it is assumed, as he described it, that the letters were put in his pocket to facilitate carrying other bulky items, handicapped as he was by having only three fingers on one hand, and that leaving the store without paying for them was done inadvertently. He had much more than enough cash on his person to make the small purchase. The point is that even he thought he had committed a crime, and the objective facts established as much. Certainly where merchandise is taken from the store without payment and there are admissions, and no exculpatory explanation, the store detective is not required to probe further the nature of the intent before making a formal arrest.

Similarly, defendants may not be held liable for the period after the police took plaintiff into custody. The jury found that the detention by Sears was reasonable and for a reasonable period of time. Under the circumstances, Sears was justified in handing plaintiff over to the police. Though not spelled out in section 218 of the General Business Law, the merchant's defense for reasonable detention extends, as a matter of implementing the policy of the statute if not as a matter of logical necessity, to the turning over of the suspect to the police under reasonable circumstances and the execution of an information or complaint necessary for his initial arraignment. Of course, the limitation that detention, to qualify under the statute, must be "on or in the immediate vicinity of the premises" does not apply to custody by the police. Moreover, the subsequent action and custody by the police was reasonable if not mandated.

Order affirmed.

CASE QUESTIONS

1. How did the court interpret the words *reasonable detention*, as found in the antishoplifting statute? Under what conditions does this interpretation assist the defendant-merchant in a suit by an alleged shoplifter?

2. What is the purpose of such antishoplifting statutes as the one in this case? What costs does it seek to reduce? What effect might such a statute have on would-be shoplifters?

3. Suppose that Jacques, upon being arrested by the store detective who had seen him place the letters in his pocket, had said that he took the letters without paying because he had forgotten about them being in his pocket. He then displayed his three-fingered hand to the store agent, saying, "This hand makes it tough for me to carry things. I made an honest mistake. Please let me go, sir." Instead, the agent detained him against his will in the security office until the police arrived. Would the court rely on this exculpatory explanation and reach a different conclusion than it did in the original case?

SUGGESTED READINGS

Prosser, *False Imprisonment: Consciousness of Confinement*, 55 COLUM.
  L. REV. 847 (1955).
Note, 15 CLEV.-MAR. L. REV. 75 (1966).
Note, 17 S.C.L. REV. 729 (1965).
Note, 50 N.C.L. REV. 188 (1971).
RESTATEMENT (SECOND) OF TORTS, § 42.

Strict Liability

When one is injured by some product or instrumentality, there are three theories of recovery in a civil action for damages. The first is the theory of negligence that was discussed at the beginning of the chapter. The second theory is breach of the warranty either expressly or impliedly contained in a contract when the product was sold. When a person buys a product, the law considers the seller to have impliedly warranted its fitness. Originally, the warranty went to the buyer only, but the trend today is to extend the warranty to nonbuyers who have been injured by a defective product.

The third theory is strict liability, or absolute liability, which imposes legal responsibilities for injuries caused by certain dangerous instrumentalities without proof of lack of due care. One who is responsible for the care of a dangerous instrumentality that is likely to cause harm is charged with the duty of taking precautions to avoid such harm. The formulation of a general definition or listing of dangerous instrumentalities that would be applicable in all jurisdictions is impossible. Poisons, explosives, airplanes, and vicious animals are examples of items that have been found to fall in this category. The possessor of a dangerous instrumentality is an ensurer of the safety of others. Strict liability in tort has been applied to product liability cases throughout the United States.

Stang v. Hertz Corp.
83 N.M. 730, 497 P.2d 732
Supreme Court of New Mexico
May 26, 1972

MCMANUS, JUSTICE
The automobile accident involved in this case occurred when a tire blew out. The tire, manufactured by Firestone Tire and Rubber Company, was mounted on a car belonging to Hertz Corporation. The car had been rented by a nun. Catherine Lavan, also a nun, was a passenger in the car when the blowout occurred. Catherine Lavan suffered injuries in the accident

resulting in her death. Prior appellate decisions were concerned with damages in wrongful death actions. *Stang v. Hertz Corporation*, 81 N.M. 69, 463 P.2d 45 (Ct. App. 1969), *aff'd* 81 N.M. 348, 467 P.2d 14 (1970). Subsequent to the appellate decisions the case was tried and submitted to a jury as against Firestone. The verdict was in favor of Firestone. There is no appeal from this verdict. The trial court directed a verdict in favor of Hertz. The dispositive issues in this appeal concern the liability of Hertz. Plaintiffs contend there were issues for the jury concerning (1) an express warranty and (2) strict liability in tort. On appeal, the court of appeals affirmed the trial court on the basis that there was no evidence of express warranty to be submitted to the jury and that strict liability is not applicable in New Mexico. *Stang v. Hertz Corporation*, 83 N.M. 217, 490 P.2d 475 (1971). We granted *certiorari* and now affirm on the issue of express warranty and reverse on the issue of strict liability.

Historically, the buyer of a defective product had two possible theories of recovery against the seller. The first was the basic theory of negligence, and in order to recover, the buyer had to establish that the seller had a duty or care and breached that duty, and that the breach was the cause of the plaintiff's injury. The second theory was based on a breach of warranty. This theory did not involve a concept of fault as found in negligence but, rather, required an agreement entered into by the seller.

The main problem with the negligence theory was the practical one of establishing the failure to exercise due care. Breach of warranty, on the other hand, involved the need of privity of contract between parties. That is, there existed a contractual relationship between the parties. The elimination of the privity requirement extended the usefulness of the breach of warranty action to a larger group of parties, and the liability for breach did not involve an element of fault as required in negligence. The law involving an action for breach of warranty was hampered, however, by contract and sales rules and other factors, such as the necessity for a sale, for notice of breach, and for disclaimers, which restricted the use of the theory of warranty in product liability cases.

Because of the shortcomings of the early theories, the courts developed a third theory of recovery which combined the strict liability of warranty with the broad reach of negligence. This theory is known as strict liability in tort and has been applied throughout the country to products liability cases. New Mexico has had very little litigation in the area of products liability. *The Restatement (Second) of Torts*, § 402A (1965), reads as follows:

1. One who sells any product in a defective condition unreasonably dangerous to the user or consumer or to his property is subject to liability for physical harm thereby caused to the ultimate user or consumer or to his property, if
   a. the seller is engaged in the business of selling such a product, and
   b. it is expected to and does reach the user or consumer without substantial change in the condition in which it is sold.

2. The rule stated in subsection 1 applies
   although
   a. the seller has exercised all possible
      care in the preparation and sale of
      his product, and
   b. the user or consumer has not bought
      the product from or entered into
      any contractual relation with the
      seller.

The New Mexico Court of Appeals made the point that if New Mexico wished to adopt the restatement view as to strict liability, then the legislature could properly do so. We agree with this contention, but we are of the opinion that we should decide whether or not strict liability is properly applicable to sellers and, as an extension, to lessors.

Since New Mexico has little to offer in the area of strict products liability, we must turn to other jurisdictions and their development of the law.

The picture of products liability law in this country was first viewed as a result of *Winterbottom v. Wright*, 10 M.&W. 109, 153 Eng. Rep. 402 (Ex. 1842), which held that only the express terms of the contract could provide a basis for recovery for injury resulting from a defect in the product. This was better known as the "privity rule," and persons not parties to the initial contract could not recover for injuries caused by one or the other contracting party. The first case to consolidate the decisions citing the exceptions to the privity rule was *MacPherson v. Buick Motor Co.*, 217 N.Y. 382, 111 N.E. 1050 (1916). It recognized that not only was privity unnecessary in cases involving things which were implements of destruction but the rule requiring

privity did not apply to cases dealing with certain products that were dangerous because of negligent manufacturing. After a thorough discussion of these cases, the court, in *MacPherson, supra*, concluded that, under the same principles, the manufacturer of an automobile was liable for negligence even in the absence of privity.

The California court abandoned the theory of implied warranty and adopted a theory of strict liability in tort. The case was *Greenman v. Yuba Power Products, Inc.*, 59 Cal. 2d 57, 27 Cal. Rptr. 697, 377 P.2d 897 (1962), and the court settled on a risk distribution approach. The basis of risk distribution was that the loss should be placed on those most able to bear it and they could then distribute the risk loss to users of the product in the form of higher prices. In *Elmore v. American Motors Corp.*, 70 Cal. 2d 578, 75 Cal. Rptr. 652, 451 P.2d 84 (1969), the California court refined the doctrine to the point that implied warranty no longer existed. In that case, the manufacturer was held liable to a bystander for injury from a defective automobile that left the road and injured the plaintiff. California has developed a theory of strict liability in tort where defective products are at issue and has completely eliminated the need for implied warranties.

This court adopts that reasoning in applying strict liability in the case now before us. The history of the evolution of strict products liability, its policy basis, and prerequisites to recovery does reveal a recognition by the courts of traditional common-law concepts of status and responsibility. It is referred to as impressive evidence of continuing reform of tort law through candidly creative judicial action. One of the great virtues of the common law is its dynamic nature that makes it adaptable to the requirements of society at the time of its application in court.

We feel that the conditions and the needs of the times make it appropriate for such changes as we are here making. Most of the states who have adopted strict liability have done so through the judicial system. This has been called "following the leader" and we see nothing wrong with this general principle if the leader is going in the right direction.

The respondent argues, in point III of the answer brief to the petition for a writ of *certiorari*, that strict liability should not be applied where the defect has arisen subsequent to the manufacture of the leased product, and that the jury verdict for Firestone established that the defect did not exist. Respondent further argues that as to Firestone, the defect did not exist at all, and if it did arise subsequent to the manufacturing, Hertz is not liable for the defect since it cannot pass the liability on to the manufacturer.

The petitioner argues, on the other hand, that Firestone's entire case was presented to the jury on the theory that the unreasonably dangerous condition arose after manufacture of the product. Hertz, however, elected to stand on the erroneous argument that strict liability did not apply to lessors and cannot now argue that the verdict for Firestone operates as *res judicata* or collateral estoppel to petitioner's theory of strict liability which was erroneously refused by the trial court.

The issues as between the petitioner and Firestone and the petitioner and Hertz are not the same. Consequently, we see no reason why the verdict for Firestone should interfere with the disposition of this case against Hertz.

For the reasons stated, the judgment for the defendant is reversed, and the cause is remanded for a new trial to be had in accordance with the views outlined.

It is so ordered.

CASE QUESTIONS

1. What was the advantage to the plaintiff of the court's decision to apply a strict liability in tort theory to the case rather than ordinary negligence theory?
2. What is the reasoning behind a court's decision to distribute the risk of losses to parties in products liability cases where the court chooses to follow strict liability in tort theory? (See *Greenman v. Yuba*, cited in *Stang*.)
3. Why wasn't Firestone held liable for the injuries suffered by the plaintiff, since it manufactured the tire involved?

SUGGESTED READINGS

W.L. PROSSER, LAW OF TORTS, §§ 96–104 (4th ed. 1971).
Dickerson, *The ABCs of Products' Liability*, 36 TENN. L. REV. 439 (1969).
RESTATEMENT (SECOND) OF TORTS, § 402 A.
Prosser, *The Assault upon the Citadel*, 69 YALE L.J. 1099, 1134 (1960).
Keeton, *Products' Liability—The Nature and Extent of Strict Liability*, 1964 U. ILL. L.F. 693.
Reitzel, *The Exploding Bottle Situation: Is There a Better Basis for Shopper Protection?* 15 AM. BUS. L.J. 187 (1977).
Jentz and Collins, *Extension of Strict Liability to All Third Persons*, 12 AM. BUS. L.J. (1975).

Chapter Questions

1. Define the following terms:
   a. agent
   b. assault
   c. assumption of risk
   d. battery
   e. contributory negligence
   f. conversions
   g. defamation
   h. false arrest, imprisonment
   i. independent contractor
   j. invitee
   k. libel
   l. malicious prosecution
   m. negligence
   n. principal
   o. proximate cause
   p. slander
   q. vicarious liability
   r. wanton misconduct
   s. warranty

2. The plaintiff became ill in the defendant's store. The defendant undertook to render medical aid to the plaintiff, keeping the plaintiff in an infirmary for six hours without medical care. When the plaintiff finally received proper medical care, it was determined that the extended lapse of time had seriously aggravated the plaintiff's illness. Discuss what action, if any, the plaintiff has.
   Zelenko v. Gimbel Bros., Inc., 158 Misc. 904, 287 N.Y.S. 134 (1935)

3. Plaintiff came into defendant's grocery store and purchased some cigarettes. He then asked if the store had any empty boxes he could use. The defendant instructed the plaintiff that he could find some in the back room and told the plaintiff to help himself. Plaintiff entered the room, which was dark. While searching for a light switch, the plaintiff fell into an open stairwell and was injured. What is the status of the plaintiff (invitee, licensee, trespasser)? How will the status af-

fect the plaintiff's ability to recover from the defendant, if at all? Do you think the fact that the defendant is operating a business should affect his duty?

Whelan v. Van Natta Grocery, 382 S.W.2d 205 (Ky. 1964)

4. Plaintiff's intestate was killed when the roof of the defendant's foundry fell in on him. Plaintiff alleges that the defendant failed to make proper repairs to the roof, and that such neglect of the defendant caused the roof to collapse. The defendant claims, however, that the roof collapsed during a violent storm, and that, even though the roof was in disrepair, the high winds caused the roof to fall. What issue is raised, and how would you resolve it?

Kimble v. Mackintosh Hemphill Co., 359 Pa. 461, 59 A.2d 68 (1948)

5. The plaintiff's intestate, who had been drinking, was crossing Broadway when he was negligently struck by one of defendant's cabs. As a result of the accident, the plaintiff's intestate was thrown about 20 feet, his thigh was broken, and his knee injured. He immediately became unconscious and was rushed to a hospital, where he died of delirium tremens (a disease characterized by violent shaking, often induced by excessive alcoholic consumption). Defendant argued that the deceased's alcoholism might have caused delirium tremens and death at a later date, even if defendant had not injured him. What is the main issue presented here? Who should prevail and why?

McCahill v. N.Y. Transportation Co., 201 N.Y. 221, 94 N.E. 616 (1911)

6. Plaintiff, while a spectator at a professional hockey game, is struck in the face by a puck. The defendant shot the puck attempting to score a goal, but shot too high, causing the puck to go into the spectator area. Plaintiff brings suit, and defendant claims assumption of risk. Who prevails? Suppose the defendant had been angry at crowd reaction and intentionally shot the puck into the crowd. Would the outcome change?

7. Clay Fruit, a life insurance salesman, was required to attend a business convention conducted by his employer. The convention included social as well as business events, and the plaintiff was encouraged to mix freely with out-of-state agents in order to learn as much as possible about sales techniques. One evening, after all scheduled business and social events had concluded, Fruit drove to a nearby bar and restaurant, looking for some out-of-state colleagues. Finding none, he drove back toward his hotel. On the journey back, he negligently struck the automobile of the plaintiff, causing serious injuries to the plaintiff's legs. Was Fruit in the course and scope of his employment at the time of the accident? From whom will the plaintiff be able to recover?

Fruit v. Schreiner, 502 P.2d 133 (Alas. 1972)

8. John Prater was employed by Roy Goodman as a general handyman in Goodman's music store, particularly to work on piano cases, deliver pianos, and keep the delivery truck in repair. One evening Goodman told Prater to take the truck home and work on the truck's body over the weekend. On the truck were a few of Goodman's trash cans, which Goodman had asked Prater to empty. The following morning, a Saturday, Prater loaded several of his own cans of garbage onto the truck. On his way back from the dump, Prater made a detour of a few blocks to pick up his daughter. On this detour, he had a collision with a car driven by W. M. Leuthold. Prater was later found to be negligent. Leuthold brought suit against Goodman for Prater's negligence. What issue comes to your mind, and how would you resolve it?
   Leuthold v. Goodman, 22 Wash. 2d 583, 157 P. 2d 326 (1945)

9. *Reader's Digest*, with a circulation in California alone of almost 2 million copies, published an article entitled "The Big Business of Hijacking." The purpose of the article was to describe various truck thefts and the efforts being made to stop such thefts. The plaintiff was mentioned by name in connection with a truck hijacking which had happened 11 years earlier in Danville, Kentucky. Nothing in the article indicated when the hijacking occurred. As a result of the publication, the plaintiff's daughter and friends learned of the incident for the first time. The plaintiff, a resident of California, filed suit against Reader's Digest Association for publishing the article, which disclosed truthful but embarrassing private facts about his past life. This case involves what intentional tort?
   Briscoe v. Reader's Digest Association, 93 Cal. Rptr. 866, 483 P.2d 34 (1971)

10. Defendant was the owner and operator of the Argonne Apartments in the city of Seattle. Plaintiff had been a tenant in one of the apartments for approximately a year prior to April 29. On this day, the plaintiff had made arrangements to move to another apartment house. When the moving men came for her furniture, the defendant landlord appeared on the scene with a pistol in hand and threatened to shoot them full of holes if they moved a single article belonging to the plaintiff. Soon thereafter, standing only a few feet from the plaintiff, the landlord pointed the pistol at her face and threatened to shoot her. What is the main question that the court must answer in deciding this case? How would you decide it?
    Allen v. Hannaford, 138 Wash. 423, 244 P. 700 (1926)

11. During lunch, several employees were seated around a table. The defendant David, in an effort to tease the plaintiff Janet, whom he knew to be shy, put his arm around her and pulled her head toward him. Immediately after his "friendly unsolicited hug," the plaintiff suffered a sharp pain in the back of her neck and ear, and sharp pains

in the base of her skull. As a result, she was paralyzed on the left side of her face and mouth. Was the "friendly unsolicited hug" an assault, battery, and/or negligence?

Spivey v. Battaglia, 258 So. 2d 815 (Fla. 1972)

12. Plaintiff, a black person, was invited to a business convention at defendant's hotel, which included a buffet luncheon. As the plaintiff was standing in line with others, one of the defendant's employees snatched the tray from his hand, and shouted that no Negro could be served in the hotel. Although the plaintiff was not actually touched, he was highly embarrassed by such conduct in the presence of his associates. What possible tort actions could be brought? Who is liable if the plaintiff succeeds in bringing suit?

Fisher v. Carrousel Motor Hotel, Inc., 424 S.W.2d 627 (Texas, 1967)

13. The defendant, while hunting ducks and other migratory birds, repeatedly discharged his rifle at fowl in flight over the plaintiff's land. Plaintiff brings a cause of action for trespass to land. Judgment for whom? Why?

Herrin v. Sutherland, 74 Mont. 587, 241 P. 328 (1925)

14. Anna Dorsey was a nurse in Joseph Larocque's employ at his home in Bernardsville, N.J. On September 26, Larocque's wife questioned Anna about the loss of certain jewelry. The following day, Anna was asked to go into a room where there were present other servants, Chief of Police Stryker, and a police officer named McGee. She was asked whether she was willing to "have your things searched." She consented. Her belongings were searched, and the lost property was not found. On October 4, Larocque subscribed and swore to an affidavit before the court recorder in Bernardsville. The affidavit accused Anna of stealing certain jewels. Stryker, the chief of police, later arrested Anna and, finding no proof of guilt on her part, released her. Anna later brought suit against Mr. Larocque for the intentional tort of malicious prosecution. Do you think she is entitled to recovery?

Larocque v. Dorsey, 299 F. 556 (2d Cir. 1924)

15. Plaintiff, who had an open account at defendant's shoe store, requested the cashier to cash her check. At the time, she explained to the cashier that she had put a notation on the check so that the bank would recognize that it was her check and was not a forged check on her account. The cashier took the check to the credit manager who had received information of recent passing of checks bearing plaintiff's forged name. The credit manager called the police and then recognized the plaintiff as a regular customer at the shoe store. When the police arrived, the credit manager did not make a full disclosure to

the police concerning plaintiff's identity. Plaintiff was arrested. She later brought suit against the store. What theory of tort law do you think she relied on? Explain the duty relationship between plaintiff and defendant.

Leon's Shoe Stores, Inc., v. Hornsby, 306 S.W.2d 402 (Tex. Civ. App. 1957)

16. While being treated at St. Joseph's Hospital, the plaintiff was given a blood transfusion. The hospital purchased the blood from Blood Services, Inc. Shortly after the transfusion, it was discovered that the plaintiff had contracted serum hepatitis, a highly contagious disease that can be transmitted by virus-infected transfused blood. Discuss the possible causes of action, parties, and theories of relief available to the plaintiff. Should strict liability be applied? Are there other products affecting your daily life that cannot be made entirely safe for use?

Hines v. St. Joseph's Hospital, 86 N.M. 763, 527 P.2d 1075 (1974)

XII Contracts

Nature and Classification of Contracts

A harmonious society and effective business community can exist only when members' rights and duties toward each other are recognized and enforced. The duties we voluntarily impose on ourselves take the form of contracts. When a self-imposed duty is not fulfilled, the person not performing the obligation is liable for breach of contract. Not only is commercial trade built on enforceable contracts, but every aspect of our lives is also affected by contractual obligations. We contract for our employment, college education, purchase or rental of the place where we live, purchases of goods, financing of our purchases, insurance, and marriage.

Definition of Contract

A *contract* is a legally enforceable agreement containing one or more promises. Not every promise is a contract—only those promises enforceable by law are contracts. The word *contract* is often used by lawyers and laymen when referring to a written document that contains the terms of the contract. In the legal sense, the word *contract* does not mean the tangible document containing evidence of an agreement, but rather the legally enforceable agreement itself.

In order to establish an enforceable contract, there must be (1) an agreement, (2) between competent parties, (3) based on genuine assent of the parties, (4) supported by consideration, (5) which does not contravene principles of law, and (6) which must be in writing in certain circumstances. Each of these requirements will be discussed in detail in this chapter.

An *agreement* is an expression of the parties' willingness to be bound to the terms of the contract. Usually, one party offers a proposal, and the other agrees to the terms by accepting it. Both parties to the contract must be *competent*. Some persons—because of age or mental disability—are not competent and thus do not have, from the legal standpoint, the capacity to bind themselves contractually. *Genuine assent* of both parties is also necessary. Genuine assent is presumed to exist unless one of the parties is induced to agree because of misrepresentation, fraud, duress, undue influence, or mistake.

Consideration on the part of both parties is an essential element of a contract. One party's promise (or consideration) must be bargained for and given in exchange for the other's act or promise (his consideration). The bargain cannot involve something that is prohibited by law or be against what is best for society. And finally, certain contracts, to be enforceable, must be evidenced by a writing.

Common law is the primary source of the law of contracts. Many statutes affect contracts, especially specific types of contracts, such as employment and insurance. But the overwhelming body of contractual principles is embodied in court decisions.

The Uniform Commercial Code (U.C.C.), which for the most part has been passed by all the states, has had the largest legislative impact on the law of contracts. As far as contract law is concerned, the U.C.C. governs only sales (and contracts to sell) goods. *Goods* are defined as movables, or personal property having tangible form. Thus the U.C.C. does not cover transactions involving realty, services, or the sale of intangibles. If a contract involves a mixed goods/services sale (for example, application of a hair product as part of a beauty treatment), courts tend to apply the U.C.C. only if the sale-of-goods aspect dominates the transaction. The U.C.C. was set up in an attempt to make the laws governing certain commercial transactions uniform among various jurisdictions. Reference will be made to it throughout the chapter where appropriate.

Valid, Void, Voidable, and Unenforceable Contracts

Contracts can be classified in terms of validity and enforceability. A *valid contract* is a binding and enforceable agreement with all the necessary contractual requirements being met. A contract is said to be valid and enforceable when a person is entitled to judicial relief in case of breach by the other party.

A *void contract* means no contract, since it has no legal effect whatsoever. When no legal obligation is created, an agreement is said to be void. When an agreement lacks a necessary contractual element—such as consideration, for example—the agreement is without legal effect, and therefore void.

A *voidable contract* exists when one or more persons can elect to avoid an obligation created by a contract. It is not wholly lacking in legal effect, since not all the parties can legally avoid their duties under it. The right of one or more parties to avoid an obligation created by the contract exists because of the manner in which the contract was brought about. For example, someone who has been induced to make a contract by fraud or duress may be able to avoid the obligation created by the contract. Contracts made by those who are not of legal age are also voidable, at the option of the party lacking legal capacity.

A contract is *unenforceable* (not void or voidable) when a defense to the enforceability of a contract is present. For example, the right of action is lost in a situation in which a sufficient writing cannot be produced when required for enforceability. Also, when a party wanting to enforce a contract waits beyond the time period prescribed by law to bring the court action (*statute of limitations*), the contract is unenforceable.

Bilateral and Unilateral Contracts

All contracts involve at least two parties. If both the parties make promises, a bilateral contract results. When only one makes a promise, then a unilateral contract comes into existence. *Bilateral contracts* consist simply of mutual promises to do some future act. The promises on both sides need not be express; one of the promises could be implied from the surrounding circumstances.

A *unilateral contract* results when one party makes a promise in exchange for another person performing an act or refraining from doing something. For example, assume that someone wants to buy an item owned by another for $100. If the buyer promises the owner to pay $100 for the item *if and when* the owner conveys legal title and possession to the buyer, a *uni*lateral contract is created. It is a promise of an act. The contract comes into existence when the act of conveying title and possession is performed. If, however, the buyer promises to pay $100 in exchange for the owner's promise to convey title and possession of the item, a bilateral contract results. A *bi*lateral contract comes into existence when mutual promises are made.

Agreement

In order for a contract to be formed, there must be a mutual *agreement* between two or more competent parties. They must manifest their intent to be bound to definite terms. The agreement is usually reached by one party making an offer and the other—expressly or impliedly—accepting the terms of the offer.

The intention of the parties is the primary factor determining the nature of the contract. The intention is ascertained not just from the words used by the parties, but also from the entire situation, including the acts and conduct of the parties. In determining the intent of the parties, the courts generally use an objective rather than a subjective test. In the objective test, the question is: What would a reasonable person in the position of one party think was meant by the words, conduct, or both, of the other party? If the subjective test were used, the question would be: What did the party actually mean by certain expressions? For example, suppose that one of the parties is not serious about creating a legal obligation, but the other party has no way of knowing this. Under the objective test, a contract would be created.

In law, invitations to social events lack contractual intention, and, when accepted, do not give rise to a binding contract. For example, when two people agree to have dinner together or go to a baseball game together, each usually feels a moral obligation to fulfill his promise. Neither, however, expects to be legally bound by the agreement. An agreement also lacks contractual intent when a party's assent to it is made in obvious anger, excitement, or jest. This is true even when the parties' expressions, if taken literally as stated, would amount to mutual assent. Sometimes proposals are made in anger, excitement, or jest, but that fact is not always obvious. Under the objective test, the surrounding circumstances and context of the expressions would be examined to determine what a reasonably prudent person would believe.

Offer

The usual manner in which parties manifest assent in the formation of a contract is that one party makes an offer and the other accepts the terms of the offer. An *offer* is a proposal to make a contract. It is a promise conditional upon a return promise, act, or forbearance being given in exchange by the offeree. The return promise, act, or forbearance is acceptance of the offer.

REQUIREMENTS OF AN OFFER

A legally effective offer must be (1) a definite proposal (2) made with the intent to contract and (3) communicated to the offeree. The terms of the offer, on acceptance, become the terms of the contract. An offer must be definite and certain, so that when the offeree accepts, both parties understand the obligations they have created.

It is important to distinguish between a definite proposal, which is an offer, and a solicitation of an offer. A willingness to make or receive an offer is not itself an offer, but an invitation to negotiate. For example, the question, ''Would you be interested in buying my television set for $100?'' is considered an invitation to negotiate. A response of Yes would not create a contract, since there was no definite proposal made.

For an offer to be effective, it need not be made to one specific named person. It can be made to the general public, in the form of an advertisement. Advertisements can be in the form of circulars, quotation sheets, displays, and announcements in publications. The publication of the fact that an item is for sale, and its price, is usually an invitation to negotiate, not an offer. Most advertisements are not definite proposals, but only an invitation to potential customers to make offers to buy the goods.

TERMINATION OF AN OFFER

The power of the offeree to bind the offeror lasts for the duration of the offer. The duration of an offer is the time period from the moment an offer is effectively communicated to the offeree until it is terminated. An offer can be terminated by (1) revocation by the offeror, (2) lapse of time, (3) subsequent illegality, (4) destruction of the subject matter, (5) death or lack of capacity, (6) rejection, (7) a counter offer, and (8) acceptance.

An offeror has the power to terminate the offer by revocation at any time before it is accepted. Even when an offeror promises to hold an offer open for a certain period of time, the offeror can revoke the offer before that time, unless consideration is given to hold the offer open. For example, a seller promises in an offer to give the offeree one week to accept the offer. The seller, *even though promising* to hold the offer open for one week, retains the power to withdraw the offer at any time.

A contract whereby an offeror is bound to hold an offer open is called an *option*. In an option contract, consideration is necessary in return for the promise to hold the offer open. For example, assume that the offeree pays the offeror $10 to hold an offer open for ten days. Since a $10 consideration was given for the promise to hold the offer open, the offeror does not have the power to withdraw the offer before the ten-day period is up.

An offer may stipulate how long it will remain open, in which case it automatically terminates with the expiration of the stated period of time. When an offer does not stipulate a time period within which it may be accepted, it is then effective for a reasonable length of time.

When an offer to enter into a contract is legal when made, but becomes illegal before accepted, the offer is void. An offer to enter into an agreement forbidden by law is ineffective and void. If the subject matter of an offer is destroyed, the offer is automatically terminated because of impossibility.

An offer is terminated at the death of either the offeror or the offeree. Adjudication of insanity usually has the same effect as death in terminating an offer. The termination is effective automatically without any need to give notice. For example, assume that a person offers to sell an item at a stated price, but dies before the offer is accepted. There can be no contract because one of the parties died before a meeting of minds took place. If the offeree had accepted the offer before the death, however, there would have been a meeting of minds. In this situation, the offeror's estate would be responsible under the contract.

An offer is also terminated by a rejection or a counter offer. When an offeree does not intend to accept an offer and so informs the offeror, the offer is said to have been terminated by rejection. If the offeree responds to an offer by making another proposal, the proposal constitutes a *counter offer*. It terminates the original offer. For example, an offer is made to sell merchandise for $300. The offeree then offers to buy the same merchandise for $250. The offeree has rejected the original offer by making a counter offer. But if the offeree had asked whether the offeror would consider reducing the price to $250, this would not terminate the original offer, since it would be merely an inquiry. An *inquiry*, or a request for additional terms, by the offeree is not a counter offer and does not terminate the offer.

Acceptance

An acceptance is an expression of agreement by the offeree to be bound by the terms of the offer. An offeror gives the offeree the power to accept the offer. There is no meeting of the minds until the offeree has consented to the proposition contained in the offer. In order for an acceptance to be effective in creating a contract, there must be (1) an unconditional consent, (2) to an open offer, (3) by the offeree only, and (4) communicated to the offeror.

For an effective acceptance, there must be some act of manifestation of the intention to contract. The act of manifestation can be in the form of (1) silence or inaction, (2) a promise, (3) an act or forbearance from an act, or (4) any other manner specifically stipulated in the offer.

In most situations, silence or inaction on the part of the offeree does not constitute acceptance. When a person receives goods or services expecting that they will have to be paid for, the act of receiving the goods or services constitutes acceptance of the offer. An offeror is usually not permitted to word the offer in such a way that silence or inaction of the offeree constitutes acceptance. However, silence or inaction *can* do so in situations in which this method of dealing has been established by agreement between the parties, or by prior dealings of the parties.

In an offer to enter into a bilateral contract, the offeree must communicate acceptance in the form of a promise to the offeror. The offeror must be made aware, by an express or implied promise, that a contract has been formed. An offer to enter into a unilateral contract calls for an acceptance in the form of an act. A mere promise to perform the act is not an effective acceptance.

The offeror has the power to stipulate the means and method of acceptance. The acceptance must comply with the stipulations. For example, an oral acceptance of an offer that called for a written acceptance would be ineffective. If nothing is stated, a reasonable means or method of acceptance is effective. An offer can provide that the acceptance is effective only on the completion of specified formalities. In such a situation, all these formalities must be complied with in order to have an effective acceptance.

At common law, an acceptance that changes the terms of an offer in any way acts only as a counter offer and has no effect as an acceptance. It must be a "mirror image" of the offer. Under U.C.C. § 2–207, covering contracts that involve the sale of goods, an acceptance that adds new or different terms is effective in creating a contract by the terms of the original offer. The new terms are proposals that must be accepted separately.

Roberts v. Buske
12 Ill. App. 3d 630, 298 N.E.2d 795
Appellate Court of Illinois
July 10, 1973

CREBS, JUSTICE
The Circuit Court of Montgomery County, sitting without a jury, rendered judgment for $358 plus costs in favor of plaintiff and against defendant. The issue involved is whether a renewal of an automobile liability policy was accepted by defendant, thereby imposing liability upon him for the annual premium prorated up to the time policy was returned and canceled.

The facts are undisputed. In September 1969, plaintiff, an insurance agent, sent defendant a policy that was a renewal of one defendant's father had previously held. Defendant had not ordered or requested issuance of this policy, but he accepted it and paid the premium. In September 1970, just prior to the expiration date of the policy, a second unsolicited renewal was sent to defendant. Attached to it was a printed notice stating that if defendant did not wish to accept it, he must return it or be liable for the premium. Defendant made no response either to this notice or to two subsequent bills mailed to him. Finally, in December, the agent telephoned defendant personally to inquire about the premium. Defendant informed him that he had purchased a policy from another company in

August, and that since he had not ordered the renewal, he felt no obligation to pay for it. The policy was then returned to the company and canceled, resulting in a loss to the agent for the prorated portion of the premium which he had advanced.

In his brief, plaintiff appears to accept the fact that the basic requisites of a valid contract are equally applicable to an insurance contract, and that a bare offer imposes no liability upon the person to whom it is made until it is accepted. However, he argues that because defendant had previously accepted a renewal policy and thereafter paid the premium, his silence in replying to the second renewal constituted an implied acceptance thereof and obligated him to pay the premium.

There do not appear to be any Illinois cases directly in point on this issue. However, other jurisdictions have considered the question. In *Preferred Risk Insurance Co. v. Central Sur. & Ins. Corp.* (*D.C. Ark.*), 191 F.Supp. 797, the facts were almost identical. After purchase of one policy, the insured accepted a renewal and paid the premium. Prior to the expiration of the renewal period, another renewal was sent to insured, but she did not pay the premium, nor did she return the policy or reply to two subsequently sent bills. She had purchased a different policy from a different company. During this time, she had an accident. The second insurance company settled on its policy and then sued the first company to recover its prorata share of the loss on the theory that its policy was also effective. The court held that the unsolicited delivery of the renewal policy was a mere offer; that insured's failure to return the policy or pay the premium did not create an implied acceptance; that her purchase of another policy from another company strongly indicated her rejection of the first company's offer; and that, therefore, no valid contract of insurance existed with the first company.

A single transaction does not establish a course of conduct or course of dealing sufficient to constitute an implied acceptance based on silence, and that acceptance cannot be presumed from a mere failure to decline a proposal. Plaintiff had sent only one other renewal to defendant and that was for a policy previously held by defendant's father. He stated that he also sent a copy of the policy to defendant's mortgagee, but that adds little to his argument. Where property is mortgaged, it is normal procedure to provide the mortgagee with a copy of the policy, attaching a mortgage clause so that the latter may be assured that his interests are protected. The same procedure would have been followed by any other insurance company and was not a singular service rendered by plaintiff. Plaintiff also argues that if defendant had had an accident, he undoubtedly would have looked to plaintiff's company for coverage. This is a pure assumption and irrelevant, and there is authority to the contrary. Defendant was covered by another policy issued by another company, and he would have no reason to look to plaintiff's company for coverage.

We recognize that the practice of sending renewals oftentimes serves the best interests of an insured; but, likewise, it serves the best business interests of the insurance agent. And it is the agent, as the offeror, who must assure himself that his offer has been accepted. Under ordinary circumstances, silence cannot be relied upon to establish an acceptance of an offer to enter into a contract. We do not preclude the possibility of an implied acceptance being established under certain circumstances. However, as held in the case above cited, we cannot find that acceptance of a single previous renewal in itself is sufficient to constitute an implied acceptance of a second renewal based solely on the silence of the offeree. Not only is the mailing of a first renewal policy insufficient to show a previous course of dealing between the parties, but plaintiff presented no evidence regarding the customary trade practice, if any, in situations similar to that presented here. It is obvious that plaintiff feels abused in that defendant did not inform him that he had bought another policy, but a simple telephone call would have revealed this fact, and there would have been no reason for plaintiff to have incurred the loss caused by his unwarranted assumption.

The judgment of the Circuit Court of Montgomery County is reversed.

Reversed

Case Questions

1. Silence in this case did not constitute acceptance. Change the facts of the case so that silence *would* constitute acceptance under the circumstances.

2. Assume that you are an insurance company executive, and your company has followed the practice of sending renewals to your customers. Should you change the practice because of the *Roberts v. Buske* decision?

Suggested Readings

J.D. Calamari and J.M. Perillo, Contracts, §§ 2–1 to 2–8 (2nd ed. 1977).

A.L. Corbin, Corbin on Contracts, §§ 1–4 (1952).

McLeod, *Exchange of Contracts by Post*, 130 New Law J. 456 (1980).

Restatement (Second) of Contracts, §§ 1–5, 13–4, 24, 25, 28, 29, 34–41, 52–73.

Taylor, *Special Developments in Commercial Law*, 11 Rut.-Cam. L. Rev. 575 (1980).

Reality of Consent

Genuine assent to be bound by a contract is not present when one of the parties' consent is obtained through duress, undue influence, fraud, or innocent misrepresentation, or when either of the parties, or both, made a mistake concerning the contract. These are defenses against the enforce-ability of a contract. They can also be used against other legal documents, such as wills, trust agreements, and executed gifts.

A contract entered into under duress, or as a result of undue influence, fraud, innocent misrepresentation, or mistake is usually voidable. The in-jured party has the right to elect to avoid or affirm the agreement.

An injured party who wishes to avoid or rescind a contract should act promptly. Silence beyond a reasonable length of time may be deemed an implied ratification. An injured party who elects to rescind a contract is entitled to the return of any property or money given in performance of the contract. The injured party must also return any property or money received through the contract. The act of restoring the property or money is called *restitution*.

Duress

Freedom of will of both parties to a contract is absolutely necessary. When one of the parties' will is overcome because of duress, the agreement is voidable. *Duress* is any unlawful constraint exercised on persons that forces their consent to an agreement which they would not otherwise have made. Unlike those situations in which people act as a result of fraud, innocent misrepresentation, or mistake, a person acting under duress does so *knowingly*. Duress is a condition of the mind produced by wrongful external pressure that causes the victim to contract without use of his own volition. Three elements are necessary for duress to exist: (1) coercion, (2) causing a loss of free will, and (3) resulting in a consent to be bound by a contract.

Any form of constraint improperly exercised in order to get another's consent to contract is sufficient for coercion. Exercise of pressure to con-tract is not enough; it must be exercised wrongfully. Advice, suggestion, or persuasion are not recognized as coercive. Causing a person to fear em-barrassment or annoyance usually does not constitute duress. In order to amount to coercion, the constraint must entail threatened injury or force. The real question is whether the pressure did in fact deprive the person of contractual volition. Any acts that do not deprive the person of the free ex-ercise of will do not constitute duress. For duress to exist, the person must enter into the agreement while under the influence of a threat.

The threat need not necessarily be to the person or the property of the contracting party. It could be exerted over a close relative. For example, a threat to injure the child of a contracting party could amount to duress. A threat of criminal prosecution gives rise to duress when fear overcomes judgment and deprives the person of the exercise of free will. Making a threat of civil action, however—with the honest belief that it may be suc-cessful—is not using duress. For example, assume that an employee embezzles an undetermined amount of money from an employer. The employer estimates that the theft amounts to about $5000, and threatens to bring a civil suit for damages unless the employee pays $5000. Even though the employee takes the threat seriously and pays the $5000, no duress exists. If the employer were to threaten to bring criminal charges under the same circumstances, duress would take place.

Economic duress or business compulsion may be grounds for duress. The court determines whether undue advantage has been taken of a person's economic distress in order to coerce the person into contracting. The surrounding circumstances of the business setting and the relative bargaining positions of the contracting parties are examined in order to determine whether duress is present. Duress is applied only when unjustified coercion is used to induce an agreement.

Austin Instrument, Inc., v. Loral Corporation
29 N.Y.2d 124, 272 N.E.2d 533
Court of Appeals of New York
July 6, 1971

FULD, CHIEF JUDGE
The defendant, Loral Corporation, seeks to recover payment for goods delivered under a contract which it had with the plaintiff, Austin Instrument, Inc., on the ground that the evidence establishes that it was forced to agree to an increase in price on the items in question under circumstances amounting to economic duress.

In July of 1965, Loral was awarded a $6 million contract by the Navy for the production of radar sets. The contract contained a schedule of deliveries, a liquidated damages clause applying to late deliveries, and a cancellation clause in case of default by Loral. The latter thereupon solicited bids for some 40 precision gear components needed to produce the radar sets and awarded Austin a subcontract to supply 23 such parts. That party commenced delivery in early 1966.

In May 1966, Loral was awarded a second Navy contract for the production of more radar sets and again went about soliciting bids. Austin bid on all 40 gear components but on July 15, a representative from Loral informed Austin's president, Mr. Krauss, that his company would be awarded the subcontract only for those items on which it was low bidder. The Austin officer refused to accept an order for less than all 40 of the gear parts. On the next day, he told Loral that Austin would cease deliveries of the parts due under the existing subcontract unless Loral consented to substantial increases in the prices provided for by that agreement—both retroactively for parts already delivered and prospectively on those not yet shipped. He placed with Austin the order for all 40 parts needed under Loral's second Navy contract. Shortly thereafter, Austin did, indeed, stop delivery. After contacting 10 manufacturers of precision gears and finding none who could produce the parts in time to meet its commitments to the Navy, Loral acceded to Austin's demands. In a letter dated July 22, Loral wrote to Austin that "we have feverishly surveyed other sources of supply and find that because of the prevailing military exigencies, were they to start from scratch as would have to be the case, they could not even remotely begin to deliver on time to meet the delivery requirements established by the government. Accordingly, we are left with no choice or alternative but to meet your conditions."

Loral thereupon consented to the price increases insisted upon by Austin under the first subcontract, and the latter was awarded a second subcontract making it the supplier of all 40 gear parts for Loral's second contract with the Navy. Although Austin was granted until September to resume deliveries, Loral did, in fact, receive parts in August and was able to produce the radar sets in time to meet its commitments to the Navy on both contracts. After Austin's last delivery under the second subcontract in July 1967, Loral notified it of its intention to seek recovery of the price increases.

On September 15, 1967, Austin instituted this action against Loral to recover an amount in excess of $17,750 which was still due on the second subcontract. On the same day, Loral commenced an action against Austin claiming damages of some $22,250—the aggregate of the price increases under the first subcontract—on the ground of economic duress. The two actions were consolidated, and following a trial, Austin was awarded the sum it requested and Loral's complaint against Austin was dismissed on the ground that it was not shown that "it could not have obtained the items in question from other sources in time to meet its commitment to the Navy under the first contract." A closely divided appellate division affirmed (35 A.D.2d 387, 316 N.Y.S.2d 528, 532). The facts are virtually undisputed, nor is there any serious question of law. The difficulty lies in the application of the law to these facts.

The applicable law is clear and, indeed, is not disputed by the parties. A contract is voidable on the ground of duress when it is established that the party making the claim was forced to agree to it by means of a wrongful threat precluding the exercise of his free will. The existence of economic duress or business compulsion is demonstrated by proof that immediate possession of needful goods is threatened or, more particularly, in cases such as the one before us, by proof that one party to a contract has threatened to breach the agreement by withholding goods unless the other party agrees to some further demand. However, a mere threat by one party to breach the contract by not delivering the required items, though wrongful, does not in itself constitute economic duress. It must also appear that the threatened party could not obtain the goods from another source of supply, and that the ordinary remedy of an action for breach of contract would not be adequate.

We find without any support in the record the conclusion reached by the courts below that Loral failed to establish that it was the victim of economic duress. On the contrary, the evidence makes out a classic case, as a matter of law, of such duress.

It is manifest that Austin's threat—to stop deliveries unless the prices were increased—deprived Loral of its free will. As bearing on this, Loral's relationship with the government is most significant. As mentioned above, its contract called for staggered monthly deliveries of the radar sets, with clauses calling for liquidated damages and possible cancellation on default. Because of its production schedule, Loral was, in July 1966, concerned with meeting its delivery requirements in September, October, and November, and it was for the sets to be delivered in those months that the withheld gears were needed. Loral had to plan ahead, and the substantial liquidated damages for which it would be liable, plus the threat of default, were genuine possibilities. Moreover, Loral did a substantial portion of its business with the government, and it feared that a failure to deliver as agreed upon would jeopardize its chances for future contracts. These genuine concerns do not merit the label "self-imposed, undisclosed, and subjective" which the appellate division majority placed upon them. It was perfectly reasonable for Loral, or any other party similarly placed, to consider itself in an emergency, duress situation.

Loral had the burden of demonstrating that it could not obtain the parts elsewhere within a reasonable time, and there can be no doubt that it met this burden. The 10 manufacturers whom Loral contacted comprised its entire list of "approved vendors" for precision gears, and none was able to commence delivery soon enough. As Loral was producing a highly sophisticated item of military machinery requiring parts made to the strictest engineering standards, it would be unreasonable to hold that Loral should have gone to other vendors, with whom it was either unfamiliar or dissatisfied, to procure the needed parts.

It is hardly necessary to add that Loral's normal legal remedy of accepting Austin's breach of the contract and then suing for damages would have been inadequate under the circumstances. Loral would still have had to obtain the gears elsewhere with all the concomitant consequences mentioned above. In other words, Loral actually had no choice when the prices were raised by Austin, except to take the gears at the "coerced" prices and then sue to get the excess back.

Austin's final argument is that Loral, even if it did enter into the contract under duress, lost any rights it had to a refund of money by waiting until July 1967, long after the termination date of the contract, to disaffirm it. It is true that one who would recover moneys allegedly paid under duress must act promptly to make his claim known.

In this case, Loral delayed making its demand for a refund until three days after Austin's last delivery on the second subcontract. Loral's reason—for waiting until that time—is that it feared another stoppage of deliveries which would again put it in an untenable situation. Considering Austin's conduct in the past, this was perfectly reasonable, as the possibility of an application by Austin of further business compulsion still existed until all the parts were delivered.

In sum, the record before us demonstrates that Loral agreed to the price increases in consequence of the economic duress employed by Austin. Accordingly, the matter should be remanded to the trial court for a computation of its damages.

CASE QUESTIONS

1. Is economic duress in keeping with modern business dealings?
2. If you were an official of Loral Corporation, how would you have handled the negotiation with Mr. Krauss, Austin's president, concerning the precision gear components?
3. If you were Mr. Krauss, Austin's president, would you have handled the negotiations with Loral Corporation's representative in the same manner?

SUGGESTED READINGS

J.D. CALAMARI AND J.M. PERILLO, CONTRACTS, §§ 9–1 to 9–8 (2nd ed. 1977).
Beatson, *Duress as a Vitiating Factor*, 33 CAMBRIDGE L. J. 97 (1974).
Sutton, *Duress by Threatened Breach of Contract*, 20 McGILL L. J. 554 (1974).

Undue Influence

Undue influence and duress are similar in that, in both, unlawful control is exerted by one party over another so as to substitute the first party's will for the volition of the injured party. An agreement can be voidable as a result of influence even though there is no coercion amounting to duress. *Undue influence* results when the will of a dominant person is substituted for that of the other party, and the substitution is done in an unlawful fashion, resulting in an unfair agreement. Usually, undue influence is found when there is (1) a confidential relationship that is used to create (2) an unfair bargain.

A confidential relationship could arise from the fact that the dominant party has some authority over another, or when the other party is mentally weak or in a situation of distress. In determining whether a confidential relationship exists, all the surrounding circumstances are examined to find out whether one of the parties dominates the other to the extent that the other is dependent on him. Family relationships, such as husband–wife or parent–child, often give rise to confidential relationships. Some relationships involving a special trust—such as trustee–beneficiary or attorney–client—entail a confidential relationship. Sometimes confidential relationships are created between business associates, neighbors, or friends. Or a person who is mentally weak—because of sickness, old age, or distress—may not be capable of resisting the dominant party's influence.

Whenever there is dominance in a confidential relationship, the court next determines whether the contract was equitable and voluntary. A contract is not invalid simply because there is a confidential relationship. A contract is voidable if one abuses the confidence in a relationship in order to obtain personal gain by substituting one's own will or interest for that of another. Whether the weaker party has had the benefit of independent advice is an important factor in determining fairness in contractual dealings. A legitimate suggestion or persuasion may influence someone, but it is not undue influence; nor, usually, is an appeal to the affections. When methods go beyond mere persuasion and prevent a person from acting freely, undue influence is present.

Fraud

The term *fraud* covers all intentional acts of deception used by one individual to gain an advantage over another. The essential elements of actionable fraud are (1) the misstatement of a material fact, (2) made with knowledge of its falsity, or in reckless disregard of its truth or falsity, (3) with the intention to deceive, (4) inducing reliance by the other party, and (5) which results or will result in injury to the other party. All five elements must be present before actionable fraud exists.

For fraud, the statement or statements must be false; hence the term *misstatement.* Such misstatements must be of a fact, a *fact* being something that existed in the past or exists at present. The misstated fact must be material. The often-used definition of a *material fact* is that it is a fact without which the contract would not have been entered into. Materiality depends on the facts and circumstances surrounding the contract. The speaker, when making the statement, must know that it is false. A statement made in reckless disregard of the truth satisfies the ''knowledge'' requirement of actionable fraud. The stating party must have the intention to deceive, and thereby induce the other party to enter into the contract. The deceived party's reliance on the misstatement must be justified and reasonable. A misstatement must be relied on to the deceived party's detriment. A party wishing to rescind a contract need not show actual damages resulting from the fraud. However, a party wishing to sue for damages in addition to rescission must prove that actual damage has been sustained.

Innocent Misrepresentation

When a party to a contract misrepresents a material fact, *even though unknowingly*, and the other party relies on and is misled by the falsehood, *innocent misrepresentation* is present. If a contract is induced by innocent misrepresentation, the deceived party has the right of rescission. Fraud and innocent misrepresentation are quite similar. The *intent* to deceive is the primary distinction between fraudulent and nonfraudulent misrepresentation. Rescission and restitution are available for both. In cases of fraud, but *not* in cases of innocent misrepresentation, damages are obtainable, in addition to rescission and restitution.

Mistake

Sometimes one or both of the parties to a contract understand the facts to be other than they are. Ignorance about some matter may influence a person to enter into a contractual relation with another. If ignorance of a fact is material to the contract, a *mistake* exists and the contract may be voidable. A mistake of material fact related to the contract is sufficient for relief, whereas a mistake of law is not. The mistake must refer to a past or present material fact, not to a future possibility.

When one enters into a plain and unambiguous contract, one cannot avoid the obligation created by proving that its terms were misunderstood. One should not be able to benefit from his ignorance resulting from lack of due diligence. Poor judgment, lack of wisdom, or a mistake as to the true value of an item contracted for are not grounds for relief. Relief based on mistake may not be had because one party to a speculative contract expected it to turn out differently than it did.

Wood v. Kalbaugh
39 Cal.App.3d 926, 114 Cal. Rptr.673
Court of Appeal, Fifth District
June 19, 1974

GARGANO, ASSOCIATE JUSTICE
This is an appeal from a judgment of the Superior Court of Kern County upholding respondents' unilateral rescission of a contract to purchase appellants' house and granting restitution. The sole question is whether the evidence supports the judgment.

In July 1970, appellants, the Kalbaughs, who had lived in their home on Glenwood Drive in Bakersfield, California, for more than five years, listed the house for sale with the Bakersfield Investment & Realty Company. Joyce Barnes, a real estate agent for the realty company, then showed the house to respondents; she told them that with the exception of the dishwasher "everything was in perfect shape." Thereupon, respondents executed a written agreement to buy the home for the purchase price of $13,400. They agreed to make a down payment of $1700, to assume a first mortgage in the amount of $8700, and to execute a promissory note in favor of appellants for the balance of the purchase price, to be secured by a second deed of trust against the property. A 30-day escrow was opened with the Title Insurance and Trust Company in Bakersfield, and respondents deposited the $1,700 down payment into the escrow. They also executed all necessary documents to complete the transaction.

On August 14, 1970, an employee of the Pacific Gas & Electric Company told respondents that he could not turn on the utilities to the Glenwood Drive house because there was a dangerous leak in the gas line. Respondents called the title company and informed the escrow officer that they were not going to go through with the escrow. The following day, respondents informed Joyce Barnes that they were not going to buy appellants' house because the gas line had a dangerous leak.

On August 15, 1970, appellant William Kalbaugh and his father, a boilermaker with plumbing experience, inspected the gas line and discovered that the leak was caused by a break in a rusted pipe running under the driveway; they pulled out the pipe and replaced it. Kalbaugh testified that after repairing the break, he pumped 15 pounds of air into the line, and that when he returned the next day, the gauge still read 15 pounds. He said he obtained a building permit from the city of Bakersfield on the following Monday and requested an inspection. The line was inspected by a city inspector and passed city safety requirements.

On August 17, 1970, the escrow closed, and thereafter, respondents failed to make any payments on the first mortgage or the second deed of trust. On October 6, 1970, appellants commenced foreclosure proceedings against respondents. Approximately seven weeks later, respondents served appellants with a notice of rescission and tendered a grant deed to the Glenwood Drive property. Appellants refused to accept the rescission or the tender of the deed. The foreclosure proceedings were completed on February 11, 1971.

In 1972, respondents brought this action in the court below for restitution. They took the position that they had rescinded the agreement to purchase appellants' house unilaterally. After court trial, the court entered judgment awarding respondents the sum of $1,804 as restitution for the down payment respondents deposited in the escrow. The court determined that the unilateral rescission was justified and declared that title to the house was vested in appellants.

It is clear that the evidence does not support the court's judgment on the theory of actual fraud. Appellants were not aware of the leak in the gas line when their agent told respondents that appellants' house was ''in perfect shape.'' Respondents' complaint for restitution was not grounded on fraud alone. It also was predicated on innocent misrepresentation, and in this state, a contract may be rescinded by a contracting party unilaterally if his consent to be bound by the agreement was induced by a material misrepresentation, though innocently made.

To justify the unilateral rescission of a contract on the ground of misrepresentation, it must be shown that the misrepresentation was of a material fact. Ordinarily, a misrepresentation is of a material fact if it would be likely to affect the conduct of a reasonable man with reference to the transaction in question. But a distinction must be drawn between a fraudulent misrepresentation and an innocent one. For example, if *A*, with knowledge of *B's* idiosyncrasy or personal belief, willfully conceals a fact related to the idiosyncrasy or belief to induce *B* to enter into a contract, *A* should not reap the fruit of his deception merely because it is unlikely that the misrepresentation would have affected a reasonable man. However, where the misrepresentation is unintentional, there are innocent parties on both sides of the contract. Materiality of the mistake induced by innocent misrepresentation is essential, whereas materiality is not essential if a mistake induced by fraud produces the intended consequences. As to innocent misrepresentations, the right to rescind is based on equitable principles, and equity dictates that in determining whether the misrepresentation was of a material fact, the objective test is applicable. In fact, it is basic that the effect of an innocent misrepresentation is destroyed if the facts subsequently accord with the representation.

We consider the misrepresentation which was made in this case with the equitable formula in mind.

Joyce Barnes's statement that appellants' house was "in perfect shape" cannot be taken in the literal sense. At the very best, it was a representation that the house was in good condition and, according to early concepts, would have been treated as commendatory language known as "sales talk" or "puffing." Under modern trend, such statements, particularly when made by builders and real estate agents, are considered representations of a material fact because they tend to induce reasonable men to purchase the property which is up for sale. Consequently, while Ms. Barnes's statement was in the nature of an opinion and cannot be viewed as a representation that appellants' house was perfect in every way, the statement obviously was intended to convey the impression that the house was in good condition and was a representation of a material fact. The question narrows to whether the leak in the gas line was a substantial defect under the objective standard so that it can be said that when the escrow closed, and later when respondents, for the first time, proceeded to effect rescission, the house was not in good condition.

We have concluded that the answer to this question is in the negative. Respondents had the burden of proof in this case, and they presented no evidence to show that the gas line in question was of inferior quality or that the leak was caused by defective workmanship. The only evidence presented on the issue shows that the leak was caused by a break in a rusted pipeline, that the rusted pipeline was replaced immediately by William Kalbaugh and his father, and that the repair work was tested by the Kalbaughs carefully and later passed city safety requirements. Nevertheless, the trial judge reasoned that respondents were entitled to rescind their contract because when the contract was entered into the gas leak created a dangerous condition, making the house uninhabitable at that time. The judge did not believe that the fact that the gas leak was readily reparable and was repaired by respondents immediately was germane to the issue involved. If this reasoning is carried to its ultimate conclusion, it would mean that a purchaser who has contracted to buy real property could rescind the contract prior to the close of escrow if he discovered a dangerous condition on the property, no matter how inconsequential or easily remediable the cause which gave rise to the condition may have been.

Breaks in underground pipelines are not rare or unusual occurrences and can be caused by rust or erosion. To hold that a house or other building, which is at least five years old, was not in good condition at the time for the performance of the contract of sale or, as in this case, when the escrow closed, because when the contract was made there was a readily reparable break in an underground gas line or sewer outlet or electrical conduit which was repaired immediately by the seller would jeopardize the integrity of contracts for the sale of property. And to declare that the purchaser could justify this unilateral rescission of the contract without even showing that the gas line or the sewer outlet or the electrical conduit, although repaired, was still in a dangerous or defective condition would place an undue restriction on good-faith sellers of property who often change their position as a result of the sale.

Furthermore, the court granted respondents restitution of their down payment without any evidence to support the implied finding that they actually relied on the representation that the house was in "perfect shape" when they agreed to buy it. For example, Mrs. Wood had been a licensed real estate saleswoman in Colorado, and she testified only that she would not have entered into the agreement had she known that there was a leak in the gas line, regardless of whether the leak was reparable. Neither Mrs. Wood nor her husband testified that they would not have purchased the house but for the representation which was made by the real estate agent. It is elementary that to justify the rescission of a contract on the ground that there was a misrepresentation of a material fact, it must be shown that the party seeking to rescind relied on the representation and that he would not have entered into the contract without it.

The judgment is reversed.

CASE QUESTIONS

1. Would there have been a different result if the seller and Joyce Barnes knew about the leak in the gas line when Barnes stated that the house was "in perfect shape"?
2. Is the statement that something is "in perfect shape" sales talk or considered a representation of material fact?

Suggested Readings

J.D. Calamari and J.M. Perillo, Contracts, §§ 9–15 to 9–30 (2d ed. 1977).

A.L. Corbin, Corbin on Contracts, §§ 27–29 (1952).

Goldberg and Thomson, *The Effect of Mistake on Contracts*, 1978 J. of Bus. L. 30 (1978).

Kronman, *Mistake, Disclosure, Information and the Law of Contracts*, 7 J. of Legal Studies 1 (1978).

Zelestis, *Misrepresentation—Doubts on Damages*, 126 New L. J. 1158 (1976).

Consideration

Consideration is simply defined as that which is bargained for and given in exchange for another's promise. Each party to a contract has a motive or price that induces the party to enter into the obligation. This cause or inducement is called consideration. A promise, an act, or forbearance is offered by one party to the contract and accepted by the other as an inducement to the other's promise or act.

A person must bargain specifically for the promise, act, or forbearance in order for it to constitute consideration. A promise is usually binding only when consideration is given in exchange. If a person promises to give another $100, this is a promise to make a gift, and it is unenforceable since the promise lacked consideration. If the promisee had given something in exchange for the promise, it would have been enforceable. For example, if the promisee had promised to convey a television set in return for the promise to convey the $100, the promise to give $100 would have been supported by consideration and therefore would be enforceable. Although a promise to make a gift is not enforceable, a person who has received a gift is not required to return it for lack of consideration.

Consideration is an obligation that usually consists of an act or a promise to do an act. Forbearance or a promise to forbear may also constitute consideration. Forbearance is refraining from doing an act, or giving up a right. Mutual obligations furnish consideration for each other when they are: (1) legally sufficient, (2) certain and possible to perform, and (3) given in exchange.

Consideration must be legally sufficient, which means that the consideration for the promise must be either a legal detriment to the promisee or a legal benefit to the promisor. One or the other must be present, although in most situations both exist. *Benefit* in the legal sense means the receipt by the promisor of some legal right that the person had not previously been entitled to. *Legal detriment* is the taking on of a legal obligation or the doing of something or giving up of a legal right by the promisee.

Assume that an uncle promises to pay a niece $1,000 if she enrolls in and graduates from an accredited college or university. If the niece graduates from an accredited college, she is entitled to the $1,000. The promisee-niece did something she was not legally obligated to do, so the promise was supported by legally sufficient consideration. The legal detriment of the niece certainly did not amount to actual detriment. It can hardly be said that the uncle received any actual benefit either.

A condition is not consideration and should not be confused with it. A *condition* is an event the happening of which qualifies the duty to perform a promise. A promise to give a person $100 if the person comes to your home to pick it up is a promise to make a gift on the condition that the person picks up the money. A promisee who shows up is not legally entitled to the $100.

When one party to an agreement makes what appears at first glance to be a promise but upon examination no real promise is made, this is called an *illusory promise.* A contract is not entered into when one of the parties makes an illusory promise, since there is no consideration. For example, a promise to work for an employer at an agreed rate for as long as the promisor wishes to work is an illusory promise. The promisor is really promising nothing and cannot be bound to do anything.

That which the parties have exchanged in their contract need not have the same value. A court will not concern itself with the terms of a contract as long as the parties have capacity and there has been genuine assent to the terms. Whether the bargain was a fair exchange is for the parties to decide when they enter into the agreement. Consideration need not have a pecuniary or money value. Assume a mother promises her son $100 if he does not drink or smoke until he reaches the age of 18. There is no pecuniary value to the abstinence; yet it is a valid consideration.

It is not necessary to state the consideration on the face of the document when an agreement is put in writing. It may be orally agreed upon or implied, but need not be written in the instrument. The recital of consideration is not final proof that it exists, but it is evidence of consideration that is *prima facie*, or sufficient on its face. Evidence that no consideration existed will overcome the presumption that the recital creates. And a statement of consideration in an instrument does not create consideration where it was really never intended or given.

If a promise is too vague or uncertain concerning time or subject matter, it will not amount to consideration. If a promise is obviously impossible to perform, it is not sufficient consideration for a return promise. When a promise is capable of being performed, even though improbable or absurd, it is consideration.

Consideration must be bargained for and given in exchange for a promise. Past consideration is not consideration. If a person performs a service for another without the other's knowledge, and later the recipient of the service promises to pay for it, the promise is not binding. The promise to pay was not supported by consideration. A promise to do what one is already legally obligated to do cannot ordinarily constitute consideration. There is no detriment. For example, a promise by a father to pay child support payments which is already an existing legal obligation determined by a court will not constitute consideration. Similarly, consideration is also lacking when a promise is made to refrain from doing what one has no legal right to do.

George W. Kistler, Inc., v. O'Brien
347 A.2d 311
Supreme Court of Pennsylvania
October 30, 1975

NIX, JUSTICE

Appellee, George W. Kistler, Inc., commenced this action seeking to enforce a restrictive covenant in a written employment contract between itself and its employee, appellant William J. O'Brien. On May 14, 1974, the court of common pleas issued a decree enjoining appellant from engaging in selling or servicing fire equipment within a 50-mile radius. This appeal followed.

Appellant seeks to vacate the ruling of the court below on several grounds. One of his contentions is that the covenant restricting appellant from engaging in a competitive business was not supported by adequate consideration. We agree with this argument and therefore reverse.

A review of the record reveals the following pertinent facts. Appellee, George W. Kistler, Inc., (Kistler) is a Pennsylvania corporation engaged in the sale and service of fire equipment and fire prevention services. About a year prior to May of 1970, appellant, William J. O'Brien (O'Brien) was contacted by representatives of Kistler with respect to O'Brien's possible employment with their company. No decision was made at that time and the matter was left open for further discussion. Subsequently, some time in the late winter or early spring of 1970, Kistler again solicited O'Brien, and after various negotiations relating to wages, duties, insurance benefits, and other terms of employment but not including any mention of a restrictive covenant, it was agreed that O'Brien would leave his present employer and work for Kistler. O'Brien gave his then employer two weeks notice and began to work for Kistler on May 11, 1970.

On or about that same day, O'Brien questioned one of the clerks at the business with regard to his insurance benefits. Upon doing so, he was handed various forms to complete and sign, among them a document entitled employment contract which contained the following clause:

In consideration of the said owner granting such requested employment to the said employee and in further consideration of the payment of one ($1.00) dollar lawful money of the United States, this day made by the owner to the employee, he, the employee, agrees with the owner that for a period of two (2) years after said employment is terminated for any cause whatsoever by either or both of the parties, that he will not directly or indirectly manufacture, sell, distribute, handle on his own account, or by association or employment by or with any other persons whomsoever within an area of fifty (50) miles, extending from the city of Allentown, Lehigh County, Pennsylvania, any product equal in character or in any way similar to the products handled, bought, sold, or serviced or to be handled, bought, sold, or serviced by said owner.

O'Brien worked at various times in the capacity of service manager and branch manager for Kistler until November 16, 1973, when he was discharged for reasons that are disputed.

Upon his departure from Kistler, O'Brien went into business for himself servicing hand portable fire extinguishers. He solicited business from concerns located in large buildings and also did service work by subcontract for distributors of hand portable fire extinguishers. This activity was to some extent in competition with the activities of his former employer.

In order for a covenant in restraint of trade to be enforceable, the covenant must (1) relate to (be ancillary to) a contract for the sale of the goodwill of a business or to a contract of employment, (2) be supported by adequate consideration, and (3) be reasonably limited in both time and territory.

Appellant asserts that the covenant is unenforceable because it lacks consideration. It is his position that the negotiations prior to May 11 constituted a complete and binding oral contract for which the consideration was the employment itself. Thus he argues that the employment as consideration was not available to support the subsequent written restrictive covenant. Moreover, he contends that the entering into an agreement containing a restrictive covenant was not a factor considered in arriving at the oral agreement of employment. It was not until O'Brien had commenced work and inquired about his Blue Cross benefit forms that he was requested by a clerk to sign the employment contract supposedly in accordance with the general practice of the firm. It is particularly significant that Kistler, who was then operating a sole proprietorship and personally participated in the final negotiations, never discussed this requirement.

Thus, we must first determine at what point a final and binding employment contract was executed before determining what, if any, consideration passed for the signing of the covenant.

The chancellor, in reviewing the evidence, rejected appellant's claim that an oral contract existed and found that the written contract was the sole agreement of employment between the parties. Based upon this premise, he concluded that the employment itself was the consideration for the covenant. The chancellor's findings must be supported by adequate evidence in order that they be affirmed on appeal. Our reading of the record, and especially the testimony of appellee, Kistler, forces us to conclude that the chancellor's finding was contrary to the evidence and that a final and binding oral contract of employment which did not contain a restrictive covenant did exist prior to the date the written contract was signed. At the hearing appellee, Kistler, testified as follows:

Q. And as a result of those meetings, I take it Mr. O'Brien decided to come work for Kistler Company?

A. That's right.

Q. During those meetings, did you discuss what his duties would be?

A. Yes.

Q. Did you discuss his amount of pay?

A. Yes.

Q. You discussed his insurance benefits and the rest of it?

A. I presume.

Q. Blue Cross, Blue Shield. You knew that he had to let his then present employer, Alpo, let them know, give them notice if he was going to leave them?

A. I believe it. I can't recall specifically.

Q. Would you agree that you were probably aware of that?

A. If it were my choice, I would have suggested he give them two weeks because I wouldn't want someone to leave and walk out the door the same day.

Q. So at some period of time two weeks before he started work physically on the job, you were aware that Mr. Kistler, or that Mr. O'Brien was coming to work for the Kistler Company?

A. I imagine, yes.

Q. That the terms of the relationship had been agreed upon. Right?

A. Yes.

Q. And that you knew that he had then, after coming to that agreement with you, notified his then employer that he was quitting that work with the Alpo Company?

A. Did you say did we notify them?

Q. You realized that he would then have to notify Alpo that he had come to an arrangement with you and that he was leaving them?

A. Yes.

Q. Now at the time that you made those arrangements with Mr. O'Brien, and prior to his notifying his then employer, Alpo, that he was leaving their employ and coming with you, did you have Mr. O'Brien sign any restrictive covenant that was a condition of his employment with the Kistler Company?

A. What's the time of this? You are saying prior to his leaving Alpo?

Q. And at the time that you made the arrangements with Mr. O'Brien for his employment with the Kistler Company, which you have now testified was at least two and maybe three to four weeks prior to his actual physical arrival on the scene, did you have Mr. O'Brien sign any alleged restrictive covenant with respect to the Kistler Company?

A. I can't think if it was signed two weeks or greater.

Q. So the answer to that is no. Correct?

A. No.

Under the law of this commonwealth, it has been held that even where a later formal document is contemplated, parties may bind themselves contractually prior to the execution of the written document through mutual manifestations of assent. Thus, evidence of mutual assent to employ and be employed which contains all the elements of a contract may be construed as a binding contract of employment, though not reduced to writing. Under this test, it is clear that the testimony recited above requires a finding of the existence of an oral contract of employment at least two weeks prior to the written contract. Not only was it agreed that O'Brien would cease working for his present employer and begin working for Kistler, but all aspects of the employment relationship such as wages, duties and benefits were also agreed upon. Kistler's testimony admits mutual assent regarding the employment. Moreover, there was no evidence that the parties understood that O'Brien was not to become a regular employee until he signed the restrictive covenant. Indeed the record establishes that both parties understood that O'Brien was to leave his then employment and become a regular employee of Kistler without any promise not to engage in a competitive enterprise.

Having concluded that a valid oral contract of employment, without a covenant not to compete, existed prior to the written contract of employment, we cannot accept the chancellor's view that the employment itself constituted the consideration for the covenant. In our judgment, such consideration would clearly be past consideration.

While a restrictive covenant, in order to be valid, need not appear in the initial contract, if it is agreed upon at some later time it must be supported by new consideration. Furthermore, continuation of the employment relationship at the time the written contract was signed was not sufficient consideration for the covenant despite the fact that the employment relationship was terminable at the will of either party. Thus, the covenant which is the basis of this action is not enforceable for lack of consideration and the decree of the court below must be reversed.

Decree reversed.

CASE QUESTIONS

1. What should Kistler have done in order to make the restrictive covenant enforceable? What effect did the $1 recited consideration in the written employment contract have?
2. When did the contract between Kistler and O'Brien take place? What did the court consider in determining when the contract took place?
3. Is there any value in having an employee sign a written employment contract after he is employed?

SUGGESTED READINGS

J.D. CALAMARI AND J.M. PERILLO, CONTRACTS, §§ 4–1 to 4–23 (2nd ed. 1977).

A.L. CORBIN, CORBIN ON CONTRACTS, §§ 109–194 (1952).

Hillman, *Contract Modification in Iowa—*Reeker v. Gustafson *and the Resurrection of the Pre-existing Duty Doctrine*, 65 IOWA L. REV. 343 (1980).

Capacity

In order to create a contract that is legally binding and enforceable, the parties must have the legal capacity to contract. All parties do not have the same legal capacity to enter into a contract. Some persons have only partial capacity; some have none. Full contractual capacity is met when a person is of legal age without mental disability or incapacity.

It is presumed that all parties to an agreement have full legal capacity to contract. Therefore any party seeking to base a claim or a defense on incapacity has the burden of alleging *and proving* the incapacity. The principal classes of persons given some degree of special protection on their contracts because of their incapacity are (1) minors, (2) insane persons, and (3) intoxicated persons.

Minors

At common law, persons remained minors until they reached the age of 21. Generally, present legislation has reduced this age to 18. The law pertaining to minors entering into contracts formerly held that those contracts were void. Now that law has been almost universally changed and holds that such contracts are voidable. This applies not only to contracts, but also to executed transactions such as a sale.

The law grants minors this right in order to protect them from their lack of judgment and experience, limited will power, and presumed immaturity. Adults contract with minors at their own peril. A contract between an adult and a minor is voidable only by the minor; the minor may legally choose to either enforce the contract or disaffirm it. The adult must fulfill the obligation, unless the minor decides to avoid the contract. Ordinarily, parents are not liable for the contracts their minor children enter into.

At first glance, the rights of minors to avoid a contract at their discretion may seem unfair to adults, but this is not necessarily the case. An adult party frequently will refuse to contract with or sell to minors because minors are incapable of giving legal assurance that they will not avoid the contract.

TRANSACTIONS A MINOR CANNOT AVOID

Many states through legislation have limited minors' ability to avoid contracts. For instance, many states provide that a contract with a college or university is binding. A purchase of life insurance has also been held to bind a minor. Some statutes take away the right of minors to avoid contracts after they are married. Most states hold that a minor engaging in a business and operating in the same manner as a person having legal capacity will not be permitted to set aside contracts arising from that business or employment. Court decisions or statutes have established this law in order to prevent minors from using the shield of minority to avoid business contracts.

Minors are liable for the reasonable value (not the contract price) of any necessary they purchase, whether goods or services, if they accept and make use of it. The reason for their being liable for the reasonable value of the necessaries, rather than their contract price, is to protect them against the possibility that the other party to the agreement has taken advantage of them by overcharging them. If the necessaries have not yet been accepted or received, the minor may disaffirm the contract without liability.

In general, the term *necessaries* includes whatever is needed for a minor's subsistence as measured by age, status, condition in life, and so on. Food, lodging, education, clothing, and medical services are the general classifications of necessaries. Objects used for pleasure and ordinary contracts relating to property or business of the minor are not classified as necessaries.

DISAFFIRMANCE OF CONTRACT

The general rule is that minors may avoid both executed and executory contracts at any time during their infancy. They may also disaffirm a contract for a reasonable period of time after they attain their majority. The justification for the privilege to disaffirm after reaching majority is that former minors should have a reasonable time in which to evaluate transactions made during their infancy. What constitutes a reasonable time depends on the nature of the property involved and the surrounding circumstances. As long as minors do not disaffirm their contracts, they are bound by the terms. They cannot refuse to carry out their part of an agreement, while at the same time requiring the adult party to perform.

Disaffirmance of a contract by a minor may be made by any expression of an intention to repudiate the contract. Disaffirmance need not be verbal or written. If a minor performs an act inconsistent with the continuing validity of a contract, that is considered a disaffirmance. For example, if a minor sells property to Gaskins and later, upon reaching majority, sells the same property to Ginger, the second sale to Ginger would be considered a disaffirmance of the contract with Gaskins.

It is clear that minors may disaffirm wholly executory contracts, that is, contracts that neither party has performed. It is also clear that if only the minors have performed, they may disaffirm and recover the money or property they have paid or transferred to an adult. A conflict arises, however, in those situations where the contract is wholly executed or where only the adult has performed and the minor has spent what he has received and, therefore, cannot make restitution. As a general rule, minors must return whatever they have in their possession of the consideration under the contract; if the consideration has been destroyed, they may nevertheless disaffirm the contract and recover the consideration they have given. For example, suppose Fay, a minor, purchases an automobile and has an accident that demolishes the car. She may obtain a full refund by disaffirming the contract and also will not be liable for the damage to the car.

A few states, however, hold that if the contract is advantageous to the minor and if the adult has been fair in every respect, the contract cannot be disaffirmed unless the minor returns the consideration. In the example above, the minor would have to replace the reasonable value of the damaged automobile before she could disaffirm the contract and receive the consideration she gave for the automobile. These states also take into account the depreciation of the property while in the possession of the minor.

From what has been discussed, we have seen that minors may disaffirm or avoid their contracts prior to reaching their majority. On the other hand, they cannot effectively ratify or approve their contracts until they have attained their majority. Ratification may consist of any expression or action that indicates an intention to be bound by the contract, and may come from the actions of the minor who has now reached majority. For example, if a minor acquired property under his contract and, after reaching majority, makes use of or sells the property, he will be deemed to have ratified the contract.

Some states have enacted statutes that prevent minors from disaffirming contracts if they have fraudulently misrepresented their age. Generally, however, the fact that minors have misrepresented their age in order to secure a contract which they could not have otherwise obtained will not later prevent them from disaffirming that contract on the basis of their minority. Most courts will hold minors liable for any resulting damage to, or deterioration of, property they received under the contract. Minors are also generally liable for their torts; consequently, in most states, the other party to the contract could recover in a tort action for deceit. In any case, the other party to the contract may avoid it because of the minor's fraud.

Insane Persons

Persons are said to be insane when they do not understand the nature and consequences of an act at the time of their entering into an agreement. If parties to agreements are insane, they lack capacity; their contracts are either void or voidable. The contracts of a person who has been judicially declared insane by a court are void. A person who has been judicially declared insane will have a judicially appointed guardian who is under a duty to transact all business for the estate of the insane person.

The general rule concerning contracts of insane persons who have not been judicially declared insane is that those contracts are voidable. Although such persons may not ratify or disaffirm a contract during their temporary insanity, they may do so once they regain their sanity. However, if the contract is executed and the sane party to the contract acts in good faith, not knowing that the other party is temporarily insane, most courts refuse to allow the temporarily insane person the right to avoid the contract, unless the consideration that has been received can be returned. On the other hand, if the sane party knows that the other party is mentally incompetent, the contract is voidable at the option of the insane person.

As in the case of minors, the party possessing capacity to contract has no right to disaffirm a contract merely because the insane party has the right to do so. The rule in regard to necessaries purchased by temporarily insane persons is the same as in the case of minors.

If persons enter into a contract when they are so intoxicated that they do not know at the time they are executing a contract, the contract is voidable at their option. The position of the intoxicated person is, therefore, much the same as that of the temporarily insane person.

Reiner v. Miller
478 S.W. 2d 283
Supreme Court of Missouri
April 10, 1972

SEILER, JUDGE
This is an action in equity by Margaret

Gahr Reiner, to set aside a deed executed by her and her husband, Charles Gahr, to Mabel Miller pursuant to a property settlement agreement. The trial court made findings and entered judgment for the defendant. We affirm.

Mr. and Mrs. Gahr, Charles and

Margaret, were married in 1946. During the marriage, the couple acquired a small amount of personal and real property, including 15 acres of rural land held in tenancy by the entirety. The couple separated on May 18, 1965. Mr. Gahr filed a divorce petition on July 21, 1965.

The two encountered one another at a tavern in Steelville on August 14, 1965, and agreed to discuss divorce matters at the office of a local lawyer. They met that afternoon with Mr. Gahr's attorney, Mr. Beckham. After some discussion, the Gahrs agreed to the following valuation of their property:

Government bonds	$ 800
1963 Chevrolet truck	1000
Land	700
Household furniture and utensils	200
	$2700

The Gahrs wanted to divide the property equally; thus, each would receive property valued at about $1350. Mrs. Gahr requested that the bonds she already had in her possession and several items from the house be included in her share. She demanded cash for the remainder, and Mr. Gahr paid her $550 in cash in order to bring her allocation to $1350. During this meeting, Mrs. Gahr signed a waiver of service and entry of appearance in the divorce proceeding and an assignment of the truck title. Both signed the property settlement and a warranty deed that conveyed the real property to the defendant, Mabel Miller. Both parties understood that the grantee was a straw party, and that following the divorce, the property would be conveyed to Mr.

Gahr. Mr. Gahr died within two weeks of this meeting, and the couple did not obtain the contemplated divorce.

This court has recognized the validity of property settlement agreements entered into between husband and wife in contemplation of or pending a divorce. Agreements in which marital rights are relinquished must be free of fraud, supported by a valid consideration, and fair, just, and equitable.

The trial court found that "the important question is: was the executed property settlement fair and equitable?" We concur in the finding of the trial court that it was.

The appellant maintains that the deed must be set aside because the settlement was not fair and equitable, since she was under the influence of alcohol, received substantially less than one-half of the property, was unrepresented by counsel, and was unduly influenced by her husband and his attorney. We will discuss each point in turn.

Mrs. Gahr testified that she was intoxicated during the meeting because she had drunk nine beers. The alcohol influenced her mental ability. She did not remember the events that occurred in the attorney's office. Her drinking companion and her daughter both testified that she was intoxicated. In contrast, Mr. Beckham, the attorney, stated that Mrs. Gahr did not appear to be under the influence of alcohol. We note that she recalled the number of beers she drank in each establishment prior to the meeting and remembered demanding that she receive the $550 in cash, not by check, before she would sign the property settlement.

A contract entered into by an intoxicated person can be voided; however, the intoxication must be such as to render the intoxicated person incapable, at the time the contract is entered into, of knowing what he is doing or of comprehending the consequences of his acts. In this case, the trial court concluded that the appellant was not so intoxicated. We agree.

The appellant maintains she did not receive one-half of the value of the property in the settlement. Mr. Beckham testified that both Mr. and Mrs. Gahr wanted to divide their property equally, that they discussed the property and agreed on the value of each item, that Mrs. Gahr selected certain specific items, and at her request, received cash as the remainder of her share. At trial, Mrs. Gahr did not directly dispute this testimony. She could not recall much of what occurred at the meeting because, she said, of her drinking. Mrs. Gahr introduced into evidence a list of personal property in which she estimated the value of the truck at $1650, the household goods at $738.30 and the bonds at $834.74. She valued the land at $1750. On these figures, her share of about $1350 would be substantially less than one-half of the property. Each party produced other witnesses, including real estate brokers and an auctioneer, whose testimony supported their respective property evaluations.

In addition to the property mentioned earlier here, there was a joint bank account, amount about $1700–$1800, which was withdrawn by the parties following separation and divided equally between them.

The trial court resolved the conflicting evidence in favor of the respondent and specifically found that "the values

placed on the property in question by the parties at the time of their agreement are substantially correct. Appellant received approximately one-half the property owned by the parties and made her own selection as to what she would take." We see no reason to disturb the finding of the trial court.

We overrule the contention that this agreement must be set aside because Mrs. Gahr was unduly influenced by her husband and his attorney. An agreement resulting from undue influence or fraud, especially in a situation where the lawyer advises both parties while employed by only one, will be found invalid. Mr. Beckham testified that he recognized an obligation to provide fairly for Mrs. Gahr in the agreement. He explained the meaning of the document to her, and she indicated that she understood. Mrs. Gahr could not recall if this discussion occurred. An unfair property settlement would be an indication of undue influence. The property here was divided fairly, and appellant has failed to show any undue influence.

The appellant argues that the property settlement never became effective because of the failure of a condition precedent that the court approve the property settlement. The property agreement provided "... it is now agreed that the following, subject to the approval of the court, will be a full and complete settlement of the property rights ..." We have recognized that a husband and wife may make a property settlement in contemplation of divorce without submitting the agreement to a court. Such a property settlement would be valid between the parties.

If this settlement agreement had been presented to the court in the divorce action, the court would have considered its terms in accordance with the same principles that we have previously discussed. We can assume that the court in the divorce action would have found the agreement valid. We overrule the contention.

Judgment affirmed.

CASE QUESTIONS

1. Are fraud, undue influence, and intoxication separate defenses to the enforcement of a contract?
2. Is defendant Miller entitled to keep the property by reason of the court's decision?

SUGGESTED READINGS

J.D. CALAMARI AND J.M. PERILLO, CONTRACTS, §§ 8–1 to 8–5 (2nd ed. 1972).

Halpern, *Civil Insanity: The New York Treatment of the Issue of Mental Incapacity in Non-Criminal Cases*, 44 CORNELL L. QUARTERLY 76 (1958).

Note, *Minor's Marriage Contract—Absolute Nullity?* 36 LA. L. REV. 826 (1976).

RESTATEMENT (SECOND) OF CONTRACTS, § 18.

Illegality

An agreement is *illegal* when either its formation or performance is criminal, tortious, or opposed to public policy. When an agreement is illegal, courts will not allow either party to sue for performance of the contract. The court will literally "leave the parties where it finds them." Generally, if one of the parties has performed, that person cannot recover either the value of the performance or any property or goods transferred to the other party. There are three exceptions to this rule, however.

First, if the law that the agreement violates is intended for the protection of one of the parties, that party may seek relief. For example, both federal and state statutes require that a corporation follow certain procedures before stocks and bonds may be offered for sale to the public. It is illegal to sell such securities without having complied with the legal requirements. Persons who have purchased securities from a corporation that has not complied with the law may obtain a refund of the purchase price if they desire to do so.

Second, when the parties are not equally at fault, the one less at fault is granted relief when the public interest is advanced by doing so. This rule is applied to illegal agreements that are induced by undue influence, duress, or fraud. In such cases, the courts do not regard the defrauded or coerced party as being an actual participant in the wrong and will, therefore, allow restitution.

A third exception occurs within very strict limits. As applied to an illegal contract, a person who repents before actually having performed any illegal part of that contract may rescind it and obtain restitution. For example, suppose James and Richards wager on the outcome of a baseball game. Each gives $500 to Smith, the stakeholder, who agrees to give $1000 to the winner. Prior to the game, either James or Richards could recover $500 from Smith through legal action, since the execution of the illegal agreement would not yet have occurred.

It is recognized everywhere that if the objectives of an agreement are illegal, the agreement is illegal and unenforceable, even though the parties were not aware, when they arrived at their agreement, that it was illegal. On the other hand, as a general rule, even if one party to an agreement knows that the other party intends to use the subject matter of the contract for illegal purposes, this fact will not make the agreement illegal unless the illegal purpose involves a serious crime.

For example, suppose Taylor lends money to Merrill, at a legal interest rate, knowing Merrill is going to use the money to gamble illegally. After Merrill loses his money, he refuses to repay Taylor on the grounds the agreement was illegal. Taylor can recover his money through court action, even though he knew Merrill was going to illegally gamble with the money he lent him.

Contracts Against Public Policy

A contract provision is contrary to public policy if it is injurious to the interests of the public, contradicts some established interests of society, violates a statute, or tends to interfere with the public health, safety, or general welfare. The term *public policy* is vague and variable; it changes as our social, economic, and political climates change. One of the most common agreements within this class is the illegal lobbying agreement. This term is used to describe an agreement by which one party uses bribery, threats of a loss of votes, or any other improper means to procure or prevent the adoption of particular legislation by a lawmaking body, such as Congress or a state legislature. Such agreements are clearly contrary to the public interest since they interfere with the workings of the democratic process. They are both illegal and void.

Miller v. Radikopf
394 Mich. 83, 228 N.W. 2d 386
Supreme Court of Michigan
May 5, 1975

LEVIN, JUSTICE

The question is whether a contract to share the proceeds of an Irish Sweepstakes ticket is judicially enforceable.

Miller claims that he and Radikopf jointly sold sweepstakes tickets. For each 20 sold, they received 2 tickets as compensation. Although each would put his name on one of the tickets, Miller claims they agreed that the tickets were jointly owned and all winnings would be divided equally. A ticket bearing Radikopf's name won and yielded in excess of $487,000. After Radikopf refused to surrender any of the proceeds, Miller commenced this action.

The trial court, stating that the alleged agreement was "spawned in violation of statute," granted Radikopf a summary judgment. The court of appeals, referring to § 372 of the Penal Code which prohibits the "setting up or promotion of a lottery," affirmed: "It is true that receiving a lottery award voluntarily paid is not prohibited. *People v. Watson*, 75 Mich. 582, 42 N.W. 1005 (1889). The general policy of this state against the holding of lotteries would be seriously compromised, however, if lottery winners were allowed to successfully bring suit for their prizes. Although the court will not interfere where a lottery prize is voluntarily given the winner, public policy demands that courts not give support to the maintenance of lotteries in this state by allowing prize winners judicial process to collect their winnings." *Miller v. Radikopf*, 51 Mich. App. 393, 395, 214 N.W.2d 897, 898 (1974).

This is not, however, an action to collect prize winnings from a lottery promoter. The narrow question to be decided is whether a contractual claim to a share of money legally paid by the Irish Sweepstakes and legally possessed by the defendant may be enforced. We would hold that the public policy of this state does not preclude Miller from attempting to enforce his claim and, accordingly, would reverse and remand for trial.

It is a crime to "set up or promote" a lottery in this state. It is similarly a crime for a person to "sell," "offer for sale," or "have in his possession with intent to sell or offer for sale" lottery tickets. However, it does not appear that Irish law prohibits the payment of money to holders of winning sweepstakes tickets. Nor does any statute or rule of law of this state prohibit the holder of a winning ticket from receiving and retaining proceeds paid voluntarily by a lottery without legal action.

There being no statute barring enforcement of the claim asserted in this case, the question whether its enforcement would be in accord with public policy is for judicial decision.

There were several contracts preceding the contract sued upon. Miller and Radikopf agreed to sell sweepstakes tickets and to accept as consideration "free" tickets. Each ticket so received by them was a separate contract binding the lottery promoters to pay the holder of a winning ticket. As neither Miller nor Radikopf is presently attempting to enforce the antecedent contracts, their possible illegality and attendant public policy ramifications need not concern us. Whatever their legality, those contractual obligations were fulfilled.

Miller in this action seeks to enforce the agreement he claims was made by him and Radikopf "that should either of the tickets win any prize, the prize would be split equally between the two of them." The consideration exchanged by each was a promise to the other to pay one-half of any proceeds won on tickets held in his name. Since receipt and retention of sweepstakes winnings voluntarily paid by the Irish promoter violates no Irish or Michigan statute or rule of law, a promise to share amounts so received constitutes legal consideration. A contract based on the exchange of legal consideration is a legal contract and its enforcement does not violate public policy.

Agreements to share possible proceeds from Irish Sweepstakes tickets are not an "essential part" of the sale and distribution of those tickets. The continued success of the Irish Sweepstakes in this state is in no way dependent on the enforceability of agreements to share winnings. Miller's and Radikopf's collateral agreement to divide their prospective winnings was not an essential part of their sale and distribution of those tickets. Nor was their agreement dependent on illegal conduct in the acquisition of the lottery tickets; they might have acquired the tickets in a manner free of any suggestion of illegality and then entered into an agreement to share proceeds.

However this case is decided, the courts of this state will continue to refuse to entertain actions seeking an accounting of proceeds obtained from illegal enterprises, such as the illegal sale of narcotics and bank robberies. Additionally, enforcement or an accounting will be denied, without regard to whether the proceeds sought to be divided have been legally obtained, if the consideration offered is illegal.

Judicial nonenforcement of agreements deemed against public policy is considered a deterrent for those who might otherwise become involved in such transactions. While nonenforcement of Miller's claim might tend to discourage people from agreeing to split their legal winnings, nonenforcement would not tend to discourage people from buying or selling Irish Sweepstakes tickets.

It is consonant with the public policy of this state to encourage performance of legal contracts and to foster the just resolution of disputes. Nonenforcement of the agreement claimed by Miller would not tend to discourage the sale of Irish Sweepstakes tickets. It could reward, without any corresponding benefit, promissory default. We conclude that public policy would not be offended by enforcement of the claimed agreement.

We would reverse and remand for trial with costs to abide the event.

COLEMAN, JUSTICE, dissenting

As a matter of law, I am compelled to dissent from my colleagues' decision. The statement of the controlling question by the majority is not as I see it. To me, it is whether a contract to share remuneration for an illegal act is judicially enforceable.

Plaintiff submits that there is no law against the ownership of an Irish

Sweepstakes ticket. He admits and correctly so that M.C.L.A. § 750.372; M.S.A. § 28.604 and M.C.L.A. § 750.373; M.S.A. § 28.605 forbid the setting up, promoting, and selling of lottery tickets. However, he finds those statutes of little consequence. Unlike the plaintiff, I do not find the statutes insignificant. They make unlawful the activity engaged in by these parties and enunciate state policy. When an agreement to share concerns the proceeds of illegal activity, the court should not be available to enforce the agreement.

Plaintiff relies strongly upon *Manning v. Bishop of Marquette*, 345 Mich. 130, 76 N.W.2d 75 (1956). Mrs. Manning, after a bingo game, had stepped into a hole in the church parking lot. She sued the bishop. In allowing her suit, the court observed that "even a rogue may have a cause of action," but the court continued to say that it did not lend its aid "to the furtherance of an unlawful project," nor would the court "decide, as between two scoundrels, who cheated whom the more." The court noted that Mrs. Manning (neither a rogue nor a scoundrel so far as we know) had ceased her illegal activity and was on her way home when she was injured. It found that there was not a substantial causal relationship between Mrs. Manning's prior bingo game and her fall in the parking lot. The bingo game was a "remote link in the chain of causation." Such is not the case here where the unlawful act was the source of the asserted "right." The prize was an integral part of the illegal sale.

Public policy will not permit a party to enforce a promise which he has obtained by an illegal act. I would "leave the parties where they have placed themselves" and hold that neither law nor equity will grant relief to violators of the law who seek to benefit as a result of their own violation.

Public policy of a state is fixed by its constitution, its statutory law, and the decisions of its court. Michigan's public policy with respect to lotteries has been fixed by statute and that policy against lotteries other than those conducted by the state has been recently reaffirmed with the enactment of the Lottery Act of 1972.

If the legislature wishes to recognize the Irish Sweepstakes as a lawful lottery, it may do so. Until then, the courts of this state should be unavailable to enforce an agreement to divide the proceeds of a ticket obtained in remuneration for illegally selling Irish Sweepstakes tickets.

The decision of the court of appeals should be affirmed.

CASE QUESTIONS

1. What was the question that had to be answered by the court as stated by the majority and as stated by the dissent?
2. What was the contractual agreement Miller and Radikopf had with Irish Sweepstakes' promoters? What was the contractual agreement be-

tween Miller and Radikopf? Were these two contracts separate or was
there a close connection between them?

3. Assume that a husband agreed to share his gross income equally with
his wife, provided that she not seek employment outside the home. During the year, he received income from several sources: (a) earnings
one-third of which was for hours he claimed he worked but did not,
(b) embezzlement from his employer, (c) the sale of marijuana, (d) prosti-
tution-related activities. Could the wife legally collect anything from her
husband based on the majority opinion of *Miller v. Radikopf?*

SUGGESTED READINGS

J.D. CALAMARI AND J.M. PERILLO, CONTRACTS, § 22–1 (2nd ed. 1977).
A.L. CORBIN, CORBIN ON CONTRACTS, § 79 (1952).
Trakman, *The Effect of Illegality in the Law of Contracts—Suggestions
for Reform*, 55 CANADA BAR REVIEW 625 (1977).

Agreements to Commit Crimes and Civil Wrongs

An agreement is illegal and therefore void when it calls for the commission of any act that constitutes a crime. Obvious examples are agreements
to commit murder, robbery, arson, burglary, and assault. An agreement
that calls for the commission of a civil wrong is also illegal and void. Examples are agreements to slander a third person, to defraud another, to
damage another's goods, or to infringe upon another's trademark or
patent.

A contract that calls for the performance of an act or the rendering of a
service may be illegal for one of two reasons. (1) The act or service itself
may be illegal (illegal *per se*), and thus any contract involving this act or
service is illegal. Prostitution is a good example. (2) Certain other service
contracts are not illegal *per se*, but may be illegal if the party performing or
contracting to perform the service is not legally entitled to do so. This
refers to the fact that a license is required before a person is entitled to perform certain functions for others. For example, doctors, dentists, lawyers,
architects, surveyors, real estate brokers, and others rendering specialized
professional services must be licensed by the appropriate body before
entering into contracts with the general public.

All the states have enacted many regulatory statutes concerning the
practice of various professions and the carrying on of business and other
activity. These statutes are not uniform either in their working or in their
scope. Many of the statutes specifically provide that all agreements that

violate them shall be void and unenforceable. No question arises in these cases. When such a provision is lacking, the court will look to the intent of the statute. If the court is of the opinion that a statute was enacted for the protection of the public, it will hold that agreements in violation of the statute are void. If, however, the court concludes that the particular statute was intended solely to raise revenue, then it will hold that contracts entered in violation of the statute are legal and enforceable.

A contract that has for its purpose the restraint of trade and nothing more is illegal and void. A contract to monopolize trade, to suppress competition, or not to compete in business, therefore, cannot be enforced because the sole purpose of the agreement would be to eliminate competition. A contract that has for its objective the establishment of a monopoly is not only unenforceable, but also renders the parties to the agreement liable to indictment for the commission of a crime. The criminal implications rest upon the parties' ability and intention to monopolize the market and also on the question of whether the restraint upon commerce and business is unreasonable.

When a business is sold, it is commonly stated in a contract that the seller shall not go into the same or similar business again within a certain geographical area, or for a certain period of time, or both. In early times, such agreements were held void since they deprived the public of the service of the person who agreed not to compete, reduced competition, and exposed the public to monopoly. Gradually, the law began to recognize the validity of such restrictive provisions. To the modern courts, the question is whether under the circumstances the restriction imposed upon one party is reasonable or whether the restriction is more extensive than is required to protect the other party. A similar situation arises when employees agree not to compete with their employers should they leave their jobs.

Diaz v. Indian Head, Inc.
402 F. Supp. 111
United States District Court, N.D. Illinois
March 12, 1975

DECKER, DISTRICT JUDGE
This is a diversity case in which a former employee seeks to have declared unenforceable a provision in his employment contract which precludes competition with his former employer for eighteen months subsequent to ter-

mination. Plaintiff Albert J. Diaz is a resident of Maryland. The defendant, Indian Head, Inc. (hereafter, Indian Head), is a Delaware corporation, also doing business as Information Handling Services in Colorado. The employment agreement specifically provides that New York law shall govern.

Indian Head is currently one in a growing field of over a hundred companies in the microform publishing business. These companies reproduce various publications on little plastic microfilm cards. Aside from gaining the ease of storing and preserving publications in this form, the buyer of these cards benefits when he desires esoteric, arcane, and hard to locate publications, because the market demand may simply be too low to justify economically conventional printing or reprinting of an item in the quantity needed. Because of this benefit, the companies in this field have to develop expertise in selecting publications to replicate and in advertising those selections to likely customers. A company which is unable to develop this expertise would either have to rely solely on unsolicited orders, or else end up replicating those very items which by definition are not in demand, and hoping to find, by chance, some one or more customers who wanted them. Because of similar considerations, these companies must develop contacts with likely customers, including libraries and universities, and they must develop marketing methods. These goals are partly accomplished through representation of the companies at booths in conventions of likely customers, such as librarians.

Plaintiff Diaz developed in himself that special expertise that is so important in this field. Indeed, there is agreement that he is one of the 10 or 15 best qualified persons in the country for selecting those subjects and titles which would be profitable to replicate in microform. Further, in working for Indian Head and other such companies, Diaz has had substantial contact with many actual and potential customers. Part of that contact arose through his attendance at various conventions and through being involved with orders actually placed. In addition, while with Indian Head and other companies, Diaz has been in a position to plan the selection and marketing of titles. There is no doubt that the services of Albert J. Diaz would be of great value to a company in this field.

In February 1975, Diaz elected to terminate his employment with Indian Head and accepted an offer of employment with the Northern Engraving Company. Diaz's position at Indian Head has since been filled. Commendably, Diaz, according to his testimony, has refrained from actually competing, pending this court's construction of the agreement.

New York law looks with disfavor upon agreements that prevent a talented person fron engaging in his or her chosen profession. In the balance between the public interest in productivity, the employer's legitimate business interest, and the employee's interest, the first weighs more heavily. The method of enforcement of noncompetition agreements is generally injunction. For these reasons, postemployment noncompetition agreements have been held void unless they threatened irreparable injury to the employer's legitimate business interest. This injury generally falls into one of three categories:

1. Trade secrets might be divulged.
2. Particular customers might be swept away by the new competitor, or there might be a loss of good will which had been bargained for at the time of employment.
3. The employee may have been special, unique, or extraordinary.

What these categories of injury all have in common is the prospect that the employee will *affirmatively* harm the former employer other than through merely being productive for another employer. The employee may be *taking away* existing customers. Where a trade secret is involved, what is at stake is a company asset which, like the business of a major customer, is not inextricably related to that special talent of the employee which New York law seeks to keep productive for the public benefit.

No issue of trade secrets is presented in this case. However, the question presented is whether, by virtue of his familiarity with the pool from which customers are drawn and with specific customers of Indian Head, competition from Diaz may amount to irreparable injury. The question must be answered in the negative. The customers, actual and potential, are already known or available to Indian Head's competitors.

The names of libraries are not secret. Even if a list of known available customers was acquired at great expense over many years, a former employee would ordinarily be free to turn to it. More importantly, Indian Head does not rely on a limited set of customers who supply most of its business, as might be the case of a medical practice in a small area, such as oral surgery. Furthermore, the small-volume-per-customer nature of Indian Head's business renders insignificant the possibility that a few extremely important clients will follow Diaz rather than stay with their current microfilm supplier, or that a particular order will be pre-empted.

The remaining major issue is whether Diaz was in some way unique or extraordinary in the sense that New York policy requires the enforcement of his agreement with Indian Head. To begin with, no New York case has been cited or discovered in which such an agreement has been enforced on this rationale in a comparable fact (managerial or sales) situation in the absence of customer solicitation or trade secrets. This qualification may of course be fulfilled where the individual is not merely very talented, but *what* he does is unique, such as the way *he* sings. The fact that Diaz excels in his professed craft does not make his services "unique." More must, of course, be shown to establish such a quality than that the employee excels at his work or that his performance is of high value to his employer.

The court is aware of *Bradford v. New York Times Company*, 501 F.2d 51 (2d Cir. 1974), which found a vice president with 16 years experience with a single newspaper to be unique enough to make a noncompetition agreement enforceable. The second circuit relied in part on the employee's high administrative position in so finding. The employee, Bradford, was being compensated for his period of noncompetition, as is Diaz. However, Diaz's 1-year association with Indian Head is much less than Bradford's 16 years. Furthermore, *Bradford* paid little attention to New York's strong policy of keeping talented people productive.

Accordingly, this court concludes that plaintiff is entitled to a declaratory judgment that the agreement between Albert J. Diaz and Indian Head, Inc., is void and unenforceable insofar as it restricts Diaz from entering into competition after his full-time employment with Indian Head terminates.

Case Questions

1. List some specific employment examples where a postemployment noncompetition agreement would be enforceable.
2. The employment contract specifically provided that New York law should govern. Why would the parties put such a provision in their contract? Could the right to choose and agree on the state law that shall govern a contract be abused?

Suggested Readings

J.D. Calimari and J.M. Perillo, Contracts, §§ 22–1 to 22–4 (2d ed. 1977).
McGarvie, *Illegality and Severability in Contracts*, 13 University of Western Australia L. Rev. 1 (1977).
Smith, *Contracts in Violation of Statutes—Necessarily Illegal?* 5 UCLA-Alaska L. Rev. 381 (1976).

Writing

Every state has statutes requiring that certain contracts be in writing to be enforceable. These statutes are called the *statutes of frauds.* Although each state's statute may differ in minor respects, they are generally in agreement as to their material provisions and are based on old English law. An Act for the Prevention of Frauds and Perjuries, passed by the English Parliament in 1677, gave rise to the modern-day statute of frauds. The impetus for the passage of this act was the prevention of fraud and perjury in the enforcement of contracts.

The kinds of contracts governed by the statute of frauds are of six types: (1) an agreement by an executor or administrator to answer for the debt of the decedent, (2) an agreement made in consideration of marriage, (3) an agreement to answer for the debt or default of another, (4) an agreement that cannot be performed in one year, (5) an agreement for the sale of an interest in real property, and (6) an agreement for the sale of goods above a certain dollar amount.

The writing required by the statute need not be in any special form or use any special language. Usually, the essential terms that must be shown on the face of the writing include the names of the parties, the terms and conditions of the contract, the consideration, a reasonably certain description of the subject matter of the contract, and the signature of the party, or the party's agent, against whom enforcement is sought. These terms need not be on one piece of paper but may be on several pieces of paper, provided that their relation or connection with each other appears on their face by the physical attachment of the papers to each other or by reference from one writing to the other. At least one, if not all of the papers must be signed by the party against whom enforcement is sought. The requirements of memorandums involving the sale of goods differ.

Agreement by Executor or Administrator

A promise by an executor or administrator to answer for the debt of the decedent is within the statute and must be in writing to be enforced. In order for the statute to operate, the executor's promise must be to pay out of the executor's own personal assets (pocket); a promise to pay a debt out of the assets of a decedent's estate, however, is not required to be in writing.

Agreement in Consideration of Marriage

Agreements made in consideraton of marriage are to be in writing. Mutual promises to marry are not within the statute, as the consideration is the exchanged promise, not the marriage itself. However, promises made to a prospective spouse or third party with marriage as the consideration are within the statute. For example, a promise by one prospective spouse to convey property to the other, provided the marriage is entered into, is required to be in writing. Similarly, if a third party, say a rich relative, promises to pay a certain sum of money to a prospective spouse if a marriage is entered into, the promise will be unenforceable unless in writing.

Agreement to Answer for the Debt of Another

Agreements to answer for the debt or default of another shall be unenforceable unless in writing. The rationale for this provision is that the guarantor or surety has received none of the benefits for which the debt was incurred and, therefore, should be bound only by the exact terms of the promise. To provide that kind of protection, the promise must be reduced to a writing. For example, Bob desires to purchase a new law text on credit. The bookstore is unsure as to Bob's ability to pay, so Bob brings in his friend, Ellen, who says, ''If Bob does not pay for the law text, I will.'' Ellen is guaranteeing payment for the book. In effect, the promise is that the bookstore must first try to collect from Bob, and after it has exhausted all possibilities of collecting from him, then it may come to Ellen to receive payment. Ellen is therefore secondarily liable. The promise by Ellen is a promise to answer for Bob's debt for which Bob is still primarily liable; therefore, it must be in writing to be enforceable.

This situation is to be distinguished from those in which the promise to answer for the debt of another is an original promise, that is, the promisor's objective is to be primarily liable. For example, Bob desires to purchase a new law text. When he takes the book to the cashier, his friend Ellen steps in and says, "Give him the book. I will pay for it." Clearly Ellen is primarily liable for the purchase price. Ellen has made an original promise to the bookstore with the objective of becoming primarily liable. Such a promise need not be in writing to be enforceable.

Situations arise in which it is difficult to ascertain whether the purpose of the promisor is to become primarily liable or secondarily liable. In resolving the issue, courts will sometimes use the leading object rule. This rule looks not only to the promise itself, but also to the individual for whose benefit the promise was made. The logic of the rule is that if the leading object of the promise is the personal benefit of the promisor, then the promisor must have intended to become primarily liable. In such a case, the promise will be deemed to be original and need not be in writing to be enforced.

Howard M. Schoor Assoc., Inc., v. Holmdel Hts. Con. Co.
68 N.J. 95, 343 A.2d 401
Supreme Court of New Jersey
July 14, 1975

MOUNTAIN, JUDGE
Plaintiffs, two engineering and surveying firms with identical or very similar management and ownership, brought this action to recover amounts due for professional services rendered by them to defendant, Holmdel Heights Construction Company. The latter is in receivership, and the suit has proceeded, in effect, solely against defendant, Alan Sugarman. Plaintiffs' claim is that Sugarman, an attorney at law of this state, personally undertook to pay for the services rendered. He defends on the factual ground that he made no promise to do so and upon the legal ground that even had he made such a promise, it would be unenforceable under the statute of frauds.

The trial judge, sitting without a jury, resolved both the factual and legal issues in favor of plaintiffs and entered judgment against defendant in the amount of $24,105.30, together with interest. On appeal to the appellate division, the judgment was reversed, with one judge dissenting. Plaintiffs have appealed to this court.

Holmdel Heights Construction Company was in the process of developing a tract of land upon which it was constructing homes. Defendant, Sugarman, owned slightly more than 18% of the capital stock of this corporation and at all relevant times acted as its attorney. Plaintiff corporations were engaged to do surveying, engineering, and professional planning work in connection with the development. Some of the invoices they submitted to the developer were paid, but others were not. The total of these unpaid charges continued to increase, and plaintiffs became concerned.

On April 14, 1970, an important conference took place in the office of Mr. Sugarman. In addition to Mr. Sugarman, there were also present at this meeting Howard M. Schoor, president of the plaintiff corporations, and Lawrence Schwartz, Esq., their attorney. The question of plaintiff's unpaid bills was a principal subject of discussion. Both Mr. Schoor and Mr. Schwartz testified that at this meeting Mr. Sugarman agreed personally to pay all outstanding bills as well as any charges that might be incurred in the future, if plaintiffs would continue with the work they were doing. The developer, Holmdel Heights Construction Company, was then busily engaged in seeking additional financing. Everyone concedes that in order to secure this financing, it was essential that further engineering work be done at once. Mr. Sugarman drew a check on his trust account for $2000 and gave it to Mr. Schoor. According to the latter, the delivery of the check was accompanied by a statement made by Mr. Sugarman that this was intended to show his good faith in giving his personal guarantee as to payment of the outstanding and continuing obligation.

Schoor and Schwartz left the meeting apparently satisfied, and the needed engineering work went forward. On June 12, 1970, Sugarman wrote a letter to Schoor, enclosing a further check in the sum of $1000. The letter stated, "I have enclosed to your order a check in the sum of $1000. The corporation does not have this money. This is my money being submitted to you in good faith because I promised it to you last week. I certainly hope you don't let us down." Plaintiffs appear to have done all the work requested, but received no further payment. Shortly thereafter, Holmdel Heights Construction Company went into receivership and this suit followed.

Defendant contends that his promise —conceding it to have been made, as we have concluded it was—is unenforceable under the statute of frauds.

It is conceded by everyone that the promise was not in writing, nor was there any written memorandum or note thereof. Defendant contends that the promise obligated him only secondarily to pay the debt owed by Holmdel Heights Construction Company in the event it should default, and that as such it comes squarely within the purview of the statute. Plaintiffs argue that the promise was made largely if not principally for defendant's personal benefit, that it did not create a suretyship relationship but rather was an original promise resting upon consideration sought by defendant for his personal ends, and that this being so the promise is not controlled by the statute. This latter argument rests upon what is sometimes referred to as the "leading object or main purpose rule." It has been stated as follows: "When the leading object of the promise or agreement is to become guarantor or surety to the promisee for a debt for which a third party is and continues to be primarily liable, the agreement, whether made before or after or at the time with the promise of the principal, is within the statute, and not binding unless evidenced by writing. On the other hand, when the leading object of the promisor is to subserve some interest or purpose of his own, notwithstanding that the effect is to pay or discharge the debt of another, his promise is not within the statute.'' (2 *Corbin on Contracts*, § 366, at 273–74 [1950])

Thus in applying this rule, it becomes important, and probably decisive, to determine what interest, purpose, or object was sought to be advanced by defendant's promise to pay plaintiff's fees. Defendant owned slightly more than 18% of the capital stock of Holmdel Heights Construction Company, for which he had paid $10,000. He was also attorney for the corporation and at the time of trial, January 18, 1973, was still owed $14,000 for legal services. Some part of this (how much we are not specifically told) was already owing to him at the time of the April 14, 1970, conference. Defendant, in the course of his testimony, agreed that had the corporation eventually been successful, the amount he would have received upon his investment, together with reasonably anticipated legal fees, would have been a substantial sum.

On the other hand, defendant was acting as counsel for the development corporation and presumably, in this capacity, was doing all he could to maintain its solvency and to further its best interests. The consideration that was sought and received from plaintiffs took the form of a continuing professional effort on their part to provide the developer with vital materials and data intended to become part of its submission to a finance agency in connection with its application for a substantial loan. Obviously, this consideration would be of benefit to defendant personally, even though indirectly, as well as to the client he served.

The present action falls factually within that category of suits where the original debtor is a corporation in which the promisor has a financial interest. Such cases are fairly numerous. Depending upon their particular facts and circumstances, they have been decided both ways.

"There are many cases in which a shareholder or officer of a corporation or other party interested in its prosperity has promised a contractor that, if he would continue to supply goods or labor under his contract with the corporation in spite of its defaults, the promisor would pay the bill. If the only expected gain to the promisor is in the protection of the value of his shares, the promise is held to be within the statute; but there are cases in which the promisor was found to have received a special benefit that constituted his "leading object" and made him an original debtor." (2 *Corbin, supra*, § 372 at 298–99)

The interest of defendant, Sugarman, in inducing plaintiffs to undertake the work that they did after the April 14 conference seems obvious. His substantial pecuniary and business interest to be furthered is abundantly clear. On the other hand, there is little to support the view that he meant to commit his personal assets to so considerable an extent to further only his client's interest. We have no difficulty in agreeing with the trial court and with the dissenting member of the appellate division that the consideration was mainly desired for his personal benefit.

Accordingly the judgment of the appellate division is reversed and the judgment of the law division is hereby reinstated.

CASE QUESTIONS

1. What percentage of a corporation would an attorney have to own before a court would find that a promise the lawyer made was for that person's own benefit?
2. What possible policy reason was beind the court's decision?

SUGGESTED READINGS

J.D. CALAMARI AND J.M. PERILLO, CONTRACTS, §§ 9–1 to 9–13 (2nd ed. 1977).
A.L. CORBIN, CORBIN ON CONTRACTS, §§ 12–16, 20 (1952).
RESTATEMENT (SECOND) OF CONTRACTS, §§ 178–193.
Note, *Statute of Frauds—The Main Purpose Doctrine in North Carolina,* 13 N. C. L. REV. 263 (1935).

Agreements Not to Be Performed in One Year

Most state statutes require to be in writing contracts that are not capable of being performed within one year from the time the contract is formed. The determination of "not capable of being performed within one year" is to be made by referring to the intentions of the parties, to the nature of the performance, and to the terms of the contract itself. For example, Jack agrees to build a house for Betty. The question becomes whether the contract is capable of being performed within one year. Houses can be built in one year. Therefore, this agreement need not be in writing even if Jack actually takes more than one year to build the house. At the time the contract was entered into, it was capable of being completed within one year. The one-year term is to be measured from the date the contract is formed.

It is important to remember that the *possibility* that the contract can be performed within one year is enough to take it out of the operation of the statute. The courts do not look at how long performance actually took; they look to see whether the contract could possibly have been performed within one year under the facts and circumstances that existed on the date the contract was entered into.

Agreement for the Sale of an Interest in Real Property

The statute of frauds generally renders unenforceable oral agreements conveying interests in real estate. Most problems center upon what an interest in real estate is and whether the agreement contemplates the transfer of any title, ownership, or possession of real property. Both must be involved to bring the statute into effect. Real property has been held to commonly include land, leaseholds, easements, standing timber, and under certain conditions, improvements and fixtures attached to the land.

Sale of Goods

Generally, a contract for the sale of goods for the price of $500 or more is not enforceable unless there is some writing to serve as evidence that a contract has been entered into. An informal or incomplete writing will be sufficient to satisfy the U.C.C. statute of frauds, providing that it (1) indicates that a contract between the parties was entered into, (2) is signed by the party against whom enforcement is sought, and (3) contains a statement of the quantity of goods sold. The price, time and place of delivery, quality of the goods, and warranties may be omitted without invalidating the writing, as the U.C.C. permits these terms to be shown by outside evidence, custom and usage, and prior dealings between the parties. Since the U.C.C. permits the omitted terms to be proved, the provisions that must be included in a writing that will conform with the U.C.C. statute of frauds are substantially less than those necessary in a writing that evidences one of the other types of contracts governed by the statute of frauds. Under the U.C.C. the contract will be enforced only as to the quantity of goods shown in the writing. (U.C.C. 2–201 [1])

Jinright v. Russell
123 Ga. App. 766, 182 S.E.2d 328
Court of Appeals of Georgia
April 28, 1971

WHITMAN, JUDGE
This is an appeal by the defendants below from the denial of their motion for a summary judgment. The complaint alleges that the parties made an oral agreement whereby the defendants agreed: "To purchase from the plaintiff all fixtures, stock, good will, and name or trade name located in the establishment known as the Bottle Shop Liquor Store ... for the sum of $6500, said money being payable $1500 down and the balance payable as soon as the license was transferred."

It is further alleged that the defendants gave the plaintiff a check in the amount of $1500 as partial payment of the contract price, but then stopped payment on the check. The defendants denied the material allegations of the complaint and set up several matters in defense.

One ground of the defendants' motion for summary judgment which is urged on appeal is that: "The alleged agreement sued upon is oral and is void and unenforceable in that it is for the sale of goods at a price of more than $500 and that no memorandum in writing was executed pursuant to the statute of frauds, and there has not been sufficient past performance so as to remove said alleged agreement from the application of the statute of frauds."

Both defendants filed an affidavit in support of their motion. The affidavits admit that there were negotiations between the parties regarding the sale of the store. It is deposed that they were quoted a price of $5500, and further that they did give plaintiff a check for $1500. But when the plaintiff mentioned a balance remaining different from what they had understood, "rather than get into a hassle over the purchase price, we stopped payment on the check and discontinued negotiations the same day it [the check] was given."

The check was before the lower court for consideration. It is for the amount of $1500 payable to the plaintiff, and is drawn on Mrs. Hurshell Jinright's account with the Fourth National Bank of Columbus, Columbus, Georgia, and is signed "Mrs. Hurshell Jinright." The check bears the notation "For Binder on Store." It is endorsed by the plaintiff. On its face the check is stamped "Payment Stopped."

U.C.C. § 2–201(1) provides: "Except as otherwise provided in this section, a contract for the sale of goods for the price of $500 or more is not enforceable by way of action or defense unless there is some writing sufficient to indicate that a contract for sale has been made between the parties and signed by the party against whom enforcement is sought or by his authorized agent or broker. A writing is not insufficient because it omits or incorrectly states terms agreed upon, but the contract is not enforceable under this paragraph beyond the quantity of goods shown in such writing."

The comment to section 2–201(1) of the 1962 official text of the U.C.C. states: "The required writing need not contain all the material terms of the contract, and such material terms as are stated need not be precisely stated. All that is required is that the writing afford a basis for believing that the offered oral evidence rests on a real transaction. It may be written in lead pencil on a scratch pad. It need not indicate which party is the buyer and which the seller. The only term which must appear is the quantity term, which need not be accurately stated, but recovery is limited to the amount stated. The price, time and place of payment or delivery, the general quality of the goods, or any particular warranties may all be omitted. . . .

"Only three definite and invariable requirements as to the memorandum are made by this subsection. First, it must evidence a contract for the sale of goods; second, it must be 'signed,' a word which includes any authentication which identifies the party to be charged; and third, it must specify a quantity."

In our view, the signed check in the present case, with its notation "For Binder on Store," meets all the requirements of a writing sufficient to indicate that a contract for sale was made between the parties. The check does not prove a contract, but it would authorize the introduction of oral evidence toward that end. The party asserting the contract still must bear the burden of proving its existence and the terms.

CASE QUESTIONS

1. What is the policy behind the decision of the court?
2. What constituted the writing in this case? What were the terms included?

SUGGESTED READINGS

J.D. CALAMARI AND J.M. PERILLO, CONTRACTS, §§ 19–14 to 19–25 (2nd ed. 1977).
A.L. CORBIN, CORBIN ON CONTRACTS, §§ 17–19, 21–23 (1952).
Kingsley, *Some Comments on the Section of the Minnesota Statute of Frauds Relating to Contracts*, 14 MINN. L. REV. 746 (1930).

Parol Evidence Rule

If parties have reduced their agreement to writing, they are presumed to have put into writing *all* their understandings on the matter. The writing is presumed to have integrated all prior matters, both oral and written. Therefore, under the parol evidence rule, evidence of prior agreements or terms not contained in the writing is not admissible in court to prove any matter within the contract. There are several exceptions to this rule. Prior evidence is admitted to address a collateral topic that is not a major part of the contract, to explain ambiguity, or to show that there is actually no contract in existence.

Aspects of Contract Performance

Accord and Satisfaction

A case may arise in which one party may agree to take something less than full performance to satisfy the agreement. For example, suppose that *A* asks *B* to pay a debt for services rendered and *B* states that he is too poor to pay the full amount. Then *A* may agree to accept payment for only half of the debt. In this situation, the parties have worked out an accord and satisfaction. An *accord* is the offer of something different from what was due under the original contract. The *satisfaction* is the agreement to take it. Since the law favors a compromise, courts try to uphold any good-faith modification agreement.

Anticipatory Repudiation

Suppose that *A*, who is one party to a contract, clearly manifests that he will not perform at the scheduled time. The other party, *B*, has a choice at common law. *B* may either sue immediately or ignore *A*'s repudiation and wait for the day of performance. If *B* waits, *A* may change his mind and still perform according to the original contract. Under U.C.C., § 2–610, the injured party may not wait until the day of performance. *B* may wait for a change of mind only for a commercially reasonable period of time after repudiation before taking action.

Warranties

A *warranty* is a contractual obligation that sets a standard by which performance of the contract is measured. If the warranties are created by the parties to the contract, they are *express*. If they are imposed by law, they are *implied*. Under U.C.C. § 2–313, express warranties exist whenever a seller affirms facts or describes goods, makes a promise about the goods, or displays a sample model.

There are two types of implied warranties under U.C.C.: § 2–314 and § 2–315. (1) When a merchant sells goods that are reputed to be fit for the ordinary purpose for which they are intended and are of average quality, properly labeled and packaged, the merchant is bound by an *implied warranty of merchantability*. (2) When the seller has reason to know some particular (nonordinary) purpose for which the buyer has relied on the seller's skill or judgment in making a selection, the seller is bound by an *implied warranty of fitness* for a particular purpose.

Implied warranties may be disclaimed by a conspicuous disclaimer statement that the goods are being sold "as is." Once an express warranty is created, it cannot be disclaimed. Any attempt to do so is void. The Magnuson–Moss Federal Warranty Act is an act requiring that written warranties for consumer products be categorized as "full" or "limited." With such a categorization, consumers can know what type of warranty protection they are getting. Under this act, a consumer may sue under both the federal and state warranties to recover actual damages.

Chapter Questions

1. Define the following terms:
   a. breach of contract   b. consideration   c. duress
   d. promise   e. rescission   f. statute of frauds
   g. Uniform Commercial Code

2. Mr. Lucy and Mr. Zehmer were talking at a restaurant. After a couple of drinks, Lucy asked Zehmer if he had sold the Ferguson farm. Zehmer replied that he had not and did not want to sell it. Lucy said, "I bet you wouldn't take $50,000 cash for that farm," and Zehmer replied, "You haven't got $50,000 cash." Lucy said, "I can get it." Zehmer said he might form a company and get it, "but you haven't got $50,000 cash to pay me tonight." Lucy asked him if he would put it in writing that he would sell him this farm. Zehmer then wrote on the back of a pad, "I agree to sell the Ferguson Place to W. O. Lucy for $50,000 cash." Lucy said, "All right, get your wife to sign it." Zehmer went to his wife and said, "You want to put your name to this?" She said no, but he said in an undertone, "It is nothing but a joke," and she signed it. At that time, Zehmer was not too drunk to make a valid contract. The Zehmers refused to convey legal title to the property, and Lucy sued for specific performance. What defense would the Zehmers use in the suit? Who should win the suit?
   Lucy v. Zehmer, 196 Va. 493, 84 S.E.2d 516 (1954)

3. National Beverages, Inc., offered to the public prizes to be awarded in a contest known as "Pepsi-Cola Streator-Chevrolet Sweepstakes." The first prize was a Chevrolet Corvair. No order of drawing was announced prior to the close of the contest. After the close of the contest, just prior to the drawing, a sign was displayed stating the order of drawing. The first tickets drawn would receive 12 cases of Pepsi-Cola and the last ticket drawn would receive the automobile. Mrs. Walter's ticket was the first ticket to be drawn from the barrel. She claims that her number being the first qualified number drawn entitles her to the first prize, the Chevrolet Corvair. She bases her claim upon the wording of the offer which listed the automobile as the first prize. She accepted the offer by entering the contest. Is Mrs. Walters entitled to the automobile?
   Walters v. National Beverages, Inc., 18 Utah 2d 301, 422 P.2d 524 (1967)

4. Mr. Green signed a roofing contract with Clay Tile, agent for Ever-Tite Roofing Company, to have a new roof put on his house. The agreement stated that this contract was subject to Ever-Tite's approval and that the agreement would become binding upon written notice of acceptance or commencement of work. Nine days later,

Clay Tile loaded up his truck and drove to Green's house, only to find that someone else was already doing the job. Ever-Tite wishes to sue on the contract for damages. Was Green's offer to Ever-Tite accepted before the offer was revoked?

Ever-Tite Roofing Corporation v. Green, 83 So.2d 449 (La.App. 1955)

5. Workers agreed to work aboard a canning ship during the salmon canning season. The contract, signed individually by each worker, was to last for the length of time it took to sail from San Francisco to Pyramid Harbor, Alaska, and back. Each worker was to receive a stated compensation. They arrived in Alaska at the height of the fishing and canning season. Knowing that every day's delay would be financially disastrous and that it would be impossible to find workers to replace them, the workers refused to work unless they were given substantial wage increases. The owner of the canning ship acceded to their demands. When the ship returned to San Francisco, the owner paid them in accordance with the original agreement. The workers now bring suit to recover the additional amounts due under the second agreement. Will the contract be upheld?

Alaska Packers Ass'n v. Domenico, 117 F.99 (9th Cir. 1902)

6. A little girl found a pretty stone about the size of a canary bird's egg. She had no idea what it was, so she took it to a jeweler who eventually bought it from her for a dollar, although he too did not know what it was. The stone turned out to be an uncut diamond worth $10,000. The girl tendered back the $1 purchase price and sued to have the sale voided on the basis of mutual mistake. Should mutual mistake be a basis of recovery?

Wood v. Boynton, 64 Wis. 265, 25 N.W. 42 (1885)

7. William E. Story agreed orally with his nephew that if he would refrain from drinking liquor, using tobacco, swearing, and playing cards or billiards for money until he became 21 years old, then he, William E. Story, would pay his nephew $5000 when the nephew reached age 21. The nephew fully performed his part of the agreement. But when he reached age 21, his uncle stated that he had earned the $5000 and that he would keep it at interest for his nephew. Twelve years later, William E. Story died, and his nephew brought an action to recover the $5000 plus interest. Was there sufficient consideration to create a contract?

Hamer v. Sidway, 124 N.Y. 538, 27 N.E. 256 (1891)

8. The Kentucky Bankers Association provided a reward of $500 for the arrest and conviction of each bank robber. Three armed men robbed First State Bank. Later in the day, they were apprehended and placed under arrest by three policemen. Two of the policemen were from the

county of the bank and the other was from a neighboring county and out of his jurisdiction. Four employees of the bank gave the officers the details of the crime and described the culprits. The information was used in capturing the robbers. After the conviction of the robbers, the employees of the bank and the policemen wanted to share in the reward. Who would be entitled to the reward?

Denney v. Reppert, 432 S.W.2d 647 (Ky. 1968)

9. Louisa Sheffield's husband was on the verge of bankruptcy. Louisa was independently wealthy but not nearly as independently intelligent. Benjamin Strong, a holder of some of her husband's notes, payable on demand, approached Louisa and convinced her to renegotiate the notes as surety even though she was not personally liable. Benjamin had been worried about her husband's financial status and sought the renegotiation as insurance that the notes would be paid. A contract was drawn up in which Louisa promised to pay the notes. In return, Benjamin promised not to collect on the notes until such time as he wanted his money. Her husband became insolvent, and Benjamin approached Louisa for payment. Is she obligated to pay under the contract?

Strong v. Sheffield, 144 N.Y. 392, 39 N.E. 330 (1895)

10. Robert Rogers turned 17, quit high school, and married his home-town sweetheart. To provide her with the style of life with which she had become accustomed, Robert went out in search of employment. He signed an agreement with the Gastonia Personnel Corp., agreeing to pay a commission of $293 to it if it was successful in procuring him a job. Gastonia found him a job, but Robert refuses to pay and denies liability on the grounds of minority. Can he avoid payment on this ground?

Gastonia Personnel Corp. v. Rogers, 276 N.C. 279, 172 S.E.2d 19 (1970)

11. Seventeen-year-old Robertson purchased a truck from Julian Pontiac Co. for $1743.85. He traded in his passenger car for which he was given a credit of $723.85, leaving a balance of $1020 payable in 24 monthly installments. Robertson was unable to get insurance because of his young age. He returned the truck to the dealer for repair of defective wiring, but the condition was not remedied. The truck caught fire and was practically destroyed. Robertson lived at home with his parents, and he did not need the truck in connection with any work. Julian Pontiac Co. disposed of the car it received in the trade and cannot restore it to Robertson. Can Robertson, who is still a minor, rescind the contract and, if so, what would be the remedy?

Robertson v. King, 225 Ark. 276, 280 S.W.2d 402 (1955)

12. Manuel Tovar was employed as a resident physician by Paxton Community Memorial Hospital in Illinois. Tovar had never been licensed to practice medicine in that state. In order to assume the position, he had had to resign his position in Kansas and move to Illinois. After two weeks of employment, the hospital discharged him. The hospital was aware of his background, professional experience, and licensing when it hired him. Should Tovar recover for breach of his employment contract?

    Tovar v. Paxton Community Memorial Hospital, 29 Ill. App.3d 218, 330 N.E.2d 247 (1975)

13. In 1941, Liebman gave Rosenthal $28,000 worth of jewels so that Rosenthal, a good friend of the Portuguese consul in France, would obtain visas for Liebman and his family so they could get out of France and into Portugal. This transaction took place during World War II, when it was illegal to obtain such visas. Rosenthal absconded to America with the jewels without procuring the visas. Many years later, Liebman and Rosenthal met in New York, where Liebman demanded the return of the jewels. Rosenthal's defense is that the agreement is illegal and, therefore, unenforceable. Is he right?

    Liebman v. Rosenthal, 57 N.Y.S.2d 875 (1945)

14. Voss approached the law firm of Preval, Wilson and Matthews to represent him in a patent-infringement suit filed by his company, V & S Ice Machine Company. Since V & S Ice Machine Company is a shell corporation, its only asset being an ice-blade patent, the law firm sought personal assurances from Voss that their firm would be paid. Voss agreed to take care of the fee and said that he expected to pay between $10,000 and $20,000 for their legal services. The suit was unsuccessful, and Voss received a bill for $14,000. He refused payment and suit is being brought for collection. Voss defends on the ground that the agreement was for him to answer for the debt of the corporation, and that it is unenforceable because it violates the statute of frauds, in that it was never reduced to writing. Is this a valid defense?

    Preval, Wilson and Matthews v. Voss, 471 F.2d 1186 (5th Cir. 1973)

15. Hedda Hopper, a famous radio and television personality, orally contracted with Lennen & Mitchell, advertising agents, to do weekly radio advertisements over a term of five years. This five-year period was divided into ten 26-week segments, and Lennen & Mitchell had the right to cancel the contract simply by giving written notice four weeks before the end of any 26-week segment. Hedda refused to perform under the contract, and Lennen & Mitchell sued for damages. Is enforcement of the contract barred by the statute of frauds?

    Hopper v. Lennen & Mitchell, 146 F.2d 364 (9th Cir. 1944)

Glossary

ABSTENTION (1) The keeping of an heir from possession. (2) The tacit renunciation of a succession by an heir. (3) A voluntary doing without.

ACCESSARY, or ACCESSORY One who is not the actual perpetrator of a felony, but is in some way concerned with the perpetration of it. He may be an accessory (a) before the fact, e.g., by inciting or counseling, or (b) after the fact, by relieving or assisting the felon.

ACCOMPLICE One concerned with others in the commission of a crime.

ACCOUNT, or ACCOMPT A detailed statement of receipts and payments of money, or of trade transactions which have taken place between two or more persons. Accounts are either (1) open or current, where the balance is not struck, or is not accepted by all the parties; (2) stated, where it has been expressly or impliedly acknowledged to be correct by all the parties; or (3) settled, where it has been accepted and discharged. To make a rest in an account, or an account with rests is, at stated periods, to strike a balance, so that interest may thenceforward be computed on the sum actually due, not merely on the original principal or debt.

ACQUITTAL A release or discharge, especially by verdict of a jury.

ACTION A lawsuit; a proceeding taken in a court of law. Its chief classifications are: civil, to enforce a right; criminal, to punish an offender. Under the modern rules of civil procedure adopted in the United States

Reprinted from *The Law Dictionary* (*Cochran's Law Lexicon*, 5th ed.), revised by Wesley Gilmer, Jr., by permission of Anderson Publishing Company, Cincinnati, Ohio.

courts and many state courts, and the codes of civil practice in most other states, the common law forms of action are abolished and one form of action, known as a *civil action,* is established. The following classifications are, therefore, significant mainly from a historical viewpoint. In rem (against a thing), to bind a thing; in personam (against a person), to bind a person; real, to recover lands, tenements, or hereditaments; personal, to recover money, damages, or specific personal property; mixed, which partake of the nature of both real and personal actions as actions of partition, actions to recover possession of property and damages, etc.; ex contractu, those which arise out of contract; and ex delicto, those which arise out of tort or the fault of the defendant. In common law pleading actions ex contractu were classed as follows: (a) covenant, being on a deed alone; (b) assumpsit, being on a simple contract only; (c) debt, being indifferently on a deed or simple contract; (d) scire facias, being on a judgment; (e) account, to compel an account and enforce the payment of the balance found due; (f) annuity, to enforce the payment of an annuity. Actions ex delicto were classed as follows: (a) trespass quare clausum fregit, to real property, or de bonis asportatis, to personal property; (b) case, being for torts which had no special writ or remedy, prior to 13 Edw. 1. c. 24, and for which, by that statute, special writs were to be framed, according to the circumstances of each case, on the lines of those already existing, such as torts committed without force, injuries resulting from negligence, abuse of legal process, etc., and injuries to reversionary, incorporeal and relative rights; (c) trover, to recover damages for the wrongful appropriation or conversion of property; (d) detinue, for the wrongful detention of property lawfully taken, and (e) replevin, to recover specific personal property, unlawfully taken.

ADJUDICATION   A judgment or decision. (2) Of bankruptcy, the declaring a debtor bankrupt. See also *Bankruptcy.*

ADMINISTRATIVE PROCEDURE ACT   An act to establish a uniform system of administering laws by and among the agencies of the United States government, and to provide for administrative and judicial review of the decisions of those agencies. 5 U.S.C. §§ 1001 *et seq.*; 60 Stat. 237 (1946).

ADVISORY OPINION   In some jurisdictions, the formal opinion of a higher court concerning a point at issue in a lower court. (2) The formal opinion of a legal officer, e.g., Attorney General, concerning a question of law submitted by a public official. (3) In some jurisdictions, the opinion of a court concerning a question submitted by a legislative body.

ADMIRALTY   The jurisdiction exercised by United States courts over maritime contracts, torts, injuries, and seizures, including cases arising on the navigable lakes and rivers. In England, this jurisdiction is exercised by the Probate, Divorce and Admiralty Division of the High Court of Justice, and is confined to cases arising on the high seas and those portions of rivers and sounds in which the tides rise and fall.

AFFIDAVIT   A written statement of fact, signed and sworn to before a person having authority to administer an oath.

AFFIRM   To make firm; to establish. (1) To ratify or confirm the judgment of a lower court. (2) To ratify or confirm a voidable contract. (3) To declare or verify as a substitute for an oath.

AFFIRMATIVE DEFENSE   A response to a claim for relief, which states information not otherwise before the court, e.g., a plea of payment, in response to a claim that a promissory note was executed and delivered. (2) A justification or avoidance.

AGENT   A person authorized by another (the principal), to do an act or transact business for him, and to bind the principal within the limits of that authority. An agent may be general, to do all business of a particular kind; or special, to do one particular act. The agent's power to bind the principal is according to the scope of his authority.

ALIEN   A person of foreign birth who is not a citizen. (2) A person who is a citizen or subject of a foreign state or who owes allegiance to a foreign government. (3) To transfer property, i.e., alienate.

ALIMONY   The allowance made to a wife out of her husband's estate for her support, either during a matrimonial suit, which is called alimony pendente lite, or at its termination, when she proves herself entitled to a separate maintenance, the fact of marriage being established. Alimony is not ordinarily granted to a husband, but under the statutes in some states, it may be awarded to the husband and ordered to be paid by the wife.

ALLEGATION   A statement of fact made in a legal proceeding, which the person stating it intends to prove. An allegation is a bare assertion, as compared with proof, which is a substantiation of the allegation.

AMBIGUITY   The quality or state of being subject to two or more different interpretations. There are two species of ambiguity (a) patent, i.e., apparent on the face of the instrument, which may occasionally be supplied or explained by extrinsic evidence, i.e., evidence not contained in the instrument itself; (b) latent, where the instrument being apparently free from obscurity, a doubt arises in carrying it into execution, e.g., from a name used in it being applicable to two persons or things. In such case, extrinsic evidence is often admissible. See also *Parol evidence rule.*

AMI'CUS CU'RIAE   Lat., "friend of the court," an attorney who, by leave of court, intervenes in pending litigation, especially arguments on appeal, in order to influence the decision in the litigation, which as a precedent is likely to affect the attorney's client. (2) A stander by, not being a party to, or interested in the cause, who informs the court of any decided case, statute, or other fact, of which it can take judicial notice.

ANSWER   In pleading, a statement of the defenses on which a party defending a lawsuit intends to rely. (2) A statement under oath, in response to written interrogatories, i.e., questions, or oral questions.

ANTI-TRUST ACTS or ANTITRUST ACTS   Various federal and state statutes intended to protect trade and commerce from unlawful restraints and monopolies.

APPEAL   An application to a higher court to correct or modify the judgment of a lower court. The person initiating the appeal is called an appellant, or petitioner, and the opposite party is called an appellee, or respondent. The manner of taking appeals, and the cases which may be appealed, are regulated by various state and federal statutes.

APPEARANCE   The initial court response by a defendant in a lawsuit. (2) A formal submission to the jurisdiction of the court by a party to a suit. It can be made in person; by the attorney, or by a guardian or next friend, where the party is an infant or under some other disability.

APPELLANT   He who initiates an appeal from one court to another.

APPELLATE JURISDICTION   The authority of a superior court to review and modify the decision of an inferior court.

APPELLEE´   The party in a lawsuit against whom an appeal has been taken.

APPURTENANCE   Something which belongs to something else, so that when the latter is transferred, the former will automatically be transferred with it. As an example, a passageway to a piece of land, i.e., an easement, is an appurtance to the land.

ARBITRATION   The voluntary submission of a matter in dispute to the non-judicial judgment of one, two, or more disinterested persons, called arbitrators, whose decision, called an award, is binding upon the parties.

ARBITRATION AND AWARD   The voluntary settlement of a controversy by mutually agreeing to submit the controversy to arbitration, so that the decision in the arbitration is binding on the parties. (2) An affirmative defense which seeks to avoid a claim because it was previously submitted to arbitration and an award was established.

ARRAIGN   To bring a prisoner to court for the purpose of having him answer the charge against him. The initial court appearance of a person who is charged with a crime. An *arraignment* consists of three parts: (a) calling the defendant by name, (b) reading him the indictment, (c) asking him if he be guilty or not guilty. He may plead "guilty" or "not guilty," or stand mute, which is, in effect, the same as pleading "not guilty."

ARREST   The seizing of a person and detaining him in custody by lawful authority, (2) The seizure and detention of personal chattels, especially of ships and vessels libeled in a Court of Admiralty.

ASSAULT   Strictly speaking, is threatening to strike or harm. (2) A threatening gesture, with or without verbal communication. If a blow is struck, it is battery (*q.v.*).

ASSUMPTION OF RISK   A defense to a claim for negligent injury to a person or property, i.e., a person who voluntarily exposes himself or his property to a known danger may not recover for injuries thereby sustained.

ATTORNEY AT LAW   A person licensed by a court to practice the profession of law. Such a license authorizes him to appear in court, give legal advice, draft written instruments, and do many other things which constitute the practice of law (*q.v.*).

BAIL To set at liberty a person arrested or imprisoned, on written security taken for his appearance on a day, and at a place named. The term is applied, as a noun, to the persons who become security for the defendant's appearance; to the act of delivering such defendant to his bondsmen; and also to the bond given by the sureties to secure his release. A person who becomes someone's bail is regarded as his jailer, to whose custody he is committed. The word "bail" is never used with a plural termination.

BAIL BOND A written undertaking, signed by a surety at the time of the release of a person who has been arrested, conditioned for the due appearance of such defendant.

BANKRUPTCY Jurisdiction exercised by United States courts and created by federal statute. It concerns the affairs of insolvent debtors and includes voluntary petitions of natural persons, wage earner plans and corporate reorganizations. Bankruptcy existed in Roman law and in English law. Congress is empowered to establish uniform laws on the subject of bankruptcies under the United States Constitution. (2) Occasionally, insolvency.

BATTERY An unlawful touching, beating, wounding or laying hold, however trifling, of another's person or clothes without his consent.

BENCH WARRANT An order issued at the direction of a court or judge, for the arrest of an individual, e.g., for contempt or where an indictment has been found.

BENEFICIARY A person who is entitled to the benefits of a trust which is administered by a trustee. Sometimes called a cestui que trust. (2) A person to whom life insurance is payable at the death of the insured.

BILL A written statement of one's claim or account against another. (2) An unconditional, written and signed, order to pay a sum certain in money to someone, drawn by a person on a third party, e.g., *a bill of exchange*, also called a draft. If it is drawn on a bank and payable on demand, it is a check. U.C.C. § 3-104. (3) The original draft of a law presented to a legislative body for enactment. It is a bill until passed, and then becomes an act, or statute. The term is applied to some special acts after their passage; e.g., *bill of attainder, bill of indemnity*, etc. (4) A document evidencing the receipt of goods for shipment, i.e., *a bill of lading*, issued by a person engaged in the business of transporting or forwarding goods. U.C.C. § 1-201. (5) The written statement of an offense charged against a person, which is presented to a grand jury. If satisfied by the evidence that the charge is probably true, it is endorsed, "a true bill," and called an indictment.

BILL OF ATTAINDER Formerly in English law, a legislative act or pronouncement which directed that a person be punished, without a court trial, for doing some act. Strictly defined, a bill of attainder directed punishment by death, and a bill of pains and penalties directed punishment of a lesser degree. The United States Constitution forbids Congress and the states to pass bills of attainder and the courts have interpreted the prohibition to also forbid them to pass bills of pains and penalties. The last such bills in England were introduced in the 18th and 19th centuries. Such acts typically made new crimes out of otherwise innocuous conduct which was politically offensive to a majority of the legislature.

BREACH   A breaking or violation.

BREACH OF CONTRACT   A flexible term for the wrongful failure to perform one or more of the promises which a person previously undertook when he made a contract, e.g., failure to deliver goods.

BULK SALES ACTS   Various state statutes which provide that the sale of all or any portion of a stock of merchandise, other than in the normal course of business, shall be fraudulent as against the seller's creditors, unless the purchaser receives from the seller a list of the seller's creditors and the purchaser notifies such creditors of the proposed sale, or pays them from its proceeds. The various state statutes have been replaced in most instances by U.C.C. §§ 6-101 to 6-111.

BURDEN OF PROOF (ONUS PROBANDI)   The duty of proving facts disputed on the trial of a case. It commonly lies on the person who asserts the affirmative of an issue, and is sometimes said to shift when sufficient evidence is furnished to raise a presumption that what is alleged is true. The shifting of the burden of proof is better characterized as the creation of a burden of going forward with the evidence; however, because the total burden of proof is not thereby changed, the burden of going forward with the evidence is apt to revert to the other party and change from time to time.

CAPITAL STOCK   The sum of money which is invested in a corporation, in exchange for which stock certificates are issued to the investors.

CASE LAW   Judicial precedent generated as a by-product of the decisions which courts have made in resolving unique disputes, as distinguished from statutes and constitutions. Case law concerns concrete facts. Statutes and constitutions are written in the abstract.

CASES AND CONTROVERSIES   A generic phrase denoting bona fide disputes or lawsuits in which something is decided either affirmatively or negatively. Controversy is usually descriptive of civil proceedings and cases usually include both criminal prosecutions and civil proceedings. Article III of the United States Constitution uses the terms, cases and controversies, to define the judicial power of the United States.

CAUSE OF ACTION   A flexible term, the definition of which is occasionally controversial. (1) An aggregation of facts which will cause a court to grant relief, and therefore entitles a person to initiate and prosecute a lawsuit. (2) The concurrence of a right belonging to a plaintiff, and a wrong committed by a defendant, which breaches the right and results in damage. Under modern rules of civil procedure, the term has been partly superseded by claim for relief (*q.v.*).

CERTIORA'RI Lat., "to be more fully informed," an original writ or action whereby a cause is removed from an inferior to a superior court for review. The record of the proceedings is then transmitted to the superior court. (2) A discretionary appellate jurisdiction that is invoked by a petition for certiorari, which the appellate court may grant or deny in its discretion. A dominant avenue to the United States Supreme Court.

CHANCELLOR A judge who presides over a court of chancery, i.e., a court of Equity.

CHANCERY, EQUITY A court exercising equitable jurisdiction. The terms equity and chancery are used synonymously in the United States. Under modern rules of civil procedure and some codes of civil practice, there is no longer any distinction between actions at law and suits in equity.

CHARITABLE USE Charitable purpose; charitable trust; charity; e.g., the establishment of colleges, schools and hospitals and the carrying on of religious and missionary enterprises.

CHATTELS Any property, except a freehold of real property. It includes personal property, e.g., furniture, automobiles and animals, and leases and other interests in land which are less than a freehold.

CITIZEN A flexible term descriptive of a person who has the freedom and privileges of a city, county, state or nation. (2) A person who is a member of a body politic, owes allegiance to its government and may claim the protection of its government.

CIVIL ACTION A lawsuit which has for its object the protection of private or civil rights or compensation for their infraction.

CIVIL REMEDY The remedy which an injured party has against a party who committed the injury, as distinguished from a criminal proceeding by which the wrongdoer is made to expiate the injury done to society.

CIVIL RIGHTS ACT OF 1964 An act to enforce the constitutional right to vote, to confer jurisdiction upon the district courts of the United States to provide injunctive relief against discrimination in public accommodations, to authorize the Attorney General to institute suits to protect constitutional rights in public facilities and public education, to extend the Commission on Civil Rights, to prevent discrimination in federally assisted programs, to establish a commission on Equal Employment Opportunity, and for other purposes. 28 U.S.C. § 1447; 42 U.S.C. § 1971, 1975a-d, 2000a-2000h-6; 78 Stat. 241 (1964).

CLAIM FOR RELIEF Under modern rules of civil procedure, a short and plain statement showing that the pleader is entitled to relief. It should give fair notice of the character of the claim asserted so as to enable the adverse party to answer and prepare for trial. It must contain a distinctive group of facts which distinguish the action from all other controversies so that the matter at issue can be later identified as *res judicata* (*q.v.*). Fed. R. Civ. P. 8(a).

CLASS ACTION, or REPRESENTATIVE ACTION   A lawsuit initiated or defended by a person, who brings it or defends it for himself, and on behalf of all other persons similarly situated. If persons constituting a class are so numerous as to make it impracticable to bring them all before the court, such of them, one or more, as will fairly insure the adequate representation of all may, on behalf of all, sue or be sued, in certain instances, depending upon the character of the right sought to be enforced. Fed. R. Civ. P. 23.

CLAYTON ACT   An act to supplement earlier laws, including the Sherman Act, against unlawful restraints and monopolies. 15 U.S.C. §§ 12 *et seq.*, 18 U.S.C. §§ 402 *et seq.*, 29 U.S.C. §§ 52, 53; 38 Stat. 730 (1914).

CLEAN HANDS   A principle that may be invoked to preclude affirmative equitable relief to someone who seeks it, and has himself been guilty of inequitable conduct, concerning the matter in which he seeks relief.

CLERICAL ERROR   A mistake made in transcribing, or in the performance of other clerical operations.

COLLATERAL ATTACK   An attempt to defeat the operation of a valid judgment in a separate proceeding, which only incidentally generates such an issue.

COLLECTIVE BARGAINING   A procedure looking toward the making of a collective agreement between the employer and the accredited representative of his employees concerning wages, hours and other conditions of employment.

COLLUSION   A secret agreement between persons apparently hostile, to do some act in order to defraud or prejudice a third person, or for some improper purpose.

COM'ITY   The practice by which one court follows the decision of another court on a like question, though not bound by the law of precedents to do so.

COMMERCIAL PAPER   Negotiable instruments, e.g., checks and promissory notes.

COMMON LAW   An ambiguous term. (1) A system of jurisprudence founded on principles of justice which are determined by reasoning and administration consistent with the usage, customs and institutions of the people and which are suitable to the genius of the people and their social, political and economic condition. The rules deduced from this system continually change and expand with the progress of society. (2) That system of law which does not rest for its authority upon any express statutes, but derives its force and authority from universal consent and immemorial usage, and which is evidenced by the decisions of the courts of law, technically so called, in contra-distinction to those of equity and the ecclesiastical courts.

COMPENSATORY DAMAGES   Such as measure the actual loss; not exemplary or punitive.

COMPLAINT   The charge made before a proper officer that an offense has been committed by a person named or described. (2) Under modern rules of civil procedure, a pleading which must be filed to commence an action.

CONFLICT OF LAWS The variance between the laws of two states or countries relating to the subject matter of a suit brought in one of them, when the parties to the suit, or some of them, or the subject matter, belong to the other. See also *lex loci*.

CONGRESS, or CONGRESS OF THE UNITED STATES The name of the legislative body of the United States, composed of the Senate and House of Representatives.

CONSIDERATION The price, motive or matter of inducement of a contract, which must be lawful in itself. The term is flexible and includes that which is bargained for and paid in return for a promise, the benefits to the party making the promise and the loss or detriment to the party to whom the promise is made. A contract derives its binding force from the existence of a valuable consideration between the parties. Consideration may be *executed*, i.e., past or performed; *executory*, i.e., to be performed; or continuing, i.e., partly both. Good or meritorious consideration is that originating in relationship and natural affection. Valuable consideration is that which has a money value.

CONSOR'TIUM Lat., "marital fellowship, company, companionship." The duties and obligations which, by marriage, the husband and wife take upon themselves toward each other.

CONSTITUTION The fundamental and basic law of a state or nation which establishes the form and limitations of government and secures the rights of the citizens. The constitution of the United States was adopted in a convention of representatives of the people, at Philadelphia, September 17, 1787, and became the law of the land on the first Wednesday in March, 1789. Each of the states composing the United States has a constitution of its own. Constitutions usually prescribe the manner in which they may be amended.

CONTEMPT A willful disregard or disobedience of public authority. Courts may punish one who disobeys the rules, orders or process, or willfully offends against the dignity and good order of the court, by fine or imprisonment. Similar authority is exercised by each house of the Congress of the United States, by state legislatures and in some instances by administrative agencies. The contempt power is usually subject to judicial review.

CONTRACT An agreement between competent parties, upon a legal consideration, to do or to abstain from doing some act. It is usually applied to simple or parol contracts, including written as well as verbal ones. Contracts may be *express*, in which the terms are stated in words; or *implied*, i.e., presumed by law to have been made from the circumstances and the relations of the parties; *mutual* and *dependent*, in which the performance by one is dependent upon the performance by the other; *independent*, when either promise may be performed without reference to the other;

entire, in which the complete performance by one is a condition precedent to demanding performance of the other; *severable,* in which the
things to be performed are capable of separation, so that on performance
of part the party performing may demand a proportionate part of the
consideration from the other; *executed,* in which the things each agrees
to perform are done at the time the contract is made; *executory,* in
which some act remains to be done by one or both of the parties; *personal,* i.e., depending on the skill or qualities of one of the parties; *contracts of beneficence,* by which only one of the contracting parties is to
be benefited, e.g., loans and deposits. (2) The total legal obligation
which results from the parties' agreement as affected by the U.C.C. and
any other applicable rules of law. U.C.C. § 1-201 (11).

CONTRIBUTORY NEGLIGENCE   The failure to exercise care by a plaintiff, which
contributed to the plaintiff's injury. Even though a defendant may have
been negligent, in the majority of jurisdictions, contributory negligence
will bar a recovery by the plaintiff.

CONVERSIONS   A flexible term. (1) The wrongful appropriation of the goods
of another. (2) Equitable conversion is the changing of the nature of
property, which may be (a) actual, e.g., by converting land into money
by selling it, or vice versa; or (b) constructive, where such an operation
is assumed to have, though it has not actually, taken place, e.g., when an
owner has agreed to sell land, and dies before executing the conveyance,
the executors are entitled to the money, and not the heirs. Property con-
structively converted assumes the same qualities as if the operation had
been actually carried out.

COPYRIGHT   A comprehensive privilege to exclusively print, reprint, publish,
copy, translate, dramatize, convert, arrange, adapt, complete, execute,
finish, deliver in public, perform and transcribe an original work. In the
United States, the privilege lasts for twenty-eight years with a provision
for renewal for twenty-eight more years under certain conditions. 17
U.S.C. §§ 1-215; 61 Stat. 652 (1947), as amended.

CORPORATION   An artificial person composed of individuals. It usually has a
corporate name and perpetual duration. Sometimes its duration is a
fixed term of years. It substitutes for the individuals who compose it.

COUNT   The statement of a cause of action. A complaint has as many *counts*
as there are causes of action, or different statements of the same cause of
action. (2) In criminal law, each part of an indictment which charges a
distinct offense.

COUNTERCLAIM   The defendant's claim against the plaintiff, which most courts
permit him to set up in his response to the complaint.

COURT   An institution for the resolving of disputes. (2) A place where justice is administered. (3) The judge or judges when performing their official duties. Courts may be classified as courts of record, those in which
a final record of the proceedings is made, which imports verity and cannot be collaterally impeached, and courts not of record, in which no final

record is made, though it may keep a docket and enter in it notes of the various proceedings; courts of original jurisdiction, in which suits are initiated, and which have power to hear and determine in the first instance, and appellate courts, which take cognizance of causes removed from other courts; courts of equity or chancery, which administer justice according to the principles of equity, and courts of law, which administer justice according to the principles of the common law; civil courts which give remedies for private wrongs; criminal courts, in which public offenders are tried, acquitted or convicted and sentenced; ecclesiastical courts, which formerly had jurisdiction over testamentary and matrimonial causes; courts of admiralty, which have jurisdiction over maritime causes, civil and criminal; courts-martial, which have jurisdiction of offenses against the military or naval laws, committed by persons in that service. In numerous instances, the various classifications of courts have been consolidated. The same court may serve as a court of equity, a court of law, a civil court, a criminal court and a court of admiralty. It may qualify as a court of record and be a court of original jurisdiction.

COURTS OF CONSCIENCE, or COURTS OF REQUEST   Formerly English courts for the recovery of debts not exceeding forty shillings. In 1846 they were abolished and their jurisdiction was transferred to the County Courts.

CRIMINAL   A person who is guilty of committing a crime. (2) *Adj.*, involving an offense against law; relating to crime.

CROSS-EXAMINATION   The questioning of a witness by the party opposed to the party which called the witness for direct examination. This usually occurs after the direct examination but on occasion may be otherwise allowed. The form of the questions on cross-examination is designed for the purpose of eliciting evidence from a hostile witness.

CUSTOMS   Taxes levied on merchandise which is imported or exported.

DAMAGES   A flexible term for the reparation in money which is allowed by law on account of damage. They may be general, such as necessarily and by implication of law arise from the act complained of; or special, such as under the peculiar circumstances of the case arise from the act complained of, but are not implied by law; compensatory, sufficient in amount to cover the loss actually sustained; exemplary, punitive, or vindictive, when in excess of the loss sustained and allowed as a punishment for torts committed with fraud, actual malice, or violence; nominal, when the act was wrong, but the loss sustained was trifling; substantial, when the loss was serious; liquidated, fixed by agreement of the parties, as when it is agreed beforehand what amount one shall receive in case of a breach of contract by the other.

DE NO'VO   Lat., "anew; afresh." A trial de novo is a trial which is held for a second time, as if there had been no former decision.

DECEIT   A type of fraud, in which facts are withheld, misrepresented or falsely intimated to be true, by which a person is misled to his injury.

(2) Formerly a common law action to recover damages for loss caused by misrepresentation or fraud.

DECLARATORY JUDGMENT, or DECLARATORY DECREE   A determination or decision by a court, which states the rights of the parties to a dispute, but does not order or coerce any performance relative to those rights. The procedural and substantive conditions of the usual action must be present. The relief which the court grants is the distinguishing characteristic.

DECREE (SC. DECREET)   A determination made by the court in a suit in equity or libel in admiralty. It is interlocutory if it does not finally dispose of the case, e.g., an order directing an accounting or a sale or appointing a receiver, or final, when it does dispose of the case. (2) Often used as a generic term for any judgment or order issued by a court.

DEFAMATION   A flexible term for the uttering of spoken or written words concerning someone, which tend to injure that person's reputation and for which an action for damages may be brought. See also *Libel; Slander.*

DEFAULT   A flexible term for the omission of that which a person ought to do. (2) The failure to plead or otherwise defend an action, by a party against whom a judgment for affirmative relief is sought.

DEFENDANT   A person against whom an action is brought, a warrant is issued or an indictment is found.

DELEGATE   A person authorized to act for another. (2) A person elected to represent others in a deliberative assembly, such as a political convention.

DEMURRER   A formal response to a pleading, which admits the allegations to be true, for the purposes of argument, but asserts that no cause of action, or defense, is stated by the allegations of the pleading. It imports that the party demurring will stay, and not proceed, until the court decides whether he is bound to do so. Demurrers are either general, where no particular cause is assigned and the insufficiency of the pleading is stated in general terms, or special, where some particular defects are pointed out. Demurrers may be to the whole or to any part of a pleading. Under modern rules of civil procedure, the demurrer has been replaced by a motion to dismiss for failure to state a claim. Fed. R. Civ. P. 12(b).

DEP'OSITION   A written record of oral testimony, in the form of questions and answers, made before a public officer, for use in a lawsuit. They are used for the purpose of discovery of information, or for the purpose of being read as evidence at a trial, or for both purposes.

DIC'TUM, or OBITER DICTUM   Lat., a statement by a judge concerning a point of law which is not necessary for the decision of the case in which it is stated. Usually, dictum is not as persuasive as is its opposite, i.e., holding (*q.v.*).

DIRECT EXAMINATION   The initial questioning of a witness by the party who calls him.

DIRECTED VERDICT   A determination by a jury made at the direction of the court, in cases where there has been a failure of evidence, an overwhelming weight of the evidence, or where the law, as applied to the facts, is for one of the parties.

DISCOVERY   A pliant method by which the opposing parties to a lawsuit may obtain full and exact factual information concerning the entire area of their controversy, via pre-trial depositions, interrogatories, requests for admissions, inspection of books and documents, physical and mental examinations and inspection of land or other property. The purpose of these pre-trial procedures is to disclose the genuine points of factual dispute and facilitate adequate preparation for trial. Either party may compel the other party to disclose the relevant facts that are in his possession, prior to the trial. Fed. R. Civ. P. 26-37.

DISCRETION   The use of private independent judgment; the authority of a trial court which is not controlled by inflexible rules, but can be exercised one way or the other as the trial judge believes to be best in the circumstances. It is subject to review, however, if it is abused. (2) Ability to distinguish between good and evil.

DISTRICT COURTS   United States trial courts established in the respective judicial districts into which the whole United States is divided. Some states constitute a single district each, but the larger states are divided into two or more. (2) Courts of some of the states established for the purpose of hearing and deciding causes in limited districts to which their jurisdiction is confined. In some of the states their jurisdiction is chiefly appellate, in others it is original.

DIVERSITY OF CITIZENSHIP   The coincidence of the parties on the opposite sides of a lawsuit being domiciled in different states, which is one of the grounds to invoke the jurisdiction of United States district courts, when the case also involves a controversy concerning $10,000.00 or more in value. 28 U.S.C. § 1332; 72 Stat. 415 (1958). Its purpose is to provide out-of-state litigants an impartial court. The definition is deceivingly simple in appearance, but the concept is very intricate because of, e.g., the mobility of parties, multiple plaintiffs and multiple defendants, nominal parties, the representative character of some actions and the interstate operations of corporations which result in their having multiple citizenship. Innumerable factors influence a court's determination as to whether diversity of citizenship exists in any particular case.

DIVORCE   A judicial severance of the tie of matrimony. It may be an absolute divorce (a vinculo matrimonii), or nullity of marriage, which is complete; or a legal separation (a mensa et thoro), which does not entitle the parties to marry again.

DOMICILE   The place where a person has his legal home or place of permanent residence. It depends on the fact of residing and on the intention of remaining. Domicile is acquired by birth, by choice, or by operation of law, e.g., the domicile of an infant is the same as that of his parents, though they are temporarily absent from it at the time of his birth.

DONOR   A person who makes a gift or confers a power of appointment.

DOUBLE JEOPARDY   A second time of danger or peril; a defense to a prosecution for crime, raising the claim that the defendant is being placed on trial for a second time for the same offense for which he has previously been tried. No person may be subject to be twice put in jeopardy of life or limb for the same offense. U.S. Const., Amend. V, and various state constitutions.

DUE PROCESS OF LAW   A flexible term for the compliance with the fundamental rules for fair and orderly legal proceedings, e.g., notice, opportunity to appear and be heard, right to effective counsel and a fair and impartial jury. (2) Legal proceedings which observe the rules designed for the protection and enforcement of individual rights and liberties. No person shall be deprived of life, liberty or property without due process of law, U.S. Const., Amendment V. No State shall deprive any person of life, liberty or property without due process of law, U.S. Const., Amendment XIV, Section I. Similar or analogous provisions are found in state constitutions.

DURESS   Imprisonment; compulsion; coercion. (2) Threats of injury or imprisonment.

DUTY   A flexible term for an obligation; the correlative to a right. (2) That which a person is obliged to do or refrain from doing. (3) A responsibility which arises from the unique relationship between particular parties. (4) What one should do, based on the probability or foreseeability of injury to a party. (5) A tax.

EASEMENT   A privilege or intangible right, which the owner of one parcel of real property, called the dominant tenement, has concerning another parcel of real property, called the servient estate, by which the owner of the latter is obligated not to interfere with the privilege. The most common easements are in the nature of passageways, e.g., road, walkway, railroad, pole line or pipeline. It is technically classified as an incorporeal hereditament.

EJECTMENT   Formerly a mixed action at common law, which depended on fictions in order to escape the inconveniences in the ancient forms of action. It was a mixed action, because it sought to recover both possession of land (a real claim), and also damages (a personal claim). Various statutory proceedings for the recovery of land, some of which bear the same name, have taken its place in most of the United States.

EMPLOY   A flexible term for the personal relationship in which one engages or uses another as an agent or substitute in transacting business, or the performance of some service; it may include skilled or unskilled labor or professional services.

EQUAL PROTECTION OF THE LAWS   A flexible term for the guaranty of uniformity of treatment under state law, of all persons in like circumstances.

U.S. Const., Amendment XIV. It usually is applied to civil and political rights. It does not create new rights where none previously existed, except insofar as it extends existing rights to such persons as may have been previously excluded from them.

EQUITY   Fairness. A type of justice that developed separately from the common law, and which tends to complement it. The current meaning is to classify disputes and remedies according to their historical relationship and development. Under modern rules of civil procedure, law and equity have been unified. Fed. R. Civ. P. 2. Historically, the courts of equity had a power of framing and adapting new remedies to particular cases, which the common law courts did not possess. In doing so, they allowed themselves latitude of construction and assumed, in certain matters such as trusts, a power of enforcing moral obligations which the courts of law did not admit or recognize. (2) A right or obligation attaching to property or a contract. In this sense, one person is said to have a better equity than another.

ERROR   A mistake in judgment. (2) An incorrect ruling or instruction made by a judge in the trial of a case.

ESTOPPEL   An admission or declaration, by which a person is concluded, i.e., prevented, from bringing evidence to controvert it, or to prove the contrary. It may be: by matter of record, which imports such absolute and incontrovertible verity that no person against whom the record is produced is permitted to deny it; by deed, because no person can dispute his own solemn deed, which is, therefore, conclusive against him, and those claiming under him, even as to facts recited in it; and by matter in pais, e.g., a tenant can not dispute his landlord's title. This includes estoppel by misrepresentation or negligence.

EVIDENCE   Proof, either written or unwritten, of allegations at issue between parties. It may be (a) direct, or indirect, which latter includes circumstantial evidence; (b) substantive, i.e., directed to proof of a distinct fact, or corroborative, i.e., in support of previous evidence; (c) intrinsic, i.e., internal; or extrinsic, i.e., not derived from anything to be found in the document itself; (d) original or derivative, i.e., which passes through some channel, e.g., parol, as opposed to original documents or evidence.

EX PAR'TE   Lat., "of the one part;" an action which is not an adverse proceeding against someone else.

EX POST FAC'TO   Lat., "made after the occurrence," e.g., legislation which has a retrospective application.

EXECUTION   The writ, order or process issued to a sheriff, directing him to carry out the judgment of a court, e.g., to make the money due on the judgment out of the property of the defendant.

EXECUTIVE   That branch of the national, state or local government which carries out and administers the laws, as distinguished from the legislative and judicial branches.

EXEMPLARY, or PUNITIVE, or VINDICTIVE DAMAGES   An award of money given because of torts committed through malice or with circumstances of aggravation, which is in addition to compensation for the injury inflicted.

EXPRESS   Something which is stated in direct words, and not left to implications, e.g., an express promise, express trust.

FALSE ARREST, or FALSE IMPRISONMENT   A tort consisting of restraint imposed on a person's liberty, without proper legal authority.

FEDERAL   Pertaining to the national government of the United States. (2) Pertaining to an association of states or nations which have various relationships with a unified or general government. Often, the states or nations will operate within specific spheres and the unified or general government will concurrently operate within other spheres.

FEDERAL TRADE COMMISSION ACTS   Acts to create a Federal Trade Commission and to define its powers and duties. 15 U.S.C. §§ 41 *et seq.*; 38 Stat. 717 (1914); 52 Stat. 111 (1938).

FELONY   A type of crime which is of a relatively serious nature, usually various offenses in various jurisdictions, for which the maximum penalty can be death or imprisonment in the state penitentiary, regardless of such lesser penalty as may in fact be imposed. Occasionally defined by various state statutes. (2) Formerly, every offensive at common law which caused a forfeiture of lands or goods, besides being punishable by death, imprisonment or other severe penalty.

FINAL DECISION, or FINAL ORDER   A decree or judgment of a court, which terminates the litigation in the court which renders it. Cf. *Interlocutory*. (2) The United States Courts of Appeals have jurisdiction of appeals from certain final decisions of United States District Courts (28 U.S.C. § 1291), but the courts have had difficulty defining final decision in that context. A decision may be final, even if it does not terminate the litigation, if the issue which is decided is fundamental to the further conduct of the case.

FOOD, DRUG AND COSMETIC ACT   An act to prohibit the movement in interstate commerce of adulterated and misbranded food, drugs and cosmetics. 21 U.S.C. §§ 301–392; 52 Stat. 1040 (1938).

FOREIGN LAWS   Those enacted and in force in a foreign state, or country.

FO'RUM   Lat., a court of justice; the place where justice must be sought. (2) Formerly, an open space in Roman cities, where the people assembled, markets were held, and the magistrates sat to transact their business.

FORUM NON CONVENIENS   Lat., an inconvenient court.

FRAUD   A broad term for all kinds of acts, which have as their objective, the gain of an advantage, to another's detriment, by deceitful or unfair means. It may be (a) actual, where there is deliberate misrepresentation or concealment; or (b) constructive, where the court implies it, either from the nature of the contract or from the relation of the parties. Some courts are reluctant to define this term, because of the myriad forms which it can take. Fraud is a ground for setting aside a transaction, at the option of the person prejudiced by it, or for recovery of damages.

FRAUDS, STATUTE OF Various state legislative acts, patterned after a 1677 English act, known by the same name. E.g., U.C.C. § 2-201. Because of the variations in each state, reference must be made to the specific state statutes. The main object was to take away the facilities for fraud, and the temptation to perjury, which arose in verbal obligations, the proof of which depended upon oral evidence. Its most common provisions are these: (a) all leases, excepting those for less than three years, shall have the force of leases at will only, unless they are in writing and signed by the parties or their agents; (b) assignments and surrenders of leases and interests in land must be in writing; (c) all declarations and assignments of trusts must be in writing, signed by the party (trusts arising by implication of law are, however, excepted); (d) no action shall be brought upon a guaranty, or upon any contract for sale of lands, or any interest in or concerning them, or upon any agreement which is not to be performed within a year, unless the agreement is in writing and signed by the party to be charged or his agent; (e) no contract for the sale of goods for a certain price or more, e.g., $500.00 U.C.C. § 2-201, shall be good, unless the buyer accept part, or give something in part payment, or some memorandum thereof be signed by the parties to be charged or their agents.

FULL FAITH AND CREDIT The requirement that the public acts, records and judicial proceedings of every state shall be given the same effect by the courts of another state that they have by law and usage in the state of origin. U.S. Const., Art. IV, Sec. I. Congress has prescribed the manner in which they may be proven. Cf. *Comity.*

GENERAL APPEARANCE A submission of the defendant to the jurisdiction of the court for all purposes.

GENERAL VERDICT The decision of the jury, when they simply find for the plaintiff or defendant, without specifying the particular facts which they found from the evidence.

GOOD FAITH Honesty of purpose, which negates an intent to defraud. A legal standard of motivation for a person's acts or conduct, in dealing with his fellow men. (2) Honesty in fact in the conduct or transaction concerned. U.C.C. § 1-201 (19). (3) In the case of a merchant, honesty in fact and the observance of reasonable commercial standards of fair dealing in the trade. U.C.C. § 2-103(1) (b).

GOOD WILL The intangible advantage or benefit which is acquired by a business, beyond the mere value of the capital or stock employed therein, in consequence of its having a body of regular customers and a favorable reputation.

GOVERNMENTAL FUNCTION A flexible term for various activities of a political entity or subdivision thereof, imposed or required for the protection and benefit of the general public, not having regard to any particular benefit to be derived as a corporate body, or to the citizens collectively, outside their relation to the state. E.g., sewage disposal, law enforcement, fire protection, public education and operation of public parks.

GRAND JURY   A body of persons, not less than twelve, nor more than twenty-four, freeholders of a county, whose duty it is, on hearing the evidence for the prosecution in each proposed bill of indictment, to decide whether a sufficient case is made out, on which to hold the accused for trial. It is a body which is convened by authority of a court and serves as an instrumentality of the court. It has authority to investigate and to accuse, but it is not authorized to try cases. It is a creature of the common law which was instituted to protect the people from governmental oppression. In a few states, it has been partially abolished, but in others it exists by constitutional mandate. No person shall be held to answer for a capital or otherwise infamous federal crime, unless on a presentment or indictment of a grand jury, except in cases arising in the land or naval forces, or in the militia, when in actual service in time of war or public danger; U.S. Const., Amendment V.

GUARDIAN   A person appointed by a court, to have the control or management of the person or property, or both, of another who is incapable of acting on his own behalf, e.g., an infant or a person of unsound mind. (2) Guardians ad litem are appointed by the court to represent such persons, who are parties to a pending action.

HA′BEAS COR′PUS   Lat., "that you have the body," words used in various writs, commanding one who detains another to have, or bring, him before the court issuing the same.

HEARING   A flexible term for a court proceeding or the trial of a suit. (2) The examination of witnesses incident to the making of a judicial determination as to whether an accused person shall be held for trial.

HEARSAY EVIDENCE   Statements offered by a witness, based upon what someone else has told him, and not upon personal knowledge or observation. Usually, such evidence is inadmissible, but exceptions are made, e.g., in questions of pedigree, custom, reputation, dying declarations, and statements made against the interest of the declarant.

HOLDING   The principle which reasonably may be drawn from the decision which a court or judge actually makes in a case; the opposite of dictum (*q.v.*). (2) The resolution of the unique dispute which is before a judge or court in a specific case. (3) A broad term for something which a person owns or possesses.

HOLDING COMPANY   A corporation, which is organized for the purpose of holding the stock of another, or other, corporations.

IMPEACH   To charge a public official with crime or misdemeanor, or with misconduct in office. (2) To prove that a witness has a bad reputation for truth and veracity, and is therefore unworthy of belief.

IN PERSO'NAM   Lat., against the person.

IN REM   Lat., against the thing; opposed to *in personam* (*q.v.*).

INCOMPETENT   A flexible term for disqualified, unable or unfit. (1) A judge or juror is incompetent, when from interest in the subject matter he is an unfit person to decide a controversy. (2) Testimony is incompetent when it is not such as by law ought to be admitted. (3) A witness is incompetent, when by law he may not testify.

INDEMNITY   A payment or promise to pay, which is given or granted, to a person to prevent his suffering damage.

INDEPENDENT CONTRACTOR   A person who agrees with another to do something for him, in the course of his occupation, but who is not controlled by the other, nor subject to the other's right to control, with respect to his performance of the undertaking, and is thereby distinguished from an employee.

INDICTMENT (DIT)   A written accusation that one or more persons have committed a crime, presented upon oath, by a grand jury. The person against whom the indictment is found is said to be indicted.

INFANT   A person who is not an adult or is not of age. (2) Under the common law, a person under twenty-one years of age, without regard to sex. The rights, privileges and disabilities of persons who are infants are defined by various state statutes.

INFORMAL   Deficient in legal form; lacking formality. An informality may, or may not, be of legal consequence. There is a tendency among courts to waive informality in some instances.

INFORMATION   Communicated knowledge. (2) A formal accusation or complaint, filed by a prosecuting attorney or other law officer, charging a person or corporation with some crime or violation of law. In certain classes of criminal cases, it may be a substitute for an indictment or presentment by a grand jury. It is often used in civil cases, to exact penalties and forfeitures for violations of law, and in proceedings in quo warranto, to deprive a corporation of its franchise. The use of an information, as a form of procedure, is regulated by various federal and state statutes, and constitutions.

INJUNCTION   A flexible, discretionary, process of preventive and remedial justice, which is exercised by courts that have equity powers. Courts issue injunctions when it appears that the ordinary remedy usually provided by the law is not a full, adequate and complete one. Injunctions are preventive, if they restrain a person from doing something, or mandatory, if they command something to be done. They are preliminary, provisional or interlocutory, if they are granted on the filing of a bill, or while the suit is pending, to restrain the party enjoined from doing or continuing to do the acts complained of, until final hearing or the further order of the court. They are final, perpetual or permanent, if they are awarded after full hearing on the merits, and as a final determination of the rights of the parties.

INSANITY   A flexible term for the various forms of mental unsoundness, aberration or impairment. It implies disease or congenital defect of the brain, and embraces idiocy, lunacy, and a great many other afflictions of the mind, e.g., mania in its various forms.

INSURANCE   The act of providing against a possible loss, by entering into a contract with a licensed corporation that is willing to bind itself to make good such loss, should it occur. The instrument by which the contract is made is called a policy; the consideration paid to the insurer, who is sometimes called an underwriter, is called a premium. Fire and marine insurance is usually by way of indemnity, i.e., only such sum is paid by the insurer as is actually lost, and, on making such payment, he is entitled to stand in the place of the assured. (2) In the case of life or accident insurance, the insurer undertakes, in consideration of a premium, to pay a certain sum to the insured, or his legal representatives, on his death or injury by an accident. (3) There are many various types of insurance, each of which are defined by the respective policies which evidence the agreements between the parties, e.g., automobile insurance, creditor life insurance, homeowner insurance, owner, landlord, and tenant insurance, and workmen's compensation insurance.

INTANGIBLES   A kind of property which is nonphysical and not subject to being sensed, e.g., touched or felt, but which exists as a concept of people's minds. E.g., promissory notes, bank accounts and corporate stock.

INTEREST   An estate or right in property. (2) Money paid for the loan or use of another sum called the principal (*q.v.*).

INTERLOC′UTORY   Incident to a suit still pending. An order or decree, made during the progress of a case, which does not amount to a final decision, is interlocutory. See also *Decree* and *Injunction.*

INTERROGATORIES   Written questions propounded on behalf of one party in an action to another party, or to someone who is not a party, before the trial thereof. The person interrogated must give his answers in writing, and upon oath. Fed. R. Civ. P. 26, 33. (2) Verbal questions put to a witness before an examiner, and answered on oath. (3) Questions in writing, annexed to a commission to take the deposition of a witness, to be put to and answered by the witness under oath, whose answers are to be reduced to writing by the commissioner.

INVALID   Not valid; of no binding force.

INVITEE   A person who goes upon land or premises of another by invitation, express or implied.

IP′SO FAC′TO   Lat., "by the very act itself," i.e., as the necessary consequence of the fact or act.

ISSUE   A flexible term for offspring or lineal descendants. (2) In the plural, the profits arising from real property. (3) The point or points which are left to be resolved by the jury or the court, at the conclusion of the pleadings. Issues may be of fact or of law. To join issue, is a technical phrase for closing the pleadings. To issue a writ or process, is for the proper officer to deliver it to the party suing it out, or to the officer to whom it is directed.

JOINT VENTURE, or JOINT ADVENTURE   An association of persons to carry out a single business enterprise for profit, for which purpose they combine their property, money and effects.

JUDGE   A public official with authority to determine a cause or question in a court of justice and to preside over the procedings therein.

JUDGMENT   The determination or decision of a court; the expression by a judge of the reasons for his decision. Judgments may be final, putting an end to the case; interlocutory, given in the progress of a case upon some matter which does not finally determine the case. They may be rendered on confession by the defendant; on default, when the defendant fails to appear, plead or otherwise defend, within the allotted time; or on the merits, after a full trial. See also *Summary judgment.*

JUDGMENT N.O.V. (NON OBSTAN′TE VEREDIC′ TO)   Notwithstanding the verdict. A type of judgment which is entered by the court, for legal cause, despite a contrary or different verdict rendered by the jury.

JUDICIAL   Relating to proceedings before a judge or in court.

JUDICIAL NOTICE   The acceptance by the court of certain notorious facts without proof.

JURISDICTION   The authority of a court to hear and decide an action or lawsuit. (2) The geographical district over which the power of a court extends. Jurisdiction is limited when the court has power to act only in certain specified cases; general, or residual, when it may act in all cases in which the parties are before it, except for those cases which are within the exclusive jurisdiction of another court; concurrent, when the same cause may be entertained by one court or another; original, when the court has power to try the case in the first instance; appellate, when the court hears cases only on appeal, certiorari, or writ of error from another court; exclusive, when no other court has power to hear and decide the same matter.

JURISPRUDENCE   Law. (2) A body of law. (3) Philosophy of law.

JURY   A body of citizens sworn to deliver a true verdict upon evidence submitted to them in a judicial proceeding. They are respectively called, jurymen or jurors. A grand jury is one summoned to consider whether the evidence, presented by the state against a person accused of crime, warrants his indictment. A petty or petit jury is the jury for the trial of cases, either civil or criminal. It usually consists of twelve persons, but by various statutes in many of the states, and in England, a lesser number may constitute a jury in some courts. A special or struck jury is one selected especially for the trial of a given cause, usually by the assistance of the parties.

JUSTICE OF THE PEACE In some jurisdictions, a minor judicial officer with specifically enumerated powers, e.g., preventing breaches of the peace, and causing the arrest and commitment of persons violating the law. Under various state statutes, they may have limited jurisdiction to try certain cases.

LACH'ES Negligence, or unreasonable delay, in pursuing a legal remedy, concurrent with a resultant prejudice to the opposing party, whereby a person forfeits his right.

LANDLORD The person from, or under, whom lands or buildings are rented.

LARCENY The unlawful taking and carrying away of personal property, without color of right, and with intent to deprive the rightful owner of the same. Larceny is commonly classified as grand or petty, according to the value of the thing taken. Usually defined and classified by various state statutes.

LAST CLEAR CHANCE A principle by which a plaintiff, who by his own fault, has caused himself to be in a perilous situation, may recover damages, notwithstanding his own negligence, if the defendant did not exercise ordinary care to avoid injuring him, after becoming aware of plaintiff's perilous situation.

LAW A method for the resolution of disputes. (2) A rule of action to which men obligate themselves to conform, via their elected representatives and other officials. (3) The principles and procedure of the common law, as distinguished from those of equity.

LEASE A transfer of real or personal property for a period of time, e.g., for years, or at will, or for life, by a person who has a greater interest in the property. The person transferring is called the landlord, or lessor; the rights or interest which he retains in his reversion; the person to whom the transfer is made is the tenant, or lessee. The consideration is usually the payment of a rent. A lease is usually drawn in duplicate, one copy being kept by the lessee, the other copy by the lessor.

LEGISLATURE A body of public officials, who collectively have the authority to make generalized law for future application. It usually consists of two branches, i.e., the upper house, or Senate, and the lower house, or House of Representatives. The Senate is usually a much smaller body and each senator represents a much larger district, or constituency, than a representative. The United States Congress is a legislature, each state has its own legislature, and cities have legislatures called, variously, boards of aldermen, city councils or common councils.

LEVY To assess, impose or require a tax. (2) The act of a sheriff in subjecting property to the satisfaction of a court judgment. (3) The act of a sheriff in subjecting property to the lien of a court attachment.

LEX FO'RI Lat., the law of the country where an action is brought. This regulates the forms of procedure and the nature of the remedy to be obtained.

LEX LO′CI   Lat., the law of the place where a contract is made, i.e., Lex loci contractus; or thing is done, i.e., Lex loci actus; tort is committed, i.e., Lex loci delicti; or where the thing, i.e., real estate, is situated, i.e., Lex loci rei sitae. It is usually applied in suits relating to such contracts, transactions, torts, and real estate.

LIABILITY   A duty, debt, obligation or responsibility. (2) A present or potential duty, debt, obligation or responsibility to pay or do something, which may arise out of a contract, tort, statute or otherwise.

LIBEL   Defamatory writing; any published matter which tends to degrade a person in the eyes of his neighbors, or to render him ridiculous, or to injure his property or business. It may be published by writing, effigy, picture, or the like. Cf. *Slander*. (2) In admiralty, the plaintiff's written statement of his case, analogous to a complaint (*q.v.*).

LICENSE   Permission or authority to do something, which would be wrongful or illegal to do, if the permission or authority were not granted. The permission or authority may pertain to a public matter, e.g., the privilege of driving a motor vehicle on the public highways, or to a private matter e.g., the privilege of manufacturing a patented article. In public matters, licenses are often required in order to regulate the activity.

LIEN   A security device, by which there is created a right (1) to retain that which is in a person's possession, belonging to another, until certain demands of the person in possession are satisfied; or (2) to charge property in another's possession with payment of a debt, e.g., a vendor's lien. It may be either (a) particular, arising out of some charge or claim connected with the identical thing; (b) general, in respect of all dealings of a similar nature between the parties; or (c) conventional, by agreement, express or implied, between the parties, e.g., a mortgage; or (d) by operation of law, e.g., a lien for taxes or an attorney's lien.

LIMITATION   A restriction; a thing which limits or restrains. (2) Various periods of time, fixed by different state and federal statutes, called statutes of limitations, within which a lawsuit must be commenced, and after the expiration of which, the claimant will be forever barred from the right to bring the action. (3) A clause in a conveyance, or will, which declares how long the estate transferred thereby, shall continue, e.g., "heirs," or "heirs of the body," are words of limitation which define the nature of the estate conveyed.

LIQUIDATED DAMAGES   The exact amount, which the parties to a contract expressly agree must be paid, or may be collected, in the event of a future default or breach of contract.

LIS PENDENS NOTICE   Information or an announcement that a lawsuit is pending which has the purpose of affecting the title to particular property described therein. Such information or announcement is filed in the public records for the purpose of preventing any transactions which would thwart the purpose of the pending lawsuit.

LITIGATION   A lawsuit, a contest in court.

LOAN   The furnishing of money to a person, upon the agreement that the person will return a like sum of money to the person who furnished it, at a specified time or according to a schedule of repayment, usually with interest. (2) A bailment (*q.v.*) of personal property for consumption or use, which must be returned in kind or redelivered. (3) The money or personal property which is the subject of a loan.

MAGISTRATE   Various public officials. (2) Various judicial officers, having limited jurisdiction in criminal offenses, and civil causes, e.g., police judges. See also *Justice of the peace*.

MALICE   Hatred; ill will; a formed design to do an unlawful act, whether another may be prejudiced by it or not. If the known and necessary consequence of the act is injury to another, the law implies malice, but express malice, i.e., actual ill feeling toward the person injured, may also be proved to exist.

MALICIOUS ARREST   Imprisonment or prosecution, a malicious setting in motion of the law, without probable cause, whereby someone is wrongfully and maliciously accused of a criminal offense or a civil wrong, and by reason of which that person sustains damage.

MASTER   An officer of a court appointed to assist the court, e.g., in taking and reporting testimony, examining and stating accounts, computing damages, and executing the decrees of the court. (2) The commander, or first officer, of a merchant ship. (3) Formerly, an employer.

MAXIM   An axiom; a general or leading principle.

MEDIATION   The settlement of disputes by the amicable intervention of an outside party who is a stranger to the controversy.

MENS REA   Criminal intent; evil intent; guilty intent.

MERGER   In real property, an absorption by operation of law, of a lesser right or estate in a greater right or estate, upon the union of their ownership in the same person. It takes place independently of the will of the party. (2) A consolidation of corporations, in which only one of two or more former corporations survives the consolidation, or which brings into existence a new corporation and destroys the former corporations.

MERITS, JUDGMENT UPON   A final resolution of a lawsuit, rendered after a hearing of the entire case on the pleadings and evidence.

MINISTERIAL FUNCTIONS   Activities which are absolute, fixed and certain and in the performance of which there is no discretion. (2) Occasionally, private corporate functions of a municipality, as distinguished from public and governmental functions. Cf. *Governmental function*.

MINORITY   Descriptive of a person or group of persons, who do not predominate in numbers within the nation, electorate or other group to which they belong, e.g., black persons or persons of Mexican descent in the United States. (2) The status of a person who is of less than full age.

MISDEMEANOR   Any crime or offense not amounting to a felony (*q.v.*).

MISREPRESENTATION   A false statement, which may variously constitute grounds for the rescission of a contract or for the recovery of damages for losses caused thereby.

MISTRIAL   An erroneous trial. Descriptive of a trial at which an event supervenes, that causes the judge to terminate the proceedings because he believes that a fair verdict cannot be obtained on account of that event.

MONOPOLY   An exclusive privilege of buying, selling, making, working, or using a particular thing. (2) The absolute and exclusive control by a person, or combination of persons, of the sale of a particular commodity. (3) A combination of producers or dealers to raise commodity prices via the more or less exclusive control of the supply or the purchasing power.

MOOT   Descriptive of something which is not genuine or concrete, something which is pretended. (2) A meeting, especially for the purpose of arguing points of law by way of exercise.

MOTION   An application to a court, by the parties or their counsel, for a rule or order, either in the progress of a lawsuit, or summarily, e.g., a motion for a writ of habeas corpus. A motion may be made either ex parte (*q.v.*), or on notice to the other side, and when based on facts not found in the record, must be supported by an affidavit, a deposition or testimony in open court, that such facts are true.

NATURAL LAW   A philosophy concerning the law of nature and the dictate of right reason, in contradistinction to positive or statute law.

NATURALIZATION   The legal act of investing aliens with the privileges and obligations of a citizen (*q.v.*).

NEGLIGENCE   A flexible term for the failure to use ordinary care, under the particular factual circumstances revealed by the evidence in a lawsuit.

NEWLY DISCOVERED EVIDENCE   Proof which could not have been discovered with reasonable diligence and produced at the trial; not newly recollected evidence.

NOL'LE PROSE'QUI, or NOL. PROS.   Lat., unwilling to prosecute; an entry made on the court record, by which the plaintiff or prosecutor declares that he will proceed no further.

NO'LO CONTEN'DERE   Lat., no contest; a plea in criminal cases whereby the defendant tacitly admits his guilt by throwing himself on the mercy of the court.

NOMINAL DAMAGES   A token sum awarded, where a breach of duty or an infraction of plaintiff's rights is shown, but no substantial injury is proven to have been sustained.

NOTICE   Information given to a person of some act done, or about to be done; knowledge. Notice may be actual, when knowledge is brought home to the party to be affected by it; or constructive, when certain acts are done in accordance with law, from which, on grounds of public policy, the party interested is presumed to have knowledge. It may be written, or oral, but written notice is preferable as avoiding disputes as to its terms. (2) A person has notice of a fact when he has actual knowledge of it, or he has received a notice or notification of it, or from all the facts and circumstances known to him at the time in question, he has reason to know that it exists. U.C.C. § 1-201(25).

NUISANCE   A flexible and imprecise term for various activities which annoy, harm, inconvenience or damage other persons, under the particular facts and circumstances proven in a lawsuit or criminal prosecution. It may be (a) private, as where one uses his property so as to damage another's or to disturb his quiet enjoyment of it; or (b) public, or common, where the whole community is annoyed or inconvenienced by the offensive acts, e.g., where a person obstructs a highway, or carries on a business that fills the air with noxious and offensive fumes.

ORDINANCE   A law, statute, or legislative enactment, particularly the legislative enactments or statutes of a municipal corporation.

ORIGINAL JURISDICTION   The authority of a court to hear and determine a lawsuit when it is initiated, as contrasted with appellate jurisdiction.

PARDON   The remission, by the chief executive of a state or nation, of a punishment which a person convicted of crime has been sentenced to undergo.

PAROL EVIDENCE RULE   A significant provision in American law, that when dealings between parties are reduced to an unambiguous written instrument, e.g., a deed, contract or lease, the instrument cannot be contradicted or modified by oral evidence. The rule is subject to various limitations and exceptions, however.

PAROLE   Supervised suspension of the execution of a convict's sentence, and release from prison, conditional upon his continued compliance with the terms of parole.

PARTNERSHIP   An association of two or more persons to carry on as co-owners a business for profit. Uniform Partnership Act § 6(1). It is usually the result of a contract to combine property or labor, or both, for the purpose of a common undertaking and the acquisition of a common profit. A partnership is dissolved by the death of any of the partners, but this and other rules applicable thereto are often modified by the agreement entered into by the partners at the outset of their undertaking.

PATENT   A flexible term for a grant of some privilege, property, or authority, by the government or sovereign to one or more individuals. (2) An instrument by which the state or national government conveys its lands. (3) An instrument granting to original inventors, the exclusive right for seventeen years to manufacture, sell and use the invention described therein.

PENALTY   Punishment. The consequence imposed upon the perpetrator, for the violation of a penal law or the violation of a personal right, e.g., the requirement of payment of a sum of money into the public treasury, or an extraordinary payment to an aggrieved person, which exceeds actual damages.

PENSION A stated allowance granted by a government or a private employer to an individual or his representative, for services previously performed.

PER CU'RIAM Lat., by the court.

PER SE Lat., by itself; alone.

PERJURY A false statement under oath or affirmation, willfully made in regard to a material matter of fact. Usually defined by various statutes.

PETITION A request made to a public official or public body that has authority to act concerning it. The right to petition the government for a redress of grievances is secured to the people by U.S. Const., Amendment I. (2) Under some codes of civil procedure, the written statement of the plaintiff's case which initiates a lawsuit.

PLAINTIFF A person who initiates a lawsuit.

PLEA The formal response of a defendant to the charge in an indictment, or to a civil lawsuit. See also *Pleadings*. (2) In England, a legal proceeding, hence (a) pleas of the Crown, criminal prosecution, and (b) common pleas, civil causes.

PLEADINGS The alternate and opposing written statements of the parties to a lawsuit. Under the Federal Rules of Civil Procedure, and analogous state rules of civil procedure, the pleadings consist of a Complaint and an Answer; a Reply to a Counterclaim denominated as such; an Answer to a Cross-claim, if the Answer contains a Cross-claim; a Third-party Complaint, if a person who was not an original party is summoned; and a Third-party Answer, if a Third-party Complaint is served. No other pleadings shall be allowed, except that the court may order a Reply to an Answer or a Third-party Answer. Fed. R. Civ. P. 7(a). Pleadings consist of simple, concise and direct averments of claims for relief, defenses and denials. Matters which constitute an avoidance or affirmative defense must be set forth affirmatively. Id. 8.

POLICE POWER A flexible term for the authority of federal and state legislatures to enact laws regulating and restraining private rights and occupations for the promotion of public health, safety, welfare and order.

PRAYER The portion of a pleading, usually at the end, which makes a specific demand for judgment for the relief to which the pleader deems himself entitled. Relief in the alternative, or of several different types, may be demanded. Fed. R. Civ. P. 8(a). See also *Pleadings*.

PREPONDERANCE OF EVIDENCE The greater weight of the evidence, in merit and in worth. (2) Sufficient evidence to overcome doubt or speculation.

PRESCRIPTION (USUCAPIO, ROM.) The transfer of rights in, or title to, real property, by enjoying it peaceably, without interruption, openly, and as if it were of right, over a long period of time, e.g., 15 years or 21 years. The period of time required for prescription was originally time out of mind, but is now the time after which a person is prevented by the statutes of limitation from recovering real property or an interest therein.

PRESUMPTION   A conclusion, or inference, drawn from the proven existence of some fact or group of facts. Presumptions may be either (a) juris et de jure (of law and by the principles of law), such as the presumption of incapacity in a minor to act, which are conclusive and irrebuttable; (b) juris (of law), which may be disproved, or rebutted, by evidence; or (c) judicis, or facti, i.e., presumptions of fact, drawn by a judge from the evidence.

PRE-TRIAL CONFERENCE, or PRE-TRIAL HEARING   A meeting between the judge and counsel for the parties, preliminary to the trial of a lawsuit. Under modern rules of civil procedure, in any lawsuit, the court may in its discretion direct the attorneys for the parties to appear before it for a conference, to consider any matters that may aid in the disposition of the lawsuit. Fed. R. Civ. P. 16.

PRICE DISCRIMINATION   As prohibited by the Robinson-Patman Act (*q.v.*), the making of a distinction in price between customers, for reasons which do not reflect differences in cost of manufacture, transportation or sale.

PRIMA FACIE EVIDENCE   Proof of a fact or collection of facts, which creates a presumption of the existence of other facts, or from which some conclusion may be legally drawn, but which presumption or conclusion may be discredited or overcome by other relevant proof.

PRINCIPAL   The leading, or most important; the original; a person, firm or corporation from whom an agent derives his authority; a person who is first responsible, and for whose fulfillment of an obligation a surety becomes bound; the chief, or actual, perpetrator of a crime, as distinguished from the accessory, who may assist him; the important part of an estate, as distinguished from incidents, or accessories; a sum of money loaned, as distinguished from the interest paid for its use.

PRIVATE   Affecting or belonging to individuals, as distinguished from the public generally, e.g., private acts or private nuisances.

PRIVATE NUISANCE   Something done to the hurt or annoyance of another's lands, tenements or hereditaments. See also *Nuisance*.

PRIVILEGE   An exceptional right, or exemption. It is either (a) personal, attached to a person or office; or (b) attached to a thing, sometimes called real. The exemption of ambassadors and members of Congress from arrest, while going to, returning from, or attending to the discharge of their public duties, is an example of the first. (2) An ordinary right.

PRIVITY   Participation in knowledge or interest. Persons who so participate are called privies. Privity in deed, i.e., by consent of the parties, is opposed to privity in law, e.g., tenant by curtesy.

PROBABLE CAUSE   A reasonable ground for suspicion, supported by circumstances sufficiently strong to warrant a cautious man to believe that an accused person is guilty of the offense with which he is charged.

PROBATE COURT   Various state courts which have jurisdiction in the matter of proving wills, appointing executors and administrators, and supervising the administration of estates.

PROBATION The delay of the imposition of punishment which has been imposed upon a person who has been convicted of a crime. It is often granted by a court, on specific conditions concerning the person's future activities. Ordinarily regulated by various federal and state statutes.

PROCEDURE The manner in which litigants proceed in the adversary conduct of a lawsuit, including the various steps by which the parties go about the litigation process. Occasionally called practice. Usually codified by rules or in codes, e.g., Fed. R. Civ. P., Fed. R. Crim. P., analogous state rules of procedure, and various state codes of practice. See also *Pleadings*.

PROCESS The means whereby a court enforces obedience to its orders. Process is termed (a) original, when it is intended to compel the appearance of the defendant; (b) mesne, when issued pending suit to secure the attendance of jurors and witnesses; and (c) final, when issued to enforce execution of a judgment. (2) In patent law, the art or method by which any particular result is produced, e.g., the smelting of ores or the vulcanizing of rubber.

PRODUCT LIABILITY The portion of American law which deals with the responsibility of a manufacturer or seller of merchandise, to the buyer and other persons affected by the merchandise, concerning the quality of the merchandise and the consequences resulting from a lack of quality in the merchandise.

PROMISE An engagement or undertaking for the performance, or nonperformance, of a particular thing. (2) In commercial paper transactions, an undertaking to pay, which is more than an acknowledgment of an obligation. U.C.C. § 3-102(1)(c).

PROPERTY A very extensive and flexible term for various rights of ownership; this may be (a) general, or absolute; (b) special, or qualified, as in the case of a bailee for a special purpose. (2) Everything that is owned. In this sense it is (a) real, or (b) personal.

PROPRIETARY FUNCTIONS Acts which are performed by a municipality, for the improvement of the territory within the corporate limits. (2) The doing of such things as inure to the benefit, pecuniarily or otherwise, of the municipality.

PROSECUTOR A person who brings an action against another, in the name of the government. A public prosecutor is an officer appointed or elected to conduct all prosecutions in behalf of the government. A private prosecutor is an individual who, not holding office, conducts an accusation against another. Occasionally, an aggrieved person will employ a private attorney to serve as such a prosecutor.

PROXIMATE CAUSE Something which produces a result, and without which, the result could not have occurred. (2) Any original event, which in natural unbroken sequence, produces a particular foreseeable result, without which the result would not have occurred.

PUBLIC POLICY A highly flexible term of imprecise definition, for the consideration of what is expedient for the community concerned. (2) The principle of law which holds that no person can do that which has a tendency to be injurious to the public, or against the public good. (3) The statutes and precedents, and not the general considerations of public interest.

QUASH   To annul or suppress, e.g., an indictment, a conviction, or an order.

QUA′SI   Lat., as if; almost. Often used to indicate significant similarity or likeness to the word that follows, while denoting that the word that follows must be considered in a flexible sense.

REAL PROPERTY, REAL ESTATE, or REALTY   All land and buildings, including estates and interests in land and buildings which are held for life, but not for years, or some greater estate therein.

RECOGNIZANCE, or RECOGNIZANCE BOND   An obligation, or acknowledgment of a debt, in a court of law, with a condition that the debt shall be void on the performance of a stipulated undertaking, e.g., to appear before the proper court, to keep the peace, or to pay the debt, interest and costs that the plaintiff may recover.

RECORD   A written memorial of the actions of a legislature or of a court. (2) The copy of a deed or other instrument relating to real property, officially preserved in a public office.

REFORMATION, or RECTIFICATION   The correction of a written instrument, via a lawsuit, so as to make it express the true agreement or intention of the parties.

RELIEF   The redress or assistance, which a court grants to a person, on account of the wrongs which another person has done to the former. See also *Remedy*. (2) Formerly, a payment which a tenant made to the lord, on coming into possession of an estate.

REMAND   To recommit a person to jail or prison. (2) To send a lawsuit back to the same court from which it came, for trial or other action.

REMEDY   The legal means to declare or enforce a right or to redress a wrong. (2) Any remedial right, to which an aggrieved party is entitled, with or without resort to a tribunal. U.C.C. § 1-201(34). See also *Relief (1)*.

REPEAL   To annul or set aside a legislative act by another legislative act. Repeals may be expressed, i.e., declared by direct language in the new act, or implied, i.e., when the new act contains provisions contrary to, or irreconcilable with, those of the former act.

REPLEVIN   A form of lawsuit which is used to recover possession of specific chattels, which have been unlawfully taken from, or withheld from, the plaintiff. It may be brought by a general owner, who has the right to immediate possession, or by someone who has a special property in the chattel, e.g., a creditor whose claim is secured by the chattel. Usually defined by various state statutes. Occasionally called claim and delivery or order of delivery.

RES GES'TAE Lat., all of the things done, including words spoken, in the course of a transaction or event.

RES JUDICA'TA Lat., a controversy already judicially decided. The decision is conclusive until the judgment is reversed.

RESCISSION The cancellation of, or putting an end to, a contract by the parties, or one of them, e.g., for any reason mutually acceptable to the parties, or on the ground of fraud.

RESPON'DEAT SUPE'RIOR Lat., let the principal be held responsible; the responsibility of an employer or a principal for the acts of his employees or agents.

RESPONDENT A party against whom a motion is filed in the course of a lawsuit; analogous to a defendant or an appellee.

RESTITUTION The restoring of property, or a right, to a person who has been unjustly deprived of it. A writ of restitution is the process by which a successful appellant may recover something of which he has been deprived under a prior judgment.

ROBINSON-PATMAN ACT An act to amend the Clayton Antitrust Act, to prevent price discrimination (*q.v.*) and other discriminatory practices, 15 U.S.C. §§ 13 *et seq.*; 49 Stat. 1526 (1936).

SANCTION The power of enforcing a statute, or inflicting a penalty for its violation. (2) Consent.

SECONDARY BOYCOTT Variously, a combination to refrain from dealing with a person, or to advise or by peaceful means persuade his customers so to refrain, or to exercise coercive pressure upon such customers, actual or prospective, in order to cause them to withhold or withdraw patronage.

SECURITY Goods or an item of property, which assures the performance of a contract, e.g., a pledge or mortgage. (2) The personal obligation of another, which assures the performance of a contract. (3) An instrument which is issued in bearer or registered form; and is of a type commonly dealt in upon securities exchanges or markets or commonly recognized in any area in which it is issued or dealt in as a medium for investment; and is either of a class or series or by its terms is divisible into a class or series of instruments; and evidences a share, participation of other interest in property or in an enterprise or evidences an obligation of the issuer. U.C.C. § 8-102(1)(a).

SEDUCTION The offense of a man deceitfully inducing a woman to have unlawful sexual intercourse with him. Often defined by various state statutes.

SEIZURE The act of taking possession of property, e.g., for a violation of law or by virtue of an execution.

SENTENCE A judgment of punishment in a criminal proceeding.

SERVICE The act of bringing a judicial proceeding to the notice of the person affected by it, e.g., by delivering to him a copy of a written summons or notice. (2) The relationship of an employee, or servant, to his employer, or master. (3) Formerly, the duty which an English tenant owed to his lord by reason of his estate, e.g., rent.

SHERMAN ACT, or SHERMAN ANTI-TRUST ACT   An act to protect trade and commerce against unlawful restraints and monopolies. 15 U.S.C. §§ 1 *et seq.;* 26 Stat. 209 (1890).

SLANDER   The malicious defamation of a person, in his reputation, profession, or business, by spoken words. To impute a criminal offense, or misconduct in business, is actionable without proof of special damage, but in any case, proof of special damage arising from the false and malicious statements of another is a sufficient ground of action. Usually, the truth of the words spoken is a defense. Occasionally defined by various state statutes. Cf. *Libel (1)*.

SOVEREIGN IMMUNITY   A rule of law holding that a nation or state, or its political subdivisions, is exempt from being sued, without its consent, in its own courts or elsewhere. Often criticized as being erroneously conceived, anachronistic and unjust. Occasionally modified by court decisions, and various state and federal statutes, e.g., Tort Claims Act.

SOVEREIGNTY   The supreme authority of an independent nation or state. It is characterized by equality of the nation or state among other nations or states, exclusive and absolute jurisdiction and self-government within its own territorial limits, and jurisdiction over its citizens beyond its territorial limits.

SPECIAL DAMAGES   Reparation in money awarded for any peculiar injury sustained by the party complaining, beyond the general damages presumed by law.

SPECIAL VERDICT   The finding by a trial jury of particular facts in a lawsuit, usually in answer to questions submitted, leaving to the court the application of the law to the facts thus found.

SPECIFIC PERFORMANCE   The actual carrying out of a contract in the particular manner agreed upon. Courts of equity will compel and coerce specific performance of a contract in many cases, where damages payable in money, the usual remedy at law, would not adequately compensate for its nonperformance, e.g., in the case of contracts concerning land, or for the sale of a unique chattel.

STA′RE DECI′SIS   Lat., to stand by decided cases; to follow precedent. A flexible doctrine of Anglo-American law that when a court expressly decides an issue of law, which is generated by the facts of a unique dispute, that decision shall constitute a precedent which should be followed by that court and by courts inferior to it, when deciding future disputes, except when the precedent's application to a particular problem case is unsuitable to the character or spirit of the people of the state or nation, and their current social, political and economic conditions.

STATUTE   A law enacted, for prospective application, by the legislative body of a nation or a state. It may be (a) declaratory, i.e., one which does not alter the existing law, as opposed to remedial or amending; (b) enabling, i.e., removing restrictions, as opposed to disabling. Statutes may also be either public, or private, the latter including those which have a special application to particular persons or places.

SUBPOENA (*sub pena*)   A court order or writ, commanding attendance in a court, under a penalty for the failure to do so. A subpoena ad testificandum is personally served upon a witness to compel him to attend a trial, or deposition, and give evidence. (2) A subpoena duces tecum is personally served upon a person who has in his possession a book, instrument, or tangible item, the production of which in evidence is desired, commanding him to bring it with him, and produce it at the trial or deposition.

SUBSTANTIAL EVIDENCE   A flexible term for more than a mere scintilla of evidence (*q.v.*); such relevant evidence as a reasonable mind might accept as adequate to support a conclusion.

SUBSTANTIVE LAW   The positive law of duties and rights.

SUIT   A lawsuit or civil action.

SUMMARY JUDGMENT   A decision of a court concerning the merits of a lawsuit, which is rendered on the motion of a party, when the pleadings, depositions, answers to interrogatories and admissions on file, together with any affidavits, show that there is no genuine issue as to any material fact, and that the party who made the motion is entitled to a judgment as a matter of law. An interlocutory summary judgment may be rendered on the issue of liability alone, although there is a genuine issue as to the amount of damages. Fed. R. Civ. P. 56

SUMMONS   A court order, or writ, commanding the sheriff to notify a party therein named to appear in court on, or before, a specified date, and defend the complaint in an action commenced against him. It should also notify the party that, in case of his failure to do so, judgment by default will be rendered against him, for the relief demanded in the complaint.

SUPERSE'DEAS   Lat., a court order or writ by which proceedings are stayed.

SURETY   A person who makes himself responsible for the fulfillment of another's obligation, in case the latter, who is called the principal, fails himself to fulfill it. It includes a guarantor. U.C.C. § 1-201(40).

TAFT-HARTLEY ACT, or LABOR MANAGEMENT RELATIONS ACT OF 1947   An act to amend the National Labor Relations Act, to provide additional facilities for the mediation of labor disputes affecting commerce, and to equalize legal responsibilities of labor organizations and employers. 29 U.S.C. §§ 141 *et seq.*; 61 Stat. 136 1947).

TANGIBLE   Descriptive of something which may be felt or touched; corporeal.

TAX   A sum of money assessed against, and collected from, a person for the support of the government. An income tax is one proportioned to the amount of his income. A poll tax is one which is assessed on all individuals alike, i.e., by the head, without reference to the value of his property, or the amount of his income. Indirect taxes are those levied on articles manufactured, or imported, e.g., excise and customs, so called because the tax is not levied on the consumer directly, but is in reality paid by him in the enhanced price of the article. (2) To fix or adjust, e.g., the amount of court costs to be paid by the losing party.

TENANT   A person who holds or has possession of real property, e.g., a lessee.

TITLE   Ownership; a valid claim of right. In this sense, it may be original, as in the case of an inventor's title to a patent, or derivative, where the owner takes from a predecessor. A marketable title to land is one which the courts will force on an unwilling person who has contracted to purchase it. A bad title is one which gives the holder no legal estate. A doubtful title is one which may not be bad, yet not so free from doubt that a court will force a purchaser to take it, pursuant to his contract. The usual covenants of title given by vendors and mortgagors are: (a) for right to convey, (b) for quiet enjoyment, (c) for freedom from incumbrances, and (d) for further assurance when called on. Under various state statutes, these covenants may be implied in a conveyance and need not be expressly inserted. (2) The distinguishing name of a writing, e.g., an act of a legislature or a book. (3) An appellation of honor or dignity. No title of nobility may be granted by the United States or any state. U.S. Const., Art. I, Sec. IX & X. No person holding any office of profit or trust under the United States shall, without the consent of Congress, accept of any present, emolument, office or title from any king, prince, or foreign state. U.S. Const., Art. I, Sec. IX.

TORT   Any one of various, legally recognized, private injuries or wrongs, which do not arise as the result of a breach of contract.

TORTFEASOR   A person who commits a tort (*q.v.*); a wrongdoer; a trespasser.

TRADE-MARK, or TRADEMARK   A distinctive mark, signature, or device, affixed to an article, or to its wrapper, package or container, to show that it is manufactured, grown, or selected by a particular person, firm or corporation. In a case of infringement, courts will enjoin the wrongdoer from using an imitation of a trade-mark.

TRADE-NAME, or TRADE NAME   The name under which a business is carried on.

TRADE SECRET   A plan, process, tool, mechanism, or compound, known only to its owner, and those of his employees to whom it is necessary to confide it, in order to apply it to the uses intended. It is distinguishable from a patent, in that it may be used by anyone who is able to discover its nature.

TRANSACTION   An item of business; a broad term for an act by one party which affects another party, and out of which a lawsuit might potentially arise.

TREASON, or LESE MAJESTY   An offense against the duty of allegiance; levy-

ing war against the United States, or adhering to their enemies, giving them aid and comfort. A person can be convicted of treason only on the testimony of two witnesses to the same overt act, or confession in open court. U.S. Const., Art. III, Sec. III.

TREATY   A written agreement between nations. On the part of the United States, it may be made by the President, by and with the advice and consent of the Senate, two-thirds of those present concurring. U.S. Const., Art. II, Sec. II.

TRESPASS   Any transgression of the law, less than treason, felony, or misprision of either. (2) Especially, trespass quare clausum fregit, i.e., entry on another's close, or land without lawful authority. (3) Trespass on the case, or Case, is a general name for torts which formerly had no special writ or remedy.

TRIAL   The examination of the issues in a civil or criminal lawsuit by an authorized tribunal; the presentation and decision of the issues of law or fact in an action. It may be by a judge or judges, with or without a jury (*q.v.*).

TRUST   A right in property held by one person, called the trustee, for the benefit of another, called the beneficiary, or cestui que trust. Trusts are divided into active, where the trustee has some duty to perform, so that the legal estate must remain in him or a successor, or the trust be defeated; passive, where the trustee simply holds the title in trust for the beneficiary, and has no duties to perform; express, where it is created by express terms in a deed, will, or other instrument; implied, including precatory, constructive, and resulting trusts, where a court will presume, from the nature of the transaction, the relations of the parties and the requirements of good faith, that a trust was intended, though no express words be employed to create it.

UNIFORM COMMERCIAL CODE   A proposal by the American Law Institute, and the National Conference of Commissioners on Uniform State Laws, for comprehensive legislation relating to commercial transactions, i.e., sales, commercial paper, bank deposits and collections, letters of credit, bulk transfers, warehouse receipts, bills of lading, other documents of title, investment securities, and secured transactions. It has been adopted in each of the states of the United States, except Louisiana, and in the District of Columbia and the Virgin Islands.

UNJUST ENRICHMENT   The doctrine which places a legal duty of restitution upon a defendant who has acquired something of value at the expense of the plaintiff.

USAGE OF TRADE   Any practice or method of dealing having such regularity of observance in a place, vocation or trade as to justify an expectation that it will be observed with respect to the transaction in question. The existence and scope of such a usage are to be proved as facts. If it is established that such a usage is embodied in a written trade code or similar writing, the interpretation of the writing is for the court. U.C.C. § 1-205(2).

VENUE (*ven'u*), or VISNE (*ven*)   The neighborhood; the county in which a particular lawsuit should be tried; the county from which the jury is taken for the trial of a lawsuit. Often regulated by various state and federal statutes. A change of venue is the sending of a lawsuit to be tried before a jury of another county, e.g., when circumstances render it impossible to have an impartial trial in the county where the cause of action arose.

VERDICT   The decision of a jury concerning the matters submitted to it in the trial of a lawsuit. It may be general, i.e., for plaintiff, fixing the amount to be recovered, or for defendant without more; or special, the latter giving the facts found, and leaving the conclusion of law to the court.

VICARIOUS LIABILITY   Substituted or indirect responsibility, e.g., the responsibility of an employer for the torts committed by his employee within the scope of his employment.

WAIVE   To forego; to decline to take advantage of, e.g., a legal right or an omission or irregularity.

WAIVER   A positive act by which a legal right is relinquished.

WANTON MISCONDUCT   Such behavior as manifests a disposition to perversity. It must be under such circumstances and conditions that the party doing the act, or failing to act, is conscious that his conduct will, in all common probability, result in injury.

WARD   An infant who is under guardianship. (2) A subdivision of a city, borough, county, or parish for election purposes.

WARRANT   Written authority. (2) An order from a court, to an officer, directing the officer to arrest a person.

WARRANTY   A guaranty concerning goods or land, which is expressly or impliedly made to a purchaser by the vendor.

WILL   The final declaration of the disposition which a person desires to have made of their property after death. It is revocable during the testator's or testatrix's lifetime. It usually must be in writing. Infants under the age of discretion and persons of unsound mind have no legal capacity to make a will. Usually regulated by various state statutes.

WITNESS   A person who sees an act or event occur, e.g., the execution of a deed. (2) A person who testifies in the trial of a lawsuit.

WORKMEN'S COMPENSATION   Various state remedies, provided for by statute, by which indemnity for injuries or death arising out of private employment is furnished to employees and their dependents. The liability of the employer is usually in a limited amount, and is determined independent of the fact of negligence or lack of negligence.

WRIT   A written court order, or a judicial process. It is issued by authority of a court, and directed to the sheriff, or other officer authorized by law to execute the same. He must return it, with a brief statement of what he has done in pursuance of it, to the court or officer who issued it. Writs are either (a) prerogative, when the granting of them is in the discretion of the court, as in the case of habeas corpus; or (b) of right, when the applicant is entitled as of course. The latter class includes original writs, by which an action is commenced, e.g., a summons, and judicial writs, under which head almost all writs at present fall, e.g., writs in aid, and writs of execution. (3) An action, e.g., the writs of waste and partition.

ZONING   The division of a city or county into separate areas, and the application to each area of regulations which limit the various purposes to which the land and buildings therein may be devoted.

The Constitution
of the United States

We the people of the United States, in order to form a more perfect union, establish justice, insure domestic tranquility, provide for the common defense, promote the general welfare, and secure the blessings of liberty to ourselves and our posterity, do ordain and establish this Constitution for the United States of America.

ARTICLE I

Section 1. All legislative powers herein granted shall be vested in a Congress of the United States, which shall consist of a Senate and House of Representatives.

Section 2. 1. The House of Representatives shall be composed of members chosen every second year by the people of the several States, and the electors in each State shall have the qualifications requisite for electors of the most numerous branch of the State legislature.

2. No person shall be a representative who shall not have attained to the age of twenty-five years, and been seven years a citizen of the United States, and who shall not, when elected, be an inhabitant of that State in which he shall be chosen.

3. Representatives and direct taxes[1] shall be apportioned among the several States which may be included within this Union, according to their respective numbers, which shall be determined by adding to the whole number of free persons, including those bound to service for a term of years, and excluding

[1] Altered by the 16th Amendment.

Indians not taxed, three fifths of all other persons.[2] The actual enumeration shall be made within three years after the first meeting of the Congress of the United States, and within every subsequent term of ten years, in such manner as they shall by law direct. The number of representatives shall not exceed one for every thirty thousand, but each State shall have at least one representative; and until such enumeration shall be made, the State of New Hampshire shall be entitled to choose three, Massachusetts eight, Rhode Island and Providence Plantations one, Connecticut five, New York six, New Jersey four, Pennsylvania eight, Delaware one, Maryland six, Virginia ten, North Carolina five, South Carolina five, and Georgia three.

4. When vacancies happen in the representation from any State, the executive authority thereof shall issue writs of election to fill such vacancies.

5. The House of Representatives shall choose their speaker and other officers; and shall have the sole power of impeachment.

Section 3. 1. The Senate of the United States shall be composed of two senators from each State, chosen by the legislature thereof,[3] for six years; and each senator shall have one vote.

2. Immediately after they shall be assembled in consequence of the first election, they shall be divided as equally as may be into three classes. The seats of the senators of the first class shall be vacated at the expiration of the second year, of the second class at the expiration of the fourth year and of the third class at the expiration of the sixth year, so that one third may be chosen every second year; and .if vacancies happen by resignation, or otheriwse, during the recess of the legislature of any State, the executive thereof may make temporary appointments until the next meeting of the legislature, which shall then fill such vacancies.[4]

3. No person shall be a senator who shall not have attained to the age of thirty years, and been nine years a citizen of the United States, and who shall not, when elected, be an inhabitant of that State for which he shall be chosen.

4. The Vice President of the United States shall be President of the Senate, but shall have no vote, unless they be equally divided.

5. The Senate shall choose their other officers, and also a president pro tempore, in the absence of the Vice President, or when he shall exercise the office of the President of the United States.

6. The Senate shall have the sole power to try all impeachments. When sitting for that purpose, they shall be on oath or affirmation. When the President of the United States is tried, the chief justice shall preside: and no person shall be convicted without the concurrence of two thirds of the members present.

7. Judgment in cases of impeachment shall not extend further than to removal from office, and disqualifications to hold and enjoy any office of honor, trust or profit under the United States: but the party convicted shall neverthe-

[2] Altered by the 14th Amendment.
[3] Superseded by the 17th Amendment.
[4] Altered by the 17th Amendment.

less be liable and subject to indictment, trial, judgment and punishment, according to law.

Section 4. 1. The times, places, and manner of holding elections for senators and representatives, shall be prescribed in each State by the legislature thereof: but the Congress may at any time by law make or alter such regulations, except as to the places of choosing senators.

2. The Congress shall assemble at least once in every year, and such meeting shall be on the first Monday in December, unless they shall by law appoint a different day.

Section 5. 1. Each House shall be the judge of the elections, returns and qualifications of its own members, and a majority of each shall constitute a quorum to do business; but a smaller number may adjourn from day to day, and may be authorized to compel the attendance of absent members, in such manner, and under such penalties as each House may provide.

2. Each House may determine the rules of its proceedings, punish its members for disorderly behavior, and, with the concurrence of two thirds, expel a member.

3. Each House shall keep a journal of its proceedings, and from time to time publish the same, excepting such parts as may in their judgment require secrecy; and the yeas and nays of the members of either House on any question shall, at the desire of one fifth of those present, be entered on the journal.

4. Neither House, during the session of Congress, shall, without the consent of the other, adjourn for more than three days, nor to any other place than that in which the two Houses shall be sitting.

Section 6. 1. The senators and representatives shall receive a compensation for their services, to be ascertained by law, and paid out of the Treasury of the United States. They shall in all cases, except treason, felony, and breach of the peace, be privileged from arrest during their attendance at the session of their respective Houses, and in going to and returning from the same; and for any speech or debate in either House, they shall not be questioned in any other place.

2. No senator or representative shall, during the time for which he was elected, be appointed to any civil office under the authority of the United States, which shall have been created, or the emoluments whereof shall have been increased, during such time; and no person holding any office under the United States shall be a member of either House during his continuance in office.

Section 7. 1. All bills for raising revenue shall originate in the House of Representatives; but the Senate may propose or concur with amendments as on other bills.

2. Every bill which shall have passed the House of Representatives and the Senate, shall, before it become a law, be presented to the President of the United States; If he approves he shall sign it, but if not he shall return it, with his objections, to that House in which it shall have originated, who shall enter the objections at large on their journal, and proceed to reconsider it. If after

such reconsideration two thirds of that House shall agree to pass the bill, it shall be sent, together with the objections, to the other House, by which it shall likewise be reconsidered, and if approved by two thirds of that House, it shall become a law. But in all such cases the votes of both Houses shall be determined by yeas and nays, and the names of the persons voting for and against the bill shall be entered on the journal of each House respectively. If any bill shall not be returned by the President within ten days (Sundays excepted) after it shall have been presented to him, the same shall be a law, in like manner as if he had signed it, unless the Congress by their adjournment prevent its return, in which case it shall not be a law.

3. Every order, resolution, or vote to which the concurrence of the Senate and the House of Representatives may be necessary (except on a question of adjournment) shall be presented to the President of the United States; and before the same shall take effect, shall be approved by him, or being disapproved by him, shall be repassed by two thirds of the Senate and House of Representatives, according to the rules and limitations prescribed in the case of a bill.

Section 8. The Congress shall have the power

1. To lay and collect taxes, duties, imposts, and excises, to pay the debts and provide for the common defense and general welfare of the United States; but all duties, imposts, and excises shall be uniform throughout the United States;

2. To borrow money on the credit of the United States;

3. To regulate commerce with foreign nations, and among the several States, and with the Indian tribes;

4. To establish an uniform rule of naturalization, and uniform laws on the subject of bankruptcies throughout the United States;

5. To coin money, regulate the value thereof, and of foreign coin, and fix the standard of weights and measures;

6. To provide for the punishment of counterfeiting the securities and current coin of the United States;

7. To establish post offices and post roads;

8. To promote the progress of science and useful arts, by securing for limited times to authors and inventors the exclusive right to their respective writings and discoveries;

9. To constitute tribunals inferior to the Supreme Court;

10. To define and punish piracies and felonies committed on the high seas, and offenses against the law of nations;

11. To declare war, grant letters of marque and reprisal, and make rules concerning captures on land and water;

12. To raise and support armies, but no appropriation of money to that use shall be for a longer term than two years;

13. To provide and maintain a navy;

14. To make rules for the government and regulation of the land and naval forces;

15. To provide for calling forth the militia to execute the laws of the Union, suppress insurrections and repel invasions;

16. To provide for organizing, arming, and disciplining the militia, and for governing such part of them as may be employed in the service of the United States, reserving to the States respectively, the appointment of the officers, and the authority of training the militia according to the discipline prescribed by Congress;

17. To exercise exclusive legislation in all cases whatsoever, over such district (not exceeding ten miles square) as may, by cession of particular States, and the acceptance of Congress, become the seat of the government of the United States, and to exercise like authority over all places purchased by the consent of the legislature of the State in which the same shall be, for the erection of forts, magazines, arsenals, dockyards, and other needful buildings; and

18. To make all laws which shall be necessary and proper for carrying into execution the foregoing powers, and all other powers vested by this Constitution in the government of the United States, or any department or officer thereof.

Section 9. 1. The migration or importation of such persons as any of the States now existing shall think proper to admit, shall not be prohibited by the Congress prior to the year one thousand eight hundred and eight, but a tax or duty may be imposed on such importation, not exceeding ten dollars for each person.

2. The privilege of the writ of habeas corpus shall not be suspended, unless when in cases of rebellion or invasion the public safety may require it.

3. No bill of attainder or ex post facto law shall be passed.

4. No capitation, or other direct, tax shall be laid, unless in proportion to the census or enumeration hereinbefore directed to be taken.[5]

5. No tax or duty shall be laid on articles exported from any State.

6. No preference shall be given by any regulation of commerce or revenue to the ports of one State over those of another: nor shall vessels bound to, or from, one State be obliged to enter, clear, or pay duties in another.

7. No money shall be drawn from the treasury, but in consequence of appropriations made by law; and a regular statement and account of the receipts and expenditures of all public money shall be published from time to time.

8. No title of nobility shall be granted by the United States: and no person holding any office of profit or trust under them, shall, without the consent of the Congress, accept of any present, emolument, office, or title, of any kind whatever, from any king, prince, or foreign State.

Section 10. 1. No State shall enter into any treaty, alliance, or confederation; grant letters of marque and reprisal; coin money; emit bills of credit; make any thing but gold and silver coin a tender in payment of debts; pass any bill of attainder, ex post facto law, or law impairing the obligation of contracts, or grant any title of nobility.

---

[5] Superseded by the 16th Amendment.

2. No State shall, without the consent of the Congress, lay any imposts or duties on imports or exports, except what may be absolutely necessary for executing its inspection laws: and the net produce of all duties and imposts laid by any State on imports or exports, shall be for the use of the treasury of the United States; and all such laws shall be subject to the revision and control of the Congress.

3. No State shall, without the consent of the Congress, lay any duty of tonnage, keep troops, or ships of war in time of peace, enter into any agreement or compact with another State, or with a foreign power, or engage in war, unless actually invaded, or in such imminent danger as will not admit of delay.

ARTICLE II

Section 1. 1. The executive power shall be vested in a President of the United States of America. He shall hold his office during the term of four years, and, together with the Vice President, chosen for the same term, be elected, as follows:

2. Each State shall appoint, in such manner as the legislature thereof may direct, a number of electors, equal to the whole number of senators and representatives to which the State may be entitled in the Congress: but no senator or representative, or person holding an office of trust or profit under the United States, shall be appointed an elector.

The electors shall meet in their respective States, and vote by ballot for two persons, of whom one at least shall not be an inhabitant of the same State with themselves. And they shall make a list of all the persons voted for, and of the number of votes for each; which list they shall sign and certify, and transmit sealed to the seat of the government of the United States, directed to the president of the Senate. The president of the Senate shall, in the presence of the Senate and House of Representatives, open all the certificates, and the votes shall then be counted. The person having the greatest number of votes shall be the President, if such number be a majority of the whole number of electors appointed; and if there be more than one who have such majority, and have an equal number of votes, then the House of Representatives shall immediately choose by ballot one of them for President; and if no person have a majority, then from the five highest on the list the said House shall in like manner choose the President. But in choosing the President, the votes shall be taken by States, the representation from each State having one vote; a quorum for this purpose shall consist of a member or members from two thirds of the States, and a majority of all the States shall be necessary to a choice. In every case, after the choice of the President, the person having the greatest number of votes of the electors shall be the Vice President. But if there should remain two or more who have equal votes, the Senate shall choose from them by ballot the Vice President.[6]

3. The Congress may determine the time of choosing the electors, and the

----

[6] Superseded by the 12th Amendment.

day on which they shall give their votes; which day shall be the same throughout the United States.

4. No person except a natural born citizen, or a citizen of the United States, at the time of the adoption of this Constitution, shall be eligible to the office of President; neither shall any person be eligible to that office who shall not have attained to the age of thirty-five years, and been fourteen years a resident within the United States.

5. In case of the removal of the President from office, or of his death, resignation, or inability to discharge the powers and duties of the said office, the same shall devolve on the Vice President, and the Congress may by law provide for the case of removal, death, resignation or inability, both of the President and Vice President, declaring what officer shall then act as President, and such officer shall act accordingly, until the disability be removed, or a President shall be elected.

6. The President shall, at stated times, receive for his services a compensation, which shall neither be increased nor diminished during the period for which he shall have been elected, and he shall not receive within that period any other emolument from the United States, or any of them.

7. Before he enter on the execution of his office, he shall take the following oath or affirmation: "I do solemnly swear (or affirm) that I will faithfully execute the office of President of the United States, and will to the best of my ability, preserve, protect, and defend the Constitution of the United States."

Section 2. 1. The President shall be commander in chief of the army and navy of the United States, and of the militia of the several States, when called into the actual service of the United States; he may require the opinion, in writing, of the principal officer in each of the executive departments, upon any subject relating to the duties of their respective offices, and he shall have power to grant reprieves and pardons for offenses against the United States, except in cases of impeachment.

2. He shall have power, by and with the advice and consent of the Senate, to make treaties, provided two thirds of the senators present concur; and he shall nominate, and by and with the advice and consent of the Senate, shall appoint ambassadors, other public ministers and consuls, judges of the Supreme Court, and all other officers of the United States, whose appointments are not herein otherwise provided for, and which shall be established by law: but the Congress may by law vest the appointment of such inferior officers, as they think proper, in the President alone, in the courts of law, or in the heads of departments.

3. The President shall have power to fill up all vacancies that may happen during the recess of the Senate, by granting commissions which shall expire at the end of their next session.

Section 3. He shall from time to time give to the Congress information of the state of the Union, and recommend to their considerations such measures as he shall judge necessary and expedient; he may, on extraordinary occasions, convene both Houses, or either of them, and in case of disagreement between them with respect to the time of adjournment, he may adjourn them to such time as he shall think proper; he shall receive ambassadors and other public ministers; he shall take care that the laws be faithfully executed, and shall commission all the officers of the United States.

Section 4. The President, Vice President, and all civil officers of the United States, shall be removed from office on impeachment for, and conviction of, treason, bribery, or other high crimes and misdemeanors.

ARTICLE III

Section 1. The judicial power of the United States shall be vested in one Supreme Court, and in such inferior courts as the Congress may from time to time ordain and establish. The judges, both of the Supreme and inferior courts, shall hold their offices during good behavior, and shall, at stated times, receive for their services, a compensation, which shall not be diminished during their continuance in office.

Section 2. 1. The judicial power shall extend to all cases, in law and equity, arising under this Constitution, the laws of the United States, and treaties made, or which shall be made, under their authority; — to all cases affecting ambassadors, other public ministers and consuls; — to all cases of admiralty and maritime jurisdiction; — to controversies to which the United States shall be a party;[7] — to controversies between two or more States; — between a State and citizens of another State; — between citizens of different States; — between citizens of the same State claiming lands under grants of different States, and between a State, or the citizens thereof, and foreign States, citizens or subjects.

2. In all cases affecting ambassadors, other public ministers and consuls, and those in which a State shall be party, the Supreme Court shall have original jurisdiction. In all the other cases before mentioned, the Supreme Court shall have appellate jurisdiction, both as to law and fact, with such exceptions, and under such regulations as the Congress shall make.

3. The trial of all crimes, except in cases of impeachment, shall be by jury; and such trial shall be held in the State where the said crimes shall have been committed; but when not committed within any State, the trial shall be at such place or places as the Congress may by law have directed.

Section 3. 1. Treason against the United States shall consist only in levying war against them, or in adhering to their enemies, giving them aid and comfort. No person shall be convicted of treason unless on the testimony of two witnesses to the same overt act, or on confession in open court.

2. The Congress shall have power to declare the punishment of treason, but no attainder of treason shall work corruption of blood, or forfeiture except during the life of the person attained.

ARTICLE IV

Section 1. Full faith and credit shall be given in each State to the public acts, records, and judicial proceedings of every other State. And the Con-

---

[7] Cf. the 11th Amendment.

gress may by general laws prescribe the manner in which such acts, records and proceedings shall be proved, and the effect thereof.

Section 2. 1. The citizens of each State shall be entitled to all privileges and immunities of citizens in the several States.[8]

2. A person charged in any State with treason, felony, or other crime, who shall flee from justice, and be found in another State, shall on demand of the executive authority of the State from which he fled, be delivered up to be removed to the State having jurisdiction of the crime.

3. No person held to service or labor in one State under the laws thereof, escaping into another, shall, in consequence of any law or regulation therein, be discharged from such service or labor, but shall be delivered up on claim of the party to whom such service or labor may be due.[9]

Section 3. 1. New States may be admitted by the Congress into this Union; but no new State shall be formed or erected within the jurisdiction of any other State; nor any State be formed by the junction of two or more States, or parts of States, without the consent of the legislatures of the States concerned as well as of the Congress.

2. The Congress shall have power to dispose of and make all needful rules and regulations respecting the territory or other property belonging to the United States; and nothing in this Constitution shall be so construed as to prejudice any claims of the United States, or of any particular State.

Section 4. The United States shall guarantee to every State in this Union a republican form of government, and shall protect each of them against invasion; and on application of the legislature, or of the executive (when the legislature cannot be convened) against domestic violence.

ARTICLE V

The Congress, whenever two thirds of both Houses shall deem it necessary, shall propose amendments to this Constitution, or, on the application of the legislatures of two thirds of the several States, shall call a convention for proposing amendments, which in either case shall be valid to all intents and purposes, as part of this Constitution, when ratified by the legislatures of three fourths of the several States, or by conventions in three fourths thereof, as the one or the other mode of ratification may be proposed by the Congress; Provided that no amendment which may be made prior to the year one thousand eight hundred and eight shall in any manner affect the first and fourth clauses in the ninth section of the first article; and that no State, without its consent, shall be deprived of its equal suffrage in the Senate.

ARTICLE VI

1. All debts contracted and engagements entered into, before the adoption of this Constitution, shall be as valid against the United States under this Constitution, as under the Confederation.

---

[8] Superseded by the 14th Amendment, Sec. 1.
[9] Voided by the 13th Amendment.

2. This Constitution, and the laws of the United States which shall be made in pursuance thereof; and all treaties made, or which shall be made, under the authority of the United States, shall be supreme law of the land; and the Judges in every State shall be bound thereby, any thing in the Constitution or laws of any State to the contrary notwithstanding.

3. The senators and representatives before mentioned, and the members of the several State legislatures, and all executive and judicial officers, both of the United States and of the several States, shall be bound by oath or affirmation to support this Constitution; but no religious test shall ever be required as a qualification to any office or public trust under the United States.

ARTICLE VII

The ratification of the conventions of nine States shall be sufficient for the establishment of this Constitution between the States so ratifying the same.

Done in Convention by the unanimous consent of the States present the seventeenth day of September in the year of our Lord one thousand seven hundred and eighty-seven, and of the independence of the United States of America the twelfth. In witness whereof we have hereunto subscribed our names. [Names omitted.]

*   *   *

Articles in addition to, and amendment of, the Constitution of the United States of America, proposed by Congress, and ratified by the legislatures of the several States, pursuant to the fifth article of the original Constitution.

AMENDMENT I [First ten amendments ratified December 15, 1791]

Congress shall make no law respecting an establishment of religion, or prohibiting the free exercise thereof; or abridging the freedom of speech, or of the press; or the right of the people peaceably to assemble, and to petition the government for a redress of grievancs.

AMENDMENT II

A well regulated militia, being necessary to the security of a free State, the right of the people to keep and bear arms, shall not be infringed.

AMENDMENT III

No soldier shall, in time of peace be quartered in any house, without the consent of the owner, nor in time of war, but in a manner to be prescribed by law.

AMENDMENT IV

The right of the people to secure in their persons, houses, papers, and effects, against unreasonable searches and seizures, shall not be violated, and no warrants shall issue, but upon probable cause, supported by oath or affirmation, and particularly describing the place to be searched, and the persons or things to be seized.

AMENDMENT V

No person shall be held to answer for a capital, or otherwise infamous crime, unless on a presentment or indictment of a grand jury, except in cases arising in the land or naval forces, or in the militia, when in actual service in time of war or public danger; nor shall any person be subject for the same offense to be twice put in jeopardy of life or limb; nor shall be compelled in any criminal case to be a witness against himself; nor be deprived of life, liberty, or property, without due process of law; nor shall private property be taken for public use, without just compensation.

AMENDMENT VI

In all criminal prosecutions, the accused shall enjoy the right to a speedy and public trial, by an impartial jury of the State and district wherein the crime shall have been committed, which district shall have been previously ascertained by law, and to be informed of the nature and cause of the accusation; to be confronted with the witnesses against him; to have compulsory process for obtaining witnesses in his favor, and to have the assistance of counsel for his defense.

AMENDMENT VII

In suits at common law, where the value in controversy shall exceed twenty dollars, the right of trial by jury shall be preserved, and no fact tried by a jury shall be otherwise reëxamined in any court of the United States, than according to the rules of the common law.

AMENDMENT VIII

Excessive bail shall not be required, nor excessive fines imposed, nor cruel and unusual punishments inflicted.

AMENDMENT IX

The enumeration in the Constitution of certain rights shall not be construed to deny or disparage others retained by the people.

AMENDMENT X

The powers not delegated to the United States by the Constitution, nor prohibited by it to the States, are reserved to the States respectively, or to the people.

AMENDMENT XI [Ratified January 8, 1798]

The judicial power of the United States shall not be construed to extend to any suit in law or equity, commenced or prosecuted against one of the United States by citizens of another State, or by citizens or subjects of any foreign State.

AMENDMENT XII [Ratified September 25, 1804]

The electors shall meet in their respective States, and vote by ballot for President and Vice President, one of whom, at least, shall not be an inhabitant of the same State with themselves; they shall name in their ballots the person voted for as President, and in distinct ballots, the person voted for as Vice President, and they shall make distinct lists of all persons voted for as President and of all persons voted for as Vice President, and of the number of votes for each, which lists they shall sign and certify, and transmit sealed to the seat of the government of the United States, directed to the President of the Senate; — The President of the Senate shall, in the presence of the Senate and House of Representatives, open all the certificates and the votes shall then be counted; — The person having the greatest number of votes for President, shall be the President, if such number be a majority of the whole number of electors appointed; and if no person have such majority, then from the persons having the highest numbers not exceeding three on the list of those voted for as President, the House of Representatives shall choose immediately, by ballot, the President. But in choosing the President, the votes shall be taken by States, the representation from each State having one vote; a quorum for this purpose shall consist of a member or members from two thirds of the States, and a majority of all the States shall be necessary to a choice. And if the House of Representatives shall not choose a President whenever the right of choice shall devolve upon them, before the fourth day of March next following, then the Vice President shall act as President, as in the case of the death or other constitutional disability of the President. The person having the greatest number of votes as Vice President shall be the Vice President, if such number be a majority of the whole number of electors appointed, and if no person have a majority, then from the two highest numbers on the list, the Senate shall choose the Vice President; a quorum for the purpose shall consist of two thirds of the whole number of Senators, and a majority of the whole number shall be necessary to a choice. But no person constitutionally ineligible to the office of President shall be eligible to that of Vice President of the United States.

AMENDMENT XIII [Ratified December 18, 1865]

Section 1. Neither slavery nor involuntary servitude, except as a punishment for crime whereof the party shall have been duly convicted, shall exist within the United States, or any place subject to their jurisdiction.

Section 2. Congress shall have power to enforce this article by appropriate legislation.

AMENDMENT XIV [Ratified July 28, 1868]

Section 1. All persons born or naturalized in the United States, and subject to the jurisdiction thereof, are citizens of the United States and of the State wherein they reside. No State shall make or enforce any law which shall abridge the privileges or immunities of citizens of the United States; nor shall any State deprive any person of life, liberty, or property, without due process of law; nor deny to any person within its jurisdiction the equal protection of the laws.

Section 2. Representatives shall be apportioned among the several States according to their respective numbers, counting the whole number of persons in each State, excluding Indians not taxed. But when the right to vote at any election for the choice of electors for President and Vice President of the United States, representatives in Congress, the executive and judicial officers of a State, or the members of the legislature thereof, is denied to any of the male inhabitants of such State, being twenty-one years of age, and citizens of the United States, or in any way abridged, except for participating in rebellion, or other crime, the basis of representation therein shall be reduced in the proportion which the number of such male citizens shall bear to the whole number of male citizens twenty-one years of age in such State.

Section 3. No person shall be a senator or representative in Congress, or elector of President and Vice President, or hold any office, civil or military, under the United States, or under any State, who having previously taken an oath, as a member of Congress, or as an officer of the United States, or as a member of any State legislature, or as an executive or judicial officer of any State, to support the Constitution of the United States, shall have engaged in insurrection or rebellion against the same, or given aid or comfort to the enemies thereof. But Congress may by a vote of two thirds of each House, remove such disability.

Section 4. The validity of the public debt of the United States, authorized by law, including debts incurred for payment of pensions and bounties for services in suppressing insurrection or rebellion, shall not be questioned. But neither the United States nor any State shall assume or pay any debt or obligation incurred in aid of insurrection or rebellion against the United States, or any claim for the loss or emancipation of any slave; but all such debts, obligations, and claims shall be held illegal and void.

Section 5. The Congress shall have power to enforce, by appropriate legislation, the provisions of this article.

AMENDMENT XV [Ratified March 30, 1870]

Section 1. The right of citizens of the United States to vote shall not be denied or abridged by the United States or by any State on account of race, color, or previous condition of servitude.

Section 2. The Congress shall have power to enforce this article by appropriate legislation.

AMENDMENT XVI [Ratified February 25, 1913]

The Congress hall have power to lay and collect taxes on incomes, from whatever source derived, without apportionment among the several States, and without regard to any census or enumeration.

AMENDMENT XVII [Ratified May 31, 1913]

The Senate of the United States shall be composed of two senators from each State, elected by the people thereof, for six years; and each senator shall have one vote. The electors in each State shall have the qualifications requisite for electors of the most numerous branch of the State legislature.

When vacancies happen in the representation of any State in the Senate, the executive authority of such State shall issue writs of election to fill such vacancies: *Provided,* That the legislature of any State may empower the executive thereof to make temporary appointments until the people fill the vacancies by election as the legislative may direct.

This amendment shall not be so construed as to affect the election or term of any senator chosen before it becomes valid as part of the Constitution.

AMENDMENT XVIII[10] [Ratified January 29, 1919]

After one year from the ratification of this article, the manufacture, sale, or transportation of intoxicating liquors within, the importation thereof into, or the exportation thereof from the United States and all territory subject to the jurisdiction thereof for beverage purposes is thereby prohibited.

The Congress and the several States shall have concurrent power to enforce this article by appropriate legislation.

This article shall be inoperative unless it shall have been ratified as an amendment to the Constitution by the legislatures of the several States, as provided in the Constitution, within seven years from the date of the submission hereof to the States by Congress.

AMENDMENT XIX [Ratified August 26, 1920]

The right of citizens of the United States to vote shall not be denied or abridged by the United States or by any State on account of sex.

Congress shall have the power to enforce this article by appropriate legislation.

AMENDMENT XX [Ratified January 23, 1933]

Section 1. The terms of the President and Vice President shall end at noon on the 20th day of January, and the terms of Senators and Representatives at noon on the 3d day of January, of the years in which such terms would have ended if this article had not been ratified; and the terms of their successors shall then begin.

Section 2. The Congress shall assemble at least once in every year, and such meeting shall begin at noon on the 3d day of January, unless they shall by law appoint a different day.

Section 3. If, at the time fixed for the beginning of the term of President, the President-elect shall have died, the Vice President-elect shall become President. If a President shall not have been chosen before the time fixed for the beginning of his term, or if the President-elect shall have failed to qualify, then the Vice President-elect shall act as President until a President shall have

[10] Repealed by the 21st Amendment.

qualified; and the Congress may by law provide for the case wherein neither a President-elect nor a Vice President-elect shall have qualified, declaring who shall then act as President, or the manner in which one who is to act shall be selected, and such person shall act accordingly until a President or Vice President shall have qualified.

Section 4. The Congress may by law provide for the case of the death of any of the persons from whom the House of Representatives may choose a President whenever the right of choice shall have devolved upon them, and for the case of the death of any of the persons from whom the Senate may choose a Vice President whenever the right of choice shall have devolved upon them.

Section 5. Sections 1 and 2 shall take effect on the 15th day of October following the ratification of this article.

Section 6. This article shall be inoperative unless it shall have been ratified as an amendment to the Constitution by the legislatures of three-fourths of the several States within seven years from the date of its submission.

AMENDMENT XXI [Ratified December 5, 1933]

Section 1. The Eighteenth Article of amendment to the Constitution of the United States is hereby repealed.

Section 2. The transportation or importation into any State, Territory, or possession of the United States for delivery or use therein of intoxicating liquors in violation of the laws thereof, is hereby prohibited.

Section 3. This article shall be inoperative unless it shall have been ratified as an amendment to the Constitution by conventions in the several States as provided in the Constitution, within seven years from the date of the submission thereof to the States by the Congress.

AMENDMENT XXII [Ratified March 1, 1951]

No person shall be elected to the office of the President more than twice, and no person who has held the office of President, or acted as President, for more than two years of a term to which some other person was elected President shall be elected to the office of the President more than once.

But this article shall not apply to any person holding the office of President when this article was proposed by the Congress, and shall not prevent any person who may be holding the office of President, or acting as President, during the term within which this article becomes operative from holding the office of President or acting as President during the remainder of such term.

This article shall be inoperative unless it shall have been ratified as an amendment to the Constitution by the legislatures of three-fourths of the several States within seven years from the date of its submission to the States by the Congress.

AMENDMENT XXIII [Ratified March 29, 1961]

Section 1. The District constituting the seat of Government of the United States shall appoint in such manner as the Congress may direct:

A number of electors of President and Vice President equal to the whole number of Senators and Representatives in Congress to which the District would be entitled if it were a State, but in no event more than the least populous State; they shall be in addition to those appointed by the States, but they shall be considered, for the purposes of the election of President and Vice President, to be electors appointed by a State; and they shall meet in the District and perform such duties as provided by the twelfth article of amendment.

Section 2. The Congress shall have power to enforce this article by appropriate legislation.

AMENDMENT XXIV [Ratified January 23, 1964]

Section 1. The right of citizens of the United States to vote in any primary or other election for President or Vice President, for electors for President or Vice President, or for Senator or Representative in Congress, shall not be denied or abridged by the United States or any State by reason of failure to pay any poll tax or other tax.

Section 2. The Congress shall have power to enforce this article by appropriate legislation.

AMENDMENT XXV [Ratified February 10, 1967]

Section 1. In case of the removal of the President from office or of his death or resignation, the Vice President shall become President.

Section 2. Whenever there is a vacancy in the office of the Vice President, the President shall nominate a Vice President who shall take office upon confirmation by a majority vote of both Houses of Congress.

Section 3. Whenever the President transmits to the President pro tempore of the Senate and the Speaker of the House of Representatives his written declaration that he is unable to discharge the powers and duties of his office, and until he transmits to them a written declaration to the contrary, such powers and duties shall be discharged by the Vice President as Acting President.

Section 4. Whenever the Vice President and a majority of either the principal officers of the executive departments or of such other body as Congress may by law provide, transmit to the President pro tempore of the Senate and the Speaker of the House of Representatives their written declaration that the President is unable to discharge the powers and duties of his office, the Vice President shall immediately assume the powers and duties of the office as Acting President.

Thereafter, when the President transmits to the President pro tempore of the Senate and the Speaker of the House of Representatives his written declaration that no inability exists, he shall resume the powers and duties of his office unless the Vice President and a majority of either the principal officers of the executive departments or of such other body as Congress may by law provide, transmit within four days to the President pro tempore of the Senate and the Speaker of the House of Representatives their written declaration that the President is unable to discharge the powers and duties of his office. Thereupon Congress shall decide the issue, assembling within forty-eight hours for that purpose if not in session. If the Congress, within twenty-one days after receipt of the latter written declaration, or, if Congress is not in session, within twenty-one days after Congress is required to assemble, determines by two-thirds vote of both Houses that the President is unable to discharge the powers and duties of his office, the Vice President shall continue to discharge the same as Acting President; otherwise, the President shall resume the powers and duties of his office.

AMENDMENT XXVI [Ratified July 1, 1971]

Section 1. The right of citizens of the United States, who are eighteen years of age or older, to vote shall not be denied or abridged by the United States or by any State on account of age.

Section 2. The Congress shall have power to enforce this article by appropriate legislation.

Index